RUNAWAY SLAVES

Runaway Slaves

REBELS ON THE PLANTATION

John Hope Franklin
Loren Schweninger

New York   Oxford
Oxford University Press
1999

Oxford University Press

Oxford   New York

Athens   Auckland   Bangkok   Bogotá   Buenos Aires   Calcutta
Cape Town   Chennai   Dar es Salaam   Delhi   Florence   Hong Kong   Istanbul
Karachi   Kuala Lumpur   Madrid   Melbourne   Mexico City   Mumbai
Nairobi   Paris   São Paulo   Singapore   Taipei   Tokyo   Toronto   Warsaw

and associated companies in
Berlin   Ibadan

Published by Oxford University Press, Inc.
198 Madison Avenue, New York, New York 10016

Oxford is a registered trademark of Oxford University Press

Library of Congress Cataloging-in-Publication Data

Franklin, John Hope, 1915–
Runaway slaves : rebels on the plantation/
John Hope Franklin and Loren Schweninger.
p.   cm.
Includes bibliographical references (p.   ) and index.
ISBN 0-19-508449-7
1. Slavery—Southern States—Insurrections, etc.   2. Fugitive
slaves—Southern States—History.   3. Southern States—
History—1775–1865.   I. Schweninger, Loren.   II. Title.
E447.F7 1999   975'.00496—dc21   98-25230

1 3 5 7 9 8 6 4 2
Printed in the United States of America
on acid-free paper

For Aurelia and
Patricia, always there

I felt assured that, if I failed in this attempt, my case would be a hopeless one—it would seal my fate as a slave forever. I could not hope to get off with anything less than the severest punishment, and being placed beyond the means of escape. It required no very vivid imagination to depict the most frightful scenes through which I should have to pass, in case I failed. The wretchedness of slavery, and the blessedness of freedom, were perpetually before me. It was life and death with me.   —Frederick Douglass

Contents

Contents

Appendix 7
Runaway Slave Database: Early Period 1790–1816; Late Period 1838–1860

Preface

OVER THE YEARS, plantation slavery has been described in many ways. Perhaps the classic description was provided by Ulrich B. Phillips. In his Pulitzer Prize–winning *Life and Labor in the Old South*, he spoke of the plantation force as "a conscript army" and the plantation as a homestead, a school, a "parish, or perhaps a chapel of ease," a pageant and variety show, and "a matrimonial bureau." Soon historians, including James Hugo Johnston, Harvey Wish, Raymond A. and Alice H. Bauer, and Herbert Aptheker, began to show that there was another way to view slavery. It was becoming clear that the plantation was not the smooth, well-managed operation described by Phillips.[1] Missing from his romantic description were the harsh realities of everyday plantation life, the severe punishments for dereliction of duties, branding, mutilation, stealing, arson, murder, rape, and division of families, including the sale of children. No discussion of plantation life can be complete without a discussion of these and similar matters.

Some forty years ago, Kenneth M. Stampp succeeded in correcting earlier descriptions of plantation life such as those set forth by Phillips. He called slaves "a troublesome property" and reminded his readers of the unrest and unhappiness that were all too prevalent even among the most passive slaves. In turn, they retaliated against unreasonable demands by refusing to obey or even running away.[2]

The revisionist trend was not altogether in one direction. In 1959, the psychological model presented by Stanley Elkins in *Slavery: A Problem in American Institutional and Intellectual Life* portrayed slaves as not unlike Jewish inmates in concentration camps during World War II. In order to survive they developed childlike, loyal, and docile dispositions. Eugene Genovese, among others, found Elkins's model disturbing. He noted that "we must recognize that all psychological models may only be used suggestively for flashes of insight or as aids in forming hypotheses and they cannot substitute for empirical investigation." George M. Fredrickson and Christopher Lasch added that the entire issue of slave resistance needed clarification. The problem was not whether plantation slaves were happy or discontent, or even that they failed to cooperate. Rather, they said, it was a question of whether or not they "actively resisted" their owners' commands.[3]

Meanwhile, pursuing his own line of inquiry, Larry Gara looked at the myths surrounding the Underground Railroad. Although the Underground Railroad was a reality, Gara said, "much of the material relating to it belongs in the realm of folklore rather than history." It was not, he asserted, a well-organized transportation system offering multitudes of slaves safe passage to the "Promised Land of freedom." Indeed, most runaways remained in the South, few were aided by abolitionists or anyone else, and many fled with a sense of terrible urgency.[4]

In the decades that followed, a large number of books and articles about slavery appeared. During the 1970s most of the literature focused on black culture and black consciousness and on slave communities and slave family life. Some of these authors argued that the emergence of a unique African American culture—extended kinship systems, folk tales, spirituals, Afro-Christianity—was an important vehicle for resisting slavery. Only a few of them discussed the importance of runaways. John Blassingame, for example, dedicated a chapter in his seminal study *The Slave Community* to rebels and runaways, and Gerald W. Mullin broke new ground in *Flight and Rebellion* with an imaginative use of runaway advertisements.[5]

Despite the large number of books and articles touching on the subject, there is still no full-length study of runaway slaves. In fact, much of the scholarship about slave resistance continues to be dominated by the conceptual framework and the focus presented by Herbert Aptheker more than a half-century ago: "The Machinery of Control," "Early Plots and Rebellions," "The Turner Cataclysm and Some Repercussions," and "The Civil War Years." Perhaps no book has "exercised such dominion over a subject of prime importance," Genovese writes, as *American Negro Slave Revolts*. Peter Kolchin recently observed, however, that Aptheker probably exaggerated the extent of slave unrest. He lamented that there is still no adequate study of slave resistance or slave flight.[6]

We have undertaken an extensive examination of "slave flight" between 1790 and 1860. It reveals, among other things, some problems of management of the South's "peculiar institution." It shows how a significant number of slaves challenged the system and how the great majority of them struggled to attain their freedom even if they failed.

The price they paid for their unwillingness to submit was obviously enormous. This study reveals how slave owners marshaled considerable effort to prevent the practice of running away, meted out punishments to slaves who disregarded the rules, and established laws and patrols to control the movement of slaves. It also exposes the violence and cruelty that were inherent in the slave system. Indeed, it shows, perhaps better than any other approach, how slaves resisted with various forms of violence and how slave owners responded, at times brutally, to demonstrate their authority over their human chattel.

Even today important aspects of the history of slavery remain shrouded in myth and legend. Many people still believe that slaves were generally content, that racial violence on the plantation was an aberration, and that the few who ran away struck out for the Promised Land in the North or Canada. We have carefully scrutinized those who challenged the system; when, where, and how they ran away; how long they remained out; how they survived away from the plantation; and how and when they were brought back and punished. We examine the motives of absentees, or those who left the farm or plantation for a few days or weeks; the incentives of outlyers, or those who hid out in the woods for months, sometimes years; and the activities of maroons, who established camps in remote swamps and bayous. We also examine how "term slaves," or those to be emancipated at a future date, responded to their status and how free blacks assisted their brethren and on occasion themselves became runaways.

Of equal importance, we seek to analyze the motives and responses of the slaveholding class and other whites. How did owners react to such intransigence in their midst? How did they attempt to halt the flow of runaways? What laws did they seek to enact? What punishments did they administer? How successfully did they curtail such dissidence? Indeed, it is less important to discover what happened to individual slaves than to understand the relationship between the owners and the runaways who challenged the system, a relationship that reveals perhaps as well as any perspective the true nature of the South's peculiar institution.

Acknowledgments

THE FIRST EXPLORATION of this subject appeared as the James W. Richard Lectures at the University of Virginia in 1980. The comments and encouraging response led to a much more extensive examination of the subject that culminated in the present work. Many individuals have assisted in bringing this work to completion. At the Alabama Department of Archives and History, Edwin Bridges, the director, and his colleagues gave their time and assistance as we explored the rich collections there. Don Carleton, Director of the Center for American History at the University of Texas, and his colleagues, especially Sara Clark, were helpful as we undertook to unlock the treasures in the remarkable Natchez Trace Slaves and Slavery Collection. The staff in the Manuscript Department at the Hill Memorial Library of Louisiana State University guided us to several important groups of papers that are valuable for this study. Other state archivists and staffs who assisted us were Richard Belding, Barbara Teague, and Jane Julian of the Kentucky Department for Libraries and Archives, Edward C. Papenfuse and Patricia V. Melville of the Maryland State Archives, Kenneth H. Winn and Patsy Luebbert of the Missouri State Archives, Jeffrey Crow of the North Carolina Division of Archives and History, Steven D. Tuttle of the South Carolina Department of Archives and History, Ann Alley and Wayne Moore of the Tennessee State Library and Archives, and Conley Edwards of the Virginia State Archives. Prosser Gifford and Deborah Newman Ham were gracious and generous during a six-week tenure in the Manuscripts Division of the Library of Congress.

Thomas D. Morris, Stanley Harrold, and Cheryl Jumk provided important material from their own research. William Scarborough, currently working on a study of the South's largest planters, generously shared with us his analysis of runaway slaves on Morville Plantation.

An earlier version of chapter 9, "Profile of a Runaway," was presented at the 1996 annual meeting of the Association for the Study of Afro-American Life and History in Charleston, South Carolina. Chapter 10, "Managing Human Property," was presented in an earlier stage at the 1996 annual meeting of the St. George Tucker Society in Atlanta, Georgia. Members of the audience and commentators at both meetings offered helpful criticisms.

Margaret Fitzsimmons, Michael Huber, and David F. Herr transcribed or photocopied more than six thousand runaway newspaper notices. David F. Herr also coded, inputted, and ran preliminary computer analyses on the notices in a database. Several colleagues at the University of North Carolina at Greensboro, David G. Herr, Marty Skinner, and Judy Martin, assisted in formatting, coding, and analyzing the data. Research assistants Denise Ettenger, Jim Giesen, Jeanette Jennings, and Tania Taylor assisted in numerous ways. Adrienne Middlebrooks expertly compiled the bibliography. Denise Kohn, Robert Shelton, and Marguerite Ross Howell proofread page proofs with great care. From the beginning of this study, Margaret Fitzsimmons served as researcher, typist, and editor. To all those who have assisted us we are deeply grateful.

Most of the petitions cited in this study are part of the Race and Slavery Petitions Project at the University of North Carolina at Greensboro. The project has received generous support from the National Historical Publications and Records Commission, National Endowment for the Humanities, and Charles Stewart Mott Foundation, for which we express our sincere appreciation. We are also indebted to the many county court officials who made their records available for examination. While we shall always value the assistance that numerous persons, including our wives, Aurelia and Patricia, gave, we assume full responsibility for the contents of this work.

RUNAWAY SLAVES

1

Dissidents in the Conscript Army

ON 17 AUGUST 1840, the day of a great Whig political convention in Nashville, Tennessee, Jake, a slave owned by an old and respected farmer, Robert Bradford, refused to go to work. Like other blacks in the neighborhood, he wanted to go to the convention, listen to the speeches, and attend the celebrations. The overseer informed Bradford that Jake was "in an ugly mood" and asked him what to do. Bradford said he would speak with Jake and see if he could calm him down. Bradford was unable to placate the black man and ordered his overseer to tie him up for a whipping. Jake quickly drew a knife. "Whether he aimed to cut the rope or the Overseer no one knew," a Nashville slave recalled, "but he made a wild thrust which killed Mr. Bradford on the spot."[1]

Jake absconded into the woods. Nine days later a notice appeared in the *Nashville Whig*: a thirty-year-old slave named Jake, a raw-boned, quick-spoken man of "bright complexion," weighing about 160 or 170 pounds, had murdered old man Bradford. When he escaped he was dressed in white homespun "linsey pantaloons, and roundabouts." A short time later, Governor James K. Polk offered a reward for the slave's apprehension. Despite concerted efforts by constables, justices of the peace, and local citizens, Jake remained at large for a number of months. Finally, however, he was captured, tried, convicted, and hanged. Few lamented his passing, but the death of the esteemed Bradford was universally mourned by whites in the community.[2]

Murders such as the one on the Bradford farm in 1840 were rare under the slave regime, but the incident revealed undercurrents that were quite common. Like Jake, other slaves were frustrated, alienated, defiant, sometimes violent; indeed, Jake's anger and hostility represented a far greater proportion of the slave population than might be suspected. Echoing the words of others, one Maryland slave master described his female slave as "turbulent, disobedient and impudent beyond endurance," and worse, when excited by passion "is perfectly deranged."[3]

To examine the discontent of enslaved and illiterate people is not without its hazards, not the least of which is that the most reliable and objective sources—in our case county court records and newspaper advertisements—are nearly always written by whites. But careful use of this evidence and other sources reveals the depth of hostility many slaves felt toward their owners and overseers.

The evidence shows that slaves engaged in a remarkable variety of acts to demonstrate their discontent. Many openly defied the system. Although historians have examined slave resistance from a number of vantage points—ranging from finding solace in a "black community" to outright revolt—the tensions, conflicts, and often violent confrontations between master and servant, or overseer and slave, have received less attention.[4] They, nevertheless, deserve close study if one is to understand fully the problem of managing slaves in a rural or urban setting.

Day to Day Resistance

Most of what historians have termed "day to day" resistance involved "crimes" against property. Slaves pulled down fences, sabotaged farm equipment, broke implements, damaged boats, vandalized wagons, ruined clothing, and committed various other destructive acts. They set fires to outbuildings, barns, and stables; mistreated horses, mules, cattle, and other livestock. They stole with impunity: sheep, hogs, cattle, poultry, money, watches, produce, liquor, tobacco, flour, cotton, indigo, corn, nearly anything that was not under lock and key—and they occasionally found the key. "He is a great old scamp," a Kentucky man wrote a relative about an elderly slave. He "took many things that were left by you." Viewing the master's property as an extension of the master himself, the destructive impulses bordered at times on the sadistic. "I have had a very seveer time a mong my negros," a cotton planter on Bayou Mason in Louisiana wrote in 1829; "they have bin Swinging my hogs and pigs." He caught two of his slaves, Harry and Roberson, tying the rear legs of his pigs together, throwing the end of the rope over a tree, pulling the animals into the air, and swinging them as they squealed in pain. Two of the pigs, the owner lamented, were badly crippled.[5]

Some blacks worked slowly, or indifferently, took unscheduled respites, performed careless or sloppy labor when planting, hoeing, and harvesting crops. Some chopped cotton so nonchalantly that they cut the young plants nearly into fodder, while others harvested rice or sugar with such indifference that they damaged the crop. Slaves feigned illness, hid in outbuildings, did not complete their assigned tasks, and balked at performing dangerous work. It was difficult to sneak off for an entire day, but on some plantations slaves did so. An eighteen-year-old Louisiana female slave managed to slip off and remain in the woods, at least until the overseer found her one morning lying on her stomach in some bushes at the bottom of a gully. The overseer got off his horse and, holding the reins with his left hand, struck her thirty or forty stripes across the shoulders. He continued to whip her until, groveling and screaming, she cried for mercy. "Oh, don't, sir! oh, please stop, master! please, sir!" The overseer eventually stopped. "She meant to cheat me out of a day's work—and she has done it, too," the overseer complained; "Oh, you have no idea how lazy these niggers are." They would not work at all, he believed, if it were not for the whipping they would receive if they refused.[6]

Other slaves turned to whiskey or other "ardent spirits" as an expression of their frustration. The number of blacks who drank regularly will never be known, but the comments of planters and complaints of whites who sought to curb the illicit traffic of whiskey, rum, beer, wine, and other spirits indicate that alcohol was more available than is generally believed. In towns and cities, grog shops and grocery stores catered to slaves, while planters and farmers found it nearly impossible to keep whiskey out of the quarters. Since selling spirits to blacks was illegal without the master's permission, the numerous prosecutions of whites who engaged in the practice reveal a good deal about the drinking habits of the slave population.

In Charleston in the mid-1830s, a resident noticed five black men walking down Market Street suddenly dart into a shed, followed by a white man carrying a decanter. When the door was forced open by authorities, they found three of them sitting at a table, with whiskey in some tumblers, and the decanter nearly empty. Such a scene was repeated often in Baltimore, Richmond, New Orleans, and other cities. It was also repeated in the quarters, as overseers and slave owners complained about black people who consumed illicit whiskey, drank to excess, were in the "habit of getting drunk," or suffered from the "vice of intemperance." By the time he was in his mid-forties, Tennessee slave Big Ike had threatened several times that he would run away. The manager of the plantation said that Ike was in the "habit of getting drunk & has become so addicted to drinking to excess" that he would undoubtedly make good on his promise to run away.[7]

The frequency of these acts—whether sabotage, carelessness, theft, or drinking—varied from plantation to plantation, region to region, depending on the responses of masters, proximity to towns and cities, interaction with free blacks, and control by overseers and owners. There is little doubt, however, that such expressions of displeasure were widespread.

Hired Slave Dissatisfaction

Although hired slaves sometimes did careless work, they could express their dissatisfaction in many other ways. Stretching back to the years before the American Revolution, the practice of renting out black workers was widespread in the South. As time passed, the practice grew even more, and by the nineteenth century a significant portion of the slave labor force was hired out at one time or another during the year. In rural areas, planters and farmers hired extra hands for harvesting the crops and sent their skilled artisans to work for neighbors who needed carpenters, coopers, or mechanics. In towns and cities or in the South's growing industries—hemp, textiles, tobacco, iron— a large proportion of the workforce was hired. In antebellum Richmond, Virginia, with its demands for road workers, tobacco hands, and laborers, nearly two-thirds of the slave labor force was hired. On the eve of the Civil War, according to one estimate, 6 percent of rural and 31 percent of urban slaves were hired.[8]

Slaves generally responded in a positive manner to being hired out by their owners. They could travel from one place to another, live more independently, perhaps earn a small amount of cash for extra work. At the same time, it also usually meant leaving their families behind for up to a year (the traditional hiring period), adjusting to a difficult, sometimes dangerous work routine, and dealing with employers who were at times harsh and ruthless. As a result, most slaves felt they should take part in decisions about how, when, and to whom they were to be hired. They wanted to know about their new employers, travel distances, work routine, days off, accommodations, clothing, wages, family visitations. When masters failed to accommodate them or when hirelings became dissatisfied with employers, conflicts arose.

The problem for slave owners was that the most talented, skilled, and proficient slaves—those who could be most easily hired at the best wages—were also the most self-confident and independent. Up to a point, both slave and master benefited if a slave took charge, demonstrated know-how, showed initiative, and worked without supervision. The difficulty occurred when slaves, at least in the minds of owners or employers, crossed the line. "My man Hansel and Mr. Brister it appears has fallen out," a slave owner in Southampton County, Virginia, wrote in 1832, a year after the Nat Turner uprising. "[W]ill you be good enough to go with Hansel home, and have the matter investigated, and if you think from all the circumstances that he ought to be corrected I am willing it should be done." But Hansel had already left, simply walked away, ironically not because of any disagreement with his employer, James Brister, a farmer near Jerusalem, but because of a conflict with one of Brister's slaves, "old Charlotte." The reason for his departure, however, was less important than the comments of an observer concerning Hansel: he was "permitted to do almost as he pleased," while what he needed was "a good whipping." Indeed, "the Negro acted more like his Master than otherwise."[9]

Some hired slaves failed to show up at an employer's business or plantation, avoided work when they got there, left without permission, kept a portion of their wages, visited families and friends without permission, and demanded concessions. "I have a boy in my employ called Jim Archer," a Vicksburg, Mississippi, man wrote in 1843; "Jim does not want to be under anyones control and says Mr. Brown has no claim on him and he wants to go home this summer." The teenage slave Ephraim seemed to care little that he had been purchased for the express purpose of providing an income for the widow Ruth Riley in her old age. Taken to the hamlet of Anderson, South Carolina, Ephraim refused to be hired to certain employers and, when hired out, would wander off and not return. Because of her "extreme old age," the widow explained, she was "unable to govern, or dispose of the said negro advantageously." In a similar case, a white widow sought to provide for herself and her three children by hiring out a slave given her in trust by her deceased father. The hired slave, named Feriley, however, kept most of the earnings that were supposed to go into the trust. The funds from the slave's hire were "very inadequate," the owner noted; her trustee failed to devote "prudent and proper attention, care and management" to Feriley, and the slave had become very willful and self-sufficient.[10]

Masters who failed to exert "prudent and proper attention" often ran into trouble with hired slaves. The hired South Carolina slave Charles, a blacksmith by trade, was proud of the fact that there was "no white man around him." When his owner announced he was moving to Mississippi, Charles refused to accompany him unless the master agreed to take his wife. At different times, he shoved one white man to the ground, threatened another, and told a third that "no white man ever had or ever would master him." When the owner's overseer attempted to whip him, he took the whip away and "struck him, and went on his way." Even when the slave was subdued and flogged "it had no effect on him; he would curse his master as soon as taken down." Apparently, Dudley, a hired field hand in Madison Parish, Louisiana, felt the same way. Ordered to work by an overseer, Dudley picked up his hoe and slashed the overseer in the face. Besides the "great physical suffering and loss of time occasioned by said act of said slave," the overseer was "impaired" for life.[11]

For some hired slaves resistance was more devious. Following the death of her master, the twenty-six-year-old slave Ellen, who was described as "a good hand, and a very good looking negro," was hired out to a family in Davidson County, Tennessee, by the minor heirs of her former owner. As a hireling, she cleaned, washed, made beds, folded linens, swept, and cooked. After being with the family a few months, "She gave my wife a roasted apple to eat," George McMurry, the slave owner who had hired Ellen, explained. Upon cutting open the apple "to divide between my Children my wife discovered that there was something unusual placed upon the inside of it." The "something unusual" was mercury, or quicksilver. Ellen had taken a knife, scraped mercury off the back side of a mirror, carefully poked a hole in the core of an apple, poured the mercury into the hole, and roasted the apple.[12]

Open Defiance

If scholars have examined covert resistance to some extent, they have devoted less attention to open individual defiance. In fact, slavery by its very nature created a milieu for interracial conflict. Slaves on occasion refused to work, demanded concessions, rejected orders, threatened whites, and sometimes reacted with violence. Verbal and physical confrontations occurred regularly, without regard to time and place. Indeed, despite severe punishments, or perhaps because of them, these challenges to white authority remained as much a part of the peculiar institution as the ubiquitous slave trader.

Slaves responded in such a manner when they were chastised and punished, witnessed the harsh treatment of loved ones, or became frustrated by their condition. They reacted to being traded or sold or to having family members traded or sold. The master of Allen, a South Carolina slave, noted the change in the black man's behavior after he had been sent to another member of the same slave-owning family in a trust estate. He became, in the words of his new owner, "unfaithful, unreliable, and vicious." Some slaves responded to new conditions by refusing to obey orders, threatening fellow blacks or overseers, or striking out against white authority. They became, owners observed, disobedient, troublesome, fractious, and violent. "I have caught him stealing meat soap and other things from my locked houses," a Maryland master said of a slave named Barton; he had also caught Barton robbing the henhouses. For three or four years, Barton had been "very insolent to me personally using threats." When called up "in a proper manner" by a white man, the slave became "very insolent" and attacked him with an axe "evidently with the intent of Killing him." The man fired at the slave and grazed his neck with a ball. "He is a vindictive bad boy," the owner confessed, "and I do not feel safe with him about me."[13]

Open defiance was not uncommon. In fact, in most sections of the South, some slaves were known by residents in the area as "vicious and violent." Burton Conner, a Kent County, Delaware, slaveholder, described his slave Caleb as "much addicted to stealing & has sustained an extremely bad character in your petitioner[']s family and throughout the neighbourhood." Caleb had committed numerous depredations, had a violent disposition, and had run away on a previous occasion for a period of eighteen months. Conner's neighbors signed a petition to have the slave sent out of the state, asserting that he was a "common plunderer and a dangerous man." The same phrase could be applied to the Charleston, South Carolina, slave Davy, who in 1800 suddenly rose up against his owner and his owner's wife. In the struggle that ensued, Davy killed them both. He then robbed the storehouse and set out across the countryside.[14]

Similarly, Big Sandy, owned by Robert Davis of Baton Rouge, Louisiana, was well known for his contempt of white authority. At six feet and 175 pounds, he was described as a "large raw boned negro," a man of unusual strength, and even at age about fifty, he was given a wide berth by most whites. When in 1856 an overseer on a plantation in West Feliciana ordered him to put down his hoe to be corrected "for some misdemeanor," Sandy said that he "would not put his hoe down, that no white man should whip him, that he would die first." The overseer drew a pistol, but Sandy refused to submit, declaring that he feared neither the white man nor his pistol.[15]

Such confrontations were not confined to farms and plantations. Slaves encountered whites in a variety of settings—on streets, sidewalks, steamboats, trains, country roads—where words might be exchanged and slaves might offer resistance. Such was the case on the back road leading from Centreville to Maplesville, Alabama, in 1834, when John Richardson, a white man, met a slave named Sam, owned by Jason Pool, and the two men argued. The exact sequence of events was not reported, but the bondsman grabbed the white man's knife and "with great force & violence wickedly willfully and maliciously assaulted & struck the Said John Richardson a great many violent strokes & blows on the head neck Shoulders arms breast hips thighs & leggs." Such attacks and other violent acts prompted a group of western Tennessee slave owners to admit that "Slaves who are dissatisfied frequently commit capital offenses."[16]

Neither age nor gender was a determining factor in predicting who might resist in such a manner. One elderly slave married couple threatened to harm their owner if he did not desist in ordering them about. The master, an older man himself, sent the two to live with his son-in-law on a plantation in an adjacent county, but apparently the new master also had difficulty controlling the slaves. They remained with him less than a year before running away and returning to their original master. At the other end of the age spectrum were two Maryland slaves—twelve-year-old Sarah of St. Mary's County, and fifteen-year-old Henny of Baltimore—who were "so bad & unmanageable," so "notoriously vicious and turbulent," that it seemed impossible to reform their behavior.[17]

Black women had a unique perspective on what was tolerable, especially when it came to protecting their children. In such cases, they were likely to refuse to do certain jobs, disobey orders, speak out, or react violently. Even though Elizabeth had "grown up" in a South Carolina slaveholding family, they could not "train her up to be useful" as a handmaiden to a white teenager. She had two children of her own, she asserted, and would not act in such a capacity. Another South Carolina slave was ordered in a deed of trust to care for a young white girl "of a weak and sickly constitution, an unfortunate cripple, incapable of assisting herself, and requiring constant care, and the best attention." The woman refused to care for the sickly white girl since it would interfere with her caring for her own son. In other instances, slave women responded after being transferred to a new owner. When Maria and her two children were transferred to a South Carolina tailor as part of a trust estate, the slave became intractable and disobedient and on one occasion Maria slapped the tailor's wife. In Frederick County, Maryland, one slaveholding man described his female slave Matilda as malevolent, a woman who had on several occasions attacked both him and his wife, "striking and otherwise acting in a vicious and turbulent manner."[18]

Even slaves who were thought to be mild mannered and obedient sometimes reached a breaking point. Having never reacted violently, the house servant of a Louisiana woman "returned the blow" as she was being physically chastised by her owner, threw her mistress to the ground, and "beat her unmercifully, on the head and face." The white woman's face swelled up and turned black. "I could not have known her, by seeing her," a visitor at the plantation said a few weeks later, "poor little woman is confined to her bed yet" and remains "dangerously ill."[19] The slaves who resisted in such a manner lived on small farms and large plantations, in towns and cities, in the Lower and Upper South; they included field hands, skilled artisans, house servants, and hirees; they were men, women, boys, girls, and the very old.

Slaves and Overseers

Slaves often bore particular resentment toward overseers. After all, overseers were white but had done little with their position of advantage and were as subject to the owners' whims as were the slaves themselves. Slaves resented being chided, scolded, chastised, punished, and whipped; they disliked being supervised during their work day by young, inexperienced white men who moved to the next plantation within a few months or years; they bitterly resented threats against their families if certain work was not completed satisfactorily within a certain period of time.[20]

On some plantations, slaves attempted to undermine the overseer's authority in subtle and surreptitious ways, while on others they criticized him openly, complaining to the owner about harsh or unfair treatment. At times, the tensions between slaves and overseers or between slaves, drivers, and overseers erupted into verbal and physical confrontations. On some plantations, such clashes occurred so often that it was difficult for overseers to inflict punishments for every incident; on other estates, interracial disputes occurred less frequently, but punishments were systematic and severe.

On a few plantations, overseers were even afraid to chastise slaves. One of the approximately thirty slaves owned by the children of a Middle Tennessee planter who died in 1851, Jim worked as a field hand on a 400-acre tract of the family property. During the 1850s, the widow hired a new overseer every one or two years. Each of them experienced difficulty with Jim, who sneaked out at night, broke into neighbors' homes, and stole various items. But it was more than the thievery that concerned the overseers. "I know the boy Jim and have known him since he was a child," Archibald J. Strickland, a fifty-seven-year-old overseer who spent most of his life in the profession, said in 1860. Jim was about twenty-five years old, large, strong, healthy, and weighed between 160 or 175 pounds. His disposition was "very bad, he is very difficult to control, and is disposed to & does resist those who control him, and it is dangerous to attempt to correct or chastise him, without being prepared with weapons to subdue him." Jim had a violent temper, and an overseer ran the risk, "in every difficulty with him, either of being killed by him, or of being compelled to kill him, or inflict upon him great personal injury in self-defense." Nor was Strickland the only overseer who had experienced difficulty in handling Jim who, a second white manager said, was violent, quarrelsome, aggressive, and "disposed to & does resist those who attempt to control him, and will fight with anything he can get."[21]

In fact, many overseers were forced to deal with slaves who were quarrelsome, difficult to control, and disposed to resist. That boldness such as Jim's persisted for so many years can only be explained by the fact that it was not especially unique. There were more than a few overseers—and masters as well—who feared a possible violent response by the slaves. Their anxiety was more than justified. When Phillip and James became dissatisfied with conditions on Chatham Plantation, Stafford County, Virginia, they assaulted William Fitzhugh's overseer and attempted to escape. Phillip was shot by a member of a local militia, and James drowned attempting to swim the Rappahannock River. Local residents called the turmoil at Chatham an "insurrection."[22]

Although violent reactions against overseers occurred in every region of the South, they were particularly widespread in the Lower Mississippi River Valley. The endless toil of clearing land, planting grains, cotton, and sugar, coupled with the unhealthy climate and the stifling heat during the summer months, made life at best a continuous, grinding routine of work. During the harvest season on sugar plantations, slaves labored in gangs sixteen hours a day, cutting stalks, grinding, boiling, and manufacturing the final product. Nor were slaveholders in the region as likely as in the rice planting sections of South Carolina and Georgia to implement the task system. Not unlike the Caribbean, some masters believed it was more profitable to buy new slaves, work them incessantly, hoping they would survive five or six years and pay for themselves before they died. As a result, there were rumors that along the Red River, and other tributaries of the Mississippi, conditions were so bad that census takers were not permitted to count the inhabitants.[23]

Most slave owners in West Feliciana Parish, Louisiana, knew that the slaves on Charles Stewart's Magnolia Plantation were "notoriously rebellious insubordinate & disorderly." It would have been a difficult task under the best of circumstances for an overseer to manage the slave labor force, but the proprietor made it even worse by failing to support his overseers, who came and went almost every winter. One of them was Samuel Cowgill [also spelled Cowgil], who was hired as superintendent in March 1826 and dismissed in September of that same year. Determined to establish discipline, Cowgill believed that it was his "duty to himself & his Employer to inflict punishment." This plan lasted less than two months when he chose the wrong slave to punish. Pompey picked up a plantation axe, swung it at Cowgill, slashed his wrist and made a "long & deep incision" cutting the tendons. Cowgill never regained the use of his hand, which, he later said, hung by his side in "a most awkward position."

Nonetheless, a month later, he again sought to perform his duty by correcting Cato, who, "armed with a long Knife & a club" sought to kill the overseer by making several passes at his body but in the end only cut the little finger off of his left hand. Indirectly, the plantation owner encouraged "overt refractory Conduct," Cowgill charged, because the owner "actually accredits & listens to every idle tale, which said slaves may carry to him about the Overseer."[24]

On some plantations, conflicts between slaves and overseers created tumult in the quarters. In 1857, a Louisiana sugar planter employed an overseer and as part of the bargain promised to pay him extra if he brought along a slave family he owned. The overseer agreed, but when he took them to the plantation they refused to work. The defiance of the overseer's slaves, one observer noted, caused great "disturbances among the negroes." On the plantation of Mary Weeks in the sugar country of the Attakapas region, two slaves were shot "and dangerously wounded by the overseer." Receiving word of the shootings, Weeks's sister in West Feliciana Parish, Rachel O'Connor, lamented that one of the slaves was Harry, whom she had once owned. "I am afraid the overseer is to blame," she said, "so many turn out bad." The accusation, however, apparently did not take into account the fact that Harry had run away twice in two years, which perhaps complicated the relationship between Harry and the overseer.[25]

In an atmosphere of such animosity it was little wonder that "so many turn out bad." Slaves confronted overseers with verbal assaults and physical force; they also attempted to intimidate their white managers. While such defiance was more common in some regions than in others, there were few plantations where slaves worked diligently and willingly under the direction of an experienced, discerning, and sagacious overseer. Far more common was an undercurrent of distrust, hostility, anger, confrontation, and periodic eruptions of violence.

Conspiracies

What slaves did and what they conspired to do, of course, were two different things. That whites became terrified at rumored conspiracies should not be cited as evidence that no such schemes existed. Indeed, some of their fears were fully justified. Several large-scale plots were uncovered before they could be implemented, including Gabriel's in 1800 and Sancho's in 1802, both in Virginia, and Denmark Vesey's in South Carolina in 1822. Two slave revolts actually took place, one in Jefferson Parish, Louisiana Territory, in 1811, and the other, the famous Nat Turner revolt in 1831.[26] But each of these spawned other conspiracies, and there were a number of instances where slaves secretly planned, or at least discussed, violent retribution against their owners and other whites.

In the same year as the Sancho conspiracy, for instance, fifteen or twenty slaves were arrested and jailed in Mecklenburg County, Virginia, following rumors that they were plotting to poison whites. Only two were found guilty: the "very artful" Frank, described as having a "vicious disposition" and being "proud & malignant, with great impudence" and Dick, who was under Frank's influence. Eight years later, in Edgefield District, South Carolina, a slave was charged with having knowledge of a planned slave rebellion. Another South Carolina plot was discovered in 1829 on the testimony of a slave owned by Ann Paisley of Georgetown District. As the accused were being held under sentence of death, whites heard that a slave "Connected with the plot in Charleston in 1822" was planning to rally his brethren at the gallows on the day of the scheduled executions and rescue those condemned. As a consequence, between July 23, when the plot was uncovered, and November, the court ordered special guard units of ten men to watch over the town twenty-four hours a day.[27]

Also in 1829, but not connected with the Vesey plot, was a scheme uncovered in West Feliciana Parish, Louisiana. During the Christmas holidays, slaves from several plantations living along Thompson's Creek began to make plans for an insurrection. Before the design could be brought to fruition, however, a black woman who had overheard the plotting informed her master. The slave owners responded quickly, and according to a local planter, put a halt to the "wickedness by hanging two negroes." A search was made for one or two white men who might have been involved, but by January 1830 nothing had been proved. Two more slaves were later caught. They, too, would have been hanged "if justice had taken place," a local man observed, but their owners "were rich, which proved excuse enough to save them."[28]

There is little doubt that some of the insurrection scares were the result of panic-stricken whites fearing the worst. Such was the case in October 1831, in the wake of the Nat Turner revolt, when a Louisiana white woman spread the word that "all the Negroes on little Robert Barrow's plantation had armed themselves and claimed there [sic] liberty." Upon hearing the news, one plantation mistress "instantly started screaming & crying as loud as she could" and the general of the local militia rode off to the plantation "where he found the overseer, and the negroes very busy gathering in the crop, as peaceable as lambs, and not one word of truth in the report." An observer said that the slaves were all "shockingly frightened at the Patrols being ordered out."[29]

But there were probably as many actual plots as imagined plots. The uncovering of several conspiracies in the early 1840s was probably no mere coincidence. In 1840, Kentucky antislavery leader James G. Birney ran for president on the Liberty Party ticket. During the campaign, the debates about halting the expansion of slavery into the territories and the gradual abolition of slavery filtered into slave quarters. There was a remarkable communication network among slaves, and such debates may well have contributed directly to several conspiracies.[30]

"Since you left we have information that a number of Negros in the neighborhood of the Barrow settlement and Bayou Sarah [West Feliciana Parish] have been detected in a conspiracy and rebellion," Moses Liddell, a Louisiana planter, wrote to a relative 21 July 1841. The relative, John Liddell, owned a plantation on Black River near Harrisonburg, Catahoula Parish, a safe distance away, but both planters were very much concerned about such news and how it might affect their slaves. About eighty had already been captured and jailed, and several white men had offered "confessions and disclosures." The discovery was made in mid-July, but in all probability more conspirators would be exposed since, as Liddell wrote, "the second of August was the time appointed by them" to put their plan into operation.[31]

Standing near a slave cabin in 1841, a visitor at John D. Thomasson's sugar plantation in West Baton Rouge Parish, Louisiana, accidentally overheard a conversation between a black man and woman. He was surprised when the woman asked the man, Harry, who was visiting from a neighboring plantatation, if he had "made use of the barrel of powder." He replied that he had; she asked him how many musket balls he had made. He said that if Jerry, a slave, had made five the night before "there must be one hundred and fifty." She asked where the powder and balls were hidden. The powder was "in the Sugar house under the cooler in the ground" and the balls were in Jerry's cabin, hidden in the loft covered by corn, as well as in the sugarhouse. A noise prevented the listener from hearing whether or not the slaves had "a weapon," presumably a musket or knives, but he did hear the end of the conversation:[32]

She asked him, "are your going to Kill every body?"
And he answered "Yes."

She Said "it would be a pity to Kill the little children."
And he said "we will burn the roofs down on them."

If the chances of a white man's eavesdropping outside a slave cabin
and hearing a conversation about plans to burn down roofs over the
heads of women and children seemed remote, perhaps even more far-
fetched was the possibility of black conspirators *writing letters* about
a planned insurrection. Considering that only a small fraction of the
slave population was literate, and writing down any plan was extremely dangerous, the letter written 6 October 1845 by an anonymous North Carolina slave was truly unique. Though at times difficult
to decipher, the meaning was clear:

> we rite to you to let you know that we have concluded to wate
> till the night before the jeneral muster before we make the trial
> to get aur freedom. thar was a good manny black wons from
> rowan aver here last night evry thing is redy thar they ar all a
> gaing to meet Sailsbory and brake the jail apen the first thing
> they doo and take the pepl out and then come to river and gard
> the bride and all the ferreys they will shot evry man that wont
> go with them

He said they would obtain guns, powder, and shot in Salisbury. He
expected three hundred slaves to participate, the plotters having appointed unit captains. When they arrived in Lexington, they "must
tye all the whites the first thing," he instructed; "dont kill nun if you
can help it." He said that the slaves should be provided with liquor—
"make all the men drunk an you can make em doo any thing"—and
told his coconspirators to "be reddy by dark and we will com by midnight all the runaway blacks jines us that night." Meanwhile, he
added gravely, "dont let a Single whit person see this or we will all
get Killed the blacks is redy all over the cuntry."[33]

While few slaves wrote out their plans, there were a number of
other plots. "We had a small move towards an insurrection not long
since but we stopped it instanter," a Louisiana planter wrote in 1848,
"no damage done." In the same year, however, some damage was done
when seventy-six slaves from the District of Columbia slipped on
board the schooner *Pearl* in the early morning hours. They forced the
three white seamen to cast off and, catching a good wind, sailed silently
down the Potomac River toward the Chesapeake Bay. When it was
discovered the following morning that the slaves were missing, a group
of slave owners expressed fear that if the fugitives were overtaken they
would offer a "desperate resistance," but a large force of armed men

on the steamboat *Salem* overtook the schooner and "succeeded in re-capturing and securing" the slaves.[34]

In the fall of 1856, an insurrection panic swept across the South from Texas to Virginia. Many slave owners were certain that the rumors were true, and so, too, were political leaders. At John Bell's iron-works along the Cumberland River in Tennessee, sixty-five slaves were arrested and nine executed. "Quite an excitement here at this time about the insurrection of the negroes," a Virginia man wrote his brother a few days before Christmas. "It was to have taken place to-morrow night but I hope it has been timely arrested." The scheme was known to slaves "all over the state," he said, and Governor Henry Wise had sent cannon and ammunition to Alexandria "to quell the Negroes in that place."[35]

The Price of Dissidence

Neither the "trial to git aur freedom" outlined by the anonymous North Carolina slave in 1845 nor subsequent movements toward insurrection ever came to fruition. Even so, they were more than figments of any master's imagination. There is little doubt that slaves conspired at various times to seek retribution against their owners and obtain their freedom. Some of the plans never went beyond a slave cabin or a small group of conspirators, while others were known about by tens and hundreds of possible recruits. A case in point is free black David Walker, a Boston resident formerly of North Carolina. His *Appeal, in Four Articles* in 1829 not only condemned slavery but urged on all people in bondage to rise up against their masters. Although the *Appeal* did not result in any known conspiracies, it caused fear and consternation throughout the South. In 1830, Walker died rather mysteriously, and some believed that he came to his end "otherwise than by the usual visitation of the providence of God."[36]

It was not known exactly how many slaves were influenced in 1839 by Virginia slave Jarrett, who circulated a "certain writing denying the right of Masters to property in their slaves and inculcating the duty of resistance to such rights." The Loudoun County Court believed his influence was significant. The five justices found Jarrett guilty and sentenced him to be "transported and Sold beyond the Limits of the United States."[37]

Most plots and conspiracies were either discovered or collapsed in the early stages of planning. That only a few revolts came to fruition was not due to the "paternalistic" attitudes of masters who permitted slaves so much autonomy that few wanted to rebel. Rather, they found other means to demonstrate their dissatisfaction. That so many did individually or in small groups reflected their conviction that the chances of success were significantly greater than with large-scale resistance.

Whether alone or with others, however, those who challenged the system paid a heavy price. The argument that slaves were not treated harshly because they were valuable property ignores the conviction among most slave owners and many other whites that severe chastisement would serve as a deterrent. Those who openly defied the owner, plantation manager, or overseer were usually dealt with quickly and ruthlessly. They were whipped, beaten, cropped, branded, and sometimes tortured. They were sold away from their families or watched as their children were turned over to slave traders. Those found guilty or sometimes merely accused of serious "crimes"—arson, assault, rape, attempted murder, conspiracy, poisoning—were banished or hanged.[38]

Typical responses of whites to some of the slave rebels were the following:

"Harry & Roberson I caught," a Louisiana owner wrote, "I stake Harry and gave him 175 lashes and Roberson 150."

Despite his "getting old," and the master's lament that he would bring only $850, Tennessee slave Big Ike was auctioned off to a slave trader for $1,110.

The young South Carolina man Ephraim was sold.

A receipt told of Davy's fate: "To Materials viz. Wood, tar, post & chains &cet: furnished for the Execution of a Negro fellow named Davey found Guilty of & Sentenced to be burnt for Robbery & Murder."

The overseer on the Louisiana plantation where Big Sandy worked said: "I had him secured and flogged him."

The Alabama slave Sam was sentenced to be hanged.

The man who administered the punishment on the South Carolina slave Elizabeth for refusing to serve a young white girl said he whipped her until she was in excruciating pain.

Shortly after slapping her mistress's face, South Carolina slave Maria was sold away from her children. The tailor used the money to purchase a new sewing machine.[39]

2

On the Run

ALONG THE WESTERN shore of Chesapeake Bay, the winter months of 1831–32 were harsh. The ground froze early and remained frozen until early spring. Although plowing and planting were delayed, the slaves on Doughoregan Manor (the House of Kings) in Anne Arundel County, the favorite plantation of Charles Carroll of Carrollton, went about their other daily chores much as in previous years. The last to survive among the signers of the Declaration of Independence, Carroll was an immensely wealthy man, owning a number of plantations, residential and business properties in Baltimore and Annapolis, stock certificates in banks and incorporated companies, outstanding debts and claims, herds of livestock, and a great many slaves. Indeed, during the late winter and early spring, more than 215 black men and women at the Manor were tending the horses, cattle, sheep, and hogs, mending fences, hauling rails, and making ready to plant wheat, rye, corn, and tobacco.[1]

Like other patriarchs of his generation, Carroll had struggled with the paradox of fighting for liberty with Great Britain while maintaining chattel slavery at home. And like many others, he considered himself a kind master who cared for "his people." He believed "his people" were contented with their lot, and it was best for them to remain in bondage since few would be able to survive on their own. On his plantation most slaves lived as families, and nineteen were either extremely old (in their seventies and eighties) or crippled or suffered from other maladies. As listed in Carroll's inventory, the nineteen were considered nearly worthless, appraised at one penny each.

When Carroll died quietly on 14 November 1832 at age ninety-five, it seemed as if the transition from the old order to the new would be smooth. He had written a will, added codicils, and provided generously for his children, grandchildren, and their families. But ten days after his death, Charles Carroll of Homewood, an heir, arrived and demanded the keys to "the Pantry &c" as well as a listing of all the personal holdings and rental incomes. When the plantation manager, William Gibbons, who had been at the Manor for eleven years, refused, the younger Carroll ordered him off the property, threatening to use force if necessary.[2]

The breakdown of order among the slaves following the departure of Gibbons was so rapid and widespread that even the most ardent abolitionist would have been astonished. The new supervisor quickly lost control of the situation. Negroes were "running at large," "doing nothing," or "getting drunk," a tenant farmer living on the Manor observed; they refused to work, or just milled around. Some were lying out, others escaped altogether. Among the latter were Andrew and Moses, who told others that this was their chance to break for freedom. Few were willing to go to such an extreme, but one recruit, John, joined the two runaways. The three went to nearby Homewood Plantation, hid out in the slave quarters, and began to make plans for the future.

In the midst of this turmoil, only a week and a half after younger Carroll had arrived, Gibbons was brought back and put in charge. Returning to the Manor, he was shocked by the disorder. The first order of business was to retrieve the runaways, and he immediately set out with his assistant to do so, traveling first to Baltimore, then to Homewood, where he found the three deserters. Andrew refused to be taken without a fight, and hit Gibbons's assistant in the mouth with his fist before being subdued. He was put in jail. Moses and John promised to reform themselves if they were allowed to return, and Gibbons acquiesced. No sooner had they returned, however, than Moses again ran away, and this time he, too, was incarcerated. Andrew was "always refractory," the manager said, and Moses was "very much of a desperado." What was worse, they were obviously having "a very improper influence upon the rest of the men." Andrew and Moses were sold at auction. After word of the sales spread through the quarters, Gibbons said, the "people have been in orderly conduct."[3]

That the system of bondage could disintegrate so rapidly reveals how fragile the institution was when management broke down even for a few days. As the legatees said, if the slaves were not put immediately under the supervision of "some responsible person" the estate would be "greatly wasted, injured and diminished in value, to the irreparable injury & loss of all who are interested."[4] It was not as if there were no whites in charge or that Charles Carroll of Homewood was an inexperienced planter. Rather, the brief episode indicated one of the situations in which slaves might seek a taste of freedom.

Death of the Master

The death of an owner and the replacement of an overseer or plantation manager was only one condition that prompted slaves to run away. Others included a fear of being sold or transferred, dissatisfaction with a new master, unhappiness with persons appointed by the court (guardians, trustees, administrators) to direct their work routine, and ill-treatment.[5] Of course, slaves and owners differed as to what constituted ill-treatment, as did masters among themselves and slaves among themselves. For some it took an egregious breach, for others a mere argument. The catalog of other areas of conflict that might prompt slaves to go on the run seemed endless: work routine; food allotments; spousal visitations; clothing; housing; Sunday work; incentive payments; hiring arrangements; being sold, transferred, traded to another plantation; or having a family member sold, transferred, or traded. At times it seemed as if there were no specific cause other than it would be a good or opportune time to leave. To examine the motives of those who challenged the system does injustice to the complexities of the human experience. Yet, an analysis of the conditions and factors that caused slaves to go "on the run" is one of the best ways to comprehend the attitudes of slaves, as well as the cruel, often inhuman nature of the South's peculiar institution.

As was the case at Doughoregan Manor, a master's death caused fear and apprehension in the slave quarters. Slave families were at the mercy of legatees or heirs, who might wish to transfer workers from one plantation to another, or creditors, who might merely want ready cash. Even among "benevolent" masters who left specific instructions concerning black families (most often defined in probate records as a mother and her children) slaves might find themselves in frightful circumstances. Sometimes their worst nightmares were realized when they were turned over to factors, commission merchants, or slave traders to be sold to the deep South. Also, before being sold or transferred, they were often hired out to produce income for the estate. For these reasons, slaves viewed the master's passing with great anxiety, and some among them viewed it as a time to attempt an escape.

"It is very likely that he will forge himself a free pass," the administrator of Robert Hill's estate in Buckingham County, Virginia, said in 1808 of Jack Going, a literate and privileged slave. Jack had stolen a saddle from his recently deceased owner's barn and made off on a horse. He feared being sold or sent away to relatives of his late owner. The same anxiety could be seen in the actions of three North Carolina slaves who ran into a swamp when they learned that their master had died. As it happened, their premonition was correct. The husband of an Alabama woman who had inherited the three wrote in September 1822 that the three had not been received because of their "Desertion—on or about the 10th day of Feby 1821 & had not yet bin Apprehended." Because of the "Frequent Total Loss of Negroes in that Section of the Country by Desertion being Coverd with those Immence Swamps so camman thair," the husband advised that the remaining slaves inherited by his wife be auctioned off as soon as possible. Otherwise, she would "Never reseave Any Benny fit from them." Learning of the passing of their owner, two Florida slaves, John and Tom, responded in a similar fashion, but chose the woods rather than a swamp. Their worst fears proved to be correct. With creditors clamoring for payment, a county probate judge granted Harriet Long, the owner's wife and the administrator of his estate, permission to sell the two men "as soon as they can be caught."[6]

Those who absconded following their owners' death often had the same motives as Jack Going, the three Negro men, or John and Tom. They feared a change in status, being sent away, or being sold. It was not a simple decision, however, since it often involved leaving loved ones who might not be able to accompany them or follow only with great difficulty. Sometimes slaves waited to see how things would turn out before making a determination. Such was the case for Sam, who had been with his master for seventeen years and had journeyed with him from Virginia to Kentucky in 1793. Sam's family was never mentioned, but it was clear that his loved ones lived nearby. Following his owner's death, Sam was turned over (as directed in the owner's last will and testament) to the husband of his deceased owner's sister and was to be hired out for the benefit of that family's children. The next year, in 1810, Sam fled, left the state, and remained away for three years. Yearning for his own family, he reappeared in 1813, was arrested, returned to his new owner, and hired out as originally planned. When the last of the family's children became an adult in 1818, Sam was sold to the slave brokerage firm of William H. Morton & Company for $650. A short time later, the company sold him to Levi Hart, who had many contacts in the New Orleans market.[7]

If Sam's decision came only after months of deliberation, others responded quickly when opportunities presented themselves, taking advantage of a breakdown in discipline, failure of communication, or conflicts among whites at the time of the owner's death. On large plantations, it took weeks, sometimes months, to complete a full inventory. While widows, overseers, and managers attempted to maintain control during this period, slaves could sometimes be absent for days before it was known. Indeed, those who disappeared during the mourning period usually achieved a good head start. The executor of

Richard Benbury's estate in North Carolina, for example, did not advertise one slave as a runaway for six months. He probably thought the man would return on his own, but it was also clear that the slave had been missing some time before it was discovered he was gone. When the administrator of Joseph Guthrow's property finally arrived on the scene in Baltimore County, Maryland, in 1827 and completed an inventory of the holdings, he discovered that one of the female slaves was absent. After a diligent search, he learned that she had "absconded and run away." She had too great a head start, he concluded, and should not be considered as part of the estate inventory except as a total loss.[8]

Another slave "lost" to an estate was Clarissa, a Virginia woman owned by Henry Love, who during the mid-1820s moved with his bride to Nashville, Tennessee. Clarissa and eight other slaves were left behind with Love's brother and sister until the newlyweds could get settled. When word came back that the master had suddenly and unexpectedly died, three slaves—Clarissa and Polly and her child—ran away. Love's widow later complained that the brother "never took any measures to reduce said girl to his possession," send anyone after her when he learned she had absconded, or advertised her as a runaway. As a consequence, Clarissa "is entirely lost." Polly and her child, on the other hand, were captured, returned, and auctioned off for $450.[9]

If the death of owners prompted slaves to run away, so, too, did their being turned over to slaveholders' guardians. The lives of slaves changed dramatically when they came under the management of patrons who were responsible for generating an income for their slave-owning wards—children, insane, incapacitated adults, or women bound by a trust. Previously under the direct supervision of their owners, they were now turned over to plantation managers or hired out from year to year. The response to their new circumstance was rarely one of acquiescence and often included malingering, hiding wages, refusing to hire, rejecting certain employers, truancy, or running away. The actions of forty-three-year-old Louisville slave Joshua, hired out to provide an income for an orphan, were not unusual. He "frequently absents himself," the guardian wrote, "staying away a long time." The income he produced was negligible, and at that very moment, the guardian believed, he was devising a plan to "runaway to a free state."[10]

Other slaves under the management of guardians proved to be no less diligent in their search for opportunities to stay away for "a long time." Eighteen-year-old Henry was in the habit of absconding from his employers and was "very disobedient." Others hired out by guardians were described as incorrigible, difficult to manage, obstreperous, and willing to go on the run. Isaac had "got into the habit of running away & lying out, and also committing crimes and misdemeanors in the neighbourhood," a group of trustees for a woman in Cheraw District, South Carolina, said. He became so difficult to control that it was "necessary to Keep him confined in Jail." This not only reduced his value, the trustees asserted, but operated injuriously on other slaves. Among those recently turned over to his charge, one guardian lamented in 1848, a young male had already escaped, fleeing to another state, where he was "not likely to be regained."[11]

Thus, slaves under the supervision of guardians tested the limits of white control. If the hiring process loosened the bonds between master and slave, hiring by guardians—with their varied interests, business activities, slaves of their own, and other concerns—loosened them even more. This was especially true when sizable groups of them were hired out to different employers by a single guardian. The difficulties of hiring out many slaves, guardians complained, created numerous problems of control.[12]

But even those who remained on the same farm or plantation tested the authority and resolve of guardians who resided a distance from their wards. When widower Noland M. Luckett, a Texas planter, died in the mid-1850s, a relative living in Travis County (Austin) took over the guardianship of Luckett's two minor children. The estate included a 1,665-acre farm in Williamson County, Texas, as well as landholdings in Mississippi and Louisiana. There were eleven slaves. With land, money, and blacks worth an estimated $18,800, the guardian anticipated little trouble providing for the children. But his reports to the court noted otherwise. Only a few of the slaves were of hiring age; among them, the most highly valued was Margaret, in her twenties, having a projected income of $150 a year. It was very difficult to hire Margaret at a profit. Even when she was left on the farm, she proved to be very troublesome, the guardian lamented, and was "in the habit of frequently running away." On one occasion she remained out five and a half months. She made it to Fayette County, sixty miles down the Colorado River from Williamson County, before being arrested and jailed. In all, it was nearly impossible to provide an adequate income for the children, the guardian complained, with Margaret as the most "valuable" slave.[13]

Lastly, although rare, some slaves slipped through the cracks in the system after an owner's death. They did not exactly run away, but left the premises and assumed a new identity as a hired slave or free person of color, sometimes in the same neighborhood or county. This most often occurred in urban areas, but it was not completely unknown in the countryside. One remarkable case involved the Bibb County, Alabama, slave Dick, who on the death of his master in 1850 or 1851 went out on his own without free papers or having been emancipated. Dick hired himself out as a ditcher, then opened a shoe shop in Maplesville in 1855, and later a candy-cheese-tobacco shop. He hired four whites and two blacks to work in his shoe shop and bought two "negro boys named Washington & Turner." One witness said that Dick "hired himself out made his own contracts collected the Money earned by his labor bought & Sold horses and traded & acted generally as a free man."[14]

The events surrounding the death of a master—the transfer or sale of slaves, disputes among legatees, appointment of guardians, hiring out of estate slaves—not only created anxiety and concern among bondsmen and women but sometimes provided opportunities for escape. Some feared being sold to distant lands or being turned over to a slave trader, others were apprehensive about losing their privileged positions, and not a few simply saw it as a good time to run. In any event, that blacks would choose a grieving period to break their ties with the master class suggests a combination of hostility and opportunism.

The Plantation Household

Besides an owner's death, other circumstances exposed fear and apprehension among the slaves. They watched, listened, and waited, and in the tiny world of the farm or plantation, they quickly learned about difficulties within slaveholding families. They knew when masters drank to excess, experienced health problems, encountered family and marital difficulties, or faced financial woes. They witnessed or learned about the arguments, hostilities, jealousies, and hatreds among family members, the violence of husbands against wives, and the excessive attention of some masters to their female slaves. When these problems, conflicts, and involvements impaired the ability of the masters to manage their slaves, when they became careless or lackadaisical or preoccupied, slaves then exploited the situation. In not a few instances, they responded by lying out or running away.[15]

The amount of alcohol consumed by slave-owning southerners was substantial. Whiskey could be purchased for small amounts or easily acquired through trade or barter. It was an unusual farmer or planter who did not have a few gallons on hand, and often it was a few barrels. Indeed, there were probably few communities in the South that did not have slave owners similar to John Farney, a farmer in Maury County, Tennessee. Farney's wife realized that her husband had a drinking problem, and she kept the six slaves given her by her father in a separate trust for the benefit of the children. Following her death, however, Farney became "excessively dissipated & otherwise irregular & immoral in his habits" and *"very much embarrassed"* financially. In 1834, he threatened to move to the Indian nation and take his children's slaves with him, but before he could set out, one of the slaves, a mulatto man named John, ran "& has not since been heard from." The other five slaves, the children's grandmother added, were at that very moment planning their escape.[16]

If excessive drinking gave slaves opportunities to abscond, so, too, might a master's mental or emotional problems. The North Carolina slave Jack knew from boyhood that his owner, Hugh Lamb, had exhibited strange behavior. The master's problems grew progressively worse after his wife gave birth to a "colored child." In 1832, at age fifteen, Jack attempted his first escape. He was caught and punished, but later, although his owner, described as a man of "weak intellect," was taken in by various relatives, Jack became a "runaway nearly all the time." The guardian of a South Carolina woman explained in 1849 that the woman's hired slave, George, was a great thief and runaway. Indeed, despite the utmost vigilance to control him, there was a real danger of losing the "value of the slave to the Estate" as a result of the slave's "criminal habits & dispositions." Part of the reason for these "dispositions," the guardian said, was that George's owner was completely insane. Also of "unsound mind—incapable of protecting her person and managing her property" was Maryland widow Catherine Bate, who owned forty-three slaves. Despite the appointment of her son John as a trustee, some of the slaves ran away. By the time members of the family moved to Kentucky, little remained of her once sizable estate.[17]

The problems resulting from interracial sexual liaisons also prompted slaves to run away. Slaveholding wives could be vicious toward black women they suspected of having relationships with their husbands. In the case of Dinah, however, an Alabama woman described as "yellowish" and about twenty-five, the white husband caused her flight. Dinah had been given by the father of a bride to his daughter as a wedding gift; when the newly wedded woman gave birth to a mulatto child six months later, the husband sent her back to her father but kept the slave. Dinah fled, fearing not only for herself but for *her* husband, who, as it turned out, was the father of the white woman's baby.[18]

While the scenario of Dinah and her husband and the white newlyweds in Alabama was not repeated often, marital conflicts within slaveholding families were anything but unique. The bitter and at times acrimonious and violent confrontations between plantation masters and mistresses—seldom mentioned in the literature on slavery—occurred frequently. Planters and their wives argued and fought about children, money, travel, friends, social events, and slaves. As a Greene County, Georgia, woman said about her slaveholding husband who was living with one of his slaves: he treated her "in the most cruel & unhuman manner and hath frequently beaten & whipt your petitioner and countenanced & permited the aforesaid Negro woman Slave to beat & whip" her. He drove the wife from their home without means of subsistence to depend "upon the liberality or charity of her friends & acquaintances."[19]

Such turmoil and violence in the master's household at times prompted slaves to run away. Some fled to protect themselves from the unwanted advances of white men. Others left because they feared some sort of retaliation. Still others absconded because their masters became preoccupied with personal matters. One of the best examples of this was Stephen L. Lee, a small planter who owned twenty-four slaves on the South River in Anne Arundel County, Maryland. Married for twenty-six years and the father of five children, Lee learned in 1859 from some of his slaves that his wife was having an affair with a young schoolteacher. For the next two years, Lee became obsessed with his wife's adultery. He spied on her, followed her on trips, employed a private investigator to track her movements, and uncovered a letter "disgustingly lustful and Sensual such as none but an adulterer could write to an adulteress." Meanwhile, his slaves observed their master's fixation, his extended absences, and his feelings of "dishonor and degradation." In the midst of his anguish, during the summer of 1860, a United States census taker arrived at the plantation on the South River. He discovered that six of Lee's twenty-four slaves were fugitives from the state, ranging in age from twenty to two years.[20]

Opportunity

Other opportunities also led slaves to run away. Among the most prominent was the accident of location. Slaves who lived in close proximity to free territory—near the Pennsylvania line, along the Ohio River, in the west or near the Indian nations, on the border with Florida, or in southern Texas—frequently tempted fate by striking out for freedom. The lure of possible assistance a short distance away created a heavy traffic of runaways in Frederick, Carroll, Washington, and Baltimore counties in Maryland, in western Virginia and northeastern Kentucky, in southern Georgia prior to Florida's statehood, and

in the southern sections of Texas. In 1854, the organization of slaveholders to halt runaways in Seguin, San Marcos, Yorks Creek, Geron-
imo, along the Guadalupe River, and at various other points in southern Texas did little good. "The number of negroes in the city and
indeed in all this part of the state is comparatively small," an observer
wrote from San Antonio in 1855. "They cannot be Kept here without
great risk to their running away." The country south of the city was
open and flat and uninhabited, the Mexican border was not far away,
and there were "always Mexicans who are ready and willing to help
the slaves off." Such slaves always succeeded in escaping.[21]

Slaves who lived in border areas or were hired to travel in those
areas, especially along the Upper Mississippi and Ohio rivers, had opportunities not available to others. Hired out by English-born merchant Thomas Durnford in New Orleans in 1816, the slave Jack went
on board a barge bound for Louisville, Kentucky. Jack was one of five
black persons (including a free man named Albert) hired by Durnford
to make the northward journey under the supervision of barge captain
Gilbert Morris. Jack remained aboard the barge as it stopped in Kentucky and continued up the Ohio River, berthing in Cincinnati. Once
on free soil, Jack bolted for freedom. It took considerable time and no
small expense, but Morris finally retrieved the runaway. Returning to
the Crescent City, he angrily asked Durnford why he had not informed him about Jack, who was "in the habit of running away" and
had run away on so many previous occasions.[22]

By the antebellum period, with attempts such as Jack's so frequent,
it became customary for steamboat captains to deposit hired slaves—
those who worked as servants, waiters, barkeepers, cooks, deckhands,
woodcutters—in a slave state for safekeeping before proceeding, unless
they could secure written permission from owners to take slaves to a
free port. Not only did this protect them if the slaves absconded, but
it also deterred slaves from hiring themselves on board without the
master's consent and then running away. "I have been engaged in
navigating the Western Waters for about 25 years, and have frequently had slaves hired on board of boats I command," James D.
Hamilton explained in 1851, "and Landing on the shores of the States
of Indiana & Illinois I have never considered the chances of escape
very great." Despite this, he continued, when he planned to port at
Cincinnati, he left his hired slaves in Louisville, or obtained "express
permission of the owner of such slaves to take them up with me to
those points."[23]

Such caution, shared by most captains, came from years of experience. Ironically slaves, too, were cautious about how and when they
attempted to escape, even when they lived or worked so close to free-

dom. To jump from the deck of a steamer, to attempt to swim to freedom or row a skiff across the river, was not only dangerous in the swift currents and sometimes icy waters, but the networks to return such slaves were well established. In southern Ohio, Indiana, and Illinois, many residents sympathized with the South, and some as late as the 1820s were themselves slaveholders. Fearing harsh retribution, or worse, prospective runaways required ideal conditions even in these sections. Jerry, a twenty-four-year-old Kentucky slave, described as "stout healthy and intelligent," who could earn $25 a month when hired on the river between Louisville and New Orleans, was permitted "to do as he pleased," one observer noted, "and he esteemed himself as free." Hired on board the steamer *Bunkerhill #3* as second cook in 1851, Jerry made three trips back and forth between Louisville and New Orleans. But on a fourth trip, the steamer sidetracked and went up the Illinois River about a hundred and fifty miles and docked in the town Pekin, Illinois. The next morning, the captain recounted:

> the boy was called up and went to his work, and a short time thereafter not being seen, it was discovered that he had left. That instantly the officers of the boat employed the police & a force to pursue him, offering a large reward for his recovery, and started themselves after him & in quick pursuit. That quick and Instant & active pursuit was made & Kept up for the boy for some time but he could not be found, altho he was heard of.

Rumors persisted about Jerry's whereabouts, the owner believing he had made it to Canada, the steamboat crew believing he had remained in Illinois.[24]

Other slaves were also patient, weighing their chances of success in a variety of circumstances. Employed in 1837 as a servant at the Louisville Hotel, Lemuel was summoned to carry luggage on board the steamer *Paul Jones*. The same day, he went back to the hotel, packed his small belongings, returned to the steamboat, and either booked passage or hired on as a waiter. At Cincinnati, he disembarked. The once "faithful & excellent & capable Servant," his owner lamented, "was Seduced by the hope of freedom."[25]

If proximity to free territory prompted slaves to run away, so, too, did living near areas where runaways congregated. While the number of such locations declined as southerners moved to the west, cleared new lands during the 1820s and 1830s, or sent militia units into areas to destroy "outlaw" camps, runaways continued to congregate deep in the woods or swamps. These included remote areas of the backcountry such as the Great Dismal Swamp along the border between Virginia and North Carolina; Elliott's Cut, between the Ashepoo and

Pon Pon rivers; Goose Creek, St. James Parish, South Carolina; and the Florida Everglades. To the west were the Indian nations in Alabama and Mississippi, at least until the late 1830s, and swampy areas and forests of the Lower Mississippi River Valley in Louisiana. As a group of slave owners and residents of King William County, Virginia, noted in 1843, there were sections of their county used as "the general resort of free negroes from all parts of the country" and a "harbour for runaway slaves."[26]

In some of these areas runaways coaxed fellow slaves off of plantations. Absolum and Cyrus, two of South Carolina planter Edward Brailsford's "primest fellows," were enticed away by a "body of runaway negroes" in St. James Parish along Goose Creek. They "were the property of your petitioner," Brailsford wrote, "and were young, and athletic, and truly valuable fellows." The slaves roamed into various other areas, including the vicinity around Dorchester, stealing and looting plantations and seeking to attract new converts. When a patrol was called out, the two had split up, and Absolum, along with a few other fugitives, made his way back to the Brailsford plantation. But the patrol had its orders to fire on any black person who refused to surrender. "In pursuance of these orders," Brailsford said, "some were routed in the vicinity of Dorchester, where Cyrus, the property of your petitioner was shot, and killed. Some were routed within the limits of your petitioner's plantation, when Absolum was shot, and soon after expired."[27]

The lure of freedom was clearly illustrated during the War of 1812 when the British blockaded American ports and promised freedom to fugitive slaves, as they had during the War for Independence. The Chesapeake Bay region bore the brunt of the British invasion, and raiding parties struck during the spring and summer of 1813 along the Virginia and Maryland shores. With defenses greatly weakened, the British marched on Washington in 1814 and burned the public buildings. Some owners sent their slaves across the mountains for safekeeping. A Maryland woman explained that with the British so close she was sure to lose her ward's bondsman, who was in any event "a head strong ungovernable boy." Those who failed to take precautions witnessed a large number of desertions. Slaves set out to join advancing troops, and as British ships lay at anchor in the bay, they stole their masters' canoes and small boats, guiding them out to the British war ships. The exodus became so great that the Virginia General Assembly passed a law instructing militia captains "on the approach of any part of the Enemies Naval forces to remove and secure as far as in their Power practicable out of the Reach of any slave or slaves any boat or vessel." In Matthews County, with its peninsula jutting out into the bay, canoes were put under constant guard, a virtual quarantine.[28]

In South Carolina, Elliott's Cut became so filled with outlaws and runaway slaves during the war that the governor ordered out a detachment of militia to clear this "Negro thoroughfare." The troops penetrated the dense marshlands and "with much difficulty" captured the two ringleaders, Mowby and Dunmore, who were summarily executed. Even so, the Cut remained a hideout for outlying slaves hoping to go over to the British. It was, according to local residents, "seldom if ever used but by Runaways and Negroes." In other sections of the state, the militia was used to seek out runaways who felt their chances of freedom were enhanced by the war. In 1813, Gabriel and Brister escaped from their owner, Dr. Mathew ODriscoll, who lived near Colleton, and made their way to a plantation in St. Bartholomew Parish, where they were taken in by friends. Word got out, however, that the runaways were in the vicinity. A militia detachment was sent, and when the two men fled, they were shot and killed.[29]

Farther south, along the sea island coast of Georgia, thousands deserted to the enemy, including a large contingent from Pierce Butler's plantation on St. Simons Island. Butler's overseer, Roswell King, revealed the attitudes of both races when he wrote the master in February and March 1815 about the 138 missing slaves:

> I can never git over the Baseness of your ungrateful Negroes. . . . To treat Negroes with humanity is like giving Pearls to Swine, it is throwing away Value and giting insult and ingratitude in return.
>
> It is not you, and myself, but the Inhabitants generally have all been deceived in the Ethiopian race. Your son's observation is now verified, that Negroes have neither honr or Gratitude.
>
> God cursed the Negroe by making him black. I Curse the Man that brot the first from Africa, and the Curse of God is still on them, to send them away to die a miserable death.
>
> I should have no heart to begin [planting sugarcane] for my feelings are such that I cant bare the sight of a Negro without Melancholy Irritation. Those animals must be ruled with a rod of iron, which must be painful to yourself, as well as me.
>
> But it is painful to look at such ungrateful rascals as your Negroes [who could not leave], when I know they would have gone off if they only had a chance.

What would he do if he ever regained possession of the runaways? It would give him great pleasure to "pick out one husband, one wife, one fellow, one Wench and sell them—leaving their children or parents behind."[30]

Again and again, slave owners used the same word to describe runaways: ungrateful. They had been treated well and humanely; they had been given proper food and clothing; they had been well housed and provided with other necessities; their families had been kept together. Yet, at the first opportunity they had set out on their own. They had neither honor nor gratitude; as a race, they were deceptive and deceitful.

Assisted by Whites

As strange and apparently incongruous as it might appear, some absconders were assisted by whites. Perhaps it occurred infrequently and under unique circumstances, but it did occur. Unwilling to concede that slaves would run away on their own, masters preferred to believe their slaves had been persuaded by others to run away. "On yesterday evening," a New Orleans man explained in 1839, "my boy Adam absented himself, without leave, from the *Planter's Hotel.*" He believed Adam had been "enticed away by some white man or free negro." Twice Mississippi slave Peter attempted to escape but was unsuccessful. "[T]he fellow has certainly gave him much trouble," the owner's brother-in-law wrote from Natchez, "he ran away on the first night after he bought him." On his third try, however, he was successful; he went off with the help of John Montgomery, a white man, who arranged for him to "go to a Certain place and hire himself out" until his master gave up the search. When a Tennessee slave set out with a white man for Ohio, it was not clear who was offering assistance to whom. The black man was described as clever, sensible, polite, and energetic; the white man, Simon McCaffery, was described as extremely awkward in manner and dress. "There was considerable talk the other day about the catching of Dr. Carter's runaways," William Clements of West Liberty, Virginia, wrote his brother in December 1860; "it appears that some six or eight of his negroes ran away in the early part of the year." Nearly a year later, the ones still at large were found working on a farm owned by a white man named Corbin in Hanover County. "The negroes sd [said] they had been working for him all the year."[31]

Whatever the actual circumstance, it was rare that whites did not have ulterior motives. They sought a partner in crime, payment for counterfeit papers, assistance in their own escapes from jail or debt. They sold slaves liquor and "Goods, wares, & Merchandise," promising to help get them out of bondage. In Wilmington, North Carolina, ninety-five whites petitioned the legislature to prohibit the influx of "transient traders" who invaded the city every winter and spring, trading with slaves and promising to assist them in getting to the North.[32]

Some whites helped blacks and then claimed them as their slaves. When Craven Davis, a resident of Hamilton, North Carolina, discovered that the wife of a slave he knew had been sold to Tennessee, he offered to assist the black man. He would help him run away to reunite with his wife. The slave, named Drew, agreed and the two set out across the Appalachian Mountains, but instead of taking him to Tennessee, he took him to Alabama and sold him in a private sale. As Davis made off to parts unknown, Drew escaped, but was jailed in Bedford County, Tennessee, where he remained for more than a year while his title was being settled. He was never reunited with his wife.[33]

Playing on such emotions, it was not difficult for whites to lure slaves away from plantations. At other times, white men promised freedom to those in bondage if they absconded, promised to conceal them if they stole from the master, or hatched other schemes to lure slaves away. A white man in Troup County, Georgia, "caused and procured" a slave owned by a Chambers County, Alabama, blacksmith "to runaway" across the state line. The Georgia man then "secreted and concealed said Negro for several days." Whatever the slave's hopes were at the outset, they were soon dashed when the sheriff of Troup County issued an attachment on the black man for his owner's $700 debt, and the slave was merely transferred from an owner in Alabama to one in Georgia.[34]

An example of a runaway slave's involvement in a major commercial operation can be seen in the adventure of a New Orleans female slave. The commander of the *Tecumseh*, a New York trading ship, provided the light-skinned New Orleans slave Aimee with a sailor's uniform as a disguise. The reason was not revealed until her owner, jeweler François Lebeau, discovered what was missing from his shop. The stolen property included twelve gold watches, a medallion breast pin set with diamonds, a gold bracelet ornamented with an opal and diamond, a diamond ring, diamond shirt buttons, and gold buckles, watch keys, and earrings. The jewelry, delivered by Aimee, came from Paris, and was appraised at $3,375.[35]

One of the strangest episodes of this kind occurred in Edenton, North Carolina, in 1808 when Arthur Howe, a hunchback, convinced Mustapha, or Muss, owned by Mathias Sawyer, to run away. "He is remarkable for having a *deformity* in his back," Sawyer explained; he hunched over so much that his arms fell to his knees. Moreover,

Sawyer said, the white man's countenance was "ferocious and expressive of dark angry passions." Apparently this did not bother Mustapha, who permitted the white man to sell him and resell him along the way as they moved through Virginia; after each sale he would run away and team up with Howe again. When they reached either Norfolk, Petersburg, or Richmond, Sawyer said, they would part company and then Mustapha would "make his escape to the northward."[36]

The penalties for whites caught helping slaves escape were severe. Since it was very difficult to get a conviction in the courts—blacks could not testify against whites—masters, their agents, and other whites often took matters into their own hands. The fate of a Philadelphia man named Seth Concklin who went to Alabama to retrieve a slave family for his friend Peter Still, a free black, suggests what could happen if plans were uncovered. Concklin sneaked the family off their plantation and took them on a skiff down the Tennessee River, pretending to be their master. They made it to Vincennes, Indiana, but were discovered by a group of suspicious whites. When Concklin tried to escape, he was bludgeoned, and a few days later his body was found in the river with his skull fractured. Still's wife and children were returned to their owner.[37]

Interracial sexual liaisons also produced runaways. "[She] would get up & go off & sometimes did not return until day light," a Nashville man said of his hired slave cook Esther; her "habits of sexual intercourse" were ruining her health, and now she was secretly seeing a white man. One morning the paramour came to the kitchen and the two spoke for a long time; that afternoon Esther said she would "do no one any good, & would runaway." She kept her word, and a short time later absconded. Quickly caught, returned, and put up for sale, "She repeatedly said that she never would have a child," explained James Glover, the slave trader assigned to auction her off. "I supposed that she was in the habit of taking medicine to prevent conception." While awaiting sale, her white lover visited her in jail and promised to buy her if he could raise the money, but he was unable to do so, and Esther was sold.[38]

If only veiled references were made as to why Esther ran away, it was much clearer why an attractive Maryland woman did. A young white man, described as a "gentleman," visited the house where the slave was working (for the brother of her owner) and the two had a private conversation. The following morning a carriage arrived, and the gentleman and slave drove away. A neighbor "pursued & saw her go on board the Steamboat, & went down & told Capt. Pearce of that steam boat, that he suspected she was on board." After a thorough search of the entire boat, except "the ladies cabin," however, the slave was not found. "[T]he negro was carried to Philadelphia," the owner lamented, "& has never been returned."[39]

Other slave women took advantage of similar opportunities to abscond from their masters. In New Orleans, this occurred frequently. In one case, a mulatto woman, Maria, was harbored by E. B. Cogswell, who hid her in a chest when authorities arrived to search his house. They found her and returned her to her owner. Afterwards, she was sold, and Cogswell went to the new owner. He had "the audacity to call on me and tell me," her new master said, "if I kept her she would do me no good, and immediately after [she] disappeared." Although it was not known whether they were assisted by white men, other female runaways were described as genteel in appearance, well-spoken, and possessing a large quantity of clothing.[40]

It was rare, but occasionally white women ran off with slave men. In 1832, a South Carolina woman, Eveline Crawford, nursing her child, fled with a slave named Jacob. The couple's first attempt to escape had been foiled when they were apprehended near Murray's Ferry, outside of Charleston, but now they were again missing. Jacob's owner warned sea captains to watch for the couple, who might be "lurking about" the wharves awaiting an opportunity to sail to some foreign port.[41] There is no record of their ever having been apprehended.

Dissatisfaction of Hired Slaves

Slaves who were hired out by their masters became part of the runaway army. Forced to leave their families, sent to new employers, and compelled to labor long hours, some felt their situation worse than those who remained behind on the plantation. Even when masters offered incentives, hired slaves could become dissatisfied with working conditions, visitation time, harsh treatment, and changing employers. It is true that some slaves eagerly awaited being hired out because they were given special privileges or permitted to keep a portion of their earnings. Others were so talented and able in their skilled occupations that they could demand and receive concessions from their owners. Even for these latter groups, however, there was displeasure. They were in a better position than other slaves to see the direct connection between work and wages. Those who collected their own earnings and turned them over to their owners must have felt a special pain to see the value of their labor going to their owner's comfort. As a consequence, hirelings, including some of the most talented and skilled, ran away.

Some hired slaves were auctioned off from year to year to different employers. They could be treated harshly or transported far away from their loved ones. It seems that both of these elements were present when a seventy-year-old Louisa County, Virginia, plantation owner sent his slave Ralph to Albemarle County to work for John M. Perry, a farmer with a reputation for driving his workers incessantly. To maintain discipline, Perry kept on hand a full-time slave catcher named Leitch. Shortly after arriving, Ralph ran away, returning to his home plantation and hiding in the quarters. When Leitch arrived in pursuit, he had been drinking. Riding into the yard, in a noisy "boisterous manner, [he] went round to the negro quarters, rushing into some or all of them, cursing the negroes for having (as he said) harbored Ralph, terrifying them, & threatening them violently if they did not produce him." Ralph again ran off, this time moving southeast toward Richmond. He remained out many months, but was eventually jailed in Hanover County just north of the capital. Perhaps his only consolation was that jail was better than working on Perry's plantation.[42]

Numerous hired slaves absconded because of harsh treatment that seemed never ending. Among them were Caty and her children who in 1815 were hired with "a parcel of negroes" to Boswell Lawson, a farmer in Caroline County, Virginia. The owner's niece, Fanny Roane, who lived nearby, said Caty "frequently came to her, complaining of the ill treatment of the sd. Lawson, showing the wounds & stripes given her by sd. Lawson." Roane also "heard the cries of the sd woman when Lawson was beating her." The black woman went to the niece and begged that she and her family be returned to their owner. She complained not only for herself but for her children, who were being "starved," she said. Caty's son William had been taken from her and hired out by Lawson, contrary to the hiring agreement. Another neighbor corroborated and added to the niece's testimony. At length, he said, Caty took her children and ran away and returned home, telling her master, Thomas Roane, that she had been "cruelly treated." Roane, however, returned the family to Lawson, and again Caty ran away; after the second escape, the master kept them on the plantation.[43]

As in the case of Caty's son William, it was especially difficult for young slaves to be hired out away from their parents. After being sent to an adjoining county, one youthful Kentucky slave returned to his mother. "Ely one of your Boys that I hired this year Left me as a runaway," Kentucky brickmaker John Fisher of Lexington wrote to Elizabeth Lee in nearby Woodford County in December 1810; "I hope you will not have any Impression on your mind as to my Treatment till you will heard [sic] from me." The employer, who had the same trouble with Ely before, was convinced that it was only the slave's loneliness for his mother that prompted him to abscond. The hired slave had his failings, as did many others "of his culer," the brick-maker reported, but he worked hard. In fact, the white man would be "very much acomodated" if he could rehire the young slave the next year.[44]

Whites who employed or owned black hirelings were especially frustrated when slaves ran away for no apparent reason. An eighteen-year-old Kentucky man named Henry was described by his owner as "very disobedient being in the habit of running away from the persons to whom he is hired & in the habit of getting drunk." It would not be long before he would "escape entirely from servitude." Apparently South Carolina slave George was well treated, but nonetheless it was nearly impossible to hire him out because of his "bad character and habits." He was a thief, a "great scoundrel," and a constant runaway. In Southampton County, Virginia, there was a continual flow of hired blacks who went into the woods or out of the county. Hirers and owners alike complained that slaves ran away from employers contin-ually. They absconded "without regard to masters," refused to be "rented out," ran away every chance they got, and were "constantly in the woods." The hired slave Ann ran off frequently and refused to live with anyone to whom she was hired. If Phebe had chosen to do so, a Virginia owner admitted, she could have been "a valuable ser-vant." She had "gotten in the habit" of running away, and now it was "impossible to hire her out."[45]

Although whites were often unsure why hired slaves ran away, blacks were more certain: Why should their earnings be expropriated? Why were they not permitted to keep a portion of their wages? If they were permitted to keep a part of their earnings, why were they not allowed to keep enough to provide more for their families? In short, there seemed to be no relationship between work, wages, and rewards. Moreover, hired slaves grieved that masters, including guardians, ad-ministrators of estates, and widows on fixed incomes, were not averse to turning them over to hiring agents. These agents leased them out wherever profits could be obtained. Other hirelings absconded, as one master said, simply because they were dissatisfied with their "situa-tion" or because they did not like their new employers. A young Maryland slave, who was raised in a Methodist family on terms of "PERFECT EQUALITY," ran away after he was hired out to a man in Baltimore. The "sole cause of his absconding," an observer noted, was the employer's failure to treat him as an equal, which "has given him offense."[46]

Hired slaves had good reason to resist some employers. Often those who were hired out were treated worse than they were treated by their owners. In Virginia, following the passage of a law in 1850 requiring owners rather than employers to be responsible for hired slaves who ran away, a group of hiring agents pointed out that the code actually encouraged employers to treat them cruelly and force them to run away after they had worked for some months. A large portion of the whites who hired slaves, especially in cities, the factors insisted, were foreign born, poor, and illiterate. Unlike "the respectable portion of our community," foreigners could not distinguish between right and wrong. In nine out of ten runaway cases, it was "this class of hirers" who abused the slaves to precipitate their running away. It was an easy way to get out of a contract.[47]

Some owners, of course, permitted hired slaves to keep a portion of their earnings, and a few held out the promise of freedom if overwork payments could make up the difference in their purchase price. None of the "contracts," of course, were legally binding, and whites could, and often did, renege on such "agreements." In Charleston, South Carolina, the hired man Sam made an arrangement with his owner James Thomson that after he paid him $500 he would receive emancipation papers. Working for a number of years, Sam paid the owner $450, but in 1811 the two men had a disagreement about how and when the final payments would be made. When the owner made certain demands, Sam ran away. "Sir, I have a Negro Boy confined here in gaol which has been Proved by Mr. Cross to be yours and the year will soon be up that I shall have to sell him," the sheriff of Newberry District wrote Thomson in 1812. Not wishing to confront Sam face to face, the master did not respond. Sam was sold at auction for $210; later, Thomson pocketed the profits from the sale, minus jail fees.[48]

Living and working conditions for hired slaves in southern industries were often worse and more dangerous than for agricultural workers. Long hours, strenuous and backbreaking labor, tedious routines, and dangerous conditions were commonplace for those who worked in coal mines, ore pits, iron foundries, textile mills, or on railroad, canal, and turnpike construction. Young men were sometimes hired to remote sections of Virginia, Tennessee, Alabama, and Missouri, where there were few if any women. In addition, some company owners and managers cared little about improving conditions.[49] Under such circumstances, slaves frequently ran away.

They departed from rice mills, sugar mills, grist mills, from construction and building locations, and from turpentine distilleries, flour mills, and gold mines. One sugar mill operator counted eleven runaways within a short period. With one exception, they all returned within a week or less. For a rice mill owner the situation was more serious. During one winter season, he saw his operations come to a virtual standstill when his carpenter, boatman, engineer, and two other slaves absconded. The five who left together from an ironworks in Perry County, Tennessee, in 1837—a black named Bob, a mulatto named Bob, and Daniel, Alexander, and Jim—were not unusual. In their late teens and twenties, one slave had been hired from a man in Tennessee, while the other four had been purchased by a partner in the company in Mississippi from "some negro traders, who brought them from Virginia or South Carolina." Not long after they arrived, the five made off in the middle of the night. Dislocation, long hours, severe routines, and ill-treatment prompted industrial slaves to go on the run.[50]

Although William Weaver of Rockbridge County, Virginia, one of the most successful ironmasters in the South, hired slaves every year, he also owned his own labor force. Weaver offered many incentives to his workers and was meticulous in the payment of overwork wages to his miners, ore pounders, wood cutters, colliers, teamsters, furnace carpenters, pattern makers, blacksmiths, and foundry hands. He was also careful about offering special incentives to workers who fired the furnace, kept it filled with measured layers of ore, limestone, and charcoal, and molded his iron bars. But even Weaver could not prevent slaves from running away and was forced to deal with them during the entire forty years he remained as an ironmaster in the Valley of Virginia.[51]

Merely To Be Free

Considered by his owner, William Sanders Sr. of Christ Church Parish, South Carolina, as a slave of "bad character," Tom was sold in 1802 to a neighboring planter, John Parker, for one hundred guineas. It was Parker who had approached Sanders concerning the slave: Tom was big, strong, and healthy, perfect for the arduous work required at his brickyard and plantation on Daniel's Island. Living in the neighborhood, Parker was "personally acquainted with the bad character of the said Negro" and said he was willing to purchase him nevertheless; all that was required "was a strict master and one who could manage him."

But Parker could not manage his new slave, and four days after his arrival on Daniel's Island, Tom ran away. Parker, who had signed a promissory note to purchase Tom, called on Sanders, asked to "inspect" the note, and when it was given to him put it in his pocket and walked away, telling Sanders he could "get his money as he could for the Negro had run away and he was determined not to pay the Note."

In a civil suit, Sanders argued that the "Negro was good property," and he had turned over "a good bona fide and legal title" to the purchaser and deserved full payment. In any event, it was the buyer who had approached the seller, not the other way around, and he had warned Parker specifically about Tom's propensity to run away.

In January 1803, Tom was captured and taken to the workhouse in Charleston. During the dispute over ownership, Tom remained incarcerated, "being occasionally corrected," until Parker died, sometime in late 1805 or early 1806. After Parker's death, Tom was put up for sale to defray expenses according to the city ordinance regarding runaway slaves in long confinement. Advertised by the sheriff and sold 20 July 1807 for $310, Tom was purchased by Benjamin Parker for the Estate of John Parker. One observer noted that the slave had been "unnecessarily and cruelly kept in confinement" four and a half years.[52]

The fate of habitual runaways like Tom was bleak during the nineteenth century. Described as "obdurate," "intractable," or of "bad character," these slaves struggled desperately to be free. They ran away not once or twice, but many times, and although often caught and punished, it did not seem to matter how frequent or how brutal the punishment or how many threats were made against them and their families. They simply refused to capitulate.[53] Such slaves presented a dilemma for slaveholders: How much punishment could they inflict without damaging their property? There was also the problem of how other slaves would perceive such intransigence and belligerence. What if they considered such defiance admirable? What if they tried to emulate such behavior?

Most habitual runaways began when they were in their teens. The first time he absconded, the North Carolina slave Jack was fifteen years old. Despite frequent whippings, he became a "notorious" absconder and when in his mid-thirties "he was runaway nearly all the time." "He was not a trusty negro," one witness said. Although "able active and strong" he "would not work unless you were with him." Frances, a New Orleans girl, was already a constant runaway by the time she was fifteen or sixteen. She spoke rapidly and "with much intelligence," her owner said, and usually hid out with relatives. Moving between the Ochlockonee and Appalachicola rivers in the Florida Territory, Pompey avoided detection by living in the densely wooded forests and by crossing into southwest Georgia. He sustained himself by hunting, fishing, and killing livestock. He had "run-away and remained in the Woods for a length of time," the guardian of his owner said. Indeed, whites had "come into the actual possession" of the slave for only two weeks during the entire year of 1844 before he went out again "& has been a run-away ever since."[54]

Also in his teens was an anonymous slave brought to the slave pen in Richmond in 1860. While his career as a perpetual runaway would be cut short by the Civil War, it was clear that he was destined to such a future. According to one observer in Richmond, the youngster was "City rased and has run away twice since J & Slater had him in jail." The physician who purchased the slave for $1,462.50, G. W. Brown of Perry County, Alabama, did not know the type of slave he was purchasing. "He ran right out of Jones & Slaters jail and Slater right after him a hollowing, Ketch him! Ketch him, & away they both went down the street," a bystander said. Slater caught up with "the boy" at the market. To some it was "very amusing to see Slater run and to hear him holl[er] & when he come up the street with the boy he had him by the collar & now and then he wd give him a little shake."[55]

Refusing to submit was characteristic of perpetual runaways. Purchased from Robert and Thomas Scott in Jessamine County, Kentucky, in the early 1800s, Charles ran away from his owner, Thomas M. Green, a planter who lived near Greenville in Jefferson County, Mississippi Territory, in the fall of 1803. He was taken up in Robertson County, Tennessee, in the summer of 1804, where he remained until March 1805. When a Tennessee man attempted to take the slave back to the Mississippi Territory, Charles "again made his escape." Similarly, John was a "keen artful fellow" who would no doubt attempt to pass for a free man, said a planter in Edgefield District, South Carolina. On a previous escape, John had assumed the name Lewis Matthews and tried to board a boat sailing for Amelia Island. In 1827, at age thirty, he had once again left the master's plantation on Stephens' Creek and was again probably heading for the coast.[56]

Physical handicaps did not dissuade slaves from attempting to escape. Andrew, "in the habit of absenting himself," was "lame in one leg." Not much information was needed in the runaway advertisement for Bob of New Orleans. Bob used a crutch because his leg had been amputated above the knee. The "American negro fellow DAVIS," aged about twenty-two years, dragged his left leg when he walked, another New Orleans owner said, but absconded nonetheless and remained at large five months. A notice for his return appeared first in English, then in French.[57] Other slaves ran away when they were suffering from ailments, with broken limbs, bloodied from severe flogging, and pregnant.

Neither age nor time in jail dissuaded Peter, alias John, from absconding. During seven years between 1824 and 1831, Peter spent more time away from his owners than he did in their service. In 1824–

25, he spent twelve months as a runaway in the Sumter District jail, after which he was sold at a sheriff's sale. During the next few years, he ran away twice. In July 1829, he was arrested and jailed in Wayne County, North Carolina. Remaining unclaimed for months, he was sold, resold, sold again, and finally, when the original owner learned of his whereabouts, reclaimed. In December 1830, as the master and slave passed through the Santee Canal in a boat on their way back to the plantation, Peter ran away.[58]

As the experiences of Peter suggest, many habitual runaways ignored personal safety. The Tennessee slave Jesse had always been willing to sacrifice his personal comfort for some free time in the woods, but following the death of his master in 1854, when he was to be hired out, he became a perpetual absconder. "He has as bad habits about running away as any slave I ever saw," exclaimed William Ezell, a farmer in Giles County who knew Jesse. "He is in the constant habit of running away & staying in the woods at all season & in all kinds of weather for weeks at a time without any provocation or cause." Another observer said he was in "the habit of running away, from the slightest cause & often viciously, & willfully without any cause." Another slave, twenty-four- or twenty-five-year-old Isaac, absconded five times during a single year. His health was "greatly endangered by the habit."[59]

At age twenty-two, Lucy was typical of those who would not remain in slavery. Described by her South Carolina owner as having lost her front teeth, she was of "ordinary size, trim made, rather sway b[a]cked, long arms, walks very proper, when spoken to speaks very bold, and rather impertinent." Raised in Charleston, she wore "the mark of the whip on her shoulders." She was described in one notice as having "a good figure," being "quite intelligent," and "considerably marked with the whip." Also marked by the lash was Sary, with "a scar under one of her breasts resembling the cut from a whip." Ralph lived the first two decades of his life around Richmond, Virginia, but when he was sold to James Kinkade of South Carolina, he ran away. As punishment, his owner let him languish in jail for "a considerable time." He was sold to another South Carolina man, John Jefferies, who lived at Gilkey's Waters on the Broad River in Union District. In 1808, Ralph absconded again. He went away with "an iron clog on his leg, and some of his fourteeth missing." The Charleston slave Sarah was passed from owner to owner, but with each new master it was the same: she would not remain enslaved. When one new owner discovered that Sarah was "a notorious Thief and runaway," he locked her in his sugarhouse, "where she remained for some time until she was delivered of a child." A short time later, she and her baby were taken out of the sugarhouse, sent to the city workhouse, confined until the next auction, and in 1800 sold. An elderly runaway in Charleston was described with a "mark of a burn on the end of one eye and mouth" and a "large scar on her shoulder and arm."[60]

Not only did they ignore their own health, but according to the planter class, perpetual runaways were often hostile and violent. The Maryland slave Ason, about twenty-three years old, was described as vicious and ungovernable. Other masters warned slave catchers to be cautious. "If apprehended, great care should be taken to secure him," Judge Spencer Roane of Spring Garden Plantation, near Hanover, Virginia, said of his slave in 1805, "as I expect he is desperate as well as vicious." A South Carolina planter, James D. Erwin of Barnwell District, described his slave Sam, a waiter and house servant, as "one of the worst of Negroes" he had ever known, "having repeatedly armed himself and eloped." Once he stole five or six hundred dollars. When he absconded in November 1828 with a fellow slave, he still had about a hundred buckshot in him from a previous escape attempt in July. During his escapades, the master added, "he has been guilty of conduct even more atrocious than this—in short, he is a villain of the most consummate kind."[61]

It was clear that some runaways became so desperate that they cared nothing about the consequences of their actions. How desperate they might become was shown by the response of the Alabama slave Dave, acquired in July 1822 by an Autauga County man, who had swapped a horse, saddle, bridle, and $500 note for the slave. Dave had come from Lee County, Georgia, where he had been purchased only fifteen days before. Judging from the wrinkles around his eyes, one observer said, he was about forty years old. It was clear that he had been passed from one owner to another. A few days after the sale, Dave "stole some property" and in attempting to abscond was "shot at and hit" but still managed to stay out for a few days. After being captured, the wounded man in a very few days again ran away and again in the same manner a third time. During a period of about nine months, Dave labored for his owner a total of about one week. It was on his third escape that he was captured in Dallas County, tried for robbery, convicted, and executed.[62]

From every indication, Texas slave Miles was destined for a tragic end. Working with ten or twelve other black men on the plantation of absentee owner Tempe Price in San Augustine County, he absconded on a number of occasions during the 1850s. Described by some whites as "impudent, malicious and rebellious," and by others as headstrong, willful, and obdurate, he found it extremely difficult to take orders from the succession of overseers who managed the small plan-

tation. On one occasion in April 1854, Miles responded to an order
(not even given to him but rather to another field hand) by saying
"something impudent." The overseer, Charles Brady, picked up a
fence rail and swung it at the slave, "but did not get a fair lick," and
Miles "clinched" him and took him to the ground and began choking
him before the other slaves pulled him off. As if this were standard
procedure, Miles then went to the field and began plowing. The overseer loaded his double-barreled shotgun, followed the slave to the field,
and ordered him to stop plowing. The black man ignored the order,
plowed down one furrow, turned a few feet from the overseer, and
began up the next. Brady fired a shotgun blast into the slave's back.
Even then, bleeding badly from his back full of buckshot, the slave
turned around with a knife in his hand, but threatened with further
violence, Miles put it away and followed the overseer's order to get
on a horse and return to the farmhouse. As they approached the house,
Miles "slipped around the corn-crib and ran away." A short time later,
he died from his wounds.[63]

As the fate of Miles indicates, chronic runaways were willing to fly
in the face of remarkable odds. They refused to be constrained, and
whatever the punishment, they continued to run away again and
again. This represented, one student of slavery asserted, "a spirit of
revolt."[64] Few set out for the North, as the distances were far too great.
Most could expect little more than a short respite from labor, a brief
time in the woods or in a nearby town. They were soon arrested,
imprisoned, shackled, and returned to their owners. Within a short
time, however, they were out again, running off "merely to be free."

Cruel and Unusual Punishment

Cruel and harsh punishments caused many blacks to flee. Slaves were
beaten, chained, incarcerated, ironed, and whipped; and they watched
as their wives, husbands, mothers, fathers, children, and relatives were
flogged. There were few masters in the South who did not believe that
a recalcitrant or unruly slave should pay the price for disobedience.
Masters themselves sometimes wielded the cowhide—the most common form of punishment—but often it was overseers who administered corrections. The amount of correction varied from plantation to
plantation, but many planters and farmers felt that severe chastisement, especially for running away, was the best deterrent. That would
teach slaves to be humble and submissive. A house servant on one
Louisiana plantation explained to a guest when the crack of a whip
echoed through the upstairs of the mansion house one night: it was

just the overseer whipping the slaves, "a common thing here." Described as a "man of strict integrity and very kind to negroes," another overseer flogged servants regularly, but did so away from the plantation house. The master's wife was "so opposed to whipping that he never corrects a negro in her presence." My "Hands worked verry badly," a planter recorded in his diary, "general Whipping," adding on another occasion "Whiped evry hand in the field this evening."[65]

It may be assumed in at least some of the instances where slaves received harsh, even brutal treatment, they ran away because of it. The owner of a Virginia slave said that he had "a scar on the right side of his neck below the ear; another on the left, lower on his neck; he has also a scar on the right leg a little below his knee, occasioned by a burn; his back has many scars on it from flogging he has received which he justly merited." From various parts of the South during different time periods, runaways were described in a similar manner: he had the "mark of the whip on his back," the letter 'R' branded on each cheek, "very much cut with the cow-hide," "scars on his back, occasioned by a whipping." One runaway had scars above his eye, on his left thumb, and many scars on his back "caused from a severe whipping." "I filed several notches between several of his upper fore teeth, which I expect is also very plain," one owner said in a matter-of-fact manner. "I also branded him on each cheek thus "*m*" about twelve months ago, which is not very perceivable."[66]

Nor were women spared the lash. Lucy was only twenty-three, but already she had caused her owners great trouble. Raised in Charleston, South Carolina, she was "a good figure, quite intelligent," one owner said, but "considerably marked with the whip." She was dressed in "country homespun" when she ran away in the spring of 1832. Another woman runaway had the mark of the whip on her arms, and another had two marks on her cheek, which appeared to have been caused by "a cow hide."[67]

Few contemporaries would deny the cruel and brutal treatment accorded to those who defied the system. Slaves escaped with the mark of the whip on their backs, irons on their ankles, brands on their cheeks and foreheads, and missing fingers and toes. Joe, Bill, and Isaac left the Richard Terrell farm in Roanoke County, Virginia, with "Irons around their necks." Henry, absent from his Yazoo County, Mississippi, plantation for ten months, was "much scarred from the whip," had scars from a dagger wound under his left arm, and was missing his left eye. The sheriff of Pointe Coupee Parish, Louisiana, described a captured runaway in 1826 as having "an Iron collar with three prongs extending upwards" and "many scars on his back and shoulders from the whip."[68]

Cotton planter Joseph Bieller of Louisiana, for example, noted how his slave Pompy "had Some difference" with the overseer, and "got whipped and did not show himself for one week." When he returned, he got "well whipped," the master said, and now had a "clog on his leg which he will ware untill I am Satisfied." A similar slave-overseer conflict produced different results. "Anderson ran away yesterday morning in consequence of some insolence to Mr. Vinson," sugar planter J. Palfrey wrote in July 1833, "for which he expected a whipping & the search has been & is now making for him." The owner feared he would do anything to stay out, eating green corn, melons, "or whatever he may find." When he was brought in a little after dark he had indeed eaten green corn and was very ill. "I gave him a small whipping he richly deserved a sever one," the master said. Later he gave his runaway a dose of oil that "has operated a number of times during the night, he appears to be quite well this morning ready & willing to go to work."[69]

Among the runaways who testified about the reasons for flight, a number said it was because their master was "very cruel & very hard." Contemporary defenders of slavery argued that usually the punishment was modest. Why should slaveholders want to damage their own property? In fact, however, owners often turned the management of their slaves over to others—supervisors, overseers, drivers—or hired them out to slave dealers or employers. In any case, whites were concerned primarily with discipline and had few pangs of conscience about severely whipping or punishing slaves. But beyond how whites managed their labor force was their emotional response to defiant slaves. If one slave spurned white authority, defied, resisted, or ran away, others would follow suit. As they meted out punishment, reasoned judgment often gave way to passion.[70] What might have been a moderate flogging grew into brutal retribution. There is little doubt that fiendish brutality played a significant role in the South's peculiar institution.

During times of crises, slaves were especially vulnerable to severe reprisals. In 1831, following the Nat Turner revolt, a slave owned by Charles Hall of Richmond County, Georgia, was walking along the Milledgeville Road toward the city of Augusta, when he encountered two white men. Words were exchanged and the black man fled, running for a mile along the rode before slipping into a creek and hiding behind a beaver dam. The water was icy, but the pursuers hovered near him for a long time. Escaping detection, the slave nonetheless "became wet and Chilly, and took a violent Cold and in consequence thereof, died." The owner sued the two whites, but a jury found the argument of the accused persuasive. They asserted "that if they did pursue and attempt to beat said negroe (which however they deny) they were justified in doing so by reason of impudent & impertinent language used by said Negroe towards [them]."[71]

Two case histories, both involving runaways, suggest the brutal side of human bondage. How often such incidents occurred will never be known, but there is little doubt that they were not rare. On 1 January 1835, as was the custom of a number of Montgomery County, Tennessee, slave owners, William Pope hired out four of his best young slave men to work at a local ironworks owned by Robert Baxter and William Hicks and under the management of C. W. Brawley. It was some time before Pope began to hear how poorly his slaves were being treated, but when he did, even this seasoned veteran of punishment was aghast at the reported brutality.

The difficulty began one morning when Brawley asked Pope's slave Dave why he "had staid over his time" away from the ironworks, and the slave refused to answer. A scuffle ensued, and Dave tried to escape but was caught, stripped, tied down, and whipped with a cow hide. In the midst of the whipping, Hicks salted Dave's wounds, while Brawley continued to administer stripes. He inflicted "diverse large grevious and injurious Wounds in and upon the body, head, Shoulders, neck, sides, back and legs." At times Brawley stopped, rested, drank some liquor, then continued. A witness said he "saw cuts on his privates and it was bad." Afterwards, Dave was dragged to the shop and an iron ring weighing 50 or 75 pounds was attached with a chain to his ankle. "I think I gave him about 100 or 120 lashes," the overseer said, but several whites said that the overseer boasted to them that it had been many more.

The principal cause for the excessive punishment was that Dave was "insolent and resisted." Placed under guard, eight or ten days later, despite swelling in his ankle, Dave was able somehow to work out of his chain, and even with two slaves on guard, he escaped and was never heard from again. The other three hired blacks owned by Pope were similarly whipped and beaten. Like Dave, a second absconded, the third was never returned to his owner, and the fourth returned home so "sick sore and diseased" from the wounds he had received that he languished and died.[72]

In Louisiana, another overseer was similarly intent on administering severe punishments to obdurate slaves. Hired by the Woods family in West Baton Rouge Parish, William C. Riley arrived in January 1848 to superintend operations on the sugar plantation. By the spring, Riley had become increasingly abusive to the slave workers and forced his black driver to administer many whippings. When the driver was not harsh enough, Riley whipped the driver "in a very cruel manner, for not chastising *more severely*" the slaves. A white visitor on the plantation believed that the overseer was "oppressive and cruel." One man was "whipped and paddled," he said, until the skin on his back "was entirely off" and then forced to lie naked in the hot sun. Another lay in his cabin on his stomach with his "pantaloons drawn down to the Knees" and his shirt turned up over his shoulders; the mosquito bar had fallen down and adhered to the blood on his back. He had been very severely whipped, one of his eyes was completely closed, and his face was bloated. After being absent from the plantation for a few days, the visitor returned and learned that the two slaves had died.

One of Riley's previous employers, a sugar planter in Iberville Parish, confirmed much of what had happened in West Baton Rouge. Riley was so "passionate in punishing negroes," he said, "that at times he would pick up almost anything that he could get hold of and pitch it at them, such as sugar canes, or a stick and striking them over the head with it and also often using his fist, and striking them in their faces & oftener using his fists than any thing else." He did not believe that the overseer had endangered the lives of these slaves, "but his treatment caused a great many of them to run off."[73]

To suggest that such incidents were mere aberrations in a sea of calm would be incorrect. On many plantations and farms, slaves who attempted to escape or who openly defied white authority were routinely whipped and severely beaten. Sometimes, they were cut with knives, attacked by dogs, shot with buckshot. If punishments did not usually result in death, they were often administered "cruelly and unmercifully." One overseer admitted that he tied a female slave's hands, put her head down a steep hill, placed a log under her belly, and administered several hundred lashes. He "whipped her so brutally" that the woman, who was pregnant, miscarried and "was Seriously injured and disabled." Not a small number of captured runaways refused to give accurate information about their owners, preferring to remain in jail and be sold to a new owner.[74]

The first two weeks of February 1833 were generally fair, with intermittent cool and cloudy days, perfect for plowing, planting, and burning brush. An anonymous Louisiana slave owner dutifully recorded the weather and the progress of planting; he also noted the disciplinary action meted out to one of his slaves and the response of another:

5th fair and pleasant. Started one more Plough this morning . . . Started five Ploughs yesterday at Solitude in Corn Ground

6th Somewhat Cloudy this morning Breaking up old Turnip Patch for Irish Potatoes— . . .

11th fair, Mr. David C. Thomas my Overseer whiped Leven this morning (and from all I can learn for little or no fault) to Such an Excess that he Died in less than an hour after he was untied. Thomas then Ran away

That afternoon the coroner conducted an inquest. The next day at noon, Leven was buried. The following day, February 13, the master hired a new overseer, John Hardy, at a yearly salary of $450. That night and the next morning a heavy rain soaked the fields and the slaves were called in at noon. Thomas had still not yet been found.[75]

There were similar inquests in other states. In South Carolina, for example, after a slave was found dead near the Coosawhatchie River, in Beaufort District, a coroner and later a grand jury determined that the "negro came to his death by the cruelty & violence of his master." The attending physician said it was a very disagreeable job: "putrification had commenced, & the body was approaching fast to decay." A few years later in Abbeville District, Phillida, a hired slave owned by Lucretia Finney, was similarly found dead. Dr. John Reid performed "the very unpleasant and disagreeable business of opening and examining the body in the presence of the Jury." They could not determine, however, whether Phillida's death came from "violence having been given her" by her employer.[76]

Witnessing such violence had a profound effect on slaves. Those who were still willing to defy their masters and overseers realized the possibility of dire consequences. Some slaves responded by becoming gloomy, sullen, morose, others obsequious and submissive, while others remained defiant. One runaway who stabbed a fellow slave was described as continually dissatisfied. Another, who worked as a house servant for a Maryland family, refused to take orders, disdained authority, and remained hostile and belligerent. In 1829, the overseer of a Georgia plantation noted that John absconded "for no other cause than that he did not feel disposed to be governed by the same rules & regulations that the other negroes on the land are governed by."[77]

Thus, the conditions and factors that prompted slaves to run away were as varied and numerous as the human experience. The fragility of the institution once the management broke down was vividly illustrated by the response of Charles Carroll's slaves on Doughoregan Manor, but whenever opportunities presented themselves, slaves were quick to take advantage. They left following the death of a master, after being hired out in southern industry, or after being severely punished. They absconded after being sold, traded, transferred, or carried to a new location, after being offered enticements by whites, or for a variety of other reasons, including general dissatisfaction. Whatever the specific cause or causes, tens of thousands of blacks each year demonstrated their discontent by going on the run.

3

Whither Thou Goest

RACHEL O'CONNOR, the mistress of Evergreen Plantation in West Feliciana Parish, Louisiana, felt deeply about her servants. In her correspondence she spoke fondly of her slaves, and it was clear that her affection was deep and sincere. But she could not completely divorce her feelings of good fortune from the economic gain that came with the birth of each new black baby. At the time of her death, 84 percent of her estate was human property. She wrote in 1830:

> I have sixteen little negro children a raising, the oldest of the sixteen a little turned of six years old, all very healthy children excepting my little favorite Isaac, he is subject to a cough but seldom sick enough to lay up, the poor little fellow is laying at my feet sound asleep. I wish I did not love him, as I do, but it is so, and I cannot help it.[1]

Beset by creditors during the late 1820s, however, O'Connor transferred title of seventeen slaves to her half brother and future heir David Weeks, owner of the elegant Shadows Plantation in St. Mary Parish, one hundred miles to the south. The longtime widow made the transfer to protect her slave property from confiscation and because she had already promised Weeks a portion of her estate. The slaves, however, would remain on her plantation. She had always prided herself on how well she treated her "black family," as she called them, and since her half brother owned many other slaves, she was confident that her black family would remain intact, at least during her lifetime.

But when Weeks established another plantation and asked her to send him some slaves, she did so. Her decision was not easy, but she weighed the economic needs of her half brother against the temporary dislocation of a few black families. As they were shipped down the Mississippi River, the young O'Connor slaves suffered great agony.

They were leaving behind their parents as well as the place of their youth. As others followed, they, too, felt the wrenching pain of leaving mothers and other kin. Some of the young men who were sent off attempted to return to Evergreen. Despite the lack of experience in the swamp and bayou country, Harry, Eben, and Littleton made it as far as Baton Rouge in 1833 before being captured and returned. Not long afterwards, Harry absconded again, this time with Frank. They reached the O'Connor place and were reunited with their mothers. As punishment, however, they were sent to the remote island plantation of Grand Cote in the Attakapas region.[2]

Even in this isolated wilderness, blacks struggled desperately to go and live with loved ones, but it was nearly impossible to get off the island. By 1840, runaway families had bonded together in secluded sections of the island, and when slaves absconded, they sometimes did so as entire families. "Linzy has taken to the woods with his wife and child he is well armed he has the little Double Barrelled gun and his butchers Knife," the plantation manager at Grand Cote wrote. He believed that Linzy would "Join the party" that had recently stolen a boat. He also observed "a great difference in the behaviour of several of the Blacks on the Island," and it was his opinion that they were being influenced by runaway bands. He had little doubt that the runaway family had joined Linzy and that there was some clandestine correspondence "between them and the plantation." The anxious manager said that the neighbors should be alerted and that there should be a concerted effort to hunt down the runaways. It was the only way to save whites from the "miseries that those beings is capable of brin[g]ing down on [our] heads."[3]

Breakup of Families

The efforts of slaves to reunite with loved ones is well illustrated by the runaways on Louisiana's Grand Cote Island. Elsewhere the situation was quite different. Most slaves separated by sale or transfer could neither abscond in family units nor form colonies as in the Louisiana bayou country. Usually they were sold off and never saw members of their families again. The trauma of being separated forever from kith and kin can hardly be imagined. Most slaves were sold at one time or another during their lifetime, and often it was when they were young and would bring the highest price. Seldom were they sold together in family units of mother, father, and children. The separation of family members was common, especially after 1820, as whites poured into the Tennessee and Mississippi river valleys. In the Louisiana sugar parishes, 70 percent of the slaves purchased were male; traders from Virginia and Maryland scoured the countryside to send young black men to market. In the Upper South, forcible separations probably destroyed one out of three first marriages, and one out of three slave children under fifteen years of age was probably separated from one or both parents.[4] As the prices for slaves in the west increased and the profits of the interregional trade mounted, men, women, boys, and girls were swept into the domestic slave trade. They were bought at private sales, auctions, and estate sales; transported to the west; and sold at a substantial profit. The buying and selling of children ages seven through twelve bore witness to the breaking up of families.

Although many owners denied they would ever engage in such practices, speculating in black youngsters was not uncommon. "What can be had for two (2) girls number one about seven (7) the other nine [?]" a slave trader asked. "I bought today a likely girl, I suppose she is 12 year old, 4 ft 10 inches high," another wrote Betts and Gregory, commission merchants in Richmond, Virginia, in 1861. "Do you think it a good time to sell. If so I will send her in." A third trader wrote the same firm inquiring if there was "anything doing in your negro Markette." He wanted to know what he could get for "a good girl 13 yrs old, one 12 yrs old, and a boy 10 yrs old, or wheather there wd be any certainty of my selling them at all."[5]

At its extreme, the speculation involved black babies. In a suit filed by a Scott County, Kentucky, woman in 1845 against a Virginia trader heading to New Orleans, no mention was made of the parents of the two black children. The only relevant information provided was that the Kentucky woman had foolishly traded horses for two black babies represented as being healthy, one being six or seven months old and another who "could almost walk." In fact, she complained, the first child was six weeks old, the other four months old. Both were "extremely delicate, sickly and feeble, and it is very doubtful whether they can be raised at all." The black babies were in great risk of "dying before they pass the age of childhood, bringing their value down to nothing."[6] It seems doubtful that a trader would carry two black babies from Virginia to Kentucky without their mother[s], or that the purchaser expected any short-term profits, but whatever the specific circumstances, the case shows the devastating impact of the domestic slave trade on black families.

The separation of families was an inherent part of the South's peculiar institution. Sales, trades, transfers, auctions, migration of slaveholders meant that mothers were taken from children, wives from husbands, children from parents, fathers from sons and daughters, and blood kin from one another. "I send you by Aaron *all* of Lucy's children," F. L. Hunt of Jackson, Mississippi, wrote a woman in Natchez, seeking to settle a debt. "I send them all down to be delivered on condition that you release me entirely from the whole matter." They were a "beautiful family of children," but if they were sold separately they could bring "a larger price."[7]

The fear of being sold away from family and friends caused constant apprehension and worry. When the fateful moment arrived, as it often did, slaves pleaded with masters not to separate them from loved ones. When their appeals were ignored, slaves began an arduous journey away from the connections of their past, away from the kinship and family ties that had bound them together, away from the places and feelings of their youth. Since most slaves were sold at some time during their lifetime, even when they remained in the area of their birth they could still experience the grief and misery of living apart from loved ones.[8]

A personal history narrated by Jenny reflected the changes that were occurring in the lives of other slaves. Described as "very black" and having lost her front teeth, she had been sold and resold at least six times by age sixteen or seventeen. She told her life's story in 1805 to a Scottsville, Virginia, jailer: she had been "raised" by William Gathright of Henrico County, who sold her to a Richmond butcher, who sold her to a man named Williamson, who sold her to "one Webster" of Buckingham County, who sold her to John Campbell of King and Queen County, who "left her" with a free black man in Powhatan County. She escaped from him and was later arrested and jailed.[9]

Among the many causes of slaves running away, perhaps none was more poignant or pervasive than members of families seeking to reunite. They ran to neighboring plantations to be with husbands or wives, ran away to search for mothers and fathers, and all too often in vain for their children. It was especially traumatic for youngsters to be sold away from their parents or to see their parents sent away. In the Runaway Slave Database [hereinafter known as RSDB; see appendix 7] among 505 advertised slaves during the early period (1790–1816) whose ages were indicated, 5 percent were under age thirteen and 27 percent were teenagers; among 1,047 advertised runaways during the later period (1838–60), 4 percent were under thirteen and 20 percent were in their teens.[10] Thus—at least in the five states examined—one out of three and one out of four absconders were minors, including many who were either seeking their parents or other loved ones.

Mere rumors of a possible sale could send slaves off and running. Slave owners planning to make a sale cautioned members of their own family to keep the matter confidential until the bargain was sealed to avoid possible flight. One Maryland owner put a mild mannered black woman and her child in jail prior to a private sale. Judging from the quick response of some slaves, such precautions were necessary. Sharper was a field hand working on a plantation across the Potomac River from Maryland. The moment he learned that he was to be turned over to a slave trader, he bolted out of the field and fled to his wife on a neighboring plantation. He remained at large nearly seven weeks, but in July 1831, he was apprehended, and by September he was on his way to a distant location. When she learned of the possible separation of her family in a pending sale, the Maryland slave Sophia gathered up her two children and ran to the District of Columbia. She too, was apprehended, jailed, returned, and auctioned off, along with her children. The money from the sale was used to care for her mistress, who, according to court records, suffered "great imbecility of mind." John Jones of Nash County, North Carolina, purchased "a negro fellow" and started with him to Georgia to sell him when "said negroe ran away" was captured and returned home.[11]

The fate of most who absconded to avoid being sold was similar to that of Sharper and Sophia. Without time to plan, with few provisions, running to locations where slave owners would look first—where a spouse, child, or parent lived—most of this group were apprehended. Even those who remained out for many months discovered that living on the run was extremely difficult. They could remain with relatives for only short periods, and slaves on neighboring plantations took a substantial risk harboring a fugitive. Life on the run meant slaves could not stay in one place long, and they were often forced to live by thievery. Even the most resourceful among them found that it was difficult to remain undetected. In May 1799, "a very valuable Negro Fellow" in Charleston, South Carolina, was purchased by an up-country planter. Learning of his fate, he immediately bolted from the city. Stealing food from various plantations, he remained at large for seventeen months, but in the fall of 1800 he was arrested, jailed, charged with burglary, and executed.[12]

It was not only the despair of being separated from loved ones that prompted slaves to abscond, but the fear of what awaited them in a new location. Purchased by Samuel Linton, who was traveling along the Eastern Shore looking for "a few young negroes," one Maryland slave escaped clutching her infant child. A year later she was apprehended in Delaware, returned to Maryland, and jailed until Linton could come up from South Carolina and take possession of his property. As soon as the North Carolina slave Delph learned she had been sold to a buyer from the Lower South, she ran away. She, too, remained at large for some months and during that time gave birth to a child. In fact, she remained hidden so long that by the time her new owner located her and the baby a law prohibited him from importing them into his native state of South Carolina, even though he knew he could "find said Negro and her child in the State of North Carolina." Similarly, a Virginia woman sold to a South Carolina man, "Run from him so that he was not able to go for her untill after the Act Passed to prohibit the importation of Negros into this State." She eluded him even when he returned to find her, and he was forced to purchase two other girls, bringing them "Near the line of this State" while seeking permission for entry.[13]

Being sold from a rural to an urban setting, from the Upper to the Lower South, from the east to the west, or even short distances across a river in the same state could cause enormous pain and suffering at the loss of family members. City slaves sent to plantations in remote or isolated locations often found the adjustments even more difficult. Lymus, a twenty-eight-year-old Charleston bricklayer, was sold to Thomas Butler King, a planter on St. Simons, a barrier island fronting on the Atlantic Ocean and surrounded by salt marshes and tidal streams. A few years later, the famous Englishwoman Frances Anne (Fanny) Kemble gave her impression of the condition of the slaves on St. Simons: the "filthy and wretched" quarters, the meals of corn grits and "small rice" (unfit for market), and the "inhumanity of allowing a man to strip and lash a woman, the mother of ten children; to exact from her, toil." Lymus discovered as well that the slaves on St. Simons were different from himself in dress, manner, beliefs, and speech, speaking Gullah with its African rhythm and inflections. A short time after his arrival, he managed to escape from the island and was seen on the road going from Darien to Savannah. He "will probably endeavor to make his way back to Charleston," King's agent wrote, hiring himself out at plantations along the way.[14]

For a few, even the possibility of such dislocations was too much to bear. In 1820, Jane's Tennessee owner decided to move to Missouri. She expressed great unwillingness to leave the state "and was very anxious" to be sold "to some person in the neighbourhood." She had grown up in Rutherford County, was very close to her mother and siblings, and dreaded the prospect of leaving family and friends. She beseeched her owner to sell her to someone in the area, but he refused. A few days before she was scheduled to leave, she took her master's horse, rode off, and did not return. What went through her mind during the next twenty-four hours is difficult to say: Should she hide out? Try to escape? Go to her family for help? The following day, the horse was discovered near a mill pond, her shoes were set neatly a short distance from the shore, her handkerchief tied to the limb of a tree, and her footprints led down to the edge of the water. Sixteen days later, Jane's bloated corpse rose to the surface and was found bobbing near the edge of the pond by a local farmer.[15]

Loved Ones

The weeks following a sale were especially traumatic for slaves. Shackled and taken away, placed in holding pens, beginning the journey to an unknown location, they were driven overland in coffles, chained aboard riverboats, or confined to the hold of coastal vessels, under the constant surveillance of slave traders. Any attempt to seek liberty at this point would be dealt with harshly, as the men who conducted the interregional transfer of slaves were intent on delivering their human cargo in good condition and at the designated time. The passage was nearly unbearable for many slaves. The heartbreak of leaving a husband or wife, mother or father, child or loved one behind, whom they would probably never see again, created feelings of indescribable despair and anguish.

Even as they were being transported, however, some struggled to return to loved ones. Although Moses was only about forty years old, he had "a bunch of gray hair on the right side of his head," and when he was taken away from Duplin County, North Carolina, to be sold on speculation, he was described as having "a very sullen look." He and another slave were placed in the hands of a trader, but they soon escaped. "These Negroes were purchased by me," a South Carolina speculator explained, "for the purpose of trading." They would attempt "to reach their former homes." Another North Carolina slave, Jim, faced a similar situation when he was purchased by slave trader Stephenton Page Jr., who had created a speculative partnership with two Edgecombe County slave owners. Jim and five others were to be taken to Mississippi, but shortly before their departure, Jim took off. Upon his return Page tracked down the fugitive and then sold him.[16]

To escape from slave traders was extremely difficult, but a few slaves watched and waited and, when the traders let down their guard, struck out on their own. The five who absconded in 1852 from J. N. Andrews's camp near Manchester, Virginia, en route to the Lower South, were among the few successful runaway groups in the domestic trade. They were not chained together, as usual, and it took only a few minutes relaxation on the part of those in charge before they realized that the group was missing. An extensive search was conducted to no avail. In their early to mid-twenties, the four men and woman had recently been purchased from the Baltimore slave trading firm of B. M. and Walter L. Campbell, who had a reputation for selling "quality merchandise." Andrews was especially tormented by the loss of Leanah, a dark mulatto who was pregnant, "supposed to be about four months gone."[17]

In the early weeks and months after arriving in a new location, slaves considered how they might return to their family. For the vast majority, it would be impossible, and they were forced to form new relationships and try to adjust to a new environment. But others were unwilling to accept separation, and almost as soon as they arrived, they began to plot their return home. The same day he was sold at Stone Fort, Franklin County, Tennessee, twenty-five-year-old Anthony, described as "very black—is a trim built, well-set fellow and very artful," set out to return to his family and friends across the Appalachian Mountains in Guilford County, North Carolina. He made it only the 135 miles to Knoxville before he was apprehended, jailed, and retrieved by his new owner. Two months later, in January 1814, Anthony set out again, and this time his owner was less sure where he might go. He might attempt another homeward journey, vanish "into the Indian nation, or possibly go to Nashville." In June of that year, he was still at large.[18]

Those who were transported down the Ohio, Mississippi, Tennessee, and Cumberland rivers, from the eastern seaboard around the tip of Florida and across the gulf, or by land across the Appalachian Mountains and down the Natchez Trace experienced the profound shock of a new land, new climate, and new culture. Arriving in Natchez or New Orleans, slaves from various parts of the Upper South were placed in large pens (jails) to await sale. For most of them, the final leg of their journey would be to the great plantations that lined the rivers and bayous of Louisiana and Mississippi. Nearly without exception, they longed to return to their homes and families. Elsy had been in New Orleans only three months and spoke "nothing but English" when she ran away. By the time James, a mulatto in his early thirties, absconded, he had learned a little French, but most of his life had been spent in Virginia. James "is a native of Virginia," his new owner said, and "arrived here from Norfolk about 7 months ago." In her early twenties, "stout built and large in the family way," the Tennessee slave Eliza escaped six weeks after her arrival. No doubt, the purchaser said, she would return to her former plantation. The fifteen-year-old South Carolina slave who arrived in New Orleans in 1830 on the *Dorade* ran off soon after his arrival.[19] New Orleans owners of recently arrived slaves who promptly absconded warned captains of steamboat and ocean vessels to keep watch for runaways who might be attempting to return to their homes in the upper states.

Husbands and Wives

Husbands separated from their wives accounted for a number of runaways. A house servant and personal waiter named George was on his way to "get to his wife," his Virginia master said; she belonged to a man living near the Lancaster County Court House. He was thought to have obtained a forged pass to seek out a new master or hire himself to tavern keepers in Fredericksburg, Norfolk, or Baltimore. The couple, once reunited, might strike out for New England by stowing away on a sailing vessel. Twenty-seven-year-old Sam, whose wife was owned by Jesse Parker on White's Creek in Davidson County, Tennessee, ran away, but was later seen at Parker's and was "believed to be in that neighborhood yet."[20]

Other runaways who were separated from their wives were similarly spotted at various times "lurking about" plantations or towns and cities where their wives lived. The slave Major of Lebanon, Wilson County, was "probably lurking about Nashville, as he has a wife at Mr. Joseph Wood's." A few weeks after he left, the Charleston shoemaker Turner (his master called him Zeno) was spotted in the neighborhood of Goose Creek, where his wife was a slave. The thirty-five-year-old black man was well known about Charleston as a fiddler. Another runaway, a field hand in his late thirties, was sold to a South Carolina Sea Island planter, but wasted only a few weeks before he set out to return to his wife and child on a plantation near Georgetown.[21]

Men often went to great lengths and traveled many miles to reunite with spouses. The obstacles they faced were often as great as the distances involved. Sometimes the quest meant attempting to traverse hundreds of miles. Having stolen a silver watch and some money, the twenty-two-year-old black man named January vanished from his New Orleans owner in May 1839. He could have been stolen, his owner H. F. Wade said, but was probably on his way to Vicksburg, Mississippi, to be with his wife. The escaped Alabama slave Wiley, about thirty-seven years old, would "make his way to Tennessee, where he says he has a wife." In his late thirties, tall and dark-skinned, Anthony spoke "remarkably quick when spoken to" and was "very intelligent and subtle." He had been sold to a man in Dallas County, Alabama, in 1852 and now was heading back to Spartanburg, South Carolina. Anthony had persuaded two slaves to join him, and the three

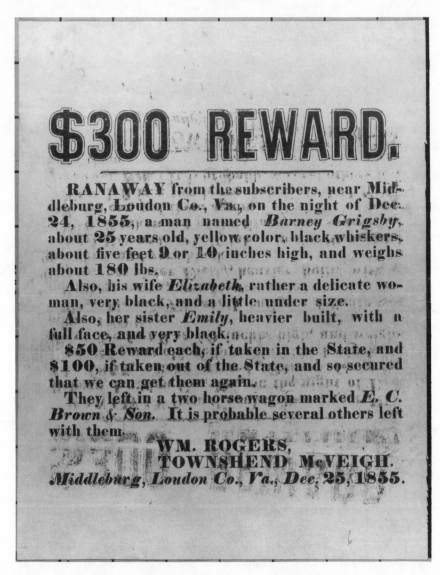

$300 REWARD.

RANAWAY from the subscribers, near Middleburg, Loudon Co., Va., on the night of Dec. 24, 1855, a man named *Barney Grigsby,* about 25 years old, yellow color, black whiskers, about five feet 9 or 10 inches high, and weighs about 180 lbs.

Also, his wife *Elizabeth,* rather a delicate woman, very black, and a little under size.

Also, her sister *Emily,* heavier built, with a full face, and very black.

$50 Reward each, if taken in the State, and $100, if taken out of the State, and so secured that we can get them again.

They left in a two horse wagon marked *E. C. Brown & Son.* It is probable several others left with them.

WM. ROGERS,
TOWNSHEND McVEIGH.
Middleburg, Loudon Co., Va., Dec. 25, 1855.

Husbands and wives often found it difficult to abscond together, but in this broadside Barney and Elizabeth Grigsby, along with Elizabeth's sister Emily and several unidentified slaves, made off in a stolen wagon. How valuable they were to their owners was suggested by the large reward and the publication of their escape within a few hours after their departure on Christmas Eve.

probably obtained forged passes "or some guarantee to travel with, as they have all taken a week's provision and all their bed clothing and apparel." Anthony had a wife in South Carolina, the owner said, "which seems to be the object of the expedition."[22]

Anthony's "expedition" was only one of many made by male slaves in search of their partners. How strong the urge was to overcome forced separations can be viewed by the frantic and continued attempts of husbands to reunite with their wives by running away. Indeed, some slaves became so obsessed with seeing their wives that they became oblivious to the most severe punishments. While the information about Thomas Taylor, a dark-freckled mulatto, is more complete than others, his case was not isolated. Sold away from his wife in Natchez down to New Orleans in April 1839, Taylor, who was "badly ruptured, and may have on Warner's Patent Truss," returned to his wife in the same month, but was captured, jailed, and returned. In August, he made a second attempt and was taken up before he left New Orleans. In October, he made a third attempt and was caught in Baton Rouge "on his way to Natchez." To avoid being returned, he lied about the name of his owner, but was still returned to the Crescent City. When his owner Thomas B. Winston advertised in May 1840—Taylor's fourth attempt in a year—he did so by berating his slave: Taylor appeared "rather dull" in countenance, and Winston offered fifty dollars if captured out of state "so that I get him delivered in New Orleans."[23]

The relationship between husbands and wives was used by some owners to control their slaves. Granting visiting privileges or permitting wives and children to visit husbands on their plantations was an advantage few blacks were willing to forsake. Some masters refused to permit visitations or required that marriages take place on the plantation; when they were permitted, the privilege was tightly controlled. But many masters believed that allowing husbands to visit their wives (or vice versa) served as a safety valve against discontent. Masters made it a point to know where their slaves' spouses lived, and very often that was the first place they looked when husbands were discovered missing.

Slaves who ran away to be with their wives were embarking on a risky and hazardous undertaking. Most were not successful, especially if the master knew where the spouse lived. But a few were able to avoid capture. When he learned in January 1817 that his wife was being taken to another state, North Carolina slave Randol ran away from his master in Franklin County, North Carolina. Randol was in his mid-twenties, "rather yellow complected," and his owner warned whites not to be taken in by his "humble" demeanor. One should look for "marks of shot about his hips, thighs, neck and face, and he has been shot at several times." More than a year later, Randol had still not been located by his master.[24]

The runaway Joe did not fare as well. Depicted as "large" and "likely," Joe belonged to William Hutt of Westmoreland County, Virginia. He had been at large for several days when a notice went out on Christmas Eve 1808 calling for patrols to suppress a rumored "Insurrection of Slaves Generally through the State." Unaware of the order, Joe remained hidden in his wife's cabin on a nearby plantation, but shortly before midnight, he was awakened by the sound of horses. When a patroller shouted for the slaves to step slowly out of their cabin, Joe bolted out the door and sprinted into the woods. "We commanded him to stop, but he continued his flight," a member of the patrol testified, and one of the men fired. Joe kept on running, however, and the whites thought that he had escaped, until they heard the cries of pain coming from the woods and found him lying severely wounded in the knee and foot. Two days later, he died.[25]

Although few husbands who sought to be with their wives were shot and killed, most ended up as did Tom, a Louisiana slave who absconded in 1822. On good and reliable intelligence, a magistrate in New Orleans explained, he had discovered that Tom was "secreted and Concealed" in the chamber of "the Negro Wench named Rose who lives in the yard of the house of Madam Cormick in Custom house Street." The magistrate ordered a constable to go to the residence and bring the slave "forthwith before me or Some other Magistrate of this City, to be dealt with according to law."[26]

Wives seeking to reunite with their husbands also ran away in a number of instances. Since children were the property of the mother's owner when they were born, it was more difficult for women than men to seek out their spouses. This, however, did not deter female slaves whose children had been sold, who were childless, or whose children were grown or owned by other slaveholders from setting out to find their partners. Owned by a woman in Jefferson Parish, Louisiana, Jane ran away on a number of occasions to be with her slave husband, John Brown, in New Orleans. Brown, a self-hired cook owned by David Bidwell, rented rooms and houses in "unfrequented portions of the City, for the purpose of more effectually concealing the whereabouts of the said slave woman."[27]

The poignant and heart-wrenching stories of women being sold away from their partners and running back to find them are numerous. Alone or clutching their children, they hid in the woods or on neighboring plantations, secluding themselves to be near their husbands.

Shortly after being sold, the South Carolina slave Sally, easily identified by her remarkably "square and flat" face, headed straight to Parker's Ferry and the plantation where her husband lived. Another slave, Nelly, owned by Isham Lowery, the captain of a coastal sloop running from Ashepoo to Charleston, left her master's plantation near Pototaligo and went straight to her husband, who concealed her for more than six months.[28]

Usually, though, those who went in search of their husbands were likely to remain at large only for brief periods, especially if they decided to take their children. Sold at auction by a man from Virginia, the forty-year-old Elvy and her two-year-old baby, Mary, were carried off by her new owner, but a short time later, she ran off with her child. The new owner said that "The above slaves are thought to be harbored in the neighborhood of the Old Church, in the lower end of Hanover county, and in the neighborhood of Dr. Webb's in the upper end of Essex, at which place she has a husband." The Virginia mulatto Martha, about thirty years old, was bought and sold twice, once to a commission house and once at auction, before she was transported to Bedford County. Originally from Chesterfield County, she left her master with a forged pass and took her nine-month-old infant. The owner believed she would return to Chesterfield County to be with her husband.[29]

As with their husbands, the treks made by female slaves were sometimes lengthy. Thirty-five-year-old Lucretia fled from her owner George R. Gibbons in Bridgewater, Rockingham County, Virginia, to be with her husband, Henry Long, who lived about one hundred and fifty miles to the east near the Farnham Church in Richmond County. A notice in the *Richmond Enquirer* in 1805 regarding Nancy, another Virginia slave, did not indicate her reason for running, but it was nonetheless obvious. She and her nine-month-old son had been sold away from her owner Laurence Ashton of King George County, who lived near the Potomac River, to Littleton Sims, a slaveholder in Greenville County, Virginia, located on the North Carolina border. Nancy got only halfway to her new home when she ran off. The man who bought her said she was heading back to her former home. She could be identified by "a very bad burn on the right side of her face."[30]

So deep were the bonds between some runaway wives and husbands that occasionally slave owners acquiesced in their desire to be together. Wenny and Easter, two slaves belonging to a woman in Northumberland County, Virginia, had attempted to escape during the War of 1812, but had been captured and sent to the western county of Rockingham. After the war, the two women, who had been hired out, had each found a husband, and Wenny had given birth to a baby boy named Isaac. It was the slaveholder's belief that Easter was "very much opposed to being separated from" her husband and if brought back would probably abscond. In the end, the owner yielded to the wishes of the slaves, selling them to masters in the west. Among those attracted to the western lands in Alabama was South Carolina planter John Garlington, who in 1833 decided to send a group of his slaves to that state, including the wife of a man who belonged to a trust established for the benefit of a neighbor's wife. "The boy had a great affection for his wife," the white woman's trustee said, "and had run away apparently determined on trying at all events" to remain with his wife. He anticipated that Abram, the slave, would cause "great trouble" if the two were separated. Another observer said that Abram had already run away once to see his wife and would probably do so in the future. "Garlington being about to send off this wench with other negroes to the State of Alabama Proposed buying the boy Abram." The trustee, after consulting with the owner and petitioning the court, sold Abram to Garlington for $650. The slave couple then went to Alabama together.[31]

Attempting to escape with a spouse was nearly as hazardous as running away with children. While there were only two people to feed, care for, seclude, and disguise, a black man and woman attempting to board a boat, riding horses, or even walking along roads together, often attracted attention. Such was the case of Isaac and Mary, who were quickly overtaken in Concordia Parish, Louisiana, in 1833 by a slave catcher named Joseph Bradshaw, who said that he "took them up in the public highway about 10 miles from the Town of Vidalia." Similarly, Caesar and Eliza made off from Edmund W. Watkins of Warren County, North Carolina, in the summer of 1852, but their master was in close pursuit. They were heading for Virginia, where Eliza had once lived, he said. "These negroes being man and wife," Watkins added, "will doubtless remain together."[32]

Whether a man and woman were husband and wife or merely ran away together was not indicated in some runaway advertisements, but often their relationship can be inferred from other information. The two slaves who were captured in Overton County, Tennessee, in December 1837 were described as "a fellow about six feet high, ordinary complexion, heavy and well made, quick and prompt in speech, open and good countenance, about 25 years of age, a Woman about 26 years old, common size, yellow complexion, open and intelligent countenance." They belonged to the estate of Samuel Hopson in Bedford County, Virginia, and they had run away together in August, crossed the Appalachian Mountains, and journeyed to Middle Tennessee. They remained together during the four months they were at large. Caesar's owner thought it strange that his thirty-five-year-old slave baker and bread carrier in New Orleans ran away about the same time as did a black woman who belonged to a planter near the city. He suspected, however, that the couple were man and wife. Nor did the St. Charles Parish plantation owner Chevalier Delhommer state the relationship between his twenty-five-year-old "creole borne negroe" woman and his twenty-five-year-old "dark complexion mulattoe" man who ran away at nearly the same time in the winter of 1830. Similarly, the New Orleans brothers who owned Frederick, a handsome thirty-year-old "griffe," did not know whether he had taken his wife and their daughter, who was "very smart for her age," but they supposed he had because they all came up missing at the same time.[33]

Among the husbands and wives who ran away together, there were touching stories of love and devotion. In 1832, Aric, or Azic, and his wife Betsey, both about thirty years old and "a long time in the country," set out from a plantation in St. Charles Parish, Louisiana, for New Orleans. They both spoke fluent French and English, Aric was dark skinned and Betsey was a mulatto. The couple was apprehended, jailed, and returned, but two months later they set out together again. Bob, a Mississippi slave, was a large man, about six feet tall, and strongly built. At age thirty, he was proud and dignified, wearing his hair plaited in locks on either side of his head, and he called himself Robert Gilmore. When Vina—a few years younger, dark, quick spoken, and attractive—was brought from St. Louis, the two fell in love. In the summer of 1839, they made plans to escape. When they fled together in September of that year their owner, Mordecai Baldwin, a ferry operator and landowner in Hinds County, thought they might have been stolen but gradually became convinced that the husband and wife ran away together. More than nine months later, they remained at large.[34]

Mothers and Children

It was not known whether other slave women absconding with their children were searching for their husbands or were simply attempting to get away or "get back home." The proportion of females fleeing with their offspring in the total runaway population was small, but they bore silent testimony to the indomitable spirit of those who rejected slavery. Pleasants took with her four children—Billey, Catey, Joe, and James—when she set out. The record does not show whether the four naked slaves were her children when they were captured and put in the Surry County, Virginia, jail. It does show, however, that

Pleasants's owner did not want to claim her or the children and that while in jail she gave birth to another child. Perhaps as punishment, Pleasants was forced to languish in jail for a year with the children and baby. In 1826, Lazette, or Elizabeth, a South Carolina slave, avoided being jailed, but her owner seemed not to be worried. She would not get far, he said in the Charleston *Mercury*, with a six-month-old baby.[35]

Mothers who departed with their children confronted special difficulties. It was not easy to feed, clothe, care for, and protect children while on the run. The physical burden of carrying babies or youngsters four or five years of age was extreme, while the seven- or eight-year-olds had trouble keeping up and often tired quickly. One runaway mother took her child despite his being "sick with a sore mouth and cannot speak." Mothers themselves often suffered from maladies. Thirty-year-old Matilda, a New Orleans black who absconded in 1832 with her seven-year-old son, had a tumor on the side of her neck. A number of the women who ran away with their children were city slaves or had recently arrived in the city. They planned to hide out, get to a suburb, or sneak aboard a sailing craft or steamboat. The owner of Jenny, a mulatto servant who departed from his house in the French Quarter carrying her two-and-a-half-month-old baby, would, the owner believed, attempt to embark on a steamboat.[36]

Pregnant women also ran away. Twenty-one-year-old Lucille, a Louisiana woman who set out in 1833, was "in an advanced stage of pregnancy." "The captains of vessels are requested not to give her shelter," the New Orleans widow who owned her threatened, "under the pain provided by law" to punish the captains. Nancy was seven or eight months pregnant and was limping because of a sore toe when she ran away in 1834, shortly before Christmas. Twenty-eight-year-old Jane, or Jinny, a mulatto slave, was "with child" when she absconded in 1835. The runaway Martha Ann, Virginia slave owner John J. Minter said in 1850, "expects to be confined in six or eight weeks." He had purchased Martha Ann—an eighteen-year-old mulatto—only two months before.[37]

Perhaps even more heartrending were children running away to find their mothers and fathers. Their chances of success were very remote, as eight-, nine-, ten-, and eleven-year-olds usually wandered in vain seeking their parents. Invariably they were caught and returned to their owners. By the time they reached their early to mid-teens, however, their chances had improved but only slightly. The runaway notices did not usually mention the motives of slaves who absconded, but for youngsters, the owners surmised that they were attempting to follow a mother or father or uncle or aunt or grandparent who had been sold. How Peter, age fourteen or fifteen, made it from the farm in northern Virginia to the mountains of Alabama without being detected seems a remarkable feat in itself. He was jailed in Tallapoosa County, however, and the jailer sent a letter to a Richmond newspaper asking his owner "to come forward, prove his property, pay expenses and take him away." Nothing was said about why the youngster was running toward the heart of the deep South, but it surely had to do with a search for his family.[38]

It was more certain why Littleton, about fourteen or fifteen, ran away from his owner Mark Robertson Cockrill, the famous Marino sheep breeder in Davidson County, Tennessee. He headed across the Appalachian Mountains to be with his mother in Virginia. He would almost surely lie about his name and about the name of his owner, Cockrill said. "I expect he has started to Richmond, Va., where he was raised." Even though the notice appeared in both the *Tennessee Republican Banner* and the *Knoxville Register*, neither apparently did any good. Eight months later, the teenager was still at large.[39]

Families and Relatives

Occasionally, siblings or father-son, father-daughter combinations ran away.[40] The newspaper advertisement telling about a father and daughter in Virginia, was very unusual. "STOP THE RUNAWAYS," the *Richmond Enquirer* commanded in 1806. The father, Jim, age about thirty-five or forty, and Sally, age thirteen or fourteen, set out from the Big Otter River, fifteen miles west of Lynchburg, in Campbell County. The man was described as "little light complected" and the girl as "tolerably bright complected." The owner believed that they would attempt "to pass as free man and wife."[41]

Learning that a loved one was in danger, injured, near death, or had died sent slaves running, sometimes great distances. Such flights were often unplanned and could prove perilous. In such cases, masters usually knew not only where to look but the reason for the slaves' absconding. Burton had been separated from his mother for many years, and at age thirty, he had come to accept the difficulties of gaining permission to visit her in Mills Point, Kentucky, about sixty miles north of where he lived in Cherryville, Tennessee. In 1838 when he learned that his mother had died, Burton fled, and his master was certain he was heading for Kentucky to grieve with his stepfather. In 1824, Maryland planter Thomas Lynch purchased Michael, already in his forties. Michael had lived in the area his entire life, and his wife lived nearby. Following a violent storm that destroyed plantation buildings, sheds, and fences, Michael, his owner complained, "left my crops to the risk of the hogs and cattle to goe to see his wife." He was not whipped, but after another absence to see her, Michael was sold.[42]

Perhaps the most difficult task was for an entire family—husband, wife, children, grandparents, grandchildren—to try to escape together. Collecting food, clothing, and other necessities before leaving, coordinating the time and place for the getaway, and traveling in a group without being detected were only a few of the obstacles entire families faced. When youngsters were involved, it took great energy and ingenuity on the part of the parents to provide for their transportation and sustenance. The larger the group, the greater the possibility of being observed. Parents had to assist youngsters, remain calm, and convey a mood of confidence. It was necessary to remain positive and encouraging despite the constant dangers. Nevertheless, families did leave together, and while they rarely made it to freedom, some were able to find refuge for extended periods.

In most instances runaway families included a husband and wife and one or two children. Other than their remarkable courage, the family groups differed in age, color, skills, literacy, and appearance. The family that absconded from Carthage, Tennessee, on the Cumberland River above Nashville, included twenty-eight-year-old Bob, his eighteen-year-old wife Hester, and their twenty-month-old daughter, who all rode off on their owner's large bay mare. They took with them a new saddle and "two large bundles." The master of a South Carolina slave Maria, a "fine tall mulatto" age about thirty, painted a unique picture of members of a runaway family in 1828: Maria left her owner on a Saturday, taking her two children—Adelaide, about seven years old and "almost white," and James, about six years old and "coal black." Accompanied by her literate black husband, Henderson, they possessed a forged pass to travel to another county. The three slaves who absconded from a Maury County plantation in 1840 included Allen, upwards of forty years old, advertised as a bright mulatto with hazel eyes who could read and write "a little" and had "no grey hairs about him"; his wife Cassy, a large woman nearly forty years of age, a dark mulatto who had lost her front teeth; and their grey-eyed daughter Emily, a "bright mulatto" about twenty-two years old.[43]

Usually it was the fear of being separated that prompted families to run away. Those who had lived for many years in one area felt great pain when they were sold away, even in the very rare instances when families were sold or transferred as a unit. A slave named July waited two years after being taken with his loved ones to South Carolina before he escaped with his wife Dolly and their four children, ranging in age from infancy to eleven years, back to North Carolina. They had previously been sold to a planter on the Black River, near Georgetown, and now they would try to make it back home, their owner said, where July was "well acquainted at different plantations." Frank and Charlotte and their four children—Morris, age sixteen; Eliza, age fourteen; Lydia, age about ten; Rosabelle, age two—felt a similar pain of separation when they were sold in an estate sale in 1824, even though they went to a planter in the same state. "Frank is thin and short; Charlotte is thick, heavy and clumsy, a long yellowish face, and a large scar on her upper lip," Cox said in a South Carolina newspaper. The parents and their four children had glided silently away in a boat late one Saturday night, he added; they went to join up with the other slaves sold in the same estate sale.[44]

If it was problematic for family groups to remain at large indefinitely, it was virtually impossible for larger groups coming from different families or groups of relatives to avoid recapture. Yet such groups made attempts. On the 6 December 1814, eleven slaves ran away from the plantation of James Austin, near the mouth of Stones River in Davidson County, Tennessee. They included Charles, Becky, and their three children; Nancy and her daughter, Betty and her son and two daughters; a woman named Hannah; and two younger girls. The relationship among them was not specified, but their ages and descriptions suggest kinship ties.[45]

One remarkable example occurred 25 May 1839, when a forty-six-year-old black woman Lettus and her husband George, also in his forties, and their three children—Adam, Susan, and Beny—absconded from a plantation in Jefferson County, Florida. They took Susan's one-year-old child Lettus, George's granddaughter, and a ten-year-old girl named Liz, whose relationship to the family was not revealed. The seven slaves, described as "very black," were owned by three masters. The runaway notice said that George was an "intelligent fellow" who had been in "charge of his master's affairs." The family set out from near Monticello, the county seat located ten miles south of the Georgia border, but whites believed they would be moving west and might try to get to Louisiana. The first two owners said that George "stole" his family. They were still at large a month later.[46]

Assistance

Slaves who remained "at large" for weeks or months were often harbored or assisted by family members or relatives. This, of course, could be hazardous for those who provided assistance. It was very difficult to keep other slaves from knowing about secreted runaways, and on small plantations or estates with especially diligent overseers, outsiders were easily uncovered. Nonetheless, slaves ran to family members, sometimes long distances, and found temporary refuge. Some owners knew that their bondspeople were being "harbored by their relatives" but were still unable to find them. Ned, his wife Bella, and their three children—Beck, age fourteen; Abel, age twelve; and Robert, age three—ran away from a plantation on the South Santee River, South Carolina. They had been sold from the Vanderhorst estate in Christ Church Parish and absconded within a few days. Absent for more than a year, their owner was convinced that they were still in the neighborhood, protected and hidden by relatives and acquaintances. The husband had even been spotted making trips to Charleston for supplies.[47]

It is clear that some runaways had a network of black friends and loved ones from whom they could expect assistance. The mulatto Julius was a sawyer, rough carpenter, and fairly good cooper who lived near Williamsburg, Virginia. When he set out in 1806, his owner thought he might go either to the plantation of Richard Byrd in York County to be near his wife, to the city of Williamsburg "where he is acquainted," or to King William County, where he had previously lived and still had "connections." The "likely mulatto woman" Kitty, of Henrico County, was married to a black man, James, a hired slave who lived near the coal pits. When they ran away together in 1808, the owners said the couple had three choices to find refuge: the husband had a "good many relations" in Chesterfield and Powhatan counties; both were "very intimate" with the slaves on Augustine Davis's plantation in Henrico; and they could find refuge with Kitty's father and mother, owned by Jesse Smith, also of Henrico. The parents of Kitty were "both very artful and designing, and as her mother has more influence than generally falls to the lot of slaves, she may perhaps be concealed by her."[48]

When he left the Cumberland Iron Works in Stewart County, Tennessee, the hired slave Charles went straight to Nashville, where his slave brother lived. The brother, Charles's owner said, was owned by "a man by the name of Beaty, on Water street." Charles was still at large two months after he allegedly arrived in the city. The Alabama owner of the slave Jim, alias Armstead, knew exactly where Jim might go when he left riding a pacing horse in 1838: he would head either for New Orleans or Nashville. The owner, George W. Lane of Limestone County, said that Jim had been raised in Nashville, had many friends there, and his free black mother, who had married Wilson Davis, lived there. Jim had spent several years in New Orleans and had friends there as well.[49] The destinations of other slaves were similar: they ran away to parents, grown children, relatives, and friends.

But owners were not always as confident as Jim's. The runaway Reuben of Giles County, Tennessee, in his early twenties, was probably heading to visit his mother in Smithland, Kentucky, but his owner could not be certain. Born about 1819 in Salem, Kentucky, Reuben had been raised in the Bluegrass State; carried to Jackson, Arkansas, where he lived for several years and had relatives; and sold into Tennessee in his mid- to late teens. He had run away before, his owner said, and had found employment on a Cumberland River steamboat, trading on the Mississippi to New Orleans. The owner sent his advertisement to the *Smithland Times* and the *Little Rock Advocate*. Caesar, "a likely black fellow"—owned by a man in St. John's Berkley, South Carolina, sold to Henry Carnes of Georgetown, sold again to a man in Charleston—was "country born." His mother, however, was a slave in Charleston, as were other relatives who might be harboring him. Another Charleston slave, a house servant, Peter, ran away without reason except that he had allegedly committed "a fault," and his owner said he would "probably go in the country, (near Ashepoo) where he has some relations."[50]

Runaways were not only assisted by relatives in slavery, but were also helped by kin who were free. Although some mothers had become free, their children who were born before they were emancipated were, of course, slaves. There are examples, nevertheless, of free mothers attempting to assist their children who were still slaves. This, too, was dangerous. It could mean that the free blacks involved could be returned to bondage. Yet a large percentage of the free black population lived in cities or were separated from whites in farming areas. Their ability to take in a fugitive without drawing attention was better than for slaves who were in proximity to whites.

The owner of Euphemie had purchased her in her mid-teens from an estate sale in St. Landry Parish and taken her to New Orleans. It was very probable, the owner said when she ran away, that she would make her way back to the area near Opelousas, where her free mother and free sisters lived. Instructions were sent to the *Opelousas Gazette* to carry the notice of Euphemie's desertion. The owner of Sarah described her as a handsome young woman with yellow skin, broad face, and large full eyes. Sarah wore an attractive calico frock with long white sleeves, black beads, earrings, and a handkerchief tied high on her head, when she ran away in December 1825 to be with her mother, Bess McIntosh, a free woman of color who lived along Swinton's Alley in Charleston. Another South Carolina slave, twenty-five-year-old Will, a hand on the schooner *Charlotte* running the South Santee

River, fled in 1826. His master believed he was heading for the residence of his free black father, John Townsend, who also lived in
Charleston.[51]

There were also older slaves who absconded to be with loved ones.
It was just as painful for slaves in their thirties, forties, and fifties to
be separated from loved ones as for younger blacks—perhaps more so.
Prior to his sale following the death of his owner, the fifty-year-old
Virginia gardener Jack elicited a promise from his new owner, a gentleman planter in Amherst County, that he would be permitted to visit
his free black wife in Richmond on a regular basis. "Jack has thought
proper to abuse this indulgence," his owner complained, "by not returning to his master." Eight months later Jack was still abusing "this
indulgence." The owner placed two different notices seeking his return. He was probably hiding out near Manchester, Chesterfield
County, where his wife's friends lived, said the first notice; he was
well-known around Richmond, had free connections in Chesterfield
County, or might be hiding in the vicinity of Williamsburg, added the
second.[52]

New Orleans, with its large free black population, was a favorite
destination for runaway slaves seeking help from free black relatives.
Slave owners in the city frequently noted in their advertisements that
their slaves "in all probability" would be hiding out in the city or a
suburb with a free black mother, daughter, father, son, or relative. The
owner of thirty-eight-year-old Eugenie was sure she was being harbored in the neighborhood where her mother, a free black, lived. A
dark-colored creole slave in the city who spoke French and "a little
English" was absent for three months when her owner, N. Wilkinson,
said that an unidentified man had stopped at his residence and said he
had seen her in the city. "She has a free colored man for husband and
is no doubt harbored by him," the owner said through the columns
of the New Orleans Picayune in 1840. He requested that the man who
had provided the intelligence "call again." When the owner of William, a twenty-three-year-old New Orleans slave, refused to grant him
his wish to be sold "to an individual of Louisville to whom he formerly
belonged" so he could be near his kin, William ran away. Later, the
owner discovered that William's brother, a free black person, was
crewman aboard the steamboat Watchman that "left here on the day
and hour of his [William's] going."[53]

Occasionally, free relatives in the North plotted to free family members remaining in bondage. Free blacks who had either escaped themselves or obtained freedom in other ways were reluctant to return to
the South. But there were other ways. Literate fugitive William Smith
of Cincinnati, Ohio, communicated with a white man in Kentucky

about what it might take to free his family. "I have the necessary papers for Andy and $15.00 You will please direct him as you think best," Smith wrote S. Pemberton in 1842. If Pemberton could somehow get him out of the "immediate neighborhood," perhaps there was a chance of escape. "Please write me whether Mr. Smith designs settling in that country or not and what he intends doing with my wife and child." Smith had considered going himself and also "trying to buy them," but had ruled out both options, the latter because "times are so hard at present." "Please do your utmost to secure the escape of Andy and the blessing of a grateful father rest upon you."[54]

Most runaway slaves who were assisted in various ways by free relatives were recaptured and returned to bondage. It was extremely difficult for them to remain for lengthy periods with free relatives, both because of the economic strains it put on the free black families and the fear of relations being caught and prosecuted for harboring fugitives. There were very few examples of success, but in the case of one Indiana free black man, luck was on his side, at least up to a point. As the father and grandfather of a family of Kentucky slaves, he assisted his son, his daughter, and his grandchildren in escaping from bondage. All of them had "fled from servitude & most likely will be lost," the guardian of an estate that contained another son, William, explained. The free black father had planned and facilitated the flight of the family members and was secretly endeavouring to help his last son escape. The guardian's information had been received from "a free man of color who communicated to him the news of the said Williams intended departure." To prevent the loss of his ward's property, the white man took twenty-five-year-old William to the Jefferson County jail in Louisville and petitioned the Circuit Court for permission to sell the slave. With unprecedented swiftness, the court ruled the same day that William was "disposed to escape from servitude and will likely be a total loss to the estate" and should be sold.[55]

Lost Forever

While some runaways ran away as a family, others were forced to leave loved ones behind. It was often a crisis—the notification that a family member would be sold, the failure of an owner to keep his word, the death of a master—that sparked this response. The voluntary family breakups, however, were as much a part of the runaway phenomenon as seeking out relatives. "One of our family," a Tennessee slave recalled, "was picked up somewhere above Louisville in Kentucky." Henry Thomas's mother had planned his escape from

Nashville, when she learned he was about to be sold. Placed in irons
and housed in the local jail, Thomas escaped the first night. He worked
off his ankle irons, sneaked down the river, unfastened a yawl, and
sculled out into the river. "The night was cold," his brother later
recalled. "[He] headed the Yawl down stream, Sculled over the falls
and made the Indiana shore. There he found a man who freed his
hands." At the time, about 1834, Henry Thomas was in his mid-teens;
he never saw his mother again, although she lived another fifteen
years, dying of cholera in Nashville in 1849.[56]

Thomas's plight was not unusual for runaways. Many others left
their parents behind in slavery. Others were forced to leave parents
who were free. Twenty-four-year-old Celeste, the daughter of a St.
Louis slave, had been promised her freedom following the death of
her master. So, too, had her mother and brothers and sisters. When
the white woman who owned them died, however, most of the family
were kept in bondage. The owner's husband, who inherited the slaves,
freed only the mother and sold the children, including Celeste. Hired
out as a chambermaid on Mississippi River steamboats, she lived with
her mother in St. Louis during layovers, but when it became apparent
the owner planned to sell her to the "Southern Market" for prosti-
tution, she left her mother and fled to Chicago.[57]

What went through a mother's mind having to part with a son or
daughter in such a manner is difficult to imagine, but she could draw
some satisfaction from the fact that the children had made it to freedom. In many cases, parents did not know whether or not runaway
children were successful. They feared the worst and were constantly
thinking about a lost child. The mother of an eighteen-year-old South
Carolina slave named Poll actually beseeched her owner to offer a
reward for the return of her runaway son. Alexander England of
Charleston and St. Paul's Parish obliged the woman, "who feels much
about her boy," and put up twenty dollars for his return. Poll, he said,
was "a foolish Negro" whose services were "of no account," but his
mother was filled with anxiety and sorrow, as he had been missing six
months. England called upon the "friends of humanity" to keep watch
out for him. The slave had one eye partially closed, was often found
along Parker's Ferry Road, and might have been carried to Walterborough.[58]

The obverse was a curious turn when parents ran away leaving
children with the master. Mothers who left without their offspring
often felt pain and remorse for many years. Wearing a sunbonnet and
a dark calico dress, Eliza, a thirty-five-year-old New Orleans slave, left
two children at her owner's residence. Twenty-one-year-old Lucretia

also left her two children behind when she absconded in 1841 wearing a dark frock, a dark handkerchief on her head, and an old pair of black stockings. Her master said she had a scar on the back of her neck and sulked when spoken to by whites.[59]

Neither distance nor time could erase the memories family members had for one another. For some, it meant attempting to traverse great distances. "STOP THE RUNAWAY. FIFTY DOLLARS REWARD," an advertisement in the *Tennessee Gazette* read. "Eloped from the subscriber living near Nashville, on the 25th of June last [1804], a Mulatto Man Slave, about thirty years old, six feet and an inch high, stout made and active, talks sensible, stoops in his walk, and has a remarkable large foot, broad across the root of the toes." Although the slave remained anonymous, the famous subscriber, Andrew Jackson, knew his slave well. He had obtained "some means" in the way of "certificates," would try to pass as a free man, and was headed for upper Louisiana or the town of Detroit, across from Canada, where he had family relations.[60]

For other runaways, even being thwarted on several attempts over many years did not dim strong family memories. The slave Billy, or Will, had lived and worked in Albemarle County for ten or twelve years when he broke away. Striking out to the west across the Blue Ridge Mountains, thence northward up the Shenandoah Valley, he was captured in Rockingham County and jailed, having made it only one-third of the distance to Winchester, where he had grown up. His owner noted that Billy had not seen his mother or other family members in a decade, but when he broke out of jail in Harrisonburg, his master thought "he will make towards Winchester."[61]

For most slaves, the yearning to reunite with mothers, fathers, children, and other kin seemed never to diminish. The twenty-two-year-old slave Isaac, owned by a man in Gallatin, Tennessee, no doubt possessed "something purporting to be free papers," and he probably absconded to see his mother, who lived on nearby Drake's Creek. Forty-five-year-old Polly, "rather thick set" and "partially gray," had lived in Richmond, Virginia, most of her life until she was traded to New Orleans. When she absconded, her new owner thought she would be "seeking passage to Virginia," where she had been raised. Her features were "well formed," the master said, but she seemed sad, despairing, and frowned constantly. Nor was Polly alone in her dejection after being sent to locations far away from family and friends. The desperate efforts of slaves to return to kinfolk often met with failure, but they never relinquished hope.[62]

The letter of a fugitive living in Canada in 1850 reveals the depth

of despair felt by some former slaves. Through a friend, Thomas Right
wrote his wife and children about his escape, his new life in freedom,
his belief in Providence, and his yearnings to see them again.[63]

> I wish you to tell All that wantes to know how I made my ascape
> That I made it in the knight when the Moon was goin away an
> their was not yet To see but god and it was throw him that I
> made my ascape and throw him that I am Know gitting along. . . .
> I feel happy in my ascape untill I thinkes about my Wife and I
> hope that you bouth will talke to her and tell Her to be not
> dichampiond [discouraged] for I thinck That I Shall See you
> again. Tell him to tell her if she is not sole at Chrismous She
> mus let me know how She an the Childrens are gatting a long.

Perhaps no aspect of slavery was more painful than the separation
of loved ones. Few families—husbands, wives, and children—were sold
together. The domestic slave trade wreaked havoc on stable family life,
and the sale of individual slaves away from parents, children, and loved
ones occurred regularly nearly everywhere in the South. Most slaves
were not able to thwart the will of owners who sought to dispose of
their property in distant markets, but a significant number responded
by running away. In the end, these attempts were largely futile, as
those seeking members of their families were captured, arrested, returned, sold, or transferred. But if the breakup of families revealed the
callous nature of many slave traders, it also bore silent testimony to
the desperate attempts to maintain family unity in the midst of constant assault on its stability.

4

A Matter of Some Urgency

AN INVENTORY OF THE BON RIDGE PLANTATION in Catahoula Parish, Louisiana, in 1852, included eleven head of mules, six horses, eighty cattle, sixty hogs, tools, wagons, carts, yokes, ploughs, coupling chains, a log chain, a double-barreled shotgun, muskets, a rifle, and twenty-nine "head of negroes." The inventory was conducted following the death of Absalom Sharp, a migrant from Pennsylvania who had built his fortune in the cotton country around Natchez using the labor of slaves. At the time of his death in 1851, the sixty-six-year-old planter owned two sizeable estates, one in Adams County, Mississippi, and Bon Ridge.[1]

Obviously, there were serious problems on the plantation even when Sharp was alive. They became accelerated following his death, and his wife Clarissa, unable to control the slaves, invested considerable power in the hands of overseers. In 1852, F. W. Ford, the overseer, described just how serious the problems were.

> I was compel to day to shoot the boy Moses to save my own life [for Moses showed] a great deal of impudence rushed upon me and I give him the whole load in his left arm he fell back a little and then rushed upon me again, and I give him the barrel of my gun over the head but could not knock him down or conquer him until he lost so much blood that he could not help himself.

The slave was not badly wounded, the overseer noted, "nor is he conquered yet." Unconquered, too, was another slave among the twenty-nine "head of negroes" on Bon Ridge. Andy ran away in September but was captured by the sheriff in Franklin Parish, sixty-five miles to the north. Despite these problems, overseer Ford reported, the fall harvest would yield one hundred and fifty bales of cotton.[2]

The next year, Ford reported that Andy ran away again, this time taking a mule. "I think he will make for Winsbourough [Franklin Parish] as he formed a good many acquaintances up there last year," the overseer noted. Ford realized now how Andy had traveled such a distance in so short a time during his previous escape. "If you recolect I wrote to you last fall that I had lost a horse," he explained. Moses had been placed in charge of the horses and mules and had reported a horse dead. "I thought no more about it until Andy carried off this mule and then I recolected the horse was missing the same time that he was!"[3]

But the difficulties with Moses and Andy paled in comparison with the problems confronted by Duncan Skinner, Ford's successor at Bon Ridge. Skinner responded to the restiveness among the hands by wielding the whip. He flailed slaves virtually every evening, at least until he became so exhausted he could not continue. Standing at a window one evening at dusk, a visitor heard the pop of the rawhide and cries of anguish and asked a slave named Henderson about the "fuss in the quarter." The slave replied that it was only Skinner whipping the slaves—"it is no uncommon thing here." The visitor, John McAllin, who viewed Skinner as a rival for the hand of Clarissa Sharp, was later reported to have told Henderson: "Well, if I was you boys, I would get rid of that Man."[4]

Whether or not McAllin made this suggestion, three slaves—Henderson, Reuben, and Anderson—did, in fact, conspire to "get rid of that Man." One night shortly before dawn, they crept into the overseer's house, tiptoed to his bedside, and bashed him on the side of his head with a club. Somehow he got out of bed and staggered into the next room, but they quickly pursued him, threw him into a corner, and beat him senseless. As they carried him off into the woods, he showed signs of life, and one of the slaves "took him by the head, and twisted it around, thereby breaking his neck."

In the soft light of early morning, they laid Skinner on the ground, retrieved his clothes, watch, gun, riding whip, and horse, washed the blood away, dressed him, lifted him on the horse, and with Anderson behind him astride the horse, rode "around through the woods, and round a beech tree, jumping the horse about the tree, skinning the roots." They then threw his body on the ground, and turned the horse loose, with the saddle turned on the horse's side. Reuben fired off one barrel of the overseer's gun and placed it within a few paces of the body, also his whip, and cap, "arranging every thing so far as to bear the appearance, of the horse having been frightened and having thrown his rider."[5]

The ruse worked so successfully that the county coroner ruled Skinner's death accidental. But the overseer's brother refused to believe that Skinner, a fine horseman, had been thrown from his steed. He began to conduct a secret investigation. After several weeks the plot began to unravel. Anderson panicked and ran away. Reuben and Henderson also planned to escape but were caught. After some days, Anderson, hiding in a cotton gin on nearby Magnolia Plantation, was captured and brought back to face his mistress. In the end, the entire charade was brought to light.[6]

Assault and Murder

If intricately planned and systematically executed murders such as the one on Bon Ridge Plantation occurred infrequently in the slave South, the plantation "crimes" that sent slaves running, as well as those committed by blacks on the run—murder, assault, arson, poisoning, rape, pillage, burglary, theft—were frequent occurrences. So, too, was the participation of runaways in a variety of clandestine economic activities, especially the bartering, trading, buying, and selling of stolen goods. These overt and covert acts of resistance brought swift responses. Malingering, laziness, lying out, and "accidental" destruction of livestock and machinery was one thing. Openly and violently defying the system and seeking to undermine planter authority was something different. For slaves and masters alike it was "a matter of some urgency."

Most slaves understood the potentially grave consequences of assaulting a white person. In the period following the American Revolution, it could mean summary execution, and even later, extreme punishment. What is surprising is the persistence of violence on the plantation. For obvious reasons, such incidents often went unreported—masters did not wish to admit a failure in governing their human property and rumors that a slave was aggressive or belligerent diminished the slave's value. But the popular myth that "slaves are more generally good tempered than other people" is not supported by the evidence. Most of the violence was spontaneous, and most of it was directed against whites—owners, members of the owner's family, overseers—although it could also be directed against fellow slaves. The South Carolina slave Sam, for example, escaped early in 1814, remained at large for six months and "plundered the Settlement" of Abbeville. At the time of his capture, Sam stabbed and killed a fellow slave who had been ordered to apprehend him. In Virginia, between 1785 and 1864, among slaves convicted of violent murder, about one-third of the victims were fellow slaves or free persons of color.[7]

Although slaves did assault other slaves or free persons of color, their animus was reserved for whites. Nearly every year, in virtually every state in the South, slaves were indicted for killing their owners. During the 1850s in Greene County, Georgia, four bondsmen and two bondswomen were tried for murdering their owners or other whites. Among them was a man who had been hiding in the woods for several months and had just been brought in when he suddenly turned on his master, grabbed a knife, and stabbed him fifteen times; the master expired almost immediately. Other slaves, either before or after they ran off, reacted in a similar manner. One Maryland man severely slashed his master on each arm before running away. Another drew a knife on his owner's wife and child "threatening to take away their lives after which he ran away." In a knife fight between a Tennessee farmer and the "large black fellow" named Sam, it was the slave who fared the worse. He was "stabbed with a knife about the time he ran away."[8] These and other cases suggest a remarkable defiance by some runaways.

Although some slaves had firearms, they usually used knives, clubs, shovels, hoes, axes, and hatchets. When the manager of one Mississippi plantation, George Croley, ordered Samuel to make himself ready for a whipping, Samuel picked up a hatchet and struck the white man on the side of the head. Croley nearly died, and when a grand jury indicted Samuel for attempted murder, the black man was at large, being cited as "late of the county aforesaid." "ROBBERY AND INTENDED MURDER!" an article in the *Richmond Enquirer* of 10 September 1805 began. The slave Moses, who worked on vessels between Richmond, Williamsburg, and Norfolk, was usually cheerful. As the slave and master traveled along the road leading to Hampton, however, a disagreement occurred, and as the master put it, Moses "made an assault upon my life, and after giving me several dangerous, perhaps fatal wounds, robbed me and escaped on my horse, leaving me helpless on the ground." When an anonymous slave in Mississippi discovered that his wife had been whipped by her owner, the black man sneaked into his house at night and clubbed him on the head. The farmer did not die, but was "badly used up," a neighbor said, and was rescued when a woman screamed and "locked the door and prevented the negro from Killing him." The assailant bolted off with his wife, but was quickly apprehended and jailed.[9]

Typical of this reaction to bondage was the response of Ned, a black man from Chambers County, Alabama, owned by Thomas A. Smith. In 1841, Ned grabbed an axe and swung it at the head of his owner. He struck the right side and split the master's skull with a "mortal wound of the breadth of three inches and the depth of three inches." As with most indictments that followed such incidents, the grand jury said the black man had feloniously, willfully, and with malice afore-thought assaulted his owner. In truth, it was a spontaneous reaction. The governor of Alabama issued a proclamation for the slave's capture. By the time the proclamation was issued, the black man was in Missouri.[10]

Most often, it was an argument over work, punishment, or treatment of loved ones that drove slaves to violence. But there were instances of long-held bitter resentment that led some slaves to plan the murder of their owners, overseers (as on Bon Ridge Plantation), or members of the owner's family. One eleven-and-a-half-year-old Maryland servant, described by her owner as notoriously vicious and turbulent, "inflicted great bodily pain" and exposed to death the owner's children, "whom she was appointed to attend and take care of." The plan of another two slaves was revealed when they walked up to their owner and shot him at point blank range and then fled. The slave owned by the father of Leonidas Jeffreys in Nottoway County, Virginia, had a clear strategy when late one Saturday night he knocked at the door of the elder Jeffreys's store. When the son opened it, the black man bludgeoned him with a heavy club. "I understand that the counting room floor was very bloody Sunday morning," one nearby resident said, noting that the slave was still out.[11]

It was not always bad feelings or altercations between whites and slaves that caused the latter to run away. Occasionally slaves attacked other slaves. When Henry ran away from Mississippi to the Choctaw Indian Nation the day after Christmas in 1830, it was not because he was accused of killing a white man. Rather it was because he had murdered a fellow slave named Peter, owned by Covington County farmer Jacob Duckworth. Remaining at large for nearly six months, Henry was finally captured in Baton Rouge, and after Duckworth obtained permission from Louisiana's governor, extradited back to Mississippi to stand trial. In Maryland, the night he ran away, an Anne Arundel County field hand "made a violent attack" on Fanny, a slave in her mid-forties. Perhaps he feared she would disclose his plan. Whatever the reason, though half Fanny's age, the runaway struck her on the arm with such force that she did not recover for nearly five weeks.[12]

Stealing

Fear, anxiety, retaliation, frustration, anger, and hatred propelled slaves toward violence. The most prevalent "crime" connected with runaways, however, was theft. Slaves, of course, viewed the master's property in a different way from how whites viewed it. The white man's wealth was earned by the labor of their slaves. In a sense, then, it was not exclusively the owner's property. For slaves, stealing was not considered theft, merely appropriating their due. The locks on the storage bins, meat houses, and tool buildings bore witness to the difficulty slaveholders had in keeping their property secure. But runaways had little hesitation breaking into buildings, and sometimes dwellings, and absconding with a wide range of property, including clothing, horses, mules, livestock, money, jewelry, gold, silver, guns, saddles, bridles, even boats, wagons, and carriages.

The most popular items were clothing. The drab homespun worn by many runaways was obviously what had been allotted them as slaves, but some slaves left with a variety of wearing apparel belonging to the owner. Garments could be sold, traded, bartered, or worn for warmth, style, or disguise. Eleven-year-old Rosa, a New Orleans slave, made off with her owner's white silk hat, sundry handkerchiefs, lace tippets, and "infant's clothing." A slave named Jim of Athens, Alabama, absconded with a brown cloth frock coat, boots, a fur cap, and a variety of other clothes, most of them belonging to his owner. He "will most likely dress very well," the owner said, "and in newest fashion." The Virginia slave Laban absconded with grey lambskin coat, white trousers, a double-breasted grey coat, a black cape, and "sundry other clothes." He would attempt to pass as a free black.[13]

A few slaves left with more substantial wardrobes. In 1814, the Tennessee slave Celia took with her a yellow calico frock, a blue calico frock, a white cambric dress, and two "homespun coarse" dresses, a pair of red morocco-eyed slippers tied with a yellow ribbon, and a "checkered gingham bonnet (or scoop)." The New Orleans cabinetmaker Delphin, whose build was nearly identical to that of his owner, took along twelve of his fine shirts, twelve stylish pairs of white pants, and his black riding coat. It is supposed, the owner added without humor, "that he will keep himself well dressed."[14]

It was not always indicated in the runaway advertisements whether or not clothing had been stolen. Most urban slaves dressed better than those from the countryside, and some were termed "dandies" because of the variety, style, and color of their coats, shirts, trousers, and hats. But the quality and quantity of apparel taken by a number of runaways strongly suggests theft. Sam absconded wearing a green frock coat with a black velvet collar, blue pants, a high-crown black hat; he carried with him a black leather trunk containing a variety of other clothing, including a reddish frock coat with a velvet collar, a green cloth coat, and a white hat. The New Orleans mulatto woman Catherine, small in stature with "tolerable straight hair," took "a great variety of clothing" as well as a feather bed, two trunks with raised tops, and two straw bonnets. The teenage mulatto Finch, owned by a farmer in Logan County, Kentucky, made his way along the Russell-ville to Bowling Green road wearing a blue cashmere coat, blue-and-white-striped cotton waistcoat, shoes and stockings, and a fur hat. He took along three extra pairs of cotton pantaloons, one blue-and-red checkered, and two white. He was described as "very likely and trim made." Other owners noted that their runaways left with "sundry clothes," "a great variety of wearing apparel," "general assortment of good clothes," and "three or four changes of clothes."[15]

If wearing apparel was most popular, runaways purloined a variety of other items. A few urban slaves made off with substantial amounts of money. The mulatto man Dick, who wore a ring on his right cheek, made off from his New Orleans owner with a pocketbook containing between $1,700 and $1,800, including $400 in "city money" and the remainder in "Mississippi paper on the Brandon Bank." It was uncertain whether Dick could convert the notes or "state paper" into specie, but there were usually free blacks or unscrupulous whites who would buy them at discount. Opportunities were better for Field, who spoke "the English and French languages fluently." He made off with a green silk purse containing $180 in gold, principally half-eagles, and $65 in silver, principally dollars and half dollars.[16]

Just as popular and often more readily available were horses. Rapid movement on horseback meant that runaways might traverse many miles before being discovered missing, as was the case of Andy of Bon Ridge, who rode sixty-five miles in two and a half days. In 1814, Jupiter and Ben, both described as dark skinned with hair combed straight up from their foreheads, rode away from a farm in Warren County, Kentucky, on two of their owner's horses. They had traveled a good distance before their owner realized they were gone. A slave blacksmith in Camden, South Carolina, similarly covered many miles by the time his master reported him missing. He was riding a six-year-old bay gelding, fifteen hands high; it raced well, trotted "when out of hand," and looked like a stallion. While his master was on a business trip to Baltimore, Dick stole a horse from a visitor at his master's farm and set out for distant points. He remained at large only four days, however, before "he was taken up as a runaway about forty five miles from Home," his owner reported, and placed in the Anne Arundel County jail.[17]

Others stole horses because they were physically unable or too weak, too young, or too old to abscond on foot. Following the death of their owner, two black men on a plantation in Jefferson County, Mississippi—Davie about twenty-five, Sandy about thirty years old—

escaped on two horses, one a slender roan, the other a sorrel mare. They could be recognized not only because of the horses, but also because Sandy had "a deformed trunk (it being no more than twelve inches from his crotch to his neck.)" Edmund, an old man who was "getting quite gray," absented himself from his owner Edwin J. Baker of Louisa County, Virginia. "On the same day one of my horses was taken from my pasture—He is a cream colored horse, with black mane and tail, and black legs up to his knees and hocks," the owner said. "I am inclined to think that Edmund rode off [on] the horse."[18]

Others pilfered whatever they could lay their hands on. A bright mulatto named William, described as very intelligent, sprightly, and quick spoken, used at least some of those attributes to escape during his trial in New Orleans for an undisclosed crime. He not only got away, but filched a valuable silver watch. The three slaves who absconded from a plantation in Jefferson Parish, Louisiana, left in their owner's skiff. The two who set out from a plantation in Barnwell District, South Carolina, in 1828 took two double-barreled shotguns, two pistols, a dirk [dagger], a violin, ten dollars in cash, and "some articles which they obtained by breaking open a store." One of the shotguns was finely finished and mounted with silver; the ivory-handled dagger was also mounted with silver. In the mid-1820s, a black man who was the slave of a Columbia, South Carolina, store owner seized "money and goods" before running away. A witness said that "the negro was a notorious runaway, thief, and housebreaker; a sullen, perverse, desperate, dangerous villain." A twelve- or thirteen-year-old black boy, Billy, purloined a miniature picture framed "in gold," Anna Byrd of Richmond, Virginia, wrote in her notice. It held the likeness of a young lady "dressed in white, of fair complexion, black eyes, and light curling hair, parted on the forehead, and flowing on the shoulders." When last seen, Billy or someone matching his description was walking along Manchester Turnpike Road, heading south.[19]

Shortly before running off from Shirley Plantation, near Hopewell, Virginia, one slave miller pilfered a large quantity of corn. The owner had taken a trip to "the springs" and, upon his return, "found that every thing had gone on tolerable well, except that Phill the miller had made way with 40 or more barrels of corn." He also robbed the barn at a neighbor's plantation of six bags of corn, assisted by the slaves "who no doubt were also engaged in making way with standing turns at the mill & were engaged in robbing the barn with Phill."[20]

Some slaves absconded after it was discovered that they had taken meat, coffee, or sugar from their master's storehouse or slaughtered poultry and livestock on neighboring plantations. Often this was done to provide extra food and provisions for their families. The kind of animals slaughtered by the South Carolina slave George to supplement his family's rations was not revealed, only that "His object in running away is the destruction of Livestock." He was "very artful" and possessed a boat, the master admitted. He left with his wife and their infant child. Other slaves killed hogs and cattle, butchering them on the spot, either eating or selling the meat. The Texas slave Asa who lived near New Braunfels, a German settlement, was in the habit of staying out at night and killing livestock, and in 1859 a grand jury indicted him for stealing a hog. When the sheriff went to his owner's farm to bring him in for trial, however, the "Negro boy could not be found."[21]

Some thefts were so brazen and so outrageous as to be almost humorous, though few masters were amused. As William Eaton Jr., stood on the deck of a steamboat going down the Roanoke River toward his plantation near Warrenton, North Carolina, in 1850, he was surprised to see his mulatto slave Solomon poling up the opposite side of the river with one of his barges. He was even more surprised when he saw a huge stack of plantation articles as well as one of his carriages tied on board his flatboat. "As he left my plantation without having had the slightest difficulty with myself or my overseer," Eaton observed, "it is probable that he is now endeavoring to get to a free State." If so, it was equally probable that he would sell the carriage and other articles as soon as he reached a place where he could do so.[22]

Violence in Defense of Freedom

The "crimes" that sent slaves running continued during the days, weeks, months they remained at large. Stealing food and clothing was often a matter of survival, but slaves on the run also purloined various other items, including horses, mules, cattle, sheep, other livestock, and poultry. They also committed violent crimes, including assault and murder. Theft and violence were serious problems for slave owners. They constantly reminded authorities that runaways were artful, cunning, articulate, intelligent, and, as one thirteen-year-old South Carolina youngster was described, "very plausible."[23] They could steal or assault a white person, and a short time afterwards calmly pose as a free person of color.

Once discovered, however, runaways possessed few options: they could surrender, attempt to escape, or fight their pursuers. Sometimes the latter two options were employed simultaneously. As he made his way across a remote section on a plantation in Concordia Parish, Louisiana, for example, John was stopped by Tilman Gilbert, an overseer.

"What are you doing?" Gilbert queried. "Hunting stray horses," for his master, he replied. Knowing that John's owner was at that very moment advertising for two runaways, the overseer ordered John to stand by "but the negro, instead of obeying made an attempt to escape." Gilbert rode after him, jumped off his horse, and the two men grappled on the ground. John got a hold of the overseer's gun, cocked it and attempted to fire several times, but the gun did not discharge. He then grabbed the overseer by the throat and began choking him. The white man pleaded with the slave to let him up—if he would let him go he would say nothing—but John responded that the white man had molested him "without cause" and "he would not release his hold." Gilbert finally extricated himself, but said later that John intended to kill him. Eventually caught and tried, John was sentenced to receive three hundred lashes, "well laid on" (evenly divided over ten days), and to wear an iron collar, weighing at least eight pounds, for one year.[24]

Other runaways, too, found it difficult to avoid confrontations. Some who fled to towns and cities, despite every effort to remain unnoticed, were discovered. Constables, magistrates, sheriffs, night watchmen in Baltimore, Richmond, Charleston, New Orleans, St. Louis, and other cities were constantly on the lookout for runaways. They stopped suspects on the street, asked to see their free papers, demanded to look at their badges, and commanded them to produce papers from their owners. Although no specifics were given, it is clear that one of these challenges was at work in an incident in Nashville, in 1842. The mayor, Samuel V. D. Stout, offered a $50 reward for the apprehension of two runaway slaves. The notice only indicated that a "bright mulatto" named Frank, the property of the estate of Thomas Martin, and a "dark mulatto" named John, the property of a "Col. Dickinson, formerly of Nashville," committed "a violent assault on one of the Watchmen of the Corporation on the night of 30th day of June." Afterwards, the slaves fled and a week later were still eluding their pursuers.[25]

Even slaves who hid out in the woods, caves, and swamps, along rivers and bayous, or in abandoned shacks were forced on occasion to fight pursuers or white farmers and overseers. As he moved rapidly across the countryside, the runaway Sandy, a slave owned by Georgia planter David Murray, was suddenly confronted by a white man. The two exchanged words, and Sandy suddenly sprang upon the man, bludgeoning him nearly to death. An anonymous South Carolina runaway similarly came across a white man, Mason Moseley, a farmer out on a hunting expedition. When interrogated, the slave could not explain himself, and the white man, after a strip search, instructed the slave to walk in front of him back to the farmhouse. Suddenly, the fugitive produced a knife, turned, thrust it into Moseley's stomach, and took off running. In another incident, farmer William B. Villard spotted "a Strange Negro Man" in a swamp along the Savannah River, who suddenly came at him with a carving knife in one hand and hatchet in the other. Villard sustained a severe contusion on the forehead and several broken ribs. In a similar incident, a North Carolina blacksmith was shot in the shoulder and disabled for life by runaways.[26]

These confrontations might occur at any time, but there was the highest probability of their taking place during the commission of a theft or burglary. In 1822, the North Carolina slave David "remained lurking about in the neighbourhood, doing & committing divers mischief and depredations." David was armed and resisted efforts to apprehend him, at least until he was discovered hiding in a farmhouse, refused to come out, and was shot and killed. Described as a first-rate sawyer and "exceedingly athletic and able," the forty-year-old Virginia slave Dave ran away in 1836, remaining at large for several months. As he roamed along the upper James River, into Albemarle County and back into Fluvanna County, pirating food from farms and plantations, he was joined by two other runaways. Late one night, the three crept through a window into the farmhouse of Joseph Wood, but suddenly the white farmer appeared in the doorway from a back room. Dave jumped on him and began beating him with his fists. He and the others continued to assault Wood until the white man's face was a bloody pulp. The assailants quickly fled, and although the farmer survived, "his life for a long time was despaired of."[27]

Equally determined to remain at large was a Mississippi slave who had been away from his master's plantation for many weeks when he was discovered by an overseer in a remote section of a neighboring plantation, suffering from malnutrition. Feeling sorry for the man, the overseer, named Staunton, took him back to his employer's plantation house and offered him a dish of food. Staunton left to take care of his horse, and the slave asked the planter's wife for another serving. While she was getting another plate, the black man, now revived, grabbed the overseer's pistols. The mistress screamed, her husband came running, "advanced towards the fellow, and recd a whole charge in his heart & fell dead. The Negro fled."[28]

Some runaways committed or were accused of committing so many outrageous acts that they were declared outlaws who could be shot on sight. Such was the case of the slave Jupiter of Lunenburg County, Virginia, who absconded from his owner's service "and lay out committing felonies and other mischief within the County of Mecklenburg." Indeed, Jupiter had "frequently runaway & was a pest to the neighbourhood where he lurked and he out hid." On 25 May 1790, the justices of the peace in Mecklenburg County issued a "Proclamation of Outlawry" against the slave authorizing "the Killing of an Out lying Slave[.]" Neither discovered nor captured by whites, Jupiter was shot and killed by a fellow slave after a robbery.[29]

Collective Resistance

At times "outlaws" such as Jupiter gathered together in bands of runaways wreaking havoc on plantations and farms. Living in isolated, heavily wooded, or swampy areas, some of these groups maintained their cohesiveness for many years, a few for more than a generation. Most, however, found it difficult to sustain themselves without being constantly on the move. Members of fugitive gangs made forays into populated farming sections for food, clothing, livestock, and trading items. Sometimes they bartered with free blacks, plantation slaves, and nonslaveholding whites, and in a few instances, white outlaws joined the outlying gangs of blacks, though this was rare. In virtually every state there were gangs of ten to twenty outlying slaves. The largest bodies of maroons, as they were sometimes called, reached only a few hundred members (with the exception of those in the Great Dismal Swamp between North Carolina and Virginia, which numbered several thousand). Despite their ephemeral nature, runaway gangs were a constant source of fear and anxiety for whites.[30]

In the aftermath of the War for Independence, Governor Thomas Pinckney of South Carolina informed the legislature that there was a serious problem concerning armed fugitive slaves who were active in the southern portion of the state, especially along the Savannah River. Some of them had fled to the British during the War for Independence and were now carrying on guerilla warfare. During the 1790s, runaways in Virginia and the Carolinas hid in woods and swamps during the day and emerged at night to commit "various depredations" on farms and plantations. In 1800, one South Carolina slave owner bitterly admitted that three of his own blacks were part of a fugitive gang. He offered $500 for the return of Cyrus, Hercules, and Tom. Cyrus and Hercules had been out for three years, he confessed, pillaging various farms and plantations along the Ashley River. Now Tom had joined them, he said, and the three were secluded somewhere in the area of the "Wappoo-cut and Ashley ferry."[31]

In each subsequent decade during the nineteenth century, outlying groups could be found in various states. In 1816, another South Car-

olina governor pointed to the difficulty in discovering the exact location of "runaway negroes" concealing themselves in the swamps and
marshes adjacent to the Combahee and Ashepoo rivers. Armed, using
hit-and-run tactics, able to disappear along creeks, inlets, bays,
marshes, islands, and waterways, they stole from slaveholders "with
impunity." Their familiarity with the surrounding area "furnished
them easy opportunities to plunder, not only the planters in open day,
but the inland coasting trade without leaving a trace of their movements by which they could be pursued."[32]

Bands of runaways sometimes became so emboldened that they sent
entire communities into panic. During the summer of 1821, an "insurrection" broke out in Onslow County, North Carolina, when "a
number of outlawed and runaway Slaves and free Negroes" banded
together. Located between the White Oak and the New rivers in the
southeastern portion of the state, the long estuaries and forested sections provided good cover. The outlying slaves "daily increased in
strength and numbers," William L. Hill, head of a militia unit, said.
Their bold acts of defiance became so alarming that "no inhabitant
could feel himself at any moment secure in his life, person or property,
from the plunder, rapine, and devastation committed by them, daily
and nightly in every corner of the County." Local inhabitants feared
for their lives to such an extent that they fled their homes. Daily
reports circulated about "violence and depredations" that the runaways committed "upon the persons and property of defenseless and
unprotected families." They were well armed, cunning, daring, and
desperate, Hill said. In broad daylight, they ravaged farms, burned
houses, broke into stores, and "ravished a number of females." It took
Hill's two-hundred-man militia unit twenty-six days searching
through "Woods, Swamps & Marshes" to subdue the "Outlaws."[33]

A similar situation existed in central Florida at about the same time.
In a fourteen-page memorial to the Territorial Governor William P.
Duval, the new Legislative Council warned of the "existing evils" following the acquisition of the region from Spain of "great numbers of
negroes belonging to the planters, availing themselves of existing dis-
orders" and running away only to take "refuge among the Indians."
They were beyond the reach of their owners, and some of them were
escaping to the island of Cuba, "from whence in all probability they
will never be recovered." This memorial was presented about 1823,
but for many years, even during the Seminole Indian War (1835–42),
groups of runaway slaves remained at large, periodically raiding plantations and farms. "I have ascertained beyond any doubt, not only
that a connection exists between a portion of the slave population and

the Seminoles," an Army officer wrote in 1837, "but that there was, before the war commenced, an understanding that a considerable force should join on the first blow being struck."[34]

At the same time, runaways in Mississippi and Alabama formed outlying encampments. In 1829, the *Woodville Republican* carried an article about "a gang of runaway negroes encamped about two miles from the village of Pinkneyville" in southwestern Mississippi. Among the fugitives were slaves from plantations along the Mississippi River in Louisiana. A patrol was immediately formed, raided the camp, and one of the slaves—the French-speaking William, who already had a scar from a gun shot on his shoulder—was mortally wounded. In 1836, residents along the Chattahoochee River in Alabama feared that a band of hostile Creek Indians were "collecting all the force they can among themselves, and from the negroes," to attack people in Georgia. In the same year, a large party of Indians "barbarously murdered" many inhabitants of a community in western Georgia, Major General William Irwin wrote Governor Clement C. Clay of Alabama. "I cannot withhold from Your Excellency my fears on account of the negroes— there are large bodies of them in this place and neighbourhood who have had uninterrupted intercourse with the Indians for a great length of time and may have matured some plan of cooperation." Most of the plantations had been abandoned, and many slaves were left "without any white authority over them." Apparently, his fears were well founded. The following year in Macon County, Alabama, a group of fifty or sixty white families complained that sections along the Cuba Hatchee River were "remarkable for the extent and impervious nature of their swamps and the morasses," and were excellent hideouts for groups of Indians and camps of "armed Negroes."[35]

During the same decade and the 1840s, groups of armed runaways in various areas remained close to populated farming areas and cities. The gangs who hid out in the cypress swamp near New Orleans raided farms and plantations along the Mississippi River. In 1837, a runaway leader, said to be responsible for killing several whites, was executed. In 1844, a group of runaways, "part of a gang," was chased and attacked by whites near Hanesville, Mississippi; and two years later, "a considerable gang of runaway negroes" was surprised by a posse in St. Landry Parish, Louisiana. During the 1840s, in Halifax County, North Carolina, on the border with Virginia, armed runaways stole seventy-five hogs from a single farmer. He was targeted because "he hunted for them," a group of farmers testified, and the slaves "sent him word, that if he would not hunt for them again—they would not Kill any more of his hogs—but if he did, they should Kill him."[36]

In Florida, Georgia, Alabama, Texas, Virginia, North and South Carolina, and other states, outlying slaves gathered in remote and isolated areas. In 1856, a North Carolina newspaper said that a gang of runaways had so intimidated local "negro hunters" that they refused to "come with their dogs unless aided from other sources." In Williamsburg District, South Carolina, an outlying slave attacked and robbed a white traveler not two miles from the town of Kingston in the middle of the day. The incident exposed the vulnerability of whites to groups of runaways who were constantly committing acts that jeopardized "the peace and safety of the people." The slave responsible for the "daring and atrocious act of high way robbery" was captured, jailed, and sentenced to death, but shortly before he was to be hanged, he "escaped by violence from the Gaol of the district."[37]

Despite such activities, however, it was extremely difficult for gangs of runaways to sustain themselves over long periods of time. Their dilemma was how to steal from farmers and planters without evoking a response from local militia or patrols. The more they pillaged, the more likely they were to arouse groups of white men to search out their encampments. Those who did sustain themselves for any length of time hid out in densely forested, swampy areas that were virtually inaccessible to anyone unfamiliar with the terrain. Even whites who knew these areas feared entering them. Even when few in number, gangs of outlyers struck fear into the hearts of white inhabitants.

Clandestine Slave Economy

More prevalent than the "outlaw" gangs were runaways who participated in what may be called the clandestine slave economic system. Most states prohibited slaves from buying and selling commodities without written permission from the owner or overseer. A Georgia law prohibited slaves from buying or selling "any quantity or amount whatever of cotton, tobacco, wheat, rye, oats, corn, rice or poultry." Tennessee slaves were prohibited from owning a pig, cow, mule, horse, "or other such like description of property." A Virginia statute stipulated that anyone who bought, sold, or received "any commodity whatsoever" from a slave would be subject to thirty-nine lashes. But such laws and prohibitions were difficult to enforce. In virtually every section of the South, slaves bought, sold, and traded a variety of goods. Property "ownership" was widespread among slaves who worked at the task system, planting and harvesting rice along the coastal areas of North and South Carolina, and Georgia, but those who worked in gangs, or a combination of gang and task systems were also able to accumulate small amounts of property, as were those who lived in towns and cities.[38]

"Every measure that may lessen the dependence of a Slave on his master ought to be opposed, as tending toward dangerous consequences," a group of South Carolina slaveholders declared in 1816. In their district, owners were far too lax in allowing bondspeople free time on Saturdays to "keep horses, raise hogs, cultivate for themselves every thing for home consumption, & for market, that their masters do." Perhaps the liberty that created the greatest loss was allowing slaves to plant, harvest, and sell cotton. This gave them the opportunity to "Steal with impunity," and those who did not plant cotton themselves found a ready market for their stolen goods among slaves who did plant and also acted as factors. Trying to locate the pilfered bales, the planters lamented, was "like looking of a drop of water lost in a river."[39]

Many runaways sustained themselves while on the run by tapping into the clandestine slave economy. Those who remained in the vicinity of their old plantation often kept in close contact with fellow slaves, who provided them with supplies from the master's storehouse. Those who moved into towns and cities brought what they had stolen to trade, barter, and sell. And those who sought to move greater distances were in regular contact with slaves who were willing to buy or sell various items or to trade stolen goods for food and clothing. Runaways took cattle, hogs, sheep, livestock, rice, cotton, corn, whiskey, poultry, grains, meats, even baskets, brooms, and farm tools. They used their loot to trade for food and other commodities. In some instances, the items pillaged wound up back on the same plantations. They also traded with free blacks and white merchants who were willing to take such risks for a profit.[40]

One striking example of this occurred in Charleston District, South Carolina, when a small colony of sixteen runaways—men, women, and children—escaped together in February 1825 and established a camp deep in the woods. Remaining close to Mowberry Plantation, owned by the Rowland family, as well as Retreat Plantation, they obtained items from fellow slaves and took them into Charleston to sell and trade. Several members of the runaway group had been seen walking among the "negroe houses" at Retreat in broad daylight, and others at Mowberry "with whose negroes they are also connected." In addition, the outlying families picked black moss, wove baskets, and took the baskets in boats to the stores on South Bay, near Bennett's Mills, where they sold their goods and purchased needed supplies. They made trips as infrequently as possible, but they had been seen several times at the Public Landing or crossing Wappoo Cut.[41]

It was not much later that three runaways in the same area launched a similar enterprise. In the early 1830s, thirty-five-year-old wharf hand Natt, his partner Tom, who belonged to an estate, and a third unidentified slave carried moss and "hoop Poles" in a twenty-five-foot canoe from the Old Town settlement to a spot near Lucas's Mills, where they found "a ready sale amongst the shops." The three were repeatedly seen in the neighborhood but avoided capture.[42] While such enterprises usually continued for short periods, outlying slaves who remained longer in the vicinity of towns and cities bought, sold, and bartered various stolen goods with slaves, free persons of color, as well as town merchants and tradesmen.

In 1854, the connection between runaways and trafficking was explained in a broadside from a group of Texas slave owners. "Whereas," they began, there were "divers instances" of slaves deserting their masters with stolen goods and seeking haven in the "territory of Mexico," it was necessary to create a vigilance committee and a police force to stop the practice. They planned to take "prompt and violent steps against any one, in our town [Seguin] or county, who will in any way trade with, or hold communication with our slaves, without permission of those having controll of them." They also demanded an investigation to see whether or not the runaways were supplied with arms, ammunition, or provisions, and if so, by whom.[43]

If trafficking between runaways and Mexicans was prevalent along the West Bank of the Rio Grande, trade also took place among absconding slaves, free blacks, and unscrupulous whites in other sections. South Carolina slave owners with plantations along the Ashepoo and Pon Pon rivers said that Elliott's Cut, which meandered between the two rivers, was "seldom if ever used but by Runaways and Negroes unlawfully trading from River to River." Outlying slaves raided plantations along the rivers, stealing food, crops, tools, and items for trade, and vanished into the "immense Swamp of impregnable and un[in]habited Marsh" along the Cut. In Mississippi, slave owners and planters decried trafficking activities among outlying slaves who traded meal, pigs, poultry, corn, and whiskey with fellow blacks and "dissolute and immoral" whites.[44]

The clandestine trade became so prevalent in southeastern Virginia that a group of slave owners demanded the death penalty for any free black convicted of harboring a fugitive slave. "Your petitioners are well aware that the penalties they propose are very severe," residents of Isle of Wight County said in 1817, but they had "long witnessed with the deepest regret the facilities furnished by base & immoral white persons & free persons of colour, to the slaves, to deprive their owners of their services & to plunder them of their property with impunity." This intercourse not only produced thievery, but promoted "insubordination & a spirit of disobedience among the slaves." Such defiance could easily lead "to insurrection & blood." More than four decades later, Virginia masters continued with the same conclusion: such interchange, they asserted, not only spawned desertion, but encouraged slaves to "revolt and massacre."[45]

If such dire predictions were meant to produce a dramatic effect, they nonetheless contained elements of truth. Masters in many sections explained how absentee and runaway slaves became involved in illicit trafficking of stolen goods and how this in turn led to brazen resistance. In sections of North Carolina, runaways came very close to "revolt and massacre." Outlying slaves in Bladen, Sampson, New Hanover, and Duplin counties "go and come when and where they please," a group of whites averred about 1830, "and if an Attempt is Made to correct them they fly to the Woods and there continue for months and years committing grievous depredations on Our Cattle hogs and Sheep and Many Other things." Horses were stolen, dogs were killed, and when patrollers mounted searches, runaways burned their homes, outhouses, and fodder stacks. The situation became so desperate that whites demanded "the privilege of Shooting and destroying all Runaway Slaves who may Refuse to Submit." Some years later, when a similar law was proposed, a committee in the General Assembly reported that it would be "unnecessarily cruel" and would "render slave property insecure and consequently diminish its value." It readily acknowledged, however, the grave problem of slaves "lying out, in the woods, swamps & other secret places" and then descending on farms and plantations, killing cattle, sheep, and hogs.[46]

Retribution

In response to such "grievous depredations," slave owners often took matters into their own hands. At times, it seemed virtually impossible to catch the culprits who stole meat, butchered livestock, and broke into storehouses. Slaves who sneaked out at night, joined up with runaways, and crept onto neighboring plantations were experienced and artful. It was difficult to trace many of the items they stole, and the meat they obtained from butchered cattle, sheep, and hogs could be identified only at the scene of the slaughter. When slaves were caught, masters and other whites often meted out extreme retribution. Several incidents in Louisiana reveal the nature of the problem and what might happen to slaves who were caught. They also indicate the types of slaves who were involved in the clandestine economy. During 1820 to 1821, Pointe Coupee slaveholder Abraham Villeret was losing cattle at an alarming rate. He strongly suspected one of his neighbor's slaves, Ephraim, a perpetual runaway, as the culprit. In 1821, Villeret went to Ephraim's owner, Judge Charles Steward, and said he would shoot any slave he found stealing his cattle. A few days later, a place was discovered where an ox had been slain; after waiting there some time, Villeret "saw two negroes getting over the fence." One of them was carrying a quarter of meat, "brought it out, laid it on a log in the act of cutting the shank bone off." Villeret snuck up on them, and when a short distance away, ordered them to remain still. The "two negroes" bolted. Villeret shot one man in the lower back, ripping a hole about two inches in diameter. He died a short time later.

Judge Steward was shocked when he learned the identity of the slain slave. It was Harry, one of the most trusted servants on his estate, described as young, intelligent, and of "great and particular value on the plantation." He had never been whipped, "for he never gave any reason to be whipped," the overseer said; and he had never run away. The man who escaped and was still at large, Harry's secret partner, was Ephraim, "a very bad slave and a great Rascal," who absconded four times in twelve months, despite being recaptured and whipped severely following each escape.[47]

The circumstances were similar for planter Isham P. Fox of East Baton Rouge Parish, Louisiana, who had been having trouble for some time with outlying slaves breaking into his storage buildings. In 1836, Little Charles, a tiny man who had been taken up several times as a runaway, was caught trying to break into Fox's meat house. The diminutive slave was chained and cuffed, and Fox's overseer and one of his slaves "whipped the boy all night." The physician who later examined him was mortified at what he saw: the skin on his back, buttocks, thighs, and hips was "literally cut off him," and his face had a number of cuts and bruises. The planter forced Charles, with a heavy iron chain around his neck, "to drag his lacerated body" from the plantation to Baton Rouge. He lingered for some time before dying.[48]

Most slaves understood the danger of sneaking out at night and killing livestock, but they still took the risk. Peter, owned by another East Baton Rouge Parish man, frequently stole away in the middle of the night to slaughter livestock. He knew the consequences, but at age twenty-six he had a good deal of experience covering his tracks. On 23 March 1837, however, about a mile and a half from his owner's farm, he was followed by a white farmer and his slave as he dragged one of the man's hogs into a thicket of palmetto trees and began adeptly butchering the dead animal. The moon was full and very high, one witness said; with a small fire, the two spies could see as if it were daylight. The farmer, Louis Pyburn, handed his shotgun to the slave and ordered him to shoot. The next moment buckshot tore into Peter's body, and he lay motionless on the ground. Pyburn commented that "he would shoot any negro whom he found Killing his hogs and that he would do it again under the same circumstances."[49] The following day, Peter died.

While these examples are from Louisiana, similar retributions occurred in other states. Indeed, most runaways who stole, threatened, or assaulted whites could expect quick reprisals. After fleeing from Burleson County, a Texas runaway named Lucky was spotted on the road leading to Austin. When a man tried to secure him, Lucky killed both the man and his wife. The slave was captured and quickly "hanged in Austin by the people of Travis county." A similar fate awaited the slave George, owned by a man in Chester District, South Carolina. Absconding in 1831, George stole two horses, broke into several homes, and "committed other offenses." Captured in Columbia, he escaped. It seemed impossible, observers said, to arrest him. After cutting a white man across his eye with a razor blade, George was finally captured and quickly tried, convicted, and executed. Others who broke into homes or fought with their pursuers, while not always suffering death, faced severe retaliation.[50]

Perhaps the quickest and most vehement response came when runaways were accused of molesting white women. Masters sought to protect white females from what was considered the lascivious nature of Africans, and by the late eighteenth and early nineteenth centuries, the fear among slaveholders concerning the black man's libidinous character seemed always near the surface. Outlying and runaway slaves "lurking" in the shadows, ready to violate unprotected women, conjured up the worst fears, especially in regions where blacks outnumbered whites. Most absconders who accosted white women paid dearly for their acts. Even those merely accused of doing so could face the most severe punishment. During the winter of 1801–2, a North Carolina runaway named Arthur was said to have caused "great terror" among women and children. The man who shot and killed the runaway said that the black man had horrified "all Women and Children in the vicinity of his range," and it was his duty to "rid the world of a daring lawless villain."[51]

If runaways could be shot and killed for frightening women and children, those accused of rape could expect even more summary "justice." In April 1799, the "Negro man" Joe, who belonged to Robert Ash of York District, South Carolina, was accused of entering Elizabeth

Woods's house and attempting "to commit a Ravishment on her Body." Though it was pitch black, the white woman said she was sure the man involved was Joe, described as "a notorious out lyer." Within hours a posse set out, inspecting Negro quarters on farms and plantations. Recalling something amiss on one farm, a member of the group doubled back and found Joe hidden in "a Negro House of a Certain Mrs. Calley." The fugitive bolted out of the house, grabbed the muzzle of the white man's gun, and attempted to wrestle it from his hand, but the gun discharged into his stomach; Joe died a short time later. In the summer of 1858, Peter, a slave railroad worker, was accused of violating "a beautiful young Lady by Committing *a Rape*," on a secluded path near Enterprise, Mississippi. The slave fled, but was caught and brought to town. The next day a group of about fifty armed men dragged him from the jail and hanged him in a public exhibition. Soon afterwards, townspeople gathered and unanimously passed resolutions "ratifying what had been done."[52]

Of course, slaves were valuable property, and if an owner had enough influence or there were mitigating circumstances, an alleged offending slave's life might be spared. This happened rarely, but it did occur. "We Find the Defendant Guilty," a Screven County, Georgia, jury proclaimed on 17 October 1844, in the case of the State vs. Guy, a slave belonging to Wyatt W. Starke. Convicted of burglary, robbery, and aggravated assault, Guy was sentenced to death. But Starke, a prominent slave owner, appealed the verdict. Guy had indeed run away, entered the home of Elizabeth Connelly, brandished a stick, used "abusive language," and left with a gun and articles of clothing. But did the slave's actions, Starke asked, constitute burglary and assault? Elizabeth Connelly testified "that said Slave Guy when he came to her house Knocked at the door, which was opened to him by one of her household, and he thereupon walked in peaceably, no objection being made to his entrance." This was not burglary, defined as forced entry. Nor were any articles of clothing "about her person" taken, nor did he attempt to "strike her or to do her any other personal violence." The superior court judge concurred, declared a mistrial, and on 22 December 1844, Guy was released to his owner.[53]

Depending on the prominence of the master or the social and economic standing of the woman in question, other runaways who assaulted white women escaped with their lives. Armstead had been at large for some time when in 1821 he forced his way into the two-room home of Betsy F. Gray and her mother in Caroline County, Virginia. The women attempted to flee, but Armstead caught them and "ordered them to go to Bed, threatening them with death [i]f they refused." Armstead "then came to the bed laying on the out side, she [the daughter] in the middle, and put the sword at the head of the Bed, when he committed the act, twice, and remained in Bed untill about day light when he left the house." Begging his master for leniency, Armstead got off with fifteen years in the penitentiary. After South Carolina authorities became convinced that an accused rapist had been unduly influenced by a slave who was "a great runaway and otherwise of bad Character," they were able to have his death sentence commuted by the governor to 250 lashes and banishment. In a few other instances, absconders owned by large slaveholders escaped death when they were accused of raping white women of low repute.[54]

Despite these exceptions, few runaways who committed violent or other "criminal acts" escaped retaliation, especially if the acts involved murder or rape. This did not, however, slow the pace of murder, stealing, and other plantation "crimes."[55] Indeed, the evidence suggests that violent resistance among runaways and other slaves increased during the 1840s and 1850s. The fear and anxiety white southerners experienced during the late antebellum period stemmed neither from the abolitionist attack nor the rise of "Black Republicans" in the North. Despite every effort at systematic control, including laws, patrols, and severe punishments, the flow of runaways and their violent assaults on persons and property not only continued but increased. Thus, the dilemma slaveholders confronted was that the more they sought to control and curb runaway violence, theft, and clandestine economic activity, the more it continued to be a matter of some urgency.

5

Where To Go?

AS PART OF THE THOMAS BOWMAN estate in Bullitt County, Kentucky, Jack (also known as John), a tanner by trade, was turned over to Bowman's widow as part of her inheritance following her husband's death. Previously, Jack had been permitted to visit his wife regularly, but when the widow moved to Louisville, the visitations ceased. In his early forties, it was a painful and difficult period, but then, a stroke of luck: H. H. Buffenmyer, a resident of Jefferson County who lived not far from the city, purchased Jack's wife.

The difficulty arose when the widow, now remarried, refused to permit Jack to visit his wife, although the black man and woman lived relatively close to one another. In response, Jack sneaked away at night, absented himself for days at a time, laid out for weeks, and when the owner still refused him visitation, ran away. As it was obvious where he was going, he was quickly picked up and returned, but the slave remained as resolute as the mistress. Running away and lying out, he became, in the mistress's words, "ungovernable and refractory," and she "did not consider him of any value" nor could she "depend on him for any valuable service." Now near fifty, suffering from rheumatism and other health problems, Jack escaped across the Ohio River but was captured, jailed, and returned. He vowed he would not serve his mistress. Finally, after years of struggle, Jack got his wish; he would be sold privately to his wife's owner. Shortly after the sale, however, he learned that the transaction was void: if any of Thomas Bowman's children were still alive (and they were), the widow could not sell any slave at a private sale. To ensure the highest price, Jack would have to be sold at public auction.[1]

How, when, and where Jack was auctioned, or whether he ever saw his wife again is not known, but Jack's response to his mistress's intransigence revealed the range of tactics employed by runaways. These included brief absenteeism, lying out for longer periods, running away in the same vicinity, and striking out to distant parts. Jack went where it might be predicted he would go—to his wife's plantation—but he also stayed out without visiting his wife, and ran away to the North to try to force his owner to grant him concessions.

Whatever their strategy, other runaways faced the same crucial question: Where to go? How and why did some slaves hide out in the vicinity of their plantations, run away to neighboring plantations, set out to the west and south as well as the north, or migrate to the nearest town or city (see chapter 6)? Every destination was fraught with risks and dangers, and there were few locations where they could avoid meeting inquisitive whites. How runaways answered this question might spell the difference between success and failure.

Absentees

The most common form of absconding was not actually running away at all, but what might be termed "truancy," "absenteeism," and in some cases, "lying out." The terms are confusing as they were used to describe a broad range of resistance, from slaves staying out a few days and coming back on their own accord to lying out in gangs and causing havoc by pillage and looting. Generally, however, those who left for short periods stayed in the vicinity of the plantation and returned on their own accord. Those who left for a few nights to be with loved ones were not technically runaways. At times, truants were hunted like runaways, and the line was sometimes blurred since any definition depended on the intention of a particular slave. After hiding in the woods, one Louisiana slave sent her child back to the plantation. The overseer noted that he now believed she (and several others with her) were "only laying out," and his previous belief that she had absconded was "groundless."[2]

Absenteeism was so common that most masters attempted to deal with it by inflicting mild punishments or ignoring it altogether. The great majority of slaves who sneaked away from their farms and plantations overnight or for a few days knew exactly where they wanted to go, namely to visit their wives, husbands, sons, daughters, other family members, and friends. They also went hunting, fishing, hid out from work, pilfered food, and consumed whiskey. One young slave owner, James Torbert, noted in his journal in 1855 that he, his father, and another man went out "hunting Some drunken negroes" who had left the plantation on a Saturday night.[3] Other slaves traveled into towns, frequented dances or religious meetings, secretly met members of the opposite sex, or went to the back rooms of grocery stores to drink and play cards. The movement of slaves from one plantation to another or into town without permission was rarely a matter of public concern or noted in newspapers. Indeed, most planters felt it better to keep such matters quiet unless they felt such movements posed a threat.

Despite its common occurrence, leaving without an owner's permission could pose a danger. Those caught trying to leave might face reprisals, and those who remained away too long might test their owner's patience. Worse still, if a slave was discovered on someone else's property, hiding in the slave quarters, that could be serious indeed. Two incidents in Georgia suggest what might happen in such cases. The first occurred in Oglethorpe County in 1849, when the slave Henry, a large man owned by John Wynne, was caught taking handouts of food from his wife, a cook on the plantation of Moses Wright. Henry was ordered not to return. Not only did he return, but the next Sunday morning he arrived at the "negro quarters and sent a desire to the house for his breakfast." Again he was ordered to leave. "After that I learned," the planter said, "he did come Secretly." Neither the owner nor his overseer, Willis Jones, knew when, at least until February 1850, when they found "where Henry and our Cook lay of nights out in the plantation." Even then, Henry avoided detection until one night when the cook was asked to remain in the master's kitchen to care for a white woman. The plantation owner related the following sequence of events:

> Mr. Jones went to the kitchen and found Henry on her bed and told him to rise and cross his hands Henry refused and Jones clenched him—Henry being much the largest, clenched Jones by the arms and Shoved him back to the wall. Jones told my negro man in the room to lay hold of him. Henry told him if he touched him he would be damned if he did not kill him. Jones then cried out for me. It was 2 O'clock A.M. and I was sound asleep; when aroused at the Third Call I ran (as it was) to his relief. I found them clenched. Jones asked me to help him tie him. He had a string [rope] in his pocket. I got it out, and we tied his hands and bucked him.

The overseer ran to the house, grabbed a cowhide whip, returned and administered about seventy-five lashes well laid on "for trying to run over him," and another thirty or forty stripes "for intruding on the Premises contrary to orders." Jones asked the owner if he "did not want to whip him Some." Wright answered no.[4]

The second incident occurred in Greene County, Georgia, when the slave Jim, owned by Gwynn Allison, went to a neighboring plantation in 1856 to spend the night with his wife. Early the next morning, according to one witness, John Broughton "took said negro from his bed while he was with his wife and then & there without any reasonable or Justifiable cause and without any legal right or any right So to do most Cruelly & unmercifully bruised beat & whiped Said Negro inflicting upon him many grievous wounds." Broughton did not even own the plantation where Jim had gone, but was determined to halt the clandestine movement of slaves from plantation to plantation.[5]

Lying Out

Staying away from the plantation for longer periods—weeks, sometimes months—was also a common practice. Those who stayed in the same vicinity as their owner's farm or plantation were said to be lying out. This could range from leaving for short periods with every intention of returning to leaving for long periods with gangs of runaways who pillaged and looted the neighborhood. Lying out tested the owner's patience to a much greater degree than did mere truancy and was usually dealt with more harshly. Slaves who "layed out" often lived by fishing, hunting, stealing, trading, and looting. Sometimes they stayed near relatives or friends, or hid in quarters on neighboring plantations. They encamped near towns and cities, along rivers and streams, or in dense forests and swamps. They stayed alone, in small groups, sometimes in large bands. Usually only those who remained at large for longer periods—a small proportion of the total—were advertised as runaways. The mulatto George, owned by a farmer in Iberville Parish, Louisiana, was typical of this group. He "absconded from my House, & has since been heard of lurking about near the plantations in this parish," the master noted. If he was not apprehended, he would "do mischief to the neighbors' property."[6]

Indeed, there were few sections of the South where farmers did not complain about vagrants in their vicinity who were lying out, "lurking about near the plantations" and doing "mischief." They sometimes moved about in broad daylight, seen by whites and other slaves. One slave owner in Lenoir County, North Carolina, said in 1818 that his outlying slave had been seen frequently roaming about "my own neighborhood," carrying a gun "and other weapons for defense." He was also known to lie out in the "Vine Swamp, in this county." If anyone would pay him $600, he would sell the black man "as he runs."[7]

Most slaves went out alone, but sometimes they did so as couples or with their children; sometimes they took several children while leaving others behind. In 1826, the slave woman Darcus, part of a trust estate established in Fairfield District, South Carolina, was about thirty-four years old. She was the mother of five children, ranging in age from about ten to less than a year. During the year she ran away twice, taking her two oldest children, remaining in the woods between three and four months on each occasion. In rare instances, entire families hid out together. In 1825, in Christ Church Parish, South Carolina, for example, a father, mother, and their three children absconded. The family was unusually successful in remaining at large, living in the woods, sneaking on to plantations at night, stealing and slaughtering livestock, retreating to their hideaway, joining up with other runaways. It was a harsh and precarious existence, living from day to day, hiding and running, fearful of discovery and capture, always worried about food and shelter for the children. But they established a successful routine of eluding slave hunters, at least until 1828, when whites mounted a determined effort to rid the countryside of the "great evil" of lying out. The family had been out for nearly three years. "They continued out until October last, when the children surrendered (one having been born in the woods)," a group of whites explained perfunctorily, "the Father & Mother both having been shot and Killed."[8]

Even under the best of circumstances, those remaining in the same area confronted many obstacles. Living conditions could be harsh, with inadequate food, water, shelter, clothing. Often the weather—stifling heat, incessant rains, and in the border states, frigid cold—could be as much a problem as finding food. In addition, the increasing density of settlement, improvements in communication, and the increasing frequency of patrols created problems. Struggling against a variety of vicissitudes, a number of lying-out slaves returned on their own. In 1829, Elisha Cain, the overseer of a plantation in Jefferson County, Georgia, reported that one of the slaves returned of his own accord after a few weeks. Another planter noted in his journal that on Saturday, 17 March 1849, "Emaline runaway." Two days later, he made a second entry: "*Emaline come home.*"[9]

Only a small portion of runaways remained out for indefinite periods. Joe was still at large six months after he absconded, despite a long-running advertisement in the *Charleston Mercury* that said he was seen "lurking in his old range" near the Saltcatcher, where he had many friends. Moses was "middle size, well made, well looking, and quite intelligent," a planter at Wiltown on the Pon Pon River in South Carolina said. The black man had acquaintances in Christ Church Parish and Charleston, where he had been secreting himself for six months. The Virginia slave Parker, according to his owner's guardian, was "of bad character, ungovernable in his disposition, in the habit of leaving the employment of his master, and remaining in the woods for considerable portions of the year."[10]

Slaves who remained in the neighborhood for extended periods were usually ingenious, daring, and unafraid of whites. They maintained contacts with friends or relatives on plantations who provided them with food, clothing, shelter, and information. One prominent South Carolina planter warned that the utmost caution and secrecy needed to be used in organizing parties to search for runaways, who, he said, maintained contact and exchanged information with slaves on his plantation. Sometimes slaves traded stolen goods with merchants and other whites or took pilfered items into towns and cities to sell. Familiar with the area, they would appear for brief periods, move about, and disappear. Such was the case for the South Carolina slave Callimus, who was in his early forties, about six feet tall, and had "good teeth." Callimus left Dean Hall Plantation on St. John's Island in November 1826. At the end of February 1828, he remained at large. Seven men, belonging to seven different owners in Chowan County, North Carolina, also remained at large for a substantial period in 1816. Escaping on the same night, they gathered outside Edenton, moved up the Chowan River, and according to local farmers and planters, stole, pillaged, looted, and committed many "acts of felony," as they moved in and out of the dense forests.[11]

A similar group of about a dozen slaves in Charleston District, South Carolina, hid out in the heavily wooded areas around their owners' plantations. There were three brothers—Sambo, Israel, and Frederick, ages twenty to twenty-six, Ned and his wife and three children, and Sancho or Sam. They moved about, maintained several base camps, and passed and repassed frequently between plantations. They also communicated with and visited town slaves. They moved in and out of slave quarters so freely that one planter issued cards to his *nonrunaway slaves,* "cards describing the bearer, which will be renewed weekly." In this way, he said, the runaways could not mix "with the other negroes on his own place" and escape detection, as they had in the past. In 1852, Francis D. Richardson, owner of Bayside Plantation in St. Mary Parish, Louisiana, reported great excitement among slaveholders in his area. As many as twenty armed runaways gathered in the swamps near Franklin, the parish seat, committing "depredations in the way of roberies." Travelers below New Orleans and on the west side of Bayou Teche, Richardson said, were being advised not to proceed without carrying weapons.[12]

Slaves who remained at large for "considerable portions of the year" were only occasionally armed with guns, but they were almost always in close communication with slaves on various plantations. The South Carolina slave Castilla had absconded and been recaptured on numerous occasions. As he grew older, he stayed out longer. Moving by boat along the Ashepoo, Combahee, and Edisto rivers, he knew slaves on plantations in nearly every backwater and bay in the triangle area between Walterborough, Charleston, and Beaufort. By about age fifty, Castilla had spent a good deal of his life on the run. In 1824, when he was arrested by the Colleton District sheriff, he had been at large for a year.[13]

At times, outlying slaves became so numerous in an area that it seemed virtually impossible to curtail their activities. In the entire "lower and middle divisions of the state," a group of South Carolina planters said about 1829, slave owners suffered from the "great evil of absconding slaves." Those lying out, at times commanded by "cunning" and "artful" leaders who were adept at avoiding capture, looted and pillaged plantations, butchered cattle, carried off sheep and hogs, stole tools and guns, and burned buildings. Several planters said it was impossible "Keeping stock of any Kind." One captured slave boasted that in less than a month he alone had butchered forty head of cattle. "In January last Eighteen slaves the property of one of Your Memorialists went off under their driver," the slave owners said in a petition to the South Carolina Senate, "and of these one fellow has been shot and Killed, while the house of the owner has been pillaged by his own Slaves, ten of whom are still out in a neighbouring parish." Some years later, in 1860, an Alabama woman wrote about "one hundred negroes taken up in Autauga County a short time since and out of the hundred there was *twenty-five hung* and also one white man was hung." It would make no difference to her, she added, if "they were all hung and the abolitionist with them."[14]

To Strike a Bargain

If these outlyers sought to conceal themselves in woods and swamps, others ran away for the opposite reason: to strike a bargain with their owners. Indeed, some left with the intention of lying out for a few days, or weeks, and then negotiating to gain concessions. It was a precarious undertaking, and it was necessary to have a good idea of how a master might respond. On some plantations, such action would have been foolhardy, but on other plantations, owners willingly negotiated with their slaves. Perhaps the most famous example was Benjamin Montgomery, who ran away in 1836 from Hurricane Plantation in Davis Bend, Mississippi, owned by Joseph Davis, the brother of Jefferson Davis. Having recently been sold from Virginia, Benjamin yearned to return home. When he was caught, however, Davis neither whipped nor punished the slave; rather the two men reached a "mutual understanding." If he vowed not to abscond, Montgomery could learn to read and write, earn money, and manage a store.[15]

Such privileges were rarely accorded slaves, but other runaways dickered with their owners about the treatment of their families, work routine, visitation privileges, overwork payments, hiring arrangements, choice of employers, food allotments, housing, clothing, and other matters. They wanted to be near their wives and husbands, live with their children, or stay on the plantation with their parents. They sought permission to visit towns and cities, stay overnight on another plantation, or travel to another county. It appears strange that members of an apparently "powerless" group would be able to negotiate with members of the slaveholding gentry. It did occur, however, and sometimes negotiations were initiated not by the slave but by the owner. "I have tried to send Pete several messages since he has been out," Mollie Mitchell of Columbiana, Alabama, wrote her sister-in-law on one occasion, "but I do not know whither he has received them or not."[16]

Some slaves ran away in order to be sold. Owned by Baker Wrather of Lebanon, Tennessee, Major journeyed twenty-eight miles to visit his wife in Nashville on numerous occasions. He often did so without the owner's permission. "Probably he is lurking about Nashville," the owner said after one such departure. "I will sell said negro—I prefer selling him in Nashville, as he has a wife there. If he will return, he shall be forgiven—I will then sell him in Nashville." When asked why he had run off, Jesse, a Maryland slave, said at first that he "could not & did not assign any reason for it," but later confessed that "he wished to be sold." One anonymous Alabama slave, about to be transferred to Mississippi as part of an estate, threatened to run away if he were not sold to someone in the same area. The guardian of the slave's owner said that "the boy had a wife in Alabama & was unwilling to come to this state." Moreover, he was literate, a person of "bad character," and had previously forged a promissory note "& procured the money on it." The black man's "intelligence and capacity to write would have enabled him to escape," the guardian said; under the circumstances, it was best to accede to the slave's wishes.[17]

Although a slave named Bug did not abscond on Bayou Mason, Louisiana, to be sold, he did want to be traded to a more sympathetic owner. Setting out during the harvest season of 1830, he went straight to the plantation house of Joseph Bieller and asked for help. It was unfortunate that he ran away, Bieller wrote a relative who owned Bug, but at least he had not "got in gaol and run you to expence."[18] He continued:

> I show like verry much to swap you one of my boys for him and give you the difference. I will give you one hundred dollars more than any other person will give. I am truly sorry to see him as a runaway. I hope you will not be so hard on him as you was the last time he came here. No one nowse but myself what fealing I have for him. Black as he is we were Raised together.

Slaves who pressed for better treatment by lying out often did so, like Major and the unnamed Alabama man, to effect improvements in their family circumstances. Of course, thousands of slaves ran away to be near loved ones or to try to follow them to distant parts, but this was different. This was an attempt to influence the action of an owner or to change a decision once it had been made. Living near or with a spouse, keeping one's children, preventing the sale of loved ones, being able to visit relatives and family members were matters of utmost importance. The motive of a Virginia family who ran away from Rose Hill Plantation in Fairfax County, Virginia, in 1804, became apparent only after they had been captured, brought back, and run away again. The first advertisement noted that Sam and his wife, Suckey, their teenage daughter Jane, and "three small Children" had left the plantation. A subsequent advertisement, noting that the father, mother, and daughter had again run away, included an offer from the owner. "If the above negroes will return home, without putting the owner to any further expense," Henry Talbutt wrote, "they will not be sold." A young Maryland servant, John Bacon, stayed out for five weeks visiting his "relatives," probably his mother and father, in Baltimore before being caught and jailed. At first, his master, William Stewart, threatened to sell him, but then changed his mind, obtained Bacon's release, and permitted him to go to Baltimore periodically. In court, he said that it was all a mistake and defended Bacon as an "alleged runaway."[19]

Although family matters were a principal concern, there were many other reasons to strike a bargain. Some slaves simply wanted to change owners. A frequent runaway, the Tennessee slave Gabriel informed his owner, Benjamin F. Moseley of Nashville, that if he were not sold he would continue to abscond. Initially, Moseley refused to give in to such a threat, but when Gabriel continued to remain out for extended periods, the owner recanted and sold him to Sarah W. Adams of Memphis. At the time of the sale, Gabriel was in the woods, and a fellow slave brought him the news, whereupon the black man went into town and turned himself over to his new owner.[20]

Bound by family, kinship, and personal history to one location, slaves also, ironically, ran away to remain in the same location. When she learned that her owner, John Butler of Adair County, Kentucky, was about to sell her to "some Natchez men," the black woman Rody "got wind of it & laid out until they were gone and then came home." Her owner said that this "could hardly be called runing away." Similarly, when she learned that her owner's husband planned to take her to Texas, an Alabama slave ran into the woods and hid. Later she was found in a neighboring county, and the white man told her that he had no intention of taking her away or leaving the state. For nearly a decade, a group of female slaves was hired out in Charleston, South Carolina, as part of a trust estate. The four women—Rachel, Sarah, Sarah's child, and Rose—lived together. After Sarah's child and Rachel died, Rose gave birth to two other children, and then Rose, Sarah, and the children made up one "family." In 1852, it was decided that the slaves would be returned to St. George's Parish, Colleton District, but the black women, "who have been accustomed always to live in town, positively refused to go into the Country and have been away." The owner's trustee and his wife were "unwilling to use coercion, and do not desire to be troubled with negroes who are not content to live where they live, and who by remaining away may put them to great trouble and expense."[21]

Sometimes the subject of arbitration was not revealed, but it was clear that the slave absconded for a specific reason and the owner agreed to a specific demand or at least was willing to seek a mutual understanding. In Maryland, Hester, a term slave, was described by her owner William Brooks of Baltimore as a runaway. He asked a local court for permission to extend her term of servitude and sell her out of the state. The next day, however, after an apparent compromise with Hester, Brooks withdrew his complaint and paid the court costs. The runaway Augustin in St. Landry Parish, Louisiana, described as "a lead slave [driver]," laid out for weeks at a time, moving eastward to hideouts along the German Coast or other sections along the Mississippi River. Using a white man as an intermediary, he sent notes back to his owner. The contents of the notes were not revealed, but it is obvious that he was seeking concessions from a master who had previously negotiated with this talented slave.[22]

On rare occasions, runaways negotiated for their own freedom. This usually occurred in the Upper South, and often in Maryland, where by the 1840s and 1850s increasing numbers were held in servitude for a period of years as term slaves. One white who held a slave in this manner became so frustrated at the black man's lying out that he told the servant that if he would pay him six dollars a month for three years, he would permit him to hire his own time and at the end of that time be "free and discharged from slavery and all manner of servitude." Moreover, the slave, James Edwards, had a buyout option: he could pay the owner $175 in cash and would be immediately "discharged from all obligations" of servitude. Another Maryland man was made the same promise, but under different circumstances. Michael ran away to be with his wife on so many occasions that his owner decided to sell him to the neighbor who owned his wife. The new owner agreed to place payments for extra work into a fund to purchase his freedom. The black man became "animated," worked diligently, and after eight years, had saved enough. The owner, however, decided against honoring the "contract." When Michael threatened a suit, the owner responded with the following explanation:[23]

> In the first place when I passed my word to Michael that he should have his freedom when he paid me the sum of $318 it was done with the view that he might become orderly obedient and subservient to my will and wishes, which he has wholly failed to doe and you cannot but see that this threat to sue me, and draw me into litigation is an instance of his disobedient contempt for my authority.

It was not only slave owners who reneged on bargains, however. Runaways were quite adept at practicing the art of deception. Once away from the plantation this would be obvious, but it was also employed when negotiating with whites, as slaves often kept their true motives hidden while convincing their masters of their good intentions. Elias Burgess of Maryland was one such slave. First, despite being a perpetual runaway, he convinced William Kriesman of Baltimore to purchase his unexpired term as a slave; second, he confessed that his past indiscretions were because he did not want to live on a farm; and third, he planned to reform. As Kriesman told it "he purchased the said boy, at the special instance and request of the said boy, that he would well and truly service your petitioner, that his desire was to live in the City, and that the reason he runaway from his former master was that he did not like to live in the Country." No sooner had he obliged him, than Elias ran away "two or three times" and each time had put Kriesman to "great trouble" and "great expense."[24]

The Virginia slave William demonstrated the same kind of deception. Despite an abundance of evidence to the contrary, he was able to convince his owner that he had good intentions. During the mid-

1850s, William became a habitual runaway—three times after being hired out in 1856 and between December 1857 and June 1858, when he remained in hiding "nearly all the year." After each episode, he would return or be brought back to his owner Elizabeth House of Brunswick County and beg for forgiveness. He was successful for several years, but finally the mistress wrote in despair that, in addition to "his incorrigible disposition to run away so often," he was untrustworthy, "having made so many promises of future good behavior—which he has not kept."[25]

Pressing for better treatment by lying out was at best a precarious undertaking, and the bargains struck were frequently abrogated on both sides. Occasionally when slaves were not able to negotiate with their masters, they ran away to neighboring plantations and sought to negotiate with other slaveholders. This was done in response to a particularly cruel master, to live with a spouse, or to be close to relatives. It was a ruse that usually ended with the return of the fugitive, but sometimes many months later. The slave Aimee and her daughter Chouchoute of St. John the Baptist Parish, Louisiana, absconded from their owner Justin Marc Rideau in the fall of 1844; nine months later, they were discovered on a neighboring plantation. Even after the discovery, they hid from authorities (ostensibly with the permission of their new "master") and remained out of the reach of their owner.[26]

In Georgia, a number of slaveholders noted that they had "casually lost" their slaves, only to discover them on a neighbor's plantation or working for someone else. In most such cases, slaves were seeking to live with loved ones, hide from their owners, or secure wages as hirelings. While on occasion farmers and planters did steal one another's slaves, they also acquiesced when runaways sought to live on their plantations or come under their control. Caroline and her child were casually lost by Jasper County slave master William Webb in 1831. They turned up two years later about seventy miles to the west in Coweta County, living on the plantation of Edward Castleberry, who now claimed title to the two slaves. In 1842, the young man George, who brought his owner $100 a year as a hired slave in Augusta, turned up in the same area after being absent for three years. He had been discovered missing 1 January 1839, the traditional hiring day in Augusta. In March 1842, George's owner, Edward Palmer of Richmond County, said the man had been lost "out of his possession," but was now discovered working for Wyatt W. Starke, who refused to return him.[27]

It appears that George was seeking a better hiring arrangement. Others changed masters to be with their loved ones. One striking example occurred in 1829 when four slaves—Casey, her two daughters,

Rose and Lucinda, and her son, John—owned by planter George Smith, in Coweta County, Georgia, ran away to the plantation of James Eckles, where Casey's husband lived. It would seem that Smith should have known where his slave's husband lived, but he did not, and the slave family remained together with the acquiescence of Eckles for many years. Indeed, Casey had given birth to three more boys— Moses, Isaac, and Jacob—and nearly a decade passed before Smith discovered their location and initiated legal action for their return.[28]

Distant Points

If the majority of runaways remained in the same vicinity of their owners' farms and plantations, others struck out for more distant parts. Where they might go depended on why they absconded. For many, the direction was less important than heading to a place where they might find loved ones, obtain assistance, secure employment, mix with other slaves or free blacks. Some simply set out in a direction they felt they would least likely be pursued; others followed the course of a river or boarded a vessel not knowing its destination. Others did not know where to go. Even among whites, there was an ignorance of geography, and blacks usually knew only what they had observed after being taken from one section to another or what they had been told by others. Some had never traveled beyond their owners' plantations. As a Tennessee fugitive who made it to Ohio admitted: "I had never been but about seventeen miles away from home in my life."[29]

There were runaways who devised a specific plan—going to a given point, hiding until advertisements ceased, then moving to another location and seeking to merge with the free black population. Armstead, an eighteen-year-old slave owned by Spotsylvania farmer William Tompkins, ran away in 1810. After some months, Tompkins concluded that Armstead was either "dead, or gone to some of the northern states." In fact, however, the slave journeyed forty miles away to Caroline County, where he took the name John Tyree and posed as a free man of color. There were many free blacks named Tyree in the county, and the wily fugitive, who could read and write, found work as a laborer. He remained at large for eleven years, being discovered only when he himself wrote his owner seeking assistance after being charged with raping a white woman.[30]

Targeting areas with free black populations was not only done to achieve anonymity, but to obtain assistance. Many slaves in the Upper South, and not a few in the Lower South as well, had friends, acquaintances, and relatives who were free. "DESERTED the premises,"

declared one Virginia owner, adding that he had reason to believe that
his slave Bob was being "harbored by free negroes." In Loudoun and
Fauquier counties, fugitives sought out free relatives and friends to
such an extent that whites petitioned the General Assembly to rid the
state of free people of color because "in many instances" they provided
food, clothing, protection, and safe haven for their brethren in bondage. A man in Norfolk, signing his petition "A Virginian," said that
areas with large numbers of free blacks were favorite hiding places for
runaways. Moreover, in these areas free women of color exerted a
great deal of influence and stubbornly refused to be deported to West
Africa, where whites wished to send free blacks. They were thus not
only willing to harbor runaways, but by rejecting emigration, they
also assisted slaves by maintaining stable free black communities
where runaways could find refuge.[31]

The interconnections between runaways and free blacks were less
frequent in the Lower South, where there were fewer free persons of
color. Nonetheless, slaves sought out relatives and friends who were
free in South Carolina, Mississippi, Louisiana, and other deep South
states. The owner of the "very likely" mulatto slave John of Charleston, South Carolina, was certain that he was being hidden by his aunt,
free woman of color Peggy Ford, as the two had been seen together
in the city. The twenty-two-year-old nurse Tenah, taken by her owner
to Charleston from the small town of Barnwell, South Carolina, immediately absconded. Her free black husband, William Lewis, living
on Grove Creek, was probably protecting her, the owner said, but "she
may have made her way towards Columbia, in this state, where it is
understood a former husband was taken and now resides."[32]

Slaves also received other types of assistance from friends and relations who were free. In 1808, following his owner's death, Giles, a
Virginia slave, was hired out to a Henrico County man named Charles
Purcell. Within three weeks, Purcell pronounced that the slave was "of
the most vile & worthless character & habits, & particularly addicted
to stealing." Giles escaped to the house of free woman of color Patsey
Whaley, who went to the executor of the deceased master's will and
asked if he would return Purcell's bond if Purcell would agree to "re-
linquish his claim to the services of said negroe." Both men agreed,
and the runaway at least for the present remained with his free black
protector. Another runaway obtained a map of the United States from
his free black father before departing. Others obtained information
about roads, river traffic, sailing vessels, routes of travel, possible hiding places, and free blacks, slaves, and whites who might assist them
along the way. The twenty-three-year-old Virginia slave Martha
Whitehead was assisted by her mother, who had become free, and by

a number of male and female free acquaintances, "all of whom," her owner believed, "doubtless had a hand in enticing her off."[33]

Great caution had to be employed when assisting runaways, and free blacks who did so sometimes paid a heavy price. In 1841, George W. Danley and Thomas Bryan, free men of color who served as mate and cook on the Philadelphia-to-New Orleans bark *B. Mezick*, assisted Jacob Francis, alias Wallace, a Louisiana slave owned by William H. Avery. The slave made it to freedom while the crewmen went to prison. Discovered during the voyage, the two free blacks vouched for Francis as a free man, one of them paying his fare, but as the *B. Mezick* sailed up the Delaware River, the runaway dove overboard, swam ashore, made it into Philadelphia, sold two of his master's gold watches, and journeyed on to Canada. When the boat returned to Louisiana, Danley and Bryan were arrested, tried, convicted, and sentenced to two years hard labor in the penitentiary.[34]

Penalties for assisting runaways could be even worse. In 1858, Maryland free black Daniel Mackey was indicted, tried, and convicted of having "persuaded, aided and assisted" a Negro man named Tom "to escape and runaway." A few days before Christmas, Mackey was sold into slavery by the sheriff of Talbot County for $950. Tom's owners, Francis and Sophia Loockerman, were then reimbursed the $200 they had paid to slave catchers to capture Mackey and retrieve Tom.[35]

The question of where to go was thus answered by runaways in a variety of ways. It was probably easier during the early nineteenth century—when transportation and communication were slow and traveling to the next county might take days—to remain within a forty- or fifty-mile radius of the owner's residence. Newspapers were not published in many towns, and the trail of an escaped slave could be cold by the time an advertisement appeared in the press. At times slave hunters would put up posters as they tracked runaways, but this was inefficient. Consequently, some shrewd runaways remained at large for years, as did Armstead, not too far from their master's plantation. Even during later decades, a few ingenious slaves found work in the same county or nearby counties. Absconding from his owner's farm on the Chickahominy River, west of Richmond, Virginia, in 1854, Barnett first returned to the upper part of Henrico County, where he had previously been hired, then moved south to Chesterfield County. Though spotted in both places, he avoided capture. One San Augustine County, Texas, slave escaped from his owner and hired himself as a well digger to a resident of the same county. It was not until a rope broke and a bucket of dirt fell on the slave's head killing him that word got back to the owner concerning his slave's whereabouts.[36]

Farther South and Elsewhere

Many slaves ran away farther south. Indeed, slaves living in the Lower Mississippi River Valley or in Mississippi and Alabama were more likely to run south and west than north. The stream of runaways moving from parishes and counties along the Mississippi River and its tributaries—especially Natchitoches, Rapides, Pointe Coupee, East and West Feliciana, East and West Baton Rouge in Louisiana and Adams, Jefferson, and Wilkinson counties in Mississippi—southward to New Orleans was relentless. "Ranaway from the subscriber's plantation, in the parish of Natchitoches," one notice read, William Chambery, about twenty years old and "well constituted." The planter not only sought Chambery, but the return of "his negro wench Louisa," "negro wench Eliza," and a black man, Henry Price. They were, he said, heading down the Cane, Red, and Mississippi rivers, to New Orleans. One slave apprentice from West Feliciana Parish went down the river so often that his employer could usually retrieve him within two weeks.[37]

Sometimes those who were seeking to return to the Upper South ventured down the Mississippi River. "He is very artful," a Pointe Coupee Parish, Louisiana, slaveholder said in 1833, concerning Davy, a thirty-three-year-old runaway brought from Virginia. One of the reasons he had been sold to the Lower South was his "habit of running away." Now he had stolen his owner's skiff and gone down the river, or crossed over it, taking with him a fifteen-day ration of pork and corn bread, a blanket capote, a change of clothes, and two hand saws. Skilled as a blacksmith and cartmaker, his owner said that he "may have taken the saws the better to impose on the community, by passing for a neighborhood carpenter." Eventually the slave would try to return to Virginia. Others went south because they believed their chances were better if they reached towns and cities along the river. The three slaves who absconded from the superintendent of public works on Bayou Boeuf in Rapides Parish in 1835 were well prepared to leave. They possessed a double-barreled shotgun, an axe, an assortment of clothes, fur hats, shoes, and "may have a pass procured from one of them who can write a fair hand." They were last seen heading down the Red River toward the Mississippi River and New Orleans.[38]

When it might be suspected that they would take to the river, some slaves who lived along the Mississippi deliberately struck out across the countryside, away from the river. The circuitous escape route of George, a field hand with two missing front teeth, was typical of this group. Leaving Wilkinson County, Mississippi, near Woodville, George ran away to the east, not to the river a few miles away, moving through the hilly and sometimes densely forested countryside to the Pearl River. He followed the river as it meandered southward forming the border between Mississippi and Louisiana. When sighted near Pearlington, a hamlet near the mouth of the river, he was heading toward the Gulf of Mexico, a few miles distant.[39]

Those who ran away from Missouri, or Kentucky, to the Lower South were often similarly attempting to confuse their owners. Who would suspect that someone living so near freedom, especially if they were close to the Ohio or Mississippi rivers, would run away to the deep South? Having served as a baker on board steamboats owned by Daniel D. Page of St. Louis, the slave Dennis did just that in 1839, when he went "down to Natchez with some person bound for Texas." The owner said, "in all probability he has gone up the Red River."[40] Most often those who went from the Upper to the Lower South in this manner were skilled and able to find employment. Dennis was not unusual in this respect, and posing as a free black, he might easily find work on his way to Texas.

Running away farther south did not always meet with such success, however. The slave Peter, taken by slave trader Miles Kelley from Kentucky to Vicksburg, escaped and moved southward along the east side of the river into Louisiana. It is not clear what happened next, but in 1846, more than seven years later, "Joe" turned himself over to the jailer in West Feliciana Parish and confessed that he was a runaway. A few days later a suit was filed by Kelley against planter Joseph Purl seeking a writ of sequestration for a "Negro slave named *Peter* alias *Joe*." The slave trader charged that the plantation owner had captured Peter and, without legal authority, forced him to work on his plantation. The court agreed, and Peter, alias Joe, was turned back to the trader.[41]

Not only to confuse their owners, but for various other reasons, some slaves in Kentucky and Tennessee absconded to the deep South. Transported from Georgia to the Flint River and thence to Warren County, Kentucky, Jupiter ran away through Kentucky and into Tennessee. "It is supposed he has lived with the Creek Indians," his owner said in 1814, "and will endeavor to get to the nation again." The young black Washington, scarred on his hand, arm, forehead, and with "a naked spot on the back of his head," made off in August 1841 from Caldwell County, in western Kentucky. Although very close to both the Tennessee and Cumberland rivers and about thirty miles from the Ohio River and the border to Illinois, Washington's owner was certain that he was heading southwest, either for Keysburg, Logan County, where he had been purchased; Nashville, where he once lived and was "very desirous to get back"; or Sumner County, Tennessee, where he had a slave uncle. He was probably helped by his aunt Sarah, a free woman of color who lived in Eddyville, Kentucky, on the east side of the Cumberland River.[42]

Not only was there a strong movement to the south and west, but depending on the circumstances, runaways headed in an easterly or southeasterly direction. Just as slaves in the Mississippi Valley followed the rivers south, in the Piedmont and Coastal Plain in states from Virginia to Georgia they went along the York, Rappahannock, Neuse, Savannah, and Saluda rivers toward the sea. Not a few absconders followed the general path of Polock, who started out ten miles below the Abbeville Court House in South Carolina. Situated between the Savannah and Saluda rivers, flowing to the southeast, Polock had several possible routes as he moved along the rivers through the rolling landscape and fields of corn and cotton toward the coast. He made it more than two hundred miles to Charleston, only to be arrested and thrown into the workhouse.[43]

As was the case elsewhere, runaways from the interior of the eastern seaboard states moved south to reunite with their families. "There is little doubt that Jim has gone to the Southward," explained a planter on the Cooper River in South Carolina in 1831 concerning his runaway carpenter who had been missing six months. Jim had been recently sold away from Colleton District and would no doubt return to that area. Leaving the plantation of Henry Carter in Halifax County, North Carolina, John moved south and west until he reached Charleston, where he was committed to the workhouse. Purchased at an auction in Richmond in 1850, Jesse was taken to Charles City County, Virginia, to work Hill Carter's Shirley Plantation. When he ran away in 1854, his owner believed he would try "to get back to North Carolina, or to the Dismal swamp, where I understand he worked before I purchased him." A slave blacksmith named Nelson, transported from Orange County, North Carolina, to Hanover County, Virginia, made a desperate attempt to return in 1856. Captured and jailed in Petersburg, he escaped and continued his southward trek, following railroad tracks as he "had been instructed" by a fellow slave.[44]

While not as strong as the other directional paths, in part because of the difficulty of travel, slaves also returned from the west to the east. Here, too, they were seeking to get back to areas where they had previously lived. As the domestic slave trade gained momentum and tens of thousands were taken across the Appalachians, some of them sought to return to Virginia, Maryland, and North and South Carolina. Many of their journeys were not unlike that of Rachel, purchased by Dr. John Newnan of Washington County, Tennessee. In 1808, the young woman struck out on foot across the Appalachian Mountains and onto the Piedmont. She managed to travel more than a hundred miles before she was captured and jailed in Salisbury, North Carolina. She was seeking to return home, but learned from the agent sent to fetch her that not only would she not be returned home but that her owner had sold her out of jail.[45]

Runaways who made it some distance from their owner's farm or plantation and headed in a direction that the master might not suspect were often not advertised in areas where captured. As a consequence, when they were jailed no one came forward to claim them as their property. In 1826, the Abbeville, South Carolina, slave Ambrose fled eastward. He was captured in Chester District, only about one hundred miles from his owner's farm, but he went unclaimed. After confinement for a year, Ambrose was sold at a sheriff's auction. The slave Anthony deserted his master in Choctaw County, Alabama, on the border of Mississippi in September 1846, making his way east and northeast across Alabama and Georgia into South Carolina. When he was arrested some months later in Union County, South Carolina, he had journeyed nearly five hundred miles. No one claimed him, however, and after his time in jail, he, too, was auctioned off to a local farmer. A few years later, he escaped again, moving eastward and northward to Halifax County, North Carolina, near the Virginia line, where he was arrested and returned to his owner in Union County.[46]

The direction others took depended on circumstances. In the period before Florida became a territory (1821), and even in later years, Georgia and South Carolina slaves moved across the border into Florida. Also in the early decades of the nineteenth century, slaves headed from every direction into Cherokee, Creek, and Choctaw territories of Georgia, Alabama, and Mississippi, favorite refuges for slaves from those states as well as Tennessee. When the land was cleared and plantations created, runaways sought more remote areas in the swamps and hills. In Alabama, the rugged hill country fifty miles north of the Black Belt was a "favorite lurking-ground for runaway negroes." The rough terrain provided them numerous "coverts for concealment" during the day, an observer noted, and at night slaves on the plantations helped "them to find the necessaries of existence." A local man said that he knew of "folks who had come here to look after niggers from plantations two hundred miles to the southward."[47]

During the 1840s and 1850s, southern Texas became a thoroughfare for slaves crossing the border to freedom in Mexico. "You are well aware of the insecurity of Slave property in this County," a group of forty-nine residents of San Antonio explained in 1851 to their Bexar County delegation in the General Assembly in Austin, "and will at once perceive the necessity of enacting an appropriate remedy." The problem was that, although the present law provided the death penalty for anyone "enticing a slave from his master," the law was only applicable to those who were convicted of actually enticing a slave away. There was no adequate punishment for those who advised or attempted to induce a slave to run away. Mexicans who assisted slaves had been brought before local authorities but were discharged because they had committed "no overt act."[48]

The Promised Land

The dream of freedom in the North or Canada—the so-called Promised Land—went unfulfilled for the vast majority of runaways. Those who headed northward from plantations along the coast of South Carolina and Georgia, the Black Belt of Alabama, or Mississippi and Louisiana faced a trek of hundreds of miles through uncharted and largely unknown territory. Even their counterparts in the upper states confronted numerous obstacles to making it to free territory. A few were able to find assistance from conductors of the Underground Railroad, Quakers, or antislavery whites. And a few others, traveling at night or hiding aboard sailing vessels and steamboats, made it to the North. But the chances of fugitives making it from the slave states into New Jersey or Pennsylvania or crossing the Ohio River were remote.[49]

Even residency in the border state of Maryland, in such proximity to freedom, did not ensure success. Most who lived in the Chesapeake region probably ended up like Willis Burgess, a slave hired out by an estate. Escaping from his employer in Anne Arundel County in 1836, Burgess headed northwest into Baltimore County, moved swiftly along the road to Hanover, and then turned toward his destination of York, Pennsylvania. Late that same night, however, he was captured and put in the Baltimore city jail. After the episode, the executor of the estate who hired Burgess out deemed it "most prudent" to sell Burgess, and a few days later, he was placed on the auction block. Sixteen-year-old Nathaniel, a Maryland slave who absconded in mid-July 1858, made it farther than had Burgess, but as he approached the Pennsylvania line, he was overtaken by a slave catcher. He, too, had been at large less than twenty-four hours. William Henry Thomas, a sixteen-year-old slave for a term of years (until he was thirty-three), was arrested in Harford County, having left Baltimore on his way to "a free state." Although teenage apprentice Melichoir Moore "was induced by designing persons" to flee from Harford County across the state line into Pennsylvania, he never made it and was ordered to be sold.[50]

Similarly, western Virginia and Kentucky slaves found the Ohio

River a formidable barrier. Authorities in counties along the river were on the lookout for those who might be trying to pass themselves off as hired hands or free persons. At certain jumping-off points and portage locations, sheriffs were particularly vigilant. Traveling more than one hundred miles through the rugged Allegheny Mountains from Greenbrier County, Virginia, Henry made it to Greenup, Kentucky, on the Ohio River, before he was caught and returned to his owner. Henry was a "likely and valuable negroe," a group of whites asserted in 1821, but also "obstinate perverse and unruly. . . . His high notions of liberty have already prompted him to make repeated attempts to go to the State of Ohio, or to some other part of the United States, in which he would expect an unmolested enjoyment of freedom." With similar "high notions of liberty," the Kentucky slave Frank traversed almost exactly the same distance—one hundred miles—to exactly the same location nearly a quarter-century later. Escaping from Pike County in eastern Kentucky near the Cumberland Mountains, the slave eluded pursuers, traversed the rugged hill country, and finally reached the Ohio River. At the last moment, however, he was discovered, arrested, and jailed.[51]

Indeed, there seemed to be no formula for success. Some runaways concealed themselves, used disguises, obtained free papers, traveled the back roads, and hid out for months, but were still captured. Others threw caution to the wind and made it to freedom. The successful District of Columbia fugitive Matilda Witherall, who ran away to Pennsylvania "or some other state or Territory," was described by her owner as a bright mulatto, with straight black hair, and a large bump protruding from her throat believed to be a goiter. She left in the middle of the day on the main road out of the city.[52]

Although no specific scheme ensured success, those who made it to the North were often among the most ingenious, persistent, and intelligent runaways. About twenty-five years old, quick spoken, articulate, and clever, the Tennessee slave Jim Lace set out in June 1839 for a free state. "This fellow has once before attempted to make his escape into a free State and was taken in Kentucky making his way to Illinois," Asa Jackson, a farmer who lived a few miles west of Lebanon, explained. "I am apprehensive that he will again make a similar attempt and probably aim for the same State." The strategy of a free black husband was to convince an elderly woman in Maryland to sell him his wife and his two boys. He signed a contract to purchase his family. When the woman died a short time later, he was on his way to Pennsylvania or New Jersey. "Annette ranaway and carried with her the two children," the administrator of the woman's estate noted; the husband "never complied with the contract," he added bitterly, nor was that ever his intention. There was no possibility, he concluded, that the mother and children would ever be returned.[53]

If Upper South runaways faced numerous obstacles in attempting to flee to the North, those in the Lower South found it virtually impossible. Most Georgia slaves heading north, for example, probably fared about the same as Isaac and William, runaways from Savannah, owned by different persons. Isaac was dark skinned and could "write a good hand," while William was "very talkative and intelligent." They were jailed at Walterborough, Colleton District, South Carolina, near the Georgia line, within a few days after they had set out. It took another slave also named Isaac a year to move northward from South Carolina to Surry County, Virginia, before he was captured and jailed. The record does not reveal what he did along the way or how long he remained in any one place or how he remained at large for so long, only that he was gradually moving northward. Setting out across the Savannah River from Wilkes County, Georgia, in February 1843, Henry Meredith moved quickly through South Carolina into North Carolina and was very close to the Virginia border when he was captured and jailed in Yanceyville, Caswell County, North Carolina. Meredith had journeyed two hundred and fifty miles. Refusing to divulge his owner's name or place of residence, the slave remained in jail for a year before being sold at a sheriff's auction in the spring of 1845 as prescribed by law.[54]

The same was true of runaways from other Lower South states. They, too, often found the journey northward hazardous, and in the great majority of cases, failed to reach their destinations. In the early years, they used the waterways by poling a skiff or barge upstream. Since this had to be done during the day and progress upstream was slow, it was easy to see them. Three slaves who escaped seventy miles above Natchez in 1814, for example, were quickly discovered by a friend of their owner's son as they went up the Mississippi River in their owner's skiff.[55] In later years, steamboats proved no better means for escape than poling skiffs. With the aid of strict state laws, local authorities searched steamboats regularly for stowaways. In New Orleans, Natchez, Vicksburg, and other ports, departing steamers were inspected, and those who could not prove their status as a freeman or hired slave were subject to arrest.

Most stowaways who sought to use the coastal trade or river systems as a means of reaching the Promised Land probably ended up as did the New Orleans slave Peter, owned by two trading partners, who sneaked aboard the steamboat *United States* in June 1822, heading for Louisville, Kentucky. Eight days into the journey, below Natchez, he was discovered hiding under the forecastle. It was probably little consolation to Peter that he was required to work for his board, remain aboard at Natchez because of a yellow fever quarantine, and, after being jailed in Louisville, be returned to his master five months later.[56] If the odds against a city slave like Peter were great, they were even greater against scantily dressed plantation hands who were unfamiliar with the surroundings.

Skilled and literate slaves probably had the best chance of making it from the Lower South to the Promised Land. The New Orleans hired slave Lydia, about twenty-four years old, left her owner, who lived on a plantation about two miles below the city, in 1831. He described the departure as if she were making applications for first-class accommodations. "She seeks, if she has not already found one an opportunity of embarking for New York." She was seen on the docks near the schooners *George* and *Joseph*, both of which were laying in cargo for New York. The skilled restaurant worker Thomas left for the same destination in 1835 after he had been sold. The partners in the firm that purchased him noted that he was dissatisfied, no longer being in the restaurant business. Some time later, they were informed the slave "had been seen in New York." A skilled and probably literate Georgia slave carpenter possessed a pass allowing him to travel across South and North Carolina, Virginia, and Maryland to a destination in Delaware. The pass said he could take any stage coach going north. When last seen he was on the road above Columbia, South Carolina, heading north.[57]

One of the most remarkable escapes occurred in 1854 when a thirty-year-old slave named Richard Shepard ran away. Ten months before, Shepard had been transported to Louisiana by slave trader Alexander Hagan, and in June he had been sold to John Henry Brown, a resident of New Orleans. Two months after the sale, Shepard escaped and made it to Mobile, Alabama, but was captured, jailed, and brought back. Within days, he escaped again, stowing away in a ship bound for Liverpool. Discovered at sea, he was "landed at Savanah and there placed in Jail as a runaway." Before news got back to Brown, however, Shepard again "made his escape and is now at large or in parts unknown."[58]

Not every slave who sought freedom in the North was as successful as Richard Shepard. After all, it was to the North that slave catchers went in search of fugitives, with the mistaken view that slaves "knew" what the North had to offer. The slave catchers, the factors, and the slave traders with northern connections served as barriers to freedom in the North that were formidable indeed. They were a match even for the limited numbers who sought freedom via the Underground Railroad. Meanwhile, slaves continued to seek freedom in southern communities or rural areas in order to be with family or to enjoy the support of free blacks or even other slaves and their chances for success were at least as great or perhaps greater in Charleston and New Orleans as Philadelphia and Boston.

In Which Direction?

Of course, the precise destination of many runaways will never be known. They were caught too soon after an attempted escape for us to be able to discern it, or they themselves were unclear about where to go. Some changed their minds in mid-flight, others wandered from one location to another. Much of the evidence of where slaves were headed comes from the owner's perceptions as reflected in runaway notices or the sheriffs' perceptions as reflected in detention notices. Some whites used terms like "suspected," "supposed," and "most likely" to indicate possible destinations. Others were even less certain. One New Orleans master said his slave might go to his friend's house, to his "usual place of resort" behind a cotton press, to one of the "negro cabarets between the two markets," or to the American burial ground.[59]

Despite their limitations, advertisements do provide at least crude *proportional estimates* of where runaways were headed, and they suggest changes over time. For the purpose of comparison, we have analyzed runaway notices that appeared in the *Nashville Whig* between January 1812 and December 1816, a five-year period, and the *Tennessee Republican Banner* between January 1840 and December 1842, a three-year period. Its central location in the state and its equidistance between the North and deep South provide an opportunity to compare runaway destinations during two time periods (see appendixes 3 and 4).

During the early period, approximately fifty-nine slaves were advertised in the *Nashville Whig* as runaways. About three out of four (73 percent) were either from Davidson County, including the city of Nashville, or six counties (Wilson, Sumner, Robertson, Rutherford, Dickson, Smith) within a fifty-mile radius of the capital. One out of four was from one of the Tennessee counties more than seventy-five miles away (White, Franklin, and Madison) or from Kentucky, Louisiana, or the Missouri Territory.

There was a similar dispersal with regard to where owners thought their slaves were heading. All of the nine Kentucky slaveholders who advertised in the Nashville newspaper had reason to believe that their slaves were moving south, either into Tennessee or beyond to the

Mississippi Territory or the Indian nations. Indeed, one owner who lived fourteen miles from Louisville in Jefferson County, Kentucky, traced his runaway into Tennessee. Another eight masters were fairly certain that their slaves were heading to Georgia, North Carolina, or Virginia, where their families lived. Others believed their slaves would remain in Davidson County or find refuge in the city. Among those who cited specific destinations (slightly more than half), nine slaves were thought to be heading north, mostly to Kentucky, where they had friends and family. Only three were thought to be fleeing to Ohio. It is clear that the so-called Promised Land to the north held only limited attraction for runaways whose owners advertised in the *Nashville Whig* during these early years. Indeed, slaves were more likely to head for the Missouri Territory, Mississippi Territory, or the Indian nations than Ohio.

During the early 1840s, approximately fifty-two slaves were advertised in the *Tennessee Republican Banner* as runaways. Now only half (54 percent) were from Davidson County, including the city of Nashville or six nearby counties (Dickson, Rutherford, Sumner, Robertson, Maury, Williamson), the remainder being from counties more distant (Stewart, Giles, Jefferson, Hamilton) or from Kentucky, Mississippi, Georgia, or Alabama. There were also changes with regard to where masters thought their slaves were heading. While the Georgia and Kentucky owners obviously thought their bondsmen and women were heading west and south, five times as many owners (25 percent of the total) believed their slaves were heading to Ohio, Indiana, "a free state," "to the Ohio River," or "down the Cumberland River." Some of them could not be sure, of course. Logan Henderson, who lived a few miles from Murfreesborough, in Rutherford County, suspected his slave would go through Kentucky and cross the Ohio River, but advertised in the *Louisville Journal, Tuscaloosa Monitor,* and *Chattanooga Gazette,* covering three points of the compass. And F. B. Pierce of Sumner County, Tennessee, said that his black man Cyrus was probably "making for a free State," but he had run away several times before and had previously been "caught in Nashville, and may be there now."[60]

But several important changes had occurred. First, the proportion of masters who cited specific destinations dropped from half in the early period to slightly more than one-third in the later period. This was not due to a lack of knowledge. Rather, slaveholders were now assuming that readers of the notices knew that owners were seeking runaways who remained in the vicinity of Nashville; owners from other parts of the state or from eastern states had reason to believe that their slaves were heading to the Tennessee capital. The largest change took place among runaways who were presumed to be going to another location in the South, compared with those heading for free states. In the early period, about one out of four runaways advertised in the *Whig* were thought to be going to another southern state; in the later period this had dropped to about one out of ten. Almost exactly the opposite had taken place with regard to those running to the North, increasing from about 5 percent to about 25 percent, as table 1 indicates (also see appendixes 3 and 4).[61] Where to go was a perplexing problem for runaways. Those who hid out for a few days or nights visiting loved ones on neighboring plantations obviously did not face this difficulty, but those who stayed out for longer periods, as well as those who struck out for distant parts, faced this problem. In which direction should they go? Where could they find even temporary safe haven? The increasing trend to head north was important, but it should be kept in the context of improved transportation and communication systems, the increased sophistication of slaves in finding out about how and where to go, and the fact that the great majority of runaways—even among those advertised in newspapers—still remained in the South. Some were more intent on striking a bargain with their masters than seeking a specific location, but lying out to gain concessions was at best a dubious proposition. In the end, the vast majority of runaways remained in the vicinity of their owner's residence. Often, they had a husband or wife, children, and parents in the area. They were also familiar with the surroundings.

For the great mass of runaways, however, the chance of remaining at large, whether in the same vicinity or a distant location, was unlikely. Indeed, as most of them realized, neither hiding in the vicinity

Table 1

Location and Possible Destinations of Runaways As Cited in Two
Nashville Newspapers

Destination	*Nashville Whig* 1812–1816		*Republican Banner* 1840–1842	
	Number	Percent	Number	Percent
In vicinity	28	47	21	40
Locations in South	13	22	4	8
North	3	5	13	25
North or other	1	2	3	6
To Nashville	14	24	11	21
Totals	59	100	52	100

of the owner's plantation nor running to the so-called Promised Land held nearly the potential for success as did going to the nearest town or city. And as the urban centers of the South expanded during the nineteenth century, increasing numbers of runaways answered the question of where to go by seeking the anonymity of the city.

6

They Seek a City

"JANE WAS YESTERDAY AFTERNOON about six o'clock arrested by Jones, a constable of this city," Charles Colcock Jones Jr. began a letter to his father from Savannah, on the first day of October 1856, "and is now in confinement in Wright the broker's yard." Owned by cotton planter Charles C. Jones Sr. of Liberty County, Georgia, Jane had been in the city more than a month before she had been discovered. She had passed herself off as a slave from the upcountry who was permitted to hire her own time, and she had found employment at $6.50 a week doing housework.

This was not the first time Jane had been arrested as a runaway. Indeed, at age eighteen, wearing "fine ear- and finger-rings," the corpulent, garrulous, self-confident black woman had traversed the thirty miles from Jones's plantation to the city on many occasions, so many that she knew the route by heart: north to the Great Ogeechee River, stealing a boat and crossing the river, then weaving her way around ponds, creeks, and drainage canals to the forests of live oaks and cypress swamps, and on to the Savannah road. On previous trips, she had found passage on coastal vessels, making part of the journey in a fishhook fashion to the mouth of the Savannah River, and thence to the city. Late summer was not a good time to run, as the summer heat lingered and the nights remained stiflingly hot, but to Jane the weather seemed to make little difference.[1]

What should the father and son do? Prosecute the woman who hired Jane? Sell the rebel away from her mother, father, brothers, and sister? With regard to prosecution, the son explained: "There are, you may say, hundreds of Negroes in this city who go about from house to house—some carpenters, some house servants, etc.—who never see their masters except at pay day, live out of their yards, hire themselves without written permit, etc." This was of course "very wrong," but "the less said and done in cases of this kind the better." To the second question the father was adamant: "We have had trouble enough, and I wish to have no more." A deeply religious and pious man, devoted to improving the spiritual well-being of his slaves, Jones felt that he could not sell Jane separately. Unlike many slaveholders, he instructed his son to sell as one group Jane, her mother, age forty-seven, father, age forty-five, and Jane's four siblings. Another field hand would also be disposed of at the same time and the eight placed on the market in Savannah should bring $6,700, including $900 for Jane, who was advertised as a "House servant, good seamstress, and field hand."[2]

Weeks passed, however, and the slaves remained unsold. An offer of $4,200 was made by George Harrison, "a gentleman of high respectability" who would "make a good master," but it was rejected as being too low. Meanwhile, it was costing Jones $10.50 a week to maintain the slaves in Savannah, and as costs mounted, Jones and his son grew apprehensive. Finally, about two months after Jane had been arrested, the now nearly desperate son sold the slaves for $4,500, far less than anticipated. The consolation was that the man who purchased them was a planter from near Macon and promised to treat the family well and keep them together. "They have been sold as we desired," the father said with relief; more money might have been made, but they were kept together. "Conscience is better than money."[3]

The sale ended a painful episode for the Jones family, or so they believed. It was a process that had occurred thousands of times, albeit with a different cast of characters, as slavery spread across the South during the nineteenth century. Tens of thousands ran away to towns and cities seeking safe haven and anonymity. As with runaways who remained near the plantation, many were caught and returned, although they probably remained at large for longer periods than blacks lying out. Even in the colonial period, towns and cities had offered slaves unique opportunities. Slave hiring and self-hire were common in the eighteenth century. By the early 1800s, the practice had grown to such an extent that there were few towns or cities in the South where there were not hundreds, in some instances, thousands, of hired bondsmen and bondswomen.

Cities offered opportunities for runaways to hide their identities, create new ones, live with relatives—slave and free—and mingle with others. They could be accosted and questioned, but control was less intrusive than in the country, where black strangers were scrutinized and often arrested. It was little wonder that the streets of southern cities—teeming with carts, buggies, wagons, drays, livestock, mules, horses, and pedestrians—lured runaway slaves.

Temporary Sojourners

Slave owners frequently advertised that their slaves were heading for one of the numerous towns and cities that dotted the southern countryside. By the antebellum period, they could point to years of experience of having their slaves run off to cities. The owners' advertisements in the *Richmond Enquirer*, 15 February 1850, were perhaps typical for the last slave decade: "the return of Jacob, hired out to work for Harvey & Company"; "FAYETTE, who ran away from my Farm in Gloucester county lately"; "RANAWAY from the subscriber, in Fluvanna county, on the 12th of December, a mulatto boy, WASHINGTON"; "RANAWAY from the plantation of Mrs. Harriet H. Hill, near King William Court-house"; and "Left my Tobacco Factory, on Saturday, the 19th inst., my Negro man, EDMUND." Nor was the allure of Richmond unlike that of Baltimore, Norfolk, Charleston, Mobile, New Orleans, Memphis, Nashville, or any number of smaller towns.[4]

It was clear that some runaways viewed the city not as a permanent refuge but as a temporary locale. As with lying out, being away from bondage for even a short period offered relief from toil on the plantation. What better place to take a holiday than a city? There were any number of slaves in various sections of the South who followed the lead of Bob, a field hand on a plantation in St. Charles Parish, Louisiana, who at age about twenty-five was "in the habit" of going to New Orleans. He was usually caught and returned within a short time. He "frequently goes to the city," is "lurking about" the suburbs, is in the "habit of going" to the city, "taken up by a Constable in the City" were constant refrains of the newspapers during the period. When Isaac left his Essex County, Virginia, master in 1852, it was clear where he was headed as "he frequently goes to the city of Richmond."[5]

Not a few runaways mingled with crowds at celebrations or sporting events in urban areas. They went to dances in the public squares, attended cockfights, and bet on horse races. The slave Lewis, from Chesterfield County, Virginia, left his owner's residence late one night in May 1806 wearing a homespun coat and homespun pants, both dyed a light olive color. A couple of weeks later, he was seen in Richmond, now wearing a black coat and a fancy vest. He was attending the horse races. "He has a pert walk, good countenance, very active," his owner said, "fond of waiting on gentlemen." It appears that Lewis and his owner differed about the latter.[6]

While slaves of all ages absconded to cities, those in their teens and early twenties found the excitement and diversity especially enticing. In the Upper South, Alexandria, the District of Columbia, Baltimore, and Annapolis became centers for runaways during the antebellum years. Their proximity to farms and plantations in eastern Maryland and northern Virginia made them attractive, as did their growing populations.[7] Some young slaves made periodic visits to cities and returned to their plantations on their own in a few days, while others hid out for weeks and months until they were arrested or captured. One young man on a farm in Anne Arundel County went to Baltimore on three different occasions. He was arrested, jailed, and returned each time, but never punished. It was obvious that he would not remain on the farm, his owner said, as he had been informed that he would be sold if he continued to run off and he ignored the admonition. With the same lament another Maryland farmer said that his youthful "Negro is well acquainted with the road to Baltimore & your petitioner believes that it will be utterly impossible to keep the said negro at work on the farm."[8]

The allure that urban areas held for slaves could been seen in the career of Hamilton, a Maryland slave who was to be emancipated at a future date. Even as a young boy, Hamilton began running away from the plantation and heading straight for Annapolis or Baltimore. By the time he was eighteen in 1846, he had already absconded a number of times, only to be found "in some House Occupied by free negroes," hiding out with other slaves, or frolicking in the city. Twice he had been arrested and held in Slatter's Jail in Baltimore. The owner had sent his overseer, his plantation manager, and on one occasion he himself had gone to fetch the runaway. "The Farm was his home," the master said, and "all kind means" were used "to prevent his going to town." But to no avail. Indeed, the master admitted that Hamilton was not his only slave who ran away to Annapolis or Baltimore. He had failed to stop a number of others.[9]

Cities in the Lower South similarly tempted slaves away from plantations and farms. The most popular city along the eastern seaboard was Charleston and its surrounding suburbs. In any given year, runaways arrived from Georgia, from along the Savannah River, from plantations along the Cooper, Ashley, and South Santee rivers. They also came from Fairfield District, above Columbia, from farms around Summerville and Wasamasaw, or from plantations on Johns Island, St. Helena Island, Edisto Island, Fenwick Island, James Island, and Goose Creek. It was rare that the Charleston Workhouse did not house groups of runaways.[10]

Most of those who streamed into the city remained only short periods before they were discovered and arrested. Two of them—Frank and Sam—living on farms about two miles apart on the Broad River, "left home together" and were arrested together a few weeks later when they arrived in Charleston. Another slave, jailed in the city within weeks after his arrival, was owned by Thomas Seabrook, who lived above the Coosawhatchie River, about seventy miles west, southwest of Charleston. A black man named March was captured in June 1826 not long after fleeing from his owner in Greenville, South Carolina. Despite the opportunity for anonymity, it was nevertheless difficult to remain at large in the city. In 1832, for instance, two African-born blacks, one with filed teeth, left their Edgefield District plantation and headed for Charleston. One of them had previously taken the same route, but had been quickly retrieved, the owner said; despite this, he believed they were again heading for Charleston.[11]

Of all the urban areas in the South, none offered a greater variety for amusement and entertainment than New Orleans. Slaves, including runaways, could attend the theater, opera, dances, cockfights, and horse racing. Merely walking the streets was an adventure; listening to the various dialects; hearing French, Spanish, and English; viewing the Old World architecture; and seeing the variety of the cafés, restaurants, boardinghouses, and hotels. "New Orleans still retained much of the old Spanish air, was strongly impregnated with French," recalled a former Tennessee slave who had first visited in the city about 1839, which "caused it to be unlike any other city in the United States." As the population grew from 27,000 in 1820 to 169,000 in 1860, including 24,000 persons of color, it also became a "most desirable place" for runaway slaves.[12]

The stream of runaways to New Orleans was enormous during the antebellum years. Quite a few were like Agnes, a field hand on a plantation on Bayou Plaquemine, an outlet of the Mississippi River about 125 miles above the Crescent City. Several times she expressed her desire "to go to town," but was denied permission. One morning at nine o'clock, she was observed cleaning fish on the bank of the river; a half hour later she vanished. Fearing she had drowned, a search was conducted, at least until it was learned that she had taken a dugout canoe and was going down river to New Orleans. Runaways came from the cotton parishes above the city and also from the sugar parishes to the south and west, from Mississippi and Alabama, even from Missouri, Arkansas, and Georgia. They were described as American, creole, and African.[13]

Not only did the city attract slaves, but by the 1820s and 1830s so, too, did the suburbs. This was especially true for urban blacks who wanted to remain near friends and family. The New Orleans slave Timothy used the name Dickson when he ran away to the suburb of St. Mary "where he keeps himself," the owner noted, and "has been often seen." The mulatto woman named Fine also remained nearby,

hiding in the suburb of Marigny. Phil's owner believed he was "lurking" around an "upper faubourg." One woman who left with her six-
year-old daughter was spotted alone near a grog shop at the corner of
Julia and Foucher streets. She had probably left the girl, the master
thought, with friends in the neighborhood of the Old Basin. The
twenty-two-year-old Elvira, "of light complexion and slender shape,"
had run away previously and "concealed herself for a long time in
suburb Washington." Jack was "very smart and intelligent," who
spoke French and English and was "studying Spanish." He was a
"straight, well made boy, but not handsome; has a large mouth, and
a scar on his upper lip, a long face, and rather a sugar-loaf sort of a
head." He had been seen frequently in the lower suburb.[14]

Towns and cities along the Mississippi River were also favorite destinations for runaways. The old ports—New Orleans, Baton Rouge,
Natchez, Vicksburg, and St. Louis—had long been destinations for
plantation hands. Many absconders were quickly arrested and jailed,
sometimes only days after they had arrived in cities.[15] It was not difficult to spot field hands because of their dress, mannerisms, behavior,
and language. Even those who attempted to act nonchalantly or don
new clothes were easily detected. Some planters noted that their runaways would undoubtedly change their clothing, but many slaves had
neither the time nor the money to do so. Rural runaways arriving in
the city for the first time were often awestruck by the diversity and
business activity. Moreover, the dialects were as numerous among
them as they were among whites, perhaps more so, and differed within
states and within regions of a state. In Savannah and Charleston, for
example, observers noted the distinct dialects within just a few miles
of the two cities. The same was true for New Orleans and for cities
in Virginia. Thus, even the most versatile runaways might have difficulty remaining at large.

Remaining at Large

Finding a place to stay was of primary importance for new arrivals. A
large black population provided opportunities in this regard. As cities
such as Baltimore, the District of Columbia, Richmond, Louisville,
Charleston, New Orleans, and St. Louis grew, it became more difficult
for local authorities to monitor closely the movements of incoming
runaways. In large urban areas, it was made even more difficult because of the residential patterns among nonwhites. Some lived in alleys behind their master's town houses; in run-down sections along
the river with working-class whites; near white residential areas, where

they worked as butlers, cooks, house servants, gardeners, and coach-men; and in the suburbs. There was very little racial separation, as regular slaves, hired slaves, free persons of color, white artisans and mechanics, and members of the planter aristocracy lived in close prox-imity. The racial and class mixing, at least in larger cities, gave run-aways opportunities to mix in and remain unnoticed.

Those who remained undiscovered for any length of time were often taken in by relatives, friends, or acquaintances, both slave and free. One observer in Camden, Delaware, described free mulatto Samuel D. Burris as "notorious" for providing protection to fugitives. Despite having been previously convicted of "harboring," Burris "still persists in the nefarious practice of enticing Servants and Slaves away from their masters." Runaways were harbored by their mothers, fathers, sons, daughters, brothers, sisters, uncles, aunts, or more distant rela-tions. The Virginia slave Billy, a collier in Chesterfield County, ran away in January 1806. He was probably "in Petersburg, or its vicin-ity," the owner said; he had been there before and would probably receive assistance from his slave father, who lived at Conjurer's Neck. On more than one occasion, the Virginia slave Lucy crossed the James River and found refuge with her two sisters, both of whom were slaves in Richmond. Slaves who absconded to other cities could also often count on relatives for assistance. "TEN DOLLARS REWARD. Ranaway, about fourteen months since, the fellow Warley," began a notice pub-lished in the *Charleston Mercury* in January 1830. He had recently been spotted at the residence of his brother, who lived on South Bay. Another South Carolina runaway had "a relation" in Charleston, where "more than probably" he would venture before he made "an attempt to leave the State." The mulatto man John was heading for Charleston, where he had "a mother and other relations." The grey-haired slave Murrea was concealed by her daughter-in-law, and then by her free black sister, Hagar McCall, who lived with Murrea's daughter on King Street, near South Bay, in Charleston.[16]

It was not only relatives and friends who helped fugitives. Many free persons of color, especially in cities of the Upper South, had vivid memories of slavery. They could recall their grandparents, parents, or even their own early years as slaves. Thus, they could understand the plight of their brethren in bondage. It was a gamble as well as dan-gerous to harbor runaways. One man—Henry Burk of Chowan County, North Carolina—provided food and lodging to a slave, but was discovered and forced to flee from his home. When indicted for "unlawfully and secretly and fraudulently" harboring and maintaining "a certain run-away slave, named Harry the property of John G. Small," Burk was listed as "late of said County."[17]

In the deep South, the urban free black population was more privileged, but there were also concentrations of slaves and those recently
freed. In towns and cities, slaves and free blacks were often willing to
provide help, despite the severe penalties for harboring fugitives. The
escape of the slave James Wilson, purchased by Plaquemines Parish
sugar planter Victor Debouchel in 1840, was not unusual in this regard. Wilson absconded a few months after he arrived at the plantation. His master said that he was "well acquainted" in New Orleans
and would certainly find refuge among free persons of color in the
city. The owner of a large plantation in St. Paul Parish, South Carolina, William Westcoat, reported that he tracked two runaways to
Charleston, only to discover that they had been hired on board out-
going vessels by "Colored Men." His neighbor, Fraser Mathewes, a
member of the Agricultural Society in the parish, said that three of
his runaways, a mother and her two children, also went to the city.
Three years after their escape, he came across them "in the yard &
employment of a Free Mulatto woman." Both men lamented that it
was almost impossible to prosecute the free blacks who hired their
slaves since convictions in such cases came only when it could be
proved beyond any doubt that the employers had knowingly hired
fugitives.[18]

Most urban migrants who remained undetected received assistance,
at least in the early days and weeks following their escape. But those
who avoided capture beyond the initial period were usually willing to
move about quickly, change residences, go from city to suburbs, or
city to city. When authorities got close to runaway Bill, who hid in
several locations in Macon, he went on to Augusta, Georgia. His decision probably extended his freedom by many months, although he
was eventually arrested. The slave Peter was also adept at moving
about. Purchased in Richmond by an agent hired by a Halifax County
planter, Peter absconded to the Portsmouth-Norfolk area, where he
stayed ahead of authorities for several years. He was arrested in 1839
but refused to divulge the name of his owner and remained in jail a
year before he was sold.[19] To avoid detection, runaways switched from
Annapolis to Baltimore, from Baltimore to the District of Columbia,
from New Bern to Wilmington in North Carolina, from Columbia to
Charleston in South Carolina, and from Baton Rouge to New Orleans.
Some of the larger cities attracted runaways from hundreds of miles
away.

Another way to avoid discovery was to pose as a free black person.
In dress, manner, language, behavior, attitudes, and appearance, most
slaves differed from free persons of color, especially in cities along the
Gulf Coast—Pensacola, Mobile, New Orleans—or up the Mississippi

River—Baton Rouge, Natchez, Vicksburg, where some free blacks owned slaves. Yet, some slaves managed to remain free for lengthy periods posing as free persons of color. Although Rosa's escape from Cuba and journey to New Orleans were unusual, her ability to adapt to a new environment was typical of runaways who remained at large. By the time she was finally discovered by her owner, Stephen Predone, in 1823, Rosa had become the mother of several children, some of whom she had sent to St. Domingo, and two of whom, teenagers Jean and Madelaine, lived with her in New Orleans. When the owner discovered them, he urged authorities to act quickly because they "would run off or secrete themselves." Indeed, when the order for their arrest was issued, they had already secreted themselves for nearly a decade-and-a-half.[20]

In South Carolina, some slaves merged into the free population and worked as barbers, bakers, butchers, masons, and builders. This group included Charleston carpenter Joseph Elwig, who eventually acquired a home on Coming Street, and Bennettsville carpenter and builder Thomas David, who negotiated contracts, hired day laborers, and supervised the construction of houses, as well as several other enterprising individuals. This occurred in other places as well. A Montgomery, Alabama, slave was discovered five years after running away to Vicksburg, Mississippi.[21]

Two slaves in Elizabeth City, North Carolina, grabbed a whip out of their owner William Glover's hand and severely flogged him and his two friends before absconding and remaining at large for two years. A subsequent investigation into how the slave rebels, Jack and Charles, lived during this time provides a profile of runaways at large. The fugitives went first to Nansemond County, Virginia, changed their names to Jack Douglass and Charles White, obtained forged freedom papers, and found jobs ($40 for three months) cutting shingles. Later, they went to Suffolk, the county seat, working on a nearby canal, then returned to North Carolina and stayed in Gatesville, Winton, and Windsor, while working on the Roanoke Railroad. They showed their false freedom papers with county seal, and everyone thought they were free. Their luck ran out, however, when a railroad agent in Weldon, North Carolina, questioned them in 1848. A short time later, they were jailed in Norfolk. When their owner was notified, he went to identify them and said they were the same "damned sons of bitches" who had whipped him and his friends.

In an effort to discover who had given Jack and Charles false papers, Glover received information from a number of people, including Virginia cotton mill owner Abram Riddick. "I spent the day yesterday in seeking out particulars about the stay of your run aways in the neighborhood of my Cotton Factory &c I am Yet keeping the matter secret, hoping to asertain who the writer of the *forged papers is*," Riddick wrote in 1848.[22]

> I am not yet satisfied about the [false free] papers you handed me & shall use all my very best endeavors to find who the base scoundrel is, and if in my power to find it out, shall see that he is rigidly dealt with, such offence stands on the lowest grade with me[.] at this time I am suffering in the same way having now 3 as likely Men as any I own in the woods—.

In New Orleans, runaways "representing" themselves as free, "pretending" to be free, using forged freedom papers, and "attempting to pass" as free, were numerous. The mulatto slave Mary was described as small in stature, light complexioned, with a flat nose, large mouth, and thick lips. She spoke very little French, but had been at large for an extended period of time. In 1829, her owner offered ten dollars for her return, noting that "she calls herself a free woman." The mulatto man who absconded from his owner in New Orleans in 1830 spoke French and English, smiled a good deal when speaking, and "pretends to be free." While not as numerous as in the Crescent City, slaves migrating to other cities sought to pass as free blacks. The "negro boy named Isaac[,] an apprentice for a term of years," ran off from his master in Anne Arundel County, Maryland, in 1859 and went to Baltimore. The owner soon learned that he "was passing as a free boy." The same phrase was used by owners searching for runaways in Richmond, Petersburg, and Norfolk, Virginia; New Bern and Raleigh, North Carolina; Columbia, South Carolina; and many other cities. After being out nearly two years, the Chesterfield County, Virginia, runaway Phill was found in Petersburg passing himself off as a free man of color.[23]

Cities also provided runaways with avenues for more distant destinations. They could board vessels moving down the river systems to the sea or go on ships destined for distant ports. A number took off for interior ports—Richmond, Virginia; Columbia, South Carolina; Montgomery, Alabama; Nashville, Tennessee—or cities on the periphery of the South with easy access to the Gulf of Mexico or the Atlantic Ocean. They used the cities as embarkation points. The "very likely well set MULATTO BOY" Paris, a teenager, was seen at the New Castle ferry; there is little doubt, his owner said, that he was destined for Richmond, "from whence he may probably attempt to get off by water." Captains of river vessels, steamboats, and oceangoing ships should be forewarned about harboring slaves, a typical advertisement in the *New Orleans Bee* said in 1829, "on peril of being prosecuted according to law." One runaway had been "bred to the sea," his owner said, and would endeavor to "get on board of some vessel or steam boat." A Piedmont South Carolina slave was on his way to Charleston, another owner said, to "enter some vessel."[24]

Runaways as Hired Slaves

For some runaways freedom lasted only a few months, but for others it was longer if they eventually merged with the free black population. Those who became successful in creating a new identity were usually able to find work. As suggested by the experiences of Jane in Savannah, the demand in southern cities for a wide range of black workers, both skilled and unskilled, remained strong during the nineteenth century. Although there were ebbs and flows in the economies of southern cities, there were few periods when hired slaves were not in demand. Wages varied, but black workers could command between $75 and $150 a year in the 1820s and 1830s and up to $20 a month during the 1850s. They worked as laborers, dockhands, domestics, laundresses, gardeners, horse tenders, servants, hod carriers, bricklayers, stonemasons, carpenters, draymen, and steamboat stewards, waiters, and cooks. In many urban areas, as competing whites pointed out, slaves dominated certain occupations.[25]

Although prohibited by law, the practice of permitting slaves to hire their own time was widespread. Primarily urban, self-hire offered advantages to both owner and slave. Bondsmen and women would gain a measure of independence by being permitted to seek out an employer, negotiate wages and working conditions, and pay the owner an agreed-upon sum. Often they were permitted to retain a portion of their wages. Owners on the other hand did not have to bother with negotiating hiring agreements and could expect a good income. The comment of Charles C. Jones Jr. that hundreds of slaves in Savannah "never see their masters except at pay day, live out of their yards, hire themselves without written permit" was applicable to most cities in the South. In fact, the demand for black workers—often with no questions asked—was so great at times that slaves earned good wages. Perhaps there is no better illustration of this than the protest meeting of Richmond freedmen following the Civil War. Their earning power, they asserted, was half what it had been as hired slaves![26]

Many runaways who fled to towns and cities tried to pass themselves off as self-hired slaves. It took self-confidence and audacity to approach whites, create a fictitious identity, and ask for employment, but some runaways convinced employers that they had been sent by their owners to find work. In cities from Baltimore to Charleston to New Orleans to Nashville, they worked as laborers, ditchdiggers, laundresses, seamstresses; as skilled artisans, carpenters, coopers, builders, and mechanics; and as fishermen and boatmen. They worked in the hemp, tobacco, and iron industries and did heavy work on road repair and canal building gangs. In Elizabeth City County, Virginia, one observer counted nearly one hundred "quasi-free" bondsmen and women who lived and worked in the Hampton area, some of whom were runaways. Employers in need of hired hands often did not ask for identification papers. How runaways might sustain themselves in towns and cities was illustrated by the flight of Sam, who left his master at Tappahannock, the port of entry for Essex County, Virginia, on the Rappahannock River, in 1805; his master said that Sam, who could read and write, would probably go to Richmond and would likely either hire himself out or try to pass as a free black. He was a "very good boot and shoe maker."[27]

In some cities, hired slaves were supposed to have a ticket or wear a badge, and everywhere they were presumed to have been given permission by their owners. But slaves could forge tickets, acquire false badges, and argue convincingly that their owner, usually located some distance away, had sent them thither to find work. If asked for written proof, slaves assured them that their masters said they did not need written permission to apply for a job. Runaways with special skills had some advantages. Working in a baker's shop on Bourbon Street in New Orleans, Francois was about twenty-four when he ran away in 1841. Sporting a goatee and a fancy coat with metal buttons and velvet collar, he had previously run away on several occasions and hired himself out to the proprietor of a boardinghouse in the city and to the captain of a Mississippi River steamboat.[28]

The advertisements in New Orleans newspapers indicated a wide range of occupations that runaways might pursue as self-hired slaves. For male slaves, they included laborers, mill hands, railroad hands, domestic servants, cotton-press hands, cigar makers, and other skilled jobs. The American black man Joe, owned by Nicholas Reggio, a planter in Plaquemines Parish, below New Orleans on the Mississippi River, was noticed "many times in the upper suburbs, close to the saw mills." The mulatto servant Thomas from Bayou St. John was a first-rate house servant. In all probability, the master said, he was working in some boardinghouse in the upper suburb; the slave John, owned by a planter across the Mississippi River from New Orleans, probably hired himself out in a cotton press. The mulatto creole slave Basile, running from a plantation in St. John the Baptist Parish, will "represent himself as free," his master said, "and will probably look for

work as a segar maker in some segar manufactory." Among the four
slaves who ran away from the Levee Steam Cotton Press Company in
July 1834 were Lloyd Hawkins, an engineer; Moses Thom, a fireman
and cook; Ben Fisher, a press hand; and Catherine, whose occupation
was not given. Black women found jobs as cooks; gardeners; market
women; fruit, vegetable, and flower hawkers; midwives; maids; laundresses; and prostitutes.[29]

In other towns and cities, fugitives found these and other types of
employment. He would probably head for Mobile, one Alabama
planter said of a Spanish-speaking slave, and find a job among the
Spaniards. He would try to pass as a free man of color, as he "is an
artful fellow and can raise a plausible story." To find employment, it
often took "a plausible story" as well as confidence, courage, poise,
and intelligence. It also took the ability to adjust to a new situation
and live by deception. All of this could be accomplished with the
greatest possibility of success in towns and cities. In cities such as
Baltimore, Washington, Richmond, Charleston, New Orleans, and St.
Louis, resourceful slaves could go about seeking work virtually unnoticed. But even in smaller towns they might secure jobs and work
unchallenged. One resident of Athens, Georgia, with its population of
under 4,000 residents, evenly divided between whites and slaves, said
in 1859 that there were more "free negroes manufactured and made
virtually free" in his town than there were "bonafide" free blacks in
Clarke and any ten surrounding counties. Among the "free negroes
manufactured" were runaway slaves who hired themselves out in a
variety of different jobs.[30]

Hired Slaves as Runaways

If plantation hands ran away to cities to find jobs, hired slaves also
joined the runaway army. They saw, perhaps more clearly than their
rural counterparts, the connection between work and wages. Slaves
who were hired in cities were sometimes paid for extra work. They
usually lived and worked away from their owners and achieved a degree of autonomy. Even under the most exploitative hiring arrangements, when they were auctioned off on New Year's Day along with
the slaves who were sold or traded, hired slaves were often permitted
to journey to and from their place of employment on their own. Sometimes slaveholders discussed with them when and where they would
be hired, the type of work they would perform, if they would be
willing to accept a particular employer, and what accommodations were
required for their families. "I have always had them hired in family,

and reference to a choice of masters made either by themselves or my agent," Virginia slave owner Joseph Anderson advised a friend concerning the best way to hire slaves, "and never extracting the largest prices that cd be obtained." Consequently, he had "lost few and perhaps fewer than any person of my acquaintance," he boasted, "nay fewer in like proportion than I have lost at my own residence in Amelia [County]."[31]

Not even Anderson's method was foolproof. His only boast was that he had *fewer* runaways than did his acquaintances. Nor was he correct in his assumption that the better they were treated the less likely they were to abscond. At times, it seemed that even those most indulged were willing to go off on their own. Often, however, slaves ran away because they were dissatisfied with working conditions, clothing or food allotments, housing, travel distance, visitation privileges, or overwork payments. They would run away, moreover, because they were forced to work in dangerous occupations such as mining, iron manufacturing, canal building, railroad construction, road building. They also objected to being required to leave home for extended periods, sent to a different employer, or turned over to a new hiring agent or manager.

The response of a group of slaves owned by a Presbyterian church in St. Paul's Parish in 1817 and of a Charleston slave belonging to a trust estate in 1854 suggested what might happen when hirelings were sent to new employers or turned over to new managers. The church fathers had hired out the church's slaves for several generations, even after many "absconded and went off with the British Army" during the American Revolution. When the hiring profits declined, the board of trustees, plantation owners William Simmons, John Ashe, and William Hayne, lamented that the slaves had become "idle and dissatisfied," and it was extremely difficult to find employers. In 1817, when they hired them out to "a man of good character," the slaves "all absconded and have declared they will not live with him." For many years, March had been hired out in Charleston, South Carolina, to produce income for a trust estate established for the benefit of Lydia Adams, but when she died and a new administrator tried to force March in 1854 to turn over more of his earnings to him, the hired slave ran away. Four years later, a trustee lamented that since the administration's action March had been "nearly three fourths of the time a runaway and is now out of the control of his legal or Equitable owner."[32]

Other slaves simply did not report to their employers, ran away shortly after arriving, or absconded during the period of the hiring contract. Tom Page, owned by Joseph K. Weisiger, a Richmond man, was hired out to a man who lived in Goochland County, but when he reached the employer, he asked to return to obtain some more clothing. His owner noted nine months later that "he has not been heard of." In this case, Page obviously did not like what he found, but in other instances, hirelings absconded apparently for no reason. Fifty-year-old Ned Robinson, a Kentucky bricklayer, was hired to a man in Richmond, Virginia, in 1805. His age and obsequious demeanor made him an unlikely candidate for overt resistance, but Ned seized an opportunity the following year and set out to the north. "I cannot give an accurate description of his person," the employer admitted, when he learned that Ned had run away in October 1806. "He is, I am induced to believe, a very artful fellow."[33]

Indeed, there were many "artful" fellows among the hirelings who ran away. The Charleston carpenter Prince Webb, purchased at age fifteen by John Hunter, grew up in the city and acquired a reputation as an intelligent, talented, and reliable artisan. With his family on an Ashepoo River plantation forty miles distant, Webb asked his owner to permit him to find a master in that vicinity. Given a ticket "to look for another owner," Webb vanished. If he would return, the owner promised, there would be "no questions asked." Even a few of those who were given a sizable portion of their earnings and had risen to the highest economic standing among urban bondsmen and women set out on their own. Hired in New Orleans as a dining room servant and barber in the City Hotel, the slave Scott wore a handsome frock coat, sported a "watch with a good deal of rigging," and boasted bushy side whiskers. It was surprising to the hotel management as well as Scott's clientele in 1840 when he did not show up for work one afternoon, and after a search, it was discovered that he had run away.[34]

Slaves who had been hired out regularly were sometimes not willing to return to the farm or plantation. Hired out to a mill owner for several years, Joe, who was about fifty-five years old and walked with a cane, left his employer shortly before Christmas in 1802 and failed to return to his owner. "I have lately been informed that he has been employed at a brick yard in or about Alexandria," the owner wrote nine months later; "his cloathing I cannot describe, as I have not seen him for upwards of two years." When owners sought to restrict the autonomy of hired urban slaves, the slaves absconded. Jim had already tried to escape once by running away to Maryland but was captured and brought back. In 1806 he was hired out to a man in Richmond, and it appeared that the slave would prove to be a profitable investment for his owner Nathaniel Hill of Hanover County. But when his owner refused to hire him out again in 1807, Jim fled.[35]

Although men comprised the bulk of the hired slave labor force, there were also a number of hired women who ran away. Those who were hired in the market or dock areas of cities or who worked in town houses and residences as cooks, maids, and house servants were knowledgeable about boat arrivals, transportation, or where they might work on their own. Hired women from the countryside who came to Charleston, Savannah, Mobile, and New Orleans to sell milk, vegetables, and poultry or to set up stalls to sell their goods were equally experienced with the workings of the cities and how they might leave their owners. Among the runaways in Charleston were a number of hired women who were either employed in the homes of affluent whites or in the markets. The black woman Hannah, well known in Charleston as a market woman, disappeared in November 1826. She was dressed in homespun and carried her mulatto child, about twelve months old, with her. For several years while owned by General Geddes, Nancy had been hired out as a cook and laundress in Charleston or sent to Sullivan's Island. She was also "a very handy house servant," her owner Mary Edings said in 1828. She probably went to the Bridge Ferry in St. Andrew's Parish to see her mother, the owner said following Nancy's failure to report back. "She is artful, and no doubt may obtain a ticket."[36]

The same was true in New Orleans. Hired runaways included Sophie, well-known as "a cake-woman"; Julie, "long known in this city as a retailer of vegetables and speaks french only"; and Lydia, who could "almost always" be found on Esplanade Street in front of the levee selling milk. The fair-skinned New Orleans–born Sally, who spoke French, English, and Spanish, ran a coffeehouse at the corner of Bourbon and Orleans streets. She ran away in mid-September 1831 but was captured and returned. The frustration of her owner could be seen in a second advertisement: "Ranaway on Friday night from the subscriber, after having broken the chains she had on, the mulatto wench name Sally, rather short, strong constitution, fair complexion, and pug nose." She had previously worked at the coffeehouse, her mistress explained, but had recently hired herself out, using the name Angelique, to a saddler in the city.[37]

Hired slaves worked for businesses, moved about, met other slaves, became acquainted with literate free blacks, and acquired some knowledge of the world beyond their locale. Some of them saved small amounts of money. When they did run, they often posed as free blacks and carried forged identification papers. One hired Virginia runaway was "known to have stolen free papers" and "may be making his way to a free State." Having small amounts of money and moving from place to place built independence, self-esteem, and confidence. For the mulatto Job, owned by the New Orleans Gas Works and hired as a steward and cook on "some of the up-river boats," another ingredient was added. He had a free mulatto wife in Vicksburg, Mississippi. During one of his trips, Job disappeared, probably "enticed off by his wife." He would not get far, an advertisement read, because the light-skinned Job had a "remarkable black mark" under his left eye stretching from his nose to his ear.[38]

Self-hired Slaves as Runaways

Self-hire placed slaves in a condition of what some contemporaries called "quasi" or "virtual" freedom. Self-hired slaves were often the most talented, skilled, industrious, and privileged among the bondsmen. They were usually permitted to find their own employers, negotiate their own wages, collect their own earnings, and pay their owners a certain sum each month or year. They rented houses, managed their own affairs, came and went as they pleased, and secured a large measure of control over their lives. Sometimes they lived with their families. From an owner's perspective, they were often the most valuable, profitable, and trusted slaves.[39]

Despite their nearly free status, a number of self-hired slaves ran off. Some did so for the same reasons as Frederick Douglass: "I was to be allowed all my time; to make all bargains for work; to find my own employment, and to collect my own wages; and, in return for this liberty, I was required, or obliged, to pay him [the master] three dollars at the end of each week, and to board and clothe myself, and buy my own calking tools." It was a hard bargain, but it "armed my love of liberty with a lash and a driver," Douglass explained, "far more efficient than any I had before known."[40]

Like Douglass, these privileged slaves found it difficult to turn over their wages. Indeed, some became so self-sufficient that the line between slavery and freedom seemed faint. The connection between skills, earnings, and autonomy was clearly on the mind of shoemaker Laban, alias Laban Lewis, who had run away once before but had been captured in Norfolk. Owned by B. H. Hilliard of New Kent County, Lewis was hired to a Richmond man who "suffered him to carry on his business of Shoe-maker." In 1807, the shoemaker "made his elopement with his Tools, Cloths, &C." Similarly, Billy who worked as a self-hired waiter, office boy, and dockworker in Charleston, realized his potential as a wage earner. Described as tall, erect, well-formed, "very intelligent and plausible," he took with him an "abundance of clothing" when he ran away. These and other self-hired slaves realized that if they could earn a good living on their own, why should they pay wages to their owners?[41]

While "a love of liberty" and economic independence were important factors in causing self-hired slaves to abscond, there were other reasons that prompted them to leave their owners. Among the most important was the attempt on the part of owners to rein in slaves who had been permitted too much freedom. When the self-hired Baltimore County slave Jim was conveyed to John N. Carroll, a minor, the boy's female guardian was amazed to discover how little the black man contributed to the estate. His occupation was not noted, but Jim obviously had little difficulty finding employment. When the guardian sought to hire Jim out herself, he "absconded from the places at which he was hired" and took it "upon himself to hire himself whenever he chooses so to do, without the consent or Knowledge" of the guardian. Such activity was setting an example that would "have an injurious effect upon the other servants of the ward."[42] Carroll's guardian was not the only person put in charge of slaves only to discover that too many "freedoms" had been granted them. The tension and ultimate break between slave and owner often occurred when new arrangements and new demands were put upon self-employed slaves.

The conflict usually occurred, as with Jim, following the transfer or sale of a slave. New owners reevaluated how best to utilize their slave property, and this often meant a close inspection of profits and losses. Privileged slaves who did not benefit a new owner or might be sold for a profit were in jeopardy. Even under the best of circumstances, new ownership would bring new rules governing where and how slaves should be hired. When masters sought to extract higher wages, limit movement or type of employment, change working conditions, or demand that urban slaves move to the countryside, slaves ran away. Owned by David Ross, master of Oxford Iron Works near Lynchburg, Virginia, John Roman was an excellent blacksmith and gunsmith who ran his own establishment at Columbia on the James River. When he was sold to Bennett Taylor of Charlestown, Virginia, it was soon made clear that Roman would be forced to give up his business and work on the farm of his new owner. A short time later, the blacksmith absconded to Maryland, but was caught and brought back by Taylor's overseer, only to run away a second time.[43]

The response of John Roman to threats against his autonomy was typical of other highly skilled slaves. A precedent had been established when they were permitted to go out on their own and keep a portion of their earnings. Any change in the original "agreement," they believed, would be considered a serious breach of master-slave relations.

In the minds of privileged slaves, not even the death of an owner or transfer or sale to a new owner altered what had been agreed upon. If a new master refused to honor an original understanding, the slave responded in kind. Twenty-four-year-old Celeste, owned by Stephen Ridgley of St. Louis, was permitted to work as a chambermaid on steamboats going from St. Louis to New Orleans or going up and down the Missouri River. She was "a very bright Yellow girl very smart & Capable spoke French & English & was a very competent servant," Ridgley said. She was allowed "to direct and control her own movements & to employ her time when and in such manner as she might choose." When she learned in 1855, however, that her owner planned to sell her as a gentleman's "Mistress" in New Orleans, she ran away to Chicago.[44]

Perhaps there is no better example of what might happen when a master went back on an original understanding than the response of James Armstrong, an extremely valuable slave owned by Kentucky farmer James Rudd, who permitted Armstrong to hire out in Louisville and keep everything he earned in excess of $5.00 a week. Between 1846 and 1853, Armstrong rarely missed a payment. He turned over to Rudd a total of $1,897.65, an average of $4.60 a week, during that period. In October 1853, however, the master demanded that the $5 be raised to $7 per week. Incensed by this "breach of contract," Armstrong ran away and was apprehended, but ran away a second time. Now captured, he was whipped, cast into irons, and early in 1854, the once highly valued slave was sold for $1,600.[45] Like Armstrong, other self-hired slaves absconded when their masters reneged on a bargain, attempted to sell or transfer them to a new owner, demanded unfair "freedom dues," or tampered with their ability to hire themselves out for the highest wages. These skilled, industrious slaves realized their value to their owners. They cherished their economic freedom. Once they were permitted to go on their own, it was extremely difficult to alter their privileged status, even when it was clear that the slave was not being forthright about reporting earnings.

The response of some masters to slaves refusing to obey orders was predictable; like James Rudd, they used the whip and the auction block. But other slaveholders sought to use the by-products of self-hire— namely, assertiveness, independence, and self-reliance—for their own benefit. One way to do this was to promise a slave his or her freedom through self-purchase and then, at the last moment, renege on the promise and sell off the slave. The profits in such a venture could be substantial. Avoiding the cost of clothing, food, lodging, and other expenses, the master could expect prompt payment of wages, plus payment of money for self-purchase. Then, after reneging on the agreed self-purchase, he could receive the price brought at auction. Within a few years, an owner could double his investment. To make sure that payments would be forthcoming, masters held family members of the self-hired slave as pawns.

In fact, it appears that a number of Maryland and Virginia masters had just such plans in mind when they made self-purchase arrangements with their slaves and permitted them to hire out in the District of Columbia. Adam Johnson, owned by Elizabeth Clarke of St. Mary's County, Maryland, worked diligently to buy himself for $360, but when he paid that amount, his new owner, Clarke's son, claimed the slave still owed him $140 in back wages not paid to the mother. Fearing he might be sold to "foreign parts" and forced to leave his wife and children, Johnson and his family went into hiding and, with the assistance of a white friend, brought a freedom suit in the district court. During the 1840s, Lucy Crawford, a slave owned by Martha A. Scott in Prince George's County, Maryland, was also permitted to hire out in the District of Columbia and purchase herself, but when she had paid all except $21, the white woman had Crawford arrested and jailed as a runaway slave. Similarly, self-hired Mary Donoho, owned by a Virginia man, was offered a self-purchase agreement, and when she had advanced her owner 86 percent of the amount agreed upon, he had her "taken up by a Constable in the City of Washington, & committed to the Jail there, by a Justice of the Peace, as a runaway negro." She was sold to traders Archibald Thompson and Henry Ryan for the southern market.[46]

The case of Letty Brown was especially heartrending. Granted "great liberties & facilities" to work for herself and raise funds to purchase herself out of bondage, Letty was described as "a steady, clever, hard working woman & a good washer & ironer." About 1823, she was sold to John H. Lowe, who also gave "her liberty to work for herself Entirely & go at large to do so." Lowe, too, thought she was an "industrious obliging good disposed creature & that he conceived it his duty as a Christian" to give her an opportunity to gain her freedom. During this time, she gave birth to two children, a daughter, owned by her first owner, Mary Greenfield, and a son, owned by Lowe. Working frantically to purchase herself, she found she could not live without her children and went to Greenfield to beseech her to let her take the girl home. When she refused, Letty swore at her, threatened her, grabbed the child and ran, whereupon Lowe, hearing of the incident, withdrew his promise of freedom. In 1826, Brown, who owed only $35.94 on her purchase price, went into hiding with her daughter. Her son, however, remained with Lowe, who claimed the boy as a slave for life.[47]

For a surprising number of self-hired slaves, it took neither a specific incident nor a series of incidents nor reneging on a promise to prompt them to run away. Within this group were slaves who were permitted to keep a substantial portion of their earnings, treated with great deference and consideration, permitted to rent their own houses, and allowed to live with their families. Many of them were intelligent, talented, hard working, skilled, experienced, and motivated. They produced significant profits for their owners and were in a sense purchasing their own autonomy. But autonomy was not freedom, and some of these self-hired slaves bided their time until the right situation presented itself. When it did, they left.

Described as slight of build, intelligent, and quick witted, Kentucky slave Weller hired himself on Ohio River steamboats as a fireman. His master, Bailey Riley, told potential employers to treat Weller well because he was "a good boy." In December 1835, however, the owner changed his mind. Weller had been "missing for two or three months," and it was clear that, after docking in Cincinnati, he had run away to Canada. Similarly, St. Louis mulatto Carter Mitchell was permitted to "go at large," "go where he pleased," hire his own time, and "act and deal as a free person." In 1849, he boarded a Mississippi River steamboat and journeyed to Illinois.[48]

Self-hired slaves in the cities of the Upper South could often gain freedom merely by crossing over to a free state. In cities of the Lower South, self-hired slaves could at times gain their freedom by simply moving from one section of a city to another. In New Orleans, self-hired men and women often went to a different section of the city or a suburb and hired themselves out. Among the throngs in such a setting, they could avoid detection for lengthy periods.[49] Both Catherine, a creole "hawker of goods," and Jacob, an American Negro who sold bread, simply moved away from their masters. The French- and English-speaking Nancy ran away on a several occasions. Described as very black, wearing an attractive blue cotton gown and a white linen apron, she sold ice cream in the streets. The last time she had absconded, her owner noted, she "was taken up behind Jean Morney's property, in a Dutch butcher's house, where she had been working for two months." Nancy was in the habit of "hiding herself" in that section of the city. The twenty-year-old self-hired milkmaid Lucy, "a negro wench of light complexion," left her owner in August 1830; "she must be still in faubourg St. Mary," he said, "where she has been seen three days ago."[50]

It was outrageous, masters felt, when slaves who were allowed so many liberties ran away. Owned by a man in Tipton County, Tennessee, along the Mississippi River, the well-dressed Squire moved back and forth between his home county and Nashville, hiring himself out as a house servant, barkeeper, hostler, and gardener. "He is fond of ardent spirits," his owner admitted and carried with him "a considerable sum of money." He was well-known by whites around Nashville and elsewhere, "as he has lived in different public houses, and generally becomes known for his attention and politeness." Another Tennessee slave, Jerry, was sent by his owner on business to Kentucky, driving a cart and hauling goods. "I am told he was in the habit of passing himself as a free man," his owner said. He left with "a considerable quantity" of clothes, "an aged sorrel horse," a pistol, and eighty dollars in cash. Also conducting business for his master was hack driver Isaac, who drove back and forth between Tuscaloosa and Selma, Alabama, during the mid-1830s. Isaac was "very intelligent, can read very well, and I believe write," the owner said. He might have acquired forged freedom papers and attempt to board a steamboat from Selma to Mobile. He "is well acquainted in every part of the state" and "very plausible."[51]

It was difficult for slaves who traveled extensively not to yearn for freedom. Many of them had a good understanding of the marketplace, conducting financial transactions, buying and selling goods, and saving money. They saw how being well dressed and "plausible" could help them pass as free persons of color. Some were literate and remained calm and poised when dealing with whites. When these trusted, talented, articulate, and self-assured slaves ran away, their masters often thought some tragedy had befallen them or they had been kidnapped or waylaid. How could a trusted, loyal, and highly privileged slave abscond?

The Urban Interlude

Towns and cities in the South attracted tens of thousands of runaway slaves during the antebellum period. For some it was a brief respite from bondage; for others the break was of longer duration. They went to cities seeking anonymity, hoping to hire out, earn wages, and establish themselves in freedom. They hoped to pass silently into the free black population. Most remained in the South, in a town or city close to their owner's plantation or in the same city as their owner. It will never be known how many runaways were successful in breaking the bonds of slavery, but it is clear that among the many absconders only a small fraction remained at large for a lengthy period. For most, the anonymity they achieved was ephemeral.

The great majority of slaves who ran away to cities, like Jane in

Savannah, were discovered, returned, and whipped or sold or both. Even in larger cities—Baltimore, Washington, Richmond, Charleston, New Orleans, St. Louis—those seeking to establish themselves in freedom encountered numerous difficulties. There were periodic crackdowns on free blacks, with officials demanding identification papers and jailing those without proper documents. In some cities all entering free persons of color were required to register with authorities. A number of states prohibited free blacks from entering the state and ordered sheriffs to arrest black "outsiders." There were also among both whites and blacks those who would turn absconders over to authorities for the reward. In addition, many owners knew the habits of their slaves and were quick to track them down when they left without permission. In 1835, free black builder Drury L. Mitchell was in the midst of framing a house in West Feliciana Parish, Louisiana, when a slave apprentice absconded. Mitchell promptly boarded a steamboat for New Orleans, and although it took him more than a week, he returned with the apprentice.[52]

Runaways who made it to cities had to keep an eye out not only for their owner or a slave catcher but for whites who might claim them as their slave. In 1821, Prince, a slave, escaped to New Orleans. Three years later, as he walked down a street, he was recognized by one of his owner's friends. "I immediately lade hold of him & was going to take him on board of a steamboat & have him Ironed down & take him home," the white man said. Prince, however, now called William, insisted that he had a new owner, a resident in the city. Nor was Prince the only runaway re-enslaved in the Crescent City. As the terminus of the domestic slave trade, New Orleans had its share of whites who kidnapped runaways and sold them to traders. The experiences of Alexis revealed what might happen to an unsophisticated field hand arriving in the city. Owned for twelve years by a planter in Iberville Parish, Alexis ran away in 1834 and made his way to New Orleans. No sooner had he arrived than he was taken up by a white man and turned over to Isaac Franklin, a partner in one of the largest slave-trading companies in the United States. He was sold at auction for $700. A few years later, he was sold to Marie Rose Hudson, a free woman of color in Jefferson Parish. By the time he was returned to his original owner, four years had passed, during which time Alexis had been kidnapped, jailed, sold, and resold.[53]

Other urban centers were similarly inhospitable to runaways. Some blacks were discovered soon after their arrival. Such was the case of the slave Simon, who ran away from his Bedford County master two days after Christmas 1843 and headed north for Nashville, about fifty

miles away. Arrested less than a week after arriving in the city, he
gave false information about his owner's name and location and remained in jail for a year. He was then sold to Toliver Dawson, who
lost him in a bet on the 1844 election. In 1845, Simon's original owner
discovered him and won a suit for his return. But even when runaways
were able to remain undetected for several months or longer, the probability was great that they would eventually be discovered and returned to their owner. The fate of Pressly, a Georgia slave, was not
unusual. Absconding from his owner of twenty years, Pressly went to
Charleston, South Carolina, changed his name to Joe Brown, and posed
as a free man of color. Nine months later, he was jailed as a fugitive
slave.[54]

If field hands and plantation slaves found it difficult to maintain
their secret identities in towns and cities, hired and self-hired slaves
also confronted problems. They were often readily identifiable because
of their special skills or talents and could be traced in that manner.
Advertisements appeared seeking the return of coopers, hostlers, midwives, barbers, gardeners, market people. "Walked off," Susan Rodg-
ers said of her "Negro man" Solomon, who had been hired out as a
gardener on Charleston Neck. He was still in the vicinity, she said,
and had been seen Sunday mornings at the market "probably selling
for some person." Nor would it be difficult to find Ned, hired out by
Andrew Jackson as cook at the Nashville Inn. He had worked at the
Inn for several years and had also served as Jackson's personal servant.[55]

The Fate of Jane

"I have learned that *Lyons* at the Boro received a *friendly* letter from
Old Cassius this evening in which he speaks of not yet being *at
home*—dated New Orleans," Charles C. Jones Sr. wrote from Mon-
tevideo Plantation in March 1857. Old Cassius was Jane's father, who
had been sold with the family a few months before. The letter related
the tragedy that had befallen the slaves. They were sold to a slave
trader, carried to New Orleans, and put up for sale. The man who had
said he was a planter from near Macon and promised to keep the
family together was, in fact, a New Orleans slave trader. "Here seems
to be deception—a wheel within a wheel!" In addition, he had now
received word about the "death of poor Jane! How soon and unexpectedly has she been cut off—the cause of all that has been done!
Would that she had lived and died at home in peace with God and

with the world! I have long prayed for those people many, many, very many times. I wish them well."[56]

Neither Jones's prayers nor his best wishes meant much to those slaves who were awaiting sale, nor could they have meant much to the intransigent Jane, who simply could not remain enslaved.

7

The Hunt

SLAVE CATCHER JAMES C. KNOX, of East Baton Rouge Parish, Louisiana, set out in July 1856 to capture Big Sandy, a slave owned by a local planter who had been hired out and had run away. A man of little means who owned no property, Knox had earned small amounts of extra cash on previous occasions hunting runaways. Borrowing a pack of hounds, he moved across the undulating countryside, along the dirt roads and into ravines, as his dogs lurched forward. An experienced hunter, Knox was confident that he could find Big Sandy, although he worried about how much resistance the black man might offer. He was confident that he could handle the situation, however, as he had on many previous occasions. He was equally confident that he would be able to collect a reward. He needed the money.

Pursuing Sandy, he accidentally came across another runaway, a field hand owned by planter Thomas Devall, and Knox interrupted his search for Sandy to take the newly found slave to Devall's overseer. Resuming his hunt, the dogs found Sandy hiding in a gully, but the slave had a Bowie knife and held the yelping hounds at bay. When Knox slid down into the gully, he slipped and fell, and Sandy leaped upon him. Even as the dogs tore at the slave's neck and arms, the black man raised his knife to stab his pursuer. "I then laid hold of the Knife with my left hand and held it," Knox said; and as they struggled he begged the black man to "get off of me and told him I would let him alone." Sandy refused, even as the dogs sunk their teeth into his back. Knox later testified:

I finally got the Knife in my right hand and then again told him to get off of me or I would Kill him with the knife—The first time I told the said Negro to get off of me he replied you have no business here and I will Kill you if I can.

The two men struggled for fifteen minutes, before Knox thrust the knife into Big Sandy's chest. The black man died a short time later.[1]

The episode involving Knox and Big Sandy symbolized the determination of slave catchers and slave owners to recover runaways. Indeed, the entire system of slavery was predicated on the ability of whites to control their property. When a slave ran away, it was necessary to make every effort to recover the "miscreant." It seemed as if the peculiar institution itself was on trial when such "breaches" occurred. To control slaves, masters established rules and regulations on each farm and plantation, but they were also aided by an elaborate system of state and local laws, patrols, militia, vigilance committees, and individuals, like Knox, who specialized in tracking runaways. In the cotton country of southwest Mississippi, for example, thirty-one-year-old B. B. Boiken, who lived on another man's farm, told census takers that he was a full-time "Negro catcher."[2]

As time passed, a sophisticated system evolved to assist slaveholders in recovering their lost property, a system that included slave catchers, patrols, traders, sheriffs, constables, jailers, justices of the peace, judges, and other state and local officials. To meet new exigencies, the laws were revised and the duties of persons involved in the process were clarified. How runaways were to be hunted, captured, jailed, and reclaimed, what the costs would be and who would pay them, and how the legal system would operate to dispose of unclaimed runaways were all questions that needed to be addressed. To examine how runaways were pursued, however, is to seek answers to questions about the fundamental nature of slavery. It reveals as well as any other focus the continual struggle between master and slave, a struggle that goes to the heart of slavery itself, a struggle that increased in intensity as the years passed.

Laws and Patrols

During the late eighteenth and nineteenth centuries, every southern state passed laws concerning runaways. While they differed slightly from state to state, the codes and the civil and criminal cases that evolved were similar in defining who were the runaways, how they should be apprehended, and what would happen to them after they were captured. Any slave "who shall be found more than twenty miles distant from the plantation, tenement, or other place where such slave is employed or required to be by his owner, overseer or employer, without a written pass or permission," was a runaway, an 1839 Arkansas statute said, mirroring those in other states. Any white person could apprehend the slave and turn him or her over to a justice of the peace. The apprehender would receive reimbursement from the county for the mileage he had traveled and was eligible for a fifteen-dollar reward. The county sheriff was then instructed to advertise the captured slave, describing him or her by name, physical appearance, wearing apparel, and name of the owner. If the runaway went unclaimed for twelve months, the sheriff was instructed to advertise and sell the slave at the courthouse to the highest bidder. After deducting expenses of apprehending, securing, advertising, maintaining, and selling the slave, the sheriff was instructed to turn the remainder of the money over to the county. Owners could reclaim their property at any time before the auction or designate others to do so.[3]

While most states passed similar statutes, there were differences from state to state. In Maryland, owners were required to inform slaves serving for a term of years who absconded that if they persisted in such action they could be sold out of the state according to the 1833 and 1845 acts of the General Assembly. In Louisiana, the buying and selling of slaves came with a legal warranty saying the slave was not a runaway. If a purchaser could prove that the seller knew about such behavior but still sold the slave, the buyer could return the slave or sue for a refund. In Tennessee, any slave taken up as a fugitive had to be "*regularly* committed" to the public jail, as opposed to jails or pens owned by private slave trading companies. In Mississippi, Indian agents were to receive thirty dollars for each runaway they captured or secured in the Indian nations. The agents could also build a jail and procure irons "for the confinement or better security of all runaway negroes." In Alabama, if a runaway were not claimed within ten days, the jailor was required to publish a description for thirty days in the nearest newspaper. If still unclaimed for the next six months, the jailer should advertise in newspapers in Mobile, Montgomery, Tuscaloosa, and Huntsville. In Texas, slave catchers who brought back runaways from west of the San Antonio River could "demand and receive the sum of fifty dollars for each and every slave." In short, every southern state had its own comprehensive legal code for identifying, capturing, jailing, advertising, returning, and selling runaway slaves.[4]

By the late antebellum period, runaway laws comprised a significant section of each state's legal code. Indeed, the importance slave owners attached to this problem was reflected in the time and energy they devoted to fashioning these laws. When the Tennessee Assembly rewrote its slave code in 1857–58, for example, it created four chapters to deal with slave crime and delinquency. These included police regulations for slaves, offenses committed by slaves or against slaves, and "Offences against The Police and Economy of Slavery," including forging passes, secreting or enticing slaves, and kidnapping slaves. Among the 131 sections in these chapters, nearly half dealt in one way or another with runaways (61 of the 131) and 1 out of 7 (19 of 131 sections) dealt specifically with runaways: how and when they were to be jailed, advertised, hired, employed, redeemed, returned, and sold. "On letting such slave to hire, the jailor, before delivering him to the hirer, shall cause an iron collar to be put on his neck stamped P. G.[Public Gaol]," one section read; "and then he shall not be answerable for his escape." Nor were Tennessee lawmakers unusual in the time and effort they spent attempting to solve this problem.[5]

Such laws were designed to control the movement of slaves when away from the plantation, to protect the master's property, and to provide an efficient means of returning or selling fugitives. The laws, of course, did not always work smoothly in practice. Disputes arose concerning payment of rewards, injuries to pursuer and pursued, even the legal ownership of runaways. In addition, some laws were poorly conceived. In 1804, a group of Virginia whites noted the inadequacy of a statute governing captains who hid slaves on their trading vessels. The penalty was adequate—death without benefit of clergy—they said, but the law "contemplates the punishment after the fact" and after a slave "has gone to sea." There were also problems in determining the penalty for killing a slave on the run. South Carolina, for example, made it a capital offense. A group of Christ Church Parish plantation owners asserted that the law increased the number of runaways. Slaves understood the statute, the planters claimed, and were willing to take more chances. "Prior to the passing of the Law of 1821 entitled an act to increase the punishment inflicted on persons convicted of murdering any slave," the memorialists asserted, blacks "were in every respect more obedient and better servants, and infinitely more trustworthy and faithful than they have been subsequently." The "evils of running away" had risen significantly since its passage.[6]

To slow the tide of runaways, southern states relied on a system of patrols. Beginning in colonial times, legislatures passed laws granting local officials, including county judges, authority to constitute patrols to control the slave population. They ranged in size from two or three to a dozen and more. They were organized in military fashion, with captains, sergeants, and patrollers [privates]; and they had legal authority to search virtually anywhere for fugitives. In times of crises, they could hold appointment through "executive authority," as in Virginia in 1808 when special patrols were formed to put down a rumored slave insurrection. As one patroller said, they were instructed to search "the negro cabins, & take every thing which we found in them, which bore a hostile aspect, such as powder, shot &c.," and were told to "apprehend every negro whom we found from his home; & if he made any resistance, or ran from us, to fire on him immediately, unless he could be stopped by other means."[7]

In many parts of the South, patrols frequently roamed across the countryside to flush out runaways. In the fall and winter of 1814, a runaway gang became so "troublesome and offensive" in the area along Goose Creek, St. James Parish, South Carolina (sixteen miles from Charleston), that members of patrols were given instructions to shoot any slave who did not surrender. Within a week, patrollers had killed two runaways, both belonging to Edward Brailsford. In South Carolina, patrollers could point to an early law giving them the legal right to kill any slave who fled. This statute was used by Lieutenant James Moore Ford, who led an armed group of men in search of Brister and Gabriel, runaways owned by a member of the House of Representatives from Colleton District. The two slaves were discovered, shot and killed. Later, a patrol captured the notorious runaway April, owned by Thomas W. Price, who it was believed had lured Brister and Gabriel away from their owner's plantation.[8]

Patrols near Charleston were similarly successful in pursuing Stephon, a runaway owned by Dr. Jean Lewis Raoul, who was quickly "apprehended, tried & Convicted, of divers felonies of which he had been guilty whilst he had so absconded as aforesaid from your petitioner & was executed." Another of Dr. Raoul's slaves, "a negro woman who had been forced from the Employment of your petitioner by the famous out Law Joe otherwise Called forest" was severely wounded when the patrol fired into Forest's camp. She survived, but her wound was so severe as "to render her of no value."[9]

In North and South Carolina, Virginia, Georgia, Mississippi, and Louisiana, patrols were particularly active, as planters and property owners expressed apprehension about slaves roaming about at night and committing robberies. In sections with large concentrations of slaves, these anxieties were especially acute. In addition, the laxity of some owners in dealing with slaves who left the plantation created problems for those who wished to enforce strict discipline. There was "an increased necessity under the present circumstances," James Butler, John Jackson, A. Marsh, and a group of eighteen others in Cumberland County, North Carolina, said, "for an active, prompt and efficient Patrol." They recommended that authorities appoint young men "willing to act without compensation," and that their patrol district lines be redrawn to include stretches along Rockfish Creek, the Bladen County line, and the Cape Fear River. By strengthening the patrol and redrawing the lines, they hoped to bring under control "some forty or fifty Negro Men" who had recently been "quartered" in their area and were committing "thefts and depradations upon our premises."[10]

The patrols were put on special alert when rumors circulated concerning slave unrest. In 1821, Colonel John H. Hill of Carteret County, North Carolina, called out his militia regiment to suppress "a number of slaves and free persons of colour who had collected with arms" and were scouring the countryside "committing thefts and alarming the inhabitants." A few years later, a major general in the Mississippi militia wrote: "A projected insurrection having been discovered amongst some Slaves residing in the Vicinity of Woodville You are Commanded to order the Militia Composing the 5th Regiment under Your Command to hold themselves in Complete preparation to assemble at a moments warning." He recommended that patrols consisting of an officer and six men be detached throughout the region to "apprehend all slaves under Suspicious Circumstances." It proved to be a false alarm, as it was in Georgia in 1848 when the Glynn County Rangers were given a similar order. Ranger Captain Hugh F. Grant and a quickly mobilized "cavalry company" went out "to protect the Community and County from insurrections," but it was really not necessary.[11]

Many thousands of white southerners served in these companies. Some of them, like Hugh F. Grant, were prominent members of their communities, but others were propertyless whites who joined merely for the pleasure of the hunt. Even when there were responsible members of the community riding on patrol, the fear and anxiety during certain periods could produce unanticipated results. In 1818, William Johnson, a New Orleans Customs House official, led twenty armed men onto a plantation in Plaquemines Parish, some miles below the city, "searching for armed Negroes." While Johnson took a detachment into the woods, another group entered the small plantation house, grabbed the owner by the arms, and put a pair of cocked pistols to his chest. The planter's daughter fell to her knees and begged them not to shoot. A member of the patrol struck her with the flat side of his saber and threw her out of the house on to the ground. Two of the men then broke open an upright closet and stole "a thousand Dollars in Gold" and a number of other items, including "six fine linen shirts." Suspecting a secret gathering of slaves on another plantation in St. James Parish, Louisiana, in 1835, a group of armed men rode onto the plantation. When the overseer protested against "various outrages & trespass" and refused to turn over a certain mulatto man, the riders swept the overseer up and took him off to jail.[12]

Such occurrences were not common, but they illustrate the power that patrol and militia units wielded once they were constituted. They could ride onto anyone's property, search any building or residence, and ride off. If runaways were declared outlaws, patrollers could shoot them on sight. Some slaves who were simply out without a pass could be caught in these sweeps. In August 1792, a South Carolina slave owned by John Adams was shot and killed by "a Party of Militia in pursuit of some runaways," though according to his owner the "valuable Negroe Man" had nothing to do with the fugitives. In 1819, another South Carolina planter noted that "A party of Gentm from Pineville commanded by Major S. Porcher went into the swamps to attack a party of runaway negroes supposed to be armed." They were unsuccessful, but a short time later another patrol "shot a couple negroes," both of whom died.[13]

Some years later, when a group of Texas slaves owned by James Weir of Bexar County crossed over into Guadalupe County, a patrol surrounded and captured them, tied them up, threw them on the ground, and "beat and bruised and injured and maltreated" them to such an extent that they were indisposed for a month. One became "lame and sick & unable to do and perform his usual labor & service." Defending themselves, patrollers explained that the slaves were "roaming over the country at night," "to a great extent intoxicated," and were "armed with swords Knives pistols guns and other deadly weapons."[14]

Such expeditions could also be dangerous for those who served in the patrol. In pursuit of runaways, a South Carolina "trooper" fell from his horse and was trampled to death. The trooper's wife explained that her husband, a blacksmith, was in pursuit of a "party of Negro Slaves, who had infested that neighbourhood and had recently committed a murder there." Others were injured when shot accidentally by members of their own units, when they tried to enter rugged terrain or swampy areas, or when runaways turned and fought. Described as "lawless," "desperate," and "bold," some runaways were willing to fight to the death and succeeded in wounding or killing their pursuers.[15]

Despite the strenuous efforts of patrols to curtail runaways and maintain order, they were largely ineffective. It was virtually impossible to maintain surveillance over the black population day and night in all parts of a county. There were too many places to hide and too many hours at night for runaways to move across the countryside, visiting, drinking, and stealing. A group of Chowan County, North Carolina, farmers and slaveholders asked the state legislature to increase the number of patrols and patrollers "For Keeping the Negroes in better Subjection." Only a few members of the current patrol did "their duty," the farmers noted, and there were any number of "Negroes Passing & repassing at all times of the Night Without Liberty from their Owners much to the Injury of our property."[16]

Slaveholders made similar complaints during different periods. In the wake of the Nat Turner rebellion, they argued that the patrol system should be reorganized and restructured. The proposals from slaveholders in Maury and Montgomery counties, Tennessee, called for a state law requiring the appointment of patrollers who would be more vigilant and more active, who would patrol at least three times a week, and who would be sufficiently compensated for their services. Patrols, they argued, should be organized formally by local magistrates or justices of the peace, rather than informally by militia captains. Moreover, members should be paid out of funds derived from a tax on slave owners for that specific purpose. Patrollers should be exempt from military duty, roadwork, and jury service, and they should receive fifty cents for every slave they lawfully corrected or carried back to an owner.[17]

Slave Catchers

More effective than patrols in finding runaways were slave catchers. Among this group were men who specialized in tracking slaves. They sometimes owned or could secure dogs and were willing to expend substantial effort to find their prey. They were hired by planters who could not spare their overseers, plantation managers, or other whites on the plantation to go on the frequent expeditions that might last for days, sometimes weeks. Charging by the day and mile, they were often illiterate, nonslaveholding whites who could earn what was for them a sizeable amount—ten to fifty dollars—for bringing back a runaway.

Typical of the "professional" slave catchers was Edward King of Concordia Parish, Louisiana, who in 1831 charged six cents a mile and two dollars a day, plus expenses. Another was Oliver P. Findley of Greene County, Georgia, who charged ten dollars per slave and additional amounts for administering punishment. In 1847, Findley apprehended Henry, Shack, and Randle, runaways from the plantation of Robert T. Wright, also of Greene County. He charged the owner thirty-five dollars, including five dollars for whipping Randle. Although the slaves were worth many times the payment slave catchers received, it would have taken the pursuers much longer, even as skilled laborers, to earn more than they did for capturing fugitives. A few "professionals" worked for higher stakes. Employed by a slaveholder

John Seaton of Loudoun County, Virginia, John Upp of Middleburg set out in late February 1817 to pursue a runaway. The experienced Upp journeyed east into Fairfax County, then toward the District of Columbia. He apprehended the slave after only two weeks, put him in the Alexandria jail, then carried him back to Middleburg to claim his $150 reward.[18]

It was not uncommon for slave catchers to track slaves for many miles. The group that worked out of Vidalia, Louisiana, across the river from Natchez, was typical. They roamed up and down the river and inland across the states of Louisiana and Mississippi. In 1831, Edward King wrote from Vidalia that he had found "two negroes in the woods, fifty miles from this place." King also hunted Moses, who belonged to William Helm of Natchez, capturing him some distance from the city. Lewis P. Leland apprehended Tom only a few miles across the river from his owner's plantation in Rodney, Mississippi, but was required by law to take the slave thirty miles to the parish jail. Another Vidalia-based slave catcher journeyed ninety miles in pursuit of a slave, while H. D. French captured John in 1834 on a Mississippi River raft seventy-five miles from Vidalia.[19]

Periodically the slave catchers would return to the parish seat of Vidalia to register their success with the justice of the peace. This action insured that they would receive their rewards and be reimbursed for travel and other expenses. In 1832, Lewis Hynor appeared before Edward Sanders, justice of the peace, and explained that he had taken up two runaway slaves in Concordia Parish. One was named Wesley and belonged to George Potts; the other said his name was Ross and that he belonged to Jacob Elen. Both owners lived in Natchez. Two years later, the illiterate slave hunter Joseph Faber appeared before G. W. Newton, justice of the peace, and said that he had taken "in the woods in this Parish about fifteen miles from town of Vidalia a negro boy who calls himself John & says that he belonged to a Mr. John Woodard of Kentucky, who is now deceased."[20]

Besides the professionals, there were others who occasionally went out in search of runaways. A few slave traders and slave factors were willing to find and return slaves for a price, as were special "agents" hired by companies. Some traders, factors, and commission merchants were willing to purchase slaves on the run at reduced prices and then hunt them down themselves or hire slave catchers to do so. There were also self-appointed trackers who went after runaways for a possible reward or following a violent crime. James Ross and Holloway Simmons of York District, South Carolina, tracked Tom, accused of murdering Solomon Coats, for a week before catching up with him in Sumter District.[21]

Many plantation owners kept in contact with various types of slave catchers, but unless they could summon such men quickly, they were of little value, whatever their talents. After returning from a slave-buying trip to Baltimore, one Alabama planter lamented that several slaves escaped shortly after arriving at their new home. He contacted W. N. Peeples, a slave catcher who lived some miles away. Peeples explained that he was more than willing to come up and assist in "catching your negros," but he feared it was too late to do any good. They were probably many miles away already since "their acquaintance must be limited in this country." "If you should find out certainly that they are in your neighborhood and let me Know I will come up and catch them for you," Peeples wrote. Adding a mild reproach, he said, "If I had Known when they first ranaway I think That I could have caught them easily."[22]

Not only planters but also industrialists employed slave catchers. Tennessee iron maker Montgomery Bell, who owned the Cumberland Furnace in Dickson County, a remote and isolated area, experienced constant difficulties keeping workers at the site. One of his "agents" was an experienced slave tracker who went out on numerous occasions to find and bring laborers back. In 1816, when twenty-six-year-old Cary, described as "intelligent, but not remarkable for honesty or industry," ran away, one of Bell's agents set out in pursuit. The runaway, now calling himself Buck, descended the Cumberland River on a keelboat, then slipped on board a barge going up the Ohio River, to Louisville. The agent followed him as far as Chillicothe, Ohio, and then lost him. "It is probable he has since passed to Pittsburg, or some part of the state of Pennsylvania," a subsequent advertisement said. But as he had a forged pass permitting him to hire himself out, he could have gone any number of places. Despite a huge reward of $300 and notices in at least eight newspapers, including the *Pittsburgh Mercury* and *Cincinnati Western Spy*, the agent never retrieved his prey.[23]

Some slave catchers worked primarily on the river systems. Boarding barges, sailing vessels, and steamboats on the rivers of Virginia, North Carolina, South Carolina, and Georgia or on the Cumberland, Tennessee, Ohio, and Mississippi rivers in the west, they knew boat captains, mates, company officials, jailers, sheriffs, constables, and other slave hunters. With a network of acquaintances and knowledge about water routes, they could track runaways on water as well as their plantation counterparts could track them across the countryside. Alfred Edgar, who worked out of St. Louis, was one such slave hunter. Pursuing a runaway to Lafayette County, Missouri, in 1853, Edgar arrived in Lexington, a small town on the Missouri River not far from the border with the Kansas Territory. It was there that he discovered that Marquis W. Withers, a resident of the town, had recently lost one of his house servants and a pregnant woman named Ann. A free black man had departed at the same time. Searching the vicinity unsuccessfully for his runaway, he finally connected the disappearance of the three with the departure of the steamboat *El Paso*.

Although Edgar failed to find the runaway he was hunting, he was not entirely unsuccessful. "During the following Spring," Edgar explained, "I found the girl [Ann] in St. Louis." Whereupon, the owner hired Edgar as an agent to sell her. She "had been lying in Jail five months, and never had been advertised. She had a child in Jail which died," Edgar explained. She was very delicate and "appeared bloated from being confined." Once "a likely fine looking girl" worth $850, she would not bring more than $575, but the owner said he would accept any offer.[24]

Masters who became desperate might hire amateurs to hunt their slaves. Unable to locate his runaway after four weeks but certain the man had not left the neighborhood, South Carolina planter James McKenny hired a young, inexperienced slave catcher, a mere boy, to search for his slave. Coming across the slave, the boy drew his pistol. Seeing he could not escape, the slave gave himself up and began walking toward his captor. The frightened boy, however, pulled the trigger and shot the black man in the chest. "He only survived a few days," the owner lamented.[25]

Some owners sent slave catchers to the North to retrieve their property. This was not only costly, but the chances of success were slim. One man who went to Cincinnati, "& on towards the Canada line, in pursuit of runaway slaves," said in 1835 that a number of residents along the way were "opposed to slavery" and "disposed to throw objections in the way of retaking runaway slaves." Indeed, some residents were actually helping the fugitives. Even "if a runaway slave was found in that state [Ohio]," he said, "it was very difficult to get him." Other owners decided against sending agents to the North. In 1840, Virginia slave owner Richard Reed lamented that he had lost his total investment following a slave's escape to New York. Attempting to reclaim him would be "altogether fruitless." "The recovery of slaves who have escaped to the non slaveholding states is, even in ordinary cases, when the individual has been all his life a slave, uniformly attended with the utmost danger & difficulty," Reed said, and more often than not "altogether impracticable." In his case, it was made worse because the slave was being protected by his black friends, and if any attempt were made to retrieve him, his friends would offer resistance in the form of "mobs that are always raised upon such occasions.[26]

The difficulties faced by slaveholders like Reed drew national attention in 1832 when ten slaves fled from Northampton County, Virginia, to New York City. The governor of Virginia demanded that the governor of New York return the fugitives, arguing that they had stolen a whaleboat and were, therefore, guilty of a felony. He said that if the slaves were not returned "the whole slave property on our SeaBoard, on the Bay, and on our Northern and Western frontier, becomes wholly valueless." The governor's arguments, however, carried little weight in New York City, where his agents were suing for a return of the runaways. During the trial in 1837, "not less than five hundred Negroes" mounted a protest outside the courtroom. As a consequence, the lawyer arguing the case for the return of the slaves was unable to get a writ served. He later confessed that at the "very moment I was exulting in my supposed victory, I was thrown entirely back to be laden a new with costs, vexations, and deep disappointment."[27]

But it was neither antislavery sentiment nor black protest that dissuaded other slaveholders from sending slave catchers to the North in pursuit of runaways. Rather, as suggested by the New York City incident, retrieving slaves in the North could be extremely time-consuming and costly. Once slaves made it to free soil, some owners conceded that their property was "entirely lost." Even those who successfully pursued their runaways were often startled at the costs. Following the death of Sherwood Haywood in Wake County, North Carolina, in 1829, several of his slaves "ran off and escaped to a free State." The widow and executrix of his estate quickly dispatched a group of slave hunters, who after a lengthy search "recaptured and brought home" the fugitives. When they were sold a short time later, they brought less than the expense of their recapture.[28]

Negro Dogs

One of the most widespread methods of tracking runaways was to use highly trained so-called "negro dogs." Frederick Law Olmsted observed that no particular breed was used in the hunt—bloodhounds, foxhounds, bulldogs, Scotch staghounds, curs—but slave hunters and planters had a method of training each breed to be effective. The dogs were locked up and "never allowed to see a negro except while training to catch him." They were given the scent of a black man or woman's shoe or article of clothing and taught to follow the scent. Slaves were sent out as trainees, and when the dogs treed them, they were given meat as a reward. "Afterwards they learn to follow any particular negro by scent."[29]

Despite Olmsted's assertions, specially bred bloodhounds were easily the dogs of choice. Charles Stearns's 1848 political tract, *Facts in the Life of Gen. Taylor; the Cuba Blood-Hound Importer, the Extensive Slave-Holder, and the Hero of the Mexican War*, noted how Louisiana slave owner and presidential candidate Zachary Taylor imported hounds from the Caribbean trained to chase slaves. The dogs were fierce hunters, and if not constrained at the end of the chase, they would tear a man to pieces.[30]

"I had rather a negro would do anything Else than runaway," Louisiana planter David Barrow once admitted, but the "drives" he and his neighbors mounted to find runaways in West Feliciana Parish were sometimes undertaken "with the zest of sport." The "Negro hunters" would arrive in the morning with their dogs, the planters would mount their horses, and a band of hunters, planters, overseers would set out behind the pack of yelping hounds. They would ride at a gallop until the dogs began baying, and then they would slow to a trot. On one occasion they trailed a male slave "about a mile[,] *treed* him, made the dogs pull him out of the tree, Bit him badly, think he will stay home a while." On another occasion, Barrow said that the "dogs soon

In this 1861 oil painting titled "The Hunted Slaves," English artist Richard Ansdell (1815–1885) depicts dogs imported from Cuba catching up with slaves in the Great Dismal Swamp of North Carolina.

tore him naked, took him home Before the negro[es] at dark & made
the dogs give him another overhauling."[31]

Such vicious attacks were against the law in a number of states. The
penal code of Georgia, for instance, provided that "any owner or employer of a slave or slaves, who shall cruelly treat such slave or slaves"
shall be guilty of a misdemeanor. This included using attack dogs to
track runaways. In 1855, in a case involving the drowning death of a
fugitive fleeing from a pack of hounds, the Georgia Supreme Court
ruled it was lawful "to track runaway negroes with dogs, and follow
them up until they are caught, provided it be done with due degree
of caution and circumspection." Dogs could be used if they did not
"lacerate or otherwise materially injure the slave."[32] In fact, however,
most dogs trained to track runaways were vicious, fearsome beasts.

At times, slaves attempted to throw off the scent by going into
streams or spreading pepper or spices on the ground, but these ploys
usually were successful only in buying time. The dogs moved quickly
up and down river banks or off in different directions to pick up the
trail again. Even if slaves did escape for a time, they returned to see
their families or obtain supplies, and as soon as this was learned, owners would "find their tracks and put the dogs on again." One master
boasted that the longest period any of his slaves remained out was

In the above drawing, "Shooting Scene," ca. 1860, a group of pursuers on horseback
with a pack of hounds has treed a runaway slave.

two months. He had "dogs trained on purpose to run after niggers, and never let out for anything else." A farmer in the cotton country of the Piedmont said that in his area there were many men "who made a business of nigger-hunting," and they trained their horses and dogs to go over any fence. From the time they were pups, the "nigger dogs," as they were called, were trained to follow runaways. Usually only two were "kept kennelled all the time—these were old, keen ones, who led the rest when they were out; they were always kept coupled together with a chain, except when trailing."[33]

Slave catchers who owned Negro dogs were quick to advertise the fact. Slave hunter David Turner, who lived a few miles from Bolivar, the county seat of Hardeman County, Tennessee, advertised in the *Western Tennessee Democrat*: "BLOOD-HOUNDS.—I have TWO of the FINEST DOGS for CATCHING NEGROES in the Southwest. They can take the trail TWELVE HOURS after the NEGRO HAS PASSED, and catch him with ease." He ended: "I am ready at all times to catch runaway negroes." They were also quick to make certain that their charges reflected the fact that they possessed the finest dogs for catching runaways. Upon receiving word that a slave had escaped from a plantation owned by William L. Balfour in Yazoo County, Mississippi, in 1857, Thomas Hamberlin quickly set out in pursuit; within a short time, he apprehended and returned the fugitive. In presenting his bill to the estate, Hamberlin charged twenty dollars "for Catching with dogs— Negro *Ed*, upon the order of E D Cox, dated Nov, er 8th 1857, for the Estate of Dr. Balfour on Woodside plantation." During the 1850s, George W. Null, who owned three slaves, hired himself and his four "Negro Dogs" out to his neighbors to hunt runaways. He could earn five dollars a day to conduct his chases. When he died in early 1862, his wife sought permission to sell "a pack of Negro dogs which are now useless to his estate or family." When the sale occurred in May 1862, the four highly trained hounds were auctioned off to William B. Wilkerson for $300, a remarkably high price even considering the early inflation of Confederate currency.[34]

Like Hamberlin, most dog-owning slave catchers worked as farmers or in other occupations, but were ready to respond at a moment's notice. Often slave owners and local sheriffs called on them when a slave ran away. In Laurens District, South Carolina, William W. Simpson was known to have "an uncommon and extraordinary dog for trailing." When a white man convicted of horse stealing and two black men sentenced to death for poisoning their master broke out of jail about 1823, Simpson on horseback with his "extraordinary dog" brought back the white man and one of the slaves. "[A] few days afterwards the negro broke gaol a second time," a report noted. Simpson and his dog "punctually attended and caught him again after a severe heat, and brought him back and he was executed according to his sentence."[35]

Runaways had reason to fear the hounds following on their heels. If they caught up with them before the pursuers on horseback, a slave could receive severe injuries. One absentee planter in Philadelphia wrote his overseer in Alabama that, while he regretted a slave was off again in the woods, "I wish you to try to get him back, but dont want *dogs* to go and Ketch him. It is to dangerous. They may kill a man in a very short time. Last time they had nearly torn him up."[36]

At times runaways were forced to stop and fight the dogs. One fleeing Mississippi slave who had assaulted a white man was taken "with much difficulty." The pursuers and the runaway had "quite a fight," and some of the dogs "were badly cut." Another slave who turned and fought was Peyton, who was hiding in an orchard behind the hotel in Columbiana, Alabama, until a fellow slave told whites where he was hiding. Late the same afternoon, ten men on horseback burst into the orchard behind a pack of dogs, and Peyton sprinted 400 yards when the dogs "bayed him." Peyton then drew his knife, quickly killed the lead dog, and ran off into a thicket. "He is so bold," a white woman commented; "Pate is a mean negro."[37]

To teach "mean negroes" a lesson, planters often used dogs in the chase, and when they had a chance to show them what might happen if they tried to run away, they were quick to use their hounds for demonstration. Out with a large pack of dogs in a fox chase, two Alabama gentlemen accidentally came across a slave who had absconded several days before. The dogs surprised Toney, one of the gentlemen explained, "put him up a fence where he made a surrender—& upon learning who he belonged to—dogs were called off—but they escorted him home, with the *entire pack* of hounds to the horror of all the plantation—I hope it will have a good effect."[38]

Masters in Pursuit

Hiring slave catchers and using "Negro dogs" were only two methods slaveholders employed to pursue runaways. They also corresponded with fellow slaveholders, kept records about the location of relatives and friends of their slaves, sent overseers and plantation managers in pursuit of runaways, advertised and offered rewards for the return of their property. A few slave owners hired special agents to take care of the problem, sent relatives or friends to search out fugitives, or persuaded privileged slaves to spy on fellow slaves. Depending on the size of the farm or plantation, owners themselves sometimes joined the chase or hunted runaways. In short, slave owners were involved in every aspect of the hunt.

Related by marriage and kinship, the families of the planter aristocracy communicated often with one another. In their correspondence and social visits, they discussed a wide range of topics, including runaways. They conferred about how, when, and why their slaves absconded, shared information about possible destinations, and offered assistance to one another in locating or returning fugitives. When a slave was captured some distance from his owner's plantation, they would provide one another with information and assistance. "I have just ascertained that a boy belonging to you has been take up as a runaway," George Connelly of Port Gibson, Mississippi, wrote fellow planter Robert Cochran of Natchez in 1846. The slave had been sent from Tallahatchie County to Cochran's Wilkinson County plantation. The black man "says you gave instructions to the overseer to treat him well but that he was very hard on him." Another planter apologized for not being able to help a fellow planter sooner in securing his boy, who was still in the woods. "I will send him down as soon as I can get him but can't say when that will be." In 1822, a rice planter, who "startled a runaway negroe" during a hunting expedition, was able to offer immediate help. He caught the slave and delivered him to his owner, who lived some twenty-five miles distant.[39]

Slave owners also shared with one another their surprise, sadness, and anger at being "betrayed" by runaways. "Ike absconded on the morning after you left, and we have not heard one word from him since," wrote Sarah W. Kittrell Goree, of Trinity Bend, Texas, to her son, Thomas Goree, in 1853. "Your Pa does not say anything about it one way or another," she added. It was her opinion that Ike left "Without any cause." After losing her favorite female slave, one plantation mistress wrote that the servant was "so honest, so faithful, so truthful, so devoted to my interests that I trusted everything to her and now I have to depend on those so entirely different from her. Such eye servants whose truth is perfect deceit."[40]

Among the most important questions owners discussed was the possible destination to which their slaves might flee. Despite their efforts to keep track of family members, friends, and acquaintances of their slaves, they were often wrong about where runaways were headed. James Morton, for example, said he was positive his slave Tobe would go to Nashville, as the twelve-year-old boy had been there several times driving his owner's wagon and had once stayed in the city several days with the owner's son.[41] Tobe was still at large six months after his escape.

Others admitted they were unsure about where their slaves might go. One planter sent a letter to a friend explaining that he planned to send his son in pursuit of three runaways but was not sure where to start. "If you have heard of my fellows be so kind as to let me know," he said. If so, his son Berry would set out in the morning, if not "pleased to give me your opinion whether it is best to start after them or wait until we hear the course they have taken." John Peck, who lived in Weakley County near the Kentucky border in west Tennessee, said his slave Wilson might move west across the Mississippi River or north across the Ohio River, but he also might be "lurking about Nashville" or near the Mississippi. C. T. Baylor of Petersburg, Virginia, created a genealogical chart for his black man George, whose father lived near Sparta, Caroline County, whose wife lived near Bestland Post Office, Essex County, and whose "other relations" resided in King and Queen County. Baylor, like Peck, however, was not sure where his slave was headed.[42]

William M. Whitehead of Livingston, Adams County, Mississippi, experienced so much difficulty with runaways that he established a network of relatives, friends, and hired slave dealers to help him regain his property. Seeking the return of Sampson and Henry—the first, a heavyset black man about forty-five years old, balding with grey hair, a Roman nose, who spoke French "tolerably well," and the second, a yellow-colored man, about thirty years old, a good carpenter with one ear "cut or bitten off"—Whitehead issued a set of instructions. If they were captured in Mississippi, Whitehead wanted them to be turned over to John T. Whitehead in Franklin County; if taken up in Louisiana, they should be turned over to William Rogers of Pointe Coupee Parish; and if found in any of the upper states, they should be transferred to M. D. Simms of Clarksville, Tennessee.[43] Such tactics were not especially effective—Sampson and Henry were still out nearly a year later—but masters still retained agents, including relatives in various locations, to be on the lookout for their slaves.

Another method employed was to offer rewards to loyal slaves if they would act as spies or assist in capturing runaways. While this was not common, it did occur, and at times runaways felt that they could trust no one. One privileged slave barber in New Bern, North Carolina, not only assisted his free black owner in returning bondsmen and women who had absconded, but acted as an informant to other slave owners. On one occasion, he provided enough information for an owner to reclaim his runaway in New York City; on another he provided useful "intelligence" concerning slave discontent and unrest in Craven County.[44]

Becoming involved in hunting runaways was especially dangerous for blacks, but some slaves either joined the hunt or went out alone to find fugitives. The South Carolina slave Sam had been absent from his master's plantation for several months when a neighboring slave-holder and a few slaves set out to capture him. "Sam, I suspected was at my Kitchen & Directed My Negroes to watch & take him or give me some Intelligence & try to Decoy him So that I could Get hold of him," William Ware of Abbeville District wrote in 1815. In endeavoring to capture Sam, one of his most prized slaves, however, "a likely Negro Man about thirty Years old" and an excellent field hand was stabbed in the heart and killed. It was a severe loss, the death of a "Negro who was doing a Laudable Act Both to State & Society" by helping to apprehend a runaway.[45]

Slaveholders would on occasion order their overseers or managers to hunt runaways. Not only did this leave the other hands without supervision but, as when slaves joined in pursuit, it could be danger-ous, especially since many slaves ran away because of an overseer's harsh or unfair treatment. In 1800, Joseph Chandler Brown and William Dunn, overseers in St. Paul's Parish, South Carolina, went out to search for "a gang of runaway negroes, the property of diverse persons . . . who infested that part of the country." Coming upon the fugitives, both men were shot. Brown died instantly, and Dunn was "desperately" wounded. Brown's widow later petitioned the legislature for an allotment to help her support her four children. Due to such incidents, it was sometimes difficult to persuade slaves or overseers to hunt runaways. It was not hard to understand why Harry and Sam, two Barnwell District, South Carolina runaways, remained at large for such a lengthy period, despite having been seen by slaves and whites in the area. Both were in their late twenties, athletic and strong, with scars on their faces; both carried a pistol and shotgun, and one flaunted an ivory-handled dagger.[46]

Despite the possible danger and disruption to the work routine, on plantations with absentee owners or in remote backcountry sections, it was often necessary for the white man in charge to pursue run-aways. Owned by David Weeks, Grand Cote Plantation remained in the family following his death in 1834, but the problems of capturing slaves in the bayou-laced sugar region of the Attakapas remained much the same as in previous years. Plantation manager John Merriman explained in 1839:

> I have not been able to Ketch that Boy as Yet I saw his sign today and find that he can run yet So I think he is not hurt Very Bad I will try to find his hiding places between this and Sunday and on that day I will drive the Island and try to take him.

In 1840 Merriman again told of a slave, Linzy, who had taken to the woods with his wife and child. This time he did not have time to go in pursuit, but recommended a "drive" through suspected hideouts.[47]

Sometimes slave owners themselves went in pursuit of runaways. This often occurred with farmers and small planters, who could not afford to hire either slave catchers, plantation managers, or overseers. The loss of a few slaves might cause severe financial difficulty, even spell economic disaster if the owner had mortgaged his chattel. Such was obviously the case for a group of Clarke County, Virginia, slave-holders who pursued their runaways across the state line to Harrisburg, Pennsylvania. While in the North, they not only failed to retrieve their property, but were indicted in Pennsylvania for "an alleged assault, tho on trial they were acquitted, yet the Court undertook to saddle them with the Costs of the prosecution!"[48]

Owners who did set out in pursuit of their property often did so with a grim determination matched only by the most fervent slave catchers. In 1817, George Hale, a farmer in Loudoun County, Virginia, for instance, went out after his slave. He journeyed west to Winchester and across the mountains to Sinclairsville, Wheeling, Greensburg, and finally to Pittsburgh, Pennsylvania, asking questions and posting reward notices along the way. Another small slaveholder, William Pickett of Louisville, displayed similar perseverance after discovering that his three black women were missing. He followed them across the Ohio River to Jeffersonville, Indiana, and found that they had boarded the steamboat *Charleston* for Cincinnati. As he later wrote, "advertising, hunting & Indeavoring to reclaim" them, he journeyed up river to Cincinnati and searched out the captain of the steamboat. There he discovered that the captain was "in the habit" of taking "Negroes on board his boat at any time from the Indiana Shore without Inquiring about them."[49]

Neither owner was successful in reclaiming his property, but they were not alone among masters who expended substantial time and effort to retrieve their fugitives. In January 1856, David L. Gray set out from Lynchburg, Virginia, for his farm in Fluvanna County, leading his slave Berry, who had been jailed as a runaway. On their way home, however, Berry again escaped. Gray searched frantically but could not find a trace of his slave. He learned a year later "that a boy answering the above description had been lodged in the Petersburg jail." Gray immediately went to investigate. Shortly before the owner arrived, however, Berry, who called himself Ned Ligon, escaped for a third time. He "says he is free, and possibly may have free papers," the frustrated owner wrote. He speculated that Berry could be in

Charles City County with his wife or in Portsmouth with a white man pretending to be his owner.[50]

Alabama owner Stewart Carter was also determined to retrieve his slave and set out himself almost immediately after the slave's escape. When he learned that Essex, a slave about forty-five or fifty, balding, and slow of speech, was leaving the state, he crossed the Tennessee River and headed north. The master remained on the slave's trail day and night until finally on 11 July 1838, he overtook him at the residence of James Bosley at Robertson's Bend, a few miles south of Nashville. They had covered more than 110 miles in six days and both were exhausted. The owner found comfort in having retrieved his property, but later that night Essex escaped and this time eluded his captor. Fourteen months later, the slave was still at large, and the owner was still offering a reward for his return.[51]

The efforts of George Hale, William Pickett, David Gray, and Stewart Carter to retrieve their lost property ended in failure, but their treks underscored the importance slave owners with only a few slaves attached to finding runaways. The remarkable time and expense devoted by Jacob Duckworth, of Covington County, Mississippi, was not to retrieve one of his own slaves, but rather one owned by a neighbor. The neighbor's slave had killed one of his prime hands and run away. Duckworth tracked the murderer into the Choctaw Indian Nation, then back into Mississippi, and eventually into Louisiana, finally catching up with him in East Baton Rouge Parish. It took him seven months before he was able to begin to bring the slave back into Mississippi. He estimated his "labor and traveling" costs at $214.50, excluding the $14.50 that he paid to lodge the runaway in a local jail for thirty-seven days while extradition papers were being sought from the governor of Louisiana. In the end, the $210.25 allotted him by the Mississippi legislature did not even meet his expenses, much less the many months it took to bring the fugitive to trial, or the loss of his own murdered slave.[52]

Most masters had neither the time nor the inclination to spend seven months stalking another man's slave. But when they did, they often did so with fanatical resolve. There were economic considerations that prompted their extreme response, but also, most of them lived and worked with their slaves. They were especially offended when slaves they trusted ran away. Sharing the large slaveholders' belief that they were good masters, they became incensed when one of their "family," as one slaveholder put it, left "without any unjust or injurious treatment."[53] When these masters set out, they remained on the trail until they were satisfied that their slaves were irretrievable

or until they had made a capture. It was not uncommon for them to
search for weeks and traverse hundreds of miles. What happened when
they caught up with their slaves usually went unsaid in the record,
but it is difficult to believe that they did not seek a harsh retribution
for such "disloyalty."

Advertisements and Rewards

Written and printed handbills offering rewards for runaway slaves
were ubiquitous in the southern states. They could be found in "nearly
every court-house, tavern, and post-office," as one perceptive traveler
said in 1856. Equally prevalent were runaway advertisements in newspapers. Indeed, it would have been difficult to travel any distance or
read any newspaper, even in sections far removed from the great plantation regions, without being reminded that there were runaway slaves
"lurking about."[54]
    Seeking the return of their property, masters (sometimes overseers)
wrote out tens of thousands of these notices. They varied from a few
lines to lengthy and detailed paragraphs. While there were things that
masters did not know, the handbills and newspaper ads were in large
measure accurate and objective in describing the demeanor, dress,
speech, character, abilities, background, and possible destination of
runaway slaves. It would not have benefited owners to include false
information. Masters often included descriptions of special facial features, speech characteristics, intellectual qualities, color, gender, age,
and other information, as well as how a slave might respond to whites.
As one master said his slave was not only "quick spoken" but a "sharp
looking fellow," and another added his slave was not only "very
smart" but "very plausible."[55]
    Generally brief and factual, the advertisements were remarkably
free of racial stereotypes so prevalent during the nineteenth century.
It is true that running away was so common and capture and return
so frequent that, despite the pervasive nature of the runaway ads,
those who were described in such a manner represented only a small
segment of runaways. They may, therefore, have been among the
most prized slaves. But whatever the reason, ironically, fugitive slaves
were described by whites with more objectivity than any other group
of slaves. They were handsome, intelligent, and articulate; they were
artful, conniving, and subtle; they were deceptive, cunning, and ruthless. Masters were quick to point out "handsome" physical features
among some of their slaves. They were described as "very black and

$50 REWARD.

NEGRO WASHINGTON eloped from my farm, the 31st of October, living in St. Mary's county, near Charlotte Hall Post Office. Said negro is about 19 years of age; yellow complexion; much freckled; he has a scar over one of his eyebrows, which not recollected; large coarse features; about five feet high; bulky made. Has taken with him several suits of clothing, both summer and winter; a snuff colored frock coat and pantaloons; a light colored short grey coat and pantaloons. His summer clothing, check domestic cotton, linen and domestic cotton shirts; bell crown furred hat, about half worn. He has been used to house work, from ten years of age. He was brought from the State of Tennessee about the month of May, and remained at Mr. Brown's Hotel during that month. He may possibly attempt to return to Winchester in Tennessee, where he lived for four or five years.

GEORGE G. ASHCOM.

November 8, 1825.

The quick response of Maryland farmer George G. Ashcom in printing and posting his broadside—three days—revealed how much he valued his nineteen-year-old "much freckled" house servant Washington.

fine looking," "rather handsome than otherwise," "very black" and possessing "handsome features," "fine looking," and having a "fine looking face." The Jefferson Parish, Louisiana, slave Sampson, a steamboat hand, was described as "a good looking negro and very intelligent." The New Orleans "American negro" Isaac was "large and strongly built," with a handsome face and nonchalant air.[56]

There were standard forms: for example, "Negro wench" was often used in the early period, but even when this phrase was coupled with comments about the slave's economic value, the advertisements were largely objective. The "Negro Wench named Beck" escaped from her owner's plantation near Georgetown, South Carolina, in 1826. "She is a remarkably prime and good looking woman, about 5 feet 6 or 7 inches high, very black complexion, and extremely plausible in her speech."[57]

Sometimes it was clear that slaveholders admired their runaways. One Louisiana master described his mulatto man Robert, age about thirty, in glowing terms: he was "a very good looking man, very intelligent and active, speaks good English a little French, but understands it very well." He could read and write, and would probably attempt to pass as a free man; he was well known "as being every day by the market." The well-dressed Charlotte, who spoke three languages—English, French, and Spanish—was "very intelligent." Not only did the description of Ursin, a small black boy who served as a body servant to a Louisiana planter, lack derogatory racial overtones, but it was filled with admiration and affection. He was a small boy, about thirteen or fourteen years old, very slender, with black skin, large eyes, long eyelids—bushy eyebrows, and a great deal of down on his upper lip. He was remarkably active, quick in his motions, enjoyed superior intelligence, and was "known in almost every parish of the state, where he always accompanied the subscriber on different trips." A similar portrait was drawn of Henry, a Negro boy about eleven or twelve years old. He was tall and slender, had smooth black skin, a full round face, and an "open pleasing countenance." He was "very intelligent."[58]

Masters often described their runaways as intelligent. The New Orleans slave Grace, or Gracy, who spoke French and English, was "very intelligent and may probably attempt to pass herself off as free." The Mulatto creole Sylvestre, about sixteen, had a "sprightly countenance" and was "very intelligent." A black man from Norfolk, Virginia, sold in New Orleans, was said to be smart and literate. The seventeen-year-old mulatto slave Richard was described by his owner, Dr. William D. Gourdin of St. John's Parish, South Carolina, in glowing terms: "very good looking," "very plausible," and "is smart, and can turn his hand to almost anything." "I think he can read and write," one New Orleans master said of Abraham, who was between twenty-four and twenty-seven years of age. "He is slender, lively, of a fine face and very black." The thirteen-year-old Charleston slave Charles was a "smart, active good looking Black Boy." A King William County, Virginia, man described his ward's slave as a very "good looking and intelligent Negro."[59]

For slaves who possessed special skills or were especially clever, active, handsome, and articulate, masters often offered substantial rewards. For a runaway married couple from Hinds County, Mississippi, the owner promised $100 each for the husband and wife if lodged in any jail within the state, and if brought to him at Baldwin's Ferry from out-of-state, "all expenses will be paid, besides reasonable compensation in addition to the above reward." "I have reason to believe that the said Negro is harbored in my neighborhood, and if any person or persons will give me information of the same, he or they shall be liberally rewarded," J. J. Frierson, a planter on the Santee River, in South Carolina, wrote. He offered $100 for the apprehension and delivery of his slave Solomon to his plantation, $25 for proof of his being harbored by a white person, and $150 for "proof his being taken out of the State by any white or free persons."[60]

"$250 REWARD, For the apprehension and confinement in Jail of my negro man ISHAM, so that I get him again," Samuel Ragland wrote from his plantation in Madison County, Alabama, to the editor of a Nashville newspaper. The reward was for any out-of-state capture; in Alabama, the owner promised $100. Isham was not only a blacksmith, but a man of many talents; he was about thirty-five years old and had a scar on his chest. The reward was so large because Isham had absconded on a previous occasion, two years before. At present, the owner confided, Isham had been at large six months. Ragland thought he would probably head into Tennessee because on his previous escape he had been captured in Columbia, Maury County.[61]

Like Ragland, other owners promised additional rewards for out-of-state capture or raised the amount when the original offering did not bring results. The owner of two mulatto slaves who absconded from the west side of the Mississippi River near New Orleans offered a $25 reward during the summer of 1832, but in mid-September raised it to $100. The master of Harriet, an eighteen-year-old hired hand, doubled the reward when she could not be found after several months. Seeking the return of "a yellow slave girl," a New Orleans owner increased her reward threefold when the girl was not discovered after some time. A Lafayette, Louisiana, woman said she would pay $35 for the return of her fifteen-year-old personal servant, who had a "downcast but at the same time roguish look." When she learned that Caroline, the slave in question, was going to see her mother in Huntsville, Alabama, the owner increased the offer to $150. At first, in March 1826, C. H. Tunis, a Charleston slaveholder, offered $20 for the return of Henry. A month later, after advertising in the *Columbia State Gazette* and the *Camden Gazette*, he increased it to $50. A plantation owner in St. John the Baptist Parish offered $50 for Jim—"(he calls himself JAMES CHRISTIAN,)"—who had a pleasing countenance, was "quick and intelligent," read and wrote script very well, and understood mathematics, but if taken out of the state, he offered $100.[62]

One of the most remarkable cases of this sort involved Joseph Allen, a planter in Goochland County, Virginia, who described his "Negro Man named WALLIS SMITH," as tall, slim, "darkbrown or gingerbread color," and about twenty-five years of age. He was slightly bowlegged, Allen said, and stammered a bit when nervous. The owner offered $20 if Smith were brought to him from farther than twenty miles away. When the notice went unheeded, he raised the reward to $50, then to $150, and finally, when after more than a year had passed, to $200, ten times the original reward. Still, Wallis Smith remained at large twenty months later.[63]

Owners also raised the amount when they learned that someone might be harboring their slave. The white man who owned a young black woman who sold cakes on Old Levee in New Orleans was typical in raising his initial offer. He would pay $20 if the woman were captured and would add another $8 "to the person who will make known to the subscriber, the person who conceals said wench, in order to have him prosecuted according to law." The hostility of owners who thought some white persons were hiding or "tampering" with their property was great, and a number of those who increased rewards also promised to prosecute those harboring runaways to the utmost limit of the law. When the possibility of slave stealing entered the picture, the rewards were often substantially increased. Speaking of one recently purchased family of six slaves, a South Carolina owner said anyone who "can carefully bring them to me, will be paid the above reward, and all reasonable expenses." The "above reward" was $10. A few days later, he learned that the family had been lured away by whites and had gone to another plantation. Now, "$100 will be given to any person or persons who will prove on conviction that they have been seduced away and harboured by white persons."[64]

On occasion, conflicts arose between masters and slave catchers about reward payments. In 1817, Edward Cowart of Screven County, Georgia, captured and carried John King's slave Harry back to the owner and asked for the advertised $20 reward, plus $2.25 he had advanced the owner. King responded by saying that he had offered no such reward, that his slave went to Cowart "and solicited him to come home with him" as a protection from being whipped, and that Cowart had given the slave credit for $2.25 and then charged the owner. Despite the owner's protestations, a jury awarded Cowart the amount he sought.[65]

Although most owners did not renege on reward payments—indeed sheriffs and justices of the peace usually did not release runaways from jail until expenses had been paid—neither did they offer sizeable rewards. In the Runaway Slave Database (RSDB) (see appendix 7) owners placed notices for the return of 695 slaves in five states during the early period (1790–1816); they offered no reward for 166, or nearly 24 percent, of the runaways. In the later period (1838–60), they offered no reward for 282, or 21 percent of the total 1,316 advertised. The numbers and percentages varied from state to state, with higher proportions of slaves advertised with rewards in Virginia than South Carolina, but a significant minority did not offer any remuneration for the return of their slaves. In addition, owners who did offer rewards were willing to promise only modest amounts: in the early period, only 13, or 2 percent, and in the later period, only 80, or 6 percent, of the slaves advertised offered a reward of $50 or more.

In 1828, for example, a South Carolina planter offered $10 and "all reasonable charges" for the "apprehension and delivery" of John, an excellent cooper and carpenter. John was in good health, "well made but slim." A Charleston resident in 1823 offered $3 to any person "who will immediately commit to the Work-house, my young Negro Fellow JOE. He is well known as one of the Oarsmen in the Printer's boat; he is thin, and has a defect in one of his eyes." The owners of an iron and brass foundry in Davidson County, Tennessee, noted in 1839 that their slave apprentice Willis Johnson had been absent for nine months. "A reward of One Dollar will be given for the apprehension and delivery of said Johnson," the owners said, "but no charges paid."[66]

The reward structure was based in part on the owner's confidence of success. When they felt there was a good chance a runaway would be quickly apprehended and returned, they usually offered modest rewards, even for highly skilled slaves. When they had reason to believe a runaway might leave the county or state, they offered larger rewards. Among slaveholders who advertised in the *Alexandria Advertiser and Commercial Intelligencer* between 1801 and 1804, for example, the average reward was only $17. They placed 123 advertisements for 142 runaways. Only 6 offered as much as $50. They all believed their slaves had either left the South, were planning to do so, or could easily find employment in a distant location. Only one offered a reward of $100. William Smit, of York District, South Carolina, said his "handsome" sixteen- or seventeen-year-old "mulatto boy" was passing as a free person and probably possessed counterfeit freedom papers. The boy had feigned being a "French barber" and had found employment as a "waitingman" for a gentleman traveling northeast. When last "heard of" the unnamed runaway was riding a horse alongside the gentleman's two-wheeled carriage on a road outside Salisbury, North Carolina, heading for Richmond or Baltimore.[67]

Even in New Orleans, during the late 1820s and 1830s, as the prices for slaves spiraled upward, the rewards remained small. For the twenty-five-year-old runaway named Samuel, the owner offered only $5 to anyone who would lodge him "in one of the jails of the state." For the two escaped field hands from St. Charles Parish, the owner promised that "Ten dollars reward will be given to the person who shall lodge them in jail." The owner of the hairdresser Caroline, who lived in New Orleans, offered $3 to anyone who arrested her and committed her to jail. Five dollars was offered in 1830 for the capture and jailing of the "American Negro JOHN," eighteen years old, coal black, speaking French and English, and working as a steward both in the city of New Orleans and on steamboats. Ten dollars was offered for the mulatto Robert, who went to the market and did other errands for his owner in New Orleans.[68]

The average reward for returning runaways in the late eighteenth and early nineteenth centuries was about $15 and in South Carolina it was only about $10. This average included those who did not offer any rewards. Even with the substantial increase in the price of slaves in subsequent years, reward averages did not increase proportionally. The averages during the later period ranged from $19 in South Carolina to $32 in Virginia. Even in Virginia during the 1850s, fewer than 10 percent of those who offered a reward said they were willing to pay $50 or more. In both periods, rewards were generally higher for men than women, for older than younger, and for mulattoes than blacks. Offerings for slaves in their twenties and thirties and persons of mixed origin were about 50 percent greater than for teenagers and blacks. The rewards advertised for African-born runaways were about half those for creoles or those born on American soil, and rewards for skilled runaways were nearly twice as much as for unskilled. Those who were valued the highest were literate runaways who were thought to have written their own passes.

Comparing average rewards with average prices of slaves reveals that generally owners offered 5 percent or less of the value of the runaway as a reward. In Virginia in 1800, the average prime field hand

Table 2
Average Rewards Offered for Slaves Advertised in Five States,
Early (1790–1816) and Late (1838–1860) Periods

State	Number Advertised		Number Offering Reward		Average Reward ($)	
	Early	Late	Early	Late	Early	Late
Virginia	95	195	84	162	18	32
North Carolina	100	132	77	113	14	27
Tennessee	138	168	116	121	20	23
South Carolina	240	458	157	298	9	19
Louisiana	122	363	95	340	17	28
	695	1,316	529	1,034	15	25

Source: RSDB. See appendix 7. Averages include slaves for whom no rewards were offered, but do not include adjustments for increases over original offers.

was selling for $350, while the average runaway reward was $18, or 5 percent of the sale price. Of course, it was not necessarily "prime" hands who absconded, but neither did the mean prices include the highly valued city slaves who joined the runaway army. Even excluding those who did not offer rewards—bringing the average up—and considering a range of prices for runaways, the fact remains that owners generally offered extremely modest rewards. Indeed, as the prices of slaves rose, the average rewards actually declined in relation to what slaves were bringing on the auction block.

That this was the case tells us a great deal about the hunters and the hunted in the slave system. Rewards declined over time in relation to the value of slaves because owners were able to rely on an increasingly sophisticated system for recovering their property. The number of advertisements for runaways rose dramatically during the 1840s and 1850s. Meanwhile, one gets the clear impression that the number of runaways for whom there was no advertisement rose even more. Absconders were so common that it was indeed impossible to advertise for even a small percentage of those who made off. Owners had to consider legal costs, transportation charges, and jail fees in addition to a reward. Newspapers were often in distant towns and cities, and the trail could be cold by the time an advertisement appeared. Considering the various means at their disposal for recovering runaways—patrols, slave catchers, hiring agents, communication with other planters, black spies, white reward seekers—it is not surprising that masters offered modest rewards.

In addition, most states required that a small reward be paid to the person who recovered a runaway. In North Carolina, an 1819 statute compelled jailers to pay $5 to anyone who captured a runaway from another county. The money was to be "taxed by the jailor" against the owner and collected with the prison fees. Tennessee also required the owner to pay the "taker up" of a runaway $5 if captured in state, and $25 if out of state. In Mississippi the amount was $6 in state with the admonition that persons who caught runaways were required by law to turn them over to the owner, agent, overseer, or jailer. Although Virginia also offered a small reward for the return of runaways, the state promised $50 for slaves captured in Ohio, Pennsylvania, and Indiana and $125 in New York, New England, and the British provinces, plus twenty cents per mile travel allowance.[69] Thus, the reward structure for slaves thought to have made it to freedom reflected the market value of the slave to a far greater extent than the rewards offered for the vast majority of runaways who, it was believed, would be caught and returned within a few weeks.

Incarceration

Runaways who were not caught or did not surrender on their own were often captured and taken to the nearest jail. Each county seat had its jailhouse, usually near the courthouse. In cities, there were usually several public and private jails for holding slaves prior to sale and shipment. The private jails, called "pens," were sometimes clean and sanitary, but public jails were often dank, foul smelling, and filthy. Some jails proved to be death bins for runaways who refused to divulge the names of their owners. One anonymous runaway jailed in Kershaw District, South Carolina, steadfastly refused to divulge the identity of his master. The jailer asserted that "every exertion was made to discover the true owner of the said fellow, that letters were Written to those to whom he stated he belonged and that to some of those letters answers were Returned denying any Knowledge of the said fellow—that the usual and legal advertisements were inserted in the Camden Gazette, but no one appeared to claim the said fellow." Locked in a tiny, vermin-ridden cell—stiflingly hot in summer and icy cold in winter—the slave grew progressively weaker. In June 1819, after 170 days, he died. Staying in the same jail slightly longer—176 days—Jim also refused to give information about himself except that he came from Georgia. In March 1822, he, too, died.[70]

Captured and jailed runaways who refused to reveal their owner's identity faced an uncertain future. Not only might they end up like the two men jailed in Kershaw District, South Carolina, but they were certain to remain in jail many months, sometimes a year or more, before being sold to pay expenses. Arrested in Chesterfield County, Virginia, in 1816, Hannibal lied about his place of origin. Although advertisements appeared in the *Richmond Enquirer*, no one claimed him, and after sixteen months, he was sold to a slave trader heading west. On his way, the trader stopped in Prince Edward County, and Hannibal confessed that he belonged to a store owner in Amelia County, but it was too late. The trader moved on with him to Nashville, then headed southwest toward Natchez and New Orleans.[71]

Their refusal to return to their owners reveals the depth of despair of some slaves, many preferring to bide their time awaiting an opportunity to escape. In the early years, jails were often crudely built, sometimes with dirt floors, wooden windows, flimsy doors, and no guards during the night. To free his friend in Vicksburg in 1819, an outlying slave sneaked up to the Warren County jail several nights in a row "with an augur and other implements and did brake open the Doors of the Jail." Both slaves were caught, and the visitor had his ears cropped and received thirty-nine lashes. Two jailed runaways in Monroe County, Mississippi, fared better. According to the sheriff they "got out and made their escape so that they could not be got." The jail was "wholly insufficient to answer the ends of public justice." Much the same could be said for many other county facilities in the west.[72]

Even when jails were more solidly constructed, ingenious slaves found ways to escape. Two Amherst County, Virginia, slaves dug their way to freedom. "In the construction of the room set apart for such prisoners," the jailer testified, "there was a deep sink dug out in the floor to be used for the purposes of a necessary." Ned and another runaway "got into this sink and by some means still unknown to any persons worked a hole under the Wall of the Jail and up to the surface of the ground on the outer side thereof." In 1854, shortly after being imprisoned in the Middlesex County jail, John burned the hinges off the jailhouse door and made his escape. A witness said that "the Jail was burning, the front door was Standing a little open, the roof was on fire, near the center." John had covered the windows with a quilt and straw mattress, used a burning stick from the stove to ignite the facings next to the hinges on the door, and escaped either by prying the back of the door open or climbing through a large hole in the burning roof.[73]

With its high brick walls and huge iron gate, Lynch's yard in St. Louis seemed virtually escapeproof. On Christmas night 1854, the slave Aaron, placed in the yard by the son of his owner because they believed he was plotting an escape, proved them right. Aaron neither scaled the wall nor assaulted the gatekeeper. He merely convinced a trusted fellow bondsman, who had been given the key to the front gate, to run away with him. Lynch "had entrusted the key of the yard to a slave he had bought sometime previous," the son of Aaron's owner testified,[74]

> his negro came to him (Lynch) about dusk in the evening & gave him a Key which Lynch thought was as usual the Key of the yard, he put it in his pocket and sometime after when he found that his own negro & the Plaintiff's had escaped together he found it was not the key of the yard.

In Charleston during the 1830s, escapes became so frequent that the city fathers passed an ordinance in 1839 to reorganize the workhouse. The statute provided for the establishment of a public market for the sale of slaves, stipulated that the master be required to admit and

Runaways and other rebellious slaves were often taken to the Charleston Work House for punishment. Early in the nineteenth century, Angelina Grimké, at age seven, heard their cries as she passed along the street. By the 1840s, city fathers decided to build a new structure, one that would better prevent escapes. Erected in 1850–51, at a cost of $35,000, the fortress-like building pictured here made it much more difficult for runaways and others to break out.

confine any slaves "delivered into his charge" and provided compensation to owners for blacks who broke out of jail. Not only would the owner be allowed "such damages as the owner of such Slave shall sustain by reason of his escape"—that is, for hiring slave catchers, sending agents, jail fees—but "also for the value of such Slave if the same be not apprehended within three months from the time of his or her escaping." Despite the law, breakouts continued and grew increasingly violent. When John, a slave owned by A. V. Toomer, escaped in 1849, he "grievously wounded" three white men before he was finally captured and executed.[75]

As the runaway traffic increased along the lower Mississippi River, the jails in New Orleans, Baton Rouge, Natchez, and Vicksburg became so overcrowded and unhealthy that slave owners complained to public authorities. In some cases, the owners said, their slaves suffered greatly during the months they were incarcerated. Even when owners received prompt notification, runaways languished in the small, cramped jails. In 1829, the Mississippi legislature passed a special act permitting runaways jailed in Vicksburg to receive daily exercise by cleaning and repairing the streets. They would work, the law said, in chain gangs. By the 1840s, the rapidly growing trade center of Memphis was experiencing the same difficulties. On any given day, a group of residents asserted, eight or ten runaways were crowded into a few small, unhealthy cells. There were more runaways arriving in the city than at any other location in Tennessee. In 1841, Memphis leaders, too, asked the state legislature to pass a law permitting them to take jailed slaves outdoors to work in chain gangs.[76]

Most incarcerated runaways, of course, did not face death, escape, or the chain gang. They were simply returned to their owners. The system that sent slaves back to their owners grew and expanded over the years as the number of patrollers increased, new jails were constructed, revised state and local laws were passed, and rewards were increased. James Knox was part of this system. A landless white, he received small rewards for hunting down runaways. Whatever the amount of the reward, however, his tenacious pursuit of Big Sandy went beyond profit. He, like Sandy's owner, was determined to keep order, maintain discipline, and curb resistance. The desperate struggle in the gully in East Baton Rouge Parish, Louisiana, in 1856 represented more than the confrontation between slave catcher and slave; it symbolized the struggle within slavery itself, a struggle involving hunters and the hunted.[77]

Backward into Bondage

"YOUR PETITIONER SHEWETH UNTO YOUR HONOUR, that he has been confined in jail without any just cause for Six long and weary months," Connecticut free black Abraham Carpenter said from his jail cell in New Bern, North Carolina. In April 1829, he had shipped out of New York City on the schooner *Fox* carrying a cargo of lime for a fort being built at Beaufort, North Carolina. Upon arrival, he had left the crew and traveled up the Neuse River to Craven County, but in August he was arrested and jailed as a fugitive slave. Advertisements were placed in newspapers and letters sent out describing Carpenter "and calling upon any person who claimed him as a Slave to come forward and shew their title to him." Yet no claimant appeared "nor has any evidence been obtained tending to shew that your Petitioner is a slave." Whatever his faults in the past, Carpenter pleaded, he was a free man, born of free parents, in a free state. Being so far from home, he feared he might never see "the face of any friend" who could vouch for his freedom.[1]

As it turned out, Carpenter was fortunate to have a loyal father who, despite his son's rebellious behavior and running away to sea, quickly came to Abraham's defense once he heard of his predicament. Sixty years old, Isaac Carpenter had struggled a lifetime to raise and care for his family. His son had been flogged at the public whipping post for theft (ten lashes) and, at age twenty, had run away from home. Meanwhile, Isaac remained an honest, hardworking, longtime resident of Greenwich, Connecticut, well known and well liked by the white residents.

When the father finally received word—in the form of a letter from the postmaster of New Bern to the postmaster of Stamford, Connecticut—in mid-February 1830 that his son might be sold as a slave, he immediately went to see Ard Reynolds, a white man whom he had known for many years, and asked him to write a letter in his son's behalf. Abraham was "a free man and a bad man," Reynolds said, "but notwithstanding his bad conduct I feel it my duty as an act of humanity to give this information to you that he may not be sold as a Slave." This letter and the other evidence convinced the authorities in North Carolina that Abraham, whom they had kept in jail for seven months, was indeed a free person. In March 1830, he was ordered to be released.[2]

Some others were not so fortunate. The economic, political, and societal pressures pushing free persons of color back into slavery were enormous. Most lived on the margins of the southern economy, especially in the Upper South, with its large free black population, working as laborers, ditchdiggers, woodchoppers, dockhands, servants, porters, seamstresses, laundresses, carters, and at other humble tasks. Without property, and with strong prejudices against them, they were vulnerable to kidnappers and traders who sought a profit in human flesh. Even those who had acquired farmland or city property were not immune from being picked up and jailed if they attempted to travel from one location to another. Some states prohibited their entrance on penalty of being sold. In other states they could be easily picked up as runaway slaves. Even free colored people who acquired large plantations, owned slaves, boasted white "protectors," and accepted the credo of the slaveholding class were sometimes mistaken for slaves.[3]

The tenuous position of free blacks in the South meant that those who had gained their freedom were forced to maintain constant vigilance against being thrust back into bondage. They remained cautious about traveling, circumspect in their dealings with whites, and sometimes even wary about their relationship with slaves. They sought to maintain cordial relations with whites who could vouch for them and they worked to fashion their own community and family networks for protection.[4]

Some were not successful, as free blacks were arrested, jailed, advertised, and sold as runaway slaves. They were transported to the deep South and placed on remote plantations. Deprived of their freedom, they sometimes toiled for years. Some ran away after being taken up; others ran away from their new owners. The number of kidnapped and falsely arrested free blacks will never be known, of course, but it was not an uncommon practice. Even some members of the slaveholding aristocracy lamented such kidnappings, although they were far more vociferous about the theft of slaves.

Taken up as Runaways

Free blacks were arrested and jailed as runaways on numerous occasions. Often illiterate, without papers, and at the mercy of whites, they found it difficult to prove that they were free men and women. In addition, the general assumption was that blacks were slaves until they could prove otherwise. As one justice of the peace said in his order to the District of Columbia jailer in 1857: "whereas the said Matilda hath adduced before me no evidence that she is not a runaway you are therefore hereby commanded to receive the said Matilda into your Jail & custody, and her safe keep, untill She Shall be discharged by due course of law." In Matilda Smith's case the warrant for her arrest "as a fugitive from labor" was issued by her former master who had sold her to the southern market, although she had been legally manumitted.[5]

If someone like Matilda Smith, who lived and worked in the same city where she was arrested, could be sold, it was no wonder that many free blacks felt apprehensive when traveling to visit family and friends. In fact, any black person could be stopped and interrogated by any white person. Free blacks were required to produce their "papers"—a copy of an emancipation deed or county court decree. In most cities, authorities were on the lookout for suspected runaways. In Richmond, Virginia, for instance, a dignified North Carolina free black, wearing a tweed coat and Glasgow pants, was taken up by authorities as a runaway. It was then that he discovered he had misplaced his freedom papers. He pleaded with his captors to write anyone in Weldon, North Carolina, and they would confirm his status, but the jailer had neither the time nor the inclination to write such a letter. "The owner, if there be any, is politely requested to come forward, prove property, pay charges and take him away," an advertisement in the *Richmond Enquirer* read, "or he will be dealt with as the law directs."[6] The law directed that he be kept in jail a year and sold at auction.

Indeed, there were constant arrests of a similar nature in various parts of the South, as free blacks were jailed despite professions of freedom. In 1816, William Delany and James Delany were arrested in Livingston County, Kentucky. They "say they are free," but were claimed by a Mr. McGee, who lived on Thompson's Creek, sixty miles below Natchez, Mississippi. "They are of yellow complexion," the jailer said, "and can read and write." "DETAINED—at the Jail of the Parish of St. John Baptiste, a MULATTO," read another notice, "who pretends that he is free." The detained man, Glober Brown, said that his papers were in the possession of a man who lived in New Orleans. Free black Harry Singer was jailed in Wilkinson County, Mississippi, in 1822 as a runaway and, as required by law, sold at a sheriff's auction when no one claimed him as their property. Singer, however, was more fortunate than many, and even after the sale, he was somehow able to bring his case before the local court. In the end, he established his status as a freeman.[7]

At other times, free persons of color were caught in crackdowns on suspected runaways. These occurred periodically in most towns and cities and in many rural communities, especially along the border with the North or at ports on the periphery of the South. In Norfolk, Wilmington, Charleston, Savannah, Mobile, New Orleans, Natchez, and Vicksburg, officials made periodic inspections of local hideouts, arresting blacks suspected of being fugitives. The same was true in Louisville; Greenup, Kentucky (a favorite crossing point for runaways); and the District of Columbia. In Washington County, Maryland—the county having the longest border in the state with Pennsylvania—sheriffs were especially diligent and alert. In mid-1855, the local sheriff arrested Thomas Rice and Hiram Good and advertised them as fugitives. They remained confined despite the fact that no claimants came forward. In December, after being imprisoned five months, they were released. A short time later, two other free blacks were jailed in the same county. They had been "wrongfully committed (as runaway slaves) to the County Jail—where they have been confined for the space of Sixty days," free blacks William Patterson and Nathan Luckett asserted in a petition to the local court. They "are free men—& have been free since their respective births," they declared. Later, they, too, were released.[8]

Even when they did obtain their freedom, free blacks who were arrested as fugitives usually remained incarcerated for months and sometimes a year or more. In September 1826, Eben Jones was committed to the Nelson County, Virginia, jail accused of being a runaway. Fourteen months later, when he was released, the court said only that his release did not preclude future claims that he was a slave. Another free black man, John Gibbs, spent two years in a Louisville, Kentucky, jail before being released. A short time later, he was arrested in Vicksburg, Mississippi. Gibbs asserted that he was "a free man and entitled to his liberty, that he knows of no one who claims him as a slave, that he was born a free man in Alexandria District of Columbia." In the spring of 1837, traveling up the Mississippi River, barber George Stewart was arrested in Baton Rouge, Louisiana, as a fugitive slave. It took him nearly a year to obtain an affidavit from William Hutson, a "Licensed Intelligence" officer in New York City, saying that he had been born in that city *of free parents.* It also took John Pedro, arrested and confined in Vicksburg as a runaway slave in 1836, a full year to prove he was born of free parents in South America.[9] While a year or two was unusual, three to six months in jail was commonplace for free blacks accused of being runaways.

The effect such arrests and incarcerations had on free black families was often devastating. Free children were taken away from parents, husbands away from wives, parents away from children, and wives and children from husbands and fathers. Born and raised in Virginia, the free black Nancy was kidnapped and sold away from her family in Virginia, to Charleston, South Carolina, transported there by the famous slave trader Austin Woolfolk. Sold to Alexander Calder, a resident of Charleston, she was unable to return to Virginia and eventually married a black man in the city. In 1823, Nancy and her husband ran away. "She may, with the assistance of her husband," her owner asserted, "endeavor to obtain free papers." A Maryland free person of color named Beale purchased his wife and children from Edward and George Calvert, Jr., of Prince George's County, over a period of years. By the 1820s, Beale had moved to the District of Columbia, found employment, rented a house, and lived comfortably with his wife and family. In 1826, however, the Calverts seized Beale's wife and children, lodged them in jail, and arranged for their sale. Beale said he was suffering from great anguish and "dreadful apprehension."[10]

When weighed against the possible profits that could be made from the sale of a free black family, such cries of anguish meant little. In 1824, the free-born daughter of an emancipated black woman was taken up by a slave trader, placed in the District of Columbia jail, and sold to a man from Tennessee or Kentucky. The panic-stricken mother sent a message to the Fairfax County, Virginia, court for proof of her status. "Agreeable to your request I have had a conversation with Mr. Joseph Sewell relative to yourself and childrens freedom," came the reply; "he informs me you were free at the age of 25 and all your children were born free except the first *Henry* which will also be at liberty at age 25." By then it was too late, and the daughter was gone.[11]

Family relationships could also be seen in the case of slaves belonging to Virginia planter Ann H. W. Harris, who stipulated in her will that three members of a black family—a mother and her two sons—should be freed and sent to Ohio. But Harris did not make arrangements for a fourth member of the family to go. Following Harris's death, it took nearly seven years to settle the estate. Finally, in 1839, the slaves were manumitted and sent North. Three years later, one of the sons, Paten Harris, returned to Richmond, Virginia, to visit his sister, left behind in slavery. Upon his arrival, he was arrested as a runaway slave. Able to find whites who knew him, he was released, but on his way north through Stafford County, he was jailed again. Sending word back, Harris was rescued a second time. But when he was jailed a third time in the District of Columbia, he found it more difficult to prove his status. It was not until the summer of 1843, fifteen months after he had started out, that Harris as a free man resumed his journey back to Ohio.[12]

Sometimes even the most well-known free blacks were taken up as runaways. Patrick McNamara wrote from his jail cell in Frederick County, Virginia, that he had spent ten weeks in a filthy, dank, fetid room, arrested "on Suspicion of being a Run Away, which I am not." In fact, he had served in the Revolutionary War, but the commander, who could have verified his status as a free man, had succumbed to severe wounds. Still, there were whites who knew he was "not a Servant." Massachusetts native Ralph Gold, jailed as a slave, asserted that he had always been free, had served in the United States Navy, and possessed an honorable discharge. British subject William Richardson, a native of New Brunswick, protested that he was not, as had been "alledged and pretended," a runaway slave.[13]

Among the most prominent free blacks arrested as a fugitive was Francis Datcher, property owner, War Department messenger, and well-known member of the District of Columbia's black community. Jailed in 1839, Datcher called upon a number of whites to testify in his behalf. Even then, it took a great deal to convince a judge of the circuit court that he was indeed entitled to his freedom: "I am satisfied by the affidavits of Thomas Fillebrown, John P. Ingle and William S. Brent Esq, and by the production of an instrument of writing signed by one Wm H. Atchison, and one Andrew Rentch, dated 25 Decr 1831 with an endorsement thereon signed also by them, and witnessed by William Price Esq, dated on the 1st of January 1834," the judge said, "that Francis Datcher is not a runaway, but is a free man."[14]

As suggested by the Datcher case, free blacks taken up as slaves were almost completely dependent upon the testimony of whites to prove their status. Thus, even the most prominent and successful free men of color in the South sought to maintain cordial relations with slave owners and others who might be needed in time of crisis. Those recently emancipated, who differed little from their brethren in slavery in manners, dress, speech, and habits, usually remained in proximity to their former owners for protection. Even with freedom papers, those who could not quickly contact whites might face problems. Jamaican-born free black Samuel Bryan discovered this when he attempted to travel from New Orleans up the Mississippi River. In Vicksburg, Mississippi, he was arrested as a runaway slave. It was not until eleven months later that a white man's testimony secured his release. A Tennessee free black named Andrew, arrested and held for several months in Mississippi, finally got word to a well-known white citizen of Nashville, Joseph Estell, about his predicament. Estell wrote authorities that he had known Andy's grandmother, mother, and Andy for many years. The grandmother had purchased Andy's mother and Andy and set them free. "You will confer a favor upon me, and do an act of justice to an injured negro boy who is free, and honest," Estell wrote in 1837, "by giving your earliest attention to this request."[15]

Another Tennessee free man of color, jailed in Mississippi, explained that he had been born of free parents. Richard Coleman had moved from Virginia, to South Carolina, to Hardin County, Tennessee, where he had a wife and child, he explained. He had traveled to Mississippi to find work. "[I] knew Dick coleman in south carolina and he past thare as a freeman," a white employer wrote; "[I] fetcht him to tennesee and he past thare as a freeman and I allso Doo beleave him to be a free man." The letter did not sway the county officials, however. It was only after Coleman's wife pleaded with John M. Clifton of Hardin County to travel to Vicksburg and testify that he had "Known him as a free man for the term of four or five years & that during the time & since my acquaintance with him" he had been a free man that Coleman was released, nearly one year after his arrest.[16]

In other sections of the South, responding to pleas of free blacks jailed as runaways, whites testified that "all the Boy has told you concerning himself is true he is free"; she had long "passed for a free woman"; "I know his mother and Father and I can say with a truth I know them to be free and him also"; he is "a free man of colour 20 years old in April last"; "he is a free man, his mother Avey is at present in my employment and has been occasionally so for years back, she I Know to be free and was born free, so of course her son Jones must also be free." Such testimony could mean the difference between slavery and freedom. About to be carried off by a slave trader, Caroline Butler got in touch with whites who acknowledged that for more than fifteen years they had "always understood that she was free." Jailed as an absconding slave in the District of Columbia in 1833, free black William Thomas, who had three aliases, presented a unique defense. He solicited the testimony of Robert Kelly, a white resident of Baltimore, to verify that he was entitled to his freedom because his mother was a "free white woman." Despite his having a black father, Kelly had never heard any statement that Thomas was not free.[17]

Even those who would not be intimidated and successfully challenged the system relied on white "protectors." In 1844, free black barge man Caleb Ogleton, who lived on a boat that traded up and

down the Potomac River between Knoxville, Maryland, and Georgetown, was jailed in Frederick County, Maryland. Ogleton was familiar
with the law and applied for a writ of habeas corpus, arguing that he
was not only free but "freeborn," that his status was well known to
a white man named John Gibson, and that he had been detained for
more than ten days, in violation of the 1831 state law. The judge
agreed and ordered the sheriff to discharge him from imprisonment.[18]
However well they knew the law, most free persons of color realized
how important it was to maintain cordial relations with whites who
would vouch for them when they were taken up as slaves.

Free Black Runaways

The reliance of free blacks on the testimony of whites was at best
unpredictable, as was attempting to convince local authorities and
county judges that they were, in fact, not slaves. In some areas of the
South, the odds against regaining their freedom after being jailed as
runaways were substantial. Numerous free blacks were arrested, jailed,
advertised, and sold. One Louisiana black was advertised as "born at
the north," a South Carolina free black was jailed in Charleston and
advertised as follows: his "friends in Columbia, if any" should come
and identify him. It was clear that little effort would be made to verify
whether or not these men and others were, in fact, entitled to their
freedom.[19]

Free blacks charged with being slaves often fared little better than
captured runaways. John Henry Doman, a free colored orphan, age
sixteen, was taken up in Baltimore County in 1856 as a fugitive slave.
Although he had an aunt living nearby, a local white man told the
Orphans Court judge that "from idleness & bad company he is con-
tracting bad habits, & is likely to become a nuisance to the neighbourhood where he resides, & a charge upon the county." He had no
visible means of support, no guardian, and had been "going about
drinking." The court apprenticed the young man to free black John
Breckinridge for five years. During that time he would work as a farm-
hand and gardener; at age twenty-one, if he gave up his "bad habits,"
Doman would be entitled to a suit of clothes or the "customary freedom dues."[20]

As a result of experiences such as Doman had, a strange, incongruous group emerged: runaway free blacks. They absconded when they
were under suspicion, during their incarceration, and after being sold.
They, like their slave brethren, attempted to conceal themselves in
towns and cities and were advertised in newspapers. Some of them

were emancipated slaves who were being kept in bondage despite freedom, others were kidnapped free people of color escaping from slave
traders, still others were running away from former owners who were
seeking to reenslave them, and a few were escaping punishment after
committing a crime. Representing only a small portion of the runaway
population, runaway free blacks were nonetheless found in almost
every section of the South.[21]

No sooner had Jinny, Milly, Lucky, Sally, "and some of their Children," including Solomon, been emancipated by a slave owner in Virginia, and "adjudged to have been regularly emancipated and free" in
Georgia, where they were living, than it became clear that they would
be kept in slavery. Even after a verdict was rendered in their favor,
they feared the worst and ran off, escaping from the sheriff of Jones
County. They were later captured by the son of the man who had
previously held them as slaves. Their white guardian, which they were
required to have under Georgia law, was able to retrieve Jinny and
Solomon, but the case remained silent about the eventual fate of Milly,
Lucky, Sally, and the other children. It appears that they remained in
bondage.[22]

The events leading up to such incidents occurred over a period of
many years and often involved betrayal by whites. One example was
the industrious William Williams of the District of Columbia, who
hired himself to Thomas C. Duvall about 1819 to earn enough money
to purchase his wife and child, both of whom were owned by Thomas
Berry. With Duvall "considerably indebted" to him for his services,
Williams approached Berry in the fall of 1829 and asked to purchase
his family. Berry agreed and set the price at $150, well below their
market value. Williams then asked Duvall to make the purchase with
the money that was owed to him, and Duvall went to Berry, paid him
the amount agreed upon, and received a bill of sale. "Upon obtaining
this bill of sale the said Duvall seized his said wife and child and had
them lodged in the Jail of this County, claiming them as his property,"
Williams agonized. Duvall proceeded "to sell them to foreign traders
in Slaves, when his said wife apprehending that such was his purpose,
refused to go with him, & succeeded in making her escape." For the
next two years Williams, his wife, and their son, ages two to four, hid
out in the city to avoid reenslavement.[23]

The wishes of slave owners as set forth in their last will and tes-
taments were sometimes challenged by heirs if the owner emancipated
a number of slaves. Heirs argued that slaves needed to be sold to pay
debts of the estate, that the master was senile when he wrote his will,
or that certain slaves had exerted undue influence on the owner. Illiterate bondspeople sometimes did not even know they had been freed,

and when they did find out, it was often too late to thwart the designs of a white family seeking to obtain the money that might accrue to the devisees if the slaves were auctioned off. Occasionally, with the assistance of a lawyer who was willing to file suit without being paid, slaves were able to bring their cases before the court, but even then there was little chance that they would succeed.

"I devise and bequeath as follows, Charles, Sylvester, William, Hanson, Albert, Washington, Laura and Henny, shall be free, and that my Executors . . . remove them from the *State of Maryland* to the *District of Columbia* or some free State and make the necessary provisions out of my personal Estate for their comfortable support for the space of Twelve months from *my death*," Henry H. Warring of Prince George's County wrote in his last will and testament. When he died in 1854, his executors, Christopher C. Hyatt and Dionysius Sheriff, moved quickly to rescind the bequest. Learning this, the emancipated slaves ran away to the District of Columbia and "employed counsel to file their Petitions for Freedom." In 1856, the executors advertised in the *National Intelligencer* for a return of "their" nine blacks (in the interim Laura had given birth to a boy named Richard), offering a $300 reward. Captured and jailed, the former slaves awaited their fate, fearing they would be sold out of the District and not be able "to secure or maintain their said right of Freedom." They were correct. After hearing the evidence, William Merrick, circuit court judge, refused to issue an injunction against the executors.[24]

Even when they understood their legal rights and lived in Louisiana, where the law was favorable for free persons of color, emancipated slaves might be reenslaved. In 1812, Rene Trudeau, a planter above New Orleans on the Mississippi River, emancipated his mulatto slave Robinette, probably his daughter by his slave Charlotte. Following Trudeau's death, when Robinette tried to act as a free person, Trudeau's son and heir to his estate ordered her arrested and imprisoned. Suing under a writ of habeas corpus, Robinette was released and afterwards won a civil action. But the son appealed to the state supreme court, which ruled that the emancipation was illegal because the slave was only twenty-four years old, not thirty or more as required by law. During the legal proceedings, the son kept Robinette either under surveillance or in jail, arguing that she awaited only an opportunity to "absent or secret herself with her children" and "embark on board of a vessel to sail to some part of the island of Cuba."[25]

For free persons of color even to be accused of a criminal act might be a harbinger for reenslavement. As much as they sought to live quiet, unobtrusive, and unexceptional lives, it was sometimes not possible. Even the most industrious and unassuming among them were forced at times to confront the consequences of a false accusation. Such was the case for William Thomas of Richmond, Virginia, who was charged with stabbing a black man. "I knew William Thomas long and well and always considered him a most peaceable and obliging negro towards persons of his own condition," a member of a group of whites supporting Thomas said. They described him as "a most submissive and faithful servant to his master." Thomas had extricated himself from slavery and acquired a reputation among residents of Richmond during the 1820s as a person "most singularly esteemed for his honest and quiet character." Everyone was shocked and surprised when Thomas was charged with attempted murder. They were even more surprised when Thomas jumped bail, ran away, and was not heard from again.[26]

Local residents in Fauquier County, Virginia, as well as members of his own family were equally surprised when free black mechanic Spencer Mavin and a slave owned by John Fant suddenly departed together for the North. Mavin's father-in-law Samuel Johnston, a respected free mulatto property owner and farmer, explained how the community had been duped: Mavin was not the person of "unimpeachable character," as everyone thought, Johnston admitted, but a black abolitionist circulating "Anti Slavery Papers." He not only deserted his wife and child and "stole" a slave, but had made every effort "to array the Black against the whites with a view to the supremacy of the former."[27]

Sold as Slaves

Perhaps no aspect of the runaway phenomenon produced more dramatic episodes or gave us a better picture of humans considered as property than the enslavement and sale of free blacks. One of the most remarkable chronicles in this regard is *Twelve Years A Slave, Narrative of Solomon Northrup, a Citizen of New York, Kidnapped in Washington City in 1841, and Rescued in 1853, from a Cotton Plantation Near the Red River in Louisiana.* But there were numerous other free blacks who were kidnapped, carried to a slave market, and auctioned off to the highest bidder. They were arrested, jailed, advertised, and sold as runaways. In most southern states, free blacks could be returned to slavery legally if they committed certain crimes, failed to pay their debts or taxes, remained in a state longer than a specified period after their emancipation (usually six to twelve months), or became a "burden" to the community. Twenty-seven black men in Prince Edward County, Virginia, for example, were listed on the county's 1847 inventory of "free Negroes to be Sold for taxes," including seven members of the Bartlett family—Joe, Henry Jr., Ben Sr., George, Samuel, Charles, and Jim.[28]

But they could also be cast back into bondage illegally, kidnapped in the North and taken to the plantations in the deep South or taken in the Upper South and transported with coffles of slaves to the lower states. Some were captured in various towns and cities and conveyed to the countryside or taken from rural areas to slave pens in towns and cities. There were penalties for illegally selling free people of color, but the profits could be substantial, and it was difficult for reenslaved free blacks to bring their cases to court. Consequently, like their brethren in slavery, reenslaved free blacks went on the run.

"I was taken up bodily by a white man," M. S. Fayman, a Louisiana free woman of color of French ancestry, recalled, "carried on the boat, put in a cabin and kept there until we got to Louisville, Kentucky." There she was sold to slave trader/planter Pierce Haynes and remained in slavery for several years before escaping to Ohio during the Civil War.[29] Most kidnapped free blacks shared the experiences of Fayman.

It is doubtful that many free blacks who were seized and enslaved were able to give testimony to a reporter as depicted in this engraving. Nor did many live in the garrets of brick houses, complete with fireplaces and wooden floors. Nonetheless, this engraving by Alex Lawson, titled "The Author writing down the narrative of several freeborn people of color who had been kidnapped," shows the phenomenon of free blacks being sold as slaves.

They were either unable to extricate themselves from their captors for lengthy periods or remained indefinitely in bondage. Traveling free blacks were especially vulnerable. Some went on a trip and simply disappeared and were not heard from again. It was dangerous for free black crewmen and sailors who docked in southern ports to leave ship, but free people of color were also kidnapped on the streets of northern cities—Buffalo, Boston, New York City, Philadelphia, Pittsburgh, Cincinnati, Cleveland, and Chicago—and taken to the South and sold.

It was especially difficult for free blacks from the North to sustain themselves as slaves in the deep South. Unfamiliar with the work, climate, and culture of the region, they suffered physical and mental anguish. A Philadelphia free black kidnapped and sold to Kentucky slave trader Thomas Roberts and later to a sugar planter in St. James Parish, Louisiana, was unable to perform the labor in the cane fields. When he failed to keep pace, the overseer would "ill treat and misuse him, by oftimes beating him cruelly, and punishing him by cutting off one of his ears, marking and scarrifying his body in diverse places with a whip and other unlawful means and by branding him on the breast with an hot iron with the letters S.T.R." After a year, he ran away to New Orleans. Others abducted in the North and sold to the lower states also suffered great physical and mental agony.[30]

In the upper states, free blacks convicted of petty theft and various misdemeanors were often sold as slaves. They, too, often attempted to escape, but often failed. Convicted of stealing a check, Maryland free black Richard Fortie was "sold" to a Maryland man, George Carman, for $150. A short time later, Fortie left Baltimore, taking the owner's horse, but was caught within a day. He escaped a second time, but was again caught and put in jail pending his sale. Convicted of stealing $5.50 in Delaware in 1828, free black William Toast, alias William Collins, was sold for a term of seven years. He ran away to Philadelphia, but later returned and was convicted again of theft, at which time he was sold as a slave for fourteen years. In 1858, Jacob Goins of Cumberland County, North Carolina, was convicted of stealing an iron pot worth less than a dollar. Unable to pay a fine, he was sentenced to five years "labor" to satisfy his "debt." During the next four years and nine months, he was hired out to various whites and eventually turned over to a slave trader who tried to sell him with a group of five slaves in South Carolina. Goins ran away in the fall of 1862, but was taken up in Lumberton and lodged in the Robeson County jail.[31]

Those convicted of more serious crimes could expect more than simply being sold. In Delaware, the record did not reveal that Isaac Tyre, a blacksmith, was a free person of color, but the sentence he received for "kidnapping" indicated he was not white. In 1832, Tyre was sentenced to receive sixty lashes on his bare back, well laid on, and three years in solitary confinement in the Sussex County jail, after which he was to be sold to the highest bidder for seven years of servitude. The governor remitted the three years in solitary, but Tyre was sold for $331 at auction. A few days after the purchase, however, he escaped. Three years later, he was still at large.[32]

In Virginia, the law required that emancipated slaves leave the state within twelve months after gaining their freedom. Since the neighboring state of North Carolina denied them permission to enter and other states restricted their movement and ability to earn a living, those freed in Virginia faced the dilemma of leaving the South entirely and abandoning loved ones or remaining in the state with the constant fear of reenslavement. Some emancipated blacks were able to elude authorities for many years, living with wives or husbands, but there was always the possibility that they might be discovered. The manumitted William remained free for nineteen years following emancipation by his owner, Charles Ewell, a planter on the eastern shore in Accomack County. In October 1838, he was found guilty of remaining in the state and sentenced to be sold. On New Year's Day 1839, he was auctioned off for $530 to a local farmer.[33]

In Maryland, too, free blacks who ran afoul of the law might find themselves thrust back into bondage. Since the free black population in the state was the largest in the South, the courts frequently issued judgments like the one for Frederick County free woman of color Caroline Sawyer, who was convicted of stealing two linen shirts, a handkerchief, and a pair of undersleeves, valued at $3.50. In 1853, she was bound over as a slave for a term of years to Caspar Mantz of Baltimore. Fleeing from her new master, she was captured eight months later and "sold" for $200. Other free blacks convicted of stealing tools, garments, small amounts of cash, linens, and other items were sold as slaves for periods of from one to five years. When they ran away, causing owners further "trouble and expense," their terms were extended.[34]

Convicted free blacks ran away so frequently that prices for those sold at auction dropped dramatically. In 1859, when young female slaves in Maryland were selling for between six and seven hundred dollars, sometimes more, William E. Beale purchased free black Maria Boston, auctioned off by order of the criminal court as a slave for four years, for only thirty-one dollars. Beale soon asked the court if he could resell her. She "stole several articles and run away," he said. When captured, she asserted that she would "run away again as soon as she got an opportunity." Emanuel C. Wade thought he got an even better deal when he purchased free Negro Emily Taylor, alias Sarah Taylor, guilty of theft, at an auction in Baltimore for twenty-six dollars "it being the highest bid." But the woman refused to work and made "several attempts to runaway and Escape." At present, Wade said in an 1859 petition seeking to sell her out of the state, "He has her chained to Keep her from escaping."[35]

When sold out of state as slaves for life, free people of color brought prices that were commensurate with prices of other slaves. There were a number of traders who stole free people of color and sold them into the interregional trade, but there were others who acted, as one said, "in strict conformity with existing Acts of the Assembly." Purchasing free blacks at auction, they mistreated them and abused them until they ran off and then obtained court decrees to dispose of them out of state. James Peters, while not described as a slave trader, "does trade in colored apprentices as good[s] and chattels," one observer noted, in strict accordance with law.[36]

Free blacks arrested as runaways were sometimes able to bring their cases before the court. While unusual in many ways, the case of John Roach reveals how unlikely it was for free Negroes to regain their freedom, even though Roach himself eventually did so. As a youngster, he had assisted his free black mother, Elizabeth, with her clothes-cleaning business in Philadelphia, collecting dirty clothes from mates and officers on board ships in the harbor. When in his teens, however, John was abducted, taken to Louisiana, and sold as a slave to a planter in St. James Parish. In late 1816 or early 1817, about a year after arriving, he ran away to New Orleans and was jailed as a fugitive. He petitioned the court *in forma pauperis* for his freedom, but he had no proof, so his alleged owner soon appeared to claim his property. At that very moment, fortuitous circumstances brought into the same jail, "on suspicion of debt," William Dixon, a seaman who recognized the young man as the same free black boy who had taken his laundry to have it cleaned years before. At the trial, despite a rigorous cross-examination, Dixon testified that he had become "acquainted with Elizabeth Roach about seven years ago—that she resided at that time in Second Street in Philadelphia—that she was a free woman of color, in the enjoyment of her liberty—that said Elizabeth Roach is the mother of the plaintiff John Roach." In the end, the court agreed; the twenty-one-year-old Roach was set free.[37]

Free blacks, especially youngsters, were fair game nearly everywhere. Those who attempted to travel alone in the South were taking an even greater risk than those who worked along the docks in northern cities. Again, it was improbable circumstances, fate, or good fortune that spared them from being sold into slavery. New York–born

William Hyden, the son of a white woman and a colored man, moved to Ohio while in his mid-teens. When the state enacted a series of repressive measures, Hyden emigrated, but passing through Virginia on his way to Washington, D.C., in 1833, he was arrested as a runaway in Prince William County and put up for sale. When he could not be sold, the sheriff asked a local trader to sell him in Richmond or Fredericksburg, but potential buyers "refused to purchase him at any price" because he was "too white." The sheriff tried to sell him on several other occasions, but no one would buy him, "alleging that his colour was too light and that he could by reason thereof too easily escape from slavery and pass himself for a free man." Even so he was not released. After nearly a year, Hyden escaped from jail. The sheriff "made every exertion in his power to regain possession" of the fugitive but was unsuccessful.[38]

Most free people of color in the North were fearful of traveling in the South. Yet, being separated from family and friends was difficult. The letter of James Roberts to his cousin Willis Roberts in Indiana about his cousin's anticipated return to friends and family in a slave state revealed the anxiety many others felt:[39]

> To think that you are a going to take your small children to that place and cant tell how soon you may be taken away from them and they may come under the hands of some cruel slaveholder, and you Know that if they can get a colored child they will use them as bad again as they will one of their own slaves. . . . I cannot do myself justice to think of living in such a country. When I think of it I cant tell how any man of color can think of going there w/small children.

Joseph Antoine's Sorrow

The sorrow, anguish, frustration, outrage, and struggle to remain free achieves a heroic dimension in the personal history of Joseph Antoine, a Cuban-born free black (emancipated by his master in Havana), who arrived at age twenty-seven in Virginia in about 1792 and fell in love with a slave owned by Jonathan Purcel. The experiences of Antoine and his wife were unique perhaps only in that their story was told in such detail by Antoine himself as he sat in a jail cell in Louisville, Kentucky, awaiting the ruling of the Jefferson County Circuit Court about his eventual fate as a runaway. Many others whose histories will never be known shared the same torments, fears, betrayals, retribution, and tortures.

When his wife's owner decided to move from Virginia to the frontier post at Fort Vincennes in the Northwest Territory, in about 1796, Antoine decided to accompany him to be with his wife. Realizing how much the two meant to each other, Purcel threatened to sell the woman "to some part of the Spanish country" if Antoine did not agree to sign an indenture committing himself to work as Purcel's servant for seven-and-a-half years. As slavery was forbidden in the territory, the white man demanded that Antoine and his wife sign identical indentures. Antoine refused. The master then forced the couple into a room and locked the door "& again insisted that they should indenture themselves for fifteen years & threatened to send them off if they refused." By "way of allurement," Purcel promised that if they did sign the indentures Antoine's wife "should be free at the expiration of that period." The black man later recalled that "being thus situated, in a state of darkness, and being apprehensive that if he refused, that [Purcel] would put him in Irons, & Send him & sell him as a slave, where he would not have it in his power to recover his freedom," he gave in, but only if at the end of that time he could "take his wife to himself."

Purcel agreed, and for the next seven years, Antoine and his wife labored on the frontier for the master. Near the end of the indentures, about 1803, Antoine reminded Purcel of the promises they had made and the papers they had signed. To their astonishment, Purcel said that the two blacks had misunderstood the terms of the agreement. Antoine and his wife were only halfway through their period of servitude. The indenture was not fifteen years in total, but *"fifteen years each."*

Despairing and distraught, Antoine now heard a rumor that Purcel had decided to sell the indentured couple anyway to Emanuel Lacey, a trader from St. Louis. When Lacey arrived at Fort Vincennes, Antoine asked him if there was any truth to the rumor; "he was informed that such was the fact." Lacey asked him if he were willing to be sold. He replied that "if he was to be sold, he would as soon be sold to him, as another," adding to himself that if he refused Purcel might very well "convey him off & place him in a worse situation."

As things evolved, it would be difficult to imagine a worse situation. Lacey took Antoine and his wife directly to the slave market in New Orleans and sold them as slaves for life. Antoine's Spanish heritage was now of benefit, however. Although Louisiana had been sold to the French in a secret treaty in 1800, at the time of its sale to the United States in 1803, the Spanish still maintained administrative control over the region. Antoine obtained an audience with the Spanish governor, Manual Juan de Salcedo, in New Orleans and produced his Deed of

Manumission. Salcedo took him and his wife into his custody, and after investigating the situation, "released them from the sale." Despite the ordeal, Antoine's wife was "anxious to return," and Antoine himself believed that his wife, despite her seven-year residence in the Northwest Territory, was legally still a slave until the two of them served out the remainder of their term of indenture. This, he admitted, "operated with him" as an additional inducement for him to return.[40]

The governor told them that if they chose to return with Emanuel Lacey "it was a matter of option with them, but that they should not be sold or taken off" by Lacey without their consent. The couple decided to go back with the man who had brought them to New Orleans only with the protection of the governor and assurances from Lacey himself that he would treat them kindly. But on the trip to St. Louis, the white man "treated him so cruelly that he could not longer remain with him." As they fled into Kentucky, Antoine's wife, exhausted and weak, said she could go no farther and collapsed by the roadside. They had met in Virginia twelve years before and had never been separated. It was perhaps fitting that the only way that they would part was through death. She died as a runaway slave on a back road in Kentucky in 1804.

Antoine continued on to Louisville but was soon captured by a slave catcher, Davis Floyd, hired by Lacey, who quickly took him across the Ohio River "& was offering to sell him." Unable to do so, he took the black man to Louisville and put him in jail "under the Act of Congress respecting Fugitives." Within three weeks, on 19 September 1804, Antoine presented his first petition to the Jefferson County Circuit Court. He feared that Floyd would "forcibly deprive him of his liberty," return him to St. Louis, and turn him over to Lacey, who would dispose of him in such a manner that he would be reduced to slavery for the balance of his life. During the next few months, he would submit an additional remonstrance to the court: "Yr Orator States that his situation is a very delicate one, he is here defenceless, that he is a free man, entitled to his freedom, & can if enabled to do so establish it [to] the satisfaction of this Hble Court." The court enjoined Lacey from "Selling Ptff as a Slave," but the case was continued at several subsequent court sessions. Finally, in June 1805, Antoine, now age forty, was released from jail.[41]

Free Black Owners of Runaways

Free blacks who controlled slaves for a profit dealt with runaways in much the same manner as their white counterparts. Eliza Pinckney, a free mulatto, for example, received in 1810 a trust conveyance for "a number of negroes" from Thomas Pinckney Jr., a member of one of South Carolina's most prominent families. During Thomas Pinckney's life the slaves were very profitable and seemingly well controlled, but when he died, Eliza, also called Elizabeth, confessed that she was "totally unable to manage the said Negroes in any way to make them productive to herself & children." This was particularly true of Harry, "who is always Runaway and pays no wages." In 1826, she petitioned the Charleston Equity Court to sell Harry, who was sold at auction for $420. But the sale did not end her troubles. In 1827, she again petitioned the court. While she did not mention absconders, it was clear that she was still having difficulties:[42]

> Your petitioner states that the said Dwelling house is at present in the most ruinous condition and is actually falling down for want of the necessary repairs thereto, that her property is so very unprofitable and her negroes yield her so little that it is impossible for her to make the necessary repairs to the said premises (which her own interests as well as that of her children requires should be done) unless this Court will allow her to use the fund now in the hands of the Commissioner of this Court (and not yet invested) for that purpose.

The largest free black slaveholder in the South, John Carruthers Stanly of North Carolina, faced a number of problems in the 1820s in dealing with the slave labor force on his three turpentine plantations in Craven County. With a total of 163 slaves, Stanly was a harsh, profit-minded taskmaster, and his field hands would run away. Stanly dealt with this through his two white overseers and with a spy network that included a few trusted slaves. Brister, his slave barber in New Bern, was responsible for relaying to his owner rumors of planned escapes. On one occasion, Stanly proudly said that "thro the agency of the Negro Man Brister he has recd such information as has enabled him to apprehend one of his slaves which had run away and to prevent the absconding of others who had manifested an intention of deserting." Nor did Stanly have any pangs of conscience about selling children away from their parents or holding free blacks in bondage. In 1832, free black Kelly Davis, also called Kelso Mabeth, petitioned the Craven County Superior Court claiming that he was being illegally held by Stanly as a slave. The court concurred and ordered Davis's release.[43]

Another large free black slaveholder, sugar planter Andrew Durnford of Louisiana, had fewer problems with runaways than his counterpart in North Carolina, but one slave named Jackson caused him particular grief. "Jackson has just left here," Durnford wrote from St. Rosalie Planation in 1836, noting that Jackson had been whipped the previous day. "He is a wicked fellow. Was he not a relic I would gett clear of him." Five days later, when Jackson had still not been caught, Durnford fumed: "I wish to lay eyes on him once more. I will fix him so the dogs will not bark at him." Seven months later, following his capture, Jackson was off again, having "the audacity to go away with all the irons I had putt on him." In the end, Durnford gave up on trying to constrain Jackson. In 1847, he noted that the slave was "a little out of his head" and believed he ran away during the fall work season because of "glands in the head at this season of the year."[44]

A large majority of profit-oriented free black slaveholders resided in the Lower South. For the most part, they were persons of mixed racial origin, often women who cohabited or were mistresses of white men, or mulatto men who claimed white and black parentage (as was the case for Eliza Pinckney, Stanly, and Durnford). Provided land and slaves by whites, they owned farms and plantations, worked their hands in the rice, cotton, and sugar fields, and like their white con- temporaries were troubled with runaways.

Free black slave owners who lived in urban areas—Charleston, Sa- vannah, Mobile, Natchez, and New Orleans—also faced difficulties with their slave property. Free mulatto barber William Johnson of Natchez was not certain what had happened to his recently purchased slave, Walker, when he disappeared in 1835. He had either been stolen or had run away to Kentucky to rejoin his wife. When on 4 July 1833, authorities in Ascension Parish, Louisiana, jailed the twelve- or fourteen-year-old black boy named Isaac taken off the steamer *Watch- man*, he admitted he was owned by "a free woman of color in New Orleans named Jane." A listing of slaves detained in the Jefferson Parish jail the same year included a slave woman owned by a free man of color. Other slaves held by free blacks absconded when they were worked too hard, hired out, or sold, as was the case with Milly, a tall, slender, and well-dressed bondswoman, who was sold by a free man of color to a white woman in New Orleans. Her face was "very pretty" and her nose "a little turned up," the new owner said shortly after the sale. She would probably be carrying counterfeit freedom papers and try to get away disguised "in men's dress." Free black slave own- ers felt few pangs of guilt selling troublesome property. Charleston free mulatto George Mathews simply let the law take its course when his slave Peggy was sold to pay jail fees.[45]

As was the case with white owners, free people of color who pur- chased slaves did not want troublesome property; when they bought a slave who then ran away, they sought reimbursement. This was a

delicate situation, but in Louisiana, they could use the court system
to obtain redress. In 1856, Jane Luke, a free woman of color in New
Orleans, hired two attorneys to get her money back from Bernard
Kendig for a twenty-year-old slave named Helena, advertised as industrious, honest, and virtuous. "The sd slave girl proves to be a thief,
a runaway and without value to the sd Jane Luke, who now desires
that you will cancel the sale and restore her the price $1,014 and take
back the slave," the attorneys, Duvant and Horner, wrote to Kendig.
The slave had been purchased with "full guarantee against the vices
and maladies prescribed by law."[46]

Slave ownership among free persons of color created strange anom-
alies with regard to runaways. Among the strangest was the case involving Baltimore freeman Jacob Guillard, a blacksmith who built up
a valuable estate with the assistance of slave apprentices and assistants.
He was a harsh taskmaster and was constantly plagued with rebellious
bondsmen. "Ran away, on Sunday 19th instant, from the subscriber,
living near Blue Ball, above Old-Town," Guillard said in one announcement, "a Mulatto boy, named John Chapman." Chapman was
quickly apprehended. A decade later, another of Guillard's slaves made
a successful break for freedom. He is a "brownish yellow Man, named
Jacob Cokkey: he sometimes calls himself *Jacob Vanlear*, at other times
Jacob Guillard," the owner wrote in 1805. "He is about 33 years of
age, 5 feet 9 or 10 inches high, straight made, and well-proportioned,
flat visage and full eyes, and has short nappy hair." Guillard explained
that still outstanding was payment of a $510 note on the slave. If
forced to pay such an amount, he would be forced to sell his property.
Only then did Guillard reveal that the runaway was his own son. "I
leave it to a generous public to judge, whether such base ingratitude
in a young man towards an aged father, can pass unnoticed." Apparently the public proved to be no more generous to Guillard than he
had been to his slave son. In the same issue as the runaway notice,
Guillard advertised: "For Sale, AN elegant two-story frame House, and
five Lots of Ground."[47]

The District of Columbia case involving a slave named John Hawkins, who belonged to his grandfather, John Griffin of Calvert County,
Maryland, also revealed an anomalous situation. As a youngster, Hawkins was taken to the District of Columbia to live. When he became
restive, John Griffin and his son went to the owner of a farm in Maryland, Henry N. Lansdale, seeking to arrange for the boy to live in the
country. In order to do this, they asked Lansdale if he would be willing
to purchase the young man until he reached age twenty-one. Samuel
and John Griffin "called on me," Lansdale wrote, "and I made all

necessary enquiries (as I knew the Laws of the State in relation to taking of a free Boy into it) and was entirely satisfied that everything was right about it." Lansdale bought young Hawkins and put him on the farm, but in June 1861 he ran away to the District of Columbia, where he was arrested and jailed as a runaway slave.

"The cause of my not having taken the Boy out of Jail," Lansdale wrote the circuit court judge William Merrick, who had summoned him to appear in court, "was that the Old Man and his Son Sam came to see me and expressed themselves as anxious to take the Boy off my hands (as he was so troublesome) and to be at the expense of taking him out of Jail &c, also to secure me moneys I had paid them, for the Boy." At that very moment, however, Hawkins was petitioning the court by his next friend, Jane Griffin, for his freedom. After reading the letter, and the petition, the judge ordered Hawkins "discharged from custody."[48]

That runaways would involve a free black father and his son and a free black grandfather and his grandson were strange aberrations in the slave system. Free black slave ownership, however, produced a number of incongruities, not the least of which was the difficulty black masters encountered with their runaway slaves.

Runaway Children in Maryland

During the early decades of the nineteenth century, as slavery spread westward to the Mississippi River and beyond, the number of free black indentured servants and apprentices declined nearly everywhere in the South. The single state where this was not the case was Maryland, where the free black population grew rapidly from 39,730 in 1820 to 83,942 in 1860, and its proportion compared with slaves rose from 27 to 49 percent. As the free black population rose, slave owners and nonslaveowning whites turned to indentured servitude. Indeed, while the remainder of the South relied on slave labor, Maryland increasingly counted on free black indentured servants, including youngsters and teenagers bound out as apprentices.[49]

By the 1840s and 1850s, significant numbers of free black children had moved from one type of bondage to another. The laws and institutions created to oversee the master-apprentice relations were not unlike the apprenticeship laws passed in other parts of the South following the Civil War.[50] Indeed, Maryland served as a training ground for the same type of labor control whites sought to implement in 1865 over freedmen and freedwomen and their children. Apprenticeship contracts written for free black youngsters before the war in Maryland and after the war in other states were similar. In 1855, eighteen-year-old Elias Burgess was apprenticed to Caleb D. Owings as follows:

The subscribers, Justices of the Peace of the State of Maryland, in and for Baltimore City by virtue of the act of Assembly, entitled, "A supplement to the act entitled an act for the better regulation of Apprentices," have bound and placed, and by these presents do bind out and place as an Apprentice, Elias Burgess Cold an Orphan aged Eighteen years, on the twenty third day of December last, unto Caleb D. Owings of Balto County until he the said Elias Burgess Cold shall arrive to the age of twenty one years: during which time he shall well and truly demean himself in every respect, as a good and faithful Apprentice; and the said Caleb D. Owings of Baltimore County shall furnish and provide for the said Apprentice, meat, drink, clothes, washing, lodging, and other suitable necessaries, during his apprenticeship; cause him to be taught and particularly teach him the art or trade of a Farmer in all the branches thereof; and when free, the said Apprentice shall be entitled to a suit of clothes, or the customary freedom dues.

While this appeared unexceptionable, the key phrase—that the apprentice would "truly demean himself in every respect as a good and faithful Apprentice"—meant that the apprentice should be humble and obedient to whites. And any deviation for this standard could result in an extension of the term of service. Three days after Owings took possession of Burgess "the said Boy absconded" and remained out for an entire week. The outraged master set out himself to find the runaway, and by the time Burgess was captured, Owings had spent nearly forty dollars for jail fees, travel expenses, and the reward he paid a police officer. No sooner had the master gone to court and obtained a four-month extension on the apprentice's period of servitude than Burgess ran away again and remained out "for some days" before being "reclaimed." Again his period of service was extended, and now the master was given permission to "sell the unexpired term of said apprentice to any person."[51]

The case of Elias Burgess was not unusual. Free black youngsters—bound out by the court with or without their parents' permission—ran away continuously in Maryland because of poor treatment, breach of contract, bad housing, inadequate food, and dissatisfaction with masters. The instances where indentured free black youngsters lived quiet, calm, and productive lives were rare, as were the situations when they learned a trade and became self-employed artisans. In most cases there were tension, conflict, and violence. Apprenticed at the age of seven to an Anne Arundel County farmer to learn the "art of Farming," free black Moses Turner absconded five times before he was twenty-one. Jerry Matthews was eleven years old when he was bound to Baltimore resident Richard Ensey for ten years. Matthews also ran away five times, causing his master "considerable expense and trouble."[52]

Some free black youngsters became so dissatisfied with their situation that they would go to great lengths to get away from their masters. Young Robert Boston was apprenticed to Maryland farmer J. B. Nichols, but in December 1854 he ran off and hid in a neighbor's fodder house. He remained there only a day or two before being discovered, but it was extremely cold at night, and his feet were frostbitten. He was "unable to work from that time," the master said in April 1855. He had been under the constant care of a physician, "is a cripple and will always be." Despite his disability, in July 1855 when the master was absent, Boston ran away, remaining out for two weeks before he was put back to work.[53]

Using the same words and phrases as slaveholders, Marylanders called their free black runaway apprentices "uncontrollable," "ungovernable," and "unmanageable." In part this language was due to the wording of the law making it necessary to show that the apprentices were not "good and faithful" servants. But masters also truly believed that their young bound workers were, as Catherine Johnson of Baltimore said of her twelve-year-old black apprentice, "in a great degree ungovernable." In her case, the youngster had not only run away, but had openly defied her, vowing he would never stay with her. This forced the woman to have the youngster "arrested and confined." William Creamer, also of Baltimore, said that teenage Henry Cornish was "disobedient and disrespectful" and refused to obey "full and proper orders and directions." He had "refused to work and has broken such things as were put in his hands to work with; and he has on four several occasions run away." Mary Jane Mason, a widow who lived in Baltimore, said her sixteen-year-old free black runaway, Margaret H. Winchester, drank, cursed, refused orders, and threatened violence. The black girl told the widow that if one of her sons ever laid a hand on her "she would cut his damned heart out," and twice she had actually slapped Mason, who was now "afraid that she may offer personal violence to her or some member of her family." Other masters said much the same: free black apprentices were angry, hostile, bad tempered, difficult to manage, and prone to running away.[54]

Those who held free blacks in apprenticeship contracts expressed their dismay that those they were trying to assist would betray them in such a manner, even though, like slaves, free black children under these contracts could be bought, sold, traded, willed, deeded, and transferred. Those holding the contracts viewed themselves as kindly masters who were deceived by their free black charges. In 1856, James S. Wilson acquired free black Augusta Sprigg, formerly bound by the Trustees of the Poor for Baltimore City and County to Joseph Merryman, who had transferred her to David H. White, who had in turn transferred her to Wilson. The transfer papers read: "sold, assigned and transferred." Wilson said that the girl had been "Kindly treated, wellfed, lodged & clothed," but nonetheless had run away from his home on several occasions. Other masters said the same thing: they treated their apprentices "well and Kindly," in a "kind and indulgent manner," with humanity and compassion; they taught them "every thing necessary & useful" to their condition in life. In return, the black children were "indifferent" and "ungrateful."[55]

What happened to free black indentured children who were "indifferent" and "ungrateful"? With remarkable precision, the courts ruled that they should continue to serve their masters for periods of time beyond the time established in the original contract. This could be as brief as four to six months, but usually the extension was for one or two years and, on occasion, five or ten years. For those who continued to run away despite warnings, their indentures were usually extended for a number of years. Twelve-year-old William Gaugh, a free boy of color who was an orphan, ran away repeatedly, but each time he was captured and returned. In 1859, to teach him "the consequence of such improper conduct," the Anne Arundel County Orphans Court extended his apprenticeship until he reached his twenty-fourth birthday in 1870. Another orphaned free black, Washington Boston, age twelve, was indentured in 1854 to David W. McKlendin to learn to be a waiter, but four years later the master transferred the indenture to John H. Toffling, who promised to teach him to be a butcher. After the transfer, Boston ran away. Toffling had him arrested, and prior to a court date, put in jail "for safe Keeping."[56]

For runaway children who remained out for extended periods, life was precarious. Not only was there the possibility of being abducted and sold into slavery or being sexually assaulted, but securing shelter and comfort was virtually impossible. In Baltimore, Louis Henry Foulks, a free boy of color, was in the "constant habit of running away" from his master. For years, the wife of the man who held the indenture said, Foulks ran "in and about the streets, lodging of nights under steps of houses, and other places offering no better protection from the cold in winter seasons, until his feet has become badly frosted, notwithstanding, he will not remain at home."[57]

In a few cases, free black parents signed indentures for their own children. They were either too poor to provide for them or thought it would be beneficial if their child learned a trade. Some could not control their boys and girls and thought the discipline of hard work would do them good. A few ironically apprenticed their children to rescue them from slavery. "NOTICE. Will be sold at the Prison of Washington county, District of Columbia, on Monday, 24 August, 1835, a Negro Girl, who calls herself NANCY JONES, committed as a runaway," a newspaper in the nation's capital read. "She is a dark mulatto, about four feet ten inches high: she says she is about sixteen or seventeen years of age. Had on when committed, a light calico dress. She says she is free, and is known to be free." She was indeed free, and shortly after she had run away from home and been jailed, her father, George Jones, apprenticed her to his employer, James Mullinax, a Baltimore shopkeeper, who secured Nancy's release.[58]

Most who apprenticed their children discovered that there were few whites who did not seek to exploit free black labor. In 1856 Hannah Powell, a free woman of color in Baltimore, bound her daughter, Hester, to Joseph Swinney until she reached the age of eighteen. A short time later, Hester absconded and went undetected for three years and nine months, although her employer hired people to look for her and spent considerable time himself searching. When she was finally discovered, she was jailed, brought to court, and her servitude extended three years. Her indenture was then transferred to John Hinesly, who, Hannah Powell agonized, "sold and disposed" of her daughter to a "Southern Negro Trader," who promptly took her out of the state.[59]

Similarly, the most obdurate free black children were sold out of the state. Having just turned fifteen, apprentice Levi Stevenson ran away from his master's farm in Anne Arundel County on two different occasions, enticing other servants to accompany him. The master complained that he had lost $135 in jail fees and lost work time. The court ruled that Stevenson, who had also been convicted of a felony, should remain in jail and be sold out of the state. When the sale of a free black apprentice did not seem practical, masters treated the obstinate ones as they might treat slaves. In 1841, farmer John Russell of Baltimore County acquired a twelve-year-old free black apprentice for seven years. Within a week, the young boy ran away and was arrested and jailed. The farmer then refused to provide him with clothing and proper maintenance and forced him "to labor at night and on the Sabbath for other persons & at periods when he was Entitled to holiday." In addition, Russell forced him to buy his own clothes and kept a heavy iron collar on his neck "for several years at a time." At the end of seven years, the white man refused to release the free black apprentice from his indenture.[60]

What might happen to even the most well-intentioned free black parents in this system of indentured servitude and child labor was clearly demonstrated in the case of Edward Johnson. In 1860, Edward's parents, poverty-ridden free blacks, bound their son as an apprentice to William Chaney of Baltimore until he reached age twenty-one. Although the youngster was supposed to remain within the jurisdiction of the court where the indenture was issued, the boy's unexpired term was sold to William Martin of Baltimore, who took the boy across Chesapeake Bay to eastern Maryland and sold Edward's indenture to a German-born couple who lived on a farm near Easton in Talbot County. In an attempt to return to his parents, the young boy ran away and was captured and ran away again and was captured and absconded for a third time. To punish "this very bad fellow," the German couple called in the local constable who, Edward testified:

> tide me with a rope put my 2 neas thrugh my hands, then and there striped me nacked, with a sticke run trugh my hands and nees pinning me down with my hed to the ground sticking my bare backside up, then and there struck me 30. licks with a heavy hickrey paddle with a number of holes bored through it brusing me in an offel manner, from that position I was tacon and plased with a rope a round my rists my back intiarly naked and swong up then and there Each of them tuck a cow hide one on Either side and beet me in such a manner when they let me down I fanted and lay on the ground 2 hours when I came too I maid out to get to the house my privits ware very much injered and swollen very large I was confined to the hous for 2 weeks my back is very much schared at this time

Later, when his master planned to whip him again, Edward escaped, but was shot in the hand as he fled. He headed straight for the county seat, Easton, and turned himself into the sheriff for protection. A few days later, the Baltimore City Orphans Court ordered Martin "to produce in this court" a certain "colored apprentice named Edward L. Johnson." It was difficult to see, however, how the court could make amends for the brutal punishment he had endured.[61]

The struggles of free blacks in some parts of the South were not unlike the struggles of their brethren in bondage, as the runaway children of Maryland indicate. But even among the most prosperous and well-known free blacks, there was always the nagging fear that some unforeseen circumstance might thrust them backward into bondage.

9

Profile of a Runaway

ON 25 OCTOBER 1816, WILLIAM W. BELL, a North Carolina farmer, placed a notice in the *North Carolina Minerva and Raleigh Advertiser* about his runaway slave. Explaining that he had purchased Frank from John Patterson of Matthews County, Virginia, Bell wrote:

> RUNAWAY, from the Subscriber, on Friday Evening last, Near Enfield Court House, a NEGRO MAN, named FRANK, pretty stout, one strait scar on his cheek passing from the under part of the ear towards the corner of the mouth, of a common dark color, something of a flat nose, a short, round chin, and a down look, about 26 or 27 years of age. Had on, brown yarn homespun Pantaloons, striped homespun waistcoat, and a white yarn roundabout. TWENTY-FIVE DOLLARS reward will be given *for lodging* said runaway in any gaol in this state or TWENTY DOLLARS if in any gaol out of the state.[1]

Forty-one years later, in the fall of 1857, a South Carolina planter, E. M. Royall, published a similar notice in the *Charleston Mercury*:

> TWENTY-FIVE DOLLARS REWARD.—Ranaway from the subscriber's plantation, in Christ Church Parish, his Negro Man TONEY. Said fellow is about 5 feet 6 inches in height; stoutly built, is very black, has a broad, full face, black eyes, and when he laughs, shows a very white set of teeth. The above reward will be paid for his apprehension and delivery to the Work House in Charleston, or to the subscriber on his place.[2]

In size, build, color, gender, age, attire, reward, probable occupation, and personality—at least as perceived by whites—the "NEGRO MAN, Named FRANK" and the "Negro Man TONEY" fit the profile of typical runaway slaves. The largest segment of the runaway army included strong, young field hands in their late teens and twenties. The two advertisements also demonstrate the continuity that existed among typical runaways from one generation to the next.

If the typical runaway was a young, male plantation hand, runaways also included a range of other slaves, young and old, black and mulatto, healthy and infirm, female and male, skilled and unskilled, urban and rural. They absconded from farms, plantations, urban residences, town houses, job sites, and riverboats. Indeed, despite the norm, runaways were a diverse lot, and judging from the comments of slave owners, it seemed impossible to predict who might abscond.

In the sections that follow, there will be an examination of the salient characteristics of runaways resulting from a statistical examination of more than two thousand slaves advertised in newspapers in five states during two time periods: early, or 1790–1816, and late, or 1838–60 (see appendix 7). It will show that, while the profile of runaways was diverse, there was a remarkable consistency over time. Indeed, as the peculiar institution evolved and changed in unprecedented ways over more than sixty years, the profile of runaways, with few exceptions, remained virtually unchanged.

Age and Gender

As the descriptions of Frank and Toney suggest, the great majority of runaways were young men in their teens and twenties. During the early period, males constituted 81 percent of those who were advertised as runaways, and among them, 78 percent were between the ages of thirteen and twenty-nine. Exactly the same proportion of males was listed during the later period and, again, about three out of four—74 percent—were in their teens and twenties. During both periods, these men were described as healthy, strong, and stout, and only about one out of six possessed skills as artisans or house servants. The proportion of men to women was slightly higher in Virginia and Louisiana than in North and South Carolina and Tennessee during the early period, and it was lower in Louisiana during the later period, when male runaways dropped to 71 percent, but the variations were less important than the remarkable consistency: the precise male-female percentage remaining exactly the same over a period of more than two generations.[3]

Young men ran away in greater numbers because often they had not yet married or, if they had married, had not yet begun a family. Those who married sometimes took their loved ones with them, but in most cases, they were forced to leave wives and children behind.

Young men also ran away more often because they were more willing to defy overseers and owners if they felt aggrieved. Once away from the plantation, young men could better defend themselves and were willing to resist recapture. The young slave Jack of Orangeburgh District, South Carolina, had been out for some time when he was discovered in 1807 by a white farmer. In the struggle that ensued, Jack slashed the white man so severely that he remained bedridden for weeks and more than a year-and-a-half later had not fully recovered. A few years later, the slave Sampson, also of South Carolina, was confronted in a similar manner by William Villard, a white farmer in Barnwell District. Sampson brandished a knife in one hand and a hatchet in the other, and as Villard approached him, he cut the white man across the forehead and swung the hatchet into his ribs. Six months later, Villard was still disabled "from the Severe Injury he sustained in the apprehension of this desperate out Law."[4]

Not only did young men offer fierce resistance, but many realized that if they did not make an attempt to escape time would run out. Death came early to slaves, and those who reached their twenty-first birthday could expect to live about sixteen or seventeen additional years. In some sections, yellow fever, dysentery, pneumonia, and cholera carried off many slaves still in their teens and twenties.[5] It was not difficult for those who survived to observe the small number of elderly slaves or know about the funerals that occurred so often on their own and nearby plantations. This, coupled with the energy and vitality of youth and the physical stamina it took to go on the run, prompted young men to leave in greatest numbers. Among the 424 runaway males whose approximate ages were given in the early period, the average age was twenty-five; among the 835 during the later

Table 3
Gender of Runaways by State, Early Period (1790–1816)

	Virginia	North Carolina	Tennessee	South Carolina	Louisiana	Total
Number of females	14	18	29	55	13	129
(percentage)	(15)	(18)	(21)	(23)	(11)	(19)
Number of males	81	82	109	185	109	566
(percentage)	(85)	(82)	(79)	(77)	(89)	(81)
Totals	95	100	138	240	122	695

Table 4

Gender of Runaways by State, Late Period (1838–1860)

	Virginia	North Carolina	Tennessee	South Carolina	Louisiana	Totals
Number of females	17	18	20	89	104	248
(percentage)	(9)	(14)	(12)	(19)	(29)	(19)
Number of males	178	114	148	369	259	1068
(percentage)	(91)	(86)	(88)	(81)	(71)	(81)
Totals	195	132	168	458	363	1316

period, the mean age was twenty-seven. The oldest runaways were in their forties and fifties, a handful in their sixties, but those forty or older represented only 5 percent in the early period and 6 percent in the later period.

Young slave women were less likely to run away because they had often begun to raise families by their late teens and early twenties. With youngsters to care for, it became difficult to contemplate either leaving them behind or taking them in an escape attempt. Lying out in the woods or fleeing to more distant points would only mean suffering, danger, and hardship for their children. As several historians have pointed out, although slave women desired freedom as much as slave men and were often as assertive and aggressive on the plantation as male slaves, the task of uprooting and carrying children in flight "was onerous, time-consuming, and exhaustive." As a result, a smaller proportion than among men decided to run away.[6]

Like their male counterparts, however, those who did abscond usually did so in their teens and twenties. These young females represented more than two-thirds of the women in both periods—69 and 68 percent respectively—who ran off. Some took their children with them or, following a sale, attempted to find their sons and daughters, despite the difficulties of such undertakings. Others ran during pregnancy. In her twenties, Letty left her owner John J. Zollicofer of Nashville in 1814. She was a "likely negro," her owner said, quick spoken, with "handsome countenance"; she was about six months pregnant. Similarly, the "American Negress *Nancy*," who ran away in New Orleans in 1828, was "with child." Purchased by a South Carolina man in Maryland in 1816, Sawney quickly fled from her new owner but remained out only a few months before being captured. By the time her owner claimed her, she had given birth to an infant. The North Carolina slave Delph also bore a child on the run. Angeline escaped from Richmond slave traders in 1836 to return to Greenbrier, Augusta County, Virginia, where she had been raised and had six children.[7] Angeline, too, was pregnant. Despite these desertions, women thought long and hard about the consequences for their families and themselves before making any decision to abscond.

Among both males and females, some did not fit the profile. Some preteen-age youngsters fled. Transferred at age ten to the household of an Anne Arundel County, Maryland, woman following the distribution of an estate, Alice was about twelve when she went "running out at night." Catherine, a French-speaking girl in New Orleans, was also about twelve when she absconded in 1831, and Henry, a "young mulatto," was about ten when he ran off two years later. In 1841, an eleven-year-old apprentice barber, Walter Scott, who traveled on steamboats, ran away. When Elias was arrested in 1828 in Charleston, he was advertised as being four feet nine inches tall and about twelve years old.[8]

At the other end of the age spectrum was a black man who worked in the kitchen at the Pontchartrain Hotel and as a hawker of hay in New Orleans. He had outlived several of his owners, and in 1830, at age fifty-five, he absconded. Although her exact age was not given, Nelly was "an elderly Negro woman" who had been sold from Virginia to South Carolina. Other slaves were described as old, decrepit, elderly, gray-haired, bent, and aged. The fifty-year-old Sumter District, South Carolina, man stooped over when walking, and was "quite grey." Some slaves were similarly described with physical defects and as being "quite gray." The Charleston carpenter Andrew was quite "elderly looking." Committed to the jail of Orangeburg, South Carolina, in 1832, another runaway was described as being "about eighty years old."[9]

Color and Physical Characteristics

Most runaways were black. They were described as having dark complexion, dark skin, black complexion, being "coal black," remarkably black, or very black. Some had "not a very black complexion" or were "not remarkably black" or "nearly quite black," but others were described as "a negro boy, perfectly black," "jet black," with a dark complexion, "very dark complexioned," or exceptionally dark. Abel was about sixteen years old and "dark complected," William B. Flowers of Smyrna, Barnwell District, South Carolina, said in his 1855 notice;

Abram was about twenty-eight years old, plausible and intelligent, and also very black, Z. B. Oakes of Charleston, said in the same issue of the *Charleston Mercury*.[10] Although at times the precise color of the runaway was not stated and "negro wench" or "negro fellow" could describe a person of mixed origin, 70 percent of the runaways in the early period were either black or their skin was so dark that readers of runaway newspaper advertisements would assume they were.*

Although a minority of runaways were mulattoes, persons of mixed racial ancestry ran away in greater numbers than their proportion in the slave population would suggest. Except for the virtual elimination of African-born blacks, the increase among mulatto runaways between the early and late periods represented one of the most significant changes that occurred in the profile of runaways. The precise proportion of mulattoes in the slave population for the early period is not known, but due to the importation of Africans at least until 1808, it was surely smaller than during the late antebellum era, when it reached 10 percent. The nearly one-third mixed blood among runaways during the early period was therefore at least three times larger than would be expected in the general population. By the later period, the proportion of advertised mulattoes had risen to 43 percent, more than four times what would be expected. Even if mixed blood slaves were more readily advertised—and there is evidence that they were—this large percentage was remarkable.[11]

Persons with light skin possessed certain advantages as runaways. The prejudices against them were generally less than against those of darker hue. They were more likely to be able to pass as free persons since the proportion of mulattoes in the free Negro group was much higher than in the slave population. The proportion of mulatto runaways in the slave population during the late period (561 of 1,316, or 43 percent) was almost exactly the same as the 41 percent of mixed racial origin in the free black population.

Sometimes they could pass as white. This was the case when the Georgia slave Coleman left his owner during a trip the two men took on the Western Atlantic Railroad in October 1839. Coleman was in his mid-twenties, with a very smooth face, straight sandy hair, blue eyes, and was "very white to be a slave." Bonaparte, a Virginia slave, possessed the physical appearance of a white man: very light skin and straight hair. A Georgia runaway named Guy would "no doubt en-

---

*In the RSDB, if "negro" was used with no additional information on color, the runaway was considered black; if no color was indicated, the runaway was also cited as black. Since owners were quick to point out those of mixed racial origin even when they used the term "negro" (i.e., "negro mulatto"), this method, which gives a color designation to all slaves in the RSDB, is probably relatively accurate.

deavor to pass himself off as a white man," and the Haywood County, Tennessee, runaway John, was described as "a bright red Mulatto" with straight hair and fashionable attire. He would certainly attempt to pass, either "for a free fellow, or perhaps a white man." Other owners described their slaves as "very nearly white," could easily pass for white, a "white mulatto boy," three-fourths white and "shows the negro blood but very little," "remarkably white for a slave," could easily "pass for a white man." "Stop Mabin!!" read the advertisement of Georgia planter Zachariah Booth in 1833, "He will pass for a white man where he is not known." Apparently, Mabin did pass, as he was still at large seven years later.[12]

Mulatto slaves were often given positions as house servants, maids, cooks, tailors, waiters, and barbers. With such skills, they could more easily attempt to pass as free blacks. Given their often privileged position as slaves, runaway mulattoes found it less difficult to affect the manners, habits, and general demeanor of free persons of color. During the later period, they were twice as likely to be literate as black runaways and more often carried freedom papers or passes. Even during the early period, when the literacy rate among runaways was only between 1 and 2 percent, nearly 10 percent of mulatto runaways possessed forged papers, compared with 6 percent among blacks.

The diversity among runaways was perhaps nowhere better illustrated than in the descriptions of mixed blood slaves who ran away. In South Carolina between 1822 and 1831, they were described as yellow, brown, mustee (brown), mulatto, pale yellow, "of rather a yellow cast," Sambo (dark), and red. In Virginia during the early and late periods, they were described as tawny, nearly black, brown, mulatto, yellow, red, reddish, yellowish, dark yellow, bright yellow, "tolerable light," "dark mulatto," and as having "a lighter complexion" than was "common among negroes." Others were a "little light complected" or "tolerably bright complected," "more of a bright mulatto than otherwise," and of a "dark ginger color." A Richmond owner said his carriage driver was of a "dark copper complexion," and other Virginia masters said their slaves were "light copper or mulatto," "pumpkin color," or "light bacon color."[13]

Louisiana owners advertised their runaways as bright yellow, very brown, "a negro, but not of the blackest cast," "a light colored black," "of a light dark color," pale yellow, rather red, and "rather light." They described their slaves also as "a dirty mulatto color," "copper colored negro man," bright mulatto, light mulatto, bright yellow mulatto, "dark freckled mulatto negro," "not very black," "dark copper color." In New Orleans, the term "griff," or "griffe," changed from a noun to an adjective. Used in the Caribbean to denote the offspring

of a black and mulatto, in New Orleans it became a color to describe
runaways. "Ranaway from the subscriber, about three weeks ago,"
one master said, "a griffe colored slave named Joe."[14]

Other physical characteristics of runaways also revealed their diversity. Owners rarely gave specific weight information, but they did
suggest size and build—slight, average, heavy, stout—in about one-
third of the notices. For men and women in the early period, the
largest proportion was described as "stout," meaning strong, sturdy,
fleshy, large—(39 percent of the females and 41 percent of the males);
in the later period, this category was still prominent although there
was wider distribution among groups. With regard to height, the data
on females are sketchy, although it does appear that they were shorter
than what was considered "average" at the time they absconded. The
information for males is much better, and in more than 55 percent of
the cases owners provided specific height data. Among the 314 males
age thirteen and over during the early period, half were five feet seven
inches or taller, a third were five feet ten inches or taller, and 12
percent were six feet or more. Among the 637 runaways males in the
same category during the later period, the figures were almost exactly
the same. In the early period, the average height of between five feet
seven inches and five feet eight inches for runaways was as tall as the
average white male height.[15] In both periods, many were tall, strong,
young men. There is little doubt that physical strength, stamina, and
size played a role in determining who was likely to flee.

A significant segment of the runaway population was identifiable
by marks, scars, and disfigurements. The list was very long, including
facial mark, cheek mark, unusual forehead mark, upper arm mark,
finger deformity, missing finger, limp, unusual gait, leg deformity,
unusual feet, missing toes, lame arm, lame hand, smallpox scars, missing ear[s], and scars from whipping and branding. It was not usually
stated how, where, or when runaways lost their fingers, toes, limbs,
or acquired their marks and brands. In the early period, African-born
slaves often acquired tribal marks before their journey to the New
World, and even in the later period some of the physical problems
described were the result of accidents or disease. Such was probably
the case for those described with "white swelling," "very remarkable
lumps," a foot "deformed and nearly half off," "a web on one of his
eyes," missing "one-half of her right foot," "lame in the left knee,"
"diseased in his left thigh." The frequent mention of missing teeth
might also be the result of natural causes.[16]

It was clear, however, that for a number slaves there was a direct
connection between deformities and prior punishment. The Virginia
slave Reuben of Culpepper County, who "eloped" in 1807, had

a scar on the right side of his neck below the ear; another on the left, lower on his neck; he has also a scar on the right leg a little below his knee, occasioned by a burn; his back has many scars on it from flogging he has received which he justly merited.

The "mark of a whip" could be seen on the arms of Celia, a fifteen-year-old girl who ran from her master in Rutherford County, Tennessee, in 1814. Fond of drinking, swearing, and fighting, the runaway Dennis had his back "very much cut with the cow-hide." Slaves had scars on their backs, shoulders, arms, legs, sides, and faces, "occasioned by the whip." Neither the young nor old were spared. Fourteen-year-old Mary, who had a "quick and lively air," had two marks on her cheek inflicted with "a cow hide." An elderly Virginia slave, transferred to South Carolina, had several marks between her shoulders caused by the lash. In 1826, the sheriff of Pointe Coupee Parish, Louisiana, described a captured slave as having "around his neck an Iron collar with three prongs extending upwards" and "many scars on his back and shoulders from the whip."[17]

In some cases it was almost possible to trace a slave's history by the various scars. By the time he reached age twenty in 1839, William had been sold from Virginia, to New Orleans, to Vicksburg, Mississippi, and finally to a plantation on Bayou Sara, near Woodville, Mississippi. "[H]e ranaway about the 1st of April," his Mississippi owner said, "was caught and put in jail in Woodville." He falsely gave the name of another man as his owner. Now he was out again, but could be recognized by a scar just above his left eye, a scar above his left thumb, and when "stripped, many scars may be seen on his back, caused from a severe whipping with a cowskin (as he says) at the time of the Southampton insurrection."[18]

The notices contain ample evidence that branding and cropping of ears continued well into the nineteenth century, especially to punish the most obdurate runaways. The Virginia slave Archie was branded on both cheeks, and the facial scars were much darker than his normal skin color. A Georgia slave had also been branded before he ran away in 1808. It was unclear whether the "R" on each cheek stood for "Runaway" or "Richard Thurmond," the Oconee River planter who claimed Joe as his slave. One Kentucky master described a runaway in 1815 as having "a black streak on his nose, which is very plain, it extends on his left cheek near the size of one little finger." "I filed several notches between several of his upper fore teeth, which I expect is also very plain," he added; "I also branded him on each cheek . . . about twelve months ago, which is not very perceivable."[19]

Similarly, advertisements in the *New Orleans Bee* during the 1820s and 1830s describe runaways with brands on their backs, hands, breasts, and faces. He "made two trips to Louisville the last time he ranaway," one notice in 1833 read. He was about thirty years old, had sunken cheeks, sulky looks, and should be easy to spot: he had a brand on his forehead of an inch-high cross, a brand on his cheek of the letter "O," and a brand on his back of the word "Orleans." He also had "the mark of the whip" on his back. The French-speaking slave Dio worked on a plantation of P. B. Marmillion, located in Orleans Parish. When he departed with two other slaves in a skiff, Marmillion warned the public to beware of Dio's "pleasing countenance" and added that the slave would be easy to recognize. "He is stamped on the forehead and on the breast," the owner commented, "with the large letters P.M." A slave who left Andry Boudousque's plantation stooped when he walked, had lost part of a thumb, and was branded "with the letter B on the left side of his breast."[20]

The scars from whippings, beatings, and branding, described by slave owners themselves, bore witness to the harsh realities of slavery. Yet there were many runaways whose marks and scars were never advertised in the newspapers. London was "neither the best nor the worst Kind of a negroe," his overseer in Natchitoches Parish, Louisiana, said; rather he was "a middling hand," or a "Very Good Second rate Negroe." London, however, ran away on numerous occasions and bore marks "of Very Violent Punishment." In August 1835, after a severe whipping, a physician wrote:

> his face was sufficiently full and round as past but on seeing the other parts of the body which were extremely poor it [his face] seemed to be swollen, that the skin on his posteriors was lank and wrinkled and that his bones protruded in such a way as to resemble more a skeleton than a living person, that not satisfied with this examination he introduced his finger into the funda-ment around which the[re] were a number of small flatulent Blis-ters that having intruded his finger as far as the intestines he found them very hard and Extremely sensitive and felt some very hard tumours & that on withdrawing his finger it was coated with putrid Matter on his finger that from the appearance of this matter that there must have been internal Tumours or Fistulaes.

A short time after the doctor's visit, London died.[21]

Among the 695 slaves listed in the runaway notices for the early period, 54 (7.8 percent) showed scars from whipping, beatings, crop-ping, torture, and other forms of severe violence. Among the 1,316 slaves listed for the later period, 76 (5.8 percent) showed the same types of scars. Only 6 slaves in the early period were obviously branded by their owners, but the 6 represented nearly 1 percent of the total, and only 15 had one or both ears cut off (a punishment usually reserved for runaways), but they represented 2.2 percent of the total. While the number of those branded by their owners in the later period dropped to 4, and those with cropped ears to 12, the fact that 1 out of 13 and 1 out of 17 fugitives (early and late periods) were identified by scars resulting from extreme forms of punishment reveals much about the peculiar institution.*

Appearance

It is doubtful that many runaways branded on the face or disfigured from the violent retribution of their masters made it to freedom. But others could and did hide their scars by wearing shirts, pants, and jackets, and the great majority of runaways, at least as indicated in the advertisements, could not be readily identified by the results of severe whipping or other violence. They could be recognized, their owners believed, by other means, and often this included a description of their clothes.

Most runaways fled in the clothing that their owners had issued them. Field hands were generally provided with a least one coarse suit of clothes per year—shirts and pants for men, dresses for women, long shirts for children. During the early period, the clothing was often homespun by black women on the plantation or sewn by them from "Negro cloth" purchased by their owners from retailers in the North. The attire of a Louisiana hand was typical: in 1830 his clothing consisted of a gray jacket, straw hat, blue striped "drilling" pantaloons, and work trousers made from "coarse cotton cloth." During the later period, hands sometimes wore ready-made clothes provided them by their masters and made or acquired special shirts, trousers, and dresses for holidays and church services.[22]

Given their limited wardrobes, what is striking about the appearance of runaways was the remarkable variety of clothing they took with them at the time of their departure. Some stole extra apparel, others made special clothes for their flight, and still others simply accumulated a selection of different garments. Even those who left wearing homespun often took other items. In 1814, the Tennessee slave Celia had a yellow calico frock, a blue calico frock, a white cambric dress,

---

*This discussion excludes slaves who had missing toes, fingers, a leg, arm, or hand, as well as those with various marks and scars, unless it was explicitly stated or obvious that these deformities were the result of severe punishment.

and two "homespun coarse" dresses, a pair of red morocco-eyed slippers tied with a yellow ribbon, and a "checkered gingham bonnet (or scoop)." The runaway Solomon wore a blue Lindsey coat with yellow metal buttons, an old fur hat, and a worn yellow waistcoat; he carried with him a buffalo robe, two or three pairs of homespun cotton pantaloons, and "several other articles of clothing." A South Carolina slave wore a "blue negro cloth round jacket with new yellow buttons, and blue pantaloons, a grey waistcoat with black velvet on the pockets, new boots, and grey worsted stockings." Another South Carolina runaway wore homespun shirt and pants and an old cloak, but carried "a large stock of Clothing." Myal, a Tennessee runaway, wore plantation-made pants, a cotton shirt, and a wool roundabout. He also had an extra pair of white woolen trousers, blue jeans, and a black fur hat. "The latter clothes are missing," the master confided, and Myal probably took them when he left.[23]

Other plantation slaves discarded their homespun altogether. The Virginia slave Laban fled with a grey lamb's skin coat, white trousers, a double-breasted grey coat, a black cape, and "sundry other clothes." A Kentucky field hand wore a cashmere coat, nice pants, shoes, stockings, and a fur hat, taking along a cotton waistcoat and three extra pairs of cotton trousers. "She is very fond of dress," one South Carolina owner said of his twenty-year-old black Hannah "and carried three or four changes of clothes with her." When he ran away from the plantation of Andre Deslondes in St. John the Baptist Parish, Louisiana, Alexander took two suits of clothes, two pairs of trousers—one dark cloth, the other striped woolen—a blue-and-white-striped jacket, shoes, and a "drab colored hat." The Mississippi plantation hand Patrick dressed "very fine" and had a "fine stock of clothes." Six feet tall, with gold rings on his fingers, Patrick was "a very fine looking negro." Else would "appear in a black Silk or white Muslin gown," her Virginia owner wrote in 1805, "as she had many very good clothes, and is fond of dress." The young North Carolina field hand Oba ran away wearing cotton trousers and a short coat "napped with black wool and cotton, wove plain." He also had two pairs of "buff casimere breeches," a grey waistcoat, a white waistcoat, a pair of ribbed, woolen stockings, and a double-breasted, grey broadcloth coat.[24]

The wardrobes of urban slaves often included a larger selection than was available to plantation hands. Those who worked as waiters, house servants, stewards, seamstresses, tailors, and barbers possessed several suits, dresses, shirts, trousers, jackets, and hats. The Richmond house servant Claiborne took with him "a great variety of wearing apparel, all of excellent quality," his master said, "much better than is usually given to servants." Despite being employed as

There is about 75 acres in cultivation; the balance
in timbered land, in point of soil is not easily
surpassed. The whole could be consolidated and
form one tract, which would make it very desirable.
I will sell the whole together, or in any quantity to
suit the convenience of those wishing to buy. I
would take young negroes in payment, or a part in
cash, and the balance in convenient instalments.—
Those wishing to purchase will call on my son Isaac
R. Eatherly on the premises, or to the subscriber,
one mile north of the mouth of Harpeth, Montgomery county. There will be about 150 or 200 barrels
of corn, and 12 or 15 stacks of fodder on the premises for sale. Should the land not be sold by the
1st of December, the stand on the road will be for
rent the ensuing year, and possession given 1st of
January next.

JESSE EATHERLY.

Oct. 24, 1838.—Wtd

Runaway,

ON the night of the 9th Nov. last, a negro man
named JIM or ARMSTEAD, aged about 22
years, about five feet ten inches high, very likely,
and when spoken to has a pleasing appearance; has
whiskers. No particular marks recollected. He
wore off when he left a fur cap, brown cloth frock
coat, boots, &c.; had with him a variety of clothing,
description not recollected, and will most likely
dress very well and in newest fashion. He also
rode off a large bay horse about 8 year old, a natural pacer, foretop has been cut off and nearly grown
out, with a Spanish saddle quilted cover, and no pad
saddle bags, &c. I think it most likely that he has
attempted to make his way for Nashville, Tenn., or
New Orleans. He has a mother in Nashville, said
to be free, the wife of a man by the name of Wilson Davis, and was raised in that place and has many acquaintances there: he has lived for the last
fewe years in New Orleans, and was a short time
since brought to Alabama by Wm. T. Gamble, who
conveyed him to me. I have but little doubt that he
will make for one of the places mentioned, and will
give a reasonable reward to any person who will
apprehend and commit him to jail, or give me such
information as will lead to the recovery of said negro and horse.

GEO. W. LANE.

Athens, Ala. Dec. 19.—W3t

The Louisville Journal will publish the above
once a week for three weeks, and charge this office.

Mrs. Burrell's Academy.

MRS. BURRELL informs her friends and the
public, that the avocations of this establishment
will be resumed on Thursday, 3rd January, on the
premises lately occupied by Dr. King (corner of Ce-
dar and High Streets.) Mrs. B. tenders her acknowl-

The Alabama runaway Jim or Armstead, who had lived five years in New Orleans, was probably heading to see his free black mother in Nashville. He took with him "a variety of clothing" and would "most likely dress very well and in newest fashion."

a carpenter and railroad hand, Jackson maintained a "general assortment of good clothes," his New Orleans owner said, and would no
doubt assume "the appearance of a dandy." When the slave Willis
boarded a steamboat in New Orleans in 1832, he wore a white shirt,
brown linen pants, a blue cloth frock coat, and a black hat. He also
took with him a bundle of clothing wrapped in a sheet. The Charleston slave George left his owner in July 1804 wearing a brown jacket,
brown calico waistcoat, and brown linen pants with suspenders.
George "is very fond of wearing a Neckcloth with a large Pad in it,"
his owner said, and although hatless, he would probably buy one
along the way. Twenty-year-old Walley, also of Charleston, wore a
blue cloth coat with yellow buttons, thin black pants, and a black fur
hat when he left in January 1828 but carried an extra jacket and two
pairs of wool pants wrapped in a carpet.[25]

Other city slaves took large wardrobes. One New Orleans owner
did not describe the dress of his slave, a waiter at the St. Charles Hotel,
but noted he was "genteel, and little on the dandy order." In 1832,
the twenty-six-year-old personal servant of Kinsey Burden of Charleston left wearing a black hat, grey wool pants, a striped gingham jacket,
and a black bombazette frock coat. In addition, he carried along a black
sealskin cap, two extra suits, two extra waistcoats—one black cassimere
and one striped gingham, two pairs of white trousers, and a worn,
light blue, broadcloth frock coat. When he left his owner in New Orleans, Nelson had on a tarpaulin hat, blue cotton calico shirt, and cotton pants, but he also possessed "an array of clothing" and might be
dressed with "a white silk hat, blue dress coat, and cloth pantaloons."
George W. Prescott's petite slave Lucy in Charleston wore a handkerchief on her head and a calico gown with wide ornamental ruffles, but,
he warned, she "may change her dress as she carried her trunk." Others took "an abundance of clothing," "an array of clothing," "a bundle
of clothing." Several owners echoed the sentiments of a New Orleans
man who complained that his slave had taken with him so many articles of clothing that "it is hard to tell what he might wear."[26]

There were practical as well as stylistic reasons for taking many
articles of apparel, as the fur or beaver hats and store-bought suits
indicated. But principally they took along changes of clothing to use
for disguise. Some slaves were best known in their communities because of their dress—Charleston and Christ Church Parish residents
knew Cyrus, a coachman, for example, by his brown frock coat and
black beaver hat—and when these slaves donned new outfits, they
could more readily slip away, as did Cyrus. "She will of course appear
in different dresses," a Johns Island, South Carolina, planter said of

his runaway in 1822. She would be in a variety of colors because shortly before leaving she was observed dying a number of white dresses.[27]

Jim was well-known around Beaufort, South Carolina, and its vicinity not for his clothing, but as "a noted thief and runaway." He frequently disguised himself as a woman and took the name Sally Turner, his master said, "having once been apprehended in women's apparel." In 1828, he had made it as far as Savannah but was captured and brought back. A short time later he ran away again. The owner believed he would again disguise himself as a woman. Just the reverse was true for the "dark griffe" Crescent City woman Mariah, who would try to pass as a boy. She frequently "dressed herself in boy's clothes, and has her hair cut short for the purpose."[28]

Color, age, gender, distinctive marks, size, and clothing were all part of the profile of runaways. So, too, were hair styles. What is striking in comparing the early and late periods is the similarity of these styles. In both periods, very few runaways were described by their hair style. Persons of mixed racial origin were far more likely to have their hair described than persons who were described as black. In the early period, among 695 slaves, only 38 (5.5 percent) were described as having unusual or distinctive hair; mulattoes were three times more likely than blacks to have their hair described (24 of 207 mulattoes, or 12 percent, compared with 14 of 488 blacks, or 3 percent). It was rare for a male slave to have his hair described as bushy, plaited, or standing high on his head. In the later period, among 1,316 slaves, only 97 (7 percent) were described by their hair style, and persons of mixed origin were nearly five times more likely than blacks to have their hair described. The most important change involved the proportion of women who were described as having unusual hair. In the early period only 1 percent of the female runaways were described by their hair style, compared with 5 percent of the males; in the later period, each group represented 7 percent of their respective totals.[29]

The similarities and differences between the two periods are reflected in newspaper advertisements. First, owners in both periods were more likely to see straight hair as distinctive; second, with the growth of the mulatto population among runaways, this distinction became more common; third, in the later period, slave women of mixed origin may well have not worn the traditional head scarves in order to advertise their straight hair; and fourth, even in the early period, bushy or long hair among male runaways was rare. These changes were more than stylistic. They pointed to cultural changes among slaves as they made the transition from Africans to African Americans.

Personality Traits and Countenance

Runaways possessed many similar personality traits. Here, too, there was diversity, but most runaways demonstrated self-confidence, self-assurance, self-possession, determination, and self-reliance. They were resourceful, willful, focused, and purposeful. A number were quick-witted, wily, and intelligent, while most were deceptive and calculating, and not a few were duplicitous and scheming when it came to dealing with whites. Perhaps the most salient characteristic, however, was courage, especially for those who ran away more than once despite severe punishments. Very few among them appeared surly, morose, or sullen. Indeed, such qualities would have exposed their deep hatred of bondage and made them, in their owner's eyes, troublemakers and potential runaways.

Among the most significant characteristics of runaways was their intelligence. Masters warned the public to beware of black persons who were able to provide credible excuses as to why they were traveling in the area. In 1804, one Virginia owner, W. Gatewood, said that his "likely negro man by the name of TOM," alias Tom Smith, alias Smith, was a "proud, artful, cunning fellow" who had a "very smooth dissembling tongue." The Georgia mulatto Sam was "a keen shrewd fellow" who would "attempt to pass for a free man, and will doubtless make for a free state." She was very "artful and talks very properly, and is capable of deceiving any person," the owner of Maria, a "fine tall mulatto" woman, about thirty years of age, explained. Her husband was literate and had probably written her a pass, and it was "therefore requested that if she should produce a pass to examine it very particularly, as she has none from me." The mulatto carpenter George was "very plausible when spoken to, and well calculated to deceive." The black cooper who left a plantation near Georgetown, South Carolina, in 1828 was "very credible" and often affected a "pleasant but bold smile." Other runaways were described in the same manner: they would change their names, produce false passes, wear fraudulent badges, profess to be free, lie about their owner, feign an illness. In short, as one master put it, they were "very smart and well calculated to deceive."[30]

In order to deceive, runaways assumed a friendly and polite countenance when dealing with whites. This was especially true for older runaways, who were often described as amicable, cordial, and congenial. The fifty-year-old Kentucky slave who was sent to Richmond, Virginia, as a hireling was remarkably polite, often repeating "master," and "making bows almost to the ground." When he absconded, the man who hired him said he was "a very artful fellow" and was probably attempting to secure a berth aboard a sailing vessel as a free man. It was also true for domestic servants and waiters who were often described in the same manner. At age twenty-two or twenty-three, Moses, the "waiting-man" for Theodore Gaillard, a Charleston gentleman, was described as pleasant, amiable, and congenial.[31]

The speech habits of runaways came under close scrutiny in the newspaper notices. About 7 and 8 percent of slaves were said to speak slowly or to a have a downcast look when they were addressed by whites. He has rather "slow speech," he speaks slowly and has "Rather a down look," she "is slow of speech," or in the words of a Louisiana master, he has "a smiling and downcast look when spoken to." Among this group were a few African-born slaves who experienced difficulty pronouncing English words. By 1833, Luck had been in the United States many years, but he still pronounced words with "difficulty as is generally the case," an observer said, "with all the Congo negroes." Others spoke in Gullah, "Savannah dialect," a Charleston dialect, or "a brogue different from Negroes raised in Eastern Virginia." Among those who spoke slowly, only a tiny number stuttered or had speech impediments. In the early period, they numbered only five; and in the later period, only twelve.[32]

Indeed, as many slaves were fluent in at least three languages as those who stuttered. Slaves in Louisiana during the 1820s and 1830s were often bilingual, and some spoke French, Spanish, and English. Advertised runaways were described as speaking English and French, English and Spanish, and as was the case of "creole *Negress* named CELESTINE," English, French, and Spanish. Others spoke English, French, and a little Spanish or French with "broken English." When masters in the region described slaves as "American creole," "American mulatto," "American negro," they were pointing not only to their American birth but to English as their principal language. In the upper states, including Maryland, Virginia, and North Carolina, a few runaways were bilingual in German and English, especially in sections where German settlers made up a significant portion of the population. Henry Kring of Rockingham County, Virginia, said that his Negro man Hons, who ran away in 1807, "speaks generally the German language."[33]

Whatever their dialect, accent, or language, runaways were generally articulate and well-spoken. They were often described as fluent and smooth with words and quick with speech. Forty-year-old Charles, who called himself Charles Wood, spoke "smooth language and will no doubt tell a good story to pass." The Mississippi slave Anthony, who absconded from Natchez in July 1803, spoke French and English "tolerably well" and was "artful in telling stories." Forty-five-year-old Tom, who eloped from Soldier's Rest, Davidson County, Tennessee, was remarkably fluent in speech and when addressed would always respond without hesitation. A man who ran away from Nashville "speaks bold and sensible." The New Orleans slave Sam spoke "very quick, and from the top of the tongue." The South Carolina slave Jacob, who was sold to Louisiana in 1834, spoke "quickly, and is rather abrupt in his manner." One twenty-two-year-old black man was "smart and active and speaks very bold in conversation." The griffe man Sam was "soft and smooth in conversation." Sixteen-year-old Frances was quick with words and "very intelligent." A runaway railroad worker spoke in "an impudent, self-confident way," while a Virginia runaway possessed "very good language indeed for a slave."[34]

The personality traits attributed to slaves by their owners and by other whites in newspaper advertisements presented only part of the picture. Though they did note that some slaves were active, bold, surly, and nervous, they rarely described them as defiant, overtly resistant, violent. Nor did they admit that they were sometimes afraid of their slaves. Runaways often demonstrated all of these traits, and owners and overseers were sometimes timid in dealing with such runaways. In their owners' opinion, these slaves were "quarrelsome," "disorderly," and "disobedient"; they were vicious, turbulent, and violent. Whites admitted that they were unable to control such slaves. As one master said, his man was "utterly disobedient and ungovernable" and despite every "admonition and threat continued to disobey him and runaway." Since this owner refused to use chains or other restraints, the only solution was a sale. When a fifteen-year-old Maryland girl

Table 5

Countenance of Slaves as Described in Runaway Advertisements

Description	Early Period, 1790–1816		Late Period, 1838–1860	
	Number	Percentage	Number	Percentage
Intelligent/Artful	81	12	142	11
Friendly/Polite	81	12	131	10
Cunning	52	8	51	4
Looks Down/Slow Speech	46	7	108	8
Active	46	7	79	6
Bold	27	4	34	3
Surly	20	3	37	3
Nervous	17	2	39	3

Source: Computed from RSDB; since some slaves were listed in more than one category, totals are not included.

named Eliza absconded, was captured, brought back, and threatened with sale to Georgia, she replied that she would "as leave go to Georgia as any where else." She ran away the next day. The owner went to Annapolis, looked up a business associate who knew Eliza's mother, and went to the associate's office. After being there a few minutes, he related, "the door opened and in walked Eliza." The master said he was glad to see her. She replied, " 'I want nothing to do with you.' " She might be forcibly taken back, she added, "but she would not stay with him." The owner sent her to jail and arranged for her sale.[35]

Such defiance was not uncommon among runaways. They were described as displaying "bad and vicious habits," refusing to obey orders, refusing to work, and refusing to "perform services required." Like Eliza, they vowed not to live on their owners' farm or plantation, threatened owners and overseers, and asserted that no amount of punishment would make them change their attitudes. The owner Cosmore Robinson said that his slave was "surly, morose and discontented," a man who was obviously "greatly dissatisfied with his state of servitude." Others were noted for their open defiance, "violent and determined temper," refusal to submit, and their threats against the master's family. When the owner of one runaway decided to sell him, he arranged for the sheriff to put him in jail. He was familiar with the slave's "Character and disposition to do harm" and believed that if the slave knew he was going to be sold the owner's family "would be in great danger."[36]

Three case studies—from South Carolina, Texas, and Maryland— illustrate this aspect of the profile of a runaway. Owned by Mary Cobb of Columbia, South Carolina, Leely ran away on numerous occasions. On one occasion when Leely was out, Cobb, who knew she was "concealed and lurking" about town, hired her out, if the hirer would "take the risk and trouble of finding and getting possession of said slave." After finding Leely, the hirer offered to purchase her, but Cobb would not sell because the black woman "was very evil disposed towards her," if "sold to any person in Columbia, she might do her mischief." A few months later, Leely insulted a member of Mary Cobb's family in the street and was arrested and publicly whipped.[37]

The testimony of a Texas overseer concerning the slave Miles, who worked on a farm in San Augustine County, suggests that runaways were often openly defiant. When a visitor arrived at the farm in 1852 searching for stolen goods, Gilbert B. McIver, the overseer, sent a slave to the field where Miles was plowing to procure the key to his locked cabin door. He refused to give it up. When this was repeated a second time, McIver broke down Miles's door but found nothing. Miles became angry and told McIver that he "was the first Man that ever sent for *his* Keys, or that broke into his house." The overseer explained:

> In the day after the occurrence of the matter about the Key, of his, I went into the field where he was ploughing, and he had a hatchet, or Hand axe, tied and swung to his Plough: and I thought at the time, that he had it for the purpose, in case he was attacked by me, or if I went to Correct him, to resist me with it. I did not go near him at the time to attempt to Correct him, but just let him plough on, as I was unarmed, and had nothing to defend myself with at the time.

Miles refused to "mind, or give obedience to his overseer," and if he were to be corrected "he would fight; he might, if he had the opportunity, run," but in any event he would resist. He was "disposed to have his own way, and if a manager ordered him to do a task he would grouse and sometimes not perform the work if he were so inclined." When a few days later, armed with a gun and accompanied by a neighbor and his dogs, McIver went to the fields where Miles was plowing to correct him, Miles darted into the woods carrying his hatchet.[38]

Such defiance was also demonstrated by "a negro slave named Peter," whose owner was regarded as kind and benevolent. The owner, John Wood of Frederick County, Maryland, had provided for the future freedom of his slaves, including Peter, who was to be manumitted when he reached age thirty. By age twenty, in 1838, however, Peter had become extremely restive. Hired out to a farmer in the area, he ran away, then ran away again, and then, on a number of different occasions, absented himself without permission. After being jailed, Peter threatened his owner's family, vowed he would never return to his owner, and asserted that being put in jail would never break his spirit. He became, his owner said, unruly, insubordinate, and disobedient. Incarceration had "no effect on his bearing or his insurrectionary spirit." Indeed, even in jail Peter boasted "of his freedom from all fear or restraint."[39]

How and When Slaves Absconded

Although the spectacular escapes depicted in slave narratives and abolitionist literature were not without their basis in fact, the great majority of runaways left neither dramatically nor in the end successfully. Rather, they sneaked off at night, on Saturday afternoon or

Sunday, or during holidays; they stowed away on sailing vessels and steamboats, crawled into the back of wagons, concealed themselves in barns, outbuildings, or abandoned houses; they camped out in the woods and swamps. A few rode off on their owners' horses or with their wagons or gigs. By the 1840s and 1850s, some slipped aboard trains or attempted to purchase tickets as free persons.[40]

Despite the unique circumstances surrounding each flight, slaves confronted a number of choices about whether they should run away alone, with members of their families, or in groups; whether they should attempt to use written passes, don a disguise, seek assistance from whites or free blacks, leave at a certain time; and whether or not they should strike out for a city, a remote area near the plantation, or to some distant land. Even in the early period, certain patterns emerged with regard to how and when slaves absconded. By then, the number of African- and West Indian–born slaves in the South had declined significantly, and American-born slaves, now second and third generation, were dominant. As in other aspects of the runaway's profile, there were only modest changes between the early and the later periods, and those that did occur were a result of virtual elimination of African-born blacks in the slave population.

In both periods, a large proportion of runaways set out alone. In the early period, nearly 80 percent in Virginia were alone, 71 percent in North Carolina, and between 51 and 57 percent in Tennessee, South Carolina, and Louisiana; the average in the five states was 60 percent. In the Lower South and Tennessee, there were eighty-eight African-born slaves, compared with none in Virginia and two in North Carolina. Africans were twice as likely as creoles to leave in groups, and their presence pulled the individual runaway percentages down in South Carolina, Louisiana, and Tennessee to slightly more than half. By the late period, the proportion of slaves who absconded alone in the five states had risen to 72 percent. This ranged from slightly more than 60 percent for Tennessee, to two-thirds in Virginia and North Carolina, to 73 percent in South Carolina and 82 percent in Louisiana. By then, those who ran away in groups were more likely to abscond with one or two others, and those in groups of five or more represented a meager 5 percent of the runaway population.[41] In short, by the 1840s and 1850s, the vast majority of runaways—95 percent—struck out on their own or with one or two others.

The "others" included slaves living on the same plantation, belonging to the same owner, working on the same projects, or hired out in the same industries. They also included slaves belonging to the same estate, to the same deceased owner, or the same new owner. Blacks absconded together after committing crimes in collusion with one another or when they were about to be sold, occasionally after plotting with fellow slaves on a neighboring plantation. The largest group of "others" in the runaway population included slaves belonging to the same owner or to members of the same family. Various family members comprised about one out of three of the "others" in the early period, and about one out of four in the late period.

Similarly, only small changes occurred in the profile among hired and skilled runaways, those who obtained false papers, or who were literate. In both periods, between 2 and 4 percent of the runaways were hired slaves and 15 percent possessed special skills as house servants, artisans, tailors, seamstresses, cooks, barbers, waiters, butlers, laundresses, or vendors. In both periods, 7 percent of the runaways were believed to be carrying forged freedom papers or owners' passes, while the literacy rate among absconders between the early and late periods rose from about 2 percent to 4 percent. It appears that the proportion of hired runaways was somewhat smaller than the proportion of hirelings in the general slave population, while the percentage of runaways who were literate was about the same, and those with special skills slightly higher than in the general population.[42]

As suggested by the small percentage who carried—or were believed to carry—false papers, it was not easy to obtain forged papers. The problem was further exacerbated if a recipient were illiterate, as most were, and his or her explanation did not coincide with what was written on the forged documents. Occasionally field hands did obtain counterfeit certificates, but it was usually city slaves who obtained papers and attempted to pose either as self-hired slaves or free blacks. The New Orleans mulatto Robert, who ran away in August 1839, produced papers saying he had permission to hire himself out. Another Crescent City slave, Lewis, secured a pass to visit his wife, and since that time, his master noted, "I have not seen him." The Charleston drayman Frank posed as a free person of color and wore a fake badge "as a protection against being committed."[43]

Slaves who obtained passes or wrote them for themselves were described as intelligent, artful, and "plausible" men and women who appeared "to be very truthful." Virginia master Hopewell Parsons told readers that his slave Eve possessed a "signed" document saying that she was Henry Cooper's emancipated slave Sally Cole. Eve used the document to her advantage, remaining at large for nearly a year. A Tennessee owner said his slave obtained a pass "from some person in the neighborhood" and was heading for Ohio or Virginia. The owner of Georgia carpenter Jacob said his slave obtained "a sealed pass, endorsed 'a pass for Jacob from Oglethorpe County Georgia, to the State of Delaware.' " It said that he should be permitted to ride any stage coach. He was last seen on the main road heading north out of Columbia, South Carolina.[44]

Literate slaves sometimes wrote their own passes. Kitt was a "very likely fellow," could read and write, and would probably "furnish himself with a pass," one New London, Virginia, owner wrote in 1805. "He is very intelligent," one advertisement said of a slave who escaped from a private jail in Richmond. The runaway could read and write very well; there was little doubt he would "have in his possession Forged Papers and Passes." The mulatto Charleston tailor Joshua, who belonged to the estate of Sabina Hall, could read and write and "may attempt to pass by forged papers as free." "There can be little doubt of his attempting to pass as a free man," the owner of Richmond slave Samuel Barker said in 1805, "as a forged certificate of his freedom was found the day after he went off."[45]

The effective use of papers is illustrated by the field hand Levi, who escaped in 1850 from a plantation near Goldsboro, North Carolina. He stole the manumission deeds of Luke and Ned Hall, free blacks in the neighborhood. Attempting to use Luke Hall's papers to board a train, he was detected and the papers confiscated. But Levi escaped, and with a second set of papers, he journeyed to the hamlet of Black Creek, about twenty miles from Goldsboro in Wayne County, where he inquired of a station master how he could get to Raleigh. This was probably a ploy, Levi's owner James G. Edwards explained, and "it is suspected that he may still be lurking somewhere in this region."[46]

The moment in time chosen by slaves to run away was in part determined by individual circumstances—sale of a child, punishment of a wife or husband, a severe whipping, the decision of a master to move, the death of an owner—but a number were biding their time until they were sure that their absence would not be immediately detected or that the weather would not be a hindrance. Among the runaways whose exact departure time could be determined from newspaper notices (611 of 695 in the early period, 1,073 of 1,316 in the late period), there were similar seasonal trends. In both periods, the number of runaways in the autumn months dropped, when harvesting made surveillance close. Between 17 and 18 percent of runaways left between late September and late December. In the winter-spring-summer, the numbers increased. Although there were variations among states, by the later period the numbers of runaways by season, excluding autumn, were almost identical: 296 in the winter, 289 in the spring, and 295 in the summer, about 27 percent per season.

African-born Runaways

In many ways, then, there was a remarkable continuity over a period of seventy years in the profile of runaways. The largest single disparity involved African-born runaways. In the late period, there were only three among the entire population, but in the early period, as indicated previously, there were 90 runaways among the 695, or 13 percent, who were Africans. As would be expected, their profile is unique. Indeed, many of the differences between the two periods were the result of the Africans, who made up a small but significant group of the early runaways.[47]

Even more than the American-born, African-born runaways were predominantly male (88 percent) and described as black or very black (90 percent), but their age groupings were not unlike other runaways, being mostly in their teens and twenties. There were none, however, who were beyond their thirties, and the proportion of those twelve or under was several times that of the American-born, as African-born parents more often took their children with them during flight. None was literate, one was said to have a pass, and one out of eight was said to be bilingual. Besides these differences, among African-born slaves nearly two-thirds (58 of 90) ran away in groups of two or more, and one-third (30 of 90) in groups of five or more; while among American-born slaves, one-third (223 of 605) ran away in groups of two or more and 14 percent (84 of 605) in groups of five or more. Among the African-born to an even greater extent than among creole slaves, those setting off together were members of the same families or kinship groups.

The physical characteristics of African-born slaves were more obvious than for any group of runaways. Described as Mandingo, Ebo, "Congo," "Guinea," or African, in most cases, their appearance was not unlike Nuncanna, a slave who lived on a farm in Tennessee. Absconding with two other African-born slaves in 1815, Nuncanna was about thirty years old, with "very long fore-teeth, appearing sharp as if the ends of them had been filed." He spoke "very bad English" and was marked "by the African mark." Other African-born runaways also had filed teeth and had marks of their "nation" on their cheeks, noses, forehead, and chins. The "Guinea negress" Rosalie in Louisiana, for example, had "marks of her country" on both sides of her face; while the Congo black Carloe had tattoos "from the ears to the eyes."[48]

Even in the 1820s and 1830s, the physical appearance of African-born slaves, now very few in number, had not changed significantly. Rosalia, alias Felicite, a forty-two-year-old woman, was owned by a New Orleans physician. Her master spoke disparagingly of her: she had "a stupid countenance," spoke almost no English and only "broken French," and had "marks of her country" on her cheeks. Despite her owner's remarks, in 1834 she left her employer, crossed the Mississippi River, journeyed to the suburb of Lafayette, then traveled to the various plantations where she had "many acquaintances." During her journey, she told anyone who questioned her that she had her owner's permission to seek a new owner. The few who spoke English or had in various ways adjusted to their new environment were still identified by their homeland: Congo-born Rose of Louisiana, who spoke French, English, and Spanish; the "African negro" Antoine who ran away from auctioneers in New Orleans; and "African" Billy who ran from a plantation South Carolina.[49]

Thus, the profile of a runaway reveals a diversity in origin, appearance, language, skills, color, physique, gender, and age. There were African-born blacks, slaves who spoke only French or Spanish, slaves who were highly skilled and privileged, others who worked in the fields. There were young boys and girls, and elderly men and women. There were some who began absconding at age eight and ten; there was a fourteen-year-old youngster who stood four feet seven and a half inches tall; and there were old men described as feeble, scared, crippled, and "quite grey."[50]

Yet, there was remarkable continuity over time and in different states in the profile of a runaway. It would probably be difficult to find any group in the United States that changed less over a period of seventy years. When one considers the expansion of slavery across the Appalachians, the growth and expanding economic base of free blacks, and the increase of the slaveholding class, the similarities among runaways—in gender, age, color, physical characteristics, appearance, personality traits, and methods of absconding—seem all the more remarkable. The persistence was not because those who ran away were successful or even because the young men who left in greatest numbers could best endure punishment following capture. Rather, it revealed the nature of slave resistance: those who could best defy the system with even a remote chance of success—young, strong, healthy, intelligent men—continued to do so relentlessly from one generation to the next.

10

Managing Human Property

ON THE THIRD SUNDAY IN JANUARY 1854, William J. Rowe took charge of Palestine, soon to be christened Morville Plantation, in Concordia Parish, Louisiana. Hired as manager and overseer by Eustace Surget, a member of one of the richest slaveholding families in Mississippi and Louisiana, Rowe found "all well" and counted 46 "negroes on the place." Located about ten miles south of Vidalia and comprising some 1,638 acres valued in 1861 at $81,000, Morville was not especially unique, boasting 17 mules, 23 horses, 10 oxen, 24 cattle, and machinery. Nor was the plantation unusual in the expansion that occurred during the 1850s. By the end of 1854, 18 slaves were added by purchase or transfer. By the end of 1855, 48 sheep were added to the livestock. By 1860, the slave force had risen to 115, while 569 bales of cotton were sent to market.

What was unusual was that Rowe, and his successor in 1855, T. D. Clement, kept a record of plantation runaways. The numerous entries created an astonishing picture of plantation turmoil and slave resistance. The notations concerning punishments were equally remarkable: both managers responded in an almost perfunctory, nonchalant manner, as if such conditions—numerous runaways and repeat offenders—were simply an unavoidable aspect of plantation life. During a four-month stretch in the late spring and summer of 1854, Rowe listed eight men who ran away at least once, including Albert, Anthony, Jerry, George, David, Lewis, Edmund, and Ellick Stallian; he listed three slaves who ran away twice, including Martha, Elisha, and Sam King. This was an average of three incidents per month. Most of the slaves remained out only a few weeks. "Martha went off this morning," Rowe wrote on 19 May 1854, noting ten days later that he retrieved her from the Vidalia jail. Rowe put some of the men in stocks for a few days. Others, like Sam King and Jerry, he took to the black-smith who "put Irons on their necks and one leg of each boy."

Apparently the punishments had little effect. The next year, despite a new overseer, the number of runaways, including repeats, continued apace. During 1855, T. D. Clement, while not as precise a record keeper as his predecessor, named eighteen slaves in thirty-six separate run-away incidents. Except for September 15–18, October 12–November 1, November 15–December 12, and December 17–21, there was at least one hand out each day. On 14 March 1855, seven slaves were gone, roughly 10 percent of the slave force. In all, fourteen of the eighteen runaways were male. George absconded nine times during the year; Edmund four times; Ellick Stallian, Elisha, and Butler three times each. Sam King remained out nearly six months, Ellick Stallian was gone for 55 days, and Elisha stayed away for 43 days. The average absence was fifteen days. In all, a total of 543 "man-days" were lost on Mor-ville in a single year.[1]

According to historian William Scarborough, this was unusual among the largest planters in the South. But the record of one plan-tation reveals a good deal about plantation management. First, plan-tation owners and managers expected a certain number of slaves to run away, as a matter of course. Firm and consistent punishment might slow such "offences" but never stop them altogether. On Mor-ville, some of the worst offenders were put in stocks for up to a week. Second, production could actually go up if slaves were driven hard enough, even in the midst of such turbulence. Working half-days Sat-urday, with Sundays and one holiday each year off, planters could produce good results. In the case of Morville, between 1854–55 and 1855–56 there was a 300 percent increase in the number of bales of cotton sent to market (60 to 250 bales) despite what an outsider might consider severe labor unrest. Lastly, managers and overseers struggled to solve this problem, tightening discipline, increasing workloads, in-creasing punishments, and honing methods of capturing and returning runaways. As they did so, more slaves ran away.

Managers and Overseers

Overseeing a plantation was at best a difficult undertaking. Managers were asked to be firm, fair, and demanding as well as vigilant, com-passionate, and strict. They were told to punish slaves who did not adhere to plantation rules but never to use threats or excessive force. They were expected to go to the fields with the hands; remain there until the end of each day; keep an eye on livestock, farm machinery, and the storehouse; and maintain accurate records of how slaves worked. They should do everything in their power, one slave owner instructed, to protect pregnant women and "sucklers"—every baby was worth several hundred dollars—and in other ways protect "the condition and value of the negroes." They should be knowledgeable about the plantation and know how and when to plant a crop, correct slaves, appoint drivers, organize a work routine, and produce a good crop. "A good crop means one that is good taking into consideration every thing," a planter in the Yazoo-Mississippi Delta wrote respecting the management of his estate, "hands, breeding women, children, mules, Stocks, provisions, farming utensils of all Sorts & Keeping up land, ditches, fences."[2]

Those who could bring in "a good crop" were in great demand, especially during the decades preceding the Civil War as the plantation system expanded in many regions. "If you have the courage to drive Negroes," a Demopolis, Alabama, man wrote a friend in North Carolina in 1859, "there are overseers about here no larger man than you are who are getting" as much as one thousand dollars a year. In Alabama, as elsewhere, they were hired almost exclusively by "planters"—those with at least twenty slaves—and even among the planters, those with twenty or twenty-five slaves could sometimes not afford to hire overseers. It was a matter of prestige, however, to have an overseer, and whenever possible, slave owners hired someone to take care of the day-to-day operations.[3] The large slaveholders—those with at least fifty in the slave force—relied almost exclusively on managers and/or overseers, men who lived on the plantation, often in small houses near the quarters, and were responsible for maintaining control, order, and discipline "among the negroes." On the largest estates there was a chain of command, with managers administering overseers, who administered slave drivers, who watched over the slaves.

Among the many problems overseers dealt with—bad weather, insects, disease, theft, low yields, owner dissatisfaction—one of the most vexing and troublesome was runaway slaves. It was a problem that confronted the vast majority of managers, and one that seemed to have no solution. It did not seem to matter whether they cajoled, chastised, or severely punished offenders; whether they threatened to sell, trade, or transfer loved ones; whether they gave cash payments, allowed special privileges, or permitted visits to town. Whatever method they tried, slaves continued to run away, alone or with their families, young and old, men and women. At times they intentionally disrupted the work routine, setting out at the peak of the planting or harvesting season. At other times, they left during a slow time or during the Christmas holiday season. It was the overseer's responsibility to prevent such transgressions, capture and return the derelicts, and punish the wrongdoers.

Prevention was a difficult undertaking. In fact, most overseers came to the conclusion that they would never be able to "eradicate the evil," even if they were to put their trust in slaves, and most did not. South Carolina overseer William Capers, who had worked for a succession of large rice planters from Georgetown to the Savannah River, recalled the advice given him by his uncle with regard to managing slaves. It was the best he had ever heard: "if a Man put his confidence in a Negro He was simply a Damned Fool." John Merriman, who managed a plantation in southern Louisiana, learned this from experience. "Linzy had no earthly grounds for leaving, nor his wife either," Merriman wrote in 1840. When he discovered that Linzy had also made off with a double-barreled shotgun, he remarked: "So much for letting the most trusty have fire arms."[4] The best way to deal with this type of behavior, a number of overseers came to believe, was by wielding the whip. To flog obdurate slaves in the presence of family members and other slaves, they said, was a good way to discourage misconduct.

But most overseers lacked experience and often found themselves being tested from the moment they arrived at the plantation. "Some of the negroes are endeavoring to try the mettle and temper of the new overseer," a Louisiana planter wrote in 1842. "Ned gave him some trouble and threatened not to live under his management." Ned was usually "a quiet well disposed negro" and was probably induced to challenge the overseer by other slaves, the master concluded. "As he escaped punishment for running away when I discharged the late overseer, I thought it best to punish him wch I did pretty severely." In other cases, new overseers seemed incapable of managing and controlling slaves and called on others to assist them. One admitted he could do little to allay "disturbances among the negroes." Many new managers were tested daily, as slaves challenged their authority and refused to obey their orders. As a result, overseers left or were fired regularly. "My Irish Overseer quit me on Sunday—and I am without an overseer," one Louisiana planter said in 1841, matching the experiences of his neighbors. It was a slow period, and he believed he was "better off without one."[5]

But even overseers as experienced and cynical as William Capers faced problems of how and when to employ extreme punishments, whether brutal reprisals might create a brooding, vengeful workforce, or worse, precipitate additional runaways. Sometimes even the mildest correction could result in an extreme response. Overseer William

Jacobs found himself in such a situation in 1837 when he disciplined a black woman, and the woman's husband threatened him with a knife. In his report to the plantation owner, Jacobs paraphrased the husband's response: "I had abused his wife and that he was not going to put up with it and that I was an unjust man and that I might go get my gun and Kill him & bury him but that he was not a going to put up with any other punishment of himself or family." A short time later, the slave vanished.[6]

At various times, overseers spent a good deal of time tracking down runaways. "I have not been able to Ketch that Boy as yet," one wrote in 1839. "I saw his sign today and find that he can run yet so I think he is not hurt very Bad." "I have not had the good luck to catch Lew yet and have offered $25 reward for him," another wrote Lew's owner in Lynchburg, Virginia. "His staying out so long will have a bad affect on the rest of the negroes and I though[t] it best to get him as soon as possible." Three weeks later, Lew was "still out beating about the place every night or two but as yet Keeps out of my reach." John Betson Traylor served as overseer for a number of planters but had the same trouble. He noted in his diary in March 1834: "Abrom runaway for nothing," and ten days later "Went to Mr. Crumton's mills to catch a runaway negro he was caut the night before and got a way agane and I did not see him his name is Abrom."[7] Overseers found it difficult to spend more than a few days pursuing slaves, and even then they were forced to leave the plantation under minimal supervision.

When they did come across outlying slaves, overseers were sometimes surprised at their fierce resistance. Archibald Hyman, an overseer in Northampton County, North Carolina, followed the slave Washington into the woods and "undertook to whip him for his Conduct." The slave, however, "raised his Hoe at Me and Swore that I Should Not whip him, I then ordered the Negros to take him, he then Swore that if one of them laid hands on him he would give them the hoe. he then left for the woods again." Others who pursued runaways carried their own weapons. The overseer of a Terrebonne Parish, Louisiana, estate spent an entire day in the woods hunting the escaped slave Isum, who had assaulted him and run off. When he discovered Isum, he did not wait for him to surrender but simply shot him four times in the hips and legs. Chandler Brown and William Dunn, overseers in St. Paul's Parish, South Carolina, were also armed when they set out to search for a gang of runaways, but the table was turned when they came upon their prey. Both were shot; Brown died from his wounds, and Dunn barely survived.[8]

If runaways avoided capture in the period immediately following their departure, overseers looked to other means to reclaim them. They hired slave catchers, with their packs of hounds; sent descriptions to local authorities; and as a last resort, placed an advertisement in newspapers that offered a reward. These actions were usually taken in consultation with plantation owners. For some overseers placing notices would have entailed a large amount of time and effort, such as on the Morville Plantation. The delay between the time when slaves set out and when advertisements were placed indicates that a significant proportion of overseers, managers, and owners spent the first few weeks hunting outlyers themselves or waiting for them to return of their own accord. In the early period, one out of four advertisers waited at least four weeks before placing their notice, and 7 percent waited more than four months. During the 1840s and 1850s, one out of three advertisers waited at least four weeks before placing a notice, and one out of ten waited at least four months. Thus, despite improved transportation and easier access to local and state newspapers, owners and managers were taking longer to place their notices. The overseer of John Henry Eaton's estate in Tennessee, for example, waited nearly a month before advertising for Claiborne, a slave about forty years old. He was among a growing number of overseers who waited for runaways to return or be captured.[9]

When these efforts failed, overseers alerted jailers, justices of the peace, sheriffs, friends, neighbors, and planters who owned relatives of runaways. They read newspaper notices for listings of recent arrests. And they sought to allay the concerns of their employers with regard to why slaves under their supervision went on the run. "I am very sorry that this difficulty has arisen with so usefull a hand," one overseer wrote his employer concerning a hired runaway; "and you may early discover Madam from what pased at the time that he left his business without any apprehention of punishment."[10]

But following his capture, it was highly likely he would indeed be punished. On most plantations, overseers were given instructions about the amount of corporal punishment to be administered, but they were also permitted a degree of latitude. The punishments for runaways included placing them in irons or shackles, putting them in stocks, leaving them in jail, and, most commonly, whipping. "The highest punishment must not exceed 100 lashes in one day," a South Carolina planter instructed his overseer. For a first offense, an overseer might administer a mild correction, but even then the number of lashes might exceed 50, and on some plantations runaways routinely received 100 stripes. Overseers whipped runaways with a leather strap, eighteen inches long and two inches wide, fastened to a wooden handle; or with a "rawhide" or "cowskin" whip, a strip of untanned ox hide three feet long and tapering to a point at the end.[11]

The problems overseers faced in attempting to deal with runaways and the difficulties this group experienced in the smooth management of a plantation were well illustrated in a report written in 1816 by Roswell King to Pierce Butler concerning the slave Jimoney, who "was out a whole week in the woods." The slave said he had been insulted by a black driver.

> His excuse for going off was mere nothing, had got affronted with his driver. After talking to him as I thot sufficient I gave him his choice to loose his next clothing, or to pay up his lost time in Sundays work. As you could not be the looser & I advised him to do the work, which he had done and all accounts Settled. I am sure that is better than to have given him 100 lashes.

After many years experience, and numerous floggings for lying out, King had come to realize that it was virtually impossible to halt the practice. He had tried the harshest punishments, administering 100 stripes on many occasions, now he would try the mildest.[12]

Few overseers were able to solve the problem of slaves running away, whatever the method of correction. Indeed, many of them were young, inexperienced men incapable of coping with the complex problems of managing a large plantation. They came and went, sometimes remaining for only a few months and rarely more than a few years. They frequently left the "profession" entirely after failing to satisfy their employers. The difficulties overseers faced were how to maintain an effective workforce in the midst of such turmoil, how to search for runaways without disrupting the plantation routine, and how to correct runaways without damaging valuable property. They never solved these dilemmas. The best they could do was to pursue, capture, and punish the many offenders.[13]

What Should Masters Do?

There was no doubt in his mind, one anonymous planter near the Georgia-Alabama line wrote in 1851, that "firmness, decision and uniformity" were the best means of governing slaves. Owners who stormed, shouted, and raged could not effectively manage their property. "He who fights most, and blusters most, and threatens most is not the man who has the most work done, or who keeps his operatives under best government," he continued; storms of passion would inevitably result in "trouble, rebellions and runaways." Owners should "keep a vigilant patrol on their own premises," a group of Virginia slaveholders added, "make frequent nightly examinations of their negro quarters and not permit any slave to leave the premises without a written permission."[14]

Other planters echoed these sentiments. In the management of slaves, there should always "be perfect uniformity of conduct toward them," punishment should be moderate but certain—nothing was worse than harsh corrections "irregularly inflicted." Yet no slave should be allowed to break plantation rules without being punished. "Every person should be made perfectly to understand what they are punished for," another planter added, "and should be made to perceive that they are not punished in anger, or through caprice."[15]

Such advice came from the pages of periodicals such as *De Bow's Review, Southern Cultivator, Farmer's Register, Carolina Planter,* and *Farmer and Planter,* in articles "On the Management of Slaves," "The Management of Negroes," "Judicious Management of the Plantation Force," "Moral Management of Negroes," and "Management of Slaves." It also came in conversations and correspondence between slaveholders. Indeed, there seemed to be no end to discussions about how to manage slaves, what incentives to offer, what liberties to grant, what penalties to inflict, and how to respond to slaves who refused to obey the rules.[16]

Yet there was almost complete silence about how to manage slaves who refused to be managed; who scoffed at punishments no matter how painful; who remained belligerent, hate-filled, and violent; and who constantly struck for freedom. The reasoned and logical discussions about management techniques bore little resemblance to conditions on most plantations. Nor did they provide much help in dealing with runaways. Even to discuss the problem, except on a case-by-case basis, would be to acknowledge the depth of discontent among slaves. It would also reveal the failure of slave owners to deal effectively with this problem.

In both the early and late periods, the great majority of slaveholders in the South were forced at one time or another to deal with runaways. It was a rare owner, large or small, who could boast that he had never had a slave abscond from his farm or plantation. It was also a rare owner, even among the largest planters, with fifty or more slaves, who did not deal with this problem personally. Those who hired managers and overseers became involved in the punishment phase or in the sale of especially recalcitrant slaves, while masters who could not afford overseers became involved in pursuing, capturing, punishing, and, if necessary, selling runaways. For most of the nonplanter class, runaways not only posed control problems but represented a significant loss in time and money.[17]

How did masters deal with this perennial problem? What actions did they take? How successful were their solutions? The largest slave-holders seemed to expect a certain number of runaways each year. Indeed, they established a routine for capturing, returning, and correcting absentees that was almost casual. For privileged slaves who ran off rarely, the punishment was usually mild. The situation with Thomas Chaplin's slave Jim was probably typical in this regard. Jim was a slave of many talents: he ginned cotton, did carpentry, and could take on a host of jobs for his South Carolina owner. He made fence gates, dug wells, fashioned shafts for ox carts, erected hog pens, and built trunks for dams to protect the fields from flooding. Though surprised when he ran away, upon his return fourteen days later, Chaplin "Gave Jim a very moderate punishment, say about 60 paddles, put on his bare hide, with my own hands." Soon after, Jim's privileges and possessions, which Chaplin had confiscated while he was out, were restored.[18]

It was clear that even with slaves constantly taking to the woods and lying out the master's production and profits would not be seriously damaged, so small was the cost of sustaining slaves compared with the profits generated from the sale of staple crops. With regard to lost labor, one response was to push harder the slaves remaining behind. One overseer, noting that on his plantation "the negroes ran away a great deal—they [dislike me] so much," explained that runaways generally returned "within a fortnight." If they did not or if too many of them went off at once, he would make the others work on Sundays and deprive them of special privileges. "The negroes on the plantation could always bring [missing slaves] in if they chose to," he said. The outlyers "depended on them for their food, and they had only to stop the supplies to oblige them to surrender." Since those who went out were usually brought back within the fortnight, they did not represent a serious economic loss nor did the temporary loss of hands mean the work could not be transferred to those who remained behind.[19]

The largest planters had the luxury of transferring slaves from one plantation to another or to a different location and different occupation. Rather than selling two slaves who ran away in 1833 from his St. Mary Parish estate in Louisiana, David Weeks sent them to his Grand Cote Plantation, located on a remote and desolate island laced with bayous and swamps. Though relatively close to their original location, escape from Grand Cote was much more difficult. The plantation was "in a remote corner of the Globe," one observer noted. Running away was not only dangerous but usually unsuccessful. In 1842, J. N. Taylor of Alabama wrote his friend and business associate Franklin H. Elmore of Columbia, South Carolina, concerning the future of several slaves. "I send also a likely young fellow by name Dick of Mr. Rhetts," Taylor said, "he is a great runaway but a prime Hand and I think at your iron works will be valuable."[20]

Some planters constructed jails or erected stocks. One traveler asked a slave about the apparatus he saw on one plantation. "Dat ting, massa?" the slave said looking at a wooden structure containing various sized holes; "well, sah, we calls that a ting to put black people, niggers in, when dey misbehaves bad, and put runaways in, sah. Heaps o' runaways, dis country, sah. Yes, sah, heaps on 'em round here."[21] The worst offenders were sent to jail, turned over to slave "breakers"—men whose business it was to break slaves of "bad" behavior— and, usually as a last resort, traded or sold. Most large owners preferred not to employ drastic solutions. Compared with the number of slaves who went out, they employed them only in extreme circumstances.

Smaller planters and farmers viewed runaways in a quite different light. Each runaway represented for them a potential loss that was far more significant. Whites who owned fewer than fifty slaves, and especially those who owned only a few families, often attempted to reform their slaves' behavior before punishing them severely or selling them or their children. "I am truly sorry to hear that he is such a villain," one slaveholder wrote to his plantation manager concerning a black man named Caesar; "he deserves and should get a proper chastisement for it—before you take him from that jail let him Know that you have the control over him, and as to his mother's threats I would soon teach her who was master of the premises." Failing this "hire him out, or as the last resort send him here and we will make him useful."[22]

When it became clear, however, that such reform efforts had failed, owners often responded with severe penalties. The scars on the backs of runaways and the severe whippings for repeat offenders bore witness to the emotion, frustration, and anger of owners who could not control intractable slaves. What might happen when masters became incensed at runaways was revealed in the responses of Georgia owner Wiley Brooks, Virginia master John Gardner, and Louisiana planter William Hamilton. In 1817, the twenty-five-year-old slave March, a constant runaway, threatened to assault his owner Wiley Brooks and absconded into the woods. Determined to put an end to such behavior, Brooks offered a reward for March's apprehension dead or alive. The slave not only threatened him, Brooks said; he "also had spite and malice against all the citizens of Pulaski County." Scouring the woods where "diverse other runaway negroes" were known to hide out, a group of whites came across March. They ordered him to surrender.

When he "attempted to effect his escape by running off," one of the
men, John Grant, shot the slave in the "legs or thighs." They carried
March back to his owner's plantation and collected their reward. After
they left, Brooks began to whip the wounded slave and, when he grew
weary, ordered "other persons" to continue the whipping. March lay
quivering on the ground, and two days later, he died.[23]

It was not revealed whether Hannah, a young black woman in
Southampton County, Virginia, had absconded before, but when her
master began to whip her for allegedly stealing eleven dollars, she ran
off. John Gardner pursued her and brought her back. He then "took
Hannah and stript her & tied her to [a] lim & whipt her," a member
of the Gardner family said, and kept flogging her for an hour and a
half or two hours. Several family members pleaded with him to stop.
The girl's tongue became "dry & white." Bystanders asked if they
might give her some water. Gardner replied that "he'd be dam'd if she
should ever eat or drink again unless he got the money." The flogging
continued until he "wore out one whip on her," and her back was
"very much lacerated," with one of her eyes swollen nearly shut.
Under such "great torture," one observer said, she cried "dreadful"
cries. At supper time, word came "the girl Hannah was dead & [the
owner] wanted assistance in laying her out."[24]

Troubled with runaways, John A. Hamilton took matters into his
own hands. "John has taken to the woods and I am afraid for good,"
Hamilton wrote to his father in 1851, "I have punished him very
severely lately for his rascality." In hunting the woods for John, he
came across a group of outlyers sitting around a campfire about to
have their supper. "I waked them up with the contents of my gun,"
he boasted; "such scampering you never did see." He killed several
slaves; indeed only "one of the flock" was saved, a young man belonging to a physician named Smith. Even the survivor was "very
badly wounded and may in all probability be disabled for life, the same
boy has been shot twice this year, and once before by me," Hamilton
explained. "I only regret it was not John."[25]

Such vehemence showed what could happen if slaves refused to
submit to authority. Other owners as well became enraged, although
punishments usually did not result in death. Besides whipping and
physical abuse, many masters also decided to put their most recalcitrant slaves on the auction block. No matter how widespread their
reputation or how many times they ran away, the intractable ones
could be sold. It was well known in Giles County, Tennessee, that the
slave man about to be sold was "in the habit of running away &
staying in the woods at all seasons of the year—that his life & health
are endangered by this habit." When the twenty-four-year-old man,

described as "very likely" except for his habit of running away, was sold in 1856 at the courthouse in Pulaski, the bidding went up to $998 before the gavel sounded. Similarly, it was well known to residents of Maury County, Tennessee, that Charlotte Wilson's slave Sam was "wild, ungovernable and of vic[i]ous habits—that he has already run away once or twice and came very near making his escape to a Free State." Described as a "likely boy about forty five years of age," he nonetheless brought a bid of $872 in 1854 at the Market House in Columbia.[26]

Some owners became so frustrated that they were willing to sell their slaves at reduced prices merely to rid themselves of the problems associated with pursuit and capture. Isaac Ferrell's slave Dick on John's Island, South Carolina, not only ran away many times, but also threatened physical resistance. In 1830, Ferrell placed an advertisement in the *Charleston Mercury* saying that Dick was out again. He was offering $100—an extremely large reward—to anyone who would deliver him to the Work House "without material injury, so that I get him." But he was also willing to sell Dick, who was worth $500, for only $300 to anyone "disposed to purchase the said Dick, as he now runs." The guardian of a slave-owning minor in Florida had made repeated attempts to retrieve a runaway named Pompey. During a three-year period, he did so only once, and then it was only for a few weeks. Informed that there were slave catchers in a nearby county who would purchase slaves "at a fair price" while they were still on the run, the guardian decided to sell Pompey as he remained in the woods. When two of his recently acquired slaves, Ned and Sampson, ran away shortly after purchase, an Alabama owner said he planned a quick resale. "I am resolved not to keep a mean negro."[27]

Not only were these slaves ungovernable, owners contended, but they exerted a pernicious influence on other slaves. A Tennessee plantation mistress explained that, in addition to her slave's own "bad conduct, he exercises a bad influence upon other negroes, especially the younger slaves." She thought it best that he "be taken out of the county & sold." Two of her overseers echoed these feelings: slaves who refused to conform had a "corrupting influence upon other negroes," particularly the younger ones, and should be auctioned off as quickly as possible. The "negro fellow named Bob," wrote estate executor George W. Allen in 1809, confined in jail after being arrested as a runaway, was a dissatisfied Negro, "and conducts himself in the gang of the said Estates Negroes highly improperly." It was important that Bob be sold since one obdurate slave might exert control over the others. He asked and received permission "to dispose of said negro at public Sale." The runaway Abner "conducted himself with such gross impropriety" and was so "incorrigible" that his example would "Corrupt the morals of the negroes." The owner of George made the same argument: he was "an ill disposed Negro . . . whose conduct may injure the morals of the other servants." It was for their benefit that the slave should be "sold to a person who lives in a remote part of the United States."[28]

Maryland owners also believed that certain evilly disposed slaves had a detrimental influence on the others. They, too, could not understand why some slaves became turbulent, disobedient, and ungovernable. Did they not treat them well? And did they not promise some of them freedom in the future? In 1843, Rezin Hammond of Anne Arundel County purchased a slave named Horace, who was to be freed by an act of a previous owner in 1855. Though treated kindly, Horace became "notoriously vicious and turbulent, often disobedient and almost useless." He ran away many times. Another owner said that his slave became "turbulent and unmanageable," and that his disposition was a "great injury to the other negroes of your petitioner and of the Negroes of his neighbours." Another said that his man Brice was "totally intractable and unmanageable and that he cannot safely keep him in his Service."[29]

Owners in Maryland responded by altering and revising the gradual manumission process. As term slaves continued to run away, owners went to court and had the length of their servitude extended, and they gained permission to sell them out of the state. Kitty Reynolds of Washington County made a bequest in her will that her slave Jacob Younker should go to a family member following her death but should be freed in 1869. Reynolds died in 1857, and Younker promptly ran away to Pennsylvania. After a good deal of expense and trouble, the heirs brought the slave back; they obtained an extension of his servitude to 1879 and obtained permission to sell him out of the state.[30]

Owners were especially angered when slaves ran away to the North. Retrieval was difficult, costly, time-consuming, and often unsuccessful. Even when fugitives were captured and returned, the cost might exceed the price of the slave. One man spent about $250 recovering a female slave when she absconded to Pennsylvania. Despite his father's wish that the slave be freed in five years, the son extended her term of slavery by a decade and sold her out of the state.[31]

If some runaways could be easily put on the auction block, it was not so simple to sell other runaways, especially when family attachments had been formed and whites believed that a slave's behavior might change. "I this morning recd your letter of the 13th inst. and have had a talk with Lewis," the cousin of an Alabama slaveholder wrote in 1859 about a runaway who had been purposely sent off to be sold away from his wife as punishment.

> [Lewis] expresses sorrow for what he has done, and I think he will be a better servant in the future for having been subjected to the fright of being sold from his family. I think he feels the separation much more than you supposed. He says if you take him back you shall never have cause to complain of him again.

The cousin recommended the slave not be sold. The owner's wife seconded this opinion. "I regret exceedingly that I left home at the time I did for I think if I had been here you would have not sent him off so hastily without finding out more," she said. Lewis's wife was so distressed about it that it made the owner's wife "perfectly miserable." A short time later, the sale was aborted, and Lewis was returned to his wife.[32]

A gift from her grandfather to Sophia Freeman of Baltimore, Maryland, the young slave girl named Rose, about twelve years old, caused her owners no end of grief. Since the granddaughter was still a minor, the mother, Rebecca Freeman, was responsible for hiring the slave out, but she found that Rose was "so bad and her habits so vicious and incorrigible" that none of her employers "would retain her in service." The mother said that Rose was in the habit of running away frequently and was "prone to falsehood & theft." In one last effort, "hoping that she might find a place where she might be governed," the mother sent Rose to an old gentleman known for his kindness toward black people, but Rose remained "so intolerably bad," the mother lamented, that even this did not make any difference. She would have to be sold. It was similarly difficult for James Luckett to dispose of Dennis Williams, who absconded in 1859 and was captured and jailed. The master had treated him with kindness, "as a master should treat his slave," but the owner was now convinced that "if he were to take him again into his family, or release him from confinement, he would again abscond" and this time "escape into some free state."[33]

Other slaveholders noted how they had made every attempt to reform their slaves' behavior. The husband of a Georgia owner complained that three of his wife's slaves were chronic runaways—they had recently been out eight months—and that he was convinced, despite his efforts, "that they cannot be broken of this habit." The court granted him permission to sell Abraham, Harris, and Jane. It was clear that J. F. Dean of Petersburg, Virginia, had reached the end of his patience with his "bright mulatto" woman who was "a very good washer & ironer." She ran off on Tuesday and returned on Thursday morning, Dean said in a letter to a Richmond slave-trading firm. He had tried to curb her stubborn behavior but failed. Dennis March, guardian of a minor, explained in a petition to the Orphans Court of Baltimore County in 1831 that his charge's black man Abraham, despite the guardian's forbearance and kind treatment, became "dissatisfied & has twice without authority left my premises & his conduct [is] altogether unpromising." John P. Thomas of Baltimore said that his "negro Slave woman Georgiana Brooks" had caused him no end of trouble, stealing away at night to the "lowest sinks of vice among the vicious and degraded of her own Color." Owners attempted to convince their slaves that they should not leave without permission, they should obey orders, and they should not become addicted to theft and running away, but many remained "incorrigible."[34] At times it seemed as if there were no easy answers to the question: What should masters do?

Self-perceptions and Managing Slaves

The vast majority of slave owners, from the middling farmers to the great planters, considered themselves kind, God-fearing, humane masters. Admittedly, it was sometimes necessary to sell black children away from parents, wives away from husbands, and older slaves away from friends and kin. Admittedly, it was necessary to correct recalcitrant slaves, as one would discipline one's own children. These actions, however, were done not out of malice or caprice but out of necessity. These were the painful aspects of an institution that had helped create the greatest civilization the world had ever known. Invariably owners looked upon themselves as decent, compassionate, and well-meaning men and women. As one Virginia planter asked his captured runaway:[35]

> Did I ever whip you?
> No, sir.
> Did I ever hire you out when you did not wish to go?
> No, sir.
> When you were sick did I not prepare a bed in my own house
> and put you on it and nurse you?
> Yes, sir.

Why, then, did so many slaves run away? They insisted, in the words of a Maryland master, that it was "not occasioned by any improper conduct" on their part. On the contrary, their treatment had always been "uniformly kind and considerate, and always that of a careful and compassionate master." Others expressed similar sentiments: they had always treated their slaves "kindly & humanely," "with the Kindness as a master should treat a Slave," "with the utmost humanity and indulgence." When a talented seamstress and personal servant ran away from Mount Vernon in 1797, George Washington expressed surprise. The girl, he wrote, had been "brought up and treated more like a child than a Servant."[36]

Like many other large slave owners, the mistress of Evergreen Plantation in West Feliciana Parish, Louisiana, was a devoutly Christian woman who devoted a great deal of time to looking after her slaves. Rachel O'Connor wrote about kind providence, a calm resignation to God's will, sanctification of daily prayer, and how her "black family" was virtually an extension of her own family. The statement of William T. Maclin was repeated by a number of others, with the same emphasis: "The boy ran off," Maclin declared, *without any provocation.*"[37]

In runaway notices published in newspapers, slave owners made similar statements. When his young slave, age eleven or twelve, absconded from a town house in New Orleans, J. A. Lyle noted that he "ranaway without cause." "Ranaway from the Subscriber," Kinsey Burden of Charleston, South Carolina, said of his nineteen-year-old house servant, "without any known cause for his absenting himself." A South Carolina owner was obviously irritated when his "Negro Boy JACK" eloped in 1824. Offering a sizable reward, he said the young man, who disappeared Christmas night, left without the slightest provocation. Another man who sought the return of his twenty-year-old slave Jim, hired out as a fireman on Savannah river steamboats, said that the slave took off without any justification. The same phrase used by another master was repeated on numerous occasions: his urban slave Jim Artope, a first rate "patron," absented himself "without any known cause." The master, however, in completing his advertisement then suggested at least a possible cause: the black man had not been "permitted to enter into contracts on his own account." Other slaveholders added that blacks "left without provocation," or "the object of their absconding is unknown," or "WALKED away" during the harvest "without any cause."[38]

Nor did the members of a society organized in Richmond, Virginia, in 1833 for the express purpose of preventing the "absconding and abduction of their slaves" believe they had any culpability in causing their bondsmen and women to leave. The society lasted for a number of years, had a board of directors, and offered rewards to discover the "means and mode" by which so many slaves effectuated their escape. In the same city some years later, another group of slave owners offered their opinion as to why so many slaves ran away, at least among the thousands of hirelings in Richmond and other cities. "A large

portion of those who hire negroes, especially in our cities," they observed, "consist of Foreigners and of poor and ignorant persons, who
have no other idea of right and wrong than that which conforms exactly to their interest." Nine out of ten hired runaways had been
abused by members of the "lower classes."[39]

One of the best revelations concerning the self-perceptions of whites
came from James Dozier, who hired Nathan, a ten- or eleven-year-old
slave who was active and intelligent "far beyond Most boys of his
age." Even as a youngster of eight or nine, Nathan's owner, a widow,
could not control him, nor could the widow's new husband. They
rented him to Dozier with the hope of reforming his behavior. "In
about two weeks, (my belief is) after I had taken possession of him,
in my absence, he ran away," Dozier testified a short time later; "And
upon inquiry as to the Cause, I was satisfied he had none."[40]

> After three or four days' inquiry I got him; [Dozier continued]
> and, being much pleased with him as a servant, and anxious to
> Keep him for a time, I resolved to pursue Such Course as would
> break the habit, if possible, and therefore, I only *talked* to him
> of the impropriety of his conduct, when I [told] him in such
> language as I am Confident he Perfectly understood—From his
> manner & his language he seemed to regret what he had done,
> & promised faithfully that he would not repeat the act—On the
> very next day, however, without any earthly cause, he absconded
> again, And after three or four days' inquiry & search I found
> him—I then joined Punishment to advice, and he again promised,
> faithfully, that he would do so no more—In six or seven days
> he repeated the offence, and eluded my search for about a week—
> when I got him, I had an iron Collar made for him & put a large
> padlock on it, and in this Condition set him about his business—
> On the same night which this was done, he eloped again and I
> resolved to have nothing more to do with him & so notified Mr.
> Grisham [the owner's husband]—

Since it was not the fault of the master that slaves ran away, or at
least many so believed, it must be due to some outside influence. A
number of owners said that their blacks must have been lured off by
some "evil-minded persons." Kentucky planter Jesse Williams found
it difficult to believe that Reuben and Tom, two "keen and sensible"
slaves, would run away only twelve days after they had been purchased. "I have no doubt but they are conducted by some villain" to
be sold," he wrote from his plantation in 1813. It was the opinion of
a Virginia farmer that his slave named John Goose, about twenty-two
years of age and six feet tall, was taken away by a white man also to
be sold. In 1827, on a Saturday night, seven slaves, including a man,

two women, and the women's four children, left Bradley Rhame's plantation in Sumter District, South Carolina. They must have been enticed away or stolen, Rhame declared, as they would never have left of their own accord. Virginia master John W. Lambeth had owned Surry for eight years, having purchased him at auction in 1845 when he was a boy of twelve. Now he was gone without a word or a trace. Lambeth had always treated his slaves kindly and fairly. Surry must have been stolen. Only recently, he explained, a wagon train moving toward Keysville had passed his farm south of the Dan River in Halifax County, Virginia, a few miles from South Boston. Surry must have been kidnapped by one of the wagoners. Other masters believed their slaves had been lured away by disreputable whites, kidnaped by slave traders, or captured and sold by thieves.[41]

Although some slaves were indeed stolen, masters often could simply not believe that their "loyal" blacks absconded of their own volition. Such beliefs had an profound effect on slave management. Many owners felt betrayed or deceived. They responded with harsh retribution. Although postslavery interviews are a dubious source of information about many aspects of slavery, there is remarkable agreement among blacks and whites about the treatment of runaways. Responding to a questionnaire developed in 1912 by Alabama educator and author Herman Clarence Nixon, two longtime residents of the state, former slave O. Z. McCann and M. T. Judge, a white man who had lived in Mobile County sixty years, had similar recollections. McCann said:

> A great many of the Slave owners were very cruel to the slaves, for that cause they feared the punishment so that they would run away they would go to the woods & live in caves and thickets, over 3/4 of them were clothed very poo[r]ly. I cant give any instances where any slave owner who never whipped their slaves.

Judge concurred:

> Runaways were given from thirty nine to one hundred [lashes] and this was often repeated at intervals of a week or ten days by a cruel master. The whipping was usually done by the Overseer, but sometimes in light cases was done by a fellow slave—As a rule the Overseer was very Cruel, often he would inflict punishment for the lightest offen[se]—The Master very seldom interfered with this man.

Like McCann, the white man did not know of any master who did not whip his slaves.[42]

Under the circumstances, it was easy to justify severe whippings, separating spouses, breaking up families, and selling blacks on the block. Had not they as masters made every effort to be gentle and generous? Had not they treated their slaves well, given them generous food allowances, provided them with comfortable living accommodations, and allowed them to visit relatives? Did they now have any other choice except to respond firmly and, if necessary, brutally to such "disloyalty"? "Poor Ignorant Devils," one master remarked, "for what do they run away? They are well cloathed, work easy, and have all kinds of Plantation produce at no alowance."[43]

Plantation Mistresses and Slave Governance

Although rarely mentioned by contemporaries or historians, single white women who lived alone had special difficulties managing slave property. These women inherited slaves from their families, deceased husbands, or relatives. In some states, they were denied certain privileges with regard to owning real and personal property and often had to have "next best [male] friends" appear with them in court to buy, sell, or transfer their holdings, but they nonetheless relied on slave labor as did their male counterparts. Those who could not afford to hire overseers or plantation managers faced unique problems with regard to governing their hands.

Indeed, it appears that widowed or unmarried women witnessed more resistance, especially among male slaves, than most men who owned slaves. When a husband died and control went to the widow, slaves considered how they might undermine the new regime. Sarah H. Childs's husband died in Maryland in the mid-1850s, and the widow inherited some slaves, including "a certain mulatto boy named Nathaniel Dorsey" who had nearly six years left in servitude as an apprentice. It was clear from the time she took over that she would have difficulty with young Dorsey. In 1855, seeking to sell his unexpired term, she confessed:

> the said boy is of a most mischievous and wicked disposition. He is always getting into trouble himself, or involving your petitioner in trouble. It is impossible for your petitioner to control him, his temper is violent and turbulent. He is continually stealing and pilfering either from your petitioner or from some of her neighbors.

More than once he ran away and "threatens to do so again." She had already been subject to great expense due to his "criminal and wicked deeds, and of his abandoning of his home." She did not wish to keep him because he would "not stay anywhere" and pilfers "everything he can reach."[44]

Other female slaveholders had great difficulty controlling male slaves following the death of their husbands. The recently widowed Alice Kelley of Northumberland County, Virginia, became so fearful of Anthony, a strong, athletic black man, that she requested he be put in jail or an insane asylum. Anthony was "more furious and ungovernable than ever," she said. He could easily escape and commit "greater outrages than he has already." She feared not only for herself but for her eleven-year-old son and neighbors. The forty-five-year-old slave Sam was kept in check by Robert Wilson, a farmer in Maury County, Tennessee, but when he died in 1851, his widow, Charlotte A. Wilson, could not control the slave. Sam sneaked out at night, caroused, drank, gambled, and worked only intermittently. He "came very near making his escape to a Free State," she said, and such a "pernicious example" undermined her ability to control her other slaves. She tried to obtain male assistance in breaking Sam of his bad habits but was unable to do so, and finally, in 1854 she sold him to a slave trader, who boasted he had never seen the slave he could not manage.[45]

In his last will and testament, South Carolina farmer Isham Goree directed that all of his property should be "kept together for the support, maintenance & education of his widow and Children until the youngest child arrives at the age of twenty one years." Some years later, when the farmer died, an estate executor took over the property, but the widow was permitted to manage the farm. As she began her duties, she learned that one of her deceased husband's runaways from four years before had been captured in Mississippi. The woman refused to permit the slave to return to her farm in South Carolina. He was an evil man, a perpetual runaway, and even her husband had great difficulty controlling him. She knew that the slave could not be kept on the farm with her, and she believed he would "induce some of the other negroes to leave with him." The court found the argument persuasive and sanctioned the slave's sale.[46]

Following the death of her husband in 1855, Margaret Mason of Giles County, Tennessee, became the administrator of her late husband's substantial property in trust for the benefit of herself and her young son. The trust included stock, cash, and a number of slaves. Most of the slaves were hired out at the Richland Cotton Mill, but a slave named Green, the widow believed, was "restive & dis[s]atisfied with the condition of slavery, and contemplates an escape from servitude." To complicate matters further, Green was nearly "white & could easily pass himself for a white man anywhere." If he "should

attempt to carry such a purpose into execution," Margaret Mason contended, "he could easily accomplish it, both from his color and general
appearance, as well as from his intelligence & shrewdness." After a
heated argument with her slave, she confessed that he needed to be
put "under the control of a vigilant Master or overseer." A short time
later, the nearly white slave was sold.[47]

When their husbands died, white women often became concerned
about controlling slaves. Some were apprehensive about giving orders
to male slaves. In some instances, relatives and friends offered assistance, but this was usually done on a short-term basis. Following the
death of her husband, Frances Blitch of Marion County, Florida, experienced great difficulty with her slave, forty-year-old Horace, who
refused to work as he had when her husband was on the farm. She
confessed that Horace had now developed the "habit of absconding"
and had been "lodged in Jail in Putnam County, having been apprehended as a runaway." The slave became "profitless troublesome and
expensive to said Estate." She could not provide for her seven children,
the widow lamented, unless Horace were immediately sold. Following
the death of her husband, Susan Price of Franklin County, Kentucky,
chose two slaves—Harry and Nelson—to remain in her possession. "I
know they were favorite negroes with the family," an observer noted;
they were energetic, intelligent, and "valued highly." Despite such
praise, taken by Price to Missouri, the pair quickly ran away to Ohio
and were never heard from again.[48]

It usually took only a short while before a widow realized that she
might have difficulty managing her human property. In a few cases,
however, many years passed before a mistress found that she was
unable to control her slaves. In the case of Jane Allen, it was, in fact,
fourteen years, by which time her slave Esther's son had grown into
manhood. By 1856, thirty-two-year-old Esther and sixteen-year-old
Henry could no longer be controlled. For several years past, the mistress said, the two slaves had been "very dishonest, of bad habits and
very impudent, and often threatened to run off to go to a free state."
Neither of them would "allow her to correct them," and she could
"not manage them at all." In August, she decided to sell the two out
of the state, but when they found out, they decided to run away.
Betrayed by a fellow slave, Henry threatened the mistress's brother
with an ax when he arrived on the scene and took control. The two
were packed and ready to make off, he said, and would have done so
had he not arrived. A few days later, the two were sold to a Mississippi
planter for $1,900.[49]

Living alone or with small children and attempting to manage a farm or plantation created emotional and psychological strains that brought some women to the edge of a breakdown. While not a few women whipped or punished slaves who displayed a bad temperament, they usually did so when an overseer or a husband was present. It was much more difficult to administer corporal punishment alone. The fear and anxiety of living in the midst of slave hands while trying to sustain a plantation alone was illustrated by planter Leah Moore, a single woman in Anderson District, South Carolina. Moore possessed "a handsome property," but Buck, one of her most valuable hands, was "insolent and highly provoking," a potential runaway. She considered selling him but feared that if he ever found out he might respond violently. For many months, Buck remained "almost alone in her contemplation." Finally, in desperation, she secretly sold him for a small fraction of his worth to a man who promised "to send him out of the state, afar off."[50]

While male slave owners were also fearful at times about selling slaves, women felt especially vulnerable. Many had relied on husbands to manage the slaves and were now cast into a new role. Others, like Leah Moore, feared certain individual slaves. The black man that Catherine Munro of Charleston District, South Carolina, purchased in 1819 was advertised as "a most capable Servant," first-rate cook, proficient house servant, "faithful & trusty." In fact, she averred, he was "morally depraved." He had a terrible temper, and Munro found it "impossible" to correct his "*moral defects.*" She arranged for a slave trader to come and take him away; the man shipped him "off to New Orleans; he was so vicious a negro." When John F. Chandler of Bedford County, Tennessee, died in 1852, the executors of his will quickly sought to sell one of his slaves. Chandler's widow was fearful for herself and her four small children. The slave in question, Jeff, was "of bad and vicious habits and cannot be controlled or managed by said widow." Indeed, the executors said, even John Chandler during his lifetime was forced to seek help from neighbors and others "to manage and control him."[51]

Women left alone by their husbands also experienced difficulty managing slaves. Unless they were kept under constant guard and supervision, Frederick Law Olmsted explained, there was a tendency toward "general insubordination." Olmsted cited an incident in Texas where the master left his wife in charge of slaves (ironically, to go on patrol). "While all the men were gone from the place, a negro described as being bare-headed, thick-set, and having on a blue blanket coat and pair of blue cottonade pants, came to the house, and seeing a double-barrel gun in the corner took it." He then ordered the mistress to get him some ammunition and threatened to kill her if she refused. When he received the shells, he took the gun and made his escape.[52]

Even women who were able to hire overseers experienced difficulties with slave governance. When her husband died in 1851, Jane B. Smith of Giles County, Tennessee, took over the management of their 400-acre farm and thirty slaves. She hired a succession of overseers, but even with their assistance, she found it almost impossible to manage a young male slave named Jim, who became increasingly turbulent. He left the farm at night, rode off on the mistress's horses, and pilfered from her neighbors. He fought with white overseers and fellow slaves, broke into cabins and forced himself on slave women, and created many "disturbances in negro families." In short, Jim "has become very troublesome on account of turbulent disposition, stubbornness, and insubordination. He is thievish, and has become annoying to the neighbors in various ways, and in fact, it is impossible for your Oratrix to control him." She feared he would be lost entirely if he were not sold.[53]

Discarding the Aged and Infirm

Once slaves became unproductive, costly, or suffered from debilitating illnesses, more than a few masters simply abandoned them. This may have been particularly true for hard-pressed, small slave owners, but others who owned larger numbers of slaves engaged in such practices as a matter of economic necessity. Wandering about from county to county, these slaves often came in contact with local authorities and were arrested as runaways. In January 1823, for instance, Milly was arrested as a runaway in Louisa County, Virginia. Upon inquiry, she confessed that she belonged to one Mr. Finlay of Richmond, but attempts to locate the owner were unsuccessful. Meanwhile, Milly remained in jail month after month. "Whilst in Confinement," John M. Price, the jailer, wrote, "I frequently applied to the County Court of Louisa for redress or relief stating that such was the infirmity of the slave Milly besides that for her advanced age that no owner would ever apply for her beside the circumstance of Severe Mental derangement." In the end, she "strayed off," and it was Price's opinion that she probably died within a short period.[54]

Despite the professions of proslavery advocates about how well they treated their human property and the fact that on some large plantations there were what might be termed nursing care facilities for the old and infirm, some masters either deliberately abandoned slaves

who reached an unproductive age or forced the mentally or physically unfit to leave their farms and plantations. Most slaves did not
reach their fifties or sixties. But some masters, for a variety of reasons,
pushed elderly, unproductive slaves out. Sometimes the abandoned slaves died a short time afterwards, but at other times, they
were arrested as runaways and languished in jail. The history of a
slave named Major Henry was not fully revealed, only that he was
jailed in Sussex County, Virginia, advertised as a runaway in the *Richmond Enquirer* and the *Petersburg Intelligencer*, and auctioned off
for $25.[55]

When Thomas Craig, a Kentucky man, sold his "negro woman slave
& her child" to a neighbor in 1806 for $400, he accepted a $50 note
and a promise that the remainder would be paid in twelve months. To
ensure payment and service the interest, Craig agreed to take Charles,
a slave owned by the buyer's brother, for his own use during the year.
Craig soon discovered, however, that Charles was "unsound and diseased," afflicted with "the King's Evil, a mortal & incurable disease."
The slave required expensive medical attention, and toward the expiration of the twelve months, he ran away, returning to his owner. But
the owner did not want him. "[T]he said Slave Charles is now going
at large," Craig said in a chancery suit. Both brothers knew about his
condition but neither would "redeem the said property."[56]

In 1824, a Georgia woman turned over twenty-seven slaves in trust
to her attorney James Smith with instructions to hire them out. Several years later, the woman discovered one of her slaves was missing.
Hannah, age about fifty, was supposed to have been sent to a man
named James Oharra, but she never went, or if she did, she ran away.
In explaining what happened to Hannah, the attorney was probably
indicating a scenario for other elderly slaves who were unable to work.
At age "fifty *or sixty*," Smith explained, Hannah was "placed" with
a "negroe man named old John" to be "put out" to the "lowest bidder,
and said Hannah and old John were bid off at public outcry as an
expense." The lowest bidder was a man named Thomas Cruthers, who
promised to provide for the couple for one year. This occurred in 1824.
The next year, Smith turned Hannah over to Oharra, but either she
did not arrive or absconded, he did not know which. He did not know
her whereabouts.[57]

Other owners simply sold slaves who were growing old or declining
in productivity. In the upper states, where slave prices remained lower
than in the deep South, such sales were not uncommon. Even older
bondsmen and women could bring profits to sellers and traders. In a
complaint to the Tennessee General Assembly in 1849, a group of
nonslaveholding whites pointed this out not because they resented

slaves being sold in such a manner, but because slaveholders paid no taxes on slaves under twelve or over fifty. They argued:[58]

> [T]he Poorman has but little to protect, but he under the present Law has to pay-taxes for every Acre of Land he owns and that as Soon as he owns it and evry dollars worth of labor he bestows that ads value to it as long as he lives; While the Rich Slave holder is Raiseing young Negros, and Speculating on his old ones free of taxation.

The concerns expressed by some planters about what might happen following their death to their elderly suggests that they were aware of slaves being set adrift or sold. At the time of a breakup of their sugar plantations in Louisiana, one partner wrote another about "old Sukey and old Nancy two faithful old and good women in whose fate I felt great interest." He wanted them to be disposed of as they might desire; he was "very anxious about them fearing that they might fall into rough hands." Despite the partner's concern, the decision was made to auction them off with the others. One of the women died before the sale, and the other was put up for sale with an "orphan child" who also died. Sometime later, one of the partners did retrieve the surviving slave.[59]

In some sections, the problem became so acute that laws were passed to prevent such occurrences. In 1798, the North Carolina Assembly passed "An act to compel owners of infirm slaves to support them." The lawmakers lamented that some owners drove their slaves off when they became unproductive. It was the duty of masters, they instructed, to furnish all slaves, whether old or disabled, with "the usual allowance of food, raiment, and lodging." In cases where this was not done, the Wardens of the Poor for each county should care for slaves "rendered incapable of service." Two years later, South Carolina prefaced its new emancipation law with an admission: for many years slave owners had pushed out elderly, infirmed, and "depraved" slaves. The new law sought to prevent such "emancipations." In 1815, Georgia passed "An act to compel owners of old and infirm slaves to maintain them." Nearly a decade later, Virginia law promised to penalize owners who abandoned their old, feeble, or insane slaves. A fine of up to fifty dollars would be levied "for every such offence." A short time later, Tennessee prohibited owners from pushing slaves out who were sick, diseased, or "unable to perform their daily labor."[60]

Anxiety, Trouble, Expense

Despite their glowing self-portrait, slave owners were continually concerned that their slaves might run away. When they refused to work,

feigned illness, argued with the overseer, or showed general dissatisfaction—described by whites as "unruly," "disobedient," and "unmanageable" behavior—slave owners and overseers realized the possibility of a slave's running away. Shortly before or shortly after a
sale or when a slave had been punished, a loved one chastised, a family
broken were also important periods for vigilance. "No negro belonging
to the plantation, will be allowed to leave it without a pass from the
proprietor, and no one from the neighborhood or elsewhere will be
permitted to frequent it without a written permission to do so," one
planter wrote to his overseer, who was required to "inspect the cabins
at different hours of the night, as often as once in every week."[61] If
the overseer suspected foul play or a possible escape attempt, he should
make more frequent inspections, the planter instructed.

But it was not always the most dissatisfied who were to be watched.
Slaves with special skills, who could read and write, who pretended to
be happy and content, or who were hired out might also be plotting
to run off. "It may be possible that Lewis and Sarah may be both
playing agreeable in order to put you off your guard," Alabama
planter William Browne wrote from Mobile to his wife on their
plantation. "I am uneasy at not having a word from you. I think that
Lewis has plenty of money laid by for his escape. Probably our
turkeys have been made to contribute to his purse and maybe the
corn crib. It is very important that the matter be thoroughly investigated."[62]

Nor was Browne the only master who remained "uneasy" at the
possibility of "agreeable" slaves plotting escapes. At various times,
other slaveholders felt that close surveillance was necessary. "Geo.
Dickey is esteemed a good Headman," Charles Ellis of Richmond explained in 1837. The black man knew the mountain areas well and was
familiar with the rivers between Lynchburg and Richmond. Owned by
an estate, he had been hired out under the management of Major
Holcombe, but Ellis, with instructions from the estate managers, now
made arrangement for his sale. "He may keep out of the way shd he
Know," Ellis warned; he asked the firm of Payne and Turner in Lynchburg to "find him out and control him so that the sale may be effected
to the greatest advantage."[63]

Such vigilance was necessary in the case of Dickey, who traveled
on his own, possessed skills, and had opportunities for self-hire. Surveillance was also necessary for Alabama slaves Isaac and Andrew, who
were to be sent to South Carolina as part of an estate transfer. "In
truth I have been obliged to deceive them as to their returning here,"
estate manager J. H. Taylor of Montgomery wrote; "and it will be
necessary that they continue to believe they are to return until they
reach their destiny."[64] Such deceptions were not isolated incidents.

Masters, mistresses, overseers, managers, slave traders, estate admin- istrators, guardians; and others were "obliged to deceive" slaves to prevent their running away.

But the anxiety caused by possible escape paled beside the trouble and expense incurred when slaves did run away. Besides the lost time in the field, there was the time spent by overseers, managers, and masters searching, advertising, traveling, and retrieving fugitives. Sometimes slave owners or overseers spent days, even weeks, tracing the whereabouts of an outlying slave. "Offering the reward you dic- tated & have made every other possible inquiry," a man sent out by slave owner Edward Telfair wrote from Augusta, Georgia, concerning a runaway named Sandy. "I am hopeful, if he is really in the neigh- bourhood, to be able to apprehend him in a short time." "I hope no more of them will run away," another owner admitted, as it was "not only very troublesome but very expensive getting them back home." "I wd have sent it sooner," a man wrote from Columbus, Georgia, referring to a check he had posted to a Richmond, Virginia, trading firm, "but have been absent after runaway negro wch I got out of jail at Perry." To claim his slave, he was forced to travel nearly two hun- dred miles.[65]

At other times, it seemed as if overseers and planters became ob- sessed with retrieving their property. Between 1838 and 1841, John M. Chapron, an absentee planter in the North who owned a plantation near Demopolis, Alabama, received frequent reports from his overseer James Martin about slave management. Chapron's letters to Martin offered various methods that might be employed to stem the tide of runaways: Harry, who stole bacon and left the plantation; Julia and Claiborn, who absconded; five field hands hiding in the woods; and Carter, who had "not forgotten his old habit." "When picking season will come," he told Martin, "you must try an experiment to give them premiums from the 1st of September in order to encourage them and to keep them from taking to the woods." When this plan did not work, he proposed providing new shirts, dresses, suits, cash payments, and giving Claiborn, who was a good shoemaker, a separate cabin for his wife and two children. "I hope that the hands will stay on the plan- tation this year," he wrote Martin, and to the physician who treated his slaves, he added more instructions: [66]

Tell them they have to obey Mr. Martin and do what he tells them to do. You have nothing to do with them. If they work well I am sure he will not whip them. Advise them to not run away. It is not Mr. Martin they wrong by doing so. It is I who is doing all I can to please them.

It appears that none of these offers was successful, however, as Chapron's slaves continued to abscond. Slaveholders often used the phrases "great trouble and expense," "considerable trouble and expense," when describing the difficulties they encountered searching for runaways. It took time and effort to arrange for trackers, hounds, notices, to alert friends and neighbors as well as local authorities that a slave was out. After a spotting, revised letters and notices needed to be sent out. Masters contacted former masters, inquired into the whereabouts of slave relatives, wrote county officials, and sent managers out to arrange for the return of their human property.[67]

When a Virginia master discovered that his trusted black, Davy, had taken a travel pass and disappeared, he wrote the slave's former owner: "May I ask the favour of you to aid me in arresting him so that he may be gotten. for your trouble and expense in doing so you shall be adequately rewarded." Davy may have returned to Culpepper County, the owner speculated, or may have gone "over the mountains" where he formerly lived or may have gone to "the place that you took him from." "Two of my negro men Jesse and Anderson left home on Sunday last," James A. Tait wrote from his plantation in Wilcox County, Alabama, to the postmaster at Greenville, Alabama. "I think they have gone back to Georgia, and through your vicinity. I wish you would let the sheriff know it, and get him to keep a look out for them."[68]

In some cases, it was necessary to take extreme measures to slow the number of runaways. Some planters imported highly trained dogs from Cuba, raised to track runaways; others kept slave catchers on their plantations; and others made periodic sweeps of areas known to be popular hiding places for outlyers. "I will try to find his hiding places between this and Sunday and on that day I will drive the Island and try to take him," one overseer wrote from an island plantation in Louisiana in 1839, adding the following year that it was necessary to station "a lookout" in areas frequented by absconders. "There is three absconded from the plantation namely John Paine, Fortune and Handy." A pioneer coal dealer in Alabama instructed his wife to "Say as little about the [runaway] negroes as possible." He was fearful of additional defections and told his wife to make arrangements with a white man to take charge of some of his slaves:

Send for O'Neil tell him on no account to give the boy Fleming the least chance to escape. it is very important. Tell Jack [a slave] to keep with him *all the time* and the chain must be kept on him *constantly* and the moment he comes home he must be handcuffd to Abrum and Kept so until he gets ready to start to [the] pit.

For some runaways, Thomas Jefferson of Monticello meted out harsh punishments. In 1812, he ordered his runaway Hubbard to be "severely flogged in the presence of his old companions." He will "never again serve any man as a slave," Jefferson admitted; "the moment he is out of jail and his irons off he will be off himself." Jefferson's premonition proved correct, and when Hubbard ran away again, he was sold in absentia.[69]

The failure of management techniques and the inability to control runaways left slave owners in a quandary.[70] It appeared that no matter how diligent, punitive, or lenient; no matter how imaginative, ingenious, or attentive; no matter how determined, compassionate, or brutal, they remained unable to halt the stream of slaves that left their plantations and farms. Although they published articles for one another about how and when to plant certain crops, use fertilizers, hire overseers, motivate and discipline their black labor force, in response to their most perplexing and intractable problem, they remained virtually silent. To begin a public discussion about how to halt runaways would be to acknowledge a problem that was at once unsolvable and at the heart of the brutal nature of human bondage. It would reveal that managing bondsmen and bondswomen required continual surveillance and coercion. Even then, most slaveholders were unable to stop the flight of their human property.

11

Counting the Costs

"Dickerson called on me to Know what Kind of a negro she was," explained William Butler, the son of a man who wanted to sell a female slave to Henry Dickerson of Barren County, Kentucky. They were sitting at the son's kitchen table in January 1819, waiting for the father to return with the slave. She was twenty-eight years old, strong and healthy, Butler said, and could be used as a field hand or house servant. "[H]e asked me how often she had runaway," the son recalled; two or three times he replied. When the father arrived with the woman, Dickerson scrutinized her closely. Discovering she had lost several toes on one foot from frostbite, he instructed her to take off her stocking and to walk across the floor. When she did so without a limp, he said he would take her home and try her out for a few days and if he liked her he would buy her. The next morning, Dickerson returned, said he would take her and promised to pay $600 in two installments for the slave woman Rody.[1]

Within a short time, Rody ran away, was captured, and ran away again. Indeed, it soon became apparent that "she was in the habit of running away & staying out . . . for weeks & months at a time." She absconded so often and stayed out so long each time that Dickerson thought she was mentally unbalanced and doubted whether she was "capable of proper reflection & judgment." If this were not enough, he now recalled what he had been told at the time of the purchase: Butler assured him that he "had never whiped said negro that she was no eye servant but was industrious & attentive to business & require no looking after." In truth, as he discovered in an interview with one of Butler's neighbors, she had been whipped repeatedly, and after each whipping, she had run away. Discovering this, he refused to pay the balance on his note. When he went to Adair County, where Butler lived, to confront Butler, he discovered that Butler himself had departed for Tennessee. There was now nothing left for him to do except send the slave to the New Orleans market. It took him a year before he sold her, and when he did, she brought only 40 percent of the original purchase price.[2] Even with his refusal to make full payment and with money from the sale, Dickerson had lost a substantial amount, paying for her capture, transportation, food and clothing, as well as the auctioneer's fees and other expenses in New Orleans.

Dishonor Among Masters

William Butler and his father's duplicity in dealing with a potential buyer was by no means unique in the slave South. Many other owners were equally deceptive. Putting slaves up for auction or approaching individual buyers, they rarely admitted, much less advertised, their slaves as habitual runaways. To do so would make a potential sale difficult, and even if it could be consummated, the price would certainly fall below market value. Slaves known as "runners" lost a significant percentage of their market value and were often difficult to sell. If word got out that a slave was rebellious or had attacked whites, it might be impossible to consummate a sale. Following the Gabriel plot, two slaves were convicted as "actors and abettors of the late insurrection" but had escaped the death penalty and were turned over to traders to be sold. They promptly escaped into the Northwest Territory but were captured after wounding a guard. Taken down the Ohio and Mississippi rivers to the Spanish Territory, the two still could not be sold. In 1829, when David McKim, a Baltimore chemical maker, sold Allen Henson, he did so at a loss because it was known that Henson had attempted to escape ten months before.[3]

The domestic slave trade was fed in part by masters seeking to rid themselves of unmanageable and unruly slaves by selling them to distant markets. Even in local markets, however, owners disguised the fact that they were selling runaways. As a number of lawsuits suggest, masters frequently sold runaways to unsuspecting buyers. In South Carolina, William Rouse paid fifty guineas in 1799 for the slave Sarah, who was represented by her owner, a man named Vernon, as "a good sound healthy & useful negro." When he ascertained that "the said Wench was a notorious Thief and runaway," Rouse filed suit. In their discussions concerning "a negro Fellow named Will," owner William Harris told the prospective buyer that the slave was "a faithful industrious and honest fellow and might be depended on as an excellent Plantation Negro." Henry Peeples, a planter in Greene County, Georgia, accepted the owner's word and purchased Will in September 1802

George R. Ghiselin and wife
and others on Petition   In chancery

                    In obedience to a decree
of the chancellor of the Louisville chancery court
rendered in the above cause I advertised as directed
by said decree on the 26th day of October 1854 to sell on
the 6th day of November 1854 to the highest bidder at
public auction about the hour of 11 oclock Am
before the court house door in the city of Louisville
a Slave man Joshua aged about 43 years on credits
of 6 & 12 months for Equal portions of the purchase
money. the Purchaser to give bond with approved
Security bearing interest from the day of Sale til paid
            And on the said 6th day of November 1854 I attended
at the court house door aforesaid about the hour
above named and offered said Slave on the above named
terms to the highest bidder at public outcry and
Henry Hawes bid the sum of two hundred Seventy five
dollars ($275) and his being the highest and best bid
offered he was struck off to him at that price
Said Hawes paid in cash ten dollars & fifty cents which was
paid to the Jailor of Jefferson county by order of
Plaintiffs attorney and executed his two bonds as required
by the terms of Sale each bond in the sum of $132 25/100
with H W Hawes his Security Said bonds are herewith
returned and made part hereof all of which is
respectfully reported
                                        H Dent M D C C

George R Ghiselin wife &c
1854   To the marshal of the chancery court
    To comd on Sale $275-   1 $13.75
                3 Sets of Printers Bills   4.00
        advertising &c in course $17.75
                Henry Dent M D C C   3.00
                                            $24.75

The guardian of Joshua's owner explained to a local court that the slave was "un-
managable and dissipated" and "frequently absents himself, staying away a long
time, paying and making no hire." Fearing he would run away to a free state, the
guardian asked for permission to sell the forty-three-year-old slave at a sheriff's sale.
Among the costs the buyer paid was a $10.50 jail fee.

for $600. It did not take him long to realize that he had been duped. The black man was "lazy rougueish & unfaithful in every respect & one whom it was impossible to keep at his work he ever being disposed to Elope." In his equity court suit, Harris noted that Will had "repeatedly runaway" and by his "profligate conduct in this and many other respects" had become entirely "useless."[4]

The same scenario was repeated in West Baton Rouge Parish, Louisiana, in 1820, when Sebastian Hiriart, a planter, crossed the Mississippi River to purchase "a certain negro fellow," about twenty-two years of age. Hiriart promised to pay $1,020 in two equal installments a year apart. The "negro fellow" was represented as a "prime specimen," and Hiriart paid nearly twice the going rate. He soon discovered, however, that he had been swindled. Not only was the slave a habitual runaway, but when brought to Hiriart's plantation, he refused to respond to any command. Indeed, the new owner thought he was deaf. The slave was "of no use or service." In Maryland, Charles Digges of Prince George's County bought the unexpired term of the twenty-three-year-old slave Enoch in 1848 for $300. In making payments of $40 a year until the term of servitude ended in 1856, there was a good possibility that the owner would make a profit. A strong, young male slave would bring three times that amount in annual hire. But he, too, quickly discovered he had been defrauded. Enoch was a habitual runaway, and Digges lost a substantial amount trying to hire him out.[5] In these and other cases, angry and hostile slave owners told of misrepresentation, deceit, and fraud. When sold, slaves were described as hardworking, trustworthy, and submissive. The new owners soon discovered just the opposite was true.

This deceit occurred not only when slaves were bought and sold but when they were hired out as well. In a suit brought in Davidson County, Tennessee, Archibald H. Harris told of the chicanery and deception practiced by Joseph Cook, the owner of "a Negro man named Harry." Cook approached him in 1814 about hiring the black man— "a good serviceable hand" and "not [a] runaway"—for a year. Shortly after Harris signed an eighty-five-dollar note for a year's hire, Harry ran away. As soon as Harris "could get him out of one Jail where he was taken up and Confined he would again escape." Harris found out that Harry was "a notorious worthless and runaway Slave."[6]

Some owners went to great lengths to conceal their slaves' behavior patterns. The conversation between the agent of a Missouri planter and a commission merchant and auctioneer in New Orleans revealed how far some owners were willing to go to rid themselves of chronic runaways. "I was about to sell said Slave Lewis to a respectable man, a friend of mine," the auctioneer reported, and he asked the owner's

MARSHAL'S SALE.

GEORGE R. GHISELIN and WIFE,
AND OTHERS, ON PETITION, } In Chancery.

By virtue of a decree of the Louisville Chancery Court, rendered in the above cause, the undersigned or one of us, will,

On MONDAY, the 6th day of NOVEMBER, 1854,

About the hour of 11 o'clock, A. M., sell to the highest bidder, at public auction, before the court house door, in the city of Louisville, a slave man JOSHUA, aged about 43 years, on credits of six and twelve months, for equal portions of the purchase money.

The purchaser to give bond with approved security, bearing interest from the day of sale until paid.

HENRY DENT, M. L. C. C.
HENRY WOLFORD, Dep.

Oct. 26th, 1854.

agent "to be candid in his representations of said slave Lewis." He wished to know his character, as the law of the state differed from the common law. He wanted a guarantee that the slave was "free of vices and maladies according to the law of Louisiana." This meant the slave had to be certified against insanity, leprosy, consumption, ill-health, and running away. The agent told the auctioneer that the slave in question had "no faults and no vices" and was "a good plantation negro."[7] The auctioneer's friend, Henry Crane, purchased Lewis in early 1851 with a full warranty.

Within days, Lewis absconded. It was an especially cold January, and by the time he was captured, after being out for some time, Lewis had developed a deep and persistent cough. Taken to the slave pen, he got dysentery. Crane was so outraged that he booked passage for the slave and himself on an upriver steamer, to return Lewis to his owner in Ste. Genevieve, Missouri. Within a short time, however, the slave died. A postmortem examination revealed that Lewis was "weak and greatly emaciated," his right lung was "absorbed and wasted in great part" with "numerous abscesses" and filled with "tuberculous matter." Though he had died of consumption, the physician said, Lewis had an enlarged liver and several ounces of a reddish fluid in the "penicardicum." In a civil litigation (for damages sought, see appendix 5), Crane charged that he been duped: he was sold a seriously ill slave who was "addicted to the habit of running away."[8]

The sale and resale of runaways reached such dimensions in Louisiana that lawmakers listed running away, along with ill-health and disease, as a "redhibitory" vice. Even if a purchaser could not prove that a slave had previously run away, the presumption of guilt on the part of the seller was assumed if the slave absconded within a few months after the sale. In 1835, for example, St. Landry Parish slaveholder Henry A. Bullard purchased in New Orleans for $1,200 "with full warranty a Negro man slave named Lewis aged twenty two years." In May 1835, "*and within two months after the said* sale, the said slave Lewis, without the slightest provocation & under circumstances which leave no doubt that he is *a runaway*, absconded & runaway from your petitioner, and has not been heard of since; altho' every precaution was used to reclaim him." In ruling for reimbursement, District Judge C. Watts, citing an act passed in 1834, asserted that if "either the vices of character viz running away or habit of theft" appeared within two months after a sale, the presumption that those vices were long-standing "repels all contrary proof or overwhelms it."[9]

To allay the fears of slave owners in the Lower Mississippi River Valley, slave traders in the upper states obtained sworn affidavits that the slaves they offered were not habitual runaways. "We, John Porter and James Porter freeholders in the County of Shelby and State aforesaid [Kentucky], do certify that a certain negro Man slave for life, aged about twenty-six years named John about five feet 7 or 8 inches high, dark complected, and is a good field hand," one such affidavit on a printed form stated in 1829, "that he has not, within their knowledge, been guilty or convicted of any crime—but that he has, on the contrary, a good moral character—and that he is not in the habit of running away." Virginia traders, too, printed up affidavits during the 1820s stating that slaves were not habitual runaways. Such documents, signed by prominent "freeholders," justices of the peace, clerks of court, and magistrates, accompanied bills of sale to Mississippi and Louisiana.[10]

Even with such safeguards, the buying and selling of runaways continued apace. Those who transported slaves from one state to another could be miles away when it was discovered that the slave sold as a "prime" and "likely" field hand was, in fact, a habitual absconder. Even when buyers were able to bring their cases to court, it was nearly impossible to recoup their losses. A Georgia planter who said he had been misled when he purchased a runaway received a favorable ruling in the Wilkes County Superior Court, but his expenses and losses far outweighed the award he received from the court. Nor were judgments easy to collect even when the seller lived in the same jurisdiction. A West Baton Rouge Parish man said he had been put to "great expense in paying charges & pursuing him the sd Slave when he has been runaway." Even with a favorable court order for repayment, he was unable to force the seller to repay what he had lost. Henry Peeples of Greene County, Georgia, lost $600 when he bought a slave who ran away. He sued William Harris, the man who sold him the perpetual runaway, but the jury awarded him only $25, out of which he was required to pay court costs. This was yet another example of duplicity and loss to the buyer of a slave who was in the habit of running away. In other instances, there were suits, countersuits, trials, retrials, appeals, temporary injunctions, confiscations of property, and years of bitter litigation.[11]

Contemporaries were well aware of misrepresentations. A group of South Carolina residents observed in 1843 that Charleston had become a dumping ground for the sale of Upper South slaves who were vicious and violent. Perpetual runaways "are palmed upon careless or confiding Citizens among us, and their mixture with our own, has had a . . . [baleful] influence upon the docility and usefulness of our slaves." Sellers and dealers engaged in these practices purposely because they reaped the largest profits by selling slaves as far away as possible from

STATE OF *Kentucky* } *Wm L Shields* and
Borbon COUNTY. } *Wm A Dickson* Freeholders in
the county of *Borbon* in the state aforesaid, this day personally appeared before me,
Wm M Baylor an acting Justice of the Peace within and for said county, and
made oath, in the due form of law, that they are well acquainted with a certain negro *man* slave,
named *Ned* aged about *Ninteen* years, about *five* feet *9* inches
high; weighing probably about *one hundred, Sixty* and of *Black* complexion.
~~Surrounding~~ = Which slave has been sold to *Jacob Allenthorp* by
Smaßy a citizen of said county, and with whom they have been intimately acquainted about *five*
years. That they have known the said slave for several years, and that *he* has not, within their knowledge, been guilty or convicted of any crimes; but that *he* has maintained a good moral character, and
is not in the habit of running away to the best of their knowledge and belief.

Sworn to and subscribed before me, this *7th*
day of *Aug* 185*5*   *Wm L Shields*
Wm M Baylor   *Wm A Dickson*

STATE OF *Kentucky* } I, *Thos P Smith* Clerk of the
Borbon COUNTY. } *Borbon* Court of said County, do hereby
certify, that the foregoing declaration, on oath, made by *Wm L Shields* and *Wm A*
Dickson Freeholders of said county, was made and signed before me at *Paris*
in said county; that said *Wm L Shields* and *Wm A Dickson* are well
known and respectable Freeholders of said county, of good character, and they are not the venders of the
slave above-mentioned in their declaration—And that *Wm M Baylor* Esq. before
whom said declaration on oath was made, is an acting Justice of the Peace for the county of *N Borbon*
aforesaid, duly authorized to administer on oath.

IN TESTIMONY WHEREOF, I, *Thos P Smith* Clerk,
of the *Borbon* Court, within and for said county, do hereunto
set my hand, and affix the seal of said court, at my office in *Paris*
this *7th* day of *Aug* A. D. 183*0* and *55* year
of American Independence.

Thos. P Smith 6 156

By Robt E Rankin DC

ky } *I, John Edwards* presiding
COUNTY. } *Judge* of the *Borbon* Court, for
said county, do hereby certify, that *Thos P Smith* Esq. before whom the foregoing
declaration, on oath, has been made and subscribed, is the Clerk of said *Borbon* Court,
over which I preside; and that due faith and credit is and ought to be given to all his official acts as such.

Given under my hand, this *7th* *Aug* 183*5*

John Edwards Judge

Slave buyers wanted a guarantee, as these affidavits reveal, that the slaves they were
purchasing were "not in the habit of running away."

COMMONWEALTH OF VIRGINIA, *Albemarle* COUNTY, to wit:

WE *Joel W. Brown and William Watson* freeholders in the county aforesaid, do hereby certify and declare that a *male* slave, named *William* aged about *Sixteen* years; about *5* feet, *3 5/10* inches in height; of a *yellow* colour; having *no marks perceivable*

was purchased from *James R. Watson* in the said county; that we have known said slave for several years; and that *he* has not within our knowledge been guilty or convicted of any crimes, but hath a good moral character; and is not in the habit of running away.

                                                        Joel W. Brown
                                                        Wm. Watson

COMMONWEALTH OF VIRGINIA, *Albemarle* COUNTY, to wit:

I *John R. Jones* a Justice of the Peace for the county aforesaid, and as such duly authorised to administer an oath, do hereby certify that *Joel W. Brown and William Watson* this day appeared before me, and made oath that the foregoing certificate and declaration contained the truth to the best of their knowledge and belief, and acknowledge the same to be their act and deed. And I further certify that the said *Joel W. Brown and William Watson* are respectable men, and men of good characters, and are not the venders of the slave described in the foregoing certificate. Given under my hand this *21st* day of *November* 1829

                                                        Jno. R. Jones

COMMONWEALTH OF VIRGINIA, *Albemarle* COUNTY, to wit:

I *Alexander Garrett* a Clerk of the county court of *Albemarle* aforesaid, do certify that *John R. Jones* is a Justice of the Peace, and as such duly authorised to administer an oath for the county aforesaid; and that *Joel W. Brown and William Watson* are well known to me to be freeholders of the said county, as appears by the records in my office. In testimony whereof, I hereunto set my hand, and affix the seal of the said court, this *21st* day of *November* 1829 *in the 54th* y. of the commonwealth

                                                        Alex Garrett C.A.C.C.

COMMONWEALTH OF VIRGINIA, *Albemarle* COUNTY, to wit:

I *Benjamin Harris* presiding Magistrate for the county of *Albemarle* do hereby certify that *Alexander Garrett* whose name is subscribed to the foregoing attestation, is now, and was at the time of subscribing the same, clerk of the said county court of *Albemarle* and that his said attestation is in due form. Given under my hand this *28th* day of *November* 1829.

                                                        Ben Harris

their "old range" where their "notorious bad character" was well known. The laws barring slave importation "merely for sale" in Alabama and Mississippi only exacerbated the problem in South Carolina. A group of Delaware residents agreed when they noted that, despite a law prohibiting the exportation of slaves from that state, the most intractable bondsmen were being exported "contrary to this law" to various parts of the Lower South.[12]

Not only did owners misrepresent their slaves, a few owner-traders dealt largely in buying and selling runaways. This was risky and highly speculative, but the profits from purchasing obstreperous slaves in one area and selling them as "prime" and "likely" hands in another could be substantial, especially during the 1840s and 1850s as demand in the west drove prices spiraling upward. The South Carolina partners of William Metts and William Bell were typical of this group. They searched out runaways, purchased them at low prices, then journeyed to slave markets in the west. In 1858, Metts learned that David Stoddard, an old farmer in Laurens District, wanted to sell a teenage slave named Sam whom he could not control. The trader went to Stoddard's farm to inspect the slave but was told not to ask Sam any questions because he might run away as he had on previous occasions. A short time later, Metts returned, purchased Sam, worth $1,000 according to his owner, for $750, and Bell co-signed the note. Then, with a coffle of slaves, Metts set out by train to Montgomery, Alabama, with Sam "heavily hand cuffed" and chained.[13]

Other masters who were in the process of buying and selling slaves kept a sharp eye out for the profits that they might gain by purchasing runaways in one section of the South and selling them in distant markets at inflated prices. In 1828, Samuel Cobun of Claiborne County, Mississippi, journeyed to Virginia to buy hands for his plantation and for speculation. He visited Henrico, Hanover, King William, King and Queen, Albemarle, and Essex counties, but hands were either "unlikely" or selling at exorbitant prices. One twenty-two-year-old slave brought $520, a boy of fourteen brought $289, and a man approaching sixty brought $150. He heard about a few "small ones," ages eight to twelve, selling at $180 each, and if they were "likely" he would buy them. "I shall be off to Maryd and should have done so before, but for difficulties there, which do not exist here," he wrote from Richmond. He was looking to buy runaways on speculation, but noted "you can't get a negro in Jail in Md. without trouble, and the titles are not good in many instances."[14]

To mislead potential buyers, false papers, improper titles, and fraudulent references could be obtained. At times, traders bought slaves without papers or abducted them for resale. It was not usually masters who became involved in such unseemly conduct, but occasionally slave owners themselves stole other owners' slaves. John Peters of Florence, Alabama, wrote Governor A. P. Bagby in 1839 about a Kentucky owner who stole several of his mother's slaves. Peters instituted a suit in Kentucky to reclaim his mother's property. "I was influenced by those considerations wch address the feeling interest and patriotism of every Southerner upon any invasion of this species of our property," Peters wrote as he sought assistance from the governor. Slaveholders must be protected in their possession of slave property "as guaranteed to us by Solemn Compact and the fundamental laws of this Govt."[15]

But slave stealing and kidnapping occurred frequently in various parts of the South. Isaac Briggs, a planter in both Maryland and Georgia, explained that there were many "avaricious and unprincipled" whites who abducted blacks—"some free, some manumitted to be free in a limited time, and some slaves." They transported them to different parts of the South, then secretly took them before a magistrate and, for a price, secured false titles and other legal documents saying that they were the owners of the slaves. If questioned, they could claim that they were bringing in a fugitive. Kidnappers carried on a brisk traffic in people of color, Briggs asserted. It was so brisk that in some sections even legitimate owners were put on the defensive. When the runaway Alabama slave Ben was sold out of the Pikeville jail in 1836, Jeremiah Pritchett, Ben's owner, not only failed to prove ownership but was accused of perfidy. "Is Pritchett held among his acquaintances as an honest, honorable man?" the court asked. "Is he a man of Known truth? Is he or not to be fully credited on his word or his oath?" Pritchett described Ben, produced a bill of sale, and brought witnesses to back up his story. "You put me to the trouble to prove my character," he wrote the judge of the Marengo County Court, assuring him that he would never lie about such a matter "for what wd it proffit me to gain the whole world and lose my own soul."[16]

Others were less concerned with quoting Scripture than profiting from the sale of runaways. In 1808, Dr. John Newnan, a physician in Johnson City, Tennessee, sold farmer Thomas Stewart a slave woman without informing him that she was in a Salisbury, North Carolina, jail under arrest as a runaway. The doctor also sold to the same farmer the woman's daughter, who had been left behind. The woman was returned to Tennessee and delivered to Stewart. When he learned he had bought a fugitive, he refused to pay, but neither would he return the slaves. Newnan hired an agent to retrieve his property. When the agent appeared, Stewart "got into a passion" and took him into the kitchen "& taking hold of said Negros by the hand Viz Rachel & Patt he said 'here I deliver these negros to you as the property of Dr.

Newnan.' " But before the agent could take them away, the farmer's son, Montgomery Stewart, appeared and refused to turn over mother and daughter. It was sometime later that Dr. Newnan himself, in the middle of the night, crept onto the Stewart farm, "kidnapped" Rachel and her daughter, and took them to Nashville for auction.[17]

That a prominent physician would sneak onto another man's farm in the middle of the night to retrieve his slave property and then set out under cover of darkness to a city halfway across the state to auction Rachel and her daughter to the highest bidder reveals the impact runaways had on the slaveholding class. The selling of runaways and the deception involved in this case were by no means unique. Indeed, one could argue that men and women who owned other human beings often found themselves in a position where even the most honorable among them were forced into acts of dishonor and deception. In the sale of runaways, such was often the case.

The Conspiracy Theory

Slave owners seemed to find it difficult to understand why so many slaves ran away. It was one thing for a few vicious, unruly, and unmanageable slaves to leave the plantation, but most, they argued, were gentle, obedient, and happy. How was it that such a contented group, sometimes even the most skilled and privileged among them, took their leave without uttering a word? Masters admitted that some slaves wanted to be with loved ones, take a holiday, and avoid hard work. They also admitted that some slaves found it difficult to make proper decisions, had some "defect" in their personalities, or suffered from depression or other mental problems. Little Charles stole away from his Louisiana plantation and broke into a meathouse on a neighboring farm. When he was caught and whipped by three white men and still ran away again, his master said he suffered from "mental alienation" and "fits of insanity."[18]

The "mental alienation" theory was given scientific authority by Dr. Samuel Cartwright, a prominent New Orleans physician. In an article in De Bow's Review in 1851, Cartwright explained that many slaves suffered from "drapetomania, or the disease causing negroes to run away." The name was derived from the Greek, δραπέτης, or a runaway slave, and μανία, mad or crazy. Absconding from service was "as much a disease of the mind as any other species of mental alienation," Cartwright wrote. It was as well understood by planters and overseers as it had been by the ancient Greeks more than two millennia ago. To cure the disease, Cartwright proposed that owners provide slaves with adequate food, housing, and fuel. If the disease persisted, however, owners should whip them until they fell "into that submissive state which it was intended for them to occupy in all after-time."[19]

Whatever the reason, slave owners believed it was not because most blacks disliked slavery or their masters and mistresses. When a Virginia runaway burned down the jail to effect his escape, his owner insisted that he did not do so out of any "malice." Some owners felt their runaways had simply made a childish mistake and would return if given an opportunity. "Should Nancy return of her own accord," a South Carolina owner explained in an advertisement, "she will be forgiven and likewise furnished with a ticket to find another owner if required." Almost exactly the same words were used by other slave owners seeking a return of their property: "If he returns of his own accord, he will be forgiven," "If Prince will return to me in two weeks, there shall be no questions asked." To a recently purchased family of six, including father, mother and their four children, George Cox of Charleston wrote: "If they return of their own accord, I will forgive them." Such "compassion" stemmed from the belief that these slaves were not unhappy with their lot but were irresponsible or unstable.[20]

Even after many months, sometimes years, owners continued to hold out hope that their runaways would come to their senses and return of their own accord. They continued to reject the notion that their slaves actually wanted to be free. Charleston owner William H. Smith tried everything to prevent his slave Tenah from running away, but nothing seemed to work. She had absconded on several occasions, each time remaining away for several months. When she left during a trip to Barnwell District in 1830, Smith offered a $100 reward. Six months later, he still could not believe she wished to be permanently free. "[I]f she comes in of her own accord, within one month from this time, no punishment will be inflicted, and she shall have a ticket to select an owner in the city." If not, however, he would have her "transported beyond the limits of the State."[21]

If it were not slave owners, then who was at fault? Masters often pointed to slaves from outside the United States, intruders from the North, free blacks, or a few lawless whites. These groups did not understand the master-slave relationship or that most slaves were contented. Rather, they sought to stir up discontent. In 1793, slave owners in South Carolina observed that slaves were becoming increasingly insolent and aggressive. The militia was put on standby. It was widely believed that "the St. Domingo negroes"—those imported from the Caribbean—were sowing the "seeds of revolt." They were doubtless influenced by black revolutionary Toussaint L'Ouverture. During the

1790s, some southern states restricted the entry of black people from the West Indies. In the early nineteenth century, slave owners pointed to "French Negroes," those from French possessions in the Caribbean, as continuing to foment unrest among the slaves in the southern states. They observed that slave revolts were often organized and planned by runaways.[22]

To others, it was not French-speaking Caribbean blacks who were inciting slaves to run away. Instead, it was whites from the North. In 1804, a group of fifty-four residents of Richmond, Virginia, accused northern ship captains of corrupting the morals of their slaves. Trading vessels from New York and the New England states frequently moved up the James, York, Rappahannock, and Potomac rivers; the captains of these ships, the group of Richmonders asserted, tried to inculcate in the "weak minds" of slaves a spirit of "discontent, tending to insurrection," and in many instances enticed them to abscond. Nor were these concerns the result of the hysteria that gripped many parts of the South following the revolt in Haiti and the Gabriel and Sancho conspiracies in Virginia. The same arguments appeared in later years, during tranquil and tumultuous times, in the Upper and Lower South, along the seaboard and in the interior. During the 1850s, southern whites expressed grave concerns about whites from the North corrupting their slaves and continued to refer to the horrors of slave revolts.[23]

The theory of meddlesome intruders corrupting the morals of slaves could be seen in the attitudes of individual slave owners. Virtually all misbehavior by slaves against their masters—violence, insurrection plots, running away—was ascribed by Rachel O'Connor, the mistress of Evergreen Plantation in Louisiana, to evil and diabolic nonslaveholding whites. When slaves absconded in the Feliciana parishes in 1835, she observed that "mean white men" were the "sole cause of all." When a slave woman assaulted her mistress on a nearby plantation, O'Connor wrote: "I have no doubt, of some mean white man being the cause of the trouble." And when a group of slaves along Thompson's Creek conspired to revolt, she had little doubt that the plot was instigated by two white men who "made their escape."[24]

In their runaway notices, some masters also revealed their belief that their slaves would never run off on their own. "I have no doubt but they are conducted by some villain," Jesse Williams said in 1813 of the two field hands he had recently purchased for his plantation in Logan County, Kentucky. They were both "keen and sensible." Why would they want to run away? A Virginia master said his slave John went off with an Englishman. He was not sure whether the white man would "endeavor to convey this fellow off [and] sell him" or entice him away with some promise, but he was certain his slave would not go off on his own. Others said they had last observed their slaves with whites, had noticed white men "lurking about the plantation" shortly before a slave absconded, had a feeling their slaves were being "persuaded away" by whites, or learned that their slaves had been promised passage "out of the state" by whites. John Saunders of Nashville was convinced that his "likely mulatto Negro Man, named GEORGE," was "coaxed off by some white man." He would simply not have gone off on his own.[25]

When some of their most "loyal" slaves ran away, masters often attributed such treachery to outside influences. In 1841, an Alabama farmer said there was little doubt that the two runaway brothers he owned had been "decoyed." An Alabama planter, James C. Coleman, of Eutaw, explained that he knew his mulatto slave Caesar well, describing him as a pleasant and contented slave. It was impossible, therefore, that Caesar, in his late twenties, well-treated, and loyal, would run away on his own. "I am apprehensive that some person induced him to run away," Coleman wrote, "as he left during my absence and without any known cause." The same was true of the four slaves who absconded from the Giles County, Tennessee, farm of John C. Reagin. They left one Sunday night in the midst of the harvest. "They are probably making their way to Ohio or Indiana—and I have reason to suspect they were enticed away by a white man, and may have free papers or passes."[26]

If slaves eluded capture, or made difficult escapes, masters said they must have done so with the aid of outsiders. Late one night, George, who managed his master's financial affairs, led his wife, three children, a grandchild, and a ten-year-old black girl away from the master's plantation in Jefferson County, Florida. His owner immediately said that George must have been "backed by some white man, who will try to carry the negroes out of the country."[27]

Rumors, innuendos, accusations, and false reports flourished following the departure of runaways who were thought to have been enticed away or hidden by "some designing white men." In some sections, even being accused of such activity could be disastrous. Georgians were no more litigious than residents of other states, but several slander suits in the state illustrate what might occur to whites imputed to have helped runaways. In 1804, John Pettit, a white man who lived in Jefferson County, was accused by a slave owner of harboring his runaway. In a $10,000 libel suit, Pettit said he had always been "a good, faithful, & honest citizen," but now had lost his "good name, fame, credit & Esteem." No one would "trust or have any connection with him." He was "a bad citizen & an harbourer of negroes." In

1821, William Jordon of Jones County was similarly impeached by Nathaniel Perrott, who said Jordon had twice concealed his "negro fellow named Sam" and provided him with meat and turnips. Jordon fell into "great discredit and distrust with those good and worthy Citizens who before that time used to desire [his] Company & Conversation." His "good name, fame Credit and reputation" were destroyed by the "false scandalous malicious and defamatory words." In 1831, John W. Hemby sought $5,000 in damages against John Appling, who said that "Wrays Runaway girl (meaning Wm Wrays Runaway female slave Susan)" was being harbored at the farm where Hemby resided. Hemby, too, experienced "public scandal infamy and disgrace."[28] Thus, the mere hint of collusion with runaway slaves could ruin a man's reputation, whether guilty or innocent. In fact, two of the three Georgia men were found by the court to be blameless, but the conspiracy theory was articulated so often that southerners came to believe that many of their runaways were indeed lured away.

Nonslaveholding whites and outside agitators, they insisted, were a major cause for slave discontent. A group of slave owners in McClennan County, Texas, contended during the 1850s that emissaries from northern organizations were distributing literature to incite slaves against their owners and to instigate desertion. Similar assertions were put forth in other parts of the South. In 1859, a group of residents in Louisa County, Virginia, said "vagrants and temporary sojourners" were inciting slaves to "desertion or conspiracy and insurrection." Under the auspices of preaching the gospel and distributing "pious works," northern fanatics were goading slaves to resist their owners. These outsiders were preaching black equality—or, as they put it, slaves were morally, socially, and politically "adequate of themselves." A member of the Virginia General Assembly asserted that the best way to combat this evil was to require that all visitors from nonslaveholding states sign a pledge promising to abide by the provisions in the Fugitive Slave law.[29]

Another strand of the conspiracy theory involved free persons of color. Many owners believed that free blacks were loyal to their slave brethren and would do anything to assist them in betraying their masters. During the 1840s and 1850s, these fears surfaced often, especially in Virginia, with its large slave population so close to the North. A group of slave owners recommended that the time period slaves be allowed to remain in the state after emancipation be reduced from twelve months to one month. That would not allow the emancipated sufficient time to become acquainted with the roads through the mountains, and they could not "purloin off our slaves and reach a free state." A free person of color was sometimes influenced by white abolitionists, but he could also have strong motives of his own, including "the liberty of his wife his child or his relation." White Virginians should also be watchful for free people of color arriving from northern cities, another group warned, for the black intruders sowed seeds of "discord and disaffection" among the slaves.[30]

It is not difficult to understand how slave owners became so attached to the conspiracy theory. It fitted neatly into their political struggle with the North; it absolved them of blame for slave discontent; and it offered a simple explanation for a complex human problem. Thus, despite the profusion of runaways in their midst, they could deny that blacks were resisting slavery.

Estimating Frequencies and Owners' Costs

Among the first things J. D. B. De Bow did after arriving in Washington, D.C., in 1853 as superintendent of the United States Census was to oversee the publication of *A Compendium of the Seventh Census*. Coming from New Orleans, where he had spent seven years as founder and editor of *De Bow's Review*, a journal strong in the defense of slavery, De Bow was now in a position to strengthen his defense. One of the questions census marshals asked slave owners in 1850 was how many bondsmen and bondswomen had run away during the previous year and had remained at large? In De Bow's opinion, the statistics compiled from the question offered further evidence of the benign nature of southern slavery: in Alabama, the number of successful fugitives stood at 29, in Arkansas 21, Florida 18, South Carolina 16, and there were fewer than a hundred each in Kentucky, Louisiana, and Georgia. Maryland led all states with 279, and the South's total stood at only 1,011. A decade later, census takers counted even fewer fugitives. During the year ending 1 June 1860, among 3,949,577 slaves, the census said, there were only 803 escaped slaves who remained at large, about one in every 5,000 blacks, or one-fiftieth of one percent.[31]

Marshals asked slaveholders to list their runaways. The replies not only produced flawed results, but the narrowly constructed question about those still at large failed even to hint at the magnitude of the problem. From various primary and secondary sources, several generalizations can be made about the size of the runaway population. First, while the number of newspaper notices for fugitives increased with the expansion of the slave population between 1790 and 1860, only a small fraction of runaways was advertised. Second, the journals, diaries, correspondence, and records of slaveholders indicate that it was a rare master who could boast that none of his slaves had absconded. In fact, the vast majority admitted just the opposite. Third, some farmers and planters owned "habitual" runaways, slaves that set out on numerous occasions and were usually sold or severely punished or both. Such slaves ran off two, three, four, or more times each year. Thus, while runaways constituted a small minority of the slave population, they were of enormous significance in the plantation universe.[32]

It will never be known how many slaves ran away at any given time, but the following examples from a group of small slaveholders, from an industrial master, and from one large plantation were unexceptional. When Maryland farmer William Biggs died and left his estate to his widow, Catherine, under the supervision of his son-in-law, one of the first things the son-in-law did was to seek to "recover some slaves who had runaway some time ago." Similarly, in the reports of guardians for children who owned slaves there is commentary on runaways. Henry Goodloe of Boyle County, Kentucky, was responsible for making the eight slaves of his ward, John R. Shannon, a clear asset. This was rendered difficult because one of the slaves was a perpetual runaway, and he was forced to sell her at auction along with her child. Among the eleven slaves in the estate of Isaac B. Nelson, a Giles County, Tennessee, farmer who died in 1854, was Isaac, who ran away five times in a single year, lying out weeks at a time during all seasons. For farmers and small planters, the record book of Basil Kiger during a two-year period reveals what many others experienced. He made the following payments, as they appeared in his record book:[33]

Sept 11th	[1849]	To cash pd. jail fees for Ezekiel	14[.]25
	[1849]	To cash pd [jail fees] Archy	17[.]17 . . .
[Oct.] 26	[1849]	To Cash paid Mrs Collins Boy For runaway	5[.]00
Augst 16	[1850]	To Cash paid. Runaway Negroes	18[.]00 . . .
[May]1st.	[1851]	To Cash Paid for catching Isham	5[.]00 . . .
Oct 12	[1851]	To Cash Paid Expenses for Runaway	13[.]00

In industrial slavery, an example of runaways exists in a mortgage deed signed in 1804 between partners of a nail factory in Havre de Grace, Maryland. In 1804, to maintain his share of equity in the enterprise, Roger Boyce mortgaged twelve of his male slaves who worked in the factory. They ranged in age from fourteen to forty-five, although half were teenagers. Within a few years, the firm folded, Boyce died, and the mortgaged slaves were put up for sale. Nearly half of them were advertised as "negroes who have runaway, and who will be sold at the risk of the purchasers." To be advertised in such a manner, and at such a reduction in price, Big and Little Jacob, Isaac, Abraham, and Harry were not merely truants but runaways.[34]

An inventory of slaves on Homestead Plantation in St. James Parish, Louisiana, in December 1860, illustrates the problem of runaways on a large plantation.[35] The slaves were owned by Reine Welham, the widow of William P. Welham, and as was the case on other sugar plantations, men outnumbered women. But among a total of 125 slaves, there were twenty-two family units. Only three women had husbands living elsewhere, and there were only five orphaned youngsters. The adults worked as cooks, gardeners, washerwomen, house servants, carpenters, nurse, cooper, hostler, driver, sugar maker, plant foreman, water carrier, and field hands. The ages of the slaves reveal a remarkably stable slave community: Old Sandy, a gardener, was eighty-five, there was one slave in her seventies, several in their sixties, eighteen in their fifties, and the same in their forties. Most labor in the cane fields was performed by the fifty slaves in their teens, twenties, and thirties.

Homestead was a typical large plantation during the late antebellum period. If anything, with 60 percent of the slaves either too young (ages one to twelve) or too old (over forty) to perform exhaustive labor in the fields, it was more benign than most, and the widow Welham more caring than a majority of her fellow planters. Among the 64 male slaves at least thirteen years of age, 4 were listed as "Runaway": twenty-three-year-old Henry Smith; Washington Jr., the same age; John Miles Jr.; and his father, forty-one-year-old John Miles Sr., a field hand who suffered with a hernia. Among the 32 women in the same age group, none was cited as a runaway. Thus, about 4 percent of slaves age thirteen and older had absconded.[36]

While it is not possible to use percentages or proportions over two generations for the South as a whole, Maryland farmer William Biggs and nail manufacturer Roger Boyce, Kentucky minor John Shannon, Tennessee farmer Isaac Nelson, and Louisiana planter Reine Welham represented typical slaveholders within their respective groups. In fact, if anything, Welham's experience with runaways would represent the conservative side of the compendium. This was certainly the case in several Mississippi counties during the 1850s, when sheriffs and magistrates used printed forms to process the volume of runaway slaves committed to jail in their jurisdictions.[37]

Touring the South during the 1850s, Frederick Law Olmsted asserted that on every large or moderate plantation he visited masters complained about runaways. Even in sections of the deep South where blacks had "no prospect of finding shelter within hundreds of miles, or of long avoiding recapture and severe punishment, many slaves had a habit of frequently making efforts to escape temporarily from their ordinary condition of subjection." This was so common that southern whites described it as "a disease—a monomania, to which the negro race is peculiarly subject." It should be kept in mind that "throughout the South," Olmsted concluded, "slaves are accustomed to 'run away.' "[38]

Olmsted was essentially correct. A close examination of planters' records, runaway advertisements, county court petitions, and other primary sources reveals that it was an unusual planter (generally defined as one with twenty or more slaves) who could boast that none of his or her slaves had ever run off. Indeed, many confronted the problem at least once or twice a year, and a few struggled to control a plague of runaways. Nor was it uncommon for blacks to flee from slaveholders who owned fewer than twenty slaves. These owners too often faced severe problems with runaways.

In 1860, there were about 385,000 slave owners in the South, among whom about 46,000 were planters. Even if only half of all planters experienced a single runaway in a year, and if only 10 or 15 percent of other slaveholders faced the same problem (both extremely conservative estimates) the number of runaways annually would exceed 50,000. Add to this the number of slaves who, like Sam King on Morville Plantation, continually ran away, and it becomes clear that Olmsted's impressionistic observation was far more accurate than the "scientific" data provided in the United States Census.

Just as the exact number of runaways will never be known, neither can we know for certain the financial losses suffered by slaveholders. But here, too, several generalizations can be made from circumstantial evidence. First, most runaways remained out only a few weeks or months and so the loss to planters was primarily a loss of labor. Second, comparatively few runaways were successful in their bid for freedom, and thus the capital losses remained minimal. Third, while running away could not be eliminated, it could be controlled with relatively modest financial outlays. Fourth, the average reward offered for advertised slaves (fifteen dollars in the early period and twenty-five dollars in the later period, including those who offered no reward) represented a tiny fraction (less than 5 percent) of the value of the slaves. The reward structure revealed how confident masters were about the return of their human property.

It was rare when the cost of retrieval amounted to more than a small percentage of a slave's value. In the early nineteenth century,

The volume of runaways in the deep South during the 1850s is suggested by the advertisements in a single issue of the New Orleans Daily Picayune. Rewards were offered for Jack, Sam, Zip or Harry, Edward, Daniel, Henrietta, Mary Mackendish, William, and Tom. The volume is also indicated by the printed, fill-in-the-blank forms (see next page) used by sheriffs in Natchez and Port Gibson, Mississippi, to collect jail fees for captured runaways.

Mrs. Maria Cooper

TO THE JAIL OF CLAIBORNE COUNTY Dr.

For Jail Fees of _Jim_ a Runaway, committed

the _23rd_ day of _September_ 18 _58_

" Committing, Releasing and Docketing, ... $2 25

" _2_ days sustenance, at 40 cents per day, ... 80

" Reward $6, Mileage, $ _____ 6 00

" Magistrate 70 cents, Constable 75 cents, ... 1 45

" Affidavit, ... 25

" Advertising in the _____ insertion,

" Writing advertisement $1, Postage, ... 1 80

" Clothing $ ____ Medical Bill $ ____

$11 75

Received Payment, _J M Girault_ Sheriff.

By _J F Girault_ D.S.

Port Gibson, _Sept 24 1858_

Rec Payment By D. H. Jones

Mrs. W. Dunbar

To the Jail of Adams County, Dr.

For Jail Fees of _Emily_ a Runaway, committed

the _12th_ day of _July_ 185 _7_.

For _2_ days sustenance, at 40¢ cents per day, ... $ " 80

" Committing and Releasing and Docketing, ... 2 25

" Magistrate 88 cents, Constable 75 cents, ... 1 63

" Reward $6, Mileage $ ____ , Postage $ ____ 6 00

" Writing Advertisement $1, Printer $ ____

" Clothing $ ____ , Medical Bill $ ____

$10 " 68

Received Payment,

Natchez, _Sept 3d_ 185 _7_.

O Metcalfe Shff

By _Joseph Frantz_ D.S.

young able-bodied field hands were valued at $350 in Richmond, $500 in Charleston, and $500 in New Orleans; in 1837, averages ranged from $900 in Richmond to $1,200 in Charleston and $1,300 in New Orleans; by 1860, averages in Richmond and Charleston were about $1,200, in New Orleans, $1,800. Women; children; the elderly; slaves who were deformed, scarred, diseased, or crippled; and babies without parents brought less, and the average for all slaves was smaller than the average for field hands. Although the costs of slave hunters, helping pay for patrols (usually assumed by the state), sending overseers in pursuit, rewards, and jail fees rose over time, the comparative costs remained small compared with the price of slaves. During the early period in the Mississippi Territory, the law required that any person bringing in a runaway receive a $6 reward and expenses. By the mid-1830s, slaveholders in various states paid a few dollars to print up handbills and to advertise in newspapers and "18 cts per day each" for "dieting negro men" in jail. It cost Franklin H. Elmore of Walterborough and Columbia, South Carolina, for example, $26.84 to retrieve Isaac and Sancho, jailed in December 1834 and claimed 7 January 1835, including capture, jailing, food and clothing. Often slaves worth several hundred dollars could be hunted, advertised, captured, jailed, and returned, for less than $50.[39]

By the 1840s and 1850s, travel costs had gone up, and professional slave hunters often charged $5 a day plus expenses, while reward offerings and jail expenses and prices for chains and handcuffs increased. But there had been a dramatic rise in the price of slaves, and expenditures for retrieval still remained relatively modest. Owners complained about "great pecuniary Loss, and personal inconvenience," the great "trouble and expense," but even some of the most troublesome runaways cost their owners small sums in lost labor and expenses. One Maryland master, who complained bitterly that his "Servant Boy Brice a slave for a term of [thirty] years" was in the "Habit of running away" and had subjected him to "much Expense trouble and inconvenience," presented a statement in 1850 showing lost labor and expenses:[40]

Absent from 16 Sept 4 Oct. 1849	Cost me	10
Absent from 26 Nov to 24 Feby 1850	Cost me	50
Incidental Expenses		15
		$75.00

A decade later, another master paid exactly the same amount to a slave catcher for the return of his property. "Mr. Roper brought down Henry today and I have put him in Jail," W. S. Cothran, president of the Bank of the Empire State in Rome, Georgia, wrote his friend

William Browne, the owner of an Alabama plantation. "Roper makes a charge against you for seventy five Dollars for catching negro etc." Such losses were not inconsequential, but compared with the value of the slaves (Brice sold for $350 a short time later, and Henry would have brought at least $1,000), even these relatively high expenses were not burdensome, especially for wealthy planters.[41]

Most retrieval costs were well below what it took to bring back Brice and Henry. R. Dunbar lost some days labor from his slave Emily, committed to the Adams County, Mississippi, jail in 1857, but when he received the notice of her incarceration, the bill included only charges for two days sustenance at 40 cents a day, a $6 reward for the person who brought her in, a magistrate's fee of 88 cents, constable fee of 75 cents, and a committing, releasing, and docket charge of $2.25, for a total cost of $10.68. Similarly, the fees for Maria Cooper's black man Jim, jailed 23 September 1858, in Claiborne County, Mississippi, was only $11.75. In Warren County one master paid an additional $5 for a branding iron.[42]

At times slave owners were able to avoid even these modest fees. It sometimes happened that runaway slaves were committed to jail by order of a justice of the peace. Michael Bruner, jailer of Adams County, Mississippi, complained in 1809 that such runaways were not always reported, and so they remained in jail for months. The jailer was subject "to considerable trouble and expense," and the masters, who were punishing their slaves, took them back at their convenience without paying "a farthing" for their incarceration. In 1807, the same situation existed in Surry County, Virginia, when a jailer took up five runaways, a woman and four children. The jailer sent word of their capture to their owner Henry Daniel but received no response. Months passed, and although the five were "regularly advertised & at the proper period offered for hire" no one wanted them. Meanwhile "their naked condition" rendered clothes and blankets necessary, and the woman, "whilst in jail, was delivered of a child, consequently gave much trouble and additional Expense." In all, when the owner finally arrived to retrieve his slaves in January 1809, the county had expended more than $422 for their care and upkeep, expenses Daniel refused to pay.[43]

As in the Surry County case, a few slaveholders found the costs of retrieval substantial. When slaves remained out over extended periods, traveled to distant locations, or had a good head start before being discovered missing, expenditures for slave catchers, dogs, transportation, advertisements, meals, rooms, horse rentals, jail fees, medical expenses, and rewards could grow large. The itemized list of charges submitted by Isaac W. Conger for a trip to Tennessee and Arkansas in May 1846 "for the purpose of recovering negroes run off" from the Kenly Plantation in Mississippi showed what might happen if fugitives had a good head start. The account included expenditures for an attorney, ferry tickets, steamboat passage, meals, rooms, intelligence reports, horse rental, a "Tavern Bill at Memphis," including $2.50 for his rental horse and $1.25 for himself, horse feed, "Passage for Horse from Memphis to Grand bluff," and a $30 "Bass Fee." The total came to $148.04, and this did not include Conger's daily charge, only "expenses." One Louisiana planter noted how he had been "obliged to lay out and expend several large sums of money to diffe[nt] persons in making search and inquiry" after his slave named Christmas, who should have been easily spotted as he left shackled with irons and branded with the word "Durnaw." Not only did he pay slave catchers, but sent along several slaves who consequently "lost a great number of days work."[44]

For small slaveholders, such expenditures could create severe hardships. The complaints of these owners concerning the "great cost and expense" of reclaiming runaways were often justified. At the time of his death about 1842, Elisha Collins of Lauderdale County, Mississippi, owned two slaves, a young man and young woman. The bills submitted to the estate by slave trackers E. Peters and M. Ethridge revealed the difficulties the owner had experienced with the man:

> To Cash paid E. Peters 4 Days With Negro Dogs to apprehe[n]d Negro Steven a $5 pr. Day 20.00 . . .
> to Cash paid E. Peters and M. Ethridge Expenses in pursuit of Negro Steven $1[.]50 pr. Day 4 Day Cash $12.00 . . .
> To Cash paid M. Ethridge 4 Days With Negro Dogs—@$5 pr Day—20.00.

For Collins such expenses were not trivial; indeed, he had not been able to pay them during his lifetime, and excluding his two slaves, who sold for $900, the $52 charge was nearly equal to the value of his entire personal estate.[45]

For a number of years, Dick and Bill labored on the small farm in Bastrop County, Texas, owned by James Alston, but following their master's death in November 1851, the two plotted an escape. When their chance came, they bolted off together, heading northeast and then southwest toward the Mexican border. The bill submitted by the administrator of Alston's estate traced the route of the slave catchers, who stopped at the Rio Grande River. In "Hunting for and traveling to hunt for, the runaway negroes Dick & Bill," they rode more than 750 miles, spent many weeks, and expended nearly $200. When Alston's estate was inventoried, it was clear why such efforts had been

An Account of expenses & disbursements (made for Mrs Kenly)
by Isaac W Conger on a trip to Arkansas for the purpose
of recovering negroes run off by D. Kenly   May. 1846

To Judge Randolph for certifying to power Atty to I W Conger	00. 50
Ferriages at Thompsons Ferry	.37½
At Grand Gulf 2 suppers & Breakfasts	1. 10
Warf Boat 2 Lodgings	.75
2 Passages to Napoleon $7.00 each	14. 00
Smith Boarding 4 days @ 1.50 per day	6 00
I. W Conger. 5 days " .. " ..	7. 50
Smiths Passage down	6. 00
Procuring Howards Reports from Enloe	1. 60
Bass Fee $30 Horse $40.00	70. 00
Ferriages across the Arkansas River & one Bayou	.50
Nights Lodging	1. 25
Tuesday Lodging & Ferriage	1. 50
Wednesday lodging & long ferriage	1. 75
Thursday Toll Bridge & lodging	1. 50
Friday lodging 1.25 long ferriage across Black 100	2. 25
Saturday 2 ferriages 50 cts	.50
Tavern Bill at Batesville 5.75 dols	5. 75
Ferriages across White River twice & lodging —	1. 75
Nights lodging and two toll gate for two Bridges	2. 00
Wednesday 1 toll gate ferriages across the St Francis & Blackfish	1. 50
Nights Lodging 1.25 Crossing Missp River 100	2. 25
Tavern Bill at Memphis for Horse 250 self 125	3. 75
Passage for Horse from Memphis to Grand Gulf 6 feed 87½ cts	6. 87
Passage for self $7.00 to G. Gulf	7. 00
	$148.04

I certify that the above is a true copy of the list of expenses
on the above trip as rendered on my return.
June 2nd. 1846.   Isaac W Conger

undertaken. Alston owned five horses worth $100, a yoke of oxen worth $35, and three slaves—Dick, valued at $900; Bill, valued at $800; and Harriett, valued at $450. In the end, the administrator noted only that the two slaves "have escaped & not [been] found."[46] After paying the slave catchers, the estate was left with a few hundred dollars.

The loss of slaves' labor was also a hardship for masters with only a few bondsmen and bondswomen. For one estate with thirteen slaves, it represented exactly 8.3 percent; twelve blacks were hired out at $50 each, or $600 per year, but the thirteenth, named Danger or Young Titas, "ran away for nearly the whole yr, and therefore was of no service." In March 1853, Peter W. Gibbons's slave John Gray of Baltimore County ran away and remained out until late November. When Gibbons listed his expenditures, he included $6 for advertising, $15 for six trips to Baltimore, including "4 different times myself in search," a $10 reward to William Snyder, $5.94 magistrate and jail fees, and $66.75 lost time at $8 per month, a total of $103.69. During one four-year period, a slave belonging to a small trust estate in South Carolina ran away so many times that he became "almost an incumbrance." The slave, the trustee asserted, was out at least three-fourths of the time. When one runaway was jailed in Vicksburg, Mississippi, in 1853, he made up a story about his owner's name. It took his real owner, R. W. Long of Montgomery, Alabama, four years to track him down. By then, the black man, known as "John," had been sold, and another man held the legal title. Long did prove ownership and received a $557 reimbursement (the sale price of $710 minus $153 expenses), but his losses were significant. Considering that the slave, in his early thirties, would have sold for at least $1,000 in 1857, and each year's labor was worth at least $100 (minus food, clothing, and housing), the $557 represented about one-third of what the owner might have expected had his slave not run away.[47]

Although financial expenditures for advertisements, rewards, slave hunters, jail fees, travel, and counting expenses can be easily measured, other costs were less readily evident. Slaveowners struggled to maintain an efficient workforce, but the time and energy they spent coping with the runaway problem caused inefficiency. This could be seen not only in the loss of labor, which for small planters could be substantial, but in the turmoil runaways created when they abandoned the plantation. In addition, owners were beset by a constant loss of their property—their own stolen slaves, items pilfered from their plantations, and runaways. Indeed, the clandestine slave economy in some sections was maintained and sustained by outlying slaves. Nor is it easy to measure the cost of living in the midst of violence, hostility, and subversive activity.

The Impact of Runaways on the Peculiar Institution

The determination of masters to rid themselves of persistent runaways, the formulation of a conspiracy theory, and costs associated
with runaways reveal only part of the impact this group had on the
institution of slavery. Masters were forced to explain how "contented"
and "well cared for" servants abandoned them in such large numbers.
Not a few owners concluded that slaves who ran away on numerous
occasions or who failed to change their behavior after severe punishments were insane, imbalanced, or suffered mental "afflictions." That
so many slaves apparently suffered from the same affliction was difficult to explain. Also difficult to understand was the flight of so many
apparently loyal and obsequious slaves. Bequeathed from father to son,
the thirty-two-year-old Maryland slave Annetta Irvine had lived with
the same family most of her life. A few years before her term of
servitude was to end, as stipulated in the father's will, she ran away
to Pennsylvania. The family expressed dismay that she would demonstrate such ingratitude after they had treated her so well. She was
soon caught and returned, however, and her term of servitude extended ten years.[48]

As suggested by the response of this Maryland family, the impact
of fugitives on the attitudes of the master class was profound. At the
heart of the slave system was the need to control laborers and produce
profits. Both seemed to be jeopardized by the behavior of runaways.
Substantial energy and time were devoted to the question of how to
control the movement of slaves. Planters prohibited them from leaving
their plantations without written permission, instructed overseers and
managers to watch the slave quarters at night, and joined militia and
patrols to keep the peace and capture runaways. They supported city
ordinances and state laws designed to regulate and control the movement of slaves. They warned ship captains and steamboat owners about
the penalties of harboring escaped slaves. Authorities in Richmond,
Charleston, Savannah, New Orleans, and other cities made concerted
efforts to prevent slaves from sneaking aboard ocean-going vessels.[49]
They watched harbors and estuaries at night for possible hideaways.
They created a system whereby slaves who ran away and were jailed
could be returned to their owners at a relatively small cost. They supported a group of professional slave hunters willing to travel substantial distances and go to great lengths to recover the owner's property.

Despite these and other attempts at control, the escapes continued.
So prevalent were runaways in some sections that whites became anxious, even fearful. Although the traveler who stopped at a Mississippi
plantation and pushed furniture up against the door of his room before

going to bed was probably atypical, it did point to how whites remained apprehensive. A man who shared the room said, "He woke me when he came in, by his efforts to barricade the door with our rather limited furniture." He took two small revolvers out of his pocket and put them "so they could be easily taken up as he lay in bed." It might be stuffy, but "he shouldn't feel safe if the door were left open." " 'You don't know,' " said he; " 'there may be runaways around.' " Some owners put it in their wills that when slaves became "disobedient," "unruly," or ran away they should be immediately sold.[50] At various times, slave owners and other whites expressed similar anxieties and fears.

They were especially apprehensive following revolts and conspiracies in the nineteenth century, such as the Gabriel plot in 1800, the revolt in Louisiana in 1811, the Denmark Vesey conspiracy in 1822, and the Nat Turner revolt in 1831. They were also anxious when groups of runaways committed various "depredations" in their neighborhoods. Despite their insistence that their own servants would never become involved in such activity, slave owners spoke of the possibility of "conspiracy" and "insurrection," of slaves who were "proud & malignant, with great impudence," of the "plotting and conspiring" to murder whites. Although not a slave owner—indeed she wrote about the "evils of slavery"—longtime North Carolina resident Frances Bumpass expressed the fears of others when she wrote in her diary in 1844 that rumors of a possible insurrection remain with her constantly. "Dwell too much on said imaginary scenes of murder— fear to sleep—when slumbering often start in dread."[51]

What weighed most heavily on the minds of slave owners and, indeed, contributed to their increasing defense of southern civilization, was the knowledge that so many slaves were neither docile nor submissive. Runaways symbolized the very aspect of bondage that they could not reconcile with their belief that slavery was beneficial for both master and slave. Few owners were unaware of the dissatisfaction or hostility among some of their slaves. Yet they could not publicly, or even privately, admit that such widespread unrest existed. To do so would undermine the very foundations of their arguments about slaves and slavery.

The influence that runaways exerted on their fellow slaves is difficult to assess. The harsh reprisals meted out to slaves who ran away and were caught and brought back were designed in part to dissuade others from following in their footsteps. There was also fear and at times resentment among those who remained behind because they were punished for the actions of absconders. Yet, most slaves had genuine sympathy, compassion, and hidden admiration for those who

defied the system in such a manner. It was painful to watch the beatings and whipping of runaways, especially if they were kin or close
friends, but those who remained on the plantation secretly cheered
their brethren who remained at large for weeks and months or never
returned.[52]

Even slaves who were captured and punished on a regular basis
could count on support from their fellow slaves. Such was the case on
James Henry Hammond's Silver Bluff Plantation on the Savannah
River in South Carolina. Between 1831 and 1855, there was an average
of two escapes per year (a total of fifty-three). The runaways did not
fit precisely into the profile described earlier, being slightly older (average age thirty-three compared with twenty-seven), slightly more
male (84 percent compared with 81 percent) and probably remaining
out longer (an average of forty-nine days). Yet, they were typical in
most respects, especially for the Lower South: not a single runaway
gained permanent freedom, one-third of them came in of their own
accord, and they received sustenance, support, and encouragement
from slaves on the plantation. This happened despite the fact that
Hammond was well aware that those who deserted were "lurking"
about in a nearby swamp. He waged a continuous but unsuccessful
battle to stop the flow of food and provisions to outlying blacks, including punishing the other slaves with more work—plantation management was "like a war without the glory" he ruefully commented—
but the blacks remained loyal to their brethren and continued to supply them.[53]

Hammond's neighbors were experiencing similar difficulties. In a
rare interview, the Georgia slave Friday explained after capture how
he remained out for several months at a time. Owned by Charles
Manigault of Gowrie Plantation on the Savannah River, Friday ran
away to a nearby swamp, hid out, then went to a store owned by a
man named Jefferson to trade for food and supplies. He spent time on
a heavily wooded island in the Savannah River, "a great hiding place,"
and in the kitchen of a nearby plantation. The house servants hid him
there because the slave quarters was often searched. In addition, Friday
said, Harry, the driver at Gowrie, "never stops a negro or tries to talk
him out of it when he knows that he is going to run away."[54]

Ironically, running away in this respect brought slaves together.
There were few slaves who could not picture themselves in the same
position as those who were striking out for freedom. At times this
commiseration and empathy, as on Silver Bluff and Gowrie plantations, translated into practical support. Plantation slaves harbored runaways from other plantations, protected, clothed, and fed them, and
offered information about routes of travel. Some fugitives hid out for

many weeks, even months, on neighboring plantations. Considering the possible reprisals for engaging in such activity, the support given in this manner was remarkable.[55] The bonds forged were strong ones, born in crisis and hardened by the fear of retribution.

Perhaps the greatest impact runaways had on the peculiar institution—among whites and blacks alike—was in their defiance of the system. Masters and slaves knew that there were blacks who were willing do almost anything to extricate themselves from bondage. They ran away again and again, and in some cases were willing to sacrifice their lives. Being transported from Jefferson Parish, Louisiana, back to New Orleans by a local sheriff, George leaped into the swift-flowing Mississippi River in 1852, swam a short distance, and went under. Others also "unexpectedly jumped overboard" and were lost when it was apparent they would be returned to their former master or sold away from a husband or wife. A few committed suicide rather than remain enslaved. Such was the case for Bush, an Arkansas slave who hid out on a mail boat going up the Ohio River from Louisville to Cincinnati but was discovered as the boat came into port. Taken into custody, he was placed in a yawl; as they rowed toward shore, Bush jumped overboard and immediately sank. "Strange story," wrote the wife of the Arkansas planter whose brother owned the runaway, "Bush such a capital swimmer, and drowned in 5 feet of water!"[56]

In their escape attempts, most slaves neither died nor committed suicide, but the number who made it as far as Bush—from the deep South to the Ohio shoreline and beyond—remained very small. Among those who did, perhaps none expressed himself more clearly and forcefully about the meaning of freedom than Frederick County, Virginia, runaway Joseph Taper, who wrote a letter to a white acquaintance in 1840 tracing his escape, near capture, stay in Pennsylvania, and arrival in Canada (see appendix 6). Forced to flee "in consequence of bad usage," Taper ran off to the North in 1837, taking his wife and children. During a two-week stay in Somerset County, Pennsylvania, he read his own runaway notice in a local newspaper. When he was in Pittsburgh, he learned of the presence of George Cremer, a slave catcher hunting "runaway servants." In August 1839, he took his family to St. Catherines, Ontario, rented a farm, and raised a crop of potatoes, corn, buckwheat, and oats, acquiring seventeen hogs and seventy chickens.

St Catherines W C, Nov 11th 1840

Dear Sir,

I now take this opportunity to inform you that I am in a land of liberty, in good health. After I left Winchester I staid in Pensylvania two years, & there met some of your neighbors who lived in the house opposite you, & they were very glad to see me; from there I moved to this place where I arrived in the month of August 1839.

I worked in Erie Penn where I met many of our neighbors from New Town. I there recieved 26 dollars a month

Since I have been in the Queens dominions I have been well contented, Yes well contented for Sure, man is as God intended he should be. That is, all are born free & equal. This is a wholesome law, not like the Southern laws which puts man made in the image of God, on level with brutes. O, what will become of the people, & where will they stand in the day of Judgment. Would that the 5th verse of the 3d chapter of Malachi were written as with the bar of iron, & the point of a diamond upon every opprossers heart that they might repent of this evil, & let the oppressed go free. I wish you might tell Addison John, & Elias to begin to serve the Lord in their youth, & be prepared for death, which they cannot escape, & if they are prepared all will be well, if not they must according to scripture be lost forever, & if we do not meet in this world I hope we shall meet in a better world when parting shall be no more. . . .

We have good schools, & all the colored population supplied with schools. My boy Edward who will be six years next January, is now reading, & I intend keeping him at school until he becomes a good scholar.

I have enjoyed more pleasure with one month here than in all my life in the land of bondage. . . .

My wife and self are sitting by a good comfortable fire happy, knowing that there are none to molest [us] or make [us] afraid. God save Queen Victoria, The Lord bless her in this life, & crown her with glory in the world to come is my prayer,

Yours With much respect
most obt, Joseph Taper[57]

A Note on Primary Sources

TO A REMARKABLE DEGREE, the recent scholarship on slavery has relied either on plantation records, planters' journals, and the testimony of prominent whites, or slave reminiscences, slave narratives, and slave autobiographies. Even authors interested in women's history have uncovered diaries of elite white women or produced monographs about black women based heavily on recollections. This is neither the time nor place to evaluate this literature. Suffice it to say that many of the persons who inhabit the pages of recent studies are either far removed in time and space from the South they describe, or, due to conventions, or the purpose of a diary, are less than candid in their observations.

In our study of runaways, we rely on two types of evidence not fully utilized by scholars: notices of runaways in newspapers and petitions to southern legislatures and county courts. Besides their contemporary nature, both sources provide a number of unique strengths. Masters who advertised for a return of their property had little reason to misinform their readers and every reason to be as precise as possible. They presented information on a range of topics concerning their slaves, including physical descriptions and family relationships. Petitions are also an excellent source. Responding to an event, situation, or potential danger, petitioners realized that it behooved them to be as forthright and candid as possible. Female petitioners, for example, knew that they would gain little by pretense or deception since most people in their communities knew their situations. Consequently, they discussed their circumstances with remarkable candor and accuracy. Moreover, the veracity of petitioners can be weighed against the response of defendants, witnesses, magistrates, and judges. Of course, all sources are biased, but when it was in the interest of individuals to state their case as clearly and truthfully as possible and to secure corroborating testimony, the primary source achieves a high degree of credibility.

The appendixes that follow provide illustrations of the types of sources used in this study. The notes reveal how we used these as well as other sources to understand the history of plantation rebels.

Appendix 1
Newspaper Advertisements

Tennessee Notice for Negro man named Sam

TWENTY DOLLARS REWARD

RUNAWAY from the subscriber living near Nashville, state of Tennessee, on the 27th of April, 1813, a negro man named SAM, about 25 years of age, nearly six feet high, stout, well proportioned, active and likely; rather of a yellow complexion, an open countenance, generally wears his hair platted before in two or three plats; is extremely proud; smokes segars, and walks with a considerable air—he is a good cook, an excellent waiter in the house, and carriage driver: he understands all kinds of farming work and the distillery; he had on when he went away a home-made cotton shirt and pantaloons, and took with him a blue broad-cloth coat about half-worn, a pair of boots, and sundry other articles of clothing which cannot now be described: he is inclined to steal, and no doubt will soon provide himself with good clothing; his back and thighs, if examined, will shew the marks of the whip. It is most likely he will make for Cincinnatti, and from thence for the Canada lines. Ten dollars will be give for securing the above negro, if taken within 60 miles of Nashville, and reasonable charges if brought home; or if further, the above reward of twenty dollars, if secured in any goal within the United States, so that I get him again.

Michl. Campbell
May 26, 1813
39-3w
[Source: *Nashville Whig*, 26 May 1813.]

Tennessee Notice for Negro man named Jim

RUNAWAY,

On the night of the 9th Nov. Inst, a negro man named JIM or ARMSTEAD, aged about 22 years, about five feet ten inches high, very likely, and when spoken to has a pleasing appearance; has whiskers. No particular marks recollected. He wore off when he left a fur cap, brown cloth frock coat, boots, &c.; had with him a variety of clothing, description not recollected, and will most likely dress very well and in newest fashion. He also rode off a large bay horse about 8 years old, a natural pacer, foretop has been cut off and nearly grown out, with a Spanish saddle quilted cover, and no padd saddle bags, &c. I think it most likely that he has attempted to make his way for Nashville, Tenn., or New Orleans. He has a mother in Nashville, said to be free, the wife of a man by the name of Wilson Davis, and was raised in that place and has many acquaintances there: he has lived for the last fewe years in New Orleans, and was a short time since brought to Alabama by WM. T. Gamble, who conveyed him to me. I have but little doubt that he will make for one of the places mentioned, and will give a reasonable reward to any person who will apprehend and commit him to jail, or give me such information as will lead to the recovery of said negro and horse.

Geo. W. Lane.

Athens, Ala. Dec. 19.—W31

The Louisville Journal will publish the above once a week for three weeks, and charge this office.

[Source: *Tennessee Republican Banner* 26 December 1838.]

Alabama Notice for Anthony, Billy, and Bartlett

RANAWAY

RANAWAY from the plantation of the subscriber, on the Alabama river, three Negro Men—ANTHONY, BILLY AND BARTLETT—of the following description, viz:

ANTHONY is apparently 38 or 39 years of age, 5 feet 10 or 11 inches high, dark complexion, and speaks remarkably quick when spoken to, very intelligent and subtle, weighing about 160 or 165 pounds. Anthony was brought from Spartansburg, or thereabouts, in South Carolina, by Mr. Underwood, a year or eighteen months since. He has a wife in that State, which seems to be an object in the expedition. He has been in the habit of going to Charleston, Savannah and Augusta. Anthony is the leader, and has persuaded the other two to go with him. It is supposed they have passes or some guarantee to travel with, as they have taken a week's provision and all their bed clothing and apparel.

BILLY was brought from Virginia during the fall of 1850 by Mr. Underwood, and sold to the subscriber in January, 1851, and ran away once since. Mrs. Catts of Lynchburg, owned him formerly, and employed him in driving an omnibus in that place for several years; and his objec[t] is to return, and thence to a free State. Billy is 28 years of age, weighing 135 or 140 pounds, mulatto complexion, and stutters very much when a question is to be answered. One of his feet (uncertain which one,) was incurably injured by frost, while driving the omnibus, so much that the skin is always seamed and cracked open remarkably. He is wearing a white hat and cassimere pantaloons of light color. He was sold by Mrs. Catts on account of his fondness for whiskey.

BARTLETT is a native of Norfolk, Va., 32 or 33 years of age, weighing 165 or 170 pounds, thick set, copper colored almost, slow spoken, and is, seemingly a companion for the rest without any object in view, unless the chance of a free State. He was brought from Norfolk when 12 years of age, and raised until that time by a Mr. Burford or Bruford. He was brought to this county by a Mr. Willis[.] If Bartlett should be taken, he will soon divulge the history of all.

A very liberal reward is offered for their apprehension, or any information concerning them, and more so for their delivery.

Anthony and Bartlett had whiskers, and Billy a Goatee, which are off probably by this time.

L. G. WEAVER.
Selma, Ala., June 30, 1853—c3t
[Source: *Richmond Enquirer*, 1 July 1853.]

South Carolina Notice for Ceely and Frances or Fanny

$500 REWARD.—RANAWAY.

about three years ago, a mulatto girly named CEELY, rather short and thickset, about 28 or 30 years of age, light complexion; has a small scar on her upper lip, near the mounth; her upper teeth bad, near gums; a fine seamstress, mantua maker and tailoress; has often been seen about the city since she went off, and is supposed to be harbored (as she has been heretofore) by some white person. Three hundred dollars will be paid for her apprehension, and fifty dollars on proof to convinction of any responsible person who may have harbored her.

ALSO,

The girl Frances, or Fanny, about 26 years of age, ranaway in December last; has been seen about town, until within the last three or four months; of good height, brown complexion, rather sharp features; her upper front teeth gone, (but she may have had fasle teeth to replace them, as she declared she would if she ran off;) talks like the North Carolina negros, where she was raised, but latterly [sic] has lived in Florida; has a pleasant expression, speaks slowly and deliberabely, and altogether a very likely girl. She, too, is supposed to be harbored by some white person in the city. One hundred dollars will be paid for her apprehension, and fifty dollars on proof to conviction of any responsible person who may have harbored her.

WM. R. TABER.

October 6

[Source: *Charleston Mercury*, 6 October 1857.]

Louisiana Notice for Molly

FIFTY DOLLARS REWARD—Ran away on the 14th September, 1859, from P. E. Beauvias, residing on S. O. Nelson's plantation, Bayou Teche, the griffe girl MOLLY, about 20 years of age, very small but well made, rather a big face for her size, with swollen eyes, very white teeth, kept very clean; dresses with taste and wears hoops; when she left, had on gold ear-rings (horse shoe shaped), and a plain flat ring on one of her fingers. She is suspected of knowing how to read and write. Will probably try to make her way to New Orleans, where she was purchased about six weeks ago from a trader. The above reward will be paid for the capture of the above described girl.

P. E. BEAUVAIS

[Source: *New Orleans Picayune*, 22 September 1859.]

Appendix 2
Petitions to State Legislatures
and County Courts

PETITION TO THE VIRGINIA GENERAL ASSEMBLY, 1817

To the Honb^le the Speaker & Members of both Houses of the General Assembly of Virginia

The Humble Petition of sundry inhabitants freeholders & Citizens of Isle of Wight County sheweth that great and serious evils have resulted to the peaceable & orderly inhabitants of this section of the state, from the black population. that these evils are encreaseing [sic] to the great annoyance, & disturbance of the peace & tranquility of society—That neither the persons, or the property, of the Citizens, can be considered in a state of safety. Within the last year several Murders have been committed in this County, by persons of that colour. Among the victims, your petitioners have to lament the loss of one of their most valuable & respectable Citizens. Your petitioners beg leave most respectfully, to invite the attention of the General Assembly to the subject—The number of slaves & free persons of colour, in this part of the state is so great—as to render it a subject of deepest solicitude to your petitioners that the most efficient laws for the restraint & controul of those persons should exist—Your petitioners are impressed with the opinion, that the laws on the subject of slaves freenegroes & Mulattoes are susceptible of many very salutary amendments, They believe the sum at present allowed by law for the apprehending of out lying & runaway slaves is entirely two [sic] low. That it might be advantageously encresed or augmented to fifteen or twenty Dollars.

That the penalty on free persons for harbouring runaway slaves, ought to be rendered as severe as would comport with the genious [sic] & principles of the Government–They most respectfully submit

to your honorable body whither, free white persons, who are so for-
getful of their own honor as to harbour runaway slaves ought not to
be deemed guilty of a misdemeanor or Crime punishable by confinement in the Jail or penetentiary House & whither free persons of
colour who are guilty of the offence of harbouring runaway slaves,
ought not to be deemed felons & punished by Death. Your petitioners
are well aware that the penalties they propose are very severe, & that
severe penalties sometimes defeat the object of the legislature, Yet
they believe that the evils of which they complain can be arrested by
the most severe & exemplary punishments only–They have long witnessed with the deepest regret the facilities furnished by base & immoral white persons & free persons of colour, to the slaves, to deprive
their owners of their services & to plunder them of their property
with impunity. That such intercourse between slaves and free persons
is calculated to produce crimes of the most serious and dreadful consequences, to promote insubordination & a spirit of disobedience
among the slaves, & finally to lead to insurrection & blood. Your
Petitioners are fully satisfied that the peace & tranquility & happiness
of the people, will always receive from the General Assembly of Virginia every security within the reach of its constitutional powers–

Your petitioners fully convinced of the truth of the last proposition
most respectfully submit to the wisdom of the legislature, the propri-
ety of passing laws on the subject above refered to. Your petitioners
Humbly pray that their situation may be taken into consideration by
the Honble. the General Assembly. That the penalty for Harbouring outlying & runaway slaves by free persons–may be greatly encreased.
That the penalty on free white persons & free persons of Colour for
dealing with slaves, be augmented, and that a larger sum be allowed
for apprehending runaways.

And that such other & further amendments be made to the laws
on the subject as shall be deemed best calculated to promote the wel-
fare, felicity & happiness of the Citizens of Virginia—

And your petitioners as in duty bound will ever pray &c

[signed] Josiah Halleman	Barthᵃ Lightfoot
Chˢ. Wrenn	Wᵐ Holleman
Arthur Smith	Bailey Davis
Joseph W Ballard	Nath P. Phillips
	[et al.]

[Source: Legislative Petitions, Petition of Josiah Halleman, et al., to
the General Assembly, 12 December 1817, Isle of Wight, VSA. Rejected.]

PETITION TO THE SOUTH CAROLINA SENATE, ca. 1824

To the Honourable, The President And The Senate of the Legislature of the State of South Carolina

We the subscribed Petitioners inhabitants of Claremont, Clarendon, St. Johns, St. Stevens and Richland Districts beg leave to offer to your honourable and enlightened Body, the following narrative as Containing the grounds of their most reasonable petition. It is now some years since M^r-[George] Ford a highly worthy and respectable Citizen of our State was murdered some where not far from Georgetown S°. Ca–by a Negroe belonging to M^r. Carroll of Richland District named Joe (or Forest) We believe that unhappy occurrence happened under the Executive administration of the honourable Thomas Bennett. The relatives of M^r.—Ford offered liberal rewards for the apprehension of this out lawed fellow.[1] The Executive offered an appropriate reward also, but neither the temptation of the private reward, nor the public reward of the Governor, nor both Combined could ^lead to the Capture. He was so cunning and artful as to elude pursuit and so daring and bold at particular times when no force was at hand as to put every thing at defiance.[2] Emboldened by his successes and his seeming good fortune he plunged deeper and deeper into Crime ^until neither fear nor danger could deter him first from threatening and then from executing a train of mischief we believe quite without a parrellel in this Country.

Most of the runaways flew to his Camp and he soon became their head and their life. He had the art and the address to inspire his followers with the most Wild and dangerous enthusiasm Such was his Cunning that but few of the enterprises for mischief planned by himself fail'd of success. We believe that nearly four years have now elapsed since the murder of M^r–Ford, the whole of which time until [Joe's] merited death was marked by Crimes, by mischiefs and by the disemination of notions the most dangerous among the blacks in of our of Sections of the Country.[3] (Such as were calculated in the end to produce insubordination and insurrections with all the hideous train

1. The reward was for $1000, an extraordinary sum at the time. *Acts and Resolutions of the General Assembly of the State of South Carolina, Passed in December, 1825* (Columbia: D. And J. M. Faust, 1826), p. 102.

2. In 1822, the Committee on Claims of the South Carolina House of Representatives awarded Meshack Williams $160.62 for the supplies he had furnished the militia as they set out to search for Joe. *Acts and Resolutions of the General Assembly of the State of South Carolina, Passed in December, 1822* (Columbia: Daniel Faust, 1823), 89.

3. The Committee on Claims in the South Carolina Senate said that Joe had terrorized inhabitants in a wide area and committed depredations "heretofore unparalleled in this State." *Acts and Resolutions of the General Assembly of the State of South Carolina, Passed in December, 1825* (Columbia: D. and J. M. Faust, 1826), 102.

of evils that usually follow.[)]] Such at length began as we believed to be the danger arising from the power and influence of this Example and such we believed were the indications given of approaching insurrection, that we deemed it ~~propper~~ expedient to call on the propper Military department to send an adequate force either to capture or destroy a species of enemy that Kept our families and neighbourhoods in a Constant state of uneasiness and alarm. This propper and justifiable application for assistance being disregarded, We made direct application to the Commander-in-Chief who taking no notice of our appeal to him We were Compelled as we conceived from the necessity of the case to associate together for the purposes of domestic safety and for the object of impressing our blacks with propper fears by the power of wholesome example We cannot but think that ∧^the state Authorities as well Civil as Military were bound not only to have aided and assisted in car[r]ying into effect these most laudable views but that they were bound also without delay to have attended to the peace and protection of an important and interesting section of the State of South Carolina, for it is held as a just and fundamental maxim of government that States are bound to give to their Citizens as adequate protection as possible in Cases of alarm and danger. We organised several companies as Infantry, from among our association, and being prepared for some days active service under persons Chosen to Com mand We or many of us scoured Santee River Swamp from the Confluence of the two rivers that form it to Munys Ferry a distance even by land of sixty miles. Notwithstanding however the zeal and alacrity with which we continued pursuit We should at length, oppressed by the sultry sun of ~~August~~ October 1823, wearied down by excessive fatigue and rendered dispirited by the number, extent and character of their places of retreat and Concealment ~~should~~ have abandoned our ~~their~~ enterprise as being likely ^to yield nothing but disappointment to ourselves and triumph to the objects of our pursuit, but for the fidelity of a slave belonging to Mrs Perrin of Richland District named Royal. He in perfect good faith conducted a select party of your Petitioners to ∧ ^the Camp of Joe and his followers, and having the Command of a boat, being its Patroon he with considerable judgment and address managed to decoy those whom we had long sought towards the Boat, where were stationed, a party expressly detailed for this duty. Soon perceiving their mistake and the danger full before them, they instantly attempted to defend themselves with well charged musquets but at a single well directed fire from the part of whites in the Boat Joe with three of his party fell dead. The rest of the gang of runaways were subsequently either killed in pursuit, hung for attempts to murder or were frightened to their respective homes. Now therefore we

your most humble and respectful Petitioners conceiving that we particularly and that the State generally ~~are~~are deeply indebted to this
Slave Royal for his fidelity and good Conduct in making himself the
immediate instrument in bringing to merited punishment an offender,
against the laws of the land,——pray that in due consideration of these
things will award to him such Compensation as may be fully adequate
and as your honourable and enlightened Body may think most com-
patible with the best interests of ∧ ^the^ State and with its dignity and
Character in rewarding those that have rendered services to it —The
good faith and honour of your Petitioners are implicated so far towards
this Slave on account of his good Conduct and faithfulness that they
are bound most earnestly to pray your honourable Body to grant their
prayer in which event they shall as in duty bound ever pray-

[signed] William D. Wilder

John Mayrant Jr.   A. P. Johnston
Rich^d^Moore   James H. Hext
Warren Mason   T. N. Johnston
John China Ju^n^   L. M. Brunson
                        [et al.]

[Source: Records of the General Assembly, Petition of Inhabitants
of Clarendon, Clarmont, St. James, St. Stephens, and Richland districts
to Senate of South Carolina, ca. 1824, ND #1874, SCDAH. Granted.
The Assembly allowed seven hundred dollars to manumit Royal so
long as it occurred within three years. See *Acts and Resolutions of the
General Assembly of the State of South Carolina, Passed in December, 1825* (Columbia: D. and J. M. Faust, 1826), 102.]

Petition to the South Carolina Senate, 1829

To the Honourable the Speaker and Members of the House of Representatives of South Carolina—
    The Memorial of the Freeholders and Other Inhabitants of the Par-
ish of Christ Church respectfully Sheweth-•-
    That Your Memorialists, Planters of South Carolina, from the
vicinity of their property to Charleston, from their parish being surrounded by navigable water leading directly to, and occasioning much
intercourse with that City, and from the great Northern road passing
through their parish in its whole length are peculiarly exposed to the
great evil of absconding slaves and their ruinous depredations—
    Your Memorialists are aware that these causes have long combined
to produce this evil, but they have within these latter Years only,
found it operate to an extent producing great irregularity and disorder
among their slaves, and now leading directly to a state of insubordi-

nation and danger affecting the lives of individuals and the security of property-•-

This State of things is operating, Your Memorialists believe, in every part of the lower and middle divisions of the State, as they are informed by the inhabitants of other parishes, and it cries aloud for the interference of your Honourable House—They think it unnecessary to say any thing of the increasing efforts made by enthusiasts out of Carolina, to poison the minds of our domestic people, these must be met in a different way, and cannot hurt us if the Southern states are true to themselves; but they would distinctly state their conviction, that great mischief has been already done, and is daily increasing by the misguided zeal and unguarded movements, acts and conversation of persons within our own State, owning little or none of the property they so earnestly and so unceasingly crave to meddle with, yet living and supported by the agriculture of the country-•-

Prior to the passing of the Law of 1821 entitled an Act to increase the punishment inflicted on persons convicted of murdering any slave, and *for other purposes therein mentioned,*$_x$ it is asserted by your Memorialists without fear of contradiction, the Slaves in this part of South Carolina were in every respect more obedient and better servants, and infinitely more trust-worthy and faithful than they have been subsequently. Since the passing of that Law, changes in the prices of our crops and consequently in the fortunes of many of our fellow Citizens have taken place, and these changes have carried to Charleston for sale, large bodies of Negroes. The unrestrained intercourse of these with free blacks and low and worthless white people, during their sojourn there, has infused into the minds of the negroes ideas of insubordination and of emancipation, which they carry with them when sold into every part of the State–

Your Memorialists have referred to the Law of 1821, as a period from which the evils of running away have increased upon them and upon the low country, and they do not hesitate to say, that this law has produced a most baneful influence on the conduct of the negroes– The persons who projected that Law stated, no doubt, that they were actuated by motives of great humanity, but Your Memorialists with much deference to Your Honorable Body undertake to assert, that they were not practical Southern Planters, otherwise they would have foreseen that the Law would be useless, and even hurtful to those whom it professes to protect; these persons were not Southern Legislators, for if they had been, they would have known that *changing the nature of the penalties in the case of negroes*—that inflicting the punishment

---

$_x$ No other purposes are mentioned in this act!

of death on a white man for killing a slave, *who is a property, instead of exacting a fine for the loss of that property,* was placing the white inhabitants on a footing which would not be admitted by Juries of our Countrymen, and hence that the penalty would never be inflicted in any case however enormous; for the very effect of the law as your Memorialists will presently shew, is to produce upon the part of the Negro, such acts of violence, as call immediate vengeance down upon him–Your Memorialists therefore deny unequivocally the policy, much less the necessity, of such a law as that of 1821, unless to satisfy the morbid feelings of those who wish to interfere with our own slaves; and they further assert that the negroes of South Carolina were better protected by the Laws and penalties which were founded by our forefathers, on the dictates of common sense and the nature of the property, than by the law of 1821; for the Old laws were practical, reasonable and therefore carried into execution, while the new law which inflicts death without benefit of clergy on a white for Killing a Slave, apparently admits of no mitigation or exception even if the slave should have ravished his daughter, attempted to Kill himself, or burnt his dwelling, and is therefore only productive of injury to the slave, to his owner and to the country.

Your Memorialists will now proceed to shew in their own case, the real and practical effect of the Law of 1821 and Your Honorable Body will not be surprised at the consequences, when the concise and artful manner in which the law has been drawn up is considered, its peculiar fitness to impress upon the minds of Slaves, (to whom it is too often read,) that they are now on a different footing as regards their owners and the whites, from what they formerly were; a footing approaching nearer to a State of emancipation from their authority, and of course to a State of unrestrained liberty and licentiousness—

And first–This Law prevents Planters and Overseers from turning out to put down even large gangs of runaways, unless under very aggravating circumstances; because they will not subject themselves to be tried for their lives by City Juries having notions and prejudices as to the property, and of course as to the principle of the law itself, different from what every planter and owner of country property must have; nor will they expose themselves to endure the expense, vexation, and loss of time, to which they may be and in some instances have been made liable under this law, although in the end honorably acquitted–

Secondly–The negroes finding a backwardness on the part of their owners and the neighbors to turn out, are encouraged to run off without Cause or with a view to commit depredations. Finding these are not closely pursued, others are encouraged to follow the same course, and those at home become disorderly and insubordinate–It is well known to Your Honorable body, *that a State of security in crime like this described,* must lead to greater and yet greater atrocities, hence the depredations upon our property, crops and cattle, have been enormous.–

Thirdly–Such negroes as have in consequence of this combination of fatal circumstances remained out for Years, at length cease to respect the whites, become reckless of consequences, and choosing their opportunities during the sickly season of the Year or when individuals are alone and supposed to be defenseless, attack them with a view to destroy them–

Fourthly the end of this chain of consequences proceeding from a most injudicious and fatal law, the act of 1821, is death to the misguided Slave and destruction to the property of your Memorialists, as will appear from the following facts supported upon the evidence of affidavits,

In 1822 a negro belonging to the Estate of Spring, but formerly the property of a Parishioner deceased, absconded and came into the parish as a runaway. In 1824 a fellow belonging to Mrs Legare joined him as a runaway was shot and killed in his company– In 1825 a family five in number purchased at the sale of A. Vanderhorst, absconded and joined the same ringleader– They continued out until October last, when the Children surrendered (one having been born in the woods) the Father and Mother having been both shot and killed– In 1827 three Negroes belonging to a Parishioners Estate returned in like manner after the sale of his effects, as runaways. One of them in January last snapped a gun heavily loaded with Slugs at one of Your Memorialists, who met him in the woods and who immediately shot the Negro. Another of these three negroes in October last attacked another of Your Memorialists with a knife fifteen inches long, stabbed him in the hand and would have cut his throat, but for assistance rendered in time to save him. In 1828, runaway slaves were collected from various parts of the Parish, one was Killed upon the spot, and another severely wounded for the second time and taken, in January last Eighteen Slaves the property of one of your Memorialists went off under their driver and of these one fellow has been shot and killed, while the house of the owner has been pillaged by his own slaves, ten of whom are still out in a neighboring parish–

The death of these negroes has been brought on them by the aggravating circumstances attending their depredations, which were no longer to be tolerated or borne with–One negro taken some months ago, declared on his trial, that he had in three weeks destroyed Forty head of Cattle, and many of Your Memorialists are altogether prevented from keeping Stock of any Kind, from these causes, after having had large gangs of cattle, sheep and hogs entirely destroyed-•-

Your Memorialists could swell this statement with many circumstances at once ruinous to them as well as most vexatious in their nature, for many of their slaves although not killed by gunshot, have been transported or have died in the woods and of diseases occasioned by running away. But they will not wear out the patience of Your Honorable Body, they would now rather, briefly, but with the utmost earnestness appeal for redress from so grievous a state of anarchy, occasioned by a spirit of infatuation which is abroad in our country touching our Negroes; they would in truth and sincerity, and in the name of humanity to their slaves, call for a repeal of a Law (the act of 1821) which lays the foundation of such waste of blood and property, and for a reestablishment of the Old State laws formerly in force-. They would ask as a means of undeceiving their misguided people, as a means of enabling Your Memorialists and all planters throughout the State, to bring their own and all other negroes into that state of subjection and perfect control, without which they speedily bring destruction on themselves and ruin on their owners—They would ask of this Honble Body, to pass an Act, declaring every Slave who shall hereafter abscond or runaway, or who may now be absent, as outlaws and deprived of the benefit of the Laws and out of the protection of the State, after the lapse of thirty days from his work without his Owners permission— And Your Memorialists as in duty bound will every pray—
[signed]

John Jonah Murrell	Joseph Maybank	I Ladson Gregorie
Henry English	J Hibber	T. H. H. Gregorie
Elisha Whilden	D Jervey	Thomas Joy
George W D Scott	A. V. Toomer	R T Morrison
Friederick Steding	Paul Weston	Daniel Legare
		[et al.]

[Source: Records of the General Assembly, Petition of John Jonah Murrell, Joseph Maybank, et al., to the Speaker and Members of the South Carolina House of Representatives, 1829, #90, SCDAH. Referred to Judiciary Committee.]

PETITION TO THE NORTH CAROLINA GENERAL ASSEMBLY, ca. 1830

To the Honourable the General Assembly of the State of North Carolina now in Session.

The petition of Sundry Inhabitants of the Counties of Sampson Bladen New Hanover and Duplin humbly Sheweth, that our Slaves are become Almost Uncontroulable they go and come when and where they please and if an Attempt is Made to correct them they fly to the Woods and there Continue for Months and years commiting grievous depredations on Our Cattle hogs and Sheep and Many Other Things. And as patrols are of no use on Account of the danger they Subject themselves to and their property.[4] Not long since three patrols two of Which for Executing their duty had their dwelling and Out houses burnt down, the Other his fodder stacks all burnt. Your petitioners pray that an Act of the General Assembly may be passed during the present Session of your honourable body Compelling Each Captain in the Afore named Counties to divide their companies into four Equal divisions which shall be Numbered 1.2.3.& 4. and One Man Shall be Chosen out of Each Company as a Captain or commander of that Company the Rest to be Submissive to his Orders under penalty of fifty Cent and the Captain or Commander on Neglect or Refusal to Comply with the duties Named in Said law Shall pay the Sum of ten dollars, and the first Company Shall be compeled so soon as appointed to search their Respective districts for Runaway Slaves in all the Suspected places houses or thicks where they may Suppose any Runaway or Runaways are concealed with the priviledge of Shooting and destroying all Runaway Slaves who may Refuse to Submit to Said Authority, And Said Company Shall Continue to make Such Search at all times when Necessary for the Space of three months and shall during the time perform all the duties Required by law for patrols to perform, and at the Expiration of three months the Company No. 2 Shall take place and perform in like manner as the first and so Continue untill the whole have served And for Compensation to said Company, the Rewards Already Offered by Owners of Slaves for Apprehending Runaways and on all Others those that have bin Runaway any time Under Six month fifteen dollars and from Six months to One year twenty five dollars and for more than One year fifty dollars which Shall be paid by the Owner of Said Runaway Slave to the Use of Said Company before they give him Up, and all property they may find in the possession of Runaways where the Owner of Said property Cannot be found.

4. Runaways and uncontrollable slaves were long-standing problems in these and other counties, dating back to the eighteenth century. In 1796, for example, the General Assembly passed a law to compensate owners of outlawed and executed slaves in Bladen, Halifax, Granville, Cumberland, Perquimans, Beaufort, and Pitt counties; the following year the act was extended to Warren, Onslow, and Chatham counties. *Laws of North-Carolina, At a General Assembly, begun and held at Raleigh, on the twentieth day of November, in the year of our Lord one thousand seven hundred and ninety-seven* ([Raleigh]: n.p., 179[8]), 4.

Whereas Many Negro Slaves are Allowed by their Owners to Raise and keep dogs and follow them at large that do great Injury to Our Stocks and if we kill there [*sic*] dogs they will then kill Our dog, Our horse, or Our Cow.

For Remedy Whereof Your petitioners humbly Request that an Act be passed Compelling all persons Owning Slaves at the time of giveing in their list of taxable property to give in on Oath all the dogs their Negroes are Allowed to Raise keep or follow them on the first day of April preceding the time of giveing in their list or Any time Since and pay a tax of five dollars on Each dog so given in. And your petitioners as in duty bound Shall Ever pray,

[signed] P. Cromartie	George A Dyer	G. Downing
Hanson W, Herring	Silas Herring	D, Melvin Senr
R W Cromartie	Richard Registe [?]	D, T, Patterson
John Cromartie	Wiley Herring	John Monroe
A. Cromartie	Phillip Herrington	Daniel Melvin Jr
D [?] Cromartie	Wiley Hall	David Cain
E. Herring	Love H Tatum	Love M Daniel
Rogers Lee		[et al.]

Your petitioners further request your Honerable Body if the method above proposed does not meet your approbation, that you will take our case into consideration & pass such a law, or grant us such relief as you in your wisdom shall think best.

[Source: General Assembly, Session Records, Petition of Inhabitants of Sampson, Bladen, New Hanover, and Duplin Counties to the General Assembly, ca. 1830, Miscellaneous Petitions, November 1830–January 1831, NCDAH.]

PETITION TO THE ORLEANS PARISH DISTRICT COURT, ca. 1821

To the honorable Joshua Lewis, District judge for the first judicial District of the State of Louisiana

The petition of Ant: Michoud of the City of New Orleans, Respectfully Sheweth

that your petitioner is the owner of one Certain Negro Slave named Robert, alias Norbonne, aged of years, or thereabout, stout, strong, of a fair complexion, healthy & possessing many good qualities such as cook, servant, —brick maker &c &c very intelligent & having twice made the voyage of East India, but very cunning and of some bad habits.

that on the 29th of December last past, your petitioner having to punish the aforesaid slave, did lodge him in the City Jail of New Orleans, then Kept by one Mr. Dom. Belaume' Gaoler; warning the aforesaid Goaler of the determined disposition of that slave to escape so soon as he can meet with the least opportunity to do it, and in consequence thereof, your said petitioner most expressly requested the said Joaler to chain the said slave and not to suffer him [to] go out of Jail even to work with the others slaves, employed by the City to repair streets, for fear that the said slave avail himself of that opportunity to attempt and effectuate his escape; to which request the Goaler answered negatively saying that the ordinances regulating his duties were contrary with the compliance of such a request, but he, at the same time, assured your petitioner that he would recommend the said slave to the overseers having charge of the slaves of the City Jail when sent at work, as an object of particular & vigilant watch & assured yr. petitr that Said Slave Should be Safely kept.

That yr petitioner relying on that assurance left his Said Slave in the said Jail and was informed that the Gaoler pointed out the Said Slave to the overseers, Ramirez, Planche, Peralte, and others, and expressly warned them of the disposition of Said Slave to make his escape, if opportunity, was left to him, and therefore ordered said overseers, carefully to watch the Said Robert alias Norbonne.

Yr petitioner further Shews that the Said overseers or Some of them were further more informed of the resolute determination of Said Slave to runaway.

Yr petitioner further Shews that the Said overseers, Ramirez, Panche, and Peralte are or were on the Second of february instant in the employment of the City in the Capacity of overseers having charge of the Slaves of the City Jail when turned out to work for the use of the Said City.

Yr petitioner further Shews that notwithstanding all his promptness, vigilance and sollicitude in warning those under the care of whom was the aforesaid Slave the Said Robert alias Norbonne, on or about the 2d of February last, through the imprudence neglect or malice of the aforesaid Overseers and namely of that of Ramirez and Peralte affectuated his escape and never Since was hear of, whereby Yr petitioner Sustained a loss of fifteen hundred dollars.

And Whereas masters and employers are by law responsible in Civil Cases for all damages and losses occasioned by their Servants and employees, yr petitioner, applied to the honorable the mayor of the City of New Orleans for the payment of the aforesaid sum of fifteen hundred dollars for the price value of Said Slave with interest from this day till paid.

Wherefore your petitioner respectfully prays your honor that all necessary process may issue in this Case and that the honorable the major aldermen and inhabitants of the City of New Orleans therein residing be cited to answer this petition and be condemned in their Capacity of body Corporate to pay unto yr petitioner the aforesaid Sum of fifteen hundred dollars for price value of Said Slave together with interests and Costs

And your petitioner as in duty bo [u]nd will ever pray & &

[illegible signature]

atty for petr

[Source: Records of the First Judicial District Court, Orleans Parish, Louisiana, Case Records, Ant. Michoud vs. Mayor, Aldermen, and Inhabitants of New Orleans, 26 February 1821, #3,370, reel 6, Louisiana Collection, New Orleans Public Library. The case was discontinued by order of the court on 3 November 1821.]

PETITION TO THE BALTIMORE COUNTY ORPHANS COURT, 1861

PERTISION

To the Oneable orpants court of Baltimore county your pertisiner bought a prentis negro boy isaac smuthers of Joshwa Zimmerman of Bal Co. may 20th 1858 and ratified by the said court the said negro boy has runway from our pertisioner 7 Seven different times as follows No 1 first time in november 1858 and was gone some four weeks and was taken up by one of the police of Baltimore No 2 second time in april 1859 and was gone some seven or eight days, and taken up by Mr Sheckels of annarundle county no 3 third time in june 1859 and was gone 6 days and taken up by Edward Bauldwin of annarandle county and brought home No 4 fourth time in april 1860, and was gone two months, and taken up by your petisioner in Baltimore

No 5 fifth time the said boy runaway the 3th day after he was brought home and your pertisioner sent after him and overtook him on his to road to Baltimor[e] No sixth time in december 1860 and was gone 4 weeks and was taken up by his [petitioner's] father in Baltimore, and was taken sick from a heavy could [cold] that he got by laying out of nights during the time he was runaway and some three or four moths before the said boy was able to worke

No 7 seventh time runaway was gone 5 or Six days and was taken up by an officer of annarundle county and brought home chargeing a fee of Six dollars the said negro boy Isaac has cost your pertisioner great deal of trouble and lost time your pertisioner asks of the Oneable Court for and extension of time cirvice of the said negro boy isaac as will pay for loss of time runing way and sick by runing way, the absent time of the said negro 3 months & 18 days excluson of the 4 months Sick and unable to worke

William Burtons bill taken up negro 6.00 Your pertisioners 4 di-

ferent times going to Baltimore after the said negro boy wich is 24
miles each way, for the court to say what it is worth the court will
please notice that this negro boy is verey small at his age, his cirvices
are but small

Yours respectfuly

James S. Wilson

[Source: Baltimore County Register of Wills (Petitions and Orders)
James Wilson vs. Isaac Smithers, 30 October 1861, reel M-11,020,
SCHWENINGER COLLECTION, MSA. Smithers's term of service was ex-
tended twelve months.]

PETITION TO THE FREDERICK COUNTY, MARYLAND, COURT, 1838

To the Honorable the Judges of Frederick County Court.

The Petition of John Wood of Frederick County humbly represents,

That your Petitioner being the owner of a negro slave named Peter, on the 17th day of July 1827, by a deed of manumission executed,
acknowledged and recorded according to law, manumitted the said Peter, when he should attain to the age of thirty years, the said Peter being
nine years old on the 15th day of March next preceding the date of said
deed, which will appear, by an authenticated copy of the said deed,
herewith exhibited, marked, Exhibit A. Your petitioner further represents, that although he has ever treated the said Peter with the utmost
humanity and indulgence, the said Peter has, for some time past, exhibited an unruly and insubordinate conduct, so much so as to set the authority of your Petitioner at defiance, and to boast of his freedom from
all fear or restraint of or from your petitioner; that your petitioner
lately hired the said Peter to one of his neighbours, who treated him
kindly, and to whom the said Peter declared that he would never return
to your petitioner, and that he never would do your petitioner any good;
that four or five months after the said Peter had been hired out, as aforesaid, he ran away from the person to whom he was hired, and was taken
up as a runaway about eighteen or twenty miles from the residence of
the person to whom he was hired, on the direct route to Pennsylvania,
and committed, as a runaway to the jail of Frederick County, as will appear, by a copy or the warrant or commitment herewith exhibited
marked exhibit B; and has remained in said jail up to this time.

Your Petitioner further represents that from the unruly and independent conduct of the said Peter, he labours under serious apprehensions for his person or the persons of his family, and his property, if
he should release him from confinement, as the said Peter has, within
a few days past, sent word to the children of your petitioner, that his
confinement in jail had no effect on his bearing; that he did not cower

under it, and used other words, not necessary to repeat here, coincide of his insurrectionary spirit. Your petitioner further represents, that the said Peter before his hiring as aforesaid, was in the habit of leaving his home, without the permission of your petitioner and returning whenever it suited his humour; and notwithstanding such idle and disobedient conduct, your petitioner chastised him in no other way, than by striking once or twice on the side of his cheek with the flat of his hand; and your petitioner avers that he never struck the said Peter, at any other time, except about seven years ago, when he inflicted a moderate punishment, for his disobedient behaviour. Your petitioner therefore, prays that your Honors will adjudge and extend the term of service of the said Peter, so as fully to indemnify your petitioner, for all expenses and loss occasioned by the absconding of the said Peter; and also, that your Honors will grant an order for the sale of all the right of your petitioner in and to the said servant, Peter, to any person or persons within or without this State; provided your Honors shall be of opinion that the absconding of the said Peter was not occasioned by improper conduct on the part of your petitioner. And your petitioner as in duty bound shall every pray &C.

Thomas C. Worthington
Attorney for Petitioner

1833. ch. 224.

[Source: Frederick County Court (Petitions), Petition of John Wood to the County Court, 31 October 1838, reel M-11,024, SC, MSA. Wood received permission to sell Peter's unexpired term "to any person within or without this State," but the court required that he be furnished with a copy of his manumission deed. Order of the Court, October Term 1838, with *ibid.*]

PETITION TO THE TENNESSEE GENERAL ASSEMBLY, 1831

To the Honble,
The Senate & House of Representatives of the State of Tennessee, Now in Session—
Your Petitioner Austin Grisham would most respectfully represent, that several years ago M^r· Henry A. Burge departed this life, leaving a widow & two infant Children, Thomas & Mary —He died without having made a will, and left Considerable property—that sometime after his death, his widow was appointed guardian for his two infant Children, and took upon herself the discharge of the duties pertaining to the appointment, which will, if Considered necessary, be proven by the order of the ~~Davidson~~ ∧ ^Williamson^ County Court, making the appointment—Your petitioner states that on the 23rd day of July 1829,

and after the s^{d.} appointment was made, he intermarried with the s^{d.} Widow of the s^{d.} Mr. Henry A. Burge; that at the time of s^{d.} marriage she had the Controul of several slaves belonging to her wards, that among them is a boy, named Nathan, Now, between eleven and twelve years old—Your Petitioner States that for three or four years back, this boy, Nathan, has been in the Constant habit ∧ ^{of} running away; that he has employed all the means he Could himself devise, to prevent it; that he has obtained the aid of other experienced persons to the same object, but has failed in every expedient—the habit is increasing—And your Petitioner doth verily believe that nothing short of actual Confinement will, or Can restrain him from an indulgence in this vice—He says that he is a boy of more than ordinary Capacity, And he doth believe if the habit Complained of, should increase with his years (and he doth believe it will) he will be lost to the heirs, perhaps, entirely, by absconding, & finding a residence in some place or County ~~where~~ they Cannot find him, or, if found, from which they Cannot take him—

Your petitioner states that by law he has no right to sell him, tho' he is Confident it would be to the advantage of the heirs that he should be sold— He further states that his wife, the guardian of the heirs, is extremely anxious that he should be sold; that her security is also desireous that it should be done

Therefore, Your Petitioner respectfully solicits Your Honorable Body that you would pass a law directing him other ∧ ^{the sd. Negro boy Nathan} to be sold, or authorising Your Petitioner to sell him, upon such terms as shall deem proper to you, and with such modification as will secure to the said heirs the money arising from the sale, and the interest thereon.

And your Petitioner as in duty bound will ever Pray.

[signed] Austin Grisham . . .

Some twelve or fifteen months ago, I was in want of a boy, and upon some inquiry was informed that I could hire one of Mr. Austin Grisham—And upon application to him he agreed to hire me a black boy named Nathan, ten or eleven years old.

I took possession of him, and was very much pleased with him.— He was ~~ob~~ obedient, active, & intelligent far beyond Most boys of his age whom I had ever seen

–In about two weeks, (my belief is) after I had taken possession of him, in my absence, he ran away. And upon inquiry as to the Cause, I was satisfied he had none—In a day or two, I saw Mr. Grisham and informed him of the boy's departure and he then told me, it was his habit, but he had hoped he would not do so, while I had him, as the boy had Promised him he would not —After three or four days' inquiry I got him; And, being much pleased with him as a servant, and anxious to Keep him for a time, I resolved to pursue Such Course as would break the habit, if possible, and therefore, I only *talked* to him of the impropriety of his conduct, when I [told] him in such language as I am Confident he Perfectly understood— From his manner & his language he seemed to regret what he had done, & promised faithfully that he would not repeat the act— On the very next day, however, without any earthly cause, he absconded again, And after three or four days' inquiry & search I found him—I then joined Punishment to advice, and he again promised, faithfully, that he would do so no more– In six or seven days he repeated the offence, and eluded my search for about a week– when I got him, I had an iron Collar made for him & put a large padlock on it, and in this Condition set him about his business— On the same night ~~on~~ which this was done, he eloped again and I resolved to have nothing more to do with him & so notified M^r. Grisham —I believe he could not be reclaimed & believe it, still.

[signed] James I. Dozier
Nov 21, 1831. . . .

I am the security of Mrs Eliza Girsham, late Burge, the Widow of M^r. H. A Burge, deceased, and Guardian for her two infant Children, Thomas & Mary Burge— I Know the Negro boy Nathan, whom Austin Grisham, the present husband of the s^d. Eliza, is anxious to sell, and have no objection to his doing so, indeed, I am of opinion that it should be done, as he is the most habitual runaway, I ever Knew of his age—He is a boy of, greatly more than Common Capacity, And I think it more than probable, that if his Cunning & disposition to runaway shall increase with his years, that he may have the adroitness, before the s^d. infant children, Thomas & Mary Burge shall have arrived at the age of twenty one to escape entirely. Given Under my hand this day of November 1831

[signed] Ja^s. Condon

[Source: Legislative Petitions, Petition of Austin Grisham to the General Assembly, ca. 1831, #18–1831, reel #18, TSLA; Deposition of James I. Dozier, 21 November 1831; Deposition of James Condon, November 1831, with *ibid.*]

Appendix 3
Location and Possible Destinations of Runaways Cited in the *Nashville Whig*, 1812–1816

Location of Runaway		Possible Destination of Runaway	
Nashville	15	Kentucky	2
		Ohio	1
		Davidson County (Duck River)	2
		Nashville or Rhea County	1
		Augusta, Georgia	3
Davidson County	11	Kentucky	2
		Rutherford County	1
		Davidson County	2
		Virginia	1
		North Carolina	1
		Missouri Territory	1
Wilson County	1	Nashville	1
Dickson County	3	Nashville	1
		Ohio	1
		Kentucky	1
Sumner County	4	Virginia or Ohio	1
		Nashville	1
Rutherford County	5	Ohio	1
Robertson County	1	North Carolina	1
Smith County	3		
Franklin County	3	North Carolina	1
		Franklin County	1
White County	1		
Madison County	1		
Kentucky	9	Tennessee	1
		Louisiana or Mississippi Territory	1
		Indian Nation	1
Missouri Territory	1		
Louisiana Territory	1		
Totals	59		30

The distance from Nashville to the county seats are as follows: Lebanon, Wilson County, 32 miles east; Charlotte, Dickson County, 38 miles west; Carthage, Smith County, 52 miles east; Gallatin, Sumner County, 26 miles northeast; Murfreesboro, Rutherford County, 34 miles southeast; Springfield, Robertson County, 26 miles north; Sparta, White County, 83 miles east; Winchester, Franklin County, 94 miles south, southeast; and Jackson, Madison County, 134 miles southwest. Daniel Haskel and J. Calvin Smith, *A Complete Descriptive and Statistical Gazetteer of the United States of America* (New York: Sherman and Smith, 1847), passim.

Appendix 4
Location and Possible Destinations of Runaways
Cited in the *Tennessee Republican Banner*
(Nashville), 1840–1842

Location of Runaway		Possible Destination of Runaway	
Nashville	10	Down the Cumberland River	3
		Richmond, Virginia	2
Davidson County	4	Kentucky	1
Dickson County	1	Davidson County	1
Rutherford County	2		
Sumner County	2	Free State or Nashville	1
Robertson County	1		
Maury County	5		
Williamson County	3	Sumner County, Tennessee	1
Stewart County	1	Nashville	1
Giles County	8	Kentucky	1
		Ohio or Indiana	4
Jefferson County	2	Nashville or Ohio River	2
Hamilton County	1		
Kentucky	3	Sumner County, Tennessee	1
Georgia			
Monroe County	1		
Walker County	1		
Madison County	1		
Alabama			
Greene County	2		
Limestone County	1		
Montgomery County	1		
Mississippi			
Noxubee County	2		
Totals	52		18

The distance from Nashville to the county seats are as follows: Charlotte, Dickson County, 38 miles west; Gallatin, Sumner County, 26 miles northeast; Murfreesboro, Rutherford County, 34 miles southeast; Franklin, Williamson County, 18 miles south; Springfield, Robertson County, 26 miles north; Columbia, Maury County, 42 miles southwest; Dallas, Hamilton County, 141 miles southeast; Dandridge, Jefferson County, 229 miles east; Dover, Stewart County, 75 miles west, northwest; and Pulaski, Giles County, 74 miles southwest. Daniel Haskel and J. Calvin Smith, *A Complete Descriptive and Statistical Gazetteer of the United States of America* (New York: Sherman and Smith, 1847), passim.

Appendix 5
Damages Sought by Henry Crane
for Runaway Lewis, 1851

1851, January 18th.

      To purchase money paid to you for a Slave
named Lewis, by Plff. at the City of New Orleans,
State of Louisiana, which said slave has since died
in consequence of disease existing before and at the
time of sale to plff. $375.00

April 7   To am't paid J. G. Gordall, M.D. & Surgeon
for professinal attendance on said Slave Lewis
including 27 visits, preseciprtions and consultation
with A. Hart $59.00

April 5   The am't paid Doct. Hart for Examination of
said Slave Lewis and consultation with Dr. Goodall $5.00

April 7   To paid for medicines for said slave Lewis
to Dr. Hyde $4.50

April 15 To 12 weeks board & lodging attendance
and nursing of said Slave Lewis at city of New
Orleans at $4 per week $48.00

April 7th To paid S. Boat Buena Vista for passage of
self & said Slave Lewis from New Orleans, La. to
Ste. Genevieve Mo. $15.00

April 17 To paid funeral Expandes—Coffin—&
burying of said Slave Lewis at Ste. Genevieve, Mo. $4.50

April 17 To paid C. R. Smyth M.D. & Surgeon for post
mortem examination of said Slave Lewis, at Ste.
Genevieve, Mo. $10.00

   "   " To pay bound bill at Ste Genevieve $1.75

   " 20 To paid S. B. Pride of the West, for passage
of myself from Ste. Genevieve, Mo. to New Orleans,
La. $12.00

"   20 To 14 days of my time spent in going from New
New Orleans, La. to Ste. Genevieve, Mo., for the
purpose of returning said slave, and back $21.00

                                                  $555.75

[Source: Records of the Circuit Court, Ste. Genevieve County, Missouri, Henry Crane vs. Toussaint Lahay and Eloy LeCompte, 3 May 1851, County Court House, Ste. Genevieve, Missouri.]

Appendix 6
Correspondence

St Catherines W C, Nov 11th 1840

Dear Sir,

I now take this opportunity to inform you that I am in a land of liberty, in good health. After I left Winchester I staid in Pensylvania two years, & there met some of your neighbors who lived in the house opposite you, & they were very glad to see me; from there I moved to this place where I arrived in the month of August 1839.

I worked in Erie Penn where I met many of our neighbors from New Town. I there recieved 26 dollars a month

Since I have been in the Queens dominions I have been well contented, Yes well contented for Sure, man is as God intended he should be. That is, all are born free & equal. This is a wholesome law, not like the Southern laws which puts man made in the image of God, on level with brutes. O, what will become of the people, & where will they stand in the day of Judgment. Would that the 5th verse of the 3d chapter of Malachi were written as with the bar of iron, & the point of a diamond upon every opprossers heart that they might repent of this evil, & let the oppressed go free. I wish you might tell Addison John, & Elias to begin to serve the Lord in their youth, & be prepared for death, which they cannot escape, & if they are prepared all will be well, if not they must according to scripture be lost forever, & if we do not meet in this world I hope we shall meet in a better world when parting shall be no more.

And now I must here inform you that I was forced away in consequence of bad usage; Only for that, & I should be been in America, though I do not regret coming, & if I had known how easy I could get along I should started 10 years sooner, for it would have been better for me. Besides having a good garden, this summer I have raised 316 bushels potatoe, 120 bushels corn, 41 bushels buckwheat, a small crop of oats, 17 Hogs, 70 chickens, I have paid 50 dolls rent this year; next year I expect to build. The Queen of England, has granted 50 acres of land, to every colored man who will accept of the gift, & Become an actual settler, also a yoke of oxen, & plough for every two families. This a very great encouragement to those who have come here for the liberty which God had designed for them. Some have already gone, & others are going to take up the said land.

When I was coming to this place I stopped at Somerset, & worked there two weeks; There was an advertissment put up there for me, 200, dolls reward while i was there. I met James Mac Near in Butler Co, Penn where I staid five months. I was in Pittsburg at the time that George Cremer was in pursuit of runaway servants. I was ostler for Isaac H. Brittner in Containion 5 Months, & in that time earned 60 dolls. I harvested while there at 115 dozen a day & then went home, & attended the stable, was counted the greatest cradler in Penn. there was no cradler known to cut that much in that part.

There was Chase Gatewood who expected to take me to the Rocky mountains, got Sadly disappointed and lost his 700 dollars.

We have good schools, & all the colored population supplied with schools. My boy Edward who will be six years next January, is now reading, & I intend keeping him at school until he becomes a good scholar.

I have enjoyed more pleasure with one month here than in all my life in the land of bondage. And now you may believe me though unwelcome as the news may be, but it is true Joseph Taper has a commission from Col Clarck of this place, & is Capt of 40 men.

After your read this I shall be very grateful to you if you will sent this to Bryan Martin Stevens. I send my respects to mrs Stevens. I thank her for her kind usage to me in time of Sickness. She acted more like a mother than a mistress. Respects to all who know me. I hope this letter will find them all well & as for old Milla, I expect she is dead & gone to the devil long ago, if she is not, I think the imps are close at her heels, & will soon put her where there are nothing else but *nasty, stinking black* dogs a plenty.

My wife and self are sitting by a good comfortable fire happy, knowing that there are none to molest or make afraid. God save Queen Victoria, The Lord bless her in this life, & crown her with glory in the world to come is my prayer,

Yours With much respect
most obt, Joseph Taper

[Source: Joseph Taper, St. Catherines, Canada West, to Joseph Long, New Town, Virginia, 11 November 1840, Joseph Long Papers, Special Collections Library, Duke University, Durham, North Carolina.]

Riddicks Ville July 22nd 1848

Mr. William Glover
  E. City N.C

Dear Sir   I spent the day yesterday in seaking out particulars about the stay of your run aways in the neighborhood of my Cotton Factory &c I am Yet keeping the matter secret, hoping to asertain who the writer of the *forged papers is*—I have only let one man into the secret of there [their] apprehensions &c And that for the purpose of gaining information, he has promised me to Keep it secret, hoping to detect a scoundrel   from the best information I can gather they were in Nansemond, about the Factory & Suffolk about 12 Months, oftener unemployed than otherwise, at the time they were employed by Mr. J. W. Everett to get shingles, there papers were examined by Mr. E. D. B. Howell— Mr Everitt & others they were closely questioned, finding there answers to correspond with there papers, the papers having the County seal, these persons come to the conclusion that they were actually free— and Mr Everitt employed them for some months to get shingles, the timber was cut out of my Mill pond & the shingles gotten on the side of the Mai[n] publicK therefore [thoroughfare] in lower Virginia, within 10 to 20 feet of all passing, they were also employed by Mr Benj Smith of Suffolk to cut a canal & when at work for Smith was frequently in the Neighborhood of my Cotton Factory— I very much regret that I did not examine there papers myself. I should most certainly have detected there being spurious, and the result would have been, that your property would have been recovered at least 12 Months sooner that it was; at the time I was called on to give them a pass & to look for work, I used, as I thought at the time all necessary precautions, not Knowing the negroes sufficiently myself, I inquired of two very respectable gentlemen, if they knew them, they both told me that they had known them for some time, had examined them, and also there papers that they had free papers with the County seal of the County where they said they were raised &c I am not yet satisfied about the papers you handed me & shall use all my very best endeavors to find who the base scountrel is, and if in my power to find it out, shall see that he is rigidly dealth with, such offence stands on the lowest grade with me at this time I am suffering in the same way having now 3 as likely Men as any I own in the woods — I shall let you hear from me again, at which time, I will enclose the pass that has the name of William Hinton signed to it. I understand Mr. Hinton lives — Gates Cty N.C and is a gentleman there is no doubt about that, as well as the others in the same hand writing, being a forgery— I very sincerely hope you will be enabled to get a hold of the rascal who furnished the seal &c

It was him who have them the chance to impose on the innocent PublicK

Yours Very Respectuflly
A Riddick

[Source: A. Riddick to William Glover, 22 July 1848, Records of the County Court, Perquimans County, North Carolina, *Slave Records 1759–1864*, NCDAH.]

Appendix 7
Runaway Slave Database: Early Period 1790–1816; Late Period 1838–1860

OUR PRIMARY GOAL in creating a computer-generated database from runaway newspaper notices was to answer two questions: How did the profile of runaways change over time? How did it differ in various sections of the South?

From a total of approximately 8,400 runaways advertised in newspapers between 1790 and 1860, including those arrested and those advertised as "stolen," we created a Runaway Slave Database (RSDB) for two periods: early (1790–1816) and late (1838–60), with emphasis on two decades, 1800–1809 and the 1850s. The geographical distribution included five states: Virginia, North and South Carolina, Tennessee, and Louisiana, chosen because of their location—two in the Upper South, one between the Upper and Lower South, and two in the Lower South, three in the east, two in the west—and because Richmond, Charleston, and New Orleans were centers of the domestic slave trade.

Among the 8,400 runaways, nearly half, or 4,084, were advertised during the two time periods. In creating the RSDB, when the number of advertised slaves was small, complete data on all advertised slaves were included; when the number became large, a random sample was drawn. The sample was generated by using SAS, or Statistical Analysis System, a widely used software package for data analyses. Considering the nature of the raw data, large samples were necessary to insure accuracy. The data were not drawn from all newspapers in a state during a time period, but rather from selected, important newspapers with extant runs that would warrant inclusion. The statistics generated by SAS include expected frequencies and a commonly used chi-square test, which tests the "hypothesis of independence." For random sampling techniques, see Sandra D. Schlotzhauer and Ramon C. Littell, *SAS System for Elementary Statistical Analysis* (Cary, N.C.: SAS Institute, 1987), 110–11. The RSDB contains information on 2,011 runawys, and can be broken down as follows:

Table 6
Number of Advertised Runaways in Database,
Early Period 1790–1816

State	Number	Total Advertised in Selected Newspapers
Virginia	95	95
North Carolina	100 sample	536
South Carolina	240 sample	516
Tennessee	138	138
Louisiana	122	122

Table 7
Number of Advertised Runaways in Database,
Late Period 1838–1860

State	Number	Total Advertised in Selected Newspapers
Virginia	195 sample	432
North Carolina	132	132
South Carolina	458 sample	717
Tennessee	168	168
Louisiana	363 sample	1,228
Totals, Tables 6 & 7	2,011	4,084

For each of the 2,011 individual runaways, a series of coded entries was typed into the RSDB. These include information on gender, age, height, weight, complexion, countenance, marks or scars, language, speech, birthplace, name, occupation, dress, literacy, method of travel, location of owner, destination, previous owner[s], reward, reason for absconding, time reported missing, length of time missing, listed as alone or with others, relation to others listed, season of running away. Within each of these general categories, a list of variables was created, including various occupations, reasons of running, reward amounts, speech patterns, skin color. There are a total of forty-seven general categories and 183 individual variables. Under the category "countenance," for example, there are 11 variables: friendly, polite, friendly and polite, nervous, surly, intelligent/artful, looks down when spoken to, inclined to drink, bold, cunning, and active; under the category "distinguishing marks," there are 39 variables, including among others unusual hair, facial mark, beard, missing teeth, finger missing, unusual feet, branded, tattoo, ear missing, smallpox scars, whipping scars, marks that represent violence to slave; and under the category "passes," there are 6 variables: suspected of having an old or invalid pass, had a pass, forged a pass, suspected of having free papers, suspected of having someone else's free papers, able to write own pass/papers. Most runaway notices, however, contained information on about only fifteen or twenty variables.

The data were drawn from twenty newspapers with the best runs in North Carolina, South Carolina, Virginia, Tennessee, and Louisiana. The data for the early sample in North Carolina were drawn from notices in Freddie Parker's *Stealing a Little Freedom: Advertisements for Slave Runaways in North Carolina, 1791–1840* (New York: Garland Publishing, 1994). The newspapers perused are the following:

Charleston Courier (South Carolina), 1806–11
Charleston Mercury, 1849–59
City Gazette and Daily Advertiser (Charleston, South Carolina),
    1790–91
Daily Picayune (New Orleans, Louisiana), 1849–58
The Edenton Gazette and North Carolina General Advertiser,
    1807–12
Louisiana Gazette (New Orleans), 1804–12
Nashville Whig (Tennessee), 1812–16
National Banner and Nashville Whig, 1849–51
North Carolina Circular (New Bern), 1802–5
North Carolina Intelligencer and Fayetteville Advertiser, 1808
North Carolina Journal (Halifax), 1799–1810
The North Carolina Whig (Charlotte), 1852–57
North Carolinian (Fayetteville), 1849–60
The North Carolina Minerva and Raleigh Advertiser, 1802–12
Raleigh Register and North Carolina Weekly Advertiser,
    1801–16
Richmond Enquirer (Virginia), 1804–9, 1849–60
The Star (Raleigh, North Carolina), 1810–11
Tennessee Gazette (Nashville), 1802–7

Tennessee Republican Banner (Nashville), 1838–42
Wilmington Gazette (North Carolina), 1799–1812

Table 8
Female Runaways by Age Group, Early Period, 1790–1816

Frequency (percent)	Virginia	North Carolina	Tennessee	South Carolina	Louisiana	Total
Ages 1–12	0	1	1	4	2	8 (10)
Teens	7	3	5	13	5	33 (41)
Twenties	2	4	4	11	2	23 (28)
Thirties	2	5	1	6	0	14 (17)
Forties and older	0	0	0	3	0	3 (4)
Total	11 (14)	13 (16)	11 (14)	37 (45)	9 (11)	81 (100)

Frequency missing = 48

Table 9
Male Runaways by Age Group, Early Period, 1790–1816

Frequency (percent)	Virginia	North Carolina	Tennessee	South Carolina	Louisiana	Total
Ages 1–12	0	2	4	7	5	18 (4)
Teens	10	15	15	42	20	102 (24)
Twenties	41	33	51	59	43	227 (54)
Thirties	13	10	5	18	9	55 (13)
Forties and older	6	6	3	5	2	22 (5)
Total	70 (16)	66 (16)	78 (18)	131 (31)	79 (19)	424 (100)

Frequency missing = 142

Table 10
Female Runaways by Age Group, Late Period, (1838–1860)

Frequency (percent)	Virginia	North Carolina	Tennessee	South Carolina	Louisiana	Total
Ages 1–12	1	0	0	4	9	14 (7)
Teens	3	4	2	20	20	49 (23)
Twenties	11	10	7	28	39	95 (45)
Thirties	0	0	7	16	22	45 (21)
Forties and older	1	1	0	5	2	9 (4)
Total	16 (8)	15 (7)	16 (8)	73 (34)	92 (43)	212 (100)

Frequency missing = 36

Table 11
Male Runaways by Age Group, Late Period, (1838–1860)

Frequency (percent)	Virginia	North Carolina	Tennessee	South Carolina	Louisiana	Total
Ages 1–12	0	2	2	13	11	28 (3)
Twenties	32	18	30	46	40	166 (20)
Twenties	76	47	68	139	119	449 (54)
Thirties	22	14	24	42	36	138 (17)
Forties and older	15	6	5	20	8	54 (6)
Total	145 (17)	87 (11)	129 (15)	260 (31)	214 (26)	835 (100)

Frequency missing = 233

Abbreviations

ADAH	Alabama Department of Archives and History, Montgomery, Alabama
DSA	Delaware State Archives, Dover, Delaware
FSA	Florida State Archives, Tallahassee, Florida
KDLA	Kentucky Department for Libraries and Archives, Frankfort, Kentucky
LC	Library of Congress, Washington, D.C.
LSU	Louisiana State University
MDAH	Mississippi Department of Archives and History, Jackson, Mississippi
MSA	Maryland State Archives, Annapolis, Maryland
NA	National Archives, Washington, D.C.
NCDAH	North Carolina Division of Archives and History, Raleigh, North Carolina
SC	Schweninger Collection
SCDAH	South Carolina Department of Archives and History, Columbia, South Carolina
TSLA	Tennessee State Library and Archives, Nashville, Tennessee
TSA	Texas State Archives, Austin, Texas
VSA	Virginia State Archives, Richmond, Virginia

Notes

PREFACE

1. Ulrich B. Phillips, *Life and Labor in the Old South* (Boston: Little, Brown, 1929), 196–203. Other historians in James Hugo Johnston, "The Participation of White Men in Virginia Negro Insurrections," *Journal of Negro History* 16 (April 1931), 158–67; Harvey Wish, "American Slave Insurrections Before 1861," ibid. 22 (July 1937), 299–320; and "The Slave Insurrection Panic of 1856," *Journal of Southern History* 5 (May 1939), 206–22; Raymond A. and Alice H. Bauer, "Day to Day Resistance to Slavery," *Journal of Negro History* 27 (October 1942), 388–419; Herbert Aptheker, "Maroons Within the Present Limits of the United States," ibid. 24 (April 1939), 167–84, and *American Negro Slave Revolts* (New York: Columbia University Press, 1943). In addition to the above authors, see Kenneth W. Porter, "Three Fighters for Freedom," *Journal of Negro History* 28 (January 1943), 51–72; and "Florida Slaves and Free Negroes in the Seminole War, 1835–1842," ibid. 28 (October 1943), 390–421; Richard Hofstadter, "U. B. Phillips and the Plantation Legend," ibid. 29 (April 1944), 109–24; John Hope Franklin, *From Slavery to Freedom: A History of American Negroes* (New York: Alfred Knopf, 1947); Marion J. R2ussell, "American Slave Discontent in Records of the High Courts," *Journal of Negro History* 31 (October 1946), 411–36.

2. Kenneth Stampp, *The Peculiar Institution: Slavery in the Ante-Bellum South* (New York: Alfred A. Knopf, 1956), 91; see Ulrich B. Phillips, *American Negro Slavery: A Survey of the Supply, Employment, and Control of Negro Labor As Determined by the Plantation Regime* (New York: D. Appleton, 1918).

3. Stanley Elkins, *Slavery: A Problem in American Institutional and Intellectual Life* (Chicago: University of Chicago Press, 1959), 20–22, 82–86; Eugene D. Genovese, "Rebelliousness and Docility in the Negro Slave: A Critique of the Elkins Thesis," *Civil War History* 4 (December 1967), 314; George M. Fredrickson and Christopher Lasch, "Resistance to Slavery," *Civil War History* 4 (December 1967), 315. Also see Marion D. de B. Kilson, "Towards Freedom: An Analysis of Slave Revolts in the United States," *Phylon* 25 (summer 1964), 175–87; Nicholas Halasz, *The Rattling Chains: Slave Unrest and Revolt in the Antebellum South* (New York: D. McKay, 1966).

4. Larry Gara, *The Liberty Line: The Legend of the Underground Railroad* (Lexington: University of Kentucky Press, 1961), 2, 10, 11, 13, 17. See also Stanley W. Campbell, *The Slave Catchers: Enforcement of the Fugitive Slave Law, 1850–1860* (Chapel Hill: University of North Carolina Press, 1968); Horatio T. Strother, *The Underground Railroad in Connecticut* (Middletown, Conn.: Wesleyan University

Press, 1962); Leon Litwack, "The Emancipation of the Negro Abolitionist," in *The Antislavery Vanguard: New Essays on the Abolitionists*, ed. Martin Duberman (Princeton: Princeton University Press, 1965), 137–55; Stanley Harrold, "Freeing the Weems Family: A New Look at the Underground Railroad," *Civil War History* 42 (December 1996), 289–306. Although historians continue to disagree about various aspects of the Underground Railroad, few deny that even today it is shrouded in myth and legend.

5. On black family and culture see, for example, Herbert G. Gutman, *The Black Family in Slavery and Freedom, 1750–1925* (New York: Pantheon Books, 1976); Lawrence W. Levine, *Black Culture and Black Consciousness: Afro-American Folk Thought from Slavery to Freedom* (New York: Oxford University Press, 1977). On runaways, see John W. Blassingame, *The Slave Community: Plantation Life in the Antebellum South* (New York: Oxford University Press, 1972; rev. ed., 1979); Gerald W. Mullin's *Flight and Rebellion: Slave Resistance in Eighteenth-Century Virginia* (New York: Oxford University Press, 1972).

6. During the 1980s and 1990s, scholars explored a wide range of topics about slavery. For a bibliographical essay on the literature, see Peter Kolchin, *American Slavery 1619–1877* (New York: Hill and Wang, 1993), 257–92. The most famous runaway, Frederick Douglass, has received a substantial amount of attention. Between 1980 and 1991, four scholars published partial or complete biographies of Douglass: Dickson J. Preston, *Young Frederick Douglass: The Maryland Years* (Baltimore: Johns Hopkins University Press, 1980); Waldo E. Martin, Jr., *The Mind of Frederick Douglass* (Chapel Hill: University of North Carolina Press, 1984); David W. Blight, *Frederick Douglass's Civil War: Keeping the Faith in Jubilee* (Baton Rouge: Louisiana State University Press, 1989); and William S. McFeely, *Frederick Douglass* (New York: W. W. Norton, 1991). On other runaways, see Daniel E. Meaders, "South Carolina Fugitives as Viewed Through Local Colonial Newspapers with Emphasis on Runaway Notices 1732–1801," *Journal of Negro History* 60 (April 1975), 288–319; Hugo Prosper Leaming, *Hidden Americans: Maroons of Virginia and the Carolinas* (New York: Garland Publishing, 1995); Michael P. Johnson, "Runaway Slaves and the Slave Communities in South Carolina, 1799 to 1830," *William and Mary Quarterly* 38 (July 1981), 418–41; Judith Kelleher Schafer, "New Orleans Slavery in 1850 as Seen in Advertisements," *Journal of Southern History* 47 (February 1981), 33–56; Freddie L. Parker, *Running for Freedom: Slave Runaways in North Carolina, 1775–1840* (New York: Garland Publishing, 1993); Paul Finkelman, ed., *Fugitive Slaves, Articles on American Slavery*, vol. 6 (New York: Garland Publishing, 1989). On various types of resistance, see Peter P. Hicks, *To Awaken My Afflicted Brethren: David Walker and the Problem of Antebellum Slave Resistance* (University Park: Pennsylvania State University Press, 1997); Norrece T. Jones, Jr., *Born a Child of Freedom, Yet a Slave: Mechanisms of Control and Strategies of Resistance in Antebellum South Carolina* (Hanover, N. H.: Wesleyan University Press, 1990); Howard Jones, *Mutiny of the Amistad: The Saga of a Slave Revolt and Its Impact on American Abolition, Law, and Diplomacy* (New York: Oxford University Press, 1987). On slave plots and uprisings, see Eugene Genovese, *From Rebellion to Revolution: Afro-American Slave Revolts in the Making of the Modern World* (Baton Rouge: Louisiana State University Press, 1979); John Lofton, *Denmark Vesey's Revolt: The Slave Plot that Lit a Fuse to Fort Sumter* (Kent, Ohio: Kent State University Press, 1983); Douglas R. Egerton, *Gabriel's Rebellion: The Virginia Slave Conspiracies of 1800 and 1802* (Chapel Hill: University of North Carolina Press, 1993); Jeffrey Crow, "Slave Rebelliousness and Social Conflict in North Carolina, 1775–1802," *William and Mary Quarterly* 37 (January 1980), 79–102.

Eugene Genovese, *The Southern Front: History and Politics in the Cultural War* (Columbia: University of Missouri Press, 1995), 205; Kolchin, *American Slavery*, 276–77. Philip J. Schwarz asserts that running away was not only the most common, but the most threatening type of resistance; it prompted continued response from slave owners. Philip J. Schwarz, *Twice Condemned: Slaves and the Criminal Laws of Virginia, 1705–1865* (Baton Rouge: Louisiana State University Press, 1988), 282.

CHAPTER 1

1. Loren Schweninger, ed., *From Tennessee Slave to St. Louis Entrepreneur: The Autobiography of James Thomas*, with foreword by John Hope Franklin (Columbia: University of Missouri Press, 1984), 58.

2. *Nashville Whig*, 26 August 1840.

3. Anne Arundel County Register of Wills (Petitions and Orders) 1851–60, 48–49, Petition of Richard J. Cowman to the Orphans Court, 17 October 1853, reel #CR 63,128-1, MSA.

4. See John W. Blassingame, *The Slave Community: Plantation Life in the Antebellum South* (New York: Oxford University Press, 1972); Lawrence W. Levine, *Black Culture and Black Consciousness: Afro-American Folk Thought from Slavery to Freedom* (New York: Oxford University Press, 1977); John Loften, *Denmark Vesey's Revolt: The Slave Plot that Lit a Fuse to Fort Sumter* (Kent, Ohio: Kent State University Press, 1983); Douglas R. Egerton, *Gabriel's Rebellion: The Virginia Slave Conspiracies of 1800 and 1802* (Chapel Hill: University of North Carolina Press, 1993).

5. Destruction of property in Legislative Records, Petition of Robert Dickinson to the Virginia General Assembly, 21 December 1825, Russell County, VSA; Petition of Thomas W. Betts, James M. Stiff, William Webb, et al. to the Virginia General Assembly, 18 February 1843, Richmond County, ibid.; Petition of the Citizens of Matthews County to the Virginia General Assembly, 10 January 1848, ibid.; Petition of Residents of Middlesex County to the Virginia General Assembly, 9 December 1850, ibid.; *The Code of Virginia* (Richmond: William F. Ritchie, 1849), 748; Alex Lichtenstein, " 'That Disposition to Theft, With Which They Have Been Branded': Moral Economy, Slave Management, and the Law," *Journal of Social History* 21 (spring 1988), 429–30; David J. McCord, *The Statutes at Large of South Carolina* (Columbia: A. S. Johnson, 1840), 434–35, 454–55.

Discussions of stealing in Helen T. Catterall, ed., *Judicial Cases Concerning American Slavery and the Negro* (Washington, D.C.: W. F. Roberts, 1932), 2:321, 333, 335, 347, 368, 460, 478; Charles Ball, *Slavery in the United States: A Narrative of the Life and Adventures of Charles Ball, a Black Man* (New York: John S. Taylor, 1837; reprint, New York: Kraus Reprint Co., 1969), 299; Peter Kolchin, *American Slavery 1619–1877* (New York: Hill and Wang, 1993), 157; William Dusinberre, *Them Dark Days: Slavery in the American Rice Swamps* (New York: Oxford University Press, 1996), 140–42, 164, 174–75, 177, 323, 335; Records of the United States District Court for the District of Columbia, Segregated Habeas Corpus Papers, Record Group 21, Petition of Susan a Slave of James Maguire, 26 August 1842, Entry #28, Box 1, NA. Susan was arrested for "unlawfully, maliciously, and violently" setting a fire at the rear of her owner's livery stable.

Quote about "old scamp" in Will S. Buford to Charles Buford, 25 November 1853, Charles Buford Papers, LC; pig "swinging" in Joseph Bieller to Jacob Bieller, 7 April 1829, in Alonzo Snyder Papers, Letters, Special Collections, Hill Memorial Library, LSU.

6. Frederick Law Olmsted, *A Journey in the Back Country* (New York: Mason Brothers, 1860), 83–87.

7. Market Street episode in Catterall, ed., *Judicial Cases Concerning American Slavery and the Negro*, 2:361. For similar instances in South Carolina, see ibid., 2: 322, 370, 371, 402, 403, 406, 410, 464, 469. Quotes on "habit" and "vice" in Records of the County Court, Davie County, North Carolina, Petition of Daniel H. Cain, Spring Term 1859, in Miscellaneous Records 1854–1864, NCDAH; *New Orleans Bee*, 6 February 1833; *Richmond Enquirer*, 28 March 1809, 27 November 1849, 5 September 1851; Records of the Equity Court, Charleston District, South Carolina, Petition of Mary Jenkins Murray Mikell, by her mother and next friend Jane E. Mikell, 12 February 1850, Case #117, Box 3, SCDAH; Eugene D. Geneovese, *Roll, Jordan, Roll: The World the Slaves Made* (New York: Pantheon Books, 1974), 599–600. Big Ike discussed in Records of the Chancery Court, Giles County, Tennessee, Case Files, Bill of Complaint of Luke H. Hancock, Virginia C. Hancock, and Achilles M. Hancock, 31 August 1858, Case #935, reel 158, frames 2,179–81, 2,184–87, 2,139–40, TSLA; Report of Sale, March Term 1859, with ibid.

8. Kolchin, *American Slavery*, 110; Claudia Goldin, *Urban Slavery in the American South, 1820–1860: A Quantitative History* (Chicago: University of Chicago Press, 1976), 36, 72–73; Robert Engs, *Freedom's First Generation: Black Hampton, Virginia, 1861–1890* (Philadelphia: University of Pennsylvania Press, 1979), 14; Randall M. Miller, "The Fabric of Control in Antebellum Textile Mills," *Business History Review* 55 (winter 1981), 475–90; Charles Dew, "Disciplining Slave Iron Workers in the Antebellum South: Coercion, Conciliation, and Accommodation," *American Historical Review* 79 (April 1974), 405–7; John T. O'Brien, "Factory, Church, and Community: Blacks in Antebellum Richmond," *Journal of Southern History* 46 (November 1978), 151; Robert S. Starobin, *Industrial Slavery in the Old South* (New York: Oxford University Press, 1970), 14–17, 134–35.

9. Records of the County Court, Southampton County, Virginia, Chancery Papers, James Brister vs. Henry Parker, 19 August 1833, Folder #1–1835, Box 40, VSA; Henry Parker to Drury Waller, 1 September 1832, with ibid.; Deposition of Augustin C. Butts, 18 August 1834, with ibid.

10. Discussion of Jim in C. J. O'Meara to Richard T. Archer, 7 May 1843, Richard Thompson Archer Family Papers, Natchez Trace Collection, Center for American History, University of Texas at Austin. Discussion of Ephraim in Records of the Equity Court, Anderson District, South Carolina, Petitions, Ruth Riley vs. John Davis, Daniel E. Riley, Jr., and Frederick K. A. Riley, 24 February 1852, Case #462—1852, SCDAH; Decree of the Court, June Term 1852, with ibid.; Report of Commissioner on Sales, 3 January 1853, with ibid. Discussion of Feriley in Records of the Equity Court, Anderson District, South Carolina, Bills, Alethea Harris vs. Oliver H. P. Jones, 15 April 1859, Case #288, Box 7, SCDAH.

11. Information on Charles is in Catterall, ed., *Judicial Cases Concerning American Slavery and the Negro*, 2:372–73. Charles ran away but was quickly caught. He was wounded during the chase and died in jail. Dudley is in Petition of Guilford Dawkins to the Madison [Louisiana] Parish Court, 3 January 1853, Special Collections, Hill Memorial Library, LSU.

12. Records of the County Court, Davidson County, Tennessee, Case Files, Petition of Edward E. Gowen, Charles H. Gowen, Tabetha J. Gowen by their Guardian Edward H. East, [November] 1856, Case #1,740, Box 15, Metropolitan Nashville-Davidson County Archives, Nashville; Deposition of George W. McMurry, 24 November 1856, with ibid.; Decree of the Court, 28 November 1856, with ibid.

13. Quotes about Allen in Records of the Equity Court, Newberry District, South

Carolina, Petitions, Frederick Werber[?] vs. Silas Johnston, 22 November 1858, Case #42, reel NB119, SCDAH. In December 1858, Allen was sold and the money reinvested in another slave named Dave.

Discussions of slaves in new conditions in Records of the Equity Court, Newberry District, South Carolina, Petition of John F. Harrington for James Alexander Pope, 14 November 1849, Case #24 in 1850, reel 113, SCDAH; Testimony of J. Harrington, 14 November 1849, with ibid.; Records of the Equity Court, Newberry District, South Carolina, Petitions, Frederick Werber[?] vs. Silas Johnston, 22 November 1858, Case #42, reel NB119, SCDAH; Records of the Chancery Court, Monroe County, Mississippi, Kemp vs. Hawkins, 13 April 1855, County Court House, Aberdeen, Mississippi; Records of the Equity Court, Laurens District, South Carolina, Petition of Thomas M. Sloan and Mary B. Sloan, 9 February 1858, Box 2, SCDAH; Records of the Equity Court, Charleston District, South Carolina, Petition of Jacob F. Schurmir[?], 11 December 1848, SCDAH.

Quotes on Barton are in Anne Arundel County Register of Wills (Petitions and Orders) 1860–74, 41, Petition of Thomas Mezick to the Orphans Court, 10 June 1861, reel #CR 63,128-2, MSA.

14. Quotes on Caleb in Records of the Court of General Quarter Sessions, Kent County, Delaware, Petition of Burton Conner, 4 May 1829, in Petitions of Servants and Slaves, reel R79.3, DSA. Davy is in Records of the General Assembly, Petition of William Simmons to the South Carolina House of Representatives, November 1802, #180, SCDAH; Copy of Receipt, William Simmons, 4, 5 December 1800; Certificate, John Johnson, Justice of the Peace, 8 November 1802, with ibid.; Sworn Statement, William Simmons, November 1802, with ibid.

15. Records of the Sixth Judicial District Court, East Baton Rouge Parish, Louisiana, Robert Davis vs. James C. Knox, 14 November 1856, #1,939, East Baton Rouge Parish Archives, Baton Rouge, Louisiana; Deposition of William McCrocklin, 28 May 1857, with ibid.

16. Records of the County Court, Bibb County, Alabama, State vs. Negro Slave Sam, Book G (October 1834), 1–8, ADAH; Legislative Petitions, Petition of Citizens of Tipton, Lauderdale, Madison, and Haywood counties to the Tennessee General Assembly, 14 January 1848, #276–1847, reel 18, TSLA.

17. Information on older slave couple in Records of the Chancery Court, Monroe County, Mississippi, Kemp vs. Hawkins, 13 April 1855, County Court House, Aberdeen, Mississippi. Sarah and Henny are in Baltimore City Register of Wills (Petitions), Petition of Lavinia Pendleton to the Orphans Court of Baltimore County, 6 March 1832, reel M-11,025, SC, MSA; St. Mary's County Court (Equity Papers), Petition of George A. Carpenter to the County Court, 10 August 1842, reel M-11,062, SC, MSA; Affidavit of C. Dorsey, 10 August 1842, ibid.

18. Discussion of Elizabeth in Records of the Equity Court, Charleston District, South Carolina, Petition of Joseph A. Landers, Trustee of his daughter Mary W. Landers, 5 February 1853, Case #340, Box 5, SCDAH; Slave refusing to care for girl in Records of the Equity Court, Charleston District, South Carolina, Petition of Jacob F. Schumir[?], 11 December 1848, SCDAH; Maria in Records of the Equity Court, Laurens District, South Carolina, George M. Auld and his wife Jane A. Auld, and her Trustee Charles Franks vs. William F. Auld, 9 August 1860, Case #11, Box 2, SCDAH; Matilda in Frederick County Circuit Court (Petitions), Petition of Ezra Shank to the Circuit Court, 24 April 1855, reel M-11,020, SC, MSA.

19. Rachel O'Connor to A. T. Conrad, 26 May 1836, Weeks (David and Family) Papers, Special Collections, Hill Memorial Library, LSU.

20. William K. Scarborough, *The Overseer: Plantation Management in the Old*

South (Baton Rouge: Louisiana State University Press, 1966), 38–39; John Spencer Bassett, *Slavery in the State of North Carolina*, Johns Hopkins University Studies in Historical and Political Science, Series 17, nos. 7,8 (Baltimore: Johns Hopkins University Press, 1899), 25.

21. Records of the Chancery Court, Giles County, Tennessee, Case Files, Jane B. Smith vs. Elizabeth E. Smith et al., 25 January 1860, Case #1,741, reel 193, frames 2,705–8, 2,698–2,700, 2,689–93, TSLA; Testimony of Archibald J. Strickland, 15 March 1860, with ibid.; Testimony of Andrew Roberts, 15 March 1860, with ibid.

22. Legislative Petitions, Petition of William Fitzhugh to the Virginia General Assembly, 19 December 1805, Stafford County, VSA. Seeking £225 for the loss of property, the petition was rejected.

23. Planters along the Sea Island coast set specific tasks for slaves to complete during the day. When the tasks were finished, slaves could tend to their own garden plots or raise their own livestock. Elsewhere, the great majority of planters employed the gang system. Slaves were taken to the fields by an overseer in the early morning. They worked until near sunset. Kolchin, *American Slavery*, 31–32; Charles Joyner, *Down By the Riverside: A South Carolina Slave Community* (Urbana: University of Illinois Press, 1984), 43, 45, 51, 59, 74, 128-29; Philip D. Morgan, "Work and Culture: The Task System and the World of Lowcountry Blacks, 1700–1800," *William and Mary Quarterly*, 3d ser., 39 (October 1982), 563–99; and "The Ownership of Property by Slaves in the Mid-Nineteenth-Century Low Country," *Journal of Southern History* 49 (August 1983), 399–420; Dylan Penningroth, "Slavery, Freedom, and Social Claims to Property among African Americans in Liberty County, Georgia, 1850–1880," *Journal of American History* 84 (September 1997), 405–35. Information on Red River in Ann Patton Malone, *Sweet Chariot: Slave Family and Household Structure in Nineteenth-Century Louisiana* (Chapel Hill: University of North Carolina Press, 1992), 51–52.

24. Records of the Parish Court, West Feliciana Parish, Louisiana, Third District Court, Samuel Cowgill vs. Charles Stewart, 11 October 1826, #369, Parish Court House, St. Francisville, Louisiana. Cowgill sued the owner for $2,000 in damages, but was awarded only $162 by a jury.

25. Records of the Parish Court, West Baton Rouge Parish, Louisiana, Sixth District Court, A. L. Dixon vs. D. P. Cain, 4 March 1858, #1,523, Parish Court House, Port Allen, Louisiana. Dixon, the overseer, who was fired, sued Cain, the planter, for his wages and the labor of his slaves. He was awarded $850. Rachel O'Connor to Mary C. Weeks, 26 December 1834, Weeks (David and Family) Papers, Special Collections, Hill Memorial Library, LSU.

26. Legislative Petitions, Petition of John Royall to the General Assembly, 21 December 1802, Nottoway County, VSA; Deposition of Richard Dennis, 9 December 1802, with ibid.; Douglas R. Egerton, *Gabriel's Rebellion*, 49–52, and idem, " 'Fly Across the River': The Easter Slave Conspiracy of 1802," *North Carolina Historical Review* 68 (April 1991), 87–110; John Lofton, *Denmark Vesey's Revolt*. The literature on black resistance is large. See Herbert Aptheker, *American Negro Slave Revolts* (New York: Columbia University Press, 1943); Joseph Carroll, *Slave Insurrections in the United States, 1800–1865* (Boston: Chapman and Grimes, 1938; reprint, New York: Negro Universities Press, 1973); Jeffrey Crow, "Slave Rebelliousness and Social Conflict in North Carolina, 1775–1802," *William and Mary Quarterly* 37 (January 1980), 79–102; Eugene Genovese, *From Rebellion to Revolution: Afro-American Slave Revolts in the Making of the Modern World* (Baton Rouge: Louisiana State University Press, 1979); James Hugo Johnston, "The Participation of White Men in Virginia

Negro Insurrections," *Journal of Negro History* 16 (April 1931), 158–67; Norrece T. Jones, Jr., *Born a Child of Freedom, Yet a Slave: Mechanisms of Control and Strategies of Resistance in Antebellum South Carolina* (Hanover, N.H.: Wesleyan University Press, 1990); Philip J. Schwarz, "Gabriel's Challenge: Slaves and Crime in Late Eighteenth-Century Virginia," *Virginia Magazine of History and Biography* 90 (July 1982), 283–309; Harvey Wish, "American Slave Insurrections Before 1861," *Journal of Negro History* 22 (July 1937), 299–320.

27. Information on Frank and Dick in Legislative Petitions, Petition of Thomas Reekes to the Speaker of the House of Representatives, 11 December 1805, Mecklenburg County, VSA; Deposition of Richard Apperson, 29 November 1805, with ibid. In the sheriff's testimony, the owner's name is spelled Reeks. The Edgefield District plot in Records of the General Assembly, Petition of Thomas Key to the South Carolina Senate, 27 November 1811, #142, SCDAH; other plot in Records of the General Assembly, Petition of the Town Council of Georgetown to the South Carolina Senate, 16 November 1829, #98, SCDAH; Petition of John Wilson, William B. Pringle, et al., to the South Carolina Senate, 1829, #131, SCDAH.

28. Rachel O'Connor to Mary Weeks, 11 January 1830, Weeks (David and Family) Papers, Special Collections, Hill Memorial Library, LSU.

29. Rachel O'Connor to David Weeks, 13 October 1831, Weeks (David and Family) Papers, Special Collections, Hill Memorial Library, LSU.

30. Historians have examined a number of false panics, but there were many actual plots. See Richard C. Wade, "The Vesey Plot: A Reconsideration," *Journal of Southern History* 30 (May 1964), 143–61; Wish, "American Slave Insurrections," 299–320; Davidson B. McKibben, "Negro Slave Insurrections in Mississippi, 1800–1865," *Journal of Negro History* 34 (January 1949), 73–90; Edwin A. Miles, "The Mississippi Slave Insurrection Scare of 1835," ibid. 42 (January 1957), 48–60; R. H. Taylor, "Slave Conspiracies in North Carolina," *North Carolina Historical Review* 5 (January 1828), 20–34; William White, "The Texas Slave Insurrection of 1860," *Southwestern Historical Quarterly* 52 (January 1949), 259–85; Genovese, *From Rebellion to Revolution*, 43–50.

31. Moses Liddell to John R. Liddell, 21 July 1841, Liddell (Moses, John R., and Family) Papers, Special Collections, Hill Memorial Library, LSU.

32. Records of the Parish Court, West Baton Rouge Parish, Louisiana, Smith vs. Blanchard, 5 July 1846, #299, Parish Court House, Port Allen, Louisiana. William B. Thomas's deposition in the criminal case of State vs. Slave Harry was attached to the above civil suit.

33. Records of the County Court, Davidson County, North Carolina, unsigned letter, 6 October 1845, in Records of Slaves and Free Persons of Color 1826–1896, NCDAH. Located in the Piedmont, Davidson and Rowan counties straddled the Yadkin River. In 1840, Davidson's population included about 2,500 and Rowan's 3,400 slaves, approximately 17 and 28 percent of their respective populations. Salisbury is the county seat of Rowan, and Lexington of Davidson. Lexington was described in 1840 as "a court house, jail, several stores and dwellings." Daniel Haskel and J. Calvin Smith, *A Complete Descriptive and Statistical Gazetteer of the United States of America* (New York: Sherman and Smith, 1847), 167, 343, 578, 594.

34. Quote of "a small move" in Levi Dearmond to D. F. O'Amand, 17 July 1848, Elizabeth Dearmond Family Papers, Natchez Trace Collection, Center for American History, University of Texas at Austin. *Pearl* incident in Records of the United States Circuit Court for the District of Columbia, Chancery Dockets and Rules Case Files, Record Group 21, Henson Ridgway et al. vs. Francis Dodge, Jr., 26 February 1849, Entry #20, Case #574, Rules 5, Box 65, NA. How the slaves organized themselves to

escape was not indicated in the civil suit above, which involved the cost of recapturing the runaways.

35. Discussion of insurrection panic in Starobin, *Industrial Slavery in the Old South,* 89; quote of "Quite an excitement" in G. Washington Powell to Brother, 22 December 1856, Isabel Grey Reddach Papers, ADAH.

36. David Walker, *David Walker's Appeal, in Four Articles; Together with a Preamble, to the Coloured Citizens of the World, But in Particular, and very Expressly, to Those of the United States of America* (Boston: David Walker, 1829); Clement Eaton, "A Dangerous Pamphlet in the Old South," *Journal of Southern History* 2 (August 1936), 322; *The Liberator,* 22 January 1831.

37. Legislative Petitions, Petition of Verlinda Perry to the Virginia Senate and House of Delegates, 11 January 1840, Loudoun County, VSA; Copy Decree in Records of the Loudoun County Court, Commonwealth vs. Negro Jarrett, Slave of Verlinda Perry, 11 July 1839, with ibid.

38. For slaveholders who sold slaves because they feared for their family's safety, see Anne Arundel County Register of Wills (Petitions and Orders) 1851–60, 349–50, Petition of Mary Crisp to the Orphans Court, 2 March 1858, reel #CR 63,128-1, MSA; Records of the Circuit Court, Jefferson County, Florida, Dorothy Burgdorff vs. Laura Burgdorff, 7 January 1858, Carton #4, FSA; Records of the Chancery Court, Bedford County, Petition of James Mullins and William Young to the Court, 30 August 1853, Chancery Court Records 1848–185[3] Vol. B, 523–24, County Court House, Shelbyville, Tennessee; Baltimore City Register of Wills (Petitions), Answer of James Graham to the Petition of William Hutchins, 30 June 1825, reel M-11,025, SC, MSA; Bill of Sale for the Negro Boy Named Sam, 29 June 1825, with ibid. For punishments meted out to slaves accused of serious crimes—poisoning in Virginia and plotting in South Carolina—see Legislative Petitions, Petition of Thomas Reekes to the Speaker of the House of Representatives, 11 December 1805, Mecklenburg County, VSA; Deposition of Richard Apperson, 29 November 1805, with ibid.; Records of the General Assembly, Petition of the Town Council of Georgetown to the South Carolina Senate, 16 November 1829, #98, SCDAH; Petition of John Wilson, William B. Pringle, et al. to the South Carolina Senate, 1829, #131, ibid.

39. Joseph Bieller to Jacob Bieller, 7 April 1829, in Alonzo Snyder Papers, Letters, Special Collections, Hill Memorial Library, LSU; Records of the Chancery Court, Giles County, Tennessee, Case Files, Bill of Complaint of Luke H. Hancock, Virginia C. Hancock, and Achilles M. Hancock, 31 August 1858, Case #935, reel 158, frames 2,179–81, 2,184–87, 2,139–40, TSLA; Report of Sale, March Term 1859, with ibid.; Records of the Equity Court, Anderson District, South Carolina, Petitions, Ruth Riley vs. John Davis, Daniel E. Riley, Jr., and Frederick K. A. Riley, 24 February 1852, Case #462–1852, SCDAH; Decree of the Court, June Term 1852, with ibid.; Report of Commissioner on Sales, 3 January 1853, with ibid.; Records of the General Assembly, Petition of William Simmons to the South Carolina House of Representatives, November 1802, #180, SCDAH; Copy of Receipt, William Simmons, 4, 5 December 1800, with ibid. Simmons was hired by Charleston authorities to provide materials for Davy's execution. In a similar case in 1842, a Natchez, Mississippi, diarist wrote "some people on the other side of the River Caught One of those Runaway Slaves that helped Kill a man by the name Todd Living near Red River—They Burned Him up soon after he was taken." William Ransom Hogan and Edwin Adams Davis, eds., *William Johnson's Natchez: The Ante-Bellum Diary of a Free Negro* (Baton Rouge: Louisiana State University Press, 1951), 386. Records of the Sixth Judicial District Court, East Baton Rouge Parish, Louisiana, Robert Davis vs. James C. Knox, 14 November 1856, #1,939, East Baton Rouge Parish Archives, Baton Rouge, Louisiana; Deposition of

William McCrocklin, 28 May 1857, with ibid. Records of the County Court, Bibb County, State of Alabama vs. Negro Slave Sam, Book G (October 1834), 1–8, ADAH. Records of the Equity Court, Charleston District, South Carolina, Petition of Joseph A. Landers, Trustee of his daughter Mary W. Landers, 5 February 1853, Case #340, Box 5, SCDAH; Records of the Equity Court, Laurens District, South Carolina, George M. Auld and his wife Jane A. Auld, and her Trustee Charles Franks vs. William F. Auld, 9 August 1860, Case #11, Box 2, SCDAH.

CHAPTER 2

1. Baltimore City Register of Wills (Petitions), Petition of Charles Carroll of Homewood et al. to the Orphans Court, 31 December 1832, reel M-11,025, SC, MSA; Deposition of William Gibbons, 21 and 22 January 1833 [filed 11 February 1833], with ibid.; Jeffrey R. Brackett, *The Negro in Maryland: A Study of the Institution of Slavery* (Baltimore: Johns Hopkins University Press, 1889), 53–54; Ellen Hart Smith, *Charles Carroll of Carrollton* (Cambridge, Mass.: Harvard University Press, 1942), 266–70; Matthew Page Andrews, *Tercentenary History of Maryland* (Chicago: S. J. Clark Publishing, 1925), 1: 525, 575, 578; ibid., 4: 9–11 (volume 4 of this set was compiled principally by Henry Fletcher Powell). There is a listing of 215 slaves in Baltimore City Register of Wills (Petitions), Petition and Order for the Sale of the Personal Estate on Doughoregan Manor, 10 May 1833, SC, MSA. See also Petition of Charles Carroll et al. to the Orphans Court for Sale of Certain Negroes on Folly Farm, 3 March 1835; Petition of Charles Carroll et al. to the Orphans Court for the Sale of Certain Negroes on Doughoregan Manor, 3 March 1835, in ibid. Folly Farm, called Folly Quarter, was part of Doughoregan Manor. In the original documents it is spelled Doughoragen. The spelling used here is from the Smith volume above.

2. Baltimore City Register of Wills (Petitions), Deposition of William Gibbons, 21 and 22 January 1833 [filed 11 February 1833], with Petition of Charles Carroll of Homewood et al. to the Orphans Court, 31 December 1832, reel M-11,025, SC, MSA. The elder Charles Carroll's benevolence was illustrated in 1817, when he emancipated thirty slaves.

3. Baltimore City Register of Wills (Petitions), Deposition of Walter Browne, 21 and 22 January 1833 [filed 11 February 1833], with Petition of Charles Carroll of Homewood et al. to the Orphans Court, 31 December 1832, reel M-11,025, SC, MSA; Deposition of William Gibbons, 21 and 22 January 1833, with ibid.

4. Baltimore City Register of Wills (Petitions), Petition of Charles Carroll of Homewood et al. to the Orphans Court, 31 December 1832, reel M-11,025, SC, MSA.

5. Legislative Petitions, Petition of Thomas Rodwell, John Darden, Ezekiel Powell, et al. to the Virginia House of Delegates, 9 December 1815, Nansemond County, VSA.

6. Quote about Jack Going in *Richmond Enquirer*, 2 September 1808; information on the three Negro men in Records of the Probate Court, Montgomery County, Alabama, Estate Case Files, Petition of R. W. Carr and Lemuel Fields to the Orphans Court, 30 September 1822, Box 50, ADAH; on John and Tom in Records of the Probate Court, Jackson County, Florida, Petition of Harriet R. Long, administratrix of the Estate of James M. Long, 27 February 1858, in Records of Estates Book D, 95–96, County Court House, Marianna, Florida.

7. Records of the Circuit Court, Jefferson County, Kentucky, Case Files, Levi Hart vs. John Nelson, 16 February 1826, Case #1,334, Box 1-18, KDLA. The suit was brought to determine who held title to Sam.

8. Records of the Equity Court, Barnwell District, South Carolina, Bills, David Platts and wife vs. Jacob Kinard and Jacob Copeland, 6 February 1834, roll BW87, frames 314–16, 331–33, 335–36, 361–62, SCDAH; disappearance during mourning in

Edenton Gazette and North Carolina General Advertiser, 16 March 1807; Guthrow estate loss in Baltimore City Register of Wills (Petitions), Petition of Simon Guthrow to the Orphans Court of Baltimore County, 25 July 1827, reel M-11,025, SC, MSA.

9. Records of the Fourth Judicial District Circuit Court, Williamson County, Tennessee, Calvin M. and Jane Smith vs. Charles and Elizabeth Love, 12 October 1827, Williamson County Archives, Franklin, Tennessee. Love's wife had remarried Calvin M. Smith, and the couple was suing her former husband's brother who was executor of the estate.

10. Records of the Circuit Court, Jefferson County, Kentucky, Case Files, Petition of George R. and Elizabeth Ghiselin, 6 July 1854, Case #9,884, Box 2-145, KDLA. The guardian complained that she was paying for the slave's upkeep but making no money from his hire. The court agreed and at a "Marshal's Sale" in Louisville in 1854, Joshua was "struck off" to the highest bidder for $275. Report of Sale, 10 November 1854, with ibid.

11. Records of the Circuit Court, Barren County, Kentucky, Equity Judgments, Petition of Thomas Morehead, Guardian of John T. Lewis et al., 5 October 1854, Case #2,117, reel 229,756, KDLA. Receiving permission to dispose of Isaac, the trustees traded him plus fifty dollars for a seventeen-year-old woman named Roda. Records of the Equity Court, Cheraw District, South Carolina, Petition of John Terrel, Josiah J. Evans, and James Forniss, 6 February 1847, SCDAH; Records of the Circuit Court, Jefferson County, Kentucky, Case Files, Series 2, F. S. J. Ronald vs. Mary Truman's Estate, 22 September 1848, Case #5,094, Box 2-88, KDAH; Copy of Last Will and Testament of Mary A. Truman, 13 May 1845, with ibid.

12. Records of the Chancery Court, Giles County, Tennessee, Case Files, Petition of James P. Nelson, 27 November 1855, Case #1,309, reel #178, frames 2,739–40, 2,765–70, TSLA; Deposition of William Ezell, 28 November 1855, with ibid; Deposition of John W. Kelly, 28 November 1855, with ibid; Records of the County Court, Davidson County, Tennessee, Case Files, Petition of B. M. Barnes, Guardian of Priscilla O'Neil, 18 April 1854, Case #1,161, Box 11, Metropolitan Nashville-Davidson County Archives, Nashville.

13. Records of the Probate Court, Travis County, Texas, Guardianship of Mary and Alfred Luckett, 16 January 1856, Case #50, County Court House, Austin; Inventory of the Property of Mary and Alfred Luckett, 8 March 1856, with ibid; Report of Leven H. Luckett, Guardian, Partition of Property, 10 May 1859, with ibid. The comments about Margaret were found in the May 1859 report. A listing of receipts paid out by the guardian included twenty-five dollars to "Jailor at Fayett."

14. Alabama Supreme Court Cases, Hugh Jones vs. William Dunlap, Jr., and Michael K. Broadhead, 6 July 1863, in Supreme Court Records, 1–10, ADAH. The case began in the circuit court of Bibb County in 1857.

15. Elizabeth Fox-Genovese, *Within the Plantation Household: Black and White Women of the Old South* (Chapel Hill: University of North Carolina Press, 1988), 9; Sally G. McMillen, *Southern Women: Black and White in the Old South* (Arlington Heights, Ill.: Harlan Davidson, 1992), 22–23; Marli F. Weiner, *Mistresses and Slaves: Plantation Women in South Carolina, 1830–80* (Urbana: University of Illinois Press, 1998), 134–43; Virginia Ingraham Burr, ed., *The Secret Eye: The Journal of Ella Gertrude Clanton Thomas, 1848–1889* (Chapel Hill: University of North Carolina Press, 1990), 45, 168–69; Suzanne Lebsock, *The Free Women of Petersburg: Status and Culture in a Southern Town, 1784–1860* (New York: W. W. Norton, 1984), 95–96. Response of a slave in Baltimore County Register of Wills (Petitions and Orders), John Lewis vs. Negro Edward, 11 October 1854, reel M-11,020, SC, MSA.

16. Records of the Sixth Judicial District Circuit Court, Maury County, Tennessee,

William R. and John D. Farney by their next friend Jemiah Sanderson vs. John Farney, 24 November 1834, Maury County Historical Society Loose Records Project, Columbia, Tennessee; Copy of Deed of Gift, John Farney to William and John D. Farney, 24 July 1826, with ibid.

17. Testimony of John Giddons, [1856], J. B. Pigford, 26 November 1856, Wiley Moore, 19 December 1854, in Records of the North Carolina Supreme Court, Lamb vs. Pigford, December 1858, Testimony and Depositions, 23, 31, 45–46, Case #7,541, NCDAH. Giddons lived a half mile from Hugh Lamb's brother-in-law Edward Pigford. He had known "Hugh Lamb's Negroes" since they were children. *Reports of Cases in Equity Argued and Determined in the Supreme Court of North Carolina, From December Term, 1853, to August Term, 1854, Both Inclusive* (Raleigh: Seaton Gales, 1855), 195–204. There are 220 pages of testimony and depositions in the original supreme court case, which involved the disposition of Lamb's estate. Despite being a habitual runaway, Jack earned so much money as a hired cooper ($80 to $100 a year) that he was not sold until 1852, at age thirty-five.

Information on George and his owner in Records of the Equity Court, Spartanburg District, South Carolina, Petition of James K. Mean, 23 May 1849, Case #2, SCDAH; on Catherine Bate's slaves in Records of the Circuit Court, Jefferson County, Kentucky, Thomas W. Wilson and John T. Buckner vs. John Bate et al., 25 April 1854, Case Files, #9,403, Box 2-140, KDLA.

18. Records of the Circuit Court, Talladega County, Alabama, Matilda Houston vs. Josiah Houston, 10 August 1839, Final Records 1839–1841, vol. 1, 226–28, 237–40, Judicial Building, Talladega, Alabama; Decree of the Court, February 1840, with ibid. The circuit court heard cases from the judicial circuit, which in this case included Benton County. For several days, the husband "hunted assiduously" for Dinah around his wife's residence without success, but he eventually discovered her hiding out and "did then & there by force take her off."

19. Records of the Chancery Court, Madison County, Alabama, Petition of Emily Cornelius to the Court, 31 August 1852 in Chancery Records 1857, 605–8, Madison County Archives, Public Library, Huntsville, Alabama; Records of the Court of Equity, Richland District, South Carolina, Bills, Anna Allen vs. John Allen, 1816, Case #141, reel RI-100, SCDAH; Records of the Court of Equity, Barnwell District, South Carolina, Bills, Eliza A. Ransom vs. Thomas S. Ransom, 1841, reel BW83, SCDAH; Records of the District Court, Brazoria County, Texas, Sarah H. Black vs. James E. Black, 26 March 1855, County Court House, Angleton, Texas.

Quote of "most cruel & unhuman manner" in Records of the Superior Court, Greene County, Georgia, Petition of Mary Jackson to the Court, 1806, in Proceedings 1808–1809, 125–27, County Court House, Greensboro, Georgia. The case was recorded in a later proceeding.

20. Anne Arundel County Circuit Court (Equity Papers) OS 298, Stephen L. Lee vs. Carolina E. Lee, 1 April 1861, reel M-11,019, SC, MSA; United States Manuscript Slave Census, Anne Arundel County, Maryland, First District, 1860, 10 [printed page number].

21. Larry E. Rivers, "A Troublesome Property: Master-Slave Relations in Florida, 1821–1865," in *The African American Heritage of Florida*, ed. David R. Coburn and Jane L. Landers (Gainesville: University Press of Florida, 1995), 104; idem, " 'Dignity and Importance': Slavery in Jefferson County, Florida—1827 to 1860," *Florida Historical Quarterly* 61 (April 1983), 425–27; idem, "Slavery in Microcosm: Leon County, Florida, 1824–1860," *Journal of Negro History* 46 (fall 1981), 244–45; Canter Brown, Jr., "The Sarrazota, or Runaway Negro Plantations: Tampa Bay's First Black Community, 1812–1821," *Tampa Bay History* 12 (fall/winter 1990), 5–19. Informa-

tion from slaveholder organization in [*Proceedings of a meeting on August 26, 1854, to take steps to put an end to trafficking with slaves and their escape beyond the Rio Grande*] (Seguin, Tex.: n.p., 1854), 1–2; "They cannot be kept here" quote in George S. Denison to his sister Eliza, 10 February 1855, George S. Denison Papers, LC.

22. Records of the First Judicial District Court, Orleans Parish, Louisiana, Case Records, Thomas Durnford vs. Gilbert Morris, 7 May 1817, #1,478, reel 3, Louisiana Collection, New Orleans Public Library. Thomas Durnford was the father of the wealthy free mulatto Andrew Durnford, a planter and slave owner during the 1840s and 1850s in Plaquemines Parish. David O. Whitten, *Andrew Durnford: A Black Sugar Planter in Antebellum Louisiana* (Natchitoches, La.: Northwestern State University Press, 1981), 3, 4, 7, 8, 12.

23. Testimony of James D. Hamilton, 8 September 1851, with Records of the Circuit Court, Jefferson County, Kentucky, Case Files, A. J. Ballard vs. Steamboat *Bunkerhill #3*, 12 April 1851, Case #7,583, Box 2-119, KDLA. For similar testimony, see Deposition of Joseph A. B. Furniss, 15 September 1851; and Deposition of N. M. Ferguson, 15 September 1851, with ibid.

24. Records of the Circuit Court, Jefferson County, Kentucky, Case Files, A. J. Ballard vs. Steamboat *Bunkerhill #3*, 12 April 1851, Case #7,583, Box 2-119, KDLA.

25. Records of the Circuit Court, Jefferson County, Kentucky, Case Files, Series 2, Ambrose D. Mann vs. Steamboat *Paul Jones*, 13 May 1837, Case #765, Box 2-14, KDLA; Deposition of Stephen Haskell, 18 September 1839, with ibid.

26. Legislative Records, Petition of the Citizens of King William County to the Virginia General Assembly, 24 January 1843, VSA; James Hugo Johnston, *Race Relations in Virginia and Miscegenation in the South, 1776–1860* (Amherst: University of Massachusetts Press, 1970), 276–77; Records of the Territorial Legislative Council of Florida, Memorial to Governor William P. Duval, [1823], Record Group 910, Series 876, Box 1, folder 6, FSA; Kenneth W. Porter, "Florida Slaves and Free Negroes in the Seminole War, 1835–1842," *Journal of Negro History* 28 (October 1943), 390–421; idem, "Negroes in the Seminole War, 1835–1842," *Journal of Southern History* 30 (November 1964), 427–50; James E. Glenn to Major John H. Howard, 29 March 1836, in Records of Alabama Governors, Administrative Files, Creek Indian War, March 1835, ADAH; Frederick Law Olmsted, *A Journey in the Seaboard Slave States, With Remarks on Their Economy* (New York: Dix and Edwards, 1856), 160–64.

27. Records of the General Assembly, Petition of Edward Brailsford to the South Carolina Senate, ca. 1822, ND #1838, SCDAH.

28. Quote of "head strong ungovernable boy" in Legislative Petitions, Petition of Catherine Nelms to the Virginia General Assembly, 12 December 1815, Northumberland County, VSA; Anne Arundel County Register of Wills (Petitions and Orders) 1814–1820, 57–58, Petition of Emily Caton to the Orphans Court, ca. November 1814, CR 63,126–2, MSA. Quote of "out of the Reach of any slave" in Legislative Petitions, Petition of Inhabitants of Matthews County to the Virginia General Assembly, 22 October 1814, Matthews County, VSA.

29. Quotes on Elliott's Cut in Records of the General Assembly, Petition of Inhabitants Along the Ashepoo and Pon Pon Rivers to the South Carolina General Assembly, ca. 1817, ND #2849, and ca. 1818, ND #2850, SCDAH; information on Gabriel and Brister in Records of the General Assembly, Petitions of Mathew ODriscoll to the South Carolina Senate, 15 November 1819, #109 and #110, SCDAH.

30. Roswell King to Pierce Butler, 12, 26 February 1815, 4 March 1815, Butler Family Papers, Historical Society of Pennsylvania, quoted in Malcolm Bell, Jr., *Major Butler's Legacy: Five Generations of a Slaveholding Family* (Athens: University of Georgia Press, 1987), 177, 178, 180, 182.

31. Records of the County Court, Prince George's County, Maryland, County Court Papers, Blacks, Bill of Indictment, 15 April 1833, Box 31, folder 40, MSA; Legislative Petitions, Petition of the Inhabitants of Culpeper County to the Virginia General Assembly, 19 December 1834, Culpeper County, VSA; John Shackelford to the Speaker of the Virginia House of Representatives, 12 December 1834, with ibid.; Records of the County Court, Prince George's County, Maryland, County Court Papers, Blacks, Presentment and Bill of Indictment, 3 September 1811, Box 31, folder 15, MSA; *New Orleans Bee*, 25 October 1834; Legislative Petitions, Petition of William A. Thrasher, Robert Powell, James Shearer, and William Dunlap to the Virginia General Assembly, 19 January 1860, VSA.

Running away attributed to whites in *New Orleans Picayune*, 11 December 1839; Philip Hill to Nathaniel Evans, 5 April 1816, Evans (Nathaniel and Family) Papers, Special Collections, Hill Memorial Library, LSU; *Tennessee Gazette*, 18 December 1802; William Martin Clements to Adams Clements, 16 December 1860, Isabel Grey Reddoch Papers, ADAH. See also Nathan, who ran away from his Maryland owner and found refuge with Thomas Smith of New Castle County, Delaware. Records of the General Assembly, Legislative Papers, Petition of J. W. Jackson, William Slaughter, Thomas Martindale, et al. to the Delaware Senate and House of Representatives, 16 February 1849, Record Group 1,111, DSA.

32. Petition of William Tolar and Robin Williams to the Mississippi Legislature, [1833,] Record Group 47, Volume 20, Petitions and Memorials, MDAH; "transient traders" quote in Records of the General Assembly, Session Records, Petition of Thomas Cowan, Thomas Callender, Thomas Macneill, et al. to the North Carolina General Assembly, 11 December 1820, House Committee Reports, November–December 1820, NCDAH.

33. Records of the Chancery Court, Bedford County, Tennessee, George W. Ruth vs. Martin Grace and Samuel Williams, 5 June 1839, Record Book 1830–1842, 195–202, County Court House, Shelbyville, Tennessee; Answer of Samuel Williams, 9 July 1839, with ibid; Final Decree, 11 February 1840, with ibid. The court ruled that Samuel Williams, of Martin County, North Carolina, was Drew's rightful owner.

34. Records of the Circuit Court, Talladega County, Alabama, Charles Simpson vs. William Freeman, 9 April 1841, in [Final Records] 1841–1842, vol. 2, 88–101, Judicial Building, Talladega, Alabama. Chambers County was part of the Fourth Judicial District of Alabama. Civil suits for this district were heard in Talladega, Alabama.

35. Records of the First Judicial District Court, Orleans Parish, Louisiana, Case Records, Francois B. Lebeau [also spelled LeBeau] vs. Captain and Owners of Ship *Tecumseh*, 18 February 1840, #18,773, reel 34, Louisiana Collection, New Orleans Public Library.

36. *Richmond Enquirer*, 8 July 1808.

37. Robert Brent Toplin, "Peter Still Versus the Peculiar Institution," *Civil War History* 13 (December 1967), 344.

38. Records of the County Court, Davidson County, Tennessee, Case Files, Petition of Bantley M. Barnes, Guardian of Priscilla O'Neal, 18 April 1854, Case #1,161, Metropolitan Nashville-Davidson County Archives, Nashville; Deposition of William H. Townsend, 3 May 1854, with ibid.; Report of Clerk and Master of Court, 3 May 1854, with ibid. The slave trader testified that Esther had told him that the white man wanted to purchase her. She was sold in January 1854 for $1,000 to the firm of Hill and Foster.

39. Records of the Court of Appeals (Judgments, Western Shore), Pennsylvania, Delaware and Maryland Steam Navigation Co. vs. Thomas B. Hungerford, December Term 1834, Series S 382, Box 130, MSA.

40. Information on Maria and Cogswell in *New Orleans Picayune*, 7 November 1838; genteel female in *Charleston Mercury*, 15 February 1832. The notice ran through 19 May 1832.

41. *Charleston Mercury*, 27 July 1832.

42. Records of the Circuit Superior Court of Law and Chancery, Albemarle County, Virginia, William Dickinson vs. John M. Perry, George W. Spooner, and William Garland, 23 October 1834, Ended Causes, 1836, Box 604, VSA.

43. Records of the General Assembly, Petition of Edward Brailsford to the South Carolina General Assembly, 26 November 1816, #100, SCDAH; Baltimore City Register of Wills (Petitions), William T. Wood vs. Aralanta, Orphans Court of Baltimore City, 23 January 1855, reel M-11,026, SC, MSA; Records of the Chancery Court, Southampton County, Virginia, Petition of James and Nancy Powell to the Judges of the County Court, [1858,] Chancery Causes Ended, 1862, Box 71, VSA; Records of the Chancery Court, Chesterfield County, Virginia, Petition of Robert Winfree to the Justices of the County Court, December 1862, Chancery Causes Ended, 1863, Box 468, VSA. Information on Caty in Records of Caroline County Chancery Court, Deposition of Fanny Roane, 6 July 1819, Deposition of Charles Taylor, 16 February 1819, Suits, Loose Papers, Box 15, VSA.

44. John Fisher to Elizabeth Lee, 14 December 1810, in Records of the Circuit Court, Fayette County, Kentucky, Case Files, John Fisher vs. Elizabeth Lee, 2 August 1811, Box 26, KDLA. In the suit, Fisher sought an injunction against Lee, who had sued him for refusing to pay his promissory note for hiring her slaves.

45. Discussion of Henry in Records of the Circuit Court, Barren County, Kentucky, Equity Judgments, Petition of Thomas Morehead, Guardian of John T. Lewis et al., 5 October 1854, Case #117, reel 229,756, KDLA; of George in Records of the Equity Court, Spartanburg District, South Carolina, Petition of James K. Mean, 23 May 1849, Case #2, SCDAH; of Virginia hires in Records of the Chancery Court, Southampton County, Virginia, Petition of Robert Barnes as Guardian of Juliet Worrell, 1860, Box 70, VSA; Records of the County Court, Southampton County, Virginia, Chancery Papers, Willis Eley's Committee vs. Eley, 1857, folder #16–1857, Box 66, VSA; Records of the Chancery Court, Southampton County, Virginia, Chancery Papers, Lewis Worrell vs. Alexander Myrick, March 1848, #40–1849, Box 56, VSA; Records of the County Court, Southampton County, Virginia, Chancery Papers, William A. Jones vs. Mary Smith, February 1847, #21–1847, Box 53, VSA; of Ann in Records of the County Court, Southampton County, Virginia, Chancery Papers, Theophilus F. Harris vs. Mary Harris et al., August 1857, folder #25–1858, Box 68, VSA; of Phebe in Records of the County Court, Henrico County, Virginia, Ended Chancery Causes, James W. Binford vs. Fanny Frayser, 5 February 1844, Box 79–13, Packet 1844, VSA.

46. Blacks' complaints in Records of the Circuit Court, Jefferson County, Kentucky, Case Files, Series 2, John P. Oldham vs. J. R. McFarland et al., 3 November 1831, Case #2,222, Box 2-39, KDLA; *New Orleans Bee*, 4 April 1829; a master's comments in Records of the Superior Circuit Court of Chancery, Lynchburg, Virginia, George Hughes vs. Jesse Abstein [also spelled Abston], 14 June 1819, Box 5, VSA; "perfect equality" quote in *Maryland Journal and Baltimore Advertiser*, 14 June 1793, in "Documents: Eighteenth Century Slaves as Advertised by Their Masters," *Journal of Negro History* 1 (April 1916), 202–3.

47. Legislative Petitions, Petition of P. M. Tabb, Edward N. Dabney, et al. to the Virginia General Assembly, 13 December 1850, Richmond City, VSA.

48. Records of the General Assembly, Petition of James Thomson to the South

Carolina General Assembly, ca. 1815, ND #1,575, SCDAH; George Warren Cross to James Thomson, 25 March 1812, with ibid.; Robert Boyce to James Thomson, 8 May 1812, with ibid.

49. *Richmond Enquirer,* 18 December 1806; *Tennessee Republican Banner,* 23 May 1839; Robert S. Starobin, *Industrial Slavery in the Old South* (New York: Oxford University Press, 1970), 81–85, 112, 114, 133, 256–57.

50. Starobin, *Industrial Slavery in the Old South,* 82; information on the five runaways in *Tennessee Republican Banner,* 6 January 1838. The notice ran through 10 July 1838.

51. Charles Dew, *Bond of Iron: Master and Slave at Buffalo Forge* (New York: W. W. Norton, 1994), 31, 43–44, 69, 70, 75, 76, 82, 108, 134, 135, 160, 162, 253–54, 274–80, 367; see also by the same author, "David Ross and the Oxford Iron Works: A Study of Industrial Slavery in the Early Nineteenth-Century South," *William and Mary Quarterly,* 3d ser., 31 (April 1974), 189–224; "Disciplining Slave Iron Workers in the Antebellum South: Coercion, Conciliation, and Accommodation," *American Historical Review* 79 (April 1974), 393–418.

52. Records of the Equity Court, Charleston District, South Carolina, William Sanders vs. Benjamin Parker, Executor for John Parker, Deceased, 17 August 1814, Case #73, SCDAH. Tom remained in jail during the controversy over ownership.

53. Baltimore City Register of Wills (Petitions), Jacob Bankard vs. Negro Jacob, Orphans Court of Baltimore City, 11 March 1861, reel M-11,026, SC, MSA; *Charleston Mercury and Morning Advertiser,* 18 April 1825; Anne Arundel County Register of Wills (Petitions and Orders) 1851–60, 843–45, Petitions of Richard Weems to the Orphans Court, 28 April 1857 and 30 April 1858, reel #CR 63,128-1, MSA; *New Orleans Bee,* 11–29 February 1828, 1–31 March 1828, 1–30 April 1828, 1–24 May 1828; *Tennessee Gazette,* 24, 31 July 1805, 2, 14 October 1805; Legislative Records, Petition of Jacob Furbee, William K. Lockwood, et al. to the Delaware General Assembly, 22 January 1810, DSA.

54. A few began as early as age seven. See Anne Arundel County Register of Wills (Petitions and Orders) 1840–51, 228–30, Stephen L. Lee vs. Clinton Wright, a colored man, 29 February 1848, reel #CR 63,127-2, MSA. Information on Jack is in Testimony of John Giddons, [1856,] J. B. Pigford, 26 November 1856, Wiley Moore, 19 December 1854, in Records of the North Carolina Supreme Court, Lamb vs. Pigford, December 1858, Testimony and Depositions, 45–46, 23, 31, Case #7,541, NCDAH; *Reports of Cases in Equity Argued and Determined in the Supreme Court of North Carolina, From December Term, 1853, to August Term, 1854, Both Inclusive* (Raleigh: Seaton Gales, 1855), 195–204. Frances is in *New Orleans Picayune,* 4 June 1839; Pompey is in Records of the Probate Court, Gadsden County, Florida, Petition of Richard Baker, 31 December 1845, in Records of the Probate Court, vol. 3, 48–49, County Court House, Quincy, Florida. Three years later the slave was still at large.

55. J. J. Price to E. H. Stokes, 11 February 1860, Chase Family Papers, Manuscript Division, LC.

56. Notices about Charles are in *Tennessee Gazette,* 24, 31 July, 7, 14 August, 12 October, 16, 30 November, 7, 14 December 1805; about John in *Charleston Mercury,* 17 March 1827.

57. Andrew is described in *New Orleans Picayune,* 24 April 1840; Bob is in *New Orleans Picayune,* 16 May 1840; Davis is in *New Orleans Bee,* 27 June 1829, 29 October 1829.

58. *Charleston Mercury,* 1 March 1831.

59. Records of the Chancery Court, Giles County, Tennessee, Case Files, Petition of James P. Nelson, 27 November 1855, Case #1,309, reel #178, frames 2,739–40, 2,765–70, TSLA; Deposition of William Ezell, 28 November 1855, with ibid.; Deposition of John W. Kelly, 28 November 1855, with ibid.

60. Quotes about Lucy in *Charleston Mercury*, 27 October 1832, 29 June 1832; about Sary in *Charleston Mercury*, 1 July 1829; about Ralph in *Richmond Enquirer*, 6 September 1808; about Sarah in Records of the Equity Court, Charleston District, South Carolina, Bills, William Rouse vs. Vernon, 21 February 1800, Case #1, SCDAH; about the elderly black woman in *Charleston Mercury*, 11 September 1828.

61. Description of Ason in Anne Arundel County Register of Wills (Petitions and Orders) 1814–20, 40, Petition of John Gibson to the Orphans Court, 21 November 1814, CR 63,126–2, MSA; of Hanover slave in *Richmond Enquirer*, 4 June 1805; of Sam in *Charleston Mercury*, 11 December 1828.

62. Records of the Alabama Supreme Court, Cases, Peter Wyatt vs. Moses Grier, #1325, in Record Book 35 (June 1833), 130–49, ADAH; Records of the Chancery Court, Shelby County, Alabama, Peter Wyatt vs. Moses Greer [*sic*], 23 November 1827, Chancery Court Record 1839–1846, 104–24, Shelby County Archives, Columbiana, Alabama. The chancery courts in the state had jurisdiction over various counties.

63. Records of the District Court, San Augustine County, Texas, Charles Brady vs. Tempe Price, 16 October 1856, Case #1,132, East Texas Research Center, Stephen F. Austin University, Nacogdoches, Texas; *Reports of Cases Argued and Decided in the Supreme Court of the State of Texas, During the Tyler Session, 1857* (St. Louis: Gilbert Book Company, 1881), 19:244–49. Similar cases can be found in Records of the General Assembly, Session Records, Testimony of Edwin Adams and Patience Johnson, 25 September 1818, with Petition of Citizens of Johnston County to the Attorney General of North Carolina, 25 September 1818, Session November–December 1818, Miscellaneous Petitions, Box 3, NCDAH; Records of the First Judicial District Court, Orleans Parish, Louisiana, Court Records, William Kincaid and Nancy Tinsley, free woman of color, vs. Frederick Buisson, 8 May 1838, #16,027, Louisiana Collection, New Orleans Public Library; Testimony of J. B. Harrison, Dr. Thomas, and Joseph Percy, free man of color, 19 December 1838, with ibid.

64. John Spencer Bassett, ed., *The Plantation Overseer As Revealed in His Letters* (Northampton, Mass.: printed for Smith College, 1925), 263.

65. Alexander K. Farrar to H. W. Drake, 5 September 1857, Farrar (Alexander K.) Papers, Special Collections, Hill Memorial Library, LSU; Richard T. Archer to Ann B. Archer, 24 February 1852, Richard Thompson Archer Family Papers, Natchez Trace Collection, Center for American History, University of Texas at Austin; Edwin Adams Davis, ed., *Plantation Life in the Florida Parishes of Louisiana, 1836–1846, As Reflected in the Diary of Bennet H. Barrow* (New York: Columbia University Press, 1943), 41.

66. *Richmond Enquirer*, 13 June 1807; 30 December 1807; *Nashville Whig*, 22 November 1814, 6 December 1814; 8, 15 August 1815; *New Orleans Picayune*, 7 June 1839; *Nashville Whig*, 8, 15 August 1815.

67. *Charleston Mercury*, 29 June 1832; *Nashville Whig*, 27 April 1814, 3, 11 May 1814; *New Orleans Bee*, 14 November 1834.

68. *Richmond Enquirer*, 30 August 1808; *Tennessee Republican Banner*, 12 September 1838; *Louisiana Journal* [St. Francisville], 26 November 1826, in *A Documentary History of American Industrial Society*, ed. Ulrich B. Phillips (Cleveland, Ohio: Arthur H. Clark, 1910), 2:88.

69. Joseph Bieller to Jacob Bieller, 8 March 1830, in Alonzo Snyder Papers, Letters,

Special Collections, Hill Memorial Library, LSU; Quotes about Anderson in J. P[alfrey] to William T. Palfrey, 16, 17 July 1833, Palfrey Family Papers, Special Collections, Hill Memorial Library, LSU.

70. Records of the Fifth Judicial District Court, Orleans Parish, Louisiana, William C. and Julietta Palmer vs. David Bidwell, 26 September 1854, #8,618, reel 26, Louisiana Collection, New Orleans Public Library; Baltimore County Register of Wills (Petitions and Orders), Carville S. Stansbury vs. Negro Nathaniel, 14 July 1858, reel M-11,020, SC, MSA; Petition of Carville S. Stansbury, 14 July 1858; Answer of Nathaniel [July 1858]; Order of the Court, 31 August 1858, with ibid. Example of reason giving way to passion in James Monette Diary, 26, 29, 30 September 1848, Special Collections, Hill Memorial Library, LSU.

71. Records of the Superior Court, Richmond County, Georgia, Charles Hall vs. Richard Mooney and Gilbert McNair, 13 December 1831, in Writs 1829–1831, 209–10, Records of the Court, Records Retention Center, Augusta, Georgia.

72. Records of the Supreme Court, Middle Tennessee, Cases, William Pope vs. Robert Baxter and William R. Hicks, 18 December 1836, Box 54, TSLA.

73. Records of the Parish Court, West Baton Rouge, Louisiana, Sixth District Court, Riley vs. Woods and Company, 26 March 1849, #1041, Parish Court House, Port Allen, Louisiana; Petition of William C. Riley to the District Court, 30 October 1848, with ibid.; Deposition of Marshall W. Courtney, 14 June 1852, with ibid.; Deposition of Paulin Dupuy, 31 August 1853, with ibid.; Indictment of West Baton Rouge Grand Jury of William C. Riley for Murder of Slave Haden, 28 September 1849, with ibid. The criminal indictment charged that Riley whipped and beat Haden "on his back legs, sides, and other parts of the body," administering "several mortal bruises, wounds, and cuts." The indictment said this had occurred 6 September 1848 and "at diverse other times." Witnesses testified that Haden had also been severely beaten in June 1848. In either case, at least three and perhaps four slaves were beaten to death by Riley before he was forced to leave the plantation. He was acquitted and awarded $248 in damages for his unpaid salary. The final decree in the civil case was not handed down until October 1860, more than twelve years after the deaths of the slaves. Dissatisfied with the amount of the award, Riley appealed his case to the state supreme court. Petition of William C. Riley to the Sixth District Court, 16 January 1861, with ibid.

74. Records of the District Court, San Augustine County, Texas, Charles W. Brady vs. Tempe Price, 16 October 1856, Case #1,132, East Texas Research Center, Stephen F. Austin University, Nacogdoches, Texas; *Reports of Cases Argued and Decided in the Supreme Court of the State of Texas, During the Tyler Session, 1857* (St. Louis: Gilbert Book Company, 1881), 19:244–49. Quote of "cruelly and unmercifully" in Records of the Parish Court, West Feliciana Parish, Louisiana, Third District Court, James A. Williams vs. Joseph L. Finley and Andrew Collins, 19 April 1826, #331, Parish Court House, St. Francisville, Louisiana; "whipped her so brutally" in Records of the Eighth Judicial District Court, Catahoula Parish, Louisiana, Albert Hendricks vs. John M. Philips, 19 February 1848, in Parish Court Record Vol. C 1840–1851, 202, Parish Court House, Harrisonburg, Louisiana. Slaves preferring jail in Records of the County Court, Robeson County, North Carolina, Order of Justice of the Peace to the Sheriff, 16 April 1861, in Records Concerning Slaves and Free Persons of Color, 1861–1862, NCDAH; Order of the Court of Pleas and Quarter Sessions, May 1862, with ibid.; Report of the Sheriff to the Robeson County Court, 1863, with ibid.

75. Plantation Diary, 5–12 February 1833, in Sterling (Lewis and Family) Papers, Accession #1,866, Special Collections, Hill Memorial Library, LSU.

76. Quotes about slave near the Coosawhatchie in Records of the General Assem-

bly, Petition of Francis Porcher to the South Carolina House of Representatives, 3 December 1822, #82, SCDAH; Certificate, Alexander Corrie, William D. Martin, 28 October 1822, with ibid.; Certificate, William Farris, 17 November 1822, with ibid.; Certificate, Francis Porcher, 17 November 1822, with ibid. Phillida information in Records of the General Assembly, Petition of John S. Reid to the South Carolina House of Representatives, 23 November 1831, #66, SCDAH; Medical Bill, 4 June 1828, with ibid.; Affidavit, John Reid, 21 November 1831 with ibid.; Affidavit, James Glasgow, 21 November 1831, with ibid.; John Reid to Treasurer of the Upper Division of South Carolina, 17 November 1831, with ibid.

77. Records of the Equity Court, Anderson District, South Carolina, Petition of Reese Bowen for the Sale of a Negro, 7 July 1855, #362, SCDAH; Baltimore City Register of Wills (Petitions), Mary M. George by her Attorney Henry F. Garey vs. William S. George, Orphans Court of Baltimore City, 31 July 1860, reel M-11,026, SC, MSA; Answer of William S. George, 21 August 1860, with ibid; Elisha Cain to Alexander Telfair, 10 October 1829, 1 November 1829, in Phillips, ed., *A Documentary History*, 2:85. The owner was in Savannah, Georgia.

CHAPTER 3

1. Ann Patton Malone, *Sweet Chariot: Slave Family and Household Structure in Nineteenth-Century Louisiana* (Chapel Hill: University of North Carolina Press, 1992), 1–2; Rachel O'Connor to Mary Weeks, 11 January 1830, Weeks (David and Family) Papers, Special Collections, Hill Memorial Library, LSU; Records of the Parish Court, West Feliciana Parish, Louisiana, Inventory of the Succession of Rachel O'Connor, 4 June 1846, in Appendix II, Avery O. Craven, *Rachel of Old Louisiana* (Baton Rouge: Louisiana State University Press, 1975), 115–22.

2. Malone, *Sweet Chariot*, 1–2, 281 n. 3, 293 n. 10; Rachel O'Connor to David Weeks, 17 March 1831, Weeks (David and Family) Papers, Special Collections, Hill Memorial Library, LSU.

3. John Merriman to Francis D. Richardson, 11 November 1840, Weeks (David and Family) Papers, Special Collections, Hill Memorial Library, LSU.

4. Donald R. Wright, *African Americans in the Early Republic, 1789–1831* (Arlington Heights, Ill.: Harlan Davidson, 1993), 38–39; Michael Tadman, *Speculators and Slaves: Masters and Slaves in the Old South* (Madison: University of Wisconsin Press, 1989), chap. 1; Donald M. Sweig, "Reassessing the Human Dimension of the Interstate Slave Trade," *Prologue* 12 (spring 1980), 5–21; Frederic Bancroft, *Slave Trading in the Old South* (Baltimore: J. H. Furst, 1931), chap. 15.

5. J. O. Stanfield to Browning and Moore, 15 February 186[1], Chase Family Papers, LC; J. O. Stanfield to Betts and Gregory, 18 February 1861, Chase Family Papers, LC; V. O. Witcher to Betts and Gregory, 22 February 1861, Chase Family Papers, LC. Also see T. H. Lipscomb to Browning, Moore and Company, 17 April 1860, ibid.; C. B. Ackiss to Browning, Moore and Company, 3 July 1860, ibid.; Bills of Sale, 21 March 1817, 27 March 1824, Alexander Steward, Augusta County, Virginia, in Sterritt Family Papers, Manuscript Division, LC.

6. Records of the Circuit Court, Scott County, Kentucky, Case Files, Willa Viley vs. Thomas McCargo, 17 November 1845, Case #3,169, Box 12, KDLA.

7. F. L. Hunt to Martha Claiborne, 17 August 1846, John Frances Claiborne Papers, Manuscript Division, LC.

8. For the breaking up of families in Maryland, see Barbara Jeanne Fields, *Slavery and Freedom on the Middle Ground: Maryland during the Nineteenth Century* (New Haven: Yale University Press, 1985), 26.

9. *Richmond Enquirer*, 17 May 1805.

10. These data are computed from the Runaway Slave Database [hereafter RSDB], which included 695 advertised runaways from five states for the early period and 1,316 for the later period. For an explanation of how the RSDB was compiled see appendix 7.

11. Anne Arundel County Register of Wills (Petitions and Orders) 1860–74, 64, Petition of Spidden V. Wilson to the Orphans Court, 12 November 1861, reel #CR 63,128-2, MSA; Records of the County Court, Westmoreland County, Virginia, Court Papers, Hiram Hardwick vs. Joseph Pierce, March 1833, Packet August 1834, Box 126, VSA; Montgomery County Circuit Court (Equity Papers), Henry Warring vs. Anna Warring [also spelled Waring], 12 November 1861, reel M-11,024, SC, MSA; Auditor's report, 27 February 1861, with ibid; Records of the General Assembly, Session Records, Petition of John Jones to the General Assembly, 9 December 1802, NCDAH.

12. Records of the General Assembly, Petition of James B. Richardson to the South Carolina Senate, 10 December 1800, #183, SCDAH.

13. Legislative Records, Petition of Samuel Linton to the South Carolina General Assembly, 1817, #136, SCDAH.

In this study, the Lower South includes the states of South Carolina, Georgia, Florida, Alabama, Mississippi, Louisiana, Texas, and Arkansas; the Upper South includes Delaware, Maryland, Virginia, North Carolina, Kentucky, Tennessee, and Missouri. Information about Delph in Legislative Records, Petition of Joseph Wardlaw to the South Carolina House of Representatives, 21 March 1817, #105, SCDAH. In 1817, the state passed a law stipulating that only under unusual circumstances, and with a special license granted by an equity court judge, could slaves be imported into South Carolina. Slave owners feared that turbulent slaves from outside the state might influence South Carolina's slave population. *The Statutes At Large of South Carolina* (Columbia: A. S. Johnston, 1840), 7:455–58. Legislative Records, Petition of Benjamin Ellis to the South Carolina Senate, 19 March 1817, #127, SCDAH.

14. Malcolm Bell, Jr., *Major Butler's Legacy: Five Generations of a Slaveholding Family* (Athens: University of Georgia Press, 1987), 132–33, 273–76, 539; *Charleston Mercury*, 10 February 1831; Frances Anne Kemble, *Journal of Residence on a Georgian Plantation in 1838–1839* (1863, reprint, with an introduction by John A. Scott, Athens: University of Georgia Press, 1984), 68–69, 99–100, 160–61, 241.

15. Tennessee Supreme Court Cases, Middle District, Robert McCombs and Gideon Thompson's administrators vs. James Allen, 1825, Box 30A, TSLA; Copy of Answer of James Allen, 13 July 1823, with ibid.

16. Moses described in *Richmond Enquirer*, 22 October 1850; Jim in Records of the County Court, Edgecombe County, North Carolina, Wyatt Moye[?] and Robert Adams vs. Stephenton Page, Jr., 10 September 1850, in Slave Papers 1790–1857, NCDAH. Even with the temporary "loss" of Jim, the partnership realized a 22 percent profit by purchasing six slaves in North Carolina for $2,762.50 and selling five of them in the west for $3,375.

17. *Richmond Enquirer*, 14 September 1852; Bancroft, *Slave Trading in the Old South*, 121, 316–17.

18. *Nashville Whig* 1, 19, 26 October 1813, 4 January 1814, 28 June 1814.

19. *New Orleans Bee*, 26 July 1831; *New Orleans Picayune*, 7 April 1839. For the activities of trading companies in the city see Bancroft, *Slave Trading in the Old South*, 38, 121, 372–74; *New Orleans Bee*, 21 May 1832, 1 June 1832. Quote about Elsy in *New Orleans Bee*, 22 April 1831, 14 May 1831; about James in *New Orleans Bee*, 9 July 1829. The notice ran through 22 September 1829; about Eliza in *New Orleans Picayune*, 22 March 1840; information about slave on the *Dorade* in *New Orleans Bee*, 21 October 1830.

20. *Richmond Enquirer*, 1 April 1806, 8, 15 April 1806; *Nashville Whig* 2, 9, 16, 23, 30 April 1816, 14, 21 May 1816.

21. *Nashville Whig*, 9, 16 April 1816; *Charleston Mercury*, 13 March 1826, *Charleston Mercury*, 23 March 1831.

22. The previously recounted two-year odyssey of the slave Drew in North Carolina, Alabama, and Tennessee was only one such attempt. Records of the Chancery Court, Bedford County, Tennessee, George W. Ruth vs. Martin Grace and Samuel Williams, 5 June 1839, Record Book 1830–1842, 195–202, County Court House, Shelbyville, Tennessee. Also see *Charleston Mercury*, 10 March 1830; *Charleston Mercury and Morning Advertiser*, 20 October 1824.

Information on January in *New Orleans Picayune*, 1 June 1839; on Wiley in *Alabama State Intelligence* [Tuscaloosa], 16 October 1837; on Anthony in *Richmond Enquirer*, 1 July 1853.

23. *New Orleans Picayune*, 26 May 1840.

24. *Raleigh Register* [North Carolina], 20 February 1818, in *A Documentary History of American Industrial Society*, ed. Ulrich B. Phillips (Cleveland, Ohio: Arthur H. Clark, 1910), 2:85–86.

25. Legislative Petitions, Petition of Samuel Templeman to the Virginia General Assembly, 21 December 1809, Westmoreland County, VSA. As executor of the estate of William Hutt, who had died "considerably in debt," Templeman was seeking compensation from the estate for the dead slave who "might have sold for at least £100." The petition was rejected.

26. Order of New Orleans Magistrate, 12 January 1822, Manuscript 44, folder 4, Historic New Orleans Collection.

27. Records of the Fifth Judicial District Court, Orleans Parish, Louisiana, William C. and Julietta Palmer vs. David Bidwell, 26 September 1854, #8,618, reel 26, Louisiana Collection, New Orleans Public Library; for other wives running away to husbands, see *New Orleans Bee*, 7 January 1832, 3 May 1830.

28. *New Orleans Picayune*, 5 January 1838; *New Orleans Bee*, 21 April 1841; *Charleston Mercury*, 14 August 1826. Information on Sally in *Charleston Mercury and Morning Advertiser*, 5 January 1825; on Nelly in *Charleston Mercury*, 8 May 1832. She ran away 20 November 1831. The notice ran until 29 May 1832.

29. *Charleston Mercury*, 26 April 1831; quote about Elvy in *Richmond Enquirer*, 6 December 1850; description of Martha in *Richmond Enquirer*, 25 January 1850.

30. *Richmond Enquirer*, 6 March 1855; *Richmond Enquirer*, 4 June 1805. Nancy escaped when they were six miles from the Hanover County Court House.

31. Information on Wenny and Easter in Legislative Petitions, Petition of Catherine Nelms to the General Assembly, 12 December 1815, Northumberland County, VSA. Abram discussed in Records of the Equity Court, Laurens District, South Carolina, Petition of Allen Barksdale, Trustee of Leanna Kennedy, 11 July 1833, Case #15, Box 1, SCDAH; Testimony of Charles Allen, ca. July 1833, with ibid.; Order of the Court, 12 July 1833, with ibid.; Commissioner's Report, 12 July 1833, with ibid. For the case of a recently freed wife forced to emigrate and the fears of whites that her slave husband would "of course go after her," see Legislative Petitions, Petition of John Flowers, Thomas Allen, John D. Lucas, et al. to the Virginia General Assembly, 11 January 1839, Harrison County, VSA.

32. Statement of Joseph Bradshaw to the Justice of the Peace in Concordia Parish, Louisiana, 9 September 1833, Natchez Trace Slaves and Slavery Collection, folder on Fugitive Slaves, Center for American History, University of Texas at Austin; *Richmond Enquirer*, 2 July 1852.

33. *Tennessee Republican Banner*, 6 January 1838; *New Orleans Bee*, 27 March

1830; *New Orleans Bee,* 1 April 1830 [in French], 6 April 1830 [in English]; *New Orleans Picayune,* 31 May 1840.

34. *New Orleans Bee,* 22 May 1832; *New Orleans Bee,* 5 July 1832; *New Orleans Picayune,* 23 June 1840. Robert and Vina absconded on 24 September 1839. The notice ran through 7 July 1840.

35. Legislative Petitions, Petition of Benjamin Browne to the Virginia General Assembly, 16 December 1809, Surry County, VSA; *Charleston Mercury,* 14 August 1826.

36. *New Orleans Bee,* 15 March 1834, 9 May 1834, 12 May 1834; *New Orleans Picayune,* 3 July 1839, 4 July 1840; *Charleston Mercury,* 4 May 1830. Quote about child "sick with a sore mouth" in *New Orleans Bee,* 30 July 1834; information on Matilda in *New Orleans Bee,* 8 September 1832; on Jenny in *New Orleans Bee,* 1 February 1833.

37. *New Orleans Bee,* 1, 2, 4, 6, 7, 8 March 1833; *New Orleans Bee,* 3 January 1835; *New Orleans Bee,* 19 November 1835; *Richmond Enquirer,* 17 May 1850.

38. *Richmond Enquirer,* 30 August 1850.

39. *Tennessee Republican Banner,* 1 October 1841, 18 April 1842; Samuel Williams, "Ann Robertson [Cockrill]: An Unsung Tennessee Heroine," *Tennessee Historical Quarterly* 3 (June 1944), 154–55. The *Banner*'s advertisement of October instructed the *Register* to insert the notice three times.

40. *Tennessee Republican Banner,* 2 June 1841; *New Orleans Bee,* 23 January 1833; *Tennessee Republican Banner,* 15 November 1839.

41. *Richmond Enquirer,* 27 May 1806.

42. *Tennessee Republican Banner,* 8 October 1838; St. Mary's County Court (Equity Papers) 86, Charles L. Gardiner vs. Edward Fenwick, 20 May 1833, reel M-11,026, SC, MSA; Testimony of Thomas Lynch, 18 October 1833, ibid.

43. *Nashville Whig,* 18, 25 December 1816; *Charleston Mercury,* 1 July 1828; *Tennessee Republican Banner,* 23, 25 November 1840, 2, 4, 7, 9, 12, 15, 17 December 1840.

44. *Charleston Mercury and Morning Advertiser,* 15 December 1824. The fear of sale was also the reason Sam, Suckey, their daughter Jane, and "three small Children" ran away in Virginia. *Alexandria Advertiser and Commercial Intelligencer,* 23 March 1804, 9 April 1804, 28 April 1804, in *Advertisements for Runaway Slaves in Virginia, 1801–1820,* ed. Daniel E. Meaders (New York: Garland Publishing, 1997), 32–33.

45. *Nashville Whig,* 13 December 1814.

46. *New Orleans Picayune,* 19 June 1839.

47. *Charleston Mercury,* 15 May 1827; *Charleston Mercury and Morning Advertiser,* 30 September 1824. Discussion of Ned and Bella's family in *Charleston Mercury,* 26 March 1828.

48. *Richmond Enquirer,* 29 July 1806, 1, 5, 12, 15 August 1806; *Richmond Enquirer,* 17 June 1808.

49. *Tennessee Republican Banner,* 1 July 1840; *Tennessee Republican Banner,* 26 December 1838.

50. *Tennessee Republican Banner,* 7 January 1841; *Charleston Mercury and Morning Advertiser,* 13 August 1824. The notice ran through 11 September 1824. *Charleston Mercury,* 4 March 1826.

51. *New Orleans Bee,* 25 November 1834; *Charleston Mercury and Morning Advertiser,* 27 December 1825; *Charleston Mercury,* 13 March 1826.

52. *Richmond Enquirer,* 11 January 1805. This notice and a second, beginning 7 June 1805, ran through 16 August 1805.

53. *New Orleans Bee*, 6 February 1833; *New Orleans Picayune*, 31 May 1840; *New Orleans Bee*, 30 August 1832.

54. William Smith to S. Pemberton, [1842], William Alexander Smith Papers, Manuscript Department, William R. Perkins Library, Duke University, Durham, North Carolina. Remarkably, Smith also wrote his son, apparently through Pemberton, about the plan. William Smith to [Andy Smith], 12 April 1842, ibid.

55. Records of the Circuit Court, Jefferson County, Kentucky, Case Files, Benjamin Lawrence, Administrator of the Estate of Elias D. Lawrence vs. J. F. Lawrence and Mary A. P. Lawrence, 20 November 1830, Case #2,698, Box 1-37, KDLA; Decree of the Jefferson County Circuit Court, 20 November 1830, with ibid. Despite the decree, there is no record of a sale, and the case was continued.

56. Loren Schweninger, ed., *From Tennessee Slave to St. Louis Entrepreneur: The Autobiography of James Thomas*, with foreword by John Hope Franklin (Columbia: University of Missouri Press, 1984), 32; *Buffalo City Directory* (Buffalo: Horatio Walker, 1844), 213; Henry K. Thomas to John Rapier, Sr., 27 October 1856, Rapier-Thomas Family Papers, Moorland-Spingarn Research Center, Howard University, Washington, D.C.; A. M. Simmons to Henry K. Thomas, 26 May 1836, ibid.

57. Missouri Supreme Court Cases, St. Louis District, Stephen Ridgley vs. Steamboat *Reindeer*, 6 October 1857, Box 598, #6, Missouri State Archives, Jefferson City, Missouri; Testimony of Stephen Ridgley, 1856, 11, in ibid.; Affidavit of George P. Strong, 17 December 1856, 14–15, in ibid.; also see Records of the Circuit Court, Jefferson County, Kentucky, Case Files, Matilda, free woman of color, vs. James H. Owen, 28 October 1852, #8,618, Box 2-131, KDLA. Rather than lose him forever, Matilda actually tried to retrieve her runaway son Lewis and return him to his owner.

58. *Charleston Mercury*, 21 January 1832.

59. *New Orleans Picayune*, 5 January 1838; *New Orleans Bee*, 21 April 1841.

60. *Tennessee Gazette*, 26 September 1804, 3, 24 October 1804, 7, 14 November 1804.

61. *Richmond Enquirer*, 19 May 1807. The notice ran through 21 July 1807.

62. *Tennessee Republican Banner*, 9 September 1842; *New Orleans Bee*, 25 July 1834. The notice ran until 26 September 1834.

63. Thomas Right to John Walker, 5 December 1850, Richard Riddick Papers, Manuscript Department, William R. Perkins Library, Duke University.

CHAPTER 4

1. Inventory of Property on Bon Ridge Plantation, 10 January 1852, Box 2, folder 58, Farrar (Alexander K.) Papers, Special Collections, Hill Memorial Library, LSU; Records of the Catahoula Parish Probate Court, Copy of Succession of Absalom Sharp, 22 December 1852, Box 2, folder 61, ibid.; Records of the Probate Court, Catahoula Parish, Louisiana, Petition for Curatorship of Clarissa Sharp, 1 February 1851, County Court House, Harrisonburg, Louisiana; Mercy Chalfant vs. Clarissa Sharp, 30 September 1853, with ibid.; John Sharp vs. Clarissa Sharp, 30 November 1855, with ibid.

2. F. W. Ford to Alexander Farrar, 14 June 1852, Box 2, folder 59, Farrar (Alexander K.) Papers, Special Collections, Hill Memorial Library, LSU; F. W. Ford to Alexander Farrar, 29 September 1852, Box 2, folder 59, ibid.; F. W. Ford to Alexander Farrar, 28 November 1852, Box 2, folder 59, ibid.

3. F. W. Ford to Alexander Farrar, 16 September 1853, Box 2, folder 61, ibid. Both in Mississippi and Louisiana, Absalom Sharp had previously confronted problems managing his slaves. A voucher in his succession papers listed a $50 expense paid to a lawyer to defend his slave Willis, and a $298.50 loss when the slave was executed

in 1851. Willis was convicted of murdering a fellow slave. Records of the Catahoula Parish Probate Court, Copy of Succession of Absalom Sharp, 22 December 1852, Box 2, folder 61, ibid.

4. Alexander K. Farrar to H. W. Drake, 5 September 1857, ibid.

5. Alexander K. Farrar to H. W. Drake, 5 September 1857, ibid.

6. Alexander K. Farrar to H. W. Drake, 4, 5 September 1857, ibid. Apparently, the slaves were hanged. In a discussion between Clarissa Sharp's lawyer, Alexander Farrar, and a friend, Farrar wrote: "I wanted to talk with you about the hanging of the Negroes." He recommended they be hanged "privately," but that they be buried by slaves so no one could say "White folks send them off and don't hang them &c &c." Another overseer was also murdered about the same time, and Farrar said that the executed slaves should be buried "by the Negroes upon the spot where the Murders were committed." Alexander K. Farrar to W. B. Foules, 6 December 1857, Box 2, folder 71, ibid.

7. Edward L. Ayers, *Vengeance and Justice: Crime and Punishment in the Nineteenth-Century American South* (New York: Oxford University Press, 1984), 132. Information on fellow slaves in Governor of Alabama, Proclamations, 22 September 1841, ADAH. On Sam, Records of the General Assembly, Petition of William Ware to the South Carolina General Assembly, 22 November 1815, #137, SCDAH; Deposition, John Robertson, Richard Stone, 22 November 1815, with ibid.; Deposition of Hector, Slave of John Robertson, July 1814, with ibid.; Oath, Thomas Ware, 22 November 1815, with ibid.; Affidavit, William Ware, 22 November 1815, with ibid.; Petition of William Ware to the South Carolina Senate, 24 November 1814, #123, with ibid.; Appraisal of Slave Jim, William Ware et al., 24 November 1814, with ibid. Discussion of Virginia convictions in Philip J. Schwarz, *Twice Condemned: Slaves and the Criminal Laws of Virginia, 1705–1865* (Baton Rouge: Louisiana State University Press, 1988), 232.

8. Records of the General Assembly, Petition of Robert Bradford to the South Carolina Senate, 3 December 1814, #46, SCDAH; *Weekly Gazette* [Greene County, Georgia], 18 May 1859, quoted in Ayers, *Vengeance and Justice*, 132, 315; Baltimore City Register of Wills (Petitions), Petitions of Job G. Stansbury to the Orphans Court of Baltimore County, 17 June 1828, 19 July 1828, reel M-11,025, SC, MSA; Howard County Register of Wills (Petitions), George Elliott vs. Anthony Boston, 16 October 1855, reel M-11,024, SC, MSA; *Nashville Whig*, 25 October 1814.

9. Some slaves did possess guns. See Helen T. Catterall, ed., *Judicial Cases Concerning American Slavery and the Negro* (Washington, D.C.: W. F. Roberts, 1932), 2:355, 369. Information on Samuel in Records of the Circuit Court, Warren County, Mississippi, State vs. Samuel, 16 June 1858, Natchez Trace Slaves and Slavery Collection, Box 2E776, folder 3, Center for American History, University of Texas at Austin; on Moses in *Richmond Enquirer*, 10 September 1805; Ann Farrar to A. K. Farrar, 3 November 1857, Farrar (Alexander K.) Papers, Box 1, folder 8, Special Collections, Hill Memorial Library, LSU.

10. Governor of Alabama, Proclamations and Writs, 20 December 1841, ADAH, for similar cases, see ibid., 7 December 1830, 20 January 1843; ibid., 30 July 1857.

11. Baltimore City Register of Wills (Petitions), Ezekiel Mills vs. Harriet Sales, Orphans Court of Baltimore City, 12 November 1858, reel M-11,026, SC, MSA. Discussion of the shooting in Records of the North Carolina Supreme Court, Harrell vs. Davenport, December 1859, Case #8,283, NCDAH; Records of the County Court, Washington County, North Carolina, Copy of Henry Harrell, Executor of William D. Davenport, vs. Polly Davenport et al., Fall Term 1859, with ibid.; *Reports of Cases in Equity Argued and Determined in The Supreme Court of North Carolina, From De-*

cember Term, 1859, to August Term, 1860 Inclusive (Salisbury, N.C.: J. J. Bruner, [1861]), 5:4–9. Bludgeoning of Leonidas Jeffreys in George W. Oliver to E. H. Stokes, 1 May 1861, Chase Family Papers, Manuscript Division, LC.

12. Petition of Jacob Duckworth to the Mississippi Legislature, 1831, Record Group 47, Volume 20, Petitions and Memorials, MDAH; Anne Arundel County Register of Wills (Petitions and Orders) 1840–51, 272–74, Petition of Richard Crisp to the Orphans Court, 14 October 1848, reel #CR 63,127-2, MSA.

13. *New Orleans Picayune*, 11 April 1837; *Tennessee Republican Banner*, 26 December 1838; *Virginia Herald*, 8 January [1805], clipping found with Legislative Petitions, Petition of Mary Bussell to the Virginia General Assembly, 14 December 1812, Stafford County, Oversize, VSA.

14. *Nashville Whig*, 27 April 1814, 3, 11 May 1814; *New Orleans Bee*, 5 August 1830.

15. *New Orleans Bee*, 8 July 1835; *New Orleans Picayune*, 22 March 1839; *Nashville Whig*, 8, 15 August 1815; comments by other owners in *Richmond Enquirer*, 13 December 1804; *New Orleans Bee*, 25 May 1832; *Charleston Mercury*, 11 October 1830.

16. *New Orleans Picayune*, 30 August 1838; *New Orleans Picayune*, 15 May 1839.

17. *Tennessee Republican Banner*, 26 December 1838; *Nashville Whig*, 6, 13 December 1814; example of Camden slave in *Charleston Mercury*, 14 January 1831; of Dick in Anne Arundel County Register of Wills (Petitions and Orders) 1840–51, 182–84, William C. Lyles vs. Negro Dick, 16 March 1847, reel #CR 63,127-2, MSA.

18. Escape of Davie and Sandy in *Tennessee Republican Banner*, 10 June 1839. The guardian of the estate said that the slaves were assisted by twenty-year-old Thomas M. Nash, an embittered heir of the deceased planter. Quote about Edmund in *Richmond Enquirer*, 30 June 1854.

19. *New Orleans Picayune*, 11 July 1837, notice ran continuously through 3 December 1837; *New Orleans Bee*, 20 October 1834; *Charleston Mercury*, 11 December 1828; Catterall, ed., *Judicial Cases Concerning American Slavery and the Negro*, 2: 333; *Richmond Enquirer*, 5 April 1808.

20. Shirley Plantation Journal, 5 October 1837, in Shirley Plantation Records, Manuscript Division, LC. Owned by Hill Carter, Shirley Plantation was located near Hopewell, Virginia. Carter was engaged primarily in raising corn, wheat, and sheep.

21. *Charleston Mercury*, 23 January 1829; Catterall, ed., *Judicial Cases Concerning American Slavery and the Negro*, 2:321, 400; Records of the District Court, Comal County, Texas, State vs. Negro Asa, Indictment for Larceny, 6 May 1859, Case #110, County Court House, New Braunfels, Texas.

22. *Richmond Enquirer*, 13 August 1850.

23. *Tennessee Gazette*, 31 May 1806; *Tennessee Republican Banner*, 28 June 1851, 1, 3, 4, 7, 8, 9, 10 14, 16, June 1851, 29 July 1851; *New Orleans Bee*, 26 October 1830, 29 March 1831, 1, 4, 5, 6, 7, 8 April 1831; *New Orleans Picayune*, 7 May 1832; *Carolina Centinel* [New Bern, North Carolina], 8 August 1818, in *A Documentary History of American Industrial Society*, ed. Ulrich B. Phillips (Cleveland, Ohio: Arthur H. Clark, 1910), 2:91. The thirteen-year-old slave was described in *Charleston Mercury*, 17 September 1832. For another example, see *Charleston Mercury*, 21 April 1831.

24. Testimony of Tilman Gilbert to the Justice of the Peace, Concordia Parish, Louisiana, 9 May 1837, Natchez Trace Slaves and Slavery Collection, folder on Fugitive Slaves, Center for American History, University of Texas at Austin. John was tried for the assault. For the court judgment in the case see Sentence of the Court,

State vs. John, a Runaway Charged with Resisting a White Person, 9 May 1837, Natchez Trace Slaves and Slavery Collection, folder on Fugitive Slaves, Center for American History, University of Texas at Austin.

25. *Tennessee Republican Banner*, 4, 6, 7, July 1842; Anita Shafer Goodstein, *Nashville 1780–1860: From Frontier to City* (Gainesville: University of Florida Press, 1989), 107, 108, 156, 152.

26. Records of the General Assembly, Petition of David Murray to the South Carolina House of Representatives, 1826, ND #511, SCDAH; Deposition, Hilray Murray, Lincoln County, Georgia, 17 October 1826; Copy of Record of Court of Justices and Freeholders, Lancaster District, State vs. Negro Sandy, December 1825, with ibid. Sandy was later captured and hanged. Records of the General Assembly, Petition of Mary Moseley to the South Carolina Senate and House of Representatives, 26 July 1806, #109, SCDAH; Statement of Support, Simeon Cushman et al., ca. 1806, with ibid.; with part of his intestine protruding through the wound, Moseley made it home but died two days later. Records of the General Assembly, Petition of William B. Villard to the South Carolina Senate, 4 December 1813, #107, SCDAH; the slave was subdued by others who came to Villard's rescue. Incident with blacksmith in Records of the General Assembly, Session Records, Petition of Henry Taylor to the North Carolina General Assembly, 1796, Miscellaneous Petitions, November–December 1796, NCDAH.

27. Records of the General Assembly, Session Records, Petition of Jarrad [also spelled Jarratt] Weaver, 24 November 1823 [date read and referred to Committee on Claims], NCDAH; Legislative Petitions, Petition of William Fontaine to the Virginia General Assembly, 1 February 1838, Fluvanna County, VSA; Copy of Proclamation, Virginia Lieutenant Governor Wyndham Robertson, 26 September 1836, with ibid. The lieutenant governor offered a $100 reward for Dave's capture. The proclamation was signed in behalf of the governor. Although the two other slaves were never caught, Dave was tracked down and killed.

28. Summary of Case of Runaway Slave and Mr. Staunton, Overseer, 17 April 1834, Adams or Wilkinson County, Mississippi, Natchez Trace Slaves and Slavery Collection, Folder on Fugitive Slaves, Center for American History, University of Texas at Austin. The testimony said "pistols" not "pistol."

29. Legislative Petitions, Petitions of Robert Wilson to the Virginia General Assembly, 21 October 1790, 22 October 1791, Lunenburg County, VSA.

30. Legislative Petitions, Petition of James Brown, Sr., William B. Brown, et al. to the Virginia General Assembly, 14 December 1809, Cumberland County, VSA; Records of the General Assembly, Petition of Edward Brailsford to the South Carolina House of Representatives, 26 November 1816, #100, SCDAH; Petition of Edward Brailsford to the South Carolina Senate, ca. 1821, ND #1,838, SCDAH; Deposition, James Hartley Hext, 12 December 1821, with ibid.; Deposition, Seth Prior, 21 November 1821, with ibid.; Petition of Edward Brailsford to the South Carolina House of Representatives, ca. 1821, ND #1,837, SCDAH; Herbert Aptheker, "Maroons Within the Present Limits of the United States," *Journal of Negro History* 24 (April 1939), 167–68; Schwarz, *Twice Condemned*, 225–26. On the difficulty capturing runaways in the Great Dismal Swamp, see *Laws of North-Carolina, Enacted by a General Assembly, begun and held at Raleigh, on the eighteenth day of November, in the year of our Lord one thousand eight hundred and twenty-two* (n.p., [1823]), 28–29; *Laws of the State of North Carolina, Passed by the General Assembly, at the Session of 1848–'49* (Raleigh: Thomas Lemay, 1849), 213–15.

31. Quote of "various depredations" in Aptheker, "Maroons Within the Present Limits of the United States," 170–71; Tom, Cyrus, and Hercules in *City Gazette and*

Daily Advertiser [Charleston, South Carolina], 5 March 1800, in "Documents: Eighteenth Century Slaves as Advertised by Their Masters," *Journal of Negro History* 1 (April 1916), 173.

32. Harvey Toliver Cook, *The Life and Legacy of David Rogerson Williams* (New York: n.p., 1916), 130.

33. Records of the General Assembly, Session Records, Petition of William L. Hill to the North Carolina General Assembly, [1823,] in Petitions (Miscellaneous), November 1823–January 1824, Box 4, NCDAH; Report of the Committee on Claims, 8 December 1823, in House Committee Reports, Box 3, ibid.; Petition of John Rhem to the North Carolina General Assembly, November 1822, in House Committee Reports, November 1823–January 1824, Box 3, NCDAH; Sworn Oaths, William Boyd and John T. Boyd, 13 November 1822, ibid.; Report of the Committee of Claims, ca. 1824, ibid. A few years later in the nearby counties, a group of outlying blacks intimidated members of patrols by threatening to burn their homes. Records of the General Assembly, Session Records, Petition of Residents of Sampson, Bladen, New Hanover, and Duplin Counties to the North Carolina General Assembly, ca. 1830, Session November 1830–January 1831, Miscellaneous Petitions, NCDAH; R. H. Taylor, "Slave Conspiracies in North Carolina," *North Carolina Historical Review* 5 (January 1928), 24.

34. Records of the Territorial Legislative Council, Memorial to Governor William P. Duval, ca. 1823, Record Group 910, Series 876, Box 1, folder 6, FSA; General Jesup to Clement C. Clay, 6 September 1837, Records of Alabama Governors, Administrative Files, Creek Indian War, ADAH.

35. *Woodville Republican*, 6 October 1829, quoted by Charles S. Syndor, in *Slavery in Mississippi* (Washington, D.C.: American Historical Association, 1933; reprint, Baton Rouge: Louisiana State University Press, 1966), 121; James E. Glenn to Major John H. Howard, 29 March 1836, Records of Alabama Governors, Administrative Files, Creek Indian War, 1836, ADAH; Major General William Irwin through Major George L. Barry to Governor Clement Comer Clay, 20 May 1836, Records of Alabama Governors, Administrative Files, Creek Indian War, ADAH; Letter Fragment, to Sir, 6 March 1837, Records of Alabama Governors, Administrative Files, Creek Indian War, ADAH.

36. Records of the General Assembly, Session Records, Petition of William M. Moody, Jr., N. M. Long, Rice B. Pierce, Lawrence C. Pierce, W. H. Day, et al. to the North Carolina General Assembly, 14 December 1844, Petitions, November 1844–January 1845, Box 5, NCDAH; Aptheker, "Maroons Within the Present Limits of the United States," 179–82; Wilmington *Journal*, 14 August 1856, cited in ibid., 182.

37. Details of Kingston incident in Legislative Records, Petition of Peter Gourdin to the House of Representatives of South Carolina, 1835, #21 and #22, SCDAH. The exact date of the robbery was not indicated.

38. *A Digest of the Laws of the State of Georgia* (Philadelphia: J. Towar and D. M. Hogan, 1831), 310; *Acts Passed at the First Session of the Twenty-third General Assembly of the State of Tennessee* (Nashville: J. George Harris, 1840), 82–83; *A Collection of All Such Acts of the General Assembly of Virginia* (Richmond: Samuel Pleasants, Jr., 1803), 188; see also Legislative Records, Report of the Judiciary Committee, South Carolina General Assembly, 1858, #93, SCDAH; *The Laws of Texas, 1822–1897* (Austin: Gamble Book Company, 1898), 5:762–63.

Enforcement of prohibitions in Philip D. Morgan, "Work and Culture: The Task System and the World of Lowcountry Blacks, 1700–1800," *William and Mary Quar-*

terly, 3d ser., 39 (October 1982), 563–66; and "The Ownership of Property by Slaves in the Mid-Nineteenth-Century Low Country," *Journal of Southern History* 49 (August 1983), 399–401; Lawrence T. McDonnell, "Money Knows No Master: Market Relations and the American Slave Community," in *Developing Dixie: Modernization in a Traditional Society,* ed. Winfred B. Moore, Jr., et al. (Westport, Conn.: Greenwood Press, 1988), 31–44; Betty Wood, *Women's Work, Men's Work: The Informal Slave Economies of Lowcountry Georgia* (Athens: University of Georgia Press, 1995), 61, 99; John T. Schlotterbeck, "The Internal Economy of Slavery in Rural Piedmont Virginia," in *The Slaves' Economy: Independent Production by Slaves in the Americas,* ed. Ira Berlin and Philip D. Morgan (London: Frank Cass, 1991), 175; Roderick A. McDonald, "Independent Economic Production by Slaves on Antebellum Louisiana Sugar Plantations," in ibid., 196; Loren Schweninger, "The Underside of Slavery: The Internal Economy, Self-Hire, and Quasi-Freedom in Virginia, 1780–1865," *Slavery and Abolition: A Journal of Comparative Studies* 12 (September 1991), 1–5.

39. Legislative Records, Petition of Edward Dudley, Timothy Barton, Jonathan Nichols, et al. to the South Carolina General Assembly, 1816, #95, SCDAH. For South Carolina, see Alex Lichtenstein, " 'That Disposition to Theft, With Which They Have Been Branded': Moral Economy, Slave Management, and the Law," *Journal of Social History* 21 (spring 1988), 429–30; David J. McCord, *The Statutes at Large of South Carolina* (Columbia: A. S. Johnson, 1840), 434–34 (1796 law), 454–55 (1817 law); David J. McCord, *Statutes at Large of South Carolina* (Columbia: A. S. Johnson, 1839), 265–66 (1825 law), 516–17 (1834 law), 529 (1835 law); Loren Schweninger, "Slave Independence and Enterprise in South Carolina, 1780–1865," *South Carolina Historical Magazine* 93 (April 1992), 116–17.

40. Information on trade on the plantation in Schlotterbeck, "The Internal Economy," 174, 176; *A Digest of Laws of the State of Georgia* (Philadelphia: J. Towar and D. M. Hogan, 1831), 310; *Acts Passed at the First Session of the Twenty-third General Assembly of the State of Tennessee* (Nashville: J. George Harris, 1840), 32–33; *Supplement to the Revised Code of the Laws of Virginia* (Richmond: Samuel Shepherd and Company, 1833), 250. Winthrop D. Jordan, *White Over Black: American Attitudes Toward the Negro, 1550–1812* (Chapel Hill: University of North Carolina Press, 1968), 380–87, 391–93; *A Collection of All Such Acts of the General Assembly of Virginia, of a Public and Permanent Nature, as are Now in Force* (Richmond: Samuel Pleasants, Jr., 1803), 137, 178, 187, 189, 191, 315; Schweninger, "The Underside of Slavery," 1–22.

41. *Charleston Mercury and Morning Advertiser,* 25 May 1825. The notice ran through 11 July 1825.

42. *Charleston Mercury,* 12 April 1832. Natt ran away in February 1832; the notice ran until 10 May 1832.

43. [*Proceedings of a meeting on August 26, 1854, to take steps to put an end to trafficking with slaves and their escape beyond the Rio Grande*] (Seguin, Tex.: n.p., 1854), 1–2.

44. Records of the General Assembly, Petition of Inhabitants Along the Ashepoo and Pon Pon Rivers to the South Carolina General Assembly, ca. 1817, ND #2849, and ca. 1818, ND #2850, SCDAH; A Memorial Addressed to the Legislature of Mississippi, Wilkinson County, Mississippi, ca. 1850s, Record Group 47, Volume 27, Petitions and Memorials, MDAH.

45. Legislative Petitions, Petitions of the Inhabitants of Isle of Wight County to the Virginia General Assembly, 9 December 1817, VSA; Petition of Propertyholders of Louisa County to the Virginia General Assembly, 21 December 1859, in ibid.;

Petition of the Citizens of Fauquier County to the Virginia General Assembly, 10 January 1860, Fauquier County, in ibid.

46. Records of the General Assembly, Session Records, Petition of Residents of Sampson, Bladen, New Hanover, and Duplin Counties to the North Carolina General Assembly, ca. 1830, Session November 1830–January 1831, Miscellaneous Petitions, NCDAH. Later proposal in Records of the General Assembly, Session Records, Report of the Select Committee, 8 January 1845, Session November 1844–January 1845, Select Committee Records, Box 4, NCDAH.

47. Records of the Parish Court, Pointe Coupee Parish, Louisiana, Fourth District Court, Charles Steward vs. Abraham Villeret, 12 September 1821, #485, Parish Court House, New Roads, Louisiana. In a civil suit, Judge Steward sued for loss of property; a jury found for the defendant. No criminal charges were brought.

48. Records of the Third Judicial District Court, East Baton Rouge Parish, Louisiana, Philip Hicky vs. Isham P. Fox, 24 December 1836, #2,258, East Baton Rouge Parish Archives, Baton Rouge, Louisiana.

49. Records of the Third Judicial District Court, East Baton Rouge Parish, Louisiana, Joseph Bernard vs. Louis Pyburn, 1 January 1838, #2,377, East Baton Rouge Parish Archives, Baton Rouge, Louisiana. The slave who fired the gun was exonerated because he was merely following orders. The jury ruled in favor of the defendant in the civil suit seeking damages.

50. In some states, whites on patrol were protected by law if they shot and killed a runaway. Even without such protection, members of patrols were rarely indicted if they shot and killed a runaway attempting to flee. See Records of the General Assembly, Petition of Matthew ODriscoll to the South Carolina Senate, 1814, #119, and 1819, #109, SCDAH; Copy of Colleton District, Record of Court of Common Pleas, ODriscoll vs. James M. Ford et al., 15 November 1819, SCDAH.

Information on Lucky in Petition of John M. Story to the Texas General Assembly, 25 September 1851, Record Group 47, Petitions and Memorials, TSA; on George in Records of the General Assembly, Petition of John Ross to the South Carolina House of Representatives, 1831, #67, SCDAH; on other slaves in Records of the Supreme Court, Middle Tennessee, Cases, William Pope vs. Robert Baxter and William R. Hicks, 18 December 1836, Box 54, TSLA; Plantation Diary, February 5–12, 1833, in Sterling (Lewis and Family) Papers, Accession #1,866, Special Collections, Hill Memorial Library, LSU.

51. Records of the General Assembly, Session Records, Petition of Inhabitants of Chatham County to the General Assembly, 1802, NCDAH. Quotes about the "daring lawless villain" in Records of the General Assembly, Session Records, Petition of Lard Sellars to the General Assembly, 18 December 1802, NCDAH. Arthur was shot on 1 March 1802, in the midst of efforts to uncover the plans of what became known as the Easter Conspiracy, led by Virginia ferryman Sancho, who moved along the Roanoke River between Halifax and Charlotte counties. Sancho was owned by John Booker of Amelia County. Douglas R. Egerton, *Gabriel's Rebellion: The Virginia Slave Conspiracies of 1800 and 1802* (Chapel Hill: University of North Carolina Press, 1993), 123–25; Jeffrey J. Crow, "Slave Rebelliousness and Social Conflict in North Carolina, 1775–1802," *William and Mary Quarterly* 37 (January 1980), 79–102.

52. Records of the General Assembly, Petitions of Robert Murphy to the South Carolina House of Representatives, 25 November 1800, #150, and ca. 1800, #151, SCDAH; Petition of the Citizens of Enterprise to the Mississippi General Assembly, 16 December 1959, Record Group 47, Volume 30, Petitions and Memorials, MDAH. The petitioners were seeking compensation of $1,400 for Peter's owner, Dr. E. A.

Miller of Wayne County. See also Records of the General Assembly, Petition of Samuel Page to the South Carolina House of Representatives, 1850, #34, SCDAH; Certificate of Value of Slave John, 8 November 1850 with ibid.; Copy of Barnwell District Court Proceedings, State vs. John, 28 February 1849, with ibid.

53. Legislative Petitions, Petition of William Tompkins to the Virginia General Assembly, 4 December 1822, Spotsylvania County, VSA; Records of the Superior Court, Carolina County, Virginia, Copy of Pleas, Court Proceedings and Testimony, October 1821, with ibid. Information on Guy in Records of the Inferior Court, Screven [spelled Scriven in the records] County, Georgia, State vs. Guy, Miscellaneous Records Court of Ordinary (17 October 1844), 1–[4], 10–17, County Court House, Sylvania, Georgia; Petition of Wyatt W. Starke to the Judge of the Superior Court of the Middle District (29 October 1844), ibid., [5]–9.

54. Legislative Petitions, Petition of William Tompkins to the Virginia General Assembly, 4 December 1822, Spotsylvania County, VSA; Records of the Superior Court, Carolina County, Virginia, Copy of Pleas, Court Proceedings, and Testimony, October 1821, with ibid. Records of the Equity Court, Newberry District, South Carolina, Petition of John B. O'Neall, Guardian of Marcus McLemore, 14 September 1855, #31, SCDAH. *New Orleans Bee*, 3 July 1835; Petition of Robert Bacot to the Mississippi General Assembly, 18 January 1854, Record Group 47, Volume 27, Petitions to the Legislature, MDAH.

55. Also see Anne Arundel County Register of Wills (Petitions and Orders) 1840–51, 161–63, Petition of Rezin Hammond to the Orphans Court, 8 September 1846, reel #CR 63,127-2, MSA; ibid., 309–10, Petition of Andrew Lynch to the Orphans Court, 31 July 1849; ibid., 313–14, Petition of Eliza Clagett to the Orphans Court, 22 October 1849; ibid., 324, Petition of William H. Bird to the Orphans Court, 11 December 1849; ibid., 261, Petition of Benjamin Carr to the Orphans Court, [September] 1855; John Merriman to Francis D. Richardson, 11 November 1840, Weeks (David and Family) Papers, Special Collections, Hill Memorial Library, LSU; *New Orleans Bee*, 31 July 1833, 4 April 1834.

CHAPTER 5

1. Records of the Circuit Court, Jefferson County, Kentucky, Case Files, Thomas Joyce, Mary [Bowman] Joyce et al. vs. H. H. Buffenmyer, 15 May 1857, Case #13,011, Box 2-178, KDLA. The case was brought when Buffenmyer refused to pay a portion of the slave's price until the title had been cleared. The court ruled that Jack, as part of the dower given to the widow, also benefited the couple's children and therefore could only be sold at auction to obtain as great a profit as possible. Copy of Mary Bowman's Dower, 15 December 1846, with ibid.

2. John Merriman to Mary Weeks, 13 November 1840, Weeks (David and Family) Papers, Special Collections, Hill Memorial Library, LSU.

3. James Monroe Torbert Journal, 29 July 1855, typescript, ADAH.

4. Records of the Superior Court, Oglethorpe County, Georgia, John Wynne vs. Moses Wright, 1 April 1851, in Minutes 1847–1853, 252–55, County Court House, Lexington, Georgia.

5. Records of the Superior Court, Greene County, Georgia, Gwynn Allison vs. John T. Broughton, August 1856, in Proceedings 1856–1858, 252–53, County Court House, Greensboro, Georgia.

6. Declaration of George de Passau to the Judge of Iberville Parish Court, Louisiana, 7 March 1810, Natchez Trace Slaves and Slavery Collection, folder on Fugitive Slaves, Center for American History, University of Texas at Austin. For other run-

aways in Iberville Parish prior to statehood, see Declaration of Nicholas Toffier to the Judge of Iberville Parish Court, 7 April 1810, and Declaration of Jacques de Villiers to the Judge of the Iberville Parish Court, 13 September 1810, with ibid.

7. *Carolina Centinel* [New Bern, North Carolina], 8 August 1818, in *A Documentary History of American Industrial Society*, ed. Ulrich B. Phillips (Cleveland, Ohio: Arthur H. Clark, 1910), 2:92.

8. Records of the Equity Court, Fairfield District, South Carolina, Testimony of Hugh Barkley and Drury Walker, 28 June 1827, in the case of James Barkley, ex parte, Trustee for Hugh and Elizabeth Smith, 1827, SCDAH; Legislative Records, Memorial of Inhabitants of Christ Church Parish to the South Carolina Senate, ca. 1829, ND #1563, SCDAH.

9. Elisha Cain to Alexander Telfair, 10 October 1829, 1 November 1829, in Phillips, ed., *A Documentary History*, 2:85; The owner was in Savannah, Georgia. Emaline quotes found in James Monroe Torbert Journal, 17, 19 March 1849, typescript, ADAH.

10. Information on Joe in *Charleston Mercury*, 17 June 1826. The notice ran continuously through 14 December 1826. Information on Moses in *Charleston Mercury*, 8 February 1832. He ran away in October 1831; the advertisement ran until 25 April 1832. Quote about Parker in Records of the County Court, Westmoreland County, Virginia, County Court Papers, Juliet W. Gawen vs. James Gawen et al., 1849, Box 134, VSA.

11. Search parties discussed in G. E. Manigault to Louis Manigault, 21 January 1861, Louis Manigault Papers, microfilm copy, Perkins Library, Duke University, Durham, North Carolina, cited by Peter Kolchin in *American Slavery, 1619–1877*, (New York: Hill and Wang, 1993), 159, 253 n. 24; Callimus mentioned in *Charleston Mercury*, 12–28 February 1828; Records of the Court of Pleas and Quarter Sessions, Chowan County, North Carolina, Writ of Outlawry vs. Negro Slaves Jacob, Dilworth, Peter, Jacob, Henry, Abraham, and Thompson, December 1816, in Miscellaneous Slave Records 1730–1866, NCDAH.

12. Issuing of cards in *Charleston Mercury*, 26 March 1828, 17 April 1828; Francis D. Richardson to Judge [Moses Liddell?], 18 July 1852, Liddell (Moses, John R., and Family) Papers, Special Collections, Hill Memorial Library, LSU.

13. *Charleston Mercury and Morning Advertiser*, 25 January 1825.

14. Legislative Records, Memorial of Inhabitants of Christ Church Parish to the South Carolina Senate, ca. 1829, ND #1,563, SCDAH; quote of "one hundred negroes" in Mollie Mitchell to Margaret Browne, 26 December 1860, William Phineas Browne Papers, ADAH.

15. Janet Sharp Hermann, *The Pursuit of a Dream* (New York: Oxford University Press, 1981), 17–18.

16. Mollie Mitchell to Margaret Browne, 21 August 1860, William Phineas Browne Papers, ADAH.

17. Quotes about Major in *Nashville Whig*, 9, 16 April 1816; quote of Jesse in Frederick County Court (Petitions), Petition of James Davis to the County Court, 6 March 1838, reel M-11,024, SC, MSA; quote of "wished to be sold" in Deposition of John Bender, [1838,] with ibid.; Deposition of Richard Cromwell [neighbor], [1838,] with ibid. Slave with "a wife in Alabama" in Petition of Thomas Boone to the Mississippi Legislature, October 1859, Record Group 47, Volume 25, Petitions and Memorials, MDAH. In fact, the guardian was so fearful that the man would run away that he sold the slave illegally, having not applied to the Carroll County Court, where his ward's estate was probated, prior to the sale. He was seeking a private act confirming the sale. The Judiciary Committee of the Mississippi General Assembly rejected the petition.

18. Joseph Bieller to Jacob Bieller, 14 September 1830, Alonzo Snyder Papers, Special Collections, Hill Memorial Library, LSU.

19. *Alexandria Advertiser and Commercial Intelligencer*, 23 March 1804, 9 April 1804, 28 April 1804, in *Advertisements for Runaway Slaves in Virginia, 1801–1820*, ed. Daniel Meaders (New York: Garland Publishing, 1997), 32–33. In the first runaway incident, two notices were placed in the newspaper. Information on John Bacon in Baltimore County Register of Wills (Petitions and Orders), William Stewart vs. Daniel Myers, jailer, 23 May 1853, reel M-11,020, SC, MSA.

20. Records of the County Court, Davidson County, Tennessee, Case Files, John Adams and Sarah W. Adams vs. Benjamin F. Moseley et al., 16 May 1853, Case #1,025, Box 10, Metropolitan Nashville-Davidson County Archives, Nashville; Decree of the Court, 19 November 1853, with ibid. Unfortunately for the slave, seventeen days later he was seized by the Davidson County sheriff for Moseley's nonpayment of a debt. Gabriel's title had not been freed from incumbrance. In her suit to reclaim the slave, Sarah Adams asked for permission to keep Gabriel in jail until he could be sold; "if he is now turned out of jail," she said, "he will be certain to runaway." Gabriel remained in jail six months—from May until November—before he was sold.

21. Petition of Henry Dickerson to the Circuit Court, in Records of the Circuit Court, Barren County, Kentucky, Equity Judgments, Henry Dickerson vs. John Butler, 9 July 1821, Case #192, reel #209,794, KDLA. Information on Alabama slave in Records of the Circuit Court, Talladega County, Alabama, Matilda Houston vs. Josiah Houston, 10 August 1839, Final Records 1839–1841 Vol. 1, 226–28, 237–40, Judicial Building, Talladega, Alabama; Decree of the Court, February 1840, with ibid. The four Charleston slaves discussed in Records of the Equity Court, Charleston District, South Carolina, Petition of James R. Felder, Trustee of Virginia Kirkland, 8 July 1852, Case #260, Box 5, SCDAH. Felder sought permission to sell the four slaves.

22. Baltimore City Register of Wills (Petitions), William Brooks vs. Hester, Orphans Court of Baltimore City, 1 November 1855, reel M-11, 026, SC, MSA. Records of the Fifth Judicial District Court, St. Landry Parish, Louisiana, David K. Markham vs. John Close, 17 June 1830, #1,689, Parish Court House, Opelousas, Louisiana.

23. Anne Arundel County Register of Wills (Petitions and Orders) 1851–60, 638–40, William Pumphrey vs. James Edwards, Negro, 10 April 1860, reel #CR 63,128-1, SC, MSA. Information on Michael in St. Mary's County Court (Equity Papers) 86, Charles L. Gardiner vs. Edward Fenwick, 20 May 1833, reel M-11,026, SC, MSA; Testimony of Thomas Lynch, 18 October 1833, ibid. St. Mary's County Court (Equity Papers) 86, Charles L. Gardiner vs. Edward Fenwich, 20 May 1833, reel M-11,026, SC, MSA; Edward Fenwich to John M. S. Causin, 11 January 1833, with ibid.; Answer of Edward Fenwich, 18 November 1833, with ibid.; Contract between Edward Fenwick and Michael, 1 October 1825, with ibid. A suit was initiated in Michael's behalf, but the contract was deemed invalid.

24. Baltimore City Register of Wills (Petitions), William Kriesman vs. Elias Burgess, Orphans Court of Baltimore City, 27 June 1855, reel M-11,026, SC, MSA.

25. Records of the Chancery Court, Brunswick County, Virginia, Chancery Suits Issued, Elizabeth House vs. John House et al., 9 June 1858, folder "Undecided Chancery Causes," Box 202, VSA.

26. Records of the Fourth Judicial District Court, St. John the Baptist Parish, Louisiana, Justin Marc Rideau vs. Jean J. Haydel, 5 February 1847, #32, Parish Court House, Edgard, Louisiana. Begun in the parish court in 1846, the case was transferred to the district court a year later.

27. Records of the Superior Court, Troup County, Georgia, William Webb vs. Edward Castleberry, January 1834, in Records Vol. B 1830–1834, 712–14, County

Court House, Newnan, Georgia. In his defense, Castleberry claimed he had earlier loaned the slaves to Webb; the jury agreed, ruling for the defendant. Records of the Superior Court, Richmond County, Georgia, Edward Palmer vs. Wyatt W. Starke, 1842, in Writs 1842–1846, 81–82, County Records Retention Center, Augusta, Georgia. The jury awarded the owner $450 in damages and ordered the slave to be returned to his master within thirty days. Also see Records of the Superior Court, Coweta County, Georgia, Jacob Brazill vs. Samuel C. Dixon, 12 February 1849, in Writs 1849–1854, 30–34, and Horatio N. Miller vs. Jacob Abraham, August 1833, Writs 1833–1837, 200–1, County Court House, Newnan, Georgia; Records of the Superior Court, Greene County, Georgia, John Dean vs. John L. Geer, [February] 1839, in Proceedings 1838–1841, 157–58, County Court House, Greensboro, Georgia.

28. Records of the Superior Court, Coweta County, Georgia, George Smith vs. James Eckles, 5 February 1838, in Writs 1837–1840, 134–37, County Court House, Newnan, Georgia.

29. Willard B. Gatewood, Jr., ed., *Slave and Freeman: The Autobiography of George L. Knox* (Lexington: University Press of Kentucky, 1979), 48.

30. Legislative Petitions, Petition of William Tompkins to the Virginia General Assembly, 4 December 1822, Spotsylvania County, VSA; Records of the Superior Court, Caroline County, Virginia, Copy of Pleas, Court Proceedings, and Testimony, October 1821, with ibid.

31. "Deserted the premises" quote in Richmond *Enquirer*, 6 November 1849; Legislative Petitions, Petitions of Citizens of Loudoun and Fauquier countries to the Virginia General Assembly, 10 December 1847, Loudoun County, VSA; Legislative Petitions, Petition of "A Virginian" to the Virginia General Assembly, 22 March 1852, Norfolk County, VSA.

32. *Charleston Mercury*, 4 April 1827; *Charleston Mercury*, 7 November 1829.

33. Records of the County Court, Henrico County, Virginia, Ended Chancery Causes, Charles Purcell vs. Parke Street, 9 August 1810, Box 79–7, Packet 1820, VSA. Information on other runaways in *Richmond Enquirer*, 8 September 1854; *Richmond Enquirer*, 21 February 1806, 11 March 1806. Quotes about Martha Whitehead in *Richmond Enquirer*, 10 August 1849.

34. *New Orleans Picayune*, 23 January 1842.

35. Talbot County Circuit Court (Petitions), Petition of Francis and Sophia Loockerman to the Court, 17 February 1859, reel M-11,026, SC, MSA

36. Barnett listed in *Richmond Enquirer*, 20 October 1854; the well digger in *Reports of Cases Argued and Decided in the Supreme Court of the State of Texas During the Latter Part of Galveston Term, 1853, and the Whole of Tyler Term, 1853* (Houston, Tex.: E. H. Cushing, 1876), 10:268–69.

37. Quotes about William Chambery and Eliza in *New Orleans Bee*, 16, 18, 19, 20, 22 November 1833; Records of the Parish Court, West Feliciana Parish, Louisiana, Third District Court, Drury L. Mitchell vs. Joseph R. Miller, 29 May 1835, #1,497, Parish Court House, St. Francisville, Louisiana; *New Orleans Bee*, 7 October 1833.

38. Quotes about Davy in *New Orleans Bee*, 22 June 1833, 1 July 1833; about others in *New Orleans Bee*, 10 July 1834; about slaves from Bayou Boeuf in *New Orleans Bee*, 22 August 1835. The notice ran continuously until 16 October 1835.

39. *New Orleans Picayune*, 25 August 1838.

40. *New Orleans Picayune*, 16 June 1839.

41. Records of the Parish Court, West Feliciana Parish, Louisiana, Seventh District Court, Miles Kelley vs. Joseph Purl, 29 August 1846, #7, Parish Court House, St. Francisville, Louisiana.

42. *Nashville Whig*, 9 August 1814; *Tennessee Republican Banner*, 1 September 1841.

43. *Charleston Mercury and Morning Advertiser*, 25 July 1825.

44. *Charleston Mercury*, 11 January 1831. Jim had absconded in June 1830, and the notice ran through 1 February 1831. *Charleston Mercury*, 31 October 1829; *Richmond Enquirer*, 2 June 1854; *Richmond Enquirer*, 16 December 1856.

45. Records of the Circuit Court, Washington County, Tennessee, John Newnan vs. Montgomery Stewart, 4 October 1815, in Civil and Criminal Cases, Accession #18, Box 74, Folder 10, Archives of Appalachia, East Tennessee State University, Johnson City, Tennessee. The events were recounted in a court case concerning title to the slave.

46. Legislative Records, Petition of Richard Todd to the South Carolina House of Representatives, ca. 1828, ND #2919, SCDAH; Legislative Records, Petition of Allen Yates of Alabama to the South Carolina General Assembly, 21 May 1859, #59, SCDAH.

47. Frederick Law Olmsted, *A Journey in the Back Country* (New York: Mason Brothers, 1860), 55.

48. Legislative Records, Petition of Citizens of San Antonio to the Members of the Bexar Delegation in the Texas General Assembly, 20 December 1851, TSA.

49. Estimates of the number of slaves who made it to freedom in the North vary considerably. It is probable, however, that perhaps one or two thousand per year were successful during the post-1830 period. Not all of them traveled along the routes of the Underground Railroad, however. Whatever the exact number, it is clear that the fugitives who made it to freedom in this manner represented, as one historian said, a "mere trickle from among the millions of slaves." By contrast, tens of thousands of slaves ran away each year into the woods, swamps, hills, backcountry, towns, and cities of the South. Indeed, running away in the South was commonplace. Charles L. Blockson, *Hippocrene Guide to The Underground Railroad* (New York: Hippocrene Books, 1994), 12–13; Larry Gara, *The Liberty Line: The Legend of the Underground Railroad* (Lexington: University of Kentucky Press, 1961), 16–17; William Dusinberre, *Them Dark Days: Slavery in the American Rice Swamps* (New York: Oxford University Press, 1996), 142; idem, *Civil War Issues in Philadelphia 1856–1865* (Philadelphia: University of Pennsylvania Press, 1965), 52–55.

50. Anne Arundel County Register of Wills (Petitions and Orders) 1820–40, 515–16, Petition of Charles R. Stewart to the Orphans Court, 26 July 1836, reel #CR 63, 127-1, SC, MSA; Baltimore County Register of Wills (Petitions and Orders), Carville S. Stansbury vs. Negro Nathaniel, 14 July 1858, reel M-11,020, SC, MSA; Baltimore City Register of Wills (Petitions), Estate of William Inloes, Orphans Court of Baltimore City, 26 August 1856, reel M-11,026, SC, MSA; Baltimore City Register of Wills (Petitions), Amos Spencer vs. Melichoir Moore, Orphans Court of Baltimore City, 27 June 1860, reel M-11,026, SC, MSA; Order of the Court, 28 June 1860, with ibid.

51. Discussion of Henry in Legislative Petitions, Petition of Sarah Welch, James Arbuckle, and John Handley, Administrators of the Estate of John Welch, to the Virginia General Assembly, 10 December 1821, Greenbrier County, VSA; of Frank in Records of the Circuit Court, Floyd County, Kentucky, Case Files, John B. Harris vs. John Spurlock et al., 21 October 1848, Case #119A, Box 1, KDLA. Though the suit was brought in Floyd County, most of Spurlock's property was in Pike County.

52. Example of a careful escape in Legislative Records, Petition of Samuel Linton to the South Carolina General Assembly, 1817, #136, SCDAH; an incautious escape in Records of the United States District Court, District of Columbia, Slavery Records, Fugitive Slave Cases, Petition of John C. Cook, 1 March 1861, Record Group 21, Entry #31, Box 1, NA.

53. Quotes about Jim Lace in *Tennessee Republican Banner*, 24 June 1839; about

Annette's husband in Baltimore City Register of Wills (Petitions), Petition of Henry Hall to the Orphans Court of Baltimore County, 29 May 1835, reel M-11,025, SC, MSA.

54. *Charleston Mercury*, 1 April 1830; Legislative Records, Petition of Charles Hammond to the South Carolina House of Representatives, ca. 1817, ND #1676, SCDAH; Records of the County Court, Caswell County, North Carolina, Petition of Nicholas Wylie of Wilkes County, Georgia, April 1845, Miscellaneous Slave Records 1836–64, NCDAH; John Codman Hurd, *The Law of Freedom and Bondage in the United States* (Boston: Little, Brown, 1862; reprint, New York: Negro Universities Press, 1968), 2:85. In a similar case, Charles Hammond's male slave April set out from Edgefield District, South Carolina, a month after he had been purchased. He made it as far as Surry County, Virginia, before being jailed. Records of the General Assembly, Petition of Charles Hammond to the South Carolina Senate, 1817, #62, SCDAH.

55. G. N. Reagan to William Willis, 18 September 1814, Barns-Willis (Family) Papers, Box 2E530, Center for American History, University of Texas at Austin.

56. Records of the First Judicial District Court, Orleans Parish, Louisiana, Case Records, Townsly and Bony vs. Rutter, 19 December 1822, #5,003, reel 10, Louisiana Collection, New Orleans Public Library; Testimony of Charles Greenleaf, [1823], and John Kinder, 22 March 1823, with ibid.

57. *New Orleans Bee*, 14 July 1831; Records of the First Judicial District Court, Orleans Parish, Louisiana, Case Records, Daquin vs. Cazenave, 17 February 1836, #12,882, reel 28, Louisiana Collection, New Orleans Public Library. Daquin was also spelled Daguin and D'Aguin. *Charleston Mercury and Morning Advertiser*, 26 June 1822.

58. Records of the Fifth District Court, New Orleans, Louisiana, John Henry Brown vs. Alexander Hagan, 26 May 1855, Case #10,001, Suit Records, reel #28, Louisiana Collection, New Orleans Public Library.

59. *Virginia Herald*, 8 January [1805], with Legislative Petitions, Petition of Mary Bussell to the Virginia General Assembly, 14 December 1812, Stafford County, Oversize, VSA; *New Orleans Bee*, 13, 14, 15, 17, 18, 19, 20 December 1832; *Tennessee Republican Banner*, 2 January 1838. This advertisement instructed the editors of the *Knoxville Register* and *Louisville Journal* to insert the notice three times. The notice ran through 23 May 1838. Quotes of the New Orleans master in *New Orleans Bee*, 5 December 1835.

60. *Tennessee Republican Banner*, 29 August 1842; *Tennessee Republican Banner*, 1 February 1841.

61. "In vicinity" refers to runaways in Nashville or surrounding counties within roughly a fifty-mile radius from the capital. Also included in this category is a Franklin County master who believed his slave remained in Franklin County. "Locations in the South" includes the Indian nations, Mississippi Territory, Missouri Territory, and the various states. "North" includes specific states and, for the later period, those going "down the Cumberland River." "To Nashville" includes those from beyond the fifty-mile radius in Tennessee and from other southern states, excluding for the later period runaways from Alabama and Mississippi, who were included with those going to the North.

CHAPTER 6

1. Charles C. Jones Jr. to Charles C. Jones Sr., 1 October 1856, in *The Children of Pride: A True Story of Georgia and the Civil War*, ed. Robert Mason Myers (New Haven: Yale University Press, 1972), 240–43.

2. Charles C. Jones Sr. to Charles C. Jones Jr., 2 October 1856, in Myers, ed., *The Children of Pride*, 243–44.

3. Charles C. Jones Sr., to Mary Jones, 10 December 1856, in Myers, ed., *The Children of Pride,* 270–71. See Charles C. Jones, *The Religious Instruction of the Negroes in the United States* (Savannah: T. Purse, 1842), 6–7; Donald G. Mathews, "Charles Colcock Jones and the Southern Evangelical Crusade to Form a Biracial Community," *Journal of Southern History* 41 (August 1975), 315.

4. *Richmond Enquirer,* 15 February 1850; information on other towns in *New Orleans Bee,* 10 June 1830, 4–30 April 1831, 2–11 May 1831, 20 March 1833. For the list, "Fugitives thought to be hiding in Norfolk, 1784–1806," see Tommy L. Bogger, *Free Blacks in Norfolk, Virginia, 1790–1860: The Darker Side of Freedom* (Charlottesville: University Press of Virginia, 1997), 184–86.

5. Comments about Bob in *New Orleans Bee,* 20 March 1833. Some other examples in *New Orleans Bee,* 20 March 1833; *New Orleans Picayune,* 11 April 1839; Records of the United States Circuit Court for the District of Columbia, Chancery Dockets and Rules Case Files, Record Group 21, Mary Donoho vs. Archibald Thompson and Henry Ryan, 8 September 1828, Case #307, Rules 2, Box 33, NA; Isaac in *Richmond Enquirer,* 23 November 1852.

6. *Richmond Enquirer,* 27 May 1806. The notice ran through 12 August 1806. The owner thought Lewis would head for Norfolk, until he received word from Richmond.

7. Howard District Register of Wills (Petitions), Petition of Charles G. Haslap to the Orphans Court of Howard District of Anne Arundel County, 8 February 1847, reel M-11,024 SC, MSA; Broadside, J. W. Thomas, Charles County, Maryland, n.d., Prints and Photographs Department, Chicago Historical Society; Broadside, John Eversfield, 31 May 1853, ibid.; Broadside, F. M. Bowie, Prince George's County, Maryland, 6 July 1857, ibid.

8. Example of periodic visits in Anne Arundel County Register of Wills (Petitions and Orders) 1860–74, 63–64, Petition of James Wilson to the Orphans Court, 5 November 1861, reel #CR 63,128-2, MSA; of persistant runaways in Anne Arundel County Register of Wills (Petitions and Orders) 1851–60, 194–95, Petition of Dennis Claude, Jr., to the Orphans Court, 3 April 1855, reel #CR 63,128-1, MSA; Anne Arundel County Register of Wills (Petitions and Orders) 1840–51, 323–25, Petition of William H. Bird to the Orphans Court, 11 December 1849, reel #CR 63,127-2, MSA. See Christopher Phillips, *Freedom's Port: The African American Community of Baltimore, 1790–1860* (Urbana: University of Illinois Press, 1997), 66–72, 80–81, 90, 136–37, 230–31.

9. Anne Arundel County Register of Wills (Petitions and Orders) 1840–51, 210–11, Dennis Claude, Jr., vs. Negro Boy Hamilton, 29 October 1847, reel #CR 63, 127-2, MSA.

10. *Charleston Mercury and Morning Advertiser,* 9 July 1824, 5 May 1825, 9 May 1825, 9, 11 20 July 1825, 23 August 1825; *Charleston Mercury,* 3, 10 July 1826, 14 February 1827, 28 February 1828, 28 June 1828, 27 July 1829, 25 February 1831.

11. Information on Frank and Sam in *Charleston Mercury and Morning Advertiser,* 8 July 1826; on Seabrook's slave in *Charleston Mercury and Morning Advertiser,* 20 July 1825; on March in *Charleston Mercury,* 27 June 1826; on the two Africans in *Charleston Mercury,* 16 April 1832.

12. *New Orleans Bee,* 4 June 1832, 15, 17, 19, 20 December 1832, 14–26 May 1834, 10 February 1835, 21 May 1835; *New Orleans Picayune,* 2 August 1838; *New Orleans Bee,* 14 January 1841. Quote about New Orleans in Loren Schweninger, ed., *From Tennessee Slave to St. Louis Entrepreneur: The Autobiography of James Thomas,* with foreword by John Hope Franklin (Columbia: University of Missouri Press, 1984), 109; statistics in Richard C. Wade, *Slavery in the Cities: The South, 1820–1860* (New York: Oxford University Press, 1964), 326.

13. Quote about Agnes in *New Orleans Bee*, 18 August 1828; the advertisement ran through 10 December 1828. Descriptions of origins in *New Orleans Bee*, 10 June 1830. "American" runaways usually spoke only English and often came from outside of Louisiana; "creole" runaways spoke French, or French and English, and were natives of the state.

14. *New Orleans Bee*, 16 November 1830; *New Orleans Bee*, 18 November 1830; *New Orleans Bee*, 30 March 1831; *New Orleans Bee*, 5 April 1841, the notice ran continuously until 30 April 1841; *New Orleans Bee*, 19 March 1836; *New Orleans Picayune*, 11 April 1839.

15. *New Orleans Bee*, 3 April 1829, 29 October 1829, 27 March 1830, 30 March 1831, 9, 11, 13 August 1831, 26 May 1832; quick arrests in Anne Arundel County Register of Wills (Petitions and Orders) 1840–51, 201–2, John Miller vs. Negro Richard, [3] August 1847, reel #CR 63,127-2, MSA.

16. Records of the General Assembly, Legislative Papers, Petition of Thomas W. Smith to the Delaware Senate and House of Representatives, 8 February 1826, Record Group 1111, DSA; *Richmond Enquirer*, 22 July 1806; *Richmond Enquirer*, 8 April 1806; *Charleston Mercury*, 28 January 1830; *Charleston Mercury*, 17 June 1830; the notice ran through 10 September 1830; *Charleston Mercury*, 28 June 1828; *Charleston Mercury*, 16 January 1828.

17. Records of the Superior Court, Chowan County, North Carolina, State vs. Henry Burk, Spring Term 1856, Slave Records, 1856, NCDAH.

18. Information on James Wilson in *New Orleans Bee*, 14 January 1841; on Westcoat's and Mathewes's slaves in Legislative Records, Petition of Fraser Mathewes, John Raven Mathewes, William Brisbane, George Morris, and members of the Agricultural Society of St. Paul Parish to the South Carolina General Assembly, 4 December 1854, #83, SCDAH.

19. Record of Bill's movement in Records of the Inferior Court, Richmond County, Georgia, Meeting of Justices James B. Bishop, Garey F. Parish, and Lambeth Hopkins, 15 March 1851, Minutes 1848–1868, 38, County Court House, Augusta, Georgia; Peter's is in Legislative Petitions, Petition of Francis Royall to the Virginia General Assembly, 19 February 1850, Halifax County, VSA. The arrest date of 1836 cited in the petition is almost surely in error. Peter was sold in April 1840 by the sheriff of Norfolk County. Runaways were usually incarcerated a year to sixteen months when they were not claimed; and it would have been highly unusual for a slave to remain in jail four years before sale. In addition, the expenses allowed by the court for $192.50 suggest a year's imprisonment. Thus, the arrest date used is 1839.

20. Records of the First Judicial District Court, Orleans Parish, Louisiana, Case Records, Joseph Lafranc vs. Rosa, 31 May 1823, #5,334, reel 12, Louisiana Collection, New Orleans Public Library. The case does not include a record of an arrest.

21. Legislative Records, Petition of Citizens of Charleston Neck to the South Carolina General Assembly, ca. 1842, ND #2,125, SCDAH; Petition of James Douglass, John Parr, John Glover, et al., Mechanics and Undertakers of Contracts, to the South Carolina General Assembly, 1820, ND #1,565, #1,566, ibid.; Petition of G. B. Stoddard, William Watson, William Doran, et al. to the South Carolina General Assembly, 1859, ND #2,916, ibid.; Allison Carll-White, "South Carolina's Forgotten Craftsmen," *South Carolina Historical Magazine* 86 (January 1985), 32–38; E. Horace Fitchett, "The Traditions of the Free Negro in Charleston, South Carolina," *Journal of Negro History* 25 (April 1940), 143; Judith Wragg Chase, "American Heritage from Ante-Bellum Black Craftsmen," *Southern Folklore Quarterly* 42 (1978), 140–41. Example of the Montgomery slave in Affidavit of H. G. Harbin, 16 January 1858, Natchez Trace Slaves and Slavery Collection, Center for American History, University of Texas at Austin.

22. Records of the County Court, Perquimans County, North Carolina, Slave Records 1759–1864, William Glover vs. Abram Riddick [ca. 1850], NCDAH; Depositions, Thomas Dunbar, Jarrett W. Everett, James E. Howell, and Edmond Howell, and John R. Lee, 27 September 1850, with ibid.; A. Riddick to William Glover, 22 July 1848, with ibid.

23. *New Orleans Picayune*, 20 August 1839; *New Orleans Picayune*, 25 June 1840; *Charleston Mercury*, 27 February 1830; *Richmond Enquirer*, 19, 22 February 1805. Example of Mary in *New Orleans Bee*, 27 October 1829. The notice ran continuously through 17 March 1830. The mulatto man is in *New Orleans Bee*, 16 September 1830; Isaac in Anne Arundel County Register of Wills (Petitions and Orders) 1851–60, 513–14, Petition of Edwin W. Duvall to the Orphans Court, 5 September 1859, reel #CR 63,128-1, MSA; some examples of same phrase in Records of the Chancery Court, Chesterfield County, Virginia, Chancery Causes Ended, Petition of James A. Clarke to the Judge of the Circuit Court, November 1863, Box 47, folder 1,867, Part 5, VSA; Phill in Records of the County Court, Chesterfield County, Virginia, Chancery Causes, Leonidas Wells vs. William A. Franklin, 12 October 1857, folder 1,857, Box 463, VSA.

24. *Richmond Enquirer*, 10 October 1804; *New Orleans Bee*, 3 April 1829; *New Orleans Bee*, 13 May 1831; *Charleston Mercury*, 16 March 1832.

25. Information on black workers in Charles Ellis to John H. Cocke, 27 December 1831, Charles Ellis to William Woods, 2 February 1832, Charles Ellis to Major Thomas Holcombe, 13 January 1835, in Ellis and Allan Company Papers, LC. Ellis was a merchant in Richmond, Virginia, who regularly hired out slaves for $120 to $130 in the 1830s. A Demopolis, Alabama, man wrote a friend: "You wished to know something about the prices of hirelings in this country. You can get $15 $20 or $25 pr. month." An experienced owner could negotiate for even more. John R. Casey to John D. Dunn, 13 July 1859, John D. Dunn Papers, Manuscripts Division, Duke University, Durham, North Carolina.

Occupations of black workers in General Assembly, Session Records, Petition of the Mechanical Society of Wilmington to the North Carolina General Assembly, 29 November 1802, NCDAH; Memorial of the Citizens of Smithville [Brunswick County] to the North Carolina General Assembly, 1856, ibid.; Peter H. Wood, "Whetting, Setting, and Laying Timbers: Black Builders in the Early South," *Southern Exposure* 8 (spring 1980), 3–7; Legislative Records, Memorial of the Mechanics of Charleston to the South Carolina General Assembly, ca. 1824 [misdated 1811], #48, SCDAH; Petition of James Rose, William J. Grayson, Benjamin Huger, et al. to the South Carolina Senate, ca. 1860, ND #2,801, ibid.; Legislative Petitions, Petition of William Walden, John Peyton, Churchill Berry, et al. to the Virginia General Assembly, 9 December 1831, Culpepper County, VSA; John T. O'Brien, "Factory, Church, and Community: Blacks in Antebellum Richmond," *Journal of Southern History* 46 (November 1978), 151.

26. John T. Trowbridge, *A Picture of the Desolated States and the Work of Restoration* (Reprint 1866; Hartford, Conn.: I. Sterbins, 1888), 330–31, quoted in *The Black Worker to 1869*, ed. Philip S. Foner and Ronald L. Lewis (Philadelphia: Temple University Press, 1978), 144; Ulrich B. Phillips, "The Slave Labor Problem in the Charleston District," in *Plantation, Town and Country: Essays on the Local History of American Slave Society*, ed. Elinor Miller and Eugene Genovese (Urbana: University of Illinois Press, 1974), 13; Frederick Douglass, *My Bondage and My Freedom* (New York: Miller, Orton and Milligan, 1855), 329–34; W. B. Cooper to Mary Carroll, 7 January 1860, Carter Woodson Collection, LC; Legislative Records, Presentment of the Grand Jury of Sumter District, South Carolina, Fall 1849, #29, SCDAH.

27. Work of self-hired slaves in *New Orleans Bee*, 11–28 November 1833, 5 February 1834, 29 January 1834, 5, 7, 9, 10 June 1834, 11–26 June 1834, 16 June 1834,

2, 3, 4, 7 July 1834, 29 November 1834, 1, 2 10, 16, 20 December 1834, 6, 7 February 1835, 18 July 1834, 9 December 1834, 9 April 1835, 11 January 1841, 13 April 1841; *Charleston Mercury*, 29 March 1832, 14 August 1830, 31 December 1830; *Charleston Mercury and Morning Advertiser*, 28 February 1824, 18 July 1825; Anne Arundel County Register of Wills (Petitions and Orders) 1820–40, 553, Petition of James Madcalf to the Orphans Court, 20 October 1837, reel #CR 63,127-1, MSA.

"Quasi-free" bondsmen in Helen T. Catterall, ed., *Judicial Cases Concerning American Slavery and the Negro* (Washington, D.C.: W. F. Roberts, 1932), 1:308–9; Robert Engs, *Freedom's First Generation: Black Hampton, Virginia, 1861–1890* (Philadelphia: University of Pennsylvania Press, 1979), 16–17; Barbara Jeanne Fields, *Slavery and Freedom on the Middle Ground: Maryland during the Nineteenth Century* (New Haven: Yale University Press, 1985), 34; Records of the County Court, Davidson County, Tennessee, Minute Book 1822–24 (July 1823), 539.

Sam in *Richmond Enquirer*, 19 February 1805.

28. Forge items in *Charleston Mercury*, 24 May 1832; Francois in *New Orleans Bee*, 11 January 1841.

29. *New Orleans Bee*, 14–26 May 1834; *New Orleans Bee*, 10 February 1835; *New Orleans Bee*, 19 March 1831, the advertisement ran until 19 April 1831; *New Orleans Bee*, 16 September 1833; *New Orleans Bee*, 18 July 1834. The notice ran until 3 September 1834.

In the case of black women, a Jefferson Parish planter, for example, noted that his slave Annette had been a runaway for two years. A large woman, of deep black complexion, she had an attractive smile, spoke excellent French and English, and, the planter believed, lived and worked in "some public house" in a suburb. *New Orleans Bee*, 31 July 1835.

30. Description of Spanish-speaking slave in *New Orleans Bee*, 28 March 1831. *Population of the United States in 1860; Compiled from the Original Returns of the Eighth Census* (Washington, D.C.: Government Printing Office, 1864), 74; *Southern Watchman*, 28 April 1859, quoted by E. Merton Coulter in "Slavery and Freedom in Athens, Georgia, 1860–66," *Georgia Historical Quarterly* 49 (September 1965), 265.

31. Joseph B. Anderson to Richard T. Archer, 24 May 1853, Richard Thompson Archer Family Papers, Natchez Trace Collection, Center for American History, University of Texas Austin.

32. Records of the Equity Court, Charleston District, South Carolina, Bills, William Simmons, John Ashe, and William Hayne, vs. William Clement, 1817, Case #55, SCDAH. The suit was brought because one of the trustees did not want to sell the slaves and invest in securities, while the other three favored a sale and reinvestment. The petitioners used the phrase "all the slaves" throughout the case, but at one point they said "both of them." The trustee's comment is in Records of the Equity Court, Charleston District, South Carolina, Petition of James W. Gray, Trustee, 5 March 1858, Case #681, Box 8, SCDAH.

33. *Richmond Enquirer*, 1 October 1852; *Richmond Enquirer*, 21 October 1806.

34. *Charleston Mercury and Morning Advertiser*, 26 July 1825; *New Orleans Picayune*, 13 March 1840. The notice ran through 3 April 1840.

35. *Alexandria Advertiser and Commercial Intelligencer*, 28 September 1803, reprinted in *Advertisements for Runaway Slaves in Virginia, 1801–1820* ed. Daniel Meaders (New York: Garland Publishing, 1997), 25; *Richmond Enquirer*, 20 June 1807.

36. Betty Wood, *Women's Work, Men's Work: The Informal Slave Economies of Lowcountry Georgia* (Athens: University of Georgia Press, 1995), 110–15; example of Hannah in *Charleston Mercury*, 24 November 1826; of Nancy in *Charleston Mercury*, 27 June 1828.

37. *New Orleans Bee*, 3 June 1831; *New Orleans Bee*, 29 June 1831; *New Orleans Bee*, 14 July 1831; *New Orleans Bee*, 6, 7, 8, 11, 13, 15 October 1831; the second advertisement is in *New Orleans Bee*, 31 October 1831.

38. *Richmond Enquirer*, 15 March 1852; *New Orleans Picayune*, 4 July 1840.

39. Records of the Probate Court, Norfolk County, Virginia, Wills, Book 2 (22 October 1804), 223, on microfilm at Museum of Early Southern Decorative Arts, Winston-Salem, North Carolina; John Liddell to Oran Mayo, 4 September 1849, and Oran Mayo to John Liddell, 4 March 1852, Liddell Family Papers, Special Collections, Hill Memorial Library, LSU; Clement Eaton, "Slave-Hiring in the Upper South: A Step Toward Freedom," *Mississippi Valley Historical Review* 46 (March 1960), 672; John Hope Franklin, "Slaves Virtually Free in Ante-Bellum North Carolina," *Journal of Negro History* 28 (July 1943), 305; Richard B. Morris, "The Measure of Bondage in the Slave States," *Mississippi Valley Historical Review* 41 (September 1954), 233–34; Loren Schweninger, "The Free-Slave Phenomenon: James P. Thomas and the Black Community in Ante-Bellum Nashville," *Civil War History* 22 (December 1976), 303; John Hebron Moore, "Simon Gray, Riverman: A Slave Who Was Almost Free," *Mississippi Valley Historical Review* 49 (December 1962), 472–74; Claudia Goldin, *Urban Slavery in the American South, 1820–1860: A Quantitative History* (Chicago: University of Chicago Press, 1976), 36; Randolph B. Campbell, "Slave Hiring in Texas," *American Historical Review* 93 (February 1988), 107–14; Sarah S. Hughes, "Slaves for Hire: The Allocation of Black Labor in Elizabeth City County, Virginia, 1782–1820," *William and Mary Quarterly*, 3d Series, 35 (April 1978), 260–86; William A. Byrne, "The Hiring of Woodson, Slave Carpenter of Savannah," *Georgia Historical Quarterly* 77 (summer 1993), 245–63.

40. Douglass, *My Bondage and My Freedom*, 328–29.

41. *Richmond Enquirer*, 6 February 1807; *Charleston Mercury and Morning Advertiser*, 3 May 1825; other self-hired slaves in *Charleston Mercury*, 17 March 1828, 8 September 1829.

42. Baltimore County Register of Wills (Petitions and Orders), Estate of John H. Carroll, 13 September 1859, reel M-11,020, SC, MSA. None of the documentation explicitly states that John N. Carroll was John H.'s son, but implicit evidence suggests that such was the case. The guardian was given permission to sell Jim "for the most money she can obtain for him." Petition of Matilda E. Carroll, Guardian, 13 September 1859 with ibid.; Order of the Court, 13 September 1859, with ibid.

43. *Richmond Enquirer*, 4 October 1808.

44. Quotes about Celeste in Missouri Supreme Court Cases, St. Louis District, Stephen Ridgley vs. Steamboat *Reindeer*, 6 October 1857, Box 598, #6, Missouri State Archives, Jefferson City, Missouri; Testimony of Stephen Ridgley, 1856, 11, ibid.; Affidavit of George P. Strong, 17 December 1856, 14–15, ibid.; Testimony of H. B. Moreland, 1856, 10, ibid.

45. James Rudd, "Account Book," 1846–53, Filson Club, Louisville, Kentucky.

46. Records of the United States Circuit Court for the District of Columbia, Chancery Dockets and Rules Case Files, Record Group 21, Adam Johnson vs. George Clarke, 26 June 1822, Entry #20, Docket #3, Case #40, Box 18, NA. In his response, Clarke argued that plaintiff was a slave, "a person incompetent at Law to be a part to a contract, & incapable of commencing & maintaining a suit in your Honorable Court against the Defendant who is entitled to possession of his person & the proceeds of his labor." Nonetheless the owner offered a twelve-hundred word reply, admitting that he had signed a deed of manumission but still should receive the back wages. The court, however, issued an injunction prohibiting Clarke from taking Johnson as his property. The final decree of the court was not in the case file. For similar cases, see

Letitia Woods Brown, *Free Negroes in the District of Columbia, 1790–1846* (New York: Oxford University Press, 1972), 121–23; Records of the United States Circuit Court for the District of Columbia, Chancery Dockets and Rules Case Files, Record Group 21, George vs. G. Adams and S. Adams, 6 February 1826, Entry #20, Rules #2, Case #168, Box 31, NA. Ibid., Lucy Crawford vs. Martha A. Scott and Alexander Hunter, 18 October 1845, Entry #20, Case #387, Rules 4, Box 58, NA. A compromise was soon reached, and the suit was within drawn by Crawford three days later. Ibid., Mary Donoho vs. Archibald Thompson and Henry Ryan, 8 September 1828, Case #307, Rules 2, Box 33, NA.

47. Records of the United States Circuit Court for the District of Columbia, Chancery Dockets and Rules Case Files, Record Group 21, Iris Smethers vs. John H. Lowe, 8 December 1826; Answer of John H. Lowe to Bill of Complaint, 5 June 1827; Testimony of John F. M. Lowe, 31 December 1827, Entry #20, Case #283, Docket #3, Box 27, NA. John F. M. Lowe was the defendant John H. Lowe's brother. Letty Brown came out of hiding to convince Iris Smethers to bring the suit. The final decree of the court was not included in the case file.

48. Records of the Circuit Court, Jefferson County, Kentucky, Case Files, Bailey Riley vs. John James, 29 December 1835, Series 2, Case #70, Box 2-2, KDLA; Deposition of Richard Love, 16 April 1836, with ibid. Records of the Missouri Supreme Court, St. Louis District, Fleming Calvert vs. Samuel Rider, 8 March 1854, Case #8, 14, 15, 27–30, Box 574, Missouri State Archives, Jefferson City, Missouri. The name of the steamboat was *Timoleon*, also spelled *Tomoleon*.

49. New Orleans discussed in Wade, *Slavery in the Cities*, 326.

50. *New Orleans Bee*, 3 June 1828; *New Orleans Bee*, 19 December 1828; *New Orleans Bee*, 5 July 1830; *New Orleans Bee*, 17 August 1830.

51. *Tennessee Republican Banner*, 18 February 1839; *Nashville Whig*, 3 January 1814; *New Orleans Picayune*, 4 February 1838. Isaac's owner offered fifty dollars for his return and advertised in the *Greensborough Beacon* [Green County, Alabama], *Mobile Chronicle*, and *New Orleans Picayune*.

52. Capture of runaways in Anne Arundel County Register of Wills (Petitions and Orders) 1840–51, 201–2, John Miller vs. Negro Richard, [3] August 1847, reel #CR 63,127-2, MSA; ibid., 1840–51, 210–11, Dennis Claude, Jr., vs. Negro Boy Hamilton, 29 October 1847, reel #CR 63,127-2, MSA; Records of the Inferior Court, Richmond County, Georgia, Meeting of Justices James B. Bishop, Garey F. Parish, and Lambeth Hopkins, 15 March 1851, in Minutes 1848–1868, 38, County Court House, Augusta, Georgia; *New Orleans Bee*, 8 March 1841. Legislative Petitions, Petition of Francis Royall to the Virginia General Assembly, 19 February 1850, VSA. The Richmond slave Peter remained at large around Portsmouth for a number of years but was eventually arrested and sold.

Crackdowns on free blacks in Grand Jury Indictments, State of Mississippi, Warren County, October and November 1842, Natchez Trace Slaves and Slavery Collection, Center for American History, University of Texas of Austin. The indictments charged whites with unlawfully permitting slaves to reside apart from their masters. Richard Tansey, "Out-of-State Free Blacks in Late Antebellum New Orleans," *Louisiana History* 22 (fall 1981), 369–86.

Records of the Parish Court, West Feliciana Parish, Louisiana, Third District Court, Drury L. Mitchell vs. Joseph R. Miller, 29 May 1835, #1,497, Parish Court House, St. Francisville, Louisiana.

53. Records of the First Judicial District Court, Orleans Parish, Louisiana, Case Records, William C. Wade vs. P. Dumee, 13 March 1824, #6,021, reel 14, Louisiana Collection, New Orleans Public Library; Testimony of John M. Dromgoole, 29 May

1824, with ibid. Another reenslaved man in Records of the First Judicial District Court, Orleans Parish, Louisiana, Case Records, Simon Presler vs. Houlder Hudgins, 3 January 1822, #4,374, reel 9, Louisiana Collection, New Orleans Public Library. Alexis's story in Records of the First Judicial District Court, Orleans Parish, Louisiana, Case Records, Auguste Christin vs. Marie Rose Hudson, 28 April 1838, #15,970, reel 31, Louisiana Collection, New Orleans Public Library; copy of Deed of Sale, Franklin to Dessalle, 8 November 1834, with ibid.; Amended Petition of Auguste Christin to the Judge of the First Judicial District Court, 12 May 1838, with ibid. The court ordered Alexis's seizure and sequestration.

54. Records of the Chancery Court, Davidson County, Tennessee, Case Files, John Woods vs. Toliver B. Dawson and Oliver P. Catron, 26 May 1845, Case #76, Box 2, Metropolitan Nashville—Davidson County Archives, Nashville; Legislative Records, Petition of Edward R. Ware to the House of Representatives of South Carolina, 28 November 1855, #24, SCDAH. Refusing to divulge correct information about his former owner, Pressly, or Joe Brown, remained in jail for a year before he was sold.

55. *New Orleans Picayune*, 13 March 1840; the notice ran through 3 April 1840; *Charleston Mercury*, 19 August 1830; *Nashville Whig*, 19 September 1815, 26 October 1815.

56. Charles C. Jones, Sr., to Charles C. Jones, Jr., 26 March 1857, in Myers, ed., *The Children of Pride*, 309–10.

CHAPTER 7

1. Records of the Sixth Judicial District Court, East Baton Rouge Parish, Louisiana, Robert Davis vs. James C. Knox, 14 November 1856, #1,939, East Baton Rouge Parish Archives, Baton Rouge, Louisiana.

2. United States Manuscript Population Census, Lauderdale County, Mississippi, Beat 5, 1860, 176.

3. *A Digest of the Statutes of Arkansas: Embracing All Laws of a General and Permanent Character, in Force at the Close of the Session of the General Assembly of 1846* (Little Rock: Reardon and Garritt, 1848), 944–47. Arkansas was chosen as an example because it was a later state that emulated the codes of older states. For other state laws concerning runaways, see *Alabama Digest: Covering Cases from State and Federal Courts* (St. Paul, Minn.: West Publishing, 1969), 17A: 252–53; John Codman Hurd, *The Law of Freedom and Bondage in the United States* (Boston: Little, Brown, 1862; reprint, New York: Negro Universities Press, 1968), 2:150, 152 (Alabama), 79–80 (Delaware), 193–94 (Florida), 105–6, 108 (Georgia), 17, 18 (Kentucky), 157–60, 162–63 (Louisiana), 21–22 (Maryland), 146–47 (Mississippi), 166 (Missouri), 85, 88 (North Carolina), 98–99 (South Carolina), 90, 92 (Tennessee), 197 (Texas), 10–12 (Virginia). *The Revised Code of the District of Columbia, Prepared Under the Authority of the Act of Congress* (Washington, D.C.: A. O. P. Nicholson, 1857), 169–72; *Code of Laws for the District of Columbia: Prepared Under the Authority of the Act of Congress* (Washington, D.C.: Davis and Force, 1819), 293–95.

4. Anne Arundel County Court (Petitions), Bill of Sale of Hugh Jenkins to Lemuel G. Taylor, 11 April 1839, with Petition of Lemuel G. Taylor to the County Court, 1 November 1839, reel M-11,019, SC, MSA; Anne Arundel County Register of Wills (Petitions and Orders) 1851–60, 98–99, Petition of Marien M. Duvall to the Orphans Court, 13 May 1854, reel #CR 63,128-1, MSA; Anne Arundel County Register of Wills (Petitions and Orders) 1851–60, 514½–515, Petition of James Wilson to the Orphans Court, 13 September 1859, reel #CR 63,128-1, MSA; Baltimore County Register of Wills (Petitions and Orders), Petition of Wa[k]eman Bryarly, 1 June 1858, reel M-11,020, SC, MSA.

Effect of the Louisiana warranty in Records of the First Judicial District Court, Orleans Parish, Louisiana, Case Records, Henry A. Bullard vs. Benjamin C. Eaton, 7 December 1835, #12,711, reel 27, Louisiana Collection, New Orleans Public Library; the Tennessee law in Records of the Chancery Court, Davidson County, Tennessee, Case Files, John Woods vs. Toliver B. Dawson and Oliver P. Catron, 26 May 1845, Case #76, Box 2, Metropolitan Nashville—Davidson County Archives, Nashville.

Runaway law of Mississippi in *Acts Passed at the First Session Second General Assembly of the State of Mississippi* (Natchez: Andrew Marschalk and Evens, 1819), 70. Also see *Laws of the State of Mississippi, Passed at the Eleventh Session of the General Assembly, Held in the Town of Jackson* (Jackson: Peter Isler, 1828), 96; *Laws of the State of Mississippi, Passed at the Twelfth Session of the General Assembly, Held in the Town of Jackson* (Jackson: Peter Isler, 1829), 41–42; *Laws of the State of Mississippi, Passed at a Regular Session of the Mississippi Legislature, Held in the City of Jackson, January, February, and March, 1850* (Jackson: Fall and Marshall, 1850), 229. Law of Alabama in *Acts, Passed at the Annual Session of the General Assembly of the State of Alabama, Begun and Held in the Town of Tuscaloosa, on the First Monday in December, One Thousand Eight Hundred and Thirty-Eight* (Tuscaloosa: Hale and Eaton, 1838), 31. Law of Texas in *The Laws of Texas 1822–1897* (Austin: Gambell Book Company, 1898), 2:950–51.

Other southern state codes in *Laws of the State of Delaware* (New Castle: Samuel and John Adams, 1797), 212; *Code of Laws for the District of Columbia: Prepared under the Authority of the Act of Congress of the 29th of April, 1816* (Washington, D.C.: Davis and Force, 1819), 438; *A Manual or Digest of the Statute Law of the State of Florida, of A General and Public Character* (Boston: Charles C. Little and James Brown, 1847), 543–45; *Acts and Resolutions of the General Assembly of the State of South-Carolina, Passed in December 1821* (Columbia: Daniel Faust, 1822), 20; *The Statutes At Large of South Carolina* (Columbia: A. S. Johnston, 1840), 430–31; *A Compilation of the Statutes of Tennessee, of a General and Permanent Nature* (Nashville: James Smith, 1836), 680; June Purcell Guild, comp., *Black Laws of Virginia: A Summary of the Legislative Acts of Virginia Concerning Negroes from Earliest Times to the Present* (originally published 1936; New York: Negro Universities Press, 1969), 44, 47, 48, 51, 53, 58, 63, 73, 77, 81–84, 86, 89, 90, 91, 195. In addition, legal practices in different states varied concerning how, when, and why slaves could be taken up, jailed, held, and sold. See Records of the Circuit Court, Jefferson County, Kentucky, Case Files, Thomas Joyce and Mary [Bowman] Joyce, et al. vs. H. H. Buffenmyer, 15 May 1857, Case #13,011, Box 2-178, KDLA; Baltimore County Register of Wills (Petitions and Orders), Petition of Wa[k]eman Bryarly, 1 June 1858, reel M-11,020, SC, MSA.

5. *The Statute Laws of the State of Tennessee, of a Public and General Nature* (Knoxville, Tenn.: S. Heiskell, 1831), 321–25; *Statute Laws of the State of Tennessee, of a General Character; passed Since the Compilation of the Statutes [in 1836]* (Nashville: J. G. Shepard, 1846), 287–88; *A Compilation of the Statutes of Tennessee, of a General and Permanent Nature, From the Commencement of the Government to the Present Time* (Nashville: James Smith, 1836), 519; *The Code of Tennessee Enacted by the General Assembly of 1857–'8* (Nashville: E. G. Eastman, 1858), 503–5 (runaways), 500–519. In addition to citations in note 4, see Hurd, *Law of Freedom and Bondage,* 2:150–52 (Alabama), 172 (Arkansas), 193–94 (Florida), 105, 107 (Georgia), 17–19 (Kentucky), 159, 162–63 (Louisiana), 20, 22 (Maryland), 146, 148 (Mississippi), 169 (Missouri), 12 (Virginia); *Acts Passed at the First Biennial Session of the General Assembly of the State of Alabama, Begun and Held in the City of Montgomery on the First Monday in December, 1847* (Montgomery: McCormick and Walshe, 1848),

130; *Acts of the Second Biennial Session of the General Assembly of Alabama, Held in the City of Montgomery, Commencing on the Second Monday in November, 1849* (Montgomery: Brittan and DeWolf, 1850), 52; *A Digest of the Laws of the State of Georgia* (Athens: Oliver H. Prince, 1837), 782–83; *The Revised Statutes of Kentucky* (Frankfort, Ky.: A. G. Hodges, 1852), 636–38; *Laws of the State of Mississippi: Passed at an Adjourned Session of the Legislature, Held in the City of Jackson, From January 7, to February 16, A.D. 1839* (Jackson: B. D. Howard, 1839), 98–99; *Laws of the State of Mississippi, Passed at a Regular Session of the Mississippi Legislature, Held in the City of Jackson, January, February, and March, 1852* (Jackson: Palmer and Pickett, 1852), 137–38.

6. Problems with laws in Records of the Chancery Court, Mobile, Alabama, Chancery Cases Not Divorces, William Magee [also spelled McGee] vs. William Byard [also spelled Bayard] and Amos C. Wilson, 6 December 1839, #541, University of South Alabama Archives, Mobile, Alabama; Legislative Petitions, Petition of Sundry Inhabitants of the City of Richmond to the Virginia General Assembly, 20 December 1804, Richmond City, VSA. A Virginia law, passed in 1753, provided the death penalty for anyone who stole a slave "out of, or from the possession of the owner or overseer." Thomas D. Morris, *Southern Slavery and the Law, 1619–1860* (Chapel Hill: University of North Carolina Press, 1996), 344.

Problems with laws on killing in Records of the Court of Pleas and Quarter Sessions, Chowan County, North Carolina, Writ of Outlawry vs. Negro Slaves Jacob, Dilworth, Peter, Jacob, Henry, Abraham, and Thompson, December 1816, in Miscellaneous Slave Records 1730–1866, NCDAH; Legislative Records, Memorial of Inhabitants of Christ Church Parish to the South Carolina Senate, ca. 1829, ND #1563, SCDAH. As indicated in the petition, the law passed in 1821 made the crime of murdering a slave punishable by death. In 1834, an appeals court judge wrote: "This change I think made a most important alteration in the law of his [the slave's] personal protection. It in a criminal point of view elevated slaves from chattels personal to human beings in the peace of society." George Rogers, "Slavery in South Carolina," in *Dictionary of Afro-American Slavery*, ed. Randall M. Miller and John David Smith (New York: Greenwood Press, 1988), 704.

7. John Hope Franklin, *The Militant South, 1800–1861* (Cambridge, Mass.: Harvard University Press, 1956), 72–73; quotes about patrols in Legislative Petitions, Petition of Samuel Templeman to the Virginia General Assembly, 21 December 1809, Westmoreland County, VSA. As executor of the estate of William Hutt, who had died in debt, Templeman was seeking compensation from the state for a slave who had been killed. The petition was rejected.

8. Records of the General Assembly, Petition of Edward Brailsford to the South Carolina General Assembly, 26 November 1816, #100, SCDAH; Records of the General Assembly, Petition of Mathew ODriscoll to the South Carolina Senate, 1814, #119, SDAH. April was tried, convicted, and executed for various crimes.

9. Records of the General Assembly, Petition of Jean Lewis Raoul to the South Carolina General Assembly, 1823, #142, SCDAH.

10. Records of the County Court, Cumberland County, North Carolina, Petition of James Butler, John Jackson, A. Marsh, et al., 1850, Miscellaneous Records, Slave Records Patrol Committees, NCDAH. The county court responded by appointing a twenty-man patrol. Report of the Patrol Committee for Willis Creek District, 15 July 1850, with ibid.

11. Records of the General Assembly, Session Records, Petition of John H. Hill to the North Carolina General Assembly, 14 December 1825, in House Committee Reports, Claims 1825–1826, NCDAH; Receipt, 22 August 1821; Returns of Officers and

Privates under Captain George H. Dudley, Sergeant George Pinser, Colonel John H. Hill, [September] 1821; Call to Arms, 15 August 1821; List of Volunteers, 22 August 1821; Minutes of Meeting, 23 August 1821; Pay Allowance, [September] 1821; Report of Committee on Claims, 20 December 1825; William Clark to John H. Hill, 20 October 1821, all with ibid.

Quotes about Mississippi patrols in Copy of Orders from Major General John Joor[?] to the Colonel Commanding the 5th Regiment Mississippi Militia, 4 October 1832, and copy of Report of George H. Gordon, 8 October 1832, Record Group 47, Box 20, Petitions and Memorials, MDAH; about Georgia patrols in Records of the Inferior Court, Glynn County, Georgia, Petition of Hugh F. Grant, June 1848, Minutes Glynn Court of Ordinary [1812–70], 119–20, 149–51. Grant sought and received an act of incorporation for his unit.

12. Records of the First Judicial District Court, Orleans Parish, Louisiana, Case Records, Martin Duplessis vs. William Johnson, 1 May 1818, #1,842, reel 4, Louisiana Collection, New Orleans Public Library; the case was discontinued by order of the court in 1820. Records of the Second Judicial District Court, St. James Parish, Louisiana, James Adlum vs. Joseph Cantrelle et al., 24 September 1835, #401, Parish Court House, Convent, Louisiana.

13. Records of the General Assembly, Petition of John Adams to the South Carolina Senate, 1795, #66, SCDAH; Petition of John Adams to the South Carolina House of Representatives, 1795, #76, SCDAH; extract from the Diary of Henry Ravenel, 12 July 1819, in *A Documentary History of American Industrial Society*, ed. Ulrich B. Phillips (Cleveland, Ohio: Arthur H. Clark, 1910), 2:91.

14. Records of the District Court, Comal County, Texas, James Weir vs. R. H. Russell et al., 16 October 1854, Case #184 [#414 was case number for Guadalupe County], County Court House, New Braunfels, Texas; Amended Answer of R. H. Russell, 1 May 1855, with ibid.

15. Information about the blacksmith in Legislative Records, Petition of Ava Culliatt to the South Carolina General Assembly, 1800, #167, SCDAH; other injuries in Legislative Records, Petition of John Anderson to the South Carolina Senate, 15 November 1823, #50, SCDAH; Legislative Records, Petition of Citizens of Georgetown District to the South Carolina House of Representatives, 1834, and accompanying Deposition of E. Waterman, 22 November 1834, #18, SCDAH; Legislative Records, Petition of Peter Gourdin to the South Carolina Senate, 1835, #21, SCDAH.

16. Records of the County Court, Chowan County, North Carolina, Petition of Lemuel Creecy, Fred Creecy, Nathan Creecy, et al., 26 September 1785, Miscellaneous Slave Records 1730–1866, NCDAH.

17. Petition of the Citizens of Maury County to the Tennessee General Assembly, 8 November 1831, in Jill Knight Garrett Collection, TSLA; Legislative Petitions, Petition of the Citizens of Montgomery County for a Patrol to Guard Against Slave Risings to the Tennessee General Assembly, 1831, roll 11, #1831-1, TSLA.

18. Statement of Edward King to the Justice of the Peace, Concordia Parish, Louisiana, 27 May 1831, Natchez Trace Slaves and Slavery Collection, folder on Fugitive Slaves, Center for American History, University of Texas at Austin; Records of the Superior Court, Greene County, Georgia, Oliver P. Findley vs. Robert T. Wright, February 1848, Proceedings 1874–1849, 351–53, County Court House, Greensboro, Georgia; Records of the Superior Court, Frederick County, Virginia, John Upp vs. Elizabeth Seaton, 15 November 1819, Ended Causes, Box 35, VSA. The owner's relatives later moved to Frederick County, where a suit was brought for payment of the reward.

19. Information on the Vidalia group in Statement of Joseph Faber to the Justice

of the Peace, Concordia Parish, Louisiana, 19 May 1834, Natchez Trace Slaves and Slavery Collection, folder on Fugitive Slaves, Center for American History, University of Texas at Austin; also see Statement of John G. Lindsey, 8 July 1834, with ibid.; Statement of Lewis Hynor to the Justice of the Peace, Concordia Parish, Louisiana, 15 June 1832, Natchez Trace Slaves and Slavery Collection, folder on Fugitive Slaves, Center for American History, University of Texas at Austin. Statement of Edward King to the Justice of the Peace, Concordia Parish, Louisiana, 25 April 1831, Natchez Trace Slaves and Slavery Collection, folder on Fugitive Slaves, Center for American History, University of Texas at Austin. Statements of Lewis P. Leland to the Justice of the Peace, Concordia Parish, Louisiana, 16 June 1832, Natchez Trace Slaves and Slavery Collection, folder on Fugitive Slaves, Center for American History, University of Texas at Austin; Statement of Samuel Clark to the Justice of the Peace, Concordia Parish, Louisiana, 24 June 1832, with ibid. Details of ninety-mile journey in Statement of Edward King to the Justice of the Peace, Concordia Parish, Louisiana, 27 May 1831, Natchez Trace Slaves and Slavery Collection, folder on Fugitive Slaves, Center for American History, University of Texas at Austin; Bill of Costs, Taking up Negro Slave Mase, n.d., with ibid. Capture of John in Statement of H. D. French to the Justice of the Peace, Concordia Parish, Louisiana, 15 June 1834, Natchez Trace Slaves and Slavery Collection, folder on Fugitive Slaves, Center for American History, University of Texas at Austin.

20. Records of Concordia Parish Court, Statement of Lewis Hynor to the Justice of the Peace, 15 June 1832, Natchez Trace Slaves and Slavery Collection, American History Center, University of Texas at Austin; Statement of Joseph Faber to the Justice of the Peace, 19 May 1834, ibid.; see also Statement of John D. Lindsey to the Justice of the Peace, 8 July 1834, ibid.

21. Records of the Hamilton District Superior Court, Knox County, Tennessee, Case Files, Francis Lea's Administration vs. George H. Hynds, September 1807, Case #1,283, Knox County Archives, Knoxville, Tennessee; Petition of George H. Hynds to the Superior Court, April 1804, with ibid.; Deposition of James P. H. Porter, 23 September 1805, with ibid. Records of the General Assembly, Petition of James Ross and Holloway Simmons to the South Carolina Senate and House of Representatives, 30 October 1830, #137, SCDAH; Certificate, Andrew McWhorter, 19 October 1830, with ibid. Tom was tried, convicted, and executed.

22. W. N. Peeples to William Phineas Browne, 10 August 1860, William Phineas Browne Papers, Correspondence, ADAH; R. A. Moseley to William Phineas Browne, 16 August 1860, ibid.

23. *Nashville Whig*, 2, 9, 16 July 1816.

24. Records of the Missouri Supreme Court, Marquis W. Withers vs. Steamer *El Paso*, July 1856, Case #23, Box 72, Missouri State Archives, Jefferson City, Missouri; Testimony of Alfred Edgar, [1855], 23–24, with ibid.

25. Records of the General Assembly, Petition of James McKenny to the South Carolina General Assembly, 17 November 1825, #120, SCDAH.

26. Information on the trip toward Canada in Records of the Circuit Court, Jefferson County, Kentucky, Case Files, Bailey Riley vs. John James, 29 December 1835, Series 2, Case #70, Box 2-2, KDLA; Opinion of George M. Bibb, Chancellor of the Louisville Chancery Court, 27 May 1836, with ibid. Reed's comments in Legislative Petitions, Petition of Richard Reed to the Virginia General Assembly, January 1840, Accomac County, VSA.

27. Legislative Petitions, Petition of Edward R. Waddey to the Virginia General Assembly, 1 January 1838, Northampton County, VSA; William Floyd to Joseph Segar, 19 January 1838, with ibid.; Copy of "Executive Journal," 6 November 1832, 4

February 1833, with ibid.; for the 1850s, see Stanley W. Campbell, *The Slave Catchers: Enforcement of the Fugitive Slave Law, 1850–1860* (Chapel Hill: University of North Carolina Press, 1972).

28. Records of the North Carolina Supreme Court, Blount vs. Hawkins, December 1858, Case #7,325, NCDAH; William Blount et al. vs. John D. Hawkins et al., Fall Term 1856, Wake County Court, with ibid.; *Reports of Cases in Equity, Argued and Determined in the Supreme Court of North Carolina, From June Term, 1858, to August Term, 1859, Inclusive* (Salisbury, N.C.: n.p., 1859), 4:160–65.

29. Frederick Law Olmsted, *A Journey in the Seaboard Slave States, With Remarks on Their Economy* (New York: Dix and Edwards, 1856), 160, 161.

30. Charles Stearns, *Facts in the Life of Gen. Taylor; The Cuba Blood-Hound Importer, the Extensive Slave-Holder, and the Hero of the Mexican War* (Boston: published by the author, 1848), 14. The authors wish to thank Robert Paquette for bringing this pamphlet to our attention.

31. Edwin Adams Davis, ed., *Plantation Life in the Florida Parishes of Louisiana, 1836–1846, As Reflected in the Diary of Bennet H. Barrow* (New York: Columbia University Press, 1943), 48–49.

32. Records of the Georgia Supreme Court, Augustus B. Moran, Trustee, Plaintiff in Error, vs. Garner Davis, Defendant in Error, *Georgia Reports*, August Term 1855, 722–23.

33. Quotes about dog training in Frederick Law Olmsted, *A Journey in the Back Country* (New York: Mason Brothers, 1860), 47–48; Piedmont farmer quotes, 214.

34. Olmsted, *A Journey in the Seaboard Slave States*, 160, 161; *West Tennessee Democrat*, 2 March 1853, in ibid, 163. Records of the County Court, Yazoo County, Mississippi, Thomas Hamberlin vs. Wallace, agent for the Estate of William L. Balfour, deceased, Summons, 11 July 1859, in Balfour (William L.) Papers, Center for American History, University of Texas at Austin; Records of the Probate Court, Lauderdale County, Mississippi, Estate of George W. Null, 28 April 1862, County Archives, Meridian, Mississippi; at the time Confederate currency was worth about 67 cents on the dollar (Douglas B. Ball, *Financial Failure and Confederate Defeat* [Urbana: University of Illinois Press, 1991], 177).

35. *Acts and Resolutions of the General Assembly of the State of South-Carolina Passed in December 1824* (Columbia: D. Faust, 1825), 83–84. Simpson requested and received $150 as compensation for his horse. Following the first chase, Simpson recounted, the horse "was of little or no account."

36. John M. Chapron to James Martin, 8 June 1841, John M. Chapron Letterbook, ADAH.

37. Quote about Mississippi slave in Ann Farrar to A. K. Farrar, 3 November 1857, Farrar (Alexander K.) Papers, Special Collections, Hill Memorial Library, LSU; about Peyton in Mollie Mitchell to Margaret Browne, 30 August 1860, William Phineas Browne Papers, Correspondence, ADAH; R. A. Moseley to William P. Browne, 30 August 1860, ibid.; Horace Ware to William P. Browne, 28 August 1860, ibid.

38. Paul Cameron to Duncan Cameron, 12 December 1845, Cameron Papers, #133, Southern Historical Collection, University of North Carolina, Chapel Hill.

39. J. J. Cochrane to Dickinson and Hill, 21 October 1861, Chase Family Papers, LC; quotes about "boy belonging to you" in George Connelly to Robert Cochran, 13 February 1846, Robert Cochran Papers, Natchez Trace Collection, Center for American History, University of Texas at Austin; about boy in the woods: John A. Scruggs to E. H. Stokes[?], 30 September 1860, Chase Family Papers, LC; about rice planter in

Plantation Journal, 1822, William Lowndes Papers, Manuscript Division, LC. The entry begins as a letter but is an entry in the Plantation Journal.

40. Sarah W. Kittrell Goree to Thomas J. Goree, 20 March 1853, in Thomas Jewett Goree Letters, Volume 1, Civil War Correspondence, Center for American History, University of Texas at Austin. Ellen Hyland to her sister, 2 September 1858, Chamberlain-Hyland-Gould Family Papers, Natchez Trace Collection, Center for American History, University of Texas at Austin.

41. *Tennessee Republican Banner*, 27 December 1839. Tobe ran away in June 1839.

42. G. N. Reagan to William Willis, 18 September 1814, Barns-Willis (Family) Papers, Box 2E530, Center for American History, University of Texas at Austin. Quotes about Wilson in *Tennessee Republican Banner*, 20 December 1839; *Tennessee Republican Banner*, 20 December 1840. Quotes about George in *Richmond Enquirer*, 30 June 1854.

43. *New Orleans Picayune*, 10 August 1839. The notice ran continuously through 19 November 1839. Sampson had run away on 2 or 3 June 1838; Henry on 15 September 1838.

44. Records of the Craven County Superior Court, Petition of John C. Stanly to the Court, ca. 1829, in Slave and Free Negro File, NCDAH; Loren Schweninger, "John Carruthers Stanly and the Anomaly of Black Slaveholding," *North Carolina Historical Review* 67 (April 1990), 177. The free black slaveholder, John Carruthers Stanly, emancipated the slave in question.

45. Records of the General Assembly, Petition of William Ware to the South Carolina General Assembly, 22 November 1815, #137, SCDAH.

46. Quotes about Joseph and William in Records of the General Assembly, Petition of Major Brown to the South Carolina House of Representatives, 1800, #165, SCDAH; "Major" was the widow's given name. Information on Harry and Sam in *Charleston Mercury*, 11 December 1828.

47. John Merriman to A. T. Conrad, 30 August 1839, Weeks (David and Family) Papers, Special Collections, Hill Memorial Library, LSU; John Merriman to F. D. Richardson, 11 November 1840, ibid.

48. Howard County Register of Wills (Petitions), Petition of Robert H. Hare to the Howard County Court, 4 May 1852, reel M-11,024, SC, MSA. Situation of the Clarke County slaveholders in Legislative Petitions, Petition of G. Mason, John A. Washington, and Dennis Johnston to the Virginia General Assembly, 14 January 1851, Fairfax County, VSA.

49. Records of the Superior Court, Frederick County, Virginia, John Upp vs. Elizabeth Seaton, 15 November 1819, Ended Causes, Box 35, VSA. The case involved two runaways, and the testimony revealed the journey of Hale to capture his slave. In Virginia and other Upper South states, owners sometimes carried with them broadsides, posting them along the way. See Broadsides, Richard Duckett, 30 March 1826, Prince George's County, Maryland, Manuscripts Division, LC; William Russell, 1 October 1847, St. Louis, Missouri, ibid.; N. I. B. Whitlocke, Essex County, Virginia, 30 May 1855, Prints and Photographs Department, Chicago Historical Society; Richard P. Helm, Fauquier County, Virginia, 9 June 1852, ibid.; A. Jackson Smoot, Charles County, Maryland, 15 July 1860, ibid.; F. M. Bowie, Prince George's County, Maryland, 6 July 1857, ibid.; Sarah Ann Talburtt, Prince George's County, Maryland, 11 June 1850, ibid. Records of the Circuit Court, Jefferson County, Kentucky, Case Files, William Pickett vs. John Norris, Jacob Funk, Joseph Griffin, et al., 12 September 1833, Case #2,903, Box 1-41, KDLA.

50. *Richmond Enquirer*, 30 January 1857.

51. *Tennessee Republican Banner*, 14 October 1839. The notice said "at the resi-

dence" of Bosley, though there was no indication that the white man was harboring the slave.

52. Petition of Jacob Duckworth to the Mississippi Legislature, 1830, Record Group 47, Volume 20, Petitions and Memorials, MDAH.

53. Howard County Register of Wills (Petitions), Petition of Robert H. Hare to the Howard County Court, 4 May 1852, reel M-11,024, SC, MSA.

54. Olmsted, *A Journey in the Seaboard Slave States*, 163.

55. *Tennessee Republican Banner*, 27 February 1840, 28 June 1851, 1, 3, 4, 7, 8, 9, 10, 14, 16, 18, 19, 21, 22, 24, 25, 28, 29, 31 July 1851.

56. *Tennessee Republican Banner*, 29 September 1841; *Tennessee Republican Banner*, 29, 30, 31 July 1842, 2, 3, 4, 8, August 1842; *Nashville Whig*, 13, 20 January 1812; *New Orleans Bee*, 28 August 1830. Description of Sampson in 23–30 March 1833, 1–13 April 1833; of Isaac in 10 July 1833.

57. *Charleston Mercury*, 28 October 1826.

58. *New Orleans Bee*, 26 October 1830; 29 March 1831, 1, 4, 5, 6, 7, 8 April 1831; 9 August 1831; 19 July 1832.

59. *New Orleans Bee*, 27 May 1831, the notice ran through 12 July 1831; 18 April 1832; 21 May 1832; *Charleston Mercury*, 17 September 1832; *New Orleans Bee*, 24 July 1834; *Charleston Mercury*, 21 April 1831; *Richmond Enquirer*, 20 February 1852.

60. *New Orleans Picayune*, 23 June 1840; *Charleston Mercury*, 25 February 1831.

61. *Tennessee Republican Banner*, 21 February 1838.

62. *New Orleans Bee*, 15 June 1832, the notice ran continuously through 18 October 1832. The $100 reward began with the 15 September 1832 issue. *New Orleans Bee*, 1, 3, 4, 5, 6, 15, 17, 19, 20, 21 December 1832; the reward was increased 15 December 1832; 26 April 1833; *New Orleans Picayune*, 14–28 June 1840, the increase occurred on 23 June 1840; *Charleston Mercury*, 22 March 1826, the notice ran through the 16 May 1826, with the increase in the reward coming on 22 April 1826; *New Orleans Daily Picayune*, 6 July 1850.

63. *Richmond Enquirer*, 21 January 185[1], 24 March 185[1], 16 September 1851, 20 July 1852. The 20 July 1852 advertisement ran through 30 November 1852.

64. *New Orleans Bee*, 8, 11, 14 April 1834; *Charleston Mercury and Morning Advertiser*, 15 December 1824; *Charleston Mercury and Morning Advertiser*, 8 January 1825.

65. Records of the Superior Court, Screven County, Georgia, John King vs. Edward Cowart, 12 January 1818, in Minutes of the Superior Court 1816–1822, 181–84, County Court House, Sylvania, Georgia. The suit was brought on appeal following a jury award to Cowart of $22.25. In 1820, at the request of the plaintiff's attorney, the appeal was discontinued.

66. *Charleston Mercury*, 29 August 1828; *Charleston Mercury and Morning Advertiser*, 10 May 1823; *Tennessee Republican Banner*, 23 May 1839.

67. Calculated from *Alexandria Advertiser and Commercial Intelligencer*, 1801–4, reprinted in *Advertisements for Runaway Slaves in Virginia, 1801–1820*, ed. Daniel Meaders (New York: Garland Publishing, 1997). For the rewards of $50, see *Alexandria Advertiser and Commercial Intelligencer*, 10 July 1801, 28 July 1803, 6 February 1804, 11 May 1804, 7 June 1804, ibid., 3, 22, 30, 34, 35; for the reward of $100, see *Alexandria Advertiser and Commercial Intelligencer*, 10 September 1804, reprinted in *Advertisements for Runaway Slaves in Virginia, 1801–1820*, ed. Daniel Meaders (New York: Garland Publishing, 1997), 39–40.

68. *New Orleans Bee*, 11 May 1830; 10 June 1830; 23 December 1831; 11 September 1830; 26 October 1830.

69. *The Laws of the State of North-Carolina, Enacted in the year 1819* (Raleigh:

Thomas Henderson, 1820), 30; *The Code of Tennessee Enacted by the General Assembly of 1857–'8* (Nashville: E. G. Eastman, 1858), 504; *Laws of the State of Mississippi, Passed at a Regular Session of the Mississippi Legislature, Held in the City of Jackson, January, February, and March, 1850* (Jackson: Fall and Marshall, 1850), 229; *Supplement to the Revised Code of the Laws of Virginia: Being a Collection of all the Acts of the General Assembly of a Public and Permanent Nature, Passed Since the year 1819* (Richmond: Samuel Shepherd, 1833), 234–35.

70. For how runaways fared in jails in various sections of the South during different time periods, see *Richmond Enquirer*, 19 May 1807; Petition of Benajah Randle to the General Assembly of the Mississippi Territory, 1815, Record Group 5, Series 524, Box 27, MDAH; *Charleston Mercury and Morning Advertiser*, 2 June 1825; *Acts and Resolutions of the General Assembly of the State of South Carolina, Passed in December, 1836* (Columbia: S. Weir, 1837), 105; Records of the United States District Court for the District of Columbia, Segregated Habeas Corpus Papers, Record Group 21, Petition of Henry Brown, 19 October 1836, Entry #28, Box 1, NA; Anne Arundel County Register of Wills (Petitions and Orders) 1851–60, 458–60, Petition of James Wilson to the Orphans Court, 16 April 1858, reel #CR 63,128-1, MSA; Baltimore County Register of Wills (Petitions and Orders), Petition of James H. Luckett, 8 March 1859, reel M-11,020, SC, MSA; *Richmond Enquirer*, 9 December 1853. For a general discussion, see John A. Hall, " 'A Rigour of Confinement Which Violates Humanity': Jail Conditions in South Carolina During the 1790s," *Southern Studies: An Interdisciplinary Journal of the South* 24 (fall 1985), 284–94.

Information on the anonymous slave in Legislative Records, Petitions of William Love to the South Carolina Senate, 15 November 1820, #74 and #75, SCDAH; on Jim in Legislative Records, Petition of William Love to the South Carolina Senate, 22 November 1822, #74, SCDAH.

71. Legislative Petitions, Petition of William Cassels to the Virginia General Assembly, 17 December 1818, Amelia County, VSA; Copy of Account of William Winfree, Jailor of Chesterfield County, to the County Court, 13 October 1817, with ibid.; Certificate [testimony] of Anderson P. Miller, 21 November 1817, concerning Hannibal's confession, with ibid.; Certificate [testimony] of Martin Baugh, 28 November 1817, concerning when Hannibal ran away, with ibid.; Petition of William Cassels to the Virginia General Assembly, 20 December 1817, Amelia County, VSA.

72. Petition of Bartlett Sims to the Mississippi General Assembly, n.d. [ca. 1820s], Record Group 47, Volume 17, Petitions and Memorials 1817–1839, MDAH; quotes about the Vicksburg jail in Records of the County Court, Warren County, Mississippi, Order of Justice of the Peace James Knowland to the Sheriff, 27 October 1819, Natchez Trace Slaves and Slavery Collection, Center for American History, University of Texas at Austin; about the Monroe County runaways in Legislative Papers, Petition of Bartlett Sims to the Mississippi Senate and House of Representatives, ca. 1820s, Petitions and Memorials 1817–1839, Record Group 47, MDAH.

73. *New Orleans Bee*, 5 September 1829; *New Orleans Bee*, 5, 8, 10, 12 19, 24, 26, 29 September 1834, 1, 3, October 1834. Information on Ned in Legislative Petitions, Petition of Lindsay Coleman to the Virginia General Assembly, 8 December 1834, Amherst County, VSA; Copy of Certificate of Lindsay Coleman, Amherst County Court, November 1834, with ibid. Ned was not heard from again. Escape of John in Legislative Petitions, Petition of the Citizens of James City, York, and surrounding counties to the Virginia General Assembly, 11 January 1858, Middlesex County, VSA; Copy of Records of Middlesex County Court, Commonwealth vs. John a slave, April and May 1854, Testimony of John Johnston, a constable, 22 May 1854, Testimony of John Parker, Thomas K. Savage, and Bradford Newcomb, with ibid.

Recaptured, tried, convicted, and condemned to death, John was afterwards "sold by the Executive, and transported beyond the limits of the United States."

74. Missouri Supreme Court Cases, St. Louis District, Russell vs. Lynch, 27 February 1858, Box 602, Case #4, Missouri State Archives, Jefferson City, Missouri; Testimony of John G. Russell, in Bill of Exceptions, 9 February 1858, 4–5, in ibid. Bernard M. Lynch established his yard, on Locust Street, between Third and Fourth, in 1849; it had walls of brick twelve feet high in front and was next to brick buildings on either side and in the rear. Lynch's "yard" was very attractive not only because it appeared escape proof, but because he charged only twenty-five cents per day per slave during the 1850s. There were several other private yards in St. Louis that competed with the one that Lynch owned.

75. Records of the Equity Court, Charleston District, South Carolina, Frederick Wesner, Master of the Work House vs. Eliza Mackey and Patience McKenzie, 21 April 1838, Bills, Case #102, and J. C. Norris, Master of the Work House vs. George Shrewsbury and James Hanscome, 5 September 1845, Bills, Case #28, SCDAH; Larry Koger, *Black Slaveowners: Free Black Slave Masters in South Carolina, 1790–1860* (Jefferson, N.C.: McFarland, 1985), 86. Example of John in Records of the General Assembly, Petition of A. V. Toomer to the South Carolina Senate, 1849, #31, SCDAH; Copy of the Record of Conviction and Sentence, State vs. John, 16 July 1849, with ibid.

76. Bond of Mayor and City Council of Vicksburg, Mississippi, unto the President of the Board of Police for Warren County, 26 December 1841, Natchez Trace Slaves and Slavery Collection, folder on Fugitive Slaves, Center for American History, University of Texas at Austin; information on Memphis difficulties in Daniel Haskel and J. Calvin Smith, *A Complete Descriptive and Statistical Gazetteer of the United States of America* (New York: Sherman and Smith, 1847), 396, 682; Legislative Petitions, Petition of the Corporation of Memphis to the Tennessee General Assembly, 29 [November] 1841, roll 16, #1842–1, TSLA. It was unclear how the chain gang would lead to a "safe and more comfortable prison," as the petitioners argued; presumably the money saved would be used to renovate or expand the Shelby County jail.

77. Records of the Sixth Judicial District Court, East Baton Rouge Parish, Louisiana, Robert Davis vs. James C. Knox, 14 November 1856, #1,939, East Baton Rouge Parish Archives, Baton Rouge, Louisiana. Robert Davis sued Knox for $2,500 in damages, arguing that the hunt was "unauthorized." The jury found for the defendant.

CHAPTER 8

1. Records of the County Court, Craven County, North Carolina, Petition of Abraham Carpenter for Habeas Corpus, 5 February 1830, Slave and Free Negro File, NCDAH.

2. Records of the County Court, Craven County, North Carolina, Petition of Abraham Carpenter for Habeas Corpus, 5 February 1830, Slave and Free Negro File, NCDAH; Ard Reynolds to Thomas Watson, 18 February 1830, with ibid.; Depositions of Jacob Dayton and Abraham Hubbard in Greenwich, Fairfield County, Connecticut, 17 February 1830, with ibid.; Subscription of Inhabitants of Greenwich, Connecticut, [February 1830], with ibid.; Writ of Habeas Corpus, 9 March 1830, Craven County, North Carolina, with ibid.

3. George Rawick, ed., *The American Slave: A Composite Autobiography* (Westport, Conn.: Greenwood Publishing, 1972–), 5 (pt. 4): 4038; United States Manuscript Agricultural Census, St. Mary Parish, Louisiana, 1850, 727; John Chinson to Ralph Gurley, 16 December 1833, Records of the American Colonization Society, reel 19, LC; James M. Johnson to Henry Ellison, 20 August 1860, Ellison Papers, South Caroliniana Library, Columbia, South Carolina; Marina Wikramanayake, *A World in*

Shadow: The Free Black in Antebellum South Carolina (Columbia: University of South Carolina Press, 1973), 58; James M. Johnson to Henry Ellison, 28 August 1860, in *No Chariot Let Down: Charleston's Free People of Color on the Eve of the Civil War*, ed. Michael P. Johnson and James L. Roark (Chapel Hill: University of North Carolina Press, 1984), 101–8. See also Carol Wilson, *Freedom At Risk: The Kidnapping of Free Blacks in America, 1780–1865* (Lexington: University of Kentucky Press, 1994), chap. 1; Leonard Curry, *The Free Black in Urban America, 1800–1850: The Shadow of the Dream* (Chicago: University of Chicago Press, 1981), 229–32; Benjamin Quarles, "Freedom Fettered: Blacks in the Constitutional Era in Maryland, 1776–1810—An Introduction," *Maryland Historical Magazine* 84 (winter 1989), 299–304; Thomas D. Morris, *Free Men All: The Personal Liberty Laws of the North, 1780–1861* (Baltimore: Johns Hopkins University Press, 1974), chap. 2.

4. In the northeastern section of the South, cases concerning reenslavement of free blacks or freed blacks who were kept in slavery occasionally reached the courts. See Records of the United States Circuit Court for the District of Columbia, Chancery Dockets and Rules Case Files, Record Group 21, Clara vs. Thomas Ewell, 12 April 1820, Case #251, Box 11, NA; Rebecca Rawlings vs. Washington Wallace [William Wallace on the Docket Page], 13 August 1828, Case #304, Rules 2, Box 33, ibid.; Delia vs. Thomas Offutt, 26 April 1814, Case #182, Box 11, ibid.; John Garrison vs. Janet Lingan and William B. Randolph, 12 December 1818, Entry #20, Case #62, Rules 1, Box 28, ibid.; Moses Foushee vs. William H. Tibbs, 30 November 1824, Case #101, Rules 2, Entry #20, Box 30, ibid. Foushee, a man of color, claimed he was "entitled to his freedom by being removed into the District of Columbia, from the State of Virginia,—contrary to the provisions of the Act of Assembly of Maryland." George Hunter vs. William M. Offutt, Zadock Offutt, and Thomas Triplett, 27 December 1824, Case #107, Rules 2, Entry #20, Box 30, ibid.; Records of the United States District Court, Segregated Habeas Corpus Papers, Record Group 21, Petitions of John McKenrey and Mulatto Mary, 31 October 1820, Entry #28, Box 1, NA. In the deep South cases brought to trial were rare, but see *Charleston Mercury and Morning Advertiser*, 29 December 1825; Records of the Inferior Court, Floyd County, Georgia, Petition of John A. Johnson, November 1856, in Minutes 1841–1857, 238, County Court House, Rome, Georgia.

5. Records of the United States District Court for the District of Columbia, Segregated Habeas Corpus Papers, Record Group 21, Petition of Matilda Smith, 26 October 1857, Entry #28, Box 2, NA. For similar cases, see Records of the United States Circuit Court for the District of Columbia, Segregated Habeas Corpus Papers, Record Group 21, Petition of George Cole, 6 July 1860, Entry #28, Box 2, NA; Petition of John H. Hawkins, 20 June 1861, Entry #28, Box 2, NA; Henry Lansdale to William Merrick, 21 June 1861, with ibid.; Order of the Court, 21 June 1861, with ibid.

6. *Richmond Enquirer*, 6 July 1850.

7. *Nashville Whig*, 25 December 1816; *New Orleans Bee*, 7 October 1833; Petition of John Bryce to the Mississippi General Assembly, 1826, Record Group 47, Volume 18, Petitions and Memorials, MDAH.

8. Records of the United States District Court for the District of Columbia, Segregated Habeas Corpus Papers, Record Group 21, Petition of Betsy Jackson, 19 September 1842, Entry #28, Box 1, NA. See also Records of the United States District Court for the District of Columbia, Segregated Habeas Corpus Papers, Record Group 21, Petition of Mary Johnson, 22 June 1839, Entry #28, Box 1, NA; Petition of William Spellman, 23 September 1839, ibid.; Petition of Elias Richards, 23 June 1838, ibid.; Petition of Mary Wilmer, 4 August 1838, ibid.; Petition of Julia Thompson, 18 July 1844, Entry #28, Box 2, ibid. Records of the United States Circuit Court for the District

of Columbia, Chancery Dockets and Rules Case Files, Record Group 21, Theresa Blackwell vs. Robert Hall, 8 January 1851, Entry #20, Case #716, Rules 5, Box 69, NA. Washington County Register of Wills (Petitions and Orders), Petition of Thomas Rice and Hiram Good, 18 December 1855, reel M-11,027 SC, MSA; Washington County Register of Wills (Petitions and Orders), Petition of William Patterson and Nathan Luckett, 23 July 1858, reel M-11,027, SC, MSA.

9. Information on Eben Jones in copy of Record of Nelson County Court, 28 November 1827, with Legislative Petitions, Petition of William Morgan to the Virginia General Assembly, 13 December 1827, Nelson County, VSA; Petition of John Gibbs to the Judge of the High Court of Errors and Appeals, Warren County, Mississippi, 9 March 1836, Natchez Trace Slaves and Slavery Collection, Box 2E773, Center for American History, University of Texas at Austin; Records of the Third Judicial District Court, East Baton Rouge Parish, Louisiana, George Stewart for Habeas Corpus, 10 February 1838, #2,427, East Baton Rouge Parish Archives, Baton Rouge, Louisiana; Deposition of William Hutson, 16 January 1838, with ibid; Deposition of Philip Bell, 16 January 1838, with ibid.; C. Satchell to George Stewart, 24 January 183[8], with ibid. The Satchell letter was misdated 1837. Records of the County Court, Warren County, Mississippi, Petition of John Pedro to the Court, 25 September 1837, Natchez Trace Slaves and Slavery Collection, Center for American History, University of Texas at Austin. See also Petition of Samuel Bryan to the Court, 4 July 1837, ibid.

10. *Charleston Mercury and Morning Advertiser*, 8 September 1823; Records of the United States Circuit Court for the District of Columbia, Chancery Dockets and Rules Case Files, Record Group 21, Negro Beale vs. Edward and George Calvert, Jr., 10 January 1826, Case #163, Entry #20, Rules 2, Box 31, NA. An injunction was issued to prevent the sale until the case could be resolved.

11. Records of the United States Circuit Court for the District of Columbia, Chancery Dockets and Rules Case Files, Record Group 21, Eliza vs. John Wetzel and Edward Smith, 11 May 1824, Case #147, Entry #20, Docket #3, Box 22, NA. For similar cases, see Records of the United States Circuit Court for the District of Columbia, Chancery Dockets and Rules Case Files, Record Group 21, Winney Cryer and child vs. Elizabeth Cocke and Peter E. Hoffman, 22 January 1847, Entry #20, Case #454, Rules 4, Box 60, NA; Joshua Cryer by his next friend Winney Cryer vs. Elizabeth Cocke and Peter E. Hoffman, 9 February 1847, Case #455, Rules 4, Box 60, ibid.

12. Records of the United States District Court for the District of Columbia, Segregated Habeas Corpus Papers, Record Group 21, Petition of Paten Harris, 8 June 1843, Entry #28, Box 1, NA; Copy of letter, Edward H. Mosely to Sir, 22 November [1842], with ibid.; Copy of Certificate of Passage out of Virginia, 14 April 1842, with ibid.; Copy of Order of the Court, Stafford County, Virginia, 9 May 1842, with ibid.

13. Frederick County Court (Petitions), Petition of Patrick McNamara, 22 March 1786, reel M-11,024, SC, MSA. Records of the United States District Court for the District of Columbia, Segregated Habeas Corpus Papers, Record Group 21, Petition of Ralph Gold, 11 June 1839, Entry #28, Box 1, NA; Gold was discharged from jail. Records of the United States District Court for the District of Columbia, Segregated Habeas Corpus Papers, Record Group 21, Petition of William Richardson, 5 December 1837, Entry #28, Box 1, NA. Richardson was discharged from jail.

14. Letitia Woods Brown, *Free Negroes in the District of Columbia, 1790–1846* (New York: Oxford University Press, 1972), 148, 152. In 1850, working as a messenger, Datcher's realty holdings were estimated at $2,100; he lived in the second ward with his wife Ellen and several children. In 1860, his holdings increased to $4,000. United States Manuscript Population Census, District of Columbia, 2nd Ward, 1850,

70 [printed page number and includes facing page]; ibid., 1860, 621. Even while a slave in 1825, Datcher owned and paid taxes on four city lots. At the time of his arrest, he was well-known as a free person of color. Affidavits on Datcher's behalf in Records of the United States District Court for the District of Columbia, Segregated Habeas Corpus Papers, Record Group 21, Petition of Francis Datcher, 24 August 1839, Entry #28, Box 1, NA; Opinion of Judge W. Cranch, 24 August 1839, with ibid.

15. Free blacks who could not contact whites in Washington County Register of Wills (Petitions and Orders), Petition of Virginia Jenkins, 22 September 1846, reel M-11,027, SC, MSA; Petition of Joseph Smallwood, 30 September 1851, with ibid. Records of the Criminal Court, Warren County, Mississippi, State vs. Samuel Bryan, 4 July 1837, Natchez Trace Slaves and Slavery Collection, Box 2E773, folder 3, Center for American History, University of Texas at Austin; Deposition of Mathew Lawson, 25 May 1837, with ibid.; Petition of Samuel Bryan, 4 July 1837, with ibid.; Deposition of William Everett, 2 March 1837, with ibid. A Writ of Habeas Corpus was issued on 7 July 1837, directing the jailer to bring Bryan before the judge. Joseph Estell to John Spence, 1 March 1837, Natchez Trace Slaves and Slavery Collection, Box 2E773, folder 3, Center for American History, University of Texas at Austin; as a result, Andrew was set free.

16. Records of the Criminal Court, Warren County, Mississippi, Petition of Richard Coleman, ca. January 1837, Natchez Trace Slaves and Slavery Collection, Box 2E773, Center for American History, University of Texas at Austin; Statement of David Atway Before the Justice of the Peace in Henderson County, Tennessee, 24 August 1836, with ibid.; Testimony of John M. Clifton, 30 January 1837, with ibid.

17. Lewis Grigsby and A. F. Young to William Everett, 26 February 1836, Natchez Trace Slaves and Slavery Collection, folder on Fugitive Slaves, Center for American History, University of Texas at Austin; Records of the United States District Court for the District of Columbia, Segregated Habeas Corpus Papers, Record Group 21, Petition of Sally Boothe, 9 November 1835, Entry #28, Box 1, NA; ibid., John Adams to Josiah Poke, 20 June 1835, with Petition of Hambleton Russell, 5 August 1835; ibid., Petition of John H. Jenkins, 27 July 1835; Copy of Registration #1,584, Hustings Court, Petersburg, Virginia, 23 July 1835, with ibid.; Robert Leslie to William L. Brent, Clerk of Court, 24 July 1835, with ibid. Leslie was responding to a letter from Brent dated 21 July 1835.

Records of the United States Circuit Court for the District of Columbia, Chancery Dockets and Rules Case Files, Record Group 21, Carolina Butler vs. Fielder Magruder, 8 December 1849, Entry #20, Case #639, Rules 5, Box 67, NA; Records of the United States District Court for the District of Columbia, Segregated Habeas Corpus Papers, Record Group 21, Petition of William Thomas, alias John Thomas, alias William Brown, alias John Brown, 13 November 1833, Entry #28, Box 1, NA; Testimony of Benjamin Lane, 13 November 1833, with ibid.; Affidavit of Robert Kelly, 11 November 1833, with ibid.

18. Frederick County Court (Petitions), Petition of Caleb Ogleton to the County Court, 20 March 1844, reel M-11,024, SC, MSA.

19. *New Orleans Bee*, 8, 11, 13 August 1834; *Charleston Mercury and Morning Advertiser*, 21 August 1824.

20. Baltimore County Register of Wills (Petitions and Orders), Petition of Frances B. Eoff, 24 October 1856, reel M-11,020, SC, MSA; Indenture of John Henry Doman to John Breckinridge, 23 October 1856, with ibid.

21. See, for example, Records of the General Assembly, Session Records, Petition of Miriam Lowe to the North Carolina General Assembly, 17 November 1795, Mis-

cellaneous Petitions, November–December 1795, NCDAH; Records of the United States District Court for the District of Columbia, Segregated Habeas Corpus Papers, Record Group 21, Petition of Granville Williams, 24 July 1855, Entry #28, Box 2, NA.

22. Records of the Superior Court, Jones County, Georgia, Aaron McKenzie vs. John Humphries, 19 January 1819, in Minute Book 1819, 227–84, County Court House, Gray, Georgia. McKenzie argued that the deed of emancipation was "condemned as insufficient and fraudulently [recorded] in the State of Virginia," although he offered no proof.

23. Records of the United States Circuit Court for the District of Columbia, Chancery Dockets and Rules Case Files, Record Group 21, William Williams vs. Thomas C. Duvall, 9 March 1831, Entry #20, Case #150, Rules 3, Box 38, NA; Testimonial of Thomas Berry, 3 March 1831, with ibid. The court issued an injunction to halt Duvall's claim.

24. Records of the United States Circuit Court for the District of Columbia, Chancery Dockets and Rules Case Files, Record Group 21, Charles Lyles et al. vs. Christopher C. Hyatt and Dionysius Sheriff, 7 October 1856, Entry #20, Case #1,205, Rules 5, Box 91, NA.

25. Records of the First Judicial District Court, Orleans Parish, Louisiana, Case Records, Trudeau vs. Robinette, 2 May 1815, #694, reel 1A, Louisiana Collection, New Orleans Public Library.

26. Legislative Petitions, Statement of W. Dandridge et al., attached to Petition of George P. Crump to the Virginia General Assembly, 19 December 1827, Richmond City, VSA.

27. Legislative Records, Petition of Samuel Johnston to the General Assembly, 19 January 1835, Fauquier County, VSA. Johnston was respected by whites. He had purchased his freedom, acquired a farm, and paid "a large sum of money" to free his family. See Legislative Records, Petition of Samuel Johnston [also spelled Johnson] to the Virginia General Assembly, 14 December 1820, Fauquier County, VSA; Certificate, F. W. Brooke et al., ca. 1820, with ibid.; Certificate, Nelson S. Hutchinson et al., 27 October 1820, with ibid.; Petitions of Samuel Johnston to the Virginia General Assembly, 12 January 1812, 16 December 1815, 17 December 1822, 4 December 1823, 25 January 1834, VSA.

28. Solomon Northrup, *Twelve Years A Slave, Narrative of Solomon Northrup, a Citizen of New York, Kidnapped in Washington City in 1841, and Rescued in 1853, from a Cotton Plantation Near the Red River in Louisiana* (Cincinnati: Henry W. Derby, 1853; reprint, edited by Sue Eakin and Joseph Logsdon, Baton Rouge: Louisiana State University Press, 1968). Some planters expressed doubts that Northrup's story was true. See Joseph D. Heacock to Sarah W. Bunting, 8 March 1855, Sarah W. Bunting Papers, Special Collections Library, Duke University, Durham, North Carolina.

Laws on the sale of free blacks in Legislative Petitions, Petition of Abner Robinson to the Virginia General Assembly, 16 February 1838, Richmond City, VSA; Records of the General Assembly, Legislative Papers, Petition of Benjamin Potter, Jr., to the Delaware Senate and House of Representatives, 7 January 1831, Record Group 1111, DSA; Records of the Sussex County Court of General Quarter Sessions, State vs. William Toast, Copy of True Bill, 16 December 1828; State vs. William Collins, Copy of True Bill, 12 December 1829, DSA. Example of the Bartlett men in Records of the County Court, Prince Edward County, Virginia, "List of free Negroes to be Sold for taxes," 1847, County Court Papers, Box 41, Packet January–April 1847, VSA.

29. Rawick, ed., *The American Slave*, 5 (pt. 4): 32–33.

30. Information on Philadelphia free black man in Records of the First Judicial

District Court, Orleans Parish, Louisiana, Case Records, John Roach vs. H. Holland [jailer], 20 February 1817, #1,353, reel 3, Louisiana Collection, New Orleans Public Library; other example in Records of the Parish Court, West Feliciana Parish, Louisiana, Third District Court, Frank Ervine, free man of color vs. Thomas Powell, 6 February 1837, Parish Court House, Francisville, Louisiana.

31. Baltimore County Register of Wills (Petitions and Orders), George H. Carman vs. Richard Fortie, 29 March 1859, reel M-11,020, SC, MSA; Baltimore County Register of Wills (Petitions and Orders), George H. Carman vs. Richard Fortie, 15 November 1859, reel M-11,020, SC, MSA. Story of William Toast in Records of the General Assembly, Legislative Papers, Petition of Benjamin Potter, Jr., to the Delaware General Assembly, 7 January 1831, Record Group 1,111, DSA; Copy of Records of Sussex County Court of Quarter Sessions, State vs. William Toast, Copy of True Bill, 16 December 1828, 12 December 1829, with ibid. Records of the County Court, Robeson County, North Carolina, Petition of Jacob Goins for Writ of Habeas Corpus, 27 November 1862, Slaves and Free Persons of Color File, NCDAH. In his petition, Goins says he was indicted in 1857. This is probably an error. See Copy of Indictment, Jacob Goins, Court of Pleas and Quarter Sessions, Cumberland County, March 1858, with ibid.

32. Records of the General Assembly, Legislative Papers, Petition of Elijah Gordy to the Delaware General Assembly, 31 January 1835, Record Group 1,111, DSA; Records of the Sussex County Court, Copy of Proceedings, State vs. Isaac Tyre, Spring Session 1832, with ibid. Gordy had purchased Tyre and was seeking compensation.

33. Legislative Petitions, Petition of Richard Reed to the Virginia General Assembly, January 1840, Accomac County, VSA. A short time later, the slave ran away to New York.

34. Baltimore City Register of Wills (Petitions), Caspar Mantz vs. Caroline Sawyer, Orphans Court of Baltimore City, 25 August 1854, reel M-11,026, SC, MSA; Copy of Proceedings of Frederick County Circuit Court, October 1853, with ibid.; Order of the Baltimore City Orphans Court, 26 August 1854, with ibid. Another "sold" free black in Baltimore City Register of Wills (Petitions), Benjamin Chaney vs. Eliza Ann Curtis, Orphans Court of Baltimore City, 25 January 1859, reel M-11,026, SC, MSA; Copy of Judgment in State vs. Eliza Ann Curtis, September 1858, with ibid.

35. Baltimore City Register of Wills (Petitions), Petition of William E. Beale to the Orphans Court of Baltimore City, 21 March 1859, reel M-11,026, SC, MSA; Receipt of Sale of Maria Boston, 17 February 1859, with ibid.; Order of the Court, 2 April 1859, with ibid. Baltimore County Register of Wills (Petitions and Orders), Petition of Emanuel C. Wade to the Orphans Court, 15 February 1859, reel M-11,020, SC, MSA. The five-year term was extended by two years, and Wade secured permission to sell Taylor out of the state.

36. Baltimore City Register of Wills (Petitions), Arthur Rich vs. James Peters, Orphans Court of Baltimore City, 10 September 1859, reel M-11,026, SC, MSA; Order of the Court, 6 September 1859, with ibid.; Arthur Rich vs. James Peters, Orphans Court of Baltimore City, 23 July 1859, with ibid.; Answer of James Peters, 29 July 1859, with ibid.

37. Records of the First Judicial District Court, Orleans Parish, Louisiana, Case Records, John Roach vs. H. Holland [Jailer], 20 February 1817, #1,353, reel 3, Louisiana Collection, New Orleans Public Library. In another court case, a free black, despite an adverse court ruling, achieved the same result. Sold as a slave to Mississippi farmer Israel Leonard for $600 in 1804, Samuel commenced a "freedom suit" in the Superior Court of Adams District, Mississippi Territory, and obtained a writ com-

manding the local sheriff to take him out of the possession of Leonard. Perhaps anticipating the decision of the court, Samuel broke out of jail and "escaped to places unknown." A short time later, the court ruled that Samuel should be returned to Leonard as a slave. Legislative Records, Petition of Israel Leonard to the Legislative Council of the Mississippi Territory, ca. 1806, Record Group 5, Series 524, Box 27, MDAH.

38. Legislative Petitions, Petition of Basil Brawner to the Virginia General Assembly, 20 February 1835, Prince William County, VSA; Testimony of James Fewell, 22 January 1835, with ibid.

39. James Roberts to Willis Roberts, 15 February 1830, Roberts Family Papers, Manuscript Division, LC. The Roberts family migrated from Northampton County, North Carolina, to Rush and Henry counties, Indiana, in 1829.

40. Antoine does not give the governor's name in recounting his story, but Spanish-born Manual Juan de Salcedo assumed office 14 July 1801 and remained governor until Pierre Clement, Baron de Laussat of France, took charge on 30 November 1803, twenty days before the transfer of Louisiana to the United States. Joseph G. Dawson III, *The Louisiana Governors: From Iberville to Edwards* (Baton Rouge: Louisiana State University Press, 1990), 74–79; Garnie William McGinty, *A History of Louisiana* (New York: Exposition Press, 1949), 95.

41. Records of the Circuit Court, Jefferson County, Kentucky, Case Files, Joseph Antoine, alias Ben, free man of color, vs. Emanuel Lacey, Jonathan Purcel [also spelled Purcell], Davis Floyd, 19 September 1804, Case #10, KDLA. Antoine wrote two petitions and began a third. The documents are unsigned, but their near illegibility points to Antoine as the author. The documents appear to have been written in 1804. The above is a composite portrait. In one petition, for instance, Antoine did not recall Emanuel Lacey's name. The basic facts set forth in the petitions, however, are nearly identical.

42. For contemporary evidence of free blacks who owned slaves, see Frederick Law Olmsted, *The Cotton Kingdom: A Traveller's Observations on Cotton and Slavery in the American Slave States*, ed. Arthur M. Schlesinger (New York: Alfred A. Knopf, 1953), 262; Andrew Durnford to John McDonogh, 25 June 1835, "Slave Buying in Virginia as Revealed by Letters of a Louisiana Negro Sugar Planter," ed. David Whitten, *Louisiana History* 11 (summer 1970), 239–40; Records of the Parish Court, Iberville Parish, Louisiana, Conveyances, Book P (18 August 1835), 85–86, County Court House, Plaquemine, Louisiana; Legislative Petitions, Petition of Christopher MacPherson to the Virginia General Assembly, 10 December 1810, Richmond City, VSA. For secondary sources, see Willard B. Gatewood, Jr., " 'To Be Truly Free': Louis Sheridan and the Colonization of Liberia," *Civil War History* 29 (December 1983), 332; John Hope Franklin, *The Free Negro in North Carolina, 1790–1860* (Chapel Hill: University of North Carolina Press, 1943), 45, 157; Luther Porter Jackson, "Free Negroes of Petersburg, Virginia," *Journal of Negro History* 12 (July 1927), 376; Loren Schweninger, "Prosperous Blacks in the South, 1790–1880," *American Historical Review* 95 (February 1990), 31–56; Michael P. Johnson and James L. Roark, *Black Masters: A Free Family of Color in the Old South* (New York: W. W. Norton, 1984).

Records of the Equity Court, Charleston, South Carolina, Petitions of Eliza Pinckney, Exparte, to the Chancellors of the Charleston District, 9 January 1826, #54, Box 8, and 12 May 1827, #43A, Box 9, SCDAH.

43. Records of the Craven County Superior Court, Petition of John C. Stanly, ca. 1829, Slave and Free Negro File, NCDAH; Records of Craven County, Petition of a Negro Man Kelso, 3 March 1832, Slave and Free Negro File, NCDAH. Also see Petition of Edmond Pasteur, free man of color, to Emancipate his Wife and Children, Spring 1827, Court Records, Bryan Collection, NCDAH.

44. Quoted in David O. Whitten, *Andrew Durnford: A Black Sugar Planter in Antebellum Louisiana* (Natchitoches: Northwestern Louisiana State University Press, 1981), 126.

45. See Larry Koger, *Black Slaveowners: Free Black Slave Masters in South Carolina, 1790–1860* (Jefferson, N.C.: McFarland and Company, 1985), 91–93. Discussion of William Johnson in Edwin Adams Davis and William Ransom Hogan, *The Barber of Natchez* (Baton Rouge: Louisiana State University Press, 1954), 64; idem., eds., *William Johnson's Natchez: The Ante-Bellum Diary of a Free Negro* (Baton Rouge: Louisiana State University Press, 1951), 72 n. 33. Information on Isaac in *New Orleans Bee*, 26 July 1833; on Jefferson Parish jail in *New Orleans Bee*, 9 August 1833; on other slaves in Records of the Parish Court, West Feliciana Parish, Louisiana, Third District Court, Drury L. Mitchell vs. Joseph R. Miller, 29 May 1835, Case #1,497, Parish Court House, St. Francisville, Louisiana; on Milly in *New Orleans Bee*, 12 September 1834; on Peggy in *Charleston Mercury*, 18 October 1827; Koger, *Black Slaveowners*, 154.

46. Statement of Attorneys Duvant and Horner in Behalf of Jane Luke, free woman of color, before Michael Hahn, Notary Public, 28 January 1856, Orleans Parish, Louisiana, in Felix Limongi Papers, LC. Luke failed to get her money back, however, when Kendig did not answer the summons.

47. *Federal Intelligencer, and Baltimore Daily Gazette*, 25 April 1795; *Maryland Journal, and Baltimore Advertiser*, 12, 19 January, 1796; *Federal Gazette and Baltimore Advertiser*, 11 April 1805, on microfilm, at Museum of Early Modern Decorative Arts, Winston-Salem, North Carolina; Leroy Graham, *Baltimore: The Nineteenth Century Black Capital* (New York: University Press of America, 1982), 261–62; Loren Schweninger, *Black Property Owners in the South, 1790–1915* (Urbana: University of Illinois Press, 1990), 24–25.

48. Records of the United States Circuit Court for the District of Columbia, Segregated Habeas Corpus Papers, Record Group 21, Petition of John H. Hawkins, 20 June 1861, Entry #28, Box 2, NA; Henry Lansdale to William Merrick, 21 June 1861, with ibid.; Order of the Court, 21 June 1861, with ibid. It seems doubtful that this had all been planned out beforehand. Apparently the grandfather could not legally free Hawkins. Without any claim of ownership, the order of the court would serve as freedom papers. Neither John nor Samuel Griffin were referred to as free blacks, but Hawkins was referred to as "colored," Samuel as his uncle, and John as Samuel's father. In the petition Jane's surname was spelled Griffith, but she was in all probability a member of the Griffin family.

49. *Charleston Mercury*, 29 September 1828, 19 November 1828; Records of the Circuit Court, Todd County, Kentucky, Equity Case Files, Simeon Clark vs. Henry Carpenter, 16 October 1832, Box 12, KDLA; Records of the Circuit Court, Todd County, Kentucky, Equity Case Files, Petition of Simeon Clark to the Circuit Court, 16 October 1832, Box 12, KDLA; Testimony of Joshua D. Austin, in Jacksonville, Morgan County, Illinois, 20 March 1833, with ibid.; Answer of Henry Carpenter to Bill in Chancery, 19 October 1832, with ibid.; for Westmoreland County, Virginia, see Mary Frances Berry and John W. Blassingame, *Long Memory: The Black Experience in America* (New York: Oxford University Press, 1982), 39–40.

Growth of free black population discussed in Ira Berlin, *Slaves Without Masters: The Free Negro in the Antebellum South* (New York: Pantheon Books, 1974), 136–37. This was also the case to a lesser degree in Delaware, where the free black population of about 17,000 in 1840 represented 87 percent of the total African American population.

50. Leon F. Litwack, *Been in the Storm So Long: The Aftermath of Slavery* (New

York: Alfred A. Knopf, 1979), 366–71; Theodore B. Wilson, *The Black Codes of the South* (University: University of Alabama Press, 1965); Richard Bardolph, ed., *The Civil Rights Record: Black Americans and the Law, 1849–1970* (New York: Thomas Y. Crowell, 1970), 35–40.

51. Baltimore County Register of Wills (Petitions and Orders), Caleb D. Owings vs. Elias Burgess, 9 January 1855, reel M-11,020, SC, MSA; copy of Elias Burgess's Indenture to Caleb D. Owings, 3 January 1855, and Petition of Caleb Owings, 12 February 1855, in ibid.

52. Anne Arundel County Register of Wills (Petitions and Orders) 1840–51, 230–31, Petition of Richard A. Harwood to the Orphans Court, 14 March 1848, reel #CR 63,127-2, MSA. Turner's indenture was extended one year. These cases were heard before the Orphans Court in each county. This court dealt with a range of equity cases, not merely ones dealing with orphans. Baltimore City Register of Wills (Petitions), Richard F. Ensey vs. Jerry Matthews, Orphans Court of Baltimore City, 14 March 1859, reel M-11,026, SC, MSA; Order of the Court, 18 March 1859, with ibid.

53. Anne Arundel County Register of Wills (Petitions and Orders) 1851–60, 203–4, Petition of J. B. Nichols to the Orphans Court, 19 April 1855, reel #CR 63,128-1, MSA; and 252, Petition of J. B. Nichols to the Orphans Court, 14 August 1855, in ibid. In each instance, Nichols was able to extend Boston's time of service.

54. Baltimore County Register of Wills (Petitions and Orders), Indenture of Charles Turner, Free Negro, to Catherine A. Johnston, 6 June 1857, reel M-11,020, SC, MSA; Petition of Catherine A. Johnston, 11 September 1860, with ibid. Baltimore City Register of Wills (Petitions), Petition of William Creamer to Orphans Court of Baltimore City, 17 August 1859, reel M-11,026, SC, MSA; Baltimore City Register of Wills (Petitions), Mary Jane Mason vs. Margaret H. Winchester, Orphans Court of Baltimore City, 15 June 1860, reel M-11,026, SC, MSA. Comment of another master in Baltimore City Register of Wills (Petitions), Jesse A. Murphy vs. Charles Henry Grandison, Orphans Court of Baltimore City, 20 February 1860, reel M-11, 026, SC, MSA.

55. Baltimore City Register of Wills (Petitions), James S. Wilson vs. Augusta Sprigg, Orphans Court of Baltimore City, 2 December 1856, reel M-11,026, SC, MSA. Quotes by other masters in Baltimore City Register of Wills (Petitions), Petition of William Creamer to Orphans Court of Baltimore City, 17 August 1859, reel M-11,026, SC, MSA; Baltimore City Register of Wills (Petitions), Mary Jane Mason vs. Margaret H. Winchester, Orphans Court of Baltimore City, 15 June 1860, reel M-11,026, SC, MSA.

56. Anne Arundel County Register of Wills (Petitions and Orders) 1851–60, 509–12, Petitions of John H. Caples to the Orphans Court, 12 July 1859, 9 August 1859, reel #CR 63,128-1, MSA; Baltimore County Register of Wills (Petitions and Orders), Thomas Biddison vs. Negro Henry Stockler, 3 August 1858, reel M-11,020, SC, MSA. Example of William Gaugh in Anne Arundel County Register of Wills (Petitions and Orders) 1851–60, 520–22, Petition of Robert H. Carr to the Orphans Court, 22 November 1859, reel #CR 63,128-1, MSA. The court granted the request. Baltimore County Register of Wills (Petitions and Orders), Indenture of Washington Boston to David W. McKlendin, 20 March 1854, reel M-11,020, SC, MSA; Petition of John H. Toffling, 18 April 1860, with ibid.; Copy of Proceedings of the Baltimore City Orphans Court, 17 June 1858, with ibid.

57. Baltimore City Register of Wills (Petitions), Margaret A. Newman vs. Louis Henry Foulks, Orphans Court of Baltimore City, 26 April 1859, reel M-11,026, SC, MSA.

58. Records of the United States District Court for the District of Columbia, Segregated Habeas Corpus Papers, Record Group 21, Petition of Nancy Jones, 24 August 1835, Entry #28, Box 1, NA; Copy of Indenture Between George Jones and James Mullinax, 27 May 1835, with ibid.; Unidentified newspaper clipping, 25 July 1835, with ibid.; J. Walsh to E. Mason, 22 August 1835, with ibid. Mullinax's name was also spelled Millinix, and Milinix.

59. Baltimore County Register of Wills (Petitions and Orders), Hezekiah Linthicum vs. Ann Marie [also spelled Maria] Carter, 6 November 1855, reel M-11,020, SC, MSA. Baltimore City Register of Wills (Petitions), Joseph Swinney vs. Hester Ann Powell, Orphans Court of Baltimore City, 6 January 1860, reel M-11,026, SC, MSA; Order of the Court, 15 February 1860, with ibid.; Petition of Hannah Powell, 10 September 1860, with Hannah Powell vs. John Hinesly, 10 September 1860, ibid.

60. Information on Levi Stevenson in Anne Arundel County Register of Wills (Petitions and Orders) 1840–51, 260–62, Petition of William H. Bird to the Orphans Court, 12 September 1848, reel #CR 63,127-2, MSA; also see Baltimore City Register of Wills (Petitions), Richard F. Ensey vs. Jerry Matthews, Orphans Court of Baltimore City, 14 March 1859, reel M-11,026, SC, MSA; Order of the Court, 18 March 1859, with ibid. Ensey received permission to sell free black Jerry Matthews at a private sale.

Baltimore City Register of Wills (Petitions), John Russell vs. Thomas Galloway, Orphans Court of Baltimore County, 21 June 1848, reel M-11,025, SC, MSA; Petition of John Russell, 21 June 1848, with ibid.; Answer of Thomas Galloway, 30 June 1848, with ibid; Deposition of William B. Perine, 5 July 1848, with ibid.; Indenture of John Russell to Thomas Galloway, 17 July 1841, with ibid. There was no final decree from the court given in this case.

61. Baltimore City Register of Wills (Petitions), Petition of Edward Johnson to the Orphans Court of Baltimore City, 8 March 1862, reel M-11,026, SC, MSA; Order of the Court, 14 March 1862, with ibid. The farmer's lawyer wrote the court: "This boy Johnson is a very bad fellow. His running away has not been because of bad treatment but because he knew he deserved punishment for stealing and other vicious conduct." None of the other black workers on the farm had ever been punished, he said, and "are within my knowledge contented." C. W. Powell to Isaac P. Cook, Register of Wills, Baltimore City, 27 March 1862, with ibid.

CHAPTER 9

1. *North Carolina Minerva and Raleigh Advertiser*, 25 October 1816, in *Stealing a Little Freedom: Advertisements for Slave Runaways in North Carolina, 1791–1840*, ed. Freddie L. Parker (New York: Garland Publishing, 1994), 120.

2. *Charleston Mercury*, 18, 21, 25 November 1857, 9, 16, 19 December 1857.

3. The statistics here and for the remainder of this chapter are computed from RSDB. For an explanation of how the data were drawn, see appendix 7. The gender delineations are comparable to those found in secondary sources. See Betty Wood, *Women's Work, Men's Work: The Informal Slave Economies of Lowcountry Georgia* (Athens: University of Georgia Press, 1995), 110; Freddie L. Parker, *Running for Freedom: Slave Runaways in North Carolina, 1775–1840* (New York: Garland Publishing, 1993), 70. Among 4,265 runaways in the South Carolina and Georgia low country between the 1730s and 1805, Michael Mullin found 867 female slaves, or 20 percent. Michael Mullin, *Africa in America: Slave Acculturation and Resistance in the American South and the British Caribbean, 1736–1831* (Urbana: University of Illinois Press, 1992), 289–91. In his analysis of advertisements in eighteenth-century Virginia and South Carolina, Lathan Windley discovered variations before and after

the American Revolution, but his 19.4 percent of female runaways (715 of 3,685) is very similar to the RSDB. Calculated from Lathan Algerna Windley, *A Profile of Runaway Slaves in Virginia and South Carolina from 1730 Through 1787* (New York: Garland Publishing, 1995), 159–60.

4. Records of the General Assembly, Petition of William Fairy to the South Carolina Senate, 1 November 1808, #37, SCDAH. Jack was later tried for assaulting a white man and executed. Records of the General Assembly, Petition of William Villard to the South Carolina Senate, 23 November 1813, #107, SCDAH. The incident occurred in 1812. Farmers who came to Villard's rescue captured Sampson. He was later executed. Villard received $300 compensation for confronting Sampson, who was described as having a "desperate and atrocious character."

5. Jeffrey R. Young, "Ideology and Death on a Savannah River Rice Plantation, 1833–1867: Paternalism amidst 'a Good Supply of Disease and Pain,'" *Journal of Southern History* 59 (November 1993), 681.

6. Parker, *Running for Freedom*, 71; Deborah White, "Female Slaves: Sex Roles and Status in the Antebellum Plantation South," *Journal of Family History* 8 (fall 1983), 251; and *Ar'n't I a Woman? Female Slaves in the Plantation South* (New York: W. W. Norton, 1985), 70–76; Eugene Genovese, *Roll, Jordan, Roll: The World the Slaves Made* (New York: Pantheon Books, 1974), 649; Stanley W. Campbell, "Runaway Slaves," in *Dictionary of Afro-American Slavery*, ed. Randall M. Miller and John David Smith (New York: Greenwood Press, 1988), 650; Judith Kelleher Schafer, "New Orleans Slavery in 1850 as Seen in Advertisements," *Journal of Southern History* 47 (February 1981), 43–44.

7. Records for Letty can be found in *Nashville Whig*, 6, 13 December 1814; for Nancy in *New Orleans Bee*, 23 September 1828. The advertisement ran through 12 November 1828. Information on Sawney in Records of the General Assembly, Petition of Samuel Linton, Sr., to the South Carolina General Assembly, 1817, #136, SCDAH; on Delph in Records of the General Assembly, Petition of Joseph Wardlaw to the South Carolina House of Representatives, 21 March 1817, #105, SCDAH. Wardlaw sought permission to bring Delph into the state following the passage of a law prohibiting the importation of slaves for sale and speculation. Discussion of Angeline in *Richmond Enquirer*, 5 August 1836, cited by Herbert Gutman in *The Black Family in Slavery and Freedom, 1750–1925* (New York: Pantheon Books, 1976), 264. See also Robert Bremner, ed., *Childhood and Youth In America: A Documentary History* (Cambridge, Mass.: Harvard University Press, 1970), 1:378.

8. For advertisements concerning black youngsters, see *Tennessee Republican Banner* [Nashville], 13 March 1838, 27 December 1839; *Alexandria Gazette, Commercial and Political*, 30 March 1815, in *Advertisements for Runaway Slaves in Virginia, 1801–1820*, ed. Daniel Meaders (New York: Garland Publishing, 1997), 230; *Richmond Enquirer*, 13 April 1816, in Meaders, ed., *Advertisements for Runaway Slaves in Virginia*, 292; also see Wilma King, *Stolen Childhood: Slave Youth in Nineteenth Century America* (Bloomington: Indiana University Press, 1995), 120. Alice is described in Baltimore City Register of Wills (Petitions), Petition of John Ven Ness Philip to the Orphans Court of Baltimore City, 5 September 1860, reel M-11,026, SC, MSA; Affidavit of Henrietta Johnson, 4 September 1860, with ibid. Catherine and Henry in *New Orleans Bee*, 16 March 1831; *New Orleans Bee*, 3 July 1833, with the latter notice running continuously through 30 September 1833. Water Scott in *New Orleans Bee*, 8 April 1841; Elias in *Charleston Mercury*, 15 December 1828.

9. *New Orleans Bee*, 12 August 1830; *Charleston Mercury and Morning Advertiser*, 29 December 1823; *Charleston Mercury*, 9 August 1828; notice running through

6 September 1828; *Charleston Mercury*, 7 June 1832; *Richmond Enquirer*, 14 May 1850; *Charleston Mercury*, 21 August 1832; *Charleston Mercury*, 11 December 1832.

10. *Richmond Enquirer*, 15 September 1804, 10 October 1804, 13, 15, 20 December 1804, 22 February 1805, 19 April 1805, 3 May 1805, 4 June 1805, 28 January 1806, 4, 11, 13, 15, 25, February 1806, 8 April 1806. Descriptions of the less black in *Richmond Enquirer*, 4 February 1808; of the very black in *Richmond Enquirer*, 15 May 1807; *New Orleans Picayune*, 4 February 1838, 30 June 1838, 14 July 1838, 7, 16, 19 June 1839, 3 July 1839, 10, 11, 31 August 1839, 3 October 1839, 5, 11, 13 December 1839, 2 January 1840, 13 March 1840; of Abel and Abram in *Charleston Mercury*, 11 January 1855.

11. For the census breakdown of blacks and mulattoes in 1850 in the United States, see Joel Williamson, *New People: Miscegenation and Mulattoes in the United States* (New York: Free Press, 1980), 24–33; also see Edward Byron Reuter, *The Mulatto in the United States: Including a Study of the Role of Mixed-Blood Races Throughout the World* (Boston: Richard G. Badger, 1918).

12. Description of Coleman in *Tennessee Republican Banner*, 22, 24, 25, 26 February 1840; of Bonaparte in *Richmond Enquirer*, 20 June 1851; of Guy in *Tennessee Republican Banner*, 22 August 1842; of John in *Tennessee Republican Banner*, 25 May 1839; *Richmond Enquirer*, 26 March 1805, 12 December 1805, 7, 14 January 1806; *Tennessee Gazette*, 31 March 1802; *Nashville Whig*, 27 April 1814, 3, 11 May 1814; *New Orleans Picayune*, 7 April 1839; *Richmond Enquirer*, 20 February 1855. In his travels in the South, Frederick Law Olmsted said he read about one hundred advertisements for runaways who were "so white they might be mistaken for white persons." Frederick Law Olmsted, *A Journey in the Seaboard Slave States, With Remarks on Their Economy* (New York: Dix and Edwards, 1856), 640–41. Discussion of Mabin in *Columbus Enquirer*, 9 February 1833, cited in William G. Proctor, Jr., "Slavery in Southwest Georgia," *Georgia Historical Quarterly* 49 (March 1965), 6.

13. South Carolina descriptions in *Charleston Mercury and Morning Advertiser*, 4 April 1822, 25 October 1822, 26 November 1823, 29 December 1823, 27 January 1824, 30 September 1824, 18, 28 April 1825, 3 May 1825; *Charleston Mercury*, 1 July 1828, 20 February 1830, 17 July 1830, 14 January 1831, 27 May 1831. Virginia ones in *Richmond Enquirer*, 28 January 1806; *Richmond Enquirer*, 4 February 1808; *Richmond Enquirer*, 23 November 1852, 14 January 1853; *Richmond Enquirer*, 15 September 1804, 10 October 1804, 13, 15, 20 December 1804, 22 February 1805, 19 April 1805, 3 May 1805, 4 June 1805, 28 January 1806, 4, 11, 13, 15, 25 February 1806, 8 April 1806; *Richmond Enquirer*, 21 February 1806, 11 March 1806; *Richmond Enquirer*, 27 May 1806; *Richmond Enquirer*, 26 July 1808; *Richmond Enquirer*, 20 February 1852; *Richmond Enquirer*, 11 February 1853; *Richmond Enquirer*, 20 July 1849; *Richmond Enquirer*, 10 August 1849.

14. *New Orleans Bee*, 16, 18 October 1834, 14, 29 November 1834, 10 February 1835, 7 March 1835, 11, 14 May 1835, 8, 20, 23 June 1835, 1 July 1835, 21 August 1835, 6, 12 January 1836, 12 March 1836. Use of "griff" in *New Orleans Picayune*, 4 February 1838, 30 June 1838, 14 July 1838, 7, 16, 19 June 1839, 3 July 1839, 10, 11, 31 August 1839, 3 October 1839, 5, 11, 13 December 1839, 2 January 1840, 13 March 1840; *New Orleans Bee*, 8 April 1841; quote about Joe in *New Orleans Bee*, 19 March 1835.

15. Slave owners sometimes used general terms to describe the height of runaways: short, medium size, tall; when these are combined with specific estimates, height categories include the following:

Estimated Heights Among Runaways: Early Period

	Number of Females	Percent in Category	Number of Males	Percent in Category
Short	21	53	71	20
Average	13	32	136	39
Tall	6	15	142	41
Total	40	100	349	100

Estimated Heights Among Runaways: Late Period

	Number of Females	Percent in Category	Number of Males	Percent in Category
Short	77	51	153	22
Average	58	38	275	39
Tall	17	11	275	39
Total	152	100	703	100

In 1857, an Edisto Island, South Carolina, planter described his slave Joe as "short—say five feet six inches." *Charleston Mercury*, 19 September 1857, 1, 6, 8, 10 October 1857. Also see the 27 September 1856 edition for a comment on height. A Virginia master described his six-foot runaway as a man of "remarkable" height. *Richmond Enquirer*, 20 July 1852.

16. Quote of "very remarkable lumps" in *Virginia Herald*, 8 January [1805], with Legislative Petitions, Petition of Mary Bussell to the Virginia General Assembly, 14 December 1812, Stafford County, Oversize, VSA; "white swelling" in *Richmond Enquirer*, 15 May 1807; *Tennessee Gazette* [Nashville], 12, 19, 26 May 1802, 9, 16 June 1802; quote about deformed foot in *Nashville Whig*, 27 December 1814, 4, 10, 17 January 1815; *Nashville Whig*, 12 December 1815; "web on one of his eyes" in *New Orleans Bee*, 17 November 1834; "lame in the left knee" in *Charleston Mercury and Morning Advertiser*, 4 April 1822; "one-half of her right foot" in *Charleston Mercury and Morning Advertiser*, 2 June 1825; quote about diseased left thigh in *Charleston Mercury*, 29 May 1830; *New Orleans Picayune*, 17 July 1840, 1 August 1840.

17. *Richmond Enquirer*, 13 June 1807; *Nashville Whig*, 27 April 1814, 3 11 May 1814; *Nashville Whig*, 22 November 1814, 6 December 1814; *New Orleans Bee*, 28 November 1832; *New Orleans Bee*, 14 November 1834; *Charleston Mercury and Morning Advertiser*, 29 December 1823; *Louisiana Journal* [St. Francisville], 26 November 1826, in *A Documentary History of American Industrial Society*, ed. Ulrich B. Phillips (Cleveland, Ohio: Arthur H. Clark, 1910), 2:88.

18. *Richmond Enquirer*, 13 January 1857; quotes about William in *New Orleans Picayune*, 7 June 1839.

19. *Richmond Enquirer*, 30 December 1807; *Georgia Express* [Athens], 17 December 1808, in Phillips, ed., *A Documentary History*, 2:92–93; *Nashville Whig*, 8, 15 August 1815.

20. *New Orleans Bee*, 21 October 1833; *New Orleans Bee*, 2 May 1835; *New Orleans Bee*, 11 November 1835. See also *New Orleans Bee*, 11–29 February 1828, 1–31 March 1828, 1–30 April 1828, 1–24 May 1828, 24 June 1831, 28 November

1832, 1 December 1832, 7 January 1833, 28 August 1833, 4 September 1833, 29 January 1834, 22 April 1834, 13 May 1834, 5–20 June 1834, 14 November 1834, 3–31 December 1834, 3–15 January 1835, 2 May 1835, 8 June 1835, 11 November 1835.

21. Records of the District Court, Natchitoches Parish, Louisiana, William H. Strong vs. Clement Rachal, 12 November 1836, #1,474, Parish Court House, Natchitoches, Louisiana.

22. *New Orleans Bee*, 21 October 1830; Peter Kolchin, *American Slavery, 1619–1877* (New York: Hill and Wang, 1993), 114; *Richmond Enquirer*, 26 March 1805, 12 December 1805; *Nashville Whig*, 4, 11, 25 January 1814, 28 June 1814; *New Orleans Bee*, 1 May 1841, 24 March 1841.

23. *Charleston Mercury and Morning Advertiser*, 4 October 1824, 10 November 1825; *Charleston Mercury*, 14 September 1829. Description of Celia in *Nashville Whig*, 27 April 1814, 3, 11 May 1814; Solomon in *Nashville Whig*, 15 August 1815, 5 September 1815; quote of "negro cloth round jacket" in *Charleston Mercury and Morning Advertiser*, 27 January 1824; "large stock of Clothing" in *Charleston Mercury*, 14 January 1831. "Myal probably took them" in *Tennessee Republican Banner*, 7 April 1838.

24. *Virginia Herald*, 8 January [1805], with Legislative Petitions, Petition of Mary Bussell to the Virginia General Assembly, 14 December 1812, Stafford County, Oversize, VSA; *Nashville Whig*, 8, 15 August, 1815; *Charleston Mercury*, 11 October 1830; *New Orleans Bee*, 14 May 1835; *New Orleans Picayune*, 30 April 1839; *Richmond Enquirer*, 13 August 1805; *Richmond Enquirer*, 12 September 1806.

25. *Richmond Enquirer*, 13 December 1804; *New Orleans Bee*, 25 May 1832; *New Orleans Bee*, 30 August 1832; *Richmond Enquirer*, 13 October 1804; *Charleston Mercury*, 14 January 1828.

26. Mention of large wardrobe in *New Orleans Bee*, 13 December 1832; *New Orleans Picayune*, 28 August 1839; *Charleston Mercury*, 27 September 1832; *New Orleans Picayune*, 5 December 1839; *Charleston Mercury*, 28 November 1827. For the dress of slave women in New Orleans, see *New Orleans Bee*, 22 April 1834, 21 January 1841. Quotes about what others took in *Charleston Mercury and Morning Advertiser*, 3 May 1825; *New Orleans Picayune*, 5 December 1839; *New Orleans Bee*, 30 August 1832; of New Orleans man in *New Orleans Bee*, 8 October 1834. The notice ran continuously through 9 December 1834.

27. *Richmond Enquirer*, 13 October 1804; *Richmond Enquirer*, 13 December 1804, 13 August 1805; *Nashville Whig*, 15 August 1815, 5 September 1815; *Charleston Mercury and Morning Advertiser*, 24 December 1822; description of Cyrus in *Charleston Mercury*, 18 March 1828; quote about Johns Island slave in *Charleston Mercury and Morning Advertiser*, 24 December 1822. She ran away "about the middle of November" and the notice appeared through 17 May 1823.

28. *Charleston Mercury*, 5 December 1829; *New Orleans Picayune*, 28 April 1837. The notice ran continuously through 28 August 1837. The $500 reward was almost certainly a misprint.

29. For a comparison with the pre-Revolutionary generation of runaways, see Shane White and Graham White, "Slave Hair and African American Culture in the Eighteenth and Nineteenth Centuries," *Journal of Southern History* 61 (February 1995), 66. In the mid-eighteenth century, a number of male slaves boasted "large bushy" heads of hair, hair worn "remarkable high," or "a large quantity of long wool"; female slaves also had "long black Hair," remarkably long hair, bushy heads of hair. Descriptions of male hair in *Richmond Enquirer*, 22 November 1805, 19 May 1807, 18 May 1807, 10 June 1807. In the early period, among 695 slaves advertised,

4 women and 34 men were described as having unusual hair. In the later period, among 1,316 slaves advertised, 18 women and 79 men were similarly described.

30. *Richmond Enquirer*, 13 December 1804; *Tennessee Republican Banner*, 21 August 1839; *Charleston Mercury*, 1 July 1828; *Charleston Mercury*, 29 August 1828; descriptions of other runaways in *Richmond Enquirer*, 4 March 1808; *Charleston Mercury*, 3 October 1831, 25 July 1832; *Richmond Enquirer*, 29 September 1854, 13 October 1854; *Tennessee Gazette*, 31 May 1806; *Tennessee Republican Banner*, 27 February 1840, 31 July 1851; *New Orleans Bee*, 29 March 1831, 4, 5, 6, 7, 8 April 1831, 27 May 1831, 9 August 1831, 19 July 1832, 23–30 March 1833, 1–13 April 1833; New *Orleans Picayune*, 7 June 1839; *Charleston Mercury*, 17 September 1832. Quote of "very smart and well calculated" in *Richmond Enquirer*, 13 October 1854.

31. *Richmond Enquirer*, 21 October 1806; *Charleston Mercury*, 14 June 1826.

32. Notices for slow speakers in *Richmond Enquirer*, 23 December 1853. Quotes cited in *New Orleans Bee*, 25 April 1834, 19 March 1835; *New Orleans Picayune*, 2 August 1838. See also *Charleston Mercury and Morning Advertiser*, 20 October 1824; *Charleston Mercury*, 12 April 1832, 7 May 1832, 29 June 1832, 27 October 1832; *New Orleans Bee*, 25 April 1834, 19 March 1835, 15 July 1835; *New Orleans Picayune*, 2 August 1838; 30 July 1838. Quotes about Luck in *New Orleans Bee*, 30 September 1833; the "Savannah dialect" is mentioned in *New Orleans Bee*, 17 February 1836; the "accent of a negress" is noted in *New Orleans Picayune*, 7 April 1839; the Virginia "brogue" is found in *Richmond Enquirer*, 31 May 1853.

33. Description of Celestine in *New Orleans Bee*, 11 February 1828, 9 April 1828; also see *New Orleans Bee*, 11 January 1831, 10, 19, 28, 29 March 1831. Descriptions of multilingual slave in *New Orleans Bee*, 21 October 1828; with the advertisement running until 12 November 1828; of American slaves in *New Orleans Bee*, 11 January 1831, 10, 19, 28, 29 March 1831; of Hons in *Staunton Eagle*, 19 November 1807, transcribed by J. Susanne Simmons in appendix 4, "They Too Were Here: African-Americans in Augusta County and Staunton, Virginia, 1745–1865," (master's thesis, James Madison University, 1994), 109.

34. *Tennessee Gazette*, 20 July 1803; *Tennessee Gazette*, 24, 31 August 1803, 7, 14, 21 September 1803; *Nashville Whig*, 2, 9 August 1814; *Nashville Whig*, 27 December 1814, 4, 10, 17 January 1815; *New Orleans Bee*, 28 August 1830; *New Orleans Bee*, 28 April 1834; *New Orleans Bee*, 11 June 1834; *New Orleans Bee*, 16 October 1834; *New Orleans Picayune*, 15 May 1839, 28 May 1840; *Richmond Enquirer*, 8 September 1854.

35. A few owners also described their runaways as having "rather dull countenance," "a broad dull face," "a downcast, stupid look." *Richmond Enquirer*, 22 February 1805; *Charleston Mercury and Morning Advertiser*, 4 April 1822; *Charleston Mercury*, 29 May 1830.

Maryland law required owners of term slaves to obtain court permission to sell them out of the state. The attitudes of owners toward rebellious slaves are therefore revealed in some detail. See Frederick County Court (Petitions), Petition of Henry Kemp to the County Court, 8 March 1836, reel 11,024, SC, MSA; Howard County Register of Wills (Petitions), Petition of A. L. Mackey to the Orphans Court, 1854, reel M-11,024, SC, MSA; Howard County Register of Wills (Petitions), Petition of George Richardson to the Orphans Court, 7 August 1855, reel M-11,024, SC; Anne Arundel County Register of Wills (Petitions and Orders) 1840–51, 274–78, Petition of James H. Watkins to the Orphans Court, 19 December 1848, reel #CR 63,127-2, MSA; Anne Arundel County Register of Wills (Petitions and Orders) 1851–60, 122–23, Petition of Charles R. Steward to the Orphans Court, 24 October 1854, reel #CR 63,128-1, MSA.

Quotes about "utterly disobedient" slave in Anne Arundel County Register of Wills (Petitions and Orders) 1851–60, 458–60, Petition of James S. Wilson to the Orphans Court, 16 April 1858, reel #CR 63,128-1, MSA; about Eliza in Anne Arundel County Register of Wills (Petitions and Orders) 1851–60, 122–23, Petition of Charles R. Steward to the Orphans Court, 24 October 1854, reel #CR 63,128-1, MSA.

36. The "violent and determined temper" quote is found in Baltimore County Register of Wills (Petitions and Orders), Petition of Richard Hutchens to the Orphans Court, 22 June 1853, reel M-11,020, SC, MSA. Also see in Baltimore County Register of Wills (Petitions and Orders), reel M-11,020, SC, MSA: James M. Brannon vs. Uriah Young, 15, April 1856; George Harryman vs. Negro Abraham, 12 July 1859; John Timanus vs. Cosmore Robinson, 1 June 1861; Petition of John Timanus to the Orphans Court, 12 November 1861; Order of the Court, 20 November 1861, with ibid., reel M-11,020, SC, MSA. Quote about slave's "disposition to do harm" in Anne Arundel County Register of Wills (Petitions and Orders) 1840–51, 161–63, Petition of Rezin Hammond to the Orphans Court, 8 September 1846, reel #CR 63,127-2, MSA.

37. Records of the Equity Court, Richland District, South Carolina, Mary Cobb vs. Ann Reynolds, 13 January 1819, microfilm reel #153, SCDAH.

38. Records of the District Court, San Augustine County, Texas, Charles W. Brady vs. Tempe Price, 16 October 1856, Case #1,132, East Texas Research Center, Stephen F. Austin University, Nacogdoches, Texas; Testimony of Gilbert B. McIver, 13 September 1856. The testimony about the earlier incident was allowed in a case involving another overseer, Charles W. Brady, who killed Miles and then sued the slave owner for back salary.

39. Frederick County Court (Petitions), Petition of John Wood to the County Court, 31 October 1838, reel M-11,024, SC, MSA. Wood received permission to sell Peter's unexpired term "to any person within or without this State," but the court required that Peter be furnished with a copy of his manumission deed. Order of the Court, October Term 1838, with ibid.

40. Discussion of spectacular escapes in Richard J. M. Blackett, *Beating Against the Barriers: Biographical Essays in Nineteenth-Century Afro-American History* (Baton Rouge: Louisiana State University Press, 1986), 87–90; Larry Gara, *The Liberty Line: The Legend of the Underground Railroad* (Lexington: University of Kentucky Press, 1961), 49–50. For slaves on trains, see Jenny Bourne Wahl, "The Bondsman's Burden: An Economic Analysis of the Jurisprudence of Slaves and Common Carriers," *Journal of Economic History* 53 (September 1993), 511–15.

41. Excluding the thirty runaways in the early period who were either stolen or absconded from Amelia Island, East Florida, and advertised in the *Nashville Whig,* 7 December 1813, the proportion of runaways in the category of four or more slaves would narrow between the two periods. Nonetheless, 17 percent in the early period and 5 percent in the later period were in this category.

42. As previously noted, according to one estimate, 6 percent of rural slaves and 31 percent of urban slaves were on hire in 1860. In addition, about three-fourths of adult slaves were field hands, and by the 1850s in the deep South, with the intense labor shortage, increasing numbers of skilled slaves were pressed into field labor. Thus, the 15 percent skilled runaways was probably slightly higher than the percentage of skilled slaves in the general population. About 5 percent of slaves were probably literate or semi-literate. See Kolchin, *American Slavery,* 105, 110, 142.

43. Legislative Petitions, Petition of Nathaniel Wilkinson to the Virginia General Assembly, 7 December 1795, Henrico County, VSA. Descriptions of slaves with fake passes in *New Orleans Picayune,* 20 August 1839; *New Orleans Picayune,* 5 December 1839; *Charleston Mercury,* 8 November 1827.

44. Quotes about appearance of slaves with fake passes in *Charleston Mercury,* 12 September 1828; *Richmond Enquirer,* 5 September 1806. Eve absconded on 15 October 1805. Forging papers for slaves was a serious offense, but it was rarely prosecuted. In the first thirty-eight years of the nineteenth century, in the entire state of Virginia, only one person went to the penitentiary for furnishing a slave with false papers. Philip J. Schwarz, *Twice Condemned, Slaves and the Criminal Laws of Virginia, 1705–1865* (Baton Rouge: Louisiana State University Press, 1988), 302–4.

Other quotes in *Nashville Whig,* 27 April 1814, 3, 11 May 1814; *Charleston Mercury and Morning Advertiser,* 26 June 1822.

45. Quotes about literate slaves in *Richmond Enquirer,* 24 May 1805; *Richmond Enquirer,* 12 August 1853, with the notice running continuously through 2 December 1853; *Charleston Mercury,* 27 February 1830; *Richmond Enquirer,* 22 February 1805.

46. *Richmond Enquirer,* 27 August 1850. Levi absconded on 29 June 1850; the notice ran through 18 October 1850.

47. For roughly comparable evidence from the Chesapeake Bay region and the Carolina low country during the eighteenth century, see Michael Mullin, *Africa in America: Slave Acculturation and Resistance in the American South and the British Caribbean, 1736–1831* (Urbana: University of Illinois Press, 1992), 289–91.

48. The male stonecutter named June, who spoke "tolerable English," for example, was described only as "a native of Africa." *Alexandria Daily Advertiser, Commercial and Political,* 23 October 1804, in Meaders, ed., *Advertisements for Runaway Slaves in Virginia,* 41. Quotes about Nuncanna in *Nashville Whig,* 29 November 1815, 12, 19 December 1815, 9, 16, 23 January 1816, 7, 27 February 1816, 5, 12 March 1816, 4, 25 June 1816, 2 July 1816. There were twenty-eight slaves in the RSDB for the early period who were not born in the United States. Their origins included various islands in the Caribbean, South America (one was cited as Portuguese), and not known. Because of their small number and diverse origins, they were excluded. Descriptions of other Africans in *New Orleans Bee,* 12 August 1830; *New Orleans Bee,* 25 April 1834; *New Orleans Bee,* 17 March 1835.

49. Quotes about Rosalia in *New Orleans Bee,* 21 July 1834. Identification of Africans in *New Orleans Bee,* 16 April 1835; *New Orleans Bee,* 7 January 1836, Antoine ran away on the 20 November 1835 and the notice continued until 14 January 1836; *Charleston Mercury,* 6 June 1827.

50. Descriptions by height in *Charleston Mercury and Morning Advertiser,* 3 December 1824; *Charleston Mercury,* 7 June 1832; *Richmond Enquirer,* 14 May 1850.

CHAPTER 10

1. Daily Journal, 1854–1855, Morville Plantation, Concordia Parish Louisiana, Surget Family Papers, MDAH.

2. William K. Scarborough, *The Overseer: Plantation Management in the Old South* (Baton Rouge: Louisiana State University Press, 1966), 68, 70; James O. Breeden, *Advice Among Masters: The Ideal in Slave Management in the Old South* (Westport, Conn.: Greenwood Press, 1980), 291–98.

3. Quote of "courage to drive Negroes" in John R. Casey to John D. Dunn, 13 July 1859, John D. Dunn Papers, Manuscript Division, Duke University, Durham, North Carolina. On the eve of the Civil War, for example, there were about 46,000 "planters" in the South, but only about 38,000 overseers. Scarborough, *The Overseer,* 10.

4. Quotes on trusting slaves in Scarborough, *The Overseer,* 164–66; John Merriman to Francis D. Richardson, 11 November 1840, Weeks (David and Family) Papers, Special Collections, Hill Memorial Library, LSU.

5. Records of the Parish Court, West Baton Rouge Parish, Louisiana, Sixth District Court, A. L. Dixon vs. D. P. Cain, 4 March 1858, #1,523, Parish Court House, Port Allen, Louisiana. Dixon, the overseer, who was fired, sued Cain, the planter, for his wages and the use of his slaves. Despite the evidence, the plaintiff was awarded $850. Description of managers being tested in Thomas Butler to Ann Butler, 22 July 1842, Butler (Thomas and Family) Papers, Special Collections, Hill Memorial Library, LSU. Quote about Irish overseer in Moses Liddell to John R. Liddell, 21 July 1841, Liddell (Moses, John R., and Family) Papers, Special Collections, Hill Memorial Library, LSU.

6. William Jacobs to Mary Weeks, 29 November 1837, Weeks (David and Family) Papers, Special Collections, Hill Memorial Library, LSU.

7. John Merriman to A. F. Conrad, 30 August 1839, Weeks (David and Family) Papers, Special Collections, Hill Memorial Library, LSU; L. Hewett to J. D. Murrell, 27 August 1848, 17 September 1848, Murrell (John D.) Papers, Special Collections, Hill Memorial Library, LSU; John Betson Traylor Diary, 11, 21 March 1834, Typescript, ADAH.

8. Hyman and Isum in Scarborough, *The Overseer*, 90–91; Records of the General Assembly, Petition of Major Brown to the South Carolina Senate, 2 December 1800, #166, SCDAH; Statement, William Fishburne et al., ca. 1800, with ibid.

9. For the time delay before advertising runaways in one Louisiana Parish, see Declaration of George de Passau to the Judge of Iberville Parish Court, Louisiana, 7 March 1810, Natchez Trace Slaves and Slavery Collection, folder on Fugitive Slaves, Center for American History, University of Texas at Austin; Declaration of Nicholas Toffier to the Judge of Iberville Parish Court, 7 April 1810, and Declaration of Jacques de Villiers to the Judge of the Iberville Parish Court, 13 September 1810, with ibid. Data on advertisers computed from RSDB. Information in *Tennessee Republican Banner*, 1 January 1838.

10. *New Orleans Bee*, 11 June 1832, 12–29 June 1832, 2–26 July 1832, 29 March 1833, 8, 10 April 1833, 4 July 1834, 19 June 1834, 12, 14, 15 July 1834; *New Orleans Picayune*, 30 June 1838, 27 May 1840; *Charleston Mercury and Morning Advertiser*, 19 June 1824, 21 August 1824; *Richmond Enquirer*, 2 April 1850; *Charleston Mercury and Morning Advertiser*, 12 January 1825; Samuel Edwards to R. W. Long, 30 December 1857, Natchez Trace Slaves and Slavery Collection, Oversize Box 2,325/v48, folder 1, Center for American History, University of Texas at Austin; *Richmond Enquirer*, 13 January 1857.

"I am very sorry" quote in William Jacobs to Mary Weeks, 29 November 1837, Weeks (David and Family) Papers, Special Collections, Hill Memorial Library, LSU.

11. Malcolm Bell, Jr., *Major Butler's Legacy: Five Generations of a Slaveholding Family* (Athens: University of Georgia Press, 1987), 219; Kenneth Stampp, *The Peculiar Institution: Slavery in the Ante-Bellum South* (New York: Vintage Books, 1956), 174–76.

12. Roswell King to Pierce Butler, 26 May 1816, quoted in Bell, *Major Butler's Legacy*, 219.

13. For the difficulties overseers had with slave violence and runaways, see Records of the Parish Court, West Feliciana Parish, Louisiana, Third District Court, Samuel Cowgill vs. Charles Stewart, 11 October 1826, #369, Parish Court House, St. Francisville, Louisiana; Rachel O'Connor to Mary C. Weeks, 26 December 1834, Weeks (David and Family) Papers, Special Collections, Hill Memorial Library, LSU; Records of the Chancery Court, Giles County, Tennessee, Case Files, Jane B. Smith vs. Elizabeth E. Smith et al., 25 January 1860, Case #1,741, reel 193, frames 2,705–8, 2,698–2,700, 2,689–93, TSLA; Testimony of Archibald J. Strickland, 15 March 1860, with

ibid.; Testimony of Andrew Roberts, 15 March 1860, with ibid.; Records of the General Assembly, Petition of Charles Carroll to the South Carolina House of Representatives, 1851, #12, SCDAH; Appraisal of Slave Paul, Barnwell District Court of Magistrates and Freeholders, 22 November 1851; G. W. Muse et al. to the Treasurer of the Upper Division of South Carolina, 22 March 1851, with ibid.

14. Breeden, *Advice Among Masters*, 42, 80, 81, 86; "Proceedings of a Meeting of Citizens of the County of Buckingham relative to Frequent Acts of Incendiaryism & for a Change in the License Law," 27 March 1852, in Legislative Petitions, Petition of Thomas F. Perkins et al. to the Virginia General Assembly, 27 March 1852, Buckingham County, VSA.

15. Breeden, *Advice Among Masters*, 42, 80, 81, 86.

16. "On the Management of Slaves," *Southern Agriculturalist* 6 (June 1833), 281–87; Pee Dee, "The Management of Negroes," *Southern Agriculturalist* 11 (October 1838), 512–14; P. T., "Judicious Management of the Plantation Force," *Southern Cultivator* 7 (May 1849), 69; Philon, "Moral Management of Negroes," *Southern Cultivator* 7 (July 1849), 105–6; "Management of Slaves," *De Bow's Review* 13 (August 1852), 193–94; see Breeden, *Advice Among Masters*, 342.

17. In 1860, those who could not afford overseers, the nonplanter class, represented about 88 percent of the 385,000 slave owners in the South. There were approximately 1.5 million white families in the region at the time.

18. Theodore Rosengarten, *Tombee: Portrait of a Cotton Planter with the Journal of Thomas B. Chaplin (1822–1890)* (New York: William Morrow, 1986), 160.

19. Frederick Law Olmsted, *A Journey in the Back Country* (New York: Mason Brothers, 1860), 87–88.

20. Ann Patton Malone, *Sweet Chariot: Slave Family and Household Structure in Nineteenth-Century Louisiana* (Chapel Hill: University of North Carolina Press, 1992), 293 n. 10; A. T. Conrad to David Weeks, 16 December 1827, Weeks (David and Family) Papers, Special Collections, Hill Memorial Library, LSU; J. N. Taylor to Franklin H. Elmore, 29 December 1842, Franklin H. Elmore Papers, LC.

21. Olmsted, *A Journey in the Back Country*, 30.

22. Joseph E. Jenkins to Dear Sir, 20 December 1858, Cornish (Reverend John Hamilton) Papers, Special Collections, Hill Memorial Library, LSU.

23. As an example of an owner's emotional response to a runaway, one master fumed: "Damned mean negro. I have not whiped him yet but I intend to give him the devil," James Monroe Torbert Journal, 3 August 1857, typescript, ADAH; March's story is in Records of the Superior Court, Pulaski County, Georgia, Wiley Brooks vs. John O. Grant, 19 September 1817, in Record Book 1815–1821, 69–71, County Court House, Hawkinsville, Georgia. Brooks accused Grant of killing his slave and sought damages. The final decree of the court was not included with the case.

24. Records of the Southampton County Circuit Court, Commonwealth vs. Gardner, Depositions of Amos Gardner and Joseph Vick, ca. 1808, Miscellaneous Papers, VSA.

25. John A. Hamilton to William S. Hamilton, 29 July 1851, William S. Hamilton Papers, Special Collections, Hill Memorial Library, LSU, quoted in James Oakes, *The Ruling Race: A History of American Slaveholders* (New York: Vintage Books, 1983), 188.

26. Records of the Chancery Court, Giles County, Tennessee, Case Files, Petition of James P. Nelson, 27 November 1855, Case #1,309, reel #178, frames 2,739–40, 2,765–70, TSLA; Report of the Clerk and Master of the Court, 28 November 1855, with ibid.; Report of the Clerk and Master of the Court, 7 January 1856, with ibid. Quotes about Sam in Records of the Chancery Court, Maury County, Tennessee,

Case Files, Petition of John and David Wilson, executors of Robert Wilson's estate, Charlotte A. Wilson, Widow of Robert Wilson, et al. vs. Margaret E. and William A. Wilson, 30 October 1854, Case #84, County Court House, Columbia, Tennessee.

27. *Charleston Mercury*, 22 April 1830; Records of the Probate Court, Gadsden County, Florida, Petition of Richard Baker, 31 December 1845, in Records of the Probate Court, vol. 3, 48–49, County Court House, Quincy, Florida; J. H. Taylor to F. H. Elmore, 24 March 1850, Franklin H. Elmore Papers, Manuscripts Division, LC.

28. Quotes about Tennessee slave in Records of the Chancery Court, Giles County, Tennessee, Case Files, Jane B. Smith vs. Elizabeth E. Smith et al., 25 January 1860, Case #1,741, reel 193, frames 2,705–8, 2,698–2,700, 2,689–93, TSLA; Testimony of Archibald J. Strickland, 15 March 1860, with ibid.; Testimony of Andrew Roberts, 15 March 1860, with ibid. Quotes about Bob in Records of the Ordinary Court, Chatham County, Georgia, Petition of George W. Allen, Executor of the Estate of Ann Mc-Knight, 7 March 1809, in Minutes 1807, 1813, 1815, 143, County Court House, Savannah, Georgia; about Abner in Anne Arundel County Register of Wills (Petitions and Orders) 1840–51, 413–14, Petition of William Cecil to the Orphans Court, 15 April 1851, reel #CR 63,127-2, MSA; about George in Anne Arundel County Register of Wills (Petitions and Orders) 1809–20, 98, Petition of Ann Dorsey to the Orphans Court, 15 March 1810, #CR 63,126, MSA. The petition did not mention specifically that George ran away.

29. Anne Arundel County Register of Wills (Petitions and Orders) 1840–51, 309–10, Petition of Andrew Lynch to the Orphans Court, 31 July 1849, reel #CR 63,127-2, MSA; Ann Arundel County Register of Wills (Petitions and Orders) 1840–51, 313–14, Petition of Eliza Clagett to the Orphans Court, 22 October 1849, reel #CR 63,127-2; Ann Arundel County Register of Wills (Petitions and Orders) 1840–51, 413–14, Petition of William Cecil to the Orphans Court, 15 April 1851, reel #CR 63,127-2; Ann Arundel County Register of Wills (Petitions and Orders) 1840–51, 309–10, Petition of Andrew Lynch to the Orphans Court, 31 July 1849, reel #CR 63,127-2; Ann Arundel County Register of Wills (Petitions and Orders) 1840–51, 261, Petition of Benjamin Carr to the Orphans Court, [September] 1855, MSA. Quotes about Horace in Anne Arundel County Register of Wills (Petitions and Orders) 1840–51, 161–63, Petition of Rezin Hammond to the Orphans Court, 8 September 1846, reel #CR 63,127-2, MSA; about the "turbulant" slave in Anne Arundel County Register of Wills (Petitions and Orders) 1840–51, 324, Petition of William H. Bird to the Orphans Court, 11 December 1849, reel #CR 63,127-2, MSA; about Brice in Anne Arundel County Register of Wills (Petitions and Orders) 1840–51, 382-83, Petition of Daniel Duvall to the Orphans Court, 30 October 1850, reel #CR 63,127-2, MSA.

30. Washington County Register of Wills (Petitions and Orders), Daniel and Eleanor Brosins et al. vs. Jacob Younker, 13 November 1857, reel M-11,027, SC, MSA; Decree of the Court, November 1857, with ibid.

31. Washington County Register of Wills (Petitions and Orders) Petition of Andrew Hagmire, 4 May 1858, reel M-11,027, SC, MSA.

32. Quotes from the cousin's letter in John B. Ives to William P. Browne, 14 May 1859, William Phineas Browne Papers, Correspondence, ADAH. Quotes of the wife in Margaret G. Browne to William P. Browne, 17 May 1859, William Phineas Browne Papers, Correspondence, ADAH; William P. Browne to Margaret Browne, 17 and 20 May 1859, ibid. Lewis was probably lured off, but there is also evidence that he was purposely trying to get away from his wife and had second thoughts. William P. Browne to Dan W. Prentice, 21 April 1859, ibid.

33. Baltimore City Register of Wills (Petitions), Petition of Rebecca Freeman to the Orphans Court of Baltimore County, 20 December 1825, reel M-11,025, SC, MSA;

Baltimore County Register of Wills (Petitions and Orders), Petition of James H. Luckett, 8 March 1859, reel M-11,020, SC, MSA.

34. Records of the Probate Court, Chatham County, Georgia, Petition of Nathaniel P. Crowell Administrator in right of his wife Mary A. Crowell, 4 February 1828, in Minutes 1823–1830 (21 July 1828), 331, County Court House, Savannah, Georgia; J. F. Dean to Betts and Gregory, 30 March 1861, Chase Family Papers, LC; Baltimore City Register of Wills (Petitions), Petition of Dennis Marsh to the Orphans Court of Baltimore County, 4 January 1831, reel M-11,025, SC, MSA; Baltimore City Register of Wills (Petitions), Petition of John P. Thomas to the Orphans Court of Baltimore City, 12 March 1861, reel M-11,026, SC, MSA; "incorrigible" slaves quote in Baltimore City Register of Wills (Petitions), Petition of Richard Younger to the Orphans Court, 14 August 1834, reel M-11,025, SC, MSA.

35. Nina Moore Tiffany, "Stories of the Fugitive Slaves[:] Anthony Burns," *New England Magazine*, new series, 2 (March–August 1890), 570. The master, who journeyed to Boston to retrieve his property in this celebrated case, was Charles F. Suttle, a planter who lived in Alexandria, Virginia.

36. Quotes of Maryland master in Anne Arundel County Register of Wills (Petitions and Orders) 1851–60, 264–66, Petition of James S. Linthicum to the Orphans Court, 4 September 1855, reel #CR 63,128-1, MSA. These comments by various masters were made after slaves ran away: Anne Arundel County Court (Petitions), Petition of Lemuel G. Taylor to the County Court, 1 November 1839, reel, M-11019, SC, MSA; Baltimore County Register of Wills (Petitions and Orders), Peter W. Gibbons vs. John Thomas Gray, 22 November 1853, and Petition of Wa[k]eman Bryarly, 1 June 1858, and James H. Luckett vs. Dennis Williams, 29 June 1859, and Juliet A. Turner vs. Mary Rebecca Henson, 9 April 1861, reel M-11,020, SC, MSA; Frederick County Court (Petitions), Petition of John Wood to the County Court, 31 October 1838, reel M-11,024, SC, MSA; Washington County Register of Wills (Petitions and Orders), Petition of George W. Post, 15 January 1856, reel M-11,027, SC, MSA. Washington quote in Fritz Hirschfeld, *George Washington and Slavery: A Documentary Portrayal* (Columbia: University of Missouri Press, 1997), 64.

37. Rachel O'Connor to Mary C. Weeks, 26 December 1834, Weeks (David and Family) Papers, Special Collections, Hill Memorial Library, LSU; Rachel O'Connor to Aldred Conrad, 3 August 1835, in Allie Bayne Windham Webb, ed., *Mistress of Evergreen Plantation: Rachel O'Connor's Legacy of Letters, 1823–1845* (Albany: State University of New York Press, 1983), 173. William T. Maclin to [?], 29 January 1846, William B. Wise Papers, Special Collections Library, Duke University, Durham, North Carolina.

38. *New Orleans Bee*, 19 July 1832; *Charleston Mercury*, 19 May 1832; *Charleston Mercury and Morning Advertiser*, 5 February 1824; *Charleston Mercury*, 10 May 1830; *Charleston Mercury*, 26 October 1830; quotes of other slaveholders in *Richmond Enquirer*, 20 July 1855, 16 October 1855.

39. Quotes on the society in Legislative Petitions, Petition of P. N. Nichols, James Boskey, John Gidden, et al. to the Virginia General Assembly, 8 March 1842, Richmond City, VSA. The petitioners asked for "An Act of Incorporation for the Protection of Slave Property in Henrico [County] & the City of Richmond." Quote about "those who hire negroes" in Legislative Petitions, Petition of P. M. Tabb, Edward N. Dabney, Richard Hill, Jr., et al. to the Virginia General Assembly, 14 December 1850, Richmond City, VSA. The petitioners addressed their remonstrance to the chairman of the Committee Upon Courts of Justice. They asked for changes in the law making owners financially responsible for hired runaways. To protect property and prevent "much inhumanity to the negro," hirers should be made responsible.

40. Legislative Petitions, Petition of Austin Grisham to the General Assembly, ca. 1831, #18–1831, reel #18, TSLA; Deposition of James Condon, November 1831, with ibid.; Deposition of James Dozier, 21 November 1831, with ibid.

41. *New Orleans Picayune*, 6 April 1839; *Nashville Whig*, 14, 21, 28 April 1813; *Richmond Enquirer*, 23 September 1806; *Charleston Mercury*, 29 March 1827; *Richmond Enquirer*, 29 April 1853.

Other masters' beliefs in *Tennessee Gazette*, 4 April 1807; *Louisiana Gazette*, 16 July 1807; *New Orleans Bee*, 7 March 1835, 19 April 1841; *Charleston Mercury and Morning Advertiser*, 22 April 1825, 23 June 1825; Anselm Anthony to Robert Menzies, 10 September 1806, Robert Menzies Papers, Special Collections Library, Duke University, Durham, North Carolina; Abram Martin to John and Wait Dunn, 9 March 1860, John D. Dunn Papers, Special Collections Library, Duke University, Durham, North Carolina. At various times, governors of southern states issued proclamations concerning slaves believed to have been "feloniously stolen." See Alabama Governors' Proclamations, 5 October 1829, 30 August 1831, 2, 21 March 1836, 6 February 1837, 28 July 1837, 14 May 1838, 29 September 1840, 5, 18 July 1842, 12, 14 September 1842, 23 January 1843, ADAH.

42. O. Z. McCann to Herman Clarence Nixon, 5 December 1912, in H. C. Nixon, Responses to Questionnaire on Slavery, 1912–1919, ADAH; M. T. Judge to Herman Clarence Nixon, 4 February 1913, with ibid. In the finding guide for this collection, McCann's initials were cited as "M. T." Judge owned a brick and concrete business in Mobile. He had grown up with former slaves and had worked with them and as their employer. "I think that I know them—their treatment during slavery and after Freedom, as well, if not better than any other man—," ibid.

43. Records of the Chancery Court, Giles County, Tennessee, Case Files, Bill of Complaint of Luke H. Hancock, Virginia C. Hancock, and Achilles M. Hancock, 31 August 1858, Case #935, reel 158, frames 2,179–81, 2,184–87, 2,139–40, TSLA; Report of Sale, March Term 1859, with ibid. "Ignorant devils" quote in Diary of William Dunbar, 12 May 1777, in *Life, Letters and Papers of William Dunbar of Elgin, Morayshire, Scotland, and Natchez, Mississippi*, comp. Eron Rowland (Jackson: Press of the Mississippi Historical Society, 1930), 46–47; Oakes, *The Ruling Race*, 188.

44. Baltimore City Register of Wills (Petitions), Sarah H. Childs vs. Nathaniel Dorsey, Orphans Court of Baltimore City, 12 November 1855, reel M-11,026, SC, MSA. Dorsey's servitude was extended and the court granted the widow permission to sell the unexpired term to any person within the state. Order of the Court, 13 November 1855, with ibid. For another example in Maryland, see Baltimore City Register of Wills (Petitions), Jane Dorman vs. Henrietta, Orphans Court of Baltimore City, 18 June 1858, reel M-11,026, SC, MSA.

45. Legislative Petitions, Petition of Alice Kelley to the Virginia Senate and House of Delegates, 23 February 1833, Northumberland County, VSA; Records of the Chancery Court, Maury County, Tennessee, Case Files, Petition of John and David Wilson, Executors of Robert Wilson's Estate, Charlotte A. Wilson, widow of Robert Wilson, et al. vs. Margaret E. and William A. Wilson, 30 October 1854, Case #84, County Court House, Columbia, Tennessee.

46. Records of the Equity Court, Newberry District, South Carolina, Petition of John B. Kinard, Executor of Isham Goree's Will, 20 May 1853, Case #24 1861, reel NB121, SCDAH.

47. Records of the Chancery Court, Giles County, Tennessee, Case Files, Margaret J. Mason vs. Willie Mason, 31 August 1857, Case #1,450, reel 175, frames 1,989–95, 1983, 1,969–72, TSLA; Deposition of John A. Jackson, 14 July 1857, with ibid.; Deposition of William Houston, 14 September 1857, with ibid.; Decree of the Court, 16

September 1857, with ibid.; Report of John A. and William H. Jackson to the Court, 17 March 1860, with ibid.

48. Records of the Probate Court, Marion County, Florida, Petition of Frances C. Blitch, 17 July 1860, Probate Packets, Series L172, reel 10, FSA; Missouri Supreme Court Cases, Susan Price vs. David Tatum, John Thornton, George Wallace, et al., owners of the Steamboat *General Leavenworth*, 8 May 1845, Box 43, #8, Missouri State Archives, Jefferson City, Missouri; Deposition of Winfrey E. Price, 1 June 1842, [5–6] in ibid.

49. Records of the County Court, Davidson County, Tennessee, Case Files, Jane D. Allen vs. Martha Allen, Sarah A. Allen, and Thomas Allen, 15 September 1856, Case #1,715, Box 15, Metropolitan Nashville-Davidson County Archives, Nashville; Deposition of James Beal Nichol, 12 November 1856, with ibid.; Deposition of Will L. Boyd, Jr., 12 November 1856, with ibid.; Deposition of Robert T. G. Hart, 12 November 1856, with ibid.; Decree of the Court, 13 November 1856, with ibid. The mother brought suit against her own children because they had no guardian and the husband's will had stipulated that the slaves should be used "for the better Support of herself and for the raising and educating of her children during her natural life."

50. Later, she sued the buyer for taking advantage of her in such a state of anxiety. The equity court agreed that in her excited frame of mind she had signed a deed she would not have signed under normal circumstances. Records of the Equity Court, Anderson District, South Carolina, Leah Moore vs. John McFall, February 1842, Case #456, Box 11, SCDAH.

51. Records of the Equity Court, Charleston District, South Carolina, Bills, Catherine Munro vs. Duke Goodman and Thomas Cochran, 19 March 1823, Case #42, SCDAH; Records of the Chancery Court, Bedford County, Tennessee, Petition of James Mullins and William Young, 30 August 1853, Chancery Court Records 1848–1851 Vol. B, 523–24, County Court House, Shelbyville, Tennessee.

52. Olmsted, *A Journey in the Back Country*, 475.

53. Records of the Chancery Court, Giles County, Tennessee, Case Files, Jane B. Smith vs. Elizabeth E. Smith et al., 25 January 1860, Case #1,741, reel 193, frames 2,705–08, 2,698–2,700, 2,689–93, TSLA; Testimony of Archibald J. Strickland, 15 March 1860, with ibid.

54. Legislative Petitions, Petition of John M. Price to the Virginia General Assembly, 11 December 1824, Louisa County, VSA.

55. Legislative Petitions, Petition of William Briggs to the Virginia General Assembly, 5 January 1843, Sussex County, VSA.

56. Records of the Circuit Court, Harrison County, Kentucky, Case Files, Thomas Craig vs. James and Walter Shropshire, 1809, Case #4,854, Drawers 164–65, County Court House, Cynthiana, Kentucky.

57. Records of the Superior Court, Jones County, Georgia, Hamutal Johnson vs. James Smith, April Term 1830, Case #5, in Writs 1829–1831, 336, 342–43, County Court House, Gray, Georgia. A jury found in favor of the plaintiff for some money owed her by Smith, but no mention was made of the two slaves.

58. Legislative Petitions, Petition of Residents of Bradley County to the General Assembly, 14 November 1849, #101–1849, reel #19, TSLA.

59. Edward Rawle to Francis Porteous Corbin, 14 March 1838, Manuscripts Division, Duke University, Durham, North Carolina. See also Francis Porteous Corbin to E. Rawle, December 1836, Edward Rawle to Francis Corbin, 15 July 1833, and James Hamilton to Dr. Joseph Maxwell, 10 January 1820, ibid.

60. Quotes from the North Carolina law in John Codman Hurd, *The Law of Freedom and Bondage in the United States* (Boston: Little, Brown, 1862; reprint, New

York: Negro University Press, 1968), 2:85; *The Public Acts of the General Assembly of North Carolina Containing the Acts from 1790–1803* (New Bern: Martin and Ogden, 1804), 120–21. The South Carolina quotes in *Acts and Resolutions of the General Assembly, of the State of South-Carolina Passed in December, 1800* (Columbia: Daniel and J. J. Faust, 1801), 39–41. The law could also involve slave children. See Records of the General Assembly, Petition of George Bellinger to the House of Representatives, ca. 1808, ND #1,804, SCDAH. Georgia quote in Hurd, *The Law of Freedom and Bondage*, 2:102. Virginia quote in *Supplement to the Revised Code of the Laws of Virginia: Being a Collection of All the Acts of the General Assembly of a Public and Permanent Nature Passed Since the Year 1819* (Richmond: Samuel Shepherd, 1833), 236. The law passed on 25 February 1824. It also stipulated that the overseers of the poor in the county or corporation "where such slave shall be found" were required to provide maintenance for the slave and charge the owner on a quarterly or annual basis.

Tennessee law in *The Statute Laws of the State of Tennessee, of a Public and General Nature* (Knoxville: S. Heiskell, 1831), 308.

61. Rules and Regulations for Plantation Management, William P. Gould, 23 December 1837, Manuscript Division, ADAH; see also Rules of J. W. Fowler for the Regulation and Treatment of his Negroes, Friars Point, Mississippi, 1859, in John W. Stovall Papers, ADAH.

62. William Phineas Browne to Margaret Browne, 22 April 1859, William Phineas Browne Papers, Correspondence, ADAH. For Browne's refusal to purchase a literate slave, see Grafton Gardner to William Phineas Browne, 18 November 1860, ibid.

63. Charles Ellis to Payne and Turner, 3 January 1837, Ellis and Allan Company Papers, LC.

64. J. H. Taylor to F. H. Elmore, 29 December 1842, Franklin H. Elmore Papers, LC. It appears that the two discovered their destiny; an inventory taken of estate slaves five weeks later in Columbia, South Carolina, included Andrew but not Isaac. The inventory was made 7 February 1843.

65. J. Meriwether to Edward Telfair, 7 March 1795, Telfair Papers, Manuscripts Division, Duke University, Durham, North Carolina; quote "no more of them will run away" in Ann Butler to Thomas Butler, 1 June 1838, Butler (Thomas and Family) Papers, Special Collections, Hill Memorial Library, LSU; "wd have sent it sooner" in C. G. McMurry to Dickinson Hill and Company, 25 February 1856, Chase Family Papers, LC. Columbus, on the Alabama state line, was about eighty-five miles west of Perry, the county seat of Houston County, Georgia, but the road mileage made the trip longer.

66. John M. Chapron to James Martin, 7 February 1839, 11 July 1838, 21, 22 August 1838, 25 May 1839, 9 August 1839, 10 September 1839, 22 July 1840, 8 September 1840, 22 April 1841, 12 May 1841, Chapron Letterbook, Manuscript Division, ADAH; John M. Chapron to Dr. L. L. Beverly, 26 April 1840; John M. Chapron to John McRae, 23 July 1840, 3 May 1841, 3, 8 June 1841, in ibid.

67. Baltimore City Register of Wills (Petitions), Michael Moan vs. William Jones, Negro Boy, Orphans Court of Baltimore City, 25 April 1855, reel M-11,026, SC, MSA; William Brooks vs. Hester, Orphans Court of Baltimore City, 26 November 1855, in ibid.; John T. Fardy vs. Daniel, 8 December 1855, in ibid; Mary B. Duvall vs. Delia, 11 February 1855, in ibid.; James A. Reed vs. Charles H. Pines, 11 February 1856, in ibid.; John Merriman to Mary Weeks, 13 November 1840, Weeks (David and Family) Papers, Special Collections, Hill Memorial Library, LSU; J. D. Terrell and Robert Hughes to Jeremiah Pritchett, 17 July 1837, John Dabney Terrell Correspondence, Manuscripts Division, ADAH; Diary of John B. Traylor, 10 March 1834, 30 March 1834, 2 April 1834, typescript, ibid.

68. Charles Ellis to A. H. Adamsborough, 26 April 1839, Ellis and Allan Company Papers, Manuscripts Division, LC; James A. Tait to Postmaster at Greenville, 7 December 1842, Charles Tait Papers, Manuscripts Division, ADAH.

69. John Merriman to A. F. Conrad, 30 August 1839, and John Merriman to F. D. Richardson, 29 December 1840, Weeks (David and Family) Papers, Special Collections, Hill Memorial Library, LSU; William Phineas Browne to Margaret Browne, 17 August 1860, William Phineas Browne Papers, Correspondence, ADAH; Jefferson quoted in Jack McLaughlin, *Jefferson and Monticello: The Biography of a Builder* (New York: Henry Holt, 1988), 96, 116.

70. See A. T. Conrad to Mary Weeks, 5 February 1841, Weeks (David and Family) Papers, Special Collections, Hill Memorial Library, LSU; Day Book and Diary of James Monette, 26, 29, 30 September 1848, typescript, Manuscript Division, LC; Journal of James Monroe Torbert, 12, 19 March 1849, typescript, Manuscript Division, ADAH.

CHAPTER 11

1. Testimony of William Butler, ca. 1821, in Records of the Circuit Court, Barren County, Kentucky, Equity Judgments, Henry Dickerson vs. John Butler, 9 July 1821, Case #192, reel #209,794, KDLA.

2. Petition of Henry Dickerson to the Circuit Court, in Records of the Circuit Court, Barren County, Kentucky, Equity Judgments, Henry Dickerson vs. John Butler, 9 July 1821, Case #192, reel #209,794, KDLA.

3. Legislative Petitions, Petition of John G. Brown and William Morris to the Virginia General Assembly, 24 December 1801, Greenbrier County, VSA. For the decline in value of slaves known to be runaways or rebellious, see Judith Kelleher Schafer, *Slavery, the Civil Law, and the Supreme Court of Louisiana* (Baton Rouge: Louisiana State University Press, 1994), 108–10, 136–46. Information on Allen Henson in T. Stephen Whitman, *The Price of Freedom: Slavery and Manumission in Baltimore and Early National Maryland* (Lexington: University of Kentucky Press, 1997), 47, 54.

4. Records of the Equity Court, Charleston District, South Carolina, Bills, William Rouse vs. Vernon, 21 February 1800, Case #1, SCDAH; Records of the Superior Court, Greene County, Georgia, Henry Peeples vs. William Harris, August 1803, in Record Book 1803–1806, 498–502, and Proceedings 1803–1806, 389–94, County Court House, Greensboro, Georgia.

5. Records of the Parish Court, West Baton Rouge, Louisiana, Fourth District Court, Pailhes vs. Hiriart, 5 June 1820, #80, Parish Court House, Port Allen, Louisiana. In civil law, "redhibitory" vices were those that made a slave "totally or virtually unusable." Pailhes "warranted against all redhibitory Diseases" and "against the claim or claims of any Person or persons whomsoever," but had said nothing about the slave's propensity to run away or about deafness. Prince George's County Court (Court Papers, Blacks), Charles Digges vs. Negro Enoch, 13 November 1848, reel M-11,024, SC, MSA; Bill of Sale, 27 June 1848, with ibid.

6. Records of the Circuit Court, Davidson County, Tennessee, Copy of Petition Archibald H. Harris vs. Joseph Cook, 1 June 1817; in Records of the Supreme Court, Middle District, Hays vs. Dale, 19 December 1817, Box 15, TSLA.

7. Prince George's County Court (Court Papers, Blacks), Petition of Thomas Baldwin to the County Court, 8 July 1850, reel M-11,024, SC, MSA; Baltimore City Register of Wills (Petitions), Michael Moan vs. William Jones, Negro Boy, Orphans Court of Baltimore City, 25 April 1855, reel M-11,026, SC, MSA; Records of the Parish Court, West Feliciana Parish, Louisiana, Third District Court, Collins Blackman vs. Matthias Wicker, 4 August 1826, #358, Parish Court House, Francisville, Louisi-

ana; Matthias Wicker vs. Mary Rice, 17 August 1826, #361, in ibid.; Copy of Petition of Cezar Jackson, free man of color, to the Circuit Court of Wilkinson County, Mississippi, 6 January 1826, with the Wicker vs. Rice suit; Records of the Circuit Court, Ste. Genevieve County, Missouri, Henry Crane vs. Toussaint Lahay and Eloy LeCompte, 3 May 1851, County Court House, Ste. Genevieve, Missouri. Information about Lewis in Records of the Circuit Court, Ste. Genevieve County, Missouri; Testimony of John P. Phillips, 25 March 1852, in Henry Crane vs. Toussaint Lahay and Eloy LeCompte, 3 May 1851, County Court House, Ste. Genevieve, Missouri.

8. Records of the Circuit Court, Ste. Genevieve County, Missouri, Henry Crane vs. Toussaint Lahay and Eloy LeCompte, 3 May 1851, County Court House, Ste. Genevieve, Missouri; Records of the Circuit Court, Ste. Genevieve County Missouri, Amended Petition of Henry Crane to the Ste. Genevieve Circuit Court, 1 December 1851, County Court House, Ste. Genevieve, Missouri. Apparently the New Orleans slave trader, Elihu Creswell, who agreed to sell Lewis, knew something was wrong because he "did not keep the negro in his yard because said Negro was not a saleable negro, or such a one as he would wish to associate with his negroes." Testimony of John P. Phillips, 25 March 1852, with ibid.

9. William Palfrey to Mary Weeks, 9 February 1841, Weeks (David and Family) Papers, Special Collections, Hill Memorial Library, LSU; Records of the Parish Court, West Baton Rouge, Louisiana, Fourth District Court, Pailhes vs. Hiriart, 5 June 1820, #80, Parish Court House, Port Allen, Louisiana. Example of the two-month rule in Records of the First District Judicial Court, Orleans Parish, Louisiana, Henry A. Bullard vs. Benjamin C. Eaton, 7 December 1835, Case #12,711, reel 27, Louisiana Collection, New Orleans Public Library.

10. Affidavit of John and James Porter, 12 December 1828, Sworn Before Clerk of Court, Shelby County, Kentucky, Natchez Trace Slaves and Slavery Collection, Center for American History, University of Texas at Austin; Virginia document in Affidavit of Benjamin F. Lipscomb and Lewis Rawlings, 19 October 1829, Sworn Before Justice of the Peace, Clerk of Court, and Magistrate, Spotsylvania County, Virginia, Natchez Trace Slaves and Slavery Collection, Center for American History, University of Texas at Austin.

11. Prince George's County Court (Court Papers, Blacks), Charles Digges vs. Negro Enoch, 13 November 1848, reel M-11,024, SC, MSA; Bill of Sale, 27 June 1848, with ibid. Records of the Superior Court, Wilkes County, Georgia, John Moss vs. Raphael Wheeler, February 1812, in Records of Suits 1817–1819, 6–8, County Court House, Washington, Georgia. The suit was brought in the inferior court and appealed to the superior court; a copy of the original petition was included in the appellate case. Records of the Parish Court, West Baton Rouge, Louisiana, Fourth District Court, Pailhes vs. Hiriart, 5 June 1820, #80, Parish Court House, Port Allen, Louisiana; Records of the Superior Court, Greene County, Georgia, Henry Peeples vs. William Harris, August 1803, in Record Book 1803–1806, 498–502, and Proceedings 1803–1806, 389–94, County Court House, Greensboro, Georgia; other instances in Records of the Equity Court, Charleston District, South Carolina, Bills, William Rouse vs. Vernon, 21 February 1800, Case #1, SCDAH.

12. Legislative Records, Petition of S. T. Robinson, Samuel Stoney, et al. to the South Carolina Senate and House of Representatives, ca. 1843, ND #2,824, SCDAH. In 1837, Mississippi passed "An act to prohibit the introduction of slaves into this State as merchandise, or for sale." The act was repealed in 1846. John Codman Hurd, *The Law of Freedom and Bondage in the United States* (Boston: Little, Brown, 1862; reprint, New York: Negro Universities Press, 1968), 2:148. In 1827, Alabama passed "An act to prohibit the importation of slaves into this state for sale or hire." In 1832,

a new law permitted specified groups (guardians, heirs, legatees, distributees, and husbands) to bring slaves into the state. *Acts Passed at the Eighth Annual Session of the General Assembly of the State of Alabama, Begun and Held in the Town of Tuscaloosa* (Tuscaloosa: Grantland and Robinson, 1827), 44–45; *Acts Passed at the Thirteenth Annual Session of the General Assembly of the State of Alabama, Begun and Held in the Town of Tuscaloosa, on the Third Monday in November, one Thousand Eight Hundred and Thirty-one* (Tuscaloosa: Wiley, McGuire and Henry, 1832), 12–18. Awareness in Delaware shown in Records of the General Assembly, Legislative Papers, Petition of Citizens of Sussex County to the Delaware Senate and House of Representatives, 10 February 1837, Record Group 1111, DSA.

13. Records of the Equity Court, Laurens District, South Carolina, Bills, William B. Bell and William T. Metts vs. David Stoddard and Thomas M. Sloan, 1860, Case #11, reel LR20, SCDAH. It was ironic that the partners, who tried to deceive buyers, were themselves deceived. Sam was neither intractable nor a runaway, Metts discovered, but a "Lunatic, imbecile and a fool." It was all a ploy, he said, to sell a "worthless" slave. During the summer, he toured Alabama and Mississippi, selling and trading human property, but he "could get no offer" for Sam.

14. Legislature Petitions, Petition of William H. Griggs to the Virginia General Assembly, 2 March 1839, Jefferson County, VSA; Anne Arundel County Register of Wills (Petitions and Orders) 1840–51, 226–28, Petition of James H. Watkins to the Orphans Court, 15 February 1848, reel #CR 63,127-2, MSA; Records of the Missouri Supreme Court, Marquis W. Withers vs. Steamer *El Paso*, July 1856, Case #23, Box 72, Missouri State Archives, Jefferson City, Missouri; Records of the Missouri Supreme Court, Deposition of Budeye M. Lynch, 19 January 1855, 35, Case #23, Box 72, Missouri State Archives, Jefferson City, Missouri; *Tennessee Republican Banner*, 14 June 1851; Records of the County Court, Caswell County, North Carolina, Petition of Nicholas Wylie of Wilkes County, Georgia, April 1845, Miscellaneous Slave Records 1836–64, NCDAH. Information on Cobun in Samuel Cobun to Abraham Barnes, 25 June 1828, 10 July 1828, Barnes-Willis Family Papers, Box 2E529, folder 5, Center for American History, University of Texas at Austin. Samuel Cobun's named is spelled Coburn in a few sources, but Cobun is the correct spelling. See *Biographical and Historical Memoirs of Mississippi*, 2 vols. (Chicago: Goodspeech Publishing, 1891), 2: 981; Harris Gaylord Warren, "Vignettes of Culture in Old Claiborne," *Journal of Mississippi History* 22 (July 1958), 129.

15. John Peters to A. P. Bagby, 3 January 1839, A. P. Bagby Papers, Correspondence, ADAH.

16. For a case in South Carolina where the plaintiff, H. Craft, won $1,000 in damages from William D. Martin, who stole his slave Charlotte, see H. Craft vs. William D. Martin, 19 November 1829, Franklin H. Elmore Papers, Manuscripts Division, LC; also see *Tennessee Gazette*, 4 April 1807; *Nashville Whig*, 14, 21, 28 April 1813; *Richmond Enquirer*, 23 September 1806, 29 April 1853; *New Orleans Bee*, 7 March 1835, 19 April 1841. Quotes on stealing in Isaac Briggs to Dudley Chase, 5 February 1817, Isaac Briggs Papers, Manuscripts Division, LC. John Dabney Terrell to Thomas Ringgold, 12 November 1836, John Dabney Terrell Papers, Correspondence, ADAH; Jeremiah Pritchett to Court of Marengo County, 21 June 1837, John Dabney Terrell Papers, Correspondence, ADAH.

17. Records of the Circuit Court, Washington County, Tennessee, John Newnan vs. Montgomery Stewart, 4 October 1815, in Civil and Criminal Cases, Accession #18, Box 74, folder 10, Archives of Appalachia, East Tennessee State University, Johnson City, Tennessee. Following the death of Thomas Stewart, the above suit was filed on appeal from a lower court case won by Montgomery for $544 in damages. The case

went to the state supreme court, which ruled in favor of Dr. Newnan. Rachel's daughter Patt is mentioned only a few times in the proceedings, but was specifically not mentioned as being in jail in North Carolina. Although Patt was not mentioned in the discussion of Dr. Newnan's repossession, the Stewart suit sought the return of both slaves, and thus the doctor probably took both slaves on the night he sneaked onto the Stewart farm. See Bill of Exceptions, An Appeal to the Supreme Court, [1816], and Transcript of Orders, John Newnan vs. Montgomery Stewart, 15 February 1817, with ibid.

18. Discussion of mental problems and personalities in Testimony of William Butler, ca. 1821, in Records of the Circuit Court, Barren County, Kentucky, Equity Judgments, Henry Dickerson vs. John Butler, 9 July 1821, Case #192, reel #209,794 KDLA; Records of the First Judicial District Court, Orleans Parish, Louisiana, Case Records, Adelaide Duvigneau vs. Louis Lanoix, 20 January 1820, #2,839, reel 5, Louisiana Collection, New Orleans Public Library; Records of the Third Judicial District Court, East Baton Rouge, Louisiana, Philip Hicky vs. Isham P. Fox, 24 December 1836, #2,258, East Baton Rouge Parish Archives, Baton Rouge, Louisiana; Testimony of T. G. Morgan, filed 13 January 1841, with ibid.

19. Samuel Cartwright, "Diseases and Peculiarities of the Negro Race," *De Bow's Southern and Western Review* 11 (September 1851), 331–33.

20. Legislative Petitions, Petition of the Citizens of James City, York, and surrounding counties to the Virginia General Assembly, 11 January 1858, Middlesex County, VSA; Certificate of A. H. Perkins, 8 November 1856, written on signature page of above petition. *Charleston Mercury and Morning Advertiser*, 14 November 1822; *Charleston Mercury*, 10 April 1826; *Charleston Mercury and Morning Advertiser*, 26 July 1825; *Charleston Mercury and Morning Advertiser*, 8 January 1825; *Charleston Mercury*, 10 August 1829.

21. *Charleston Mercury*, 17 August 1829.

22. Winthrop D. Jordan, *White Over Black: American Attitudes Toward the Negro, 1550–1812* (Chapel Hill: University of North Carolina Press, 1968), 381–82, 383 n. 14.

23. Legislative Petitions, Petition of Sundry Inhabitants of the City of Richmond to the Virginia General Assembly, 20 December 1804, Richmond City, VSA. Later arguments in *Charleston Mercury and Morning Advertiser*, 22 April 1825. Southern whites' concerns in Jordan, *White Over Black*, 383 n. 14; Legislative Records, Petition of William H. Harrison, R. G. Dunn, Richard Harrison, et al. to the Virginia General Assembly, 13 December 1859, Prince George County, and Petition of Residents and Propertyholders of Louisa County to the Virginia General Assembly, 21 December 1859, Louisa County, VSA.

24. Rachel O'Connor to A. T. Conrad, 26 May 1836, Weeks (David and Family) Papers, Special Collections, Hill Memorial Library, LSU; Rachel O'Connor to Aldred Conrad, 3 August 1835, in Allie Bayne Windham Webb, ed., *Mistress of Evergreen Plantation: Rachel O'Connor's Legacy of Letters, 1823–1845* (Albany: State University of New York Press, 1983), 173; Rachel O'Connor to Mary Weeks, 11 January 1830, and 26 December 1834, Weeks (David and Family) Papers, Special Collections, Hill Memorial Library, LSU.

25. *Nashville Whig*, 14, 21, 28 April 1813; *Richmond Enquirer*, 23 September 1806; *New Orleans Bee*, 19 March 1835; *New Orleans Picayune*, 17 July 1840; Records of the District Court, Travis County, Texas, Benjamin and Isabella Grumbles vs. John and Benjamin P. Grumbles, 29 December 1852, Case #222, reel #9, County Court House, Austin, Texas; *Tennessee Republican Banner*, 21 April 1838.

26. *Tennessee Republican Banner*, 2 June 1841; *Tennessee Republican Banner*, 2

June 1841; *Tennessee Republican Banner*, 1 October 1841. See also *New Orleans Picayune*, 2, 9 June 1839; *Charleston Mercury and Morning Advertiser*, 15 December 1824, 8 January 1825; *Charleston Mercury*, 25 February 1831.

27. *New Orleans Picayune*, 19 June 1839.

28. Records of the Superior Court, Jefferson County, Georgia, John Pettit vs. James Neely, April 1804, in Minutes 1803–1809, 112–16, County Court House, Louisville, Georgia; Records of the Superior Court, Jones County, Georgia, William Jordon vs. Nathaniel Perrott, January 1821, Case #15, in Minutes 1822, 293–95, County Court House, Gray, Georgia.

Since it was the slaveholding class being sued, the plaintiffs were rarely awarded large amounts. In *Pettit vs. Neely*, a jury awarded the plaintiff twenty-five dollars. Records of the Superior Court, Jefferson County, Georgia, John Pettit vs. James Neely, April 1804, in Minutes 1803–1809, 112–16, County Court House, Louisville, Georgia.

In the second case, *Jordon vs. Perrott*, the jury "considered the case as settled" and found for the plaintiff the cost of the suit, or $12.50. Records of the Superior Court, Jones County, Georgia, William Jordon vs. Nathaniel Perrott, January 1821, Case #15, in Minutes 1822, 293–95, County Court House, Gray, Georgia.

In the *Hemby* case, a jury found for the defendant. Records of the Superior Court, Oglethorpe County, Georgia, John W. Hemby vs. John Appling, 26 August 1831, in Minutes 1830–1833, 231–32, County Court House, Lexington, Georgia.

29. Petition of Citizens and Property Owners of McClennan County to the Texas Legislature, n.d., ca. 1850s, TSA; Legislative Petitions, Petition of Propertyholders of Louisa County to the Virginia General Assembly, 21 December 1859, VSA. For a similar remonstrance, see Legislative Petitions, Petition of P. Smith, Edward Turner, J. W. Patterson, et al. to the Virginia General Assembly, 10 January 1860, Fauquier County, VSA.

Draft Resolution to the Committee for Courts of Justice, ca. 1860, found with Legislative Petitions, Petition of George H. Burwell et al. to the Virginia Senate and House of Delegates, ca. 1860, Frederick County, VSA. This Draft Resolution was found with a group of petitions from Frederick, Jefferson, and Clarke counties seeking to exempt one slave from "all legal process for debt." This, the petitioners contend, would bring "negro property within the means of the Poor as well as the Rich." Though located with Frederick County petitions, the Resolution is attached to a petition from George H. Burwell of Clarke County. The Fugitive Slave Act of 1850 was designed to make it easier for slave owners to recapture runaways to the North. It affirmed that fugitive slaves were the owner's property and could be redeemed anywhere in the free states.

30. Quote of "the liberty of his wife" in Legislative Petitions, Petition of Rockingham and Adjacent Counties to the Virginia General Assembly, 30 January 1849, Rockingham County, VSA; "discord and disaffection" in Legislative Petitions, Petition of David M. Erwin, Thomas C. Burwell, William B. Woods, et al. to the Virginia General Assembly, ca. 1850, Greenbrier County, VSA.

31. Among the numerous articles on the subject were "Slavery and the Bible," *De Bow's Review* 9 (September 1850), 281–86; Henry H. Boardman, "The South's Power to Preserve Her Slaves," ibid. 10 (March 1851), 367–69; D. J. McCord, "How the South is Affected by Her Slave Institutions," ibid. 9 (October 1851), 349–63; J. B. D. De Bow, "Something Better for the South than the Fugitive Slave Law," ibid. 13 (July 1852), 90–93; "Management of Slaves," ibid. 13 (August 1852), 193–94; "Relation of Master and Slave in Louisiana and the South," ibid. 15 (September 1853), 275–77; "Southern Slavery and Its Assailants," ibid. 15 (November 1853), 486–96; and George Fitzhugh, "The Slave Trade," ibid. 22 (May 1857), 449–62.

Census data in *Statistical View of the United States . . . Being a Compendium of the Seventh Census* (Washington D.C.: Beverley Tucker, 1854), 64; *Population of the United States in 1860; Compiled from the Original Returns of the Eighth Census* (Washington, D.C.: Government Printing Office, 1864), xv–xvi.

32. For the small number of advertised runaways in All Saints Parish, South Carolina, see Charles Joyner, *Down By the Riverside: A South Carolina Slave Community* (Urbana: University of Illinois Press, 1984), 27–28.

33. Carroll County Court (Equity Papers) 47, Catherine Biggs vs. Daniel Poole, 2 September 1839, reel M-11,020, SC, MSA. The suit was brought because a paper ostensibly authorizing the son-in-law to return the runaways was, in fact, a deed empowering him to sell the slaves on the farm to "foreign purchasers." The illiterate Catherine signed the deed, but later obtained an injunction to block the sales. Injunction, 2 September 1839, with ibid. Records of the Circuit Court, Boyle County, Kentucky, Equity Court, Chancery Cases, Henry Goodloe vs. John R. Shannon, 10 May 1847, Box 45, KDLA; Final Decree of the Boyle County Circuit Court, March 1848, with ibid.; Records of the Chancery Court, Giles County, Tennessee, Case Files, Petition of James P. Nelson, 27 November 1855, Case #1,309, reel #178, frames 2,739–40, 2,765–70, TSLA; Plantation Record Book, 1848–1851, Kiger Family Papers, Natchez Trace Slaves and Slavery Collection, 2E636, Center for American History, University of Texas at Austin.

34. Chancery Court (Chancery Papers) 2, 764, Samuel Jay vs. Hannah Boyce, 25 July 1811, reel M 11,081, SC, MSA. The mortgage deed is quoted in the bill of complaint in the above case. See also T. Stephen Whitman, "Industrial Slavery at the Margin: The Maryland Chemical Works," *Journal of Southern History* 59 (February 1993), 46–47.

35. Reine Welham Plantation Record Book, December 1860, Special Collections, Hill Memorial Library, LSU. In 1805, listing the field hands on his plantations named Horshoe and Parker's Ferry in the Lower Mississippi River Valley, William Lowndes noted a total of seventy-two hands but added, "Primus and Cloe (m) have runaway and are not counted." List of Field Hands, William Lowndes Papers, 1805, LC.

36. Reine Welham Plantation Record Book, December 1860, Special Collections, Hill Memorial Library, LSU. The exact location of the Plantation is not given in the Record Book, but the Welham family owned two plantation tracts in St. James Parish. See Map of "Plantations on the Mississippi River from Natchez to New Orleans, 1858," at Hill Memorial Library, LSU. In all, the slave community consisted of 125 members, 81 males and 44 females. There were only 5 slaves listed ages thirteen to nineteen. The exact ages of 4 slaves listed under "Men" and 2 under "Women" (as opposed to lists for "Boys" and "Girls") were missing or illegible. John Miles, Jr., one of the runaways, was probably twenty years old, though the first numeral is not clear in the Record Book. In June 1860, a census taker listed William P. Welham, age sixty-two, as owning $150,000 in real estate on the Left Bank of the Mississippi, and $100,000 in personal property. Ninety-one-year-old Amelia Welham was also listed with personal property. The census taker counted 126 slaves (the census did not include names, only age, color, and gender and the owner's name). The ages did not match with the Record Book, but the latter is probably more accurate. The gender distribution in the census listing was 85 males and 41 females. United States Manuscript Population Census, St. James Parish, Louisiana, 1860, 18–19; United States Manuscript Slave Census, St. James Parish, Louisiana, 1860, 11.

37. Runaway Form for Slave John, 17 June 1855, Roach (Benjamin) Family Papers, Box 2E524, Center for American History, University of Texas at Austin.

38. Frederick Law Olmsted, *A Journey in the Back Country* (New York: Mason Brothers, 1860), 476.

39. Value of slaves in Ulrich B. Phillips, "The Economics of the Slave Trade, Foreign and Domestic," *The Slave Economy of the Old South: Selected Essays in Economic and Social History*, ed. Eugene D. Genovese (Baton Rouge: Louisiana State University Press, 1968), 142. Elmore's costs for retrieval in Bill for Advertising Boy Jacob, with E. W. Harrison, agent to A. R. Porter, 2 May 1838, and Franklin H. Elmore to Daniel Moorer, [1835,] Franklin H. Elmore Papers, LC. The second letter appears to be incorrectly dated 14 November 1834. In an unusual case, Col. W. Nesbitt of the Nesbitt Manufacturing Company paid $100 to get a slave out of jail. Receipt of G. Cannon to Col. W. Nesbitt, 31 October 1838, ibid.

40. Specific costs for retrieval in Account Book of E. H. Stokes, 1856, Chase Family Papers, LC. Owners' complaints in Anne Arundel County Register of Wills (Petitions and Orders) 1840–51, 179–80, 237–38, Petition of Thomas Brice to the Orphans Court, 23 February 1847, and Petition of James W. Allen to the Orphans Court, 28 April 1848, reel #CR 63,127-2, MSA; Anne Arundel County Register of Wills (Petitions and Orders) 1840–51, 238–39, Petition of James B. Stockett to the Orphans Court, 24 July 1855, reel #CR 63,128-1, MSA; Record of Expenses, 21 June 1860, Charles Bruce Family Papers, LC. A Virginia planter, Bruce paid $10, for "having a negro taken up."

Anne Arundel County Register of Wills (Petitions and Orders) 1840–51, 349–50, Stevens Gambrill vs. Negro Boy Brice, 26 February 1850, reel #CR 63,127-2, MSA.

41. W. S. Cothran to William Browne, 13 September 1860, William Phineas Browne Papers, Manuscript Division, ADAH; Anne Arundel County Register of Wills (Petitions and Orders) 1840–51, 382–83, Petition of Daniel Duvall to the Orphans Court, 30 October 1850, reel #CR 63,127-2, MSA.

42. Jail Fees, Adams County, Mississippi, for slave Emily, 12 July 1857, and Jail Fees, Claiborne County, Mississippi, for slave Jim, 23 September 1858, Natchez Trace Slaves and Slavery Collection, folder on Fugitive Slaves, Center for American History, University of Texas at Austin; Bill For Making Branding Iron, To George Hawken for Use by Samuel Edwards, n.d., Warren County, Mississippi, Natchez Trace Slaves and Slavery Collection, folder on Fugitive Slaves, Center for American History, University of Texas at Austin.

43. The Memorial of Michael Bruner to the Mississippi Legislative Council, December 1809, Record Group 5, Series 524, Box 14, MDAH; Petition of Benjamin Browne to the Virginia General Assembly, 16 December 1809, Surry County, VSA. The owner claimed he had not received any notification. The county had several options under such circumstances: suing the owner, hiring or selling the slaves, or returning the slaves to the owner. In this case, the latter was most economical.

44. Substantial costs of retrieval in Petition of Jacob Duckworth to the Mississippi Legislature, 1830, Record Group 47, Volume 20, Petitions and Memorials, MDAH; Account of Expenses and Disbursements (made for Mrs. Kenly) by Isaac W. Conger on a Trip to Arkansas, 2 June 1846, [Claiborne County], Mississippi, Natchez Trace Slaves and Slavery Collection, folder on Fugitive Slaves, Center for American History, University of Texas at Austin; Records of the Probate Court, Lauderdale County, Mississippi, Estate of Elisha Collins, 21 July 1844, Box 4, folder 37, County Archives, Meridian, Mississippi.

In the Account of Expenses and Disbursements (made for Mrs. Kenly) by Isaac W. Conger on a Trip to Arkansas, 2 June 1846, [Claiborne County], Mississippi, Natchez Trace Slaves and Slavery Collection, folder on Fugitive Slaves, Center for American History, University of Texas at Austin, the "Bass Fee" was for sleeping accommodations. "Bass" refers to the coarse mat made of bast used as a mattress. Expenses of

Louisiana planter in Records of the Parish Court, Iberville Parish, Louisiana, Old Parish Court, Andre Langlois vs. Vincent Tenant, 19 May 1807, #1, Parish Court House, Plaquemine, Louisiana.

45. Complaints of small slaveholders in Howard County Register of Wills (Petitions), Petition of W. Worthington to the Orphans Court, 16 November 1852, Petition of John R. D. Thomas, 19 September 1854, and Petition of A. L. Mackey, 1854, reel M-11,024, SC, MSA; Records of the Probate Court, Lauderdale County, Mississippi, Estate of Elisha Collins, 21 July 1844, Box 4, folder 37, County Archives, Meridian, Mississippi.

46. Records of the Probate Court, Bastrop County, Texas, E. B. Alston vs. Executors of the Estate of James Alston, 19 January 1852, County Court House, Bastrop, Texas.

47. Hardships for small slaveholders in Records of the Chancery Court, Giles County, Tennessee, Case Files, Petition of James P. Nelson, 27 November 1855, Case #1,309, reel #178, frames 2,739–40, 2,765–70, TSLA; Deposition of William Ezell, 28 November 1855, with ibid.; Anne Arundel County Register of Wills (Petitions and Orders) 1851–60, 238–39, Petition of James B. Stockett to the Orphans Court, 24 July 1855, reel #CR 63,128-1, MSA; Baltimore County Register of Wills (Petitions and Orders), William W. Glenn vs. John Bacon, 7 August 1860, reel M-11,020, SC, MSA; Petition of William W. Glenn, 9 October 1860, with ibid.; Deposition of William Glover, 3 February 1860; Order of the Court, 16 October 1860, with ibid.

Account Book, Thomas Lynch Horry with Elias Horry, March 1828, Edward Frost Papers, Manuscripts Division, LC; Baltimore County Register of Wills (Petitions and Orders), Peter W. Gibbons vs. John Thomas Gray, 22 November 1853, reel M-11,020, SC, MSA; Records of the Equity Court, Charleston District, South Carolina, Petition of James W. Gray, Trustee, 5 March 1858, Case #681, Box 8, SCDAH; Samuel Edwards to R. W. Long, 30 December 1857, Natchez Trace Slaves and Slavery Collection, Oversize Box 2,325/v48, folder 1, Center for American History, University of Texas at Austin.

48. Baltimore County Register of Wills (Petitions and Orders), Estate of William E. Grimes, 2 October 1855, reel M-11,020, SC, MSA; St. Mary's County Court Register of Wills (Petitions), Petition of Henry Hammett, 9 January 1859, reel M-11,026, ibid; Annetta Irvine's escape detailed in Washington County Register of Wills (Petitions and Orders), Petition of Andrew Hagmire, 4 May 1858, reel M-11,027, SC, MSA. The owner was also given permission to sell her out of state.

49. Records of the Circuit Court, Jefferson County, Kentucky, Case Files, Bailey Riley vs. John James, 29 December 1835, Series 2, Case #70, Box 2-2, KDLA; Deposition of Richard Love, 16 April 1836, with ibid.; Records of the Circuit Court, Jefferson County, Kentucky, Case Files, Series 2, Ambrose D. Mann vs. Steamboat *Paul Jones*, 13 May 1837, Case #765, Box 2-14, KDLA; Deposition of Stephen Haskell, 18 September 1839, with ibid.; *New Orleans Bee*, 3 April 1829, 29 October 1829, 27 March 1830, 30 March 1831, 9, 11 13 August 1831; *New Orleans Picayune*, 2 June 1839, 18 March 1840; *Charleston Mercury*, 16 March 1832; *Charleston Mercury and Morning Advertiser*, 4 April 1822, 25 January 1823. Efforts of authorities in Records of the Equity Court, Charleston District, South Carolina, Petition of Alexander W. Marshall, 31 July 1846, #800, Box 1, SCDAH; Testimony of Moses Levy, 30 July 1846, with ibid.

50. Olmsted, *A Journey in the Back Country*, 30. Instructions contained in wills in Legislative Petitions, Petition of Mary Hunt to the Tennessee General Assembly, 7 January 1846, #143–1846, reel 17, TSLA; Copy of Last Will and Testament of Spencer T. Hunt, 9 December 1843, with ibid.

51. Legislative Petitions, Petition of John Royall to the General Assembly, 21 December 1802, Nottoway County, VSA; Deposition of Richard Dennis, 9 December 1802, and Deposition of Ransom Hudgings, 3 December 1802, with ibid.; Records of the General Assembly, Petition of Thomas Key to the South Carolina Senate, 27 November 1811, #142, SCDAH; Legislative Records, Petition of the Town Council of Georgetown to the South Carolina Senate, 16 November 1829, #98, SCDAH; Petition of John Wilson, William B. Pringle, et al. to the South Carolina Senate, 1829, #131, in ibid.; Records of the Parish Court, West Baton Rouge Parish, Louisiana, Smith vs. Blanchard, 5 July 1846, #299, Parish Court House, Port Allen, Louisiana; Diary of Frances M. Bumpass, 5 August 1844, Bumpass Papers, Southern Historical Collection, Chapel Hill, North Carolina.

52. Records of North Carolina General Assembly, Session Records, Testimony of Edwin Adams and Patience Johnson, 25 September 1818, with Petition of Citizens of Johnston County to the Attorney General of North Carolina, 25 September 1818, Session November–December 1818, Miscellaneous Petitions, Box 3, NCDAH; Records of the Second District Court, St. James Parish, Louisiana, Antoine Bayon vs. J. Vavasseur, 27 December 1819, #71, Parish Court House, Convent, Louisiana; *Nashville Whig*, 5, 12, 19 September 1815; Records of the District Court, Natchitoches Parish, Louisiana, William H. Strong vs. Clement Rachal, 12 November 1836, Case #1,474, Parish Court House, Natchitoches, Louisiana.

53. See Chapter 9, pp. 210–13, for profile of runaways; Drew Gilpin Faust, *James Henry Hammond and the Old South: A Design for Mastery* (Baton Rouge: Louisiana State University Press, 1982), 94, 95, 105.

54. William Dusinberre, *Them Dark Days: Slavery in the American Rice Swamps* (New York: Oxford University Press, 1996), 144–45. Friday, a habitual runaway, was sold. Among the seventy-five slaves on Manigault's plantation, runaways were fairly common, despite the fact that between 1833 and 1861 none was successful. See also Jeffrey R. Young, "Ideology and Death on a Savannah River Rice Plantation, 1833–1867: Paternalism amidst 'a Good Supply of Disease and Pain,' " *Journal of Southern History* 59 (November 1993), 691.

55. For a slave who was whipped to death for refusing to divulge information about his runaway friend, see Records of the General Assembly, Session Records, Petition of Joel H. Lane, A. Lucas, James F. Taylor, et al. to North Carolina Governor William Miller, ca. 1819, NCDAH.

56. Affidavit of Gary Dunn, Justice of the Peace, Jefferson Parish, Louisiana, 27 April 1852, in Felix Limongi Papers, LC; Hilliard (Mrs. Isaac H.) Diary, 17–20 June 1850, Special Collections, Hill Memorial Library, LSU.

57. Joseph Taper to Joseph Long, 11 November 1840, Joseph Long Papers, Special Collections Library, Duke University, Durham, North Carolina. Long was a resident of Stephensburg, Frederick County, Virginia. He had served in the Virginia militia during the War of 1812, as a captain of the local militia during the 1820s and 1830s, and a Democratic party election commissioner in later years. Taper asks Long to pass his letter along to his former owner Bryan Martin Stevens. The authors thank Linda McCurdy of Duke University for her assistance in providing information on Long.

Bibliography

Andrews, Matthew Page. *Tercentenary History of Maryland*. 4 vols. Chicago: S. J. Clark Publishing, 1925.

Aptheker, Herbert. *American Negro Slave Revolts*. New York: Columbia University Press, 1943.

———. "Maroons Within the Present Limits of the United States." *Journal of Negro History* 24 (April 1939): 167–84.

Ayers, Edward L. *Vengeance and Justice: Crime and Punishment in the Nineteenth-Century American South*. New York: Oxford University Press, 1984.

Ball, Charles. *Slavery in the United States: A Narrative of the Life and Adventures of Charles Ball, a Black Man*. New York: John S. Taylor, 1837. Reprint, New York: Kraus Reprint, 1969.

Ball, Douglas B. *Financial Failure and Confederate Defeat*. Urbana: University of Illinois Press, 1991.

Bancroft, Frederic B. *Slave Trading in the Old South*. Baltimore: J. H. Furst, 1931.

Bardolph, Richard, ed. *The Civil Rights Records: Black Americans and the Law, 1849–1970*. New York: Thomas Y. Crowell, 1970.

Bassett, John Spencer. *Slavery in the State of North Carolina*. Johns Hopkins University Studies in Historical and Political Science Series 17, nos 7, 8. Baltimore: Johns Hopkins University Press, 1899.

———. ed. *The Plantation Overseer As Revealed in His Letters*. Northampton, Mass.: Printed for Smith College, 1925.

Bauer, Raymond A., and Alice H. Bauer. "Day to Day Resistance to Slavery." *Journal of Negro History* 27 (October 1942): 388–419.

Bell, Malcolm, Jr. *Major Butler's Legacy: Five Generations of a Slaveholding Family*. Athens: University of Georgia Press, 1987.

Berlin, Ira. *Slaves Without Masters: The Free Negro in the Antebellum South*. New York: Pantheon Books, 1974.

Berry, Mary Frances, and John W. Blassingame. *Long Memory: The Black Experience in America*. New York: Oxford University Press, 1982.

Blackett, Richard J. M. *Beating Against the Barriers: Biographical Essays in Nineteenth-Century Afro-American History*. Baton Rouge: Louisiana State University Press, 1986.

Blassingame, John W. *The Slave Community: Plantation Life in the Antebellum South*. Rev. ed., 1979. New York: Oxford University Press, 1972.

Blight, David W. *Frederick Douglass's Civil War: Keeping the Faith in Jubilee.* Baton Rouge: Louisiana State University Press, 1989.

Blockson, Charles L. *Hippocrene Guide to The Underground Railroad.* New York: Hippocrene Books, 1994.

Bogger, Tommy L. *Free Blacks in Norfolk, Virginia, 1790–1860: The Darker Side of Freedom.* Charlottesville: University Press of Virginia, 1997.

Brackett, Jeffrey R. *The Negro in Maryland: A Study of the Institution of Slavery.* Baltimore: Johns Hopkins University Press, 1889.

Breeden, James O., ed. *Advice Among Masters: The Ideal in Slave Management in the Old South.* Westport, Conn.: Greenwood Press, 1980.

Bremner, Robert, ed. *Childhood and Youth In America: A Documentary History.* 2 vols. Cambridge, Mass.: Harvard University Press, 1970.

Brown, Canter, Jr. "The Sarrazota, or Runaway Negro Plantations: Tampa Bay's First Black Community, 1812–1821." *Tampa Bay History* 12 (fall/winter 1990): 5–19.

Brown, Letitia Woods. *Free Negroes in the District of Columbia, 1790–1846.* New York: Oxford University Press, 1972.

Burr, Virginia Ingraham, ed. *The Secret Eye: The Journal of Ella Gertrude Clanton Thomas, 1848–1889.* Chapel Hill: University of North Carolina Press, 1990.

Byrne, William A. "The Hiring of Woodson, Slave Carpenter of Savannah." *Georgia Historical Quarterly* 77 (summer 1993): 245–63.

Campbell, Randolph B. "Slave Hiring in Texas." *American Historical Review* 93 (February 1988): 107–14.

Campbell, Stanley W. *The Slave Catchers: Enforcement of the Fugitive Slave Law, 1850–1860.* Chapel Hill: University of North Carolina Press, 1972.

Carll-White, Allison. "South Carolina's Forgotten Craftsmen." *South Carolina Historical Magazine* 86 (January 1985): 32–38.

Carroll, Joseph. *Slave Insurrections in the United States, 1800–1865.* Boston: Chapman and Grimes, 1938. Reprint, New York: Negro Universities Press, 1968.

Catterall, Helen T., ed. *Judicial Cases Concerning American Slavery and the Negro.* 5 vols. Washington, D.C.: W. F. Roberts, 1932.

Celeski, David S. "The Shores of Freedom: The Maritime Underground Railroad in North Carolina, 1800–1860." *North Carolina Historical Review* 71 (April 1994): 174–206.

Chase, Judith Wragg. "American Heritage from Ante-Bellum Black Craftsmen." *Southern Folklore Quarterly* 42 (1978): 140–41.

Clifton, James M., ed. *Life and Labor on Argyle Island: Letters and Documents of a Savannah River Rice Plantation, 1833–1867.* Savannah: Beehive Press, 1978.

Cody, Cheryll Ann. "Sale and Separation: Four Crises for Enslaved Women on the Ball Plantations, 1764–1854," 119–42, In *Working Toward Freedom: Slave Society and Domestic Economy in the American South,* edited by Larry E. Hudson, Jr. Rochester, N.Y.: University of Rochester Press, 1994.

Cook, Harvey Toliver. *The Life and Legacy of David Rogerson Williams.* New York: n.p., 1916.

Coulter, E. Merton. "Slavery and Freedom in Athens, Georgia, 1860–66." *Georgia Historical Quarterly* 49 (September 1965): 264–93.

Craven, Avery O. *Rachel of Old Louisiana.* Baton Rouge: Louisiana State University Press, 1975.

Crow, Jeffrey. "Slave Rebelliousness and Social Conflict in North Carolina, 1775–1802." *William and Mary Quarterly* 37 (January 1980): 79–102.

Curry, Leonard. *The Free Black in Urban America, 1800–1850: The Shadow of the Dream.* Chicago: University of Chicago Press, 1981.

Davis, Edwin Adams, ed. *Plantation Life in the Florida Parishes of Louisiana, 1836–1846, As Reflected in the Diary of Bennet H. Barrow.* New York: Columbia University Press, 1943.

Davis, Edwin Adams, and William Ransom Hogan. *The Barber of Natchez.* Baton Rouge: Louisiana State University Press, 1954.

———, eds. *William Johnson's Natchez: The Ante-Bellum Diary of a Free Negro.* Baton Rouge: Louisiana State University Press, 1951.

Dawson, Joseph G. III. *The Louisiana Governors: From Iberville to Edwards.* Baton Rouge: Louisiana State University Press, 1990.

Dew, Charles. *Bond of Iron: Master and Slave at Buffalo Forge.* New York: W. W. Norton, 1994.

———. "David Ross and the Oxford Iron Works: A Study of Industrial Slavery in the Early Nineteenth-Century South." *William and Mary Quarterly,* 3d ser., 31 (April 1974): 189–224.

———. "Disciplining Slave Iron Workers in the Antebellum South: Coercion, Conciliation, and Accommodation." *American Historical Review* 79 (April 1974): 393–418.

Douglass, Frederick. *My Bondage and My Freedom.* New York: Miller, Orton and Milligan, 1855.

Dusinberre, William. *Civil War Issues in Philadelphia, 1856–1865.* Philadelphia: University of Pennsylvania Press, 1965.

———. *Them Dark Days: Slavery in the American Rice Swamps.* New York: Oxford University Press, 1996.

Eaton, Clement. "A Dangerous Pamphlet in the Old South," *Journal of Southern History* 2 (August 1936): 322–34.

———. "Slave-Hiring in the Upper South: A Step Toward Freedom." *Mississippi Valley Historical Review* 46 (March 1960): 663–78.

Egerton, Douglas R. *Gabriel's Rebellion: The Virginia Slave Conspiracies of 1800 and 1802.* Chapel Hill: University of North Carolina Press, 1993.

———. " 'Fly Across the River': The Easter Slave Conspiracy of 1802." *North Carolina Historical Review* 68 (April 1991): 87–110.

Elkins, Stanley. *Slavery: A Problem in American Institutional and Intellectual Life.* Chicago: University of Chicago Press, 1959.

Engs, Robert. *Freedom's First Generation: Black Hampton, Virginia, 1861–1890.* Philadelphia: University of Pennsylvania Press, 1979.

Faust, Drew Gilpin. *James Henry Hammond and the Old South: A Design for Mastery.* Baton Rouge: Louisiana State University Press, 1982.

Fields, Barbara Jeanne. *Slavery and Freedom on the Middle Ground: Maryland during the Nineteenth Century.* New Haven: Yale University Press, 1985.

Finkelman, Paul, ed. *Fugitive Slaves, Articles on American Slavery.* Vol. 6. New York: Garland Publishing, 1989.

Fitchett, E. Horace. "The Traditions of the Free Negro in Charleston, South Carolina." *Journal of Negro History* 25 (April 1940): 139–52.

Fox-Genovese, Elizabeth. *Within the Plantation Household: Black and White Women of the Old South.* Chapel Hill: University of North Carolina Press, 1988.

Franklin, John Hope. *The Free Negro in North Carolina, 1790–1860.* Chapel Hill: University of North Carolina Press, 1943.

———. *From Slavery to Freedom: A History of American Negroes.* New York: Alfred Knopf, 1947.

———. *The Militant South, 1800–1861.* Cambridge, Mass.: Harvard University Press, 1956.

———. "Slaves Virtually Free in Ante-Bellum North Carolina." *Journal of Negro History* 28 (July 1943): 284–310.

Fredrickson, George M., and Christopher Lasch. "Resistance to Slavery." *Civil War History* 4 (December 1967): 315–29.

Gara, Larry. *The Liberty Line: The Legend of the Underground Railroad.* Lexington: University of Kentucky Press, 1961.

Gatewood, Willard B., Jr. " 'To Be Truly Free': Louis Sheridan and the Colonization of Liberia."*Civil War History* 29 (December 1983): 332.

———, ed. *Slave and Freeman: The Autobiography of George L. Knox.* Lexington: University Press of Kentucky, 1979.

Genovese, Eugene. *From Rebellion to Revolution: Afro-American Slave Revolts in the Making of the Modern World.* Baton Rouge: Louisiana State University Press, 1979.

———. *Roll, Jordan, Roll: The World the Slaves Made.* New York: Pantheon Books, 1974.

———. *The Southern Front: History and Politics in the Cultural War.* Columbia: University of Missouri Press, 1995.

———. "Rebelliousness and Docility in the Negro Slave: A Critique of the Elkins Thesis." *Civil War History* 4 (December 1967): 293–314.

Goldin, Claudia. *Urban Slavery in the American South, 1820–1860: A Quantitative History.* Chicago: University of Chicago Press, 1976.

Goodstein, Anita Shafer. *Nashville 1780–1860: From Frontier to City.* Gainesville: University of Florida Press, 1989.

Gordon, Asa H. "The Struggle of the Negro Slaves for Physical Freedom." *Journal of Negro History* 13 (January 1928): 22–35.

Graham, Leroy. *Baltimore: The Nineteenth Century Black Capital.* New York: University Press of America, 1982.

Guild, June Purcell, comp. *Black Laws of Virginia: A Summary of the Legislative Acts of Virginia Concerning Negroes from Earliest Times to the Present.* Richmond: Whittet and Shepperson, 1936. Reprint, New York: Negro Universities Press, 1969.

Gutman, Herbert G. *The Black Family in Slavery and Freedom, 1750–1925.* New York: Pantheon Books, 1976.

Halasz, Nicholas. *The Rattling Chains: Slave Unrest and Revolt in the Antebellum South.* New York: D. McKay, 1966.

Hall, John A. " 'A Rigour of Confinement Which Violates Humanity': Jail Conditions in South Carolina During the 1790s." *Southern Studies: An Interdisciplinary Journal of the South* 24 (fall 1985): 284–94.

Harrold, Stanley. "Freeing the Weems Family: A New Look at the Underground Railroad." *Civil War History* 42 (December 1996): 289–306.

Hermann, Janet Sharp. *The Pursuit of a Dream.* New York: Oxford University Press, 1981.

Hicks, Peter P. *To Awaken My Afflicted Brethren: David Walker and the Problem of Antebellum Slave Resistance.* University Park: Pennsylvania State University Press, 1997.

Hirschfeld, Fritz. *George Washington and Slavery: A Documentary Portrayal.* Columbia: University of Missouri Press, 1997.

Hofstadter, Richard. "U. B. Phillips and the Plantation Legend." *Journal of Negro History* 29 (April 1944): 109–24.

Hughes, Sarah S. "Slaves for Hire: The Allocation of Black Labor in Elizabeth City County, Virginia, 1782–1820." *William and Mary Quarterly*, 3d ser., 35 (April 1978): 260–86.

Hurd, John Codman. *The Law of Freedom and Bondage in the United States*, 2 vols. Boston: Little, Brown, 1862. Reprint, New York: Negro Universities Press, 1968.

Jackson, Luther Porter. "Free Negroes of Petersburg, Virginia." *Journal of Negro History* 12 (July 1927): 365–88.

Johnson, Michael P. "Runaway Slaves and the Slave Communities in South Carolina, 1799 to 1830." *William and Mary Quarterly* 38 (July 1981): 418–41.

Johnson, Michael P., and James L. Roark. *Black Masters: A Free Family of Color in the Old South*. New York: W. W. Norton, 1984.

———, eds. *No Chariot Let Down: Charleston's Free People of Color on the Eve of the Civil War*. Chapel Hill: University of North Carolina Press, 1984.

Johnston, James Hugo. *Race Relations in Virginia and Miscegenation in the South, 1776–1860*. Amherst: University of Massachusetts Press, 1970.

———. "The Participation of White Men in Virginia Negro Insurrections." *Journal of Negro History* 16 (April 1931): 158–67.

Jones, Howard. *Mutiny on the Amistad: The Saga of a Slave Revolt and Its Impact on American Abolition, Law, and Diplomacy*. New York: Oxford University Press, 1987.

Jones, Norrece T., Jr. *Born a Child of Freedom, Yet a Slave: Mechanisms of Control and Strategies of Resistance in Antebellum South Carolina*. Hanover, N. H.: Wesleyan University Press, 1990.

Jordan, Winthrop D. *White Over Black: American Attitudes Toward the Negro, 1550–1812*. Chapel Hill: University of North Carolina Press, 1968.

Joyner, Charles. *Down By the Riverside: A South Carolina Slave Community*. Urbana: University of Illinois Press, 1984.

Kemble, Frances Anne. *Journal of Residence on a Georgian Plantation in 1838–1839*. 1863. Reprint, with introduction by John A. Scott, Athens: University of Georgia Press, 1984.

Kilson, Marion D. de B. "Towards Freedom: An Analysis of Slave Revolts in the United States." *Phylon* 25 (summer 1964): 175–87.

King, Wilma. *Stolen Childhood: Slave Youth in Nineteenth Century America*. Bloomington: Indiana University Press, 1995.

Koger, Larry. *Black Slaveowners: Free Black Slave Masters in South Carolina, 1790–1860*. Jefferson, N.C.: McFarland, 1985.

Kolchin, Peter. *American Slavery 1619–1877*. New York: Hill and Wang, 1993.

Leaming, Hugo Prosper. *Hidden Americans: Maroons of Virginia and the Carolinas*. New York: Garland Publishing, 1995.

Lebsock, Suzanne. *The Free Women of Petersburg: Status and Culture in a Southern Town, 1784–1860*. New York: W. W. Norton, 1984.

Levine, Lawrence W. *Black Culture and Black Consciousness: Afro-American Folk Thought from Slavery to Freedom*. New York: Oxford University Press, 1977.

Lichtenstein, Alex. " 'That Disposition to Theft, With Which They Have Been Branded': Moral Economy, Slave Management, and the Law." *Journal of Social History* 21 (spring 1988): 429–30.

Litwack, Leon F. *Been in the Storm So Long: The Aftermath of Slavery*. New York: Alfred A. Knopf, 1979.

Lofton, John. *Denmark Vesey's Revolt: The Slave Plot that Lit a Fuse to Fort Sumter*. Kent, Ohio: Kent State University Press, 1983.

McCord, David J. *The Statutes at Large of South Carolina*. Columbia: A. S. Johnson, 1840.

McDonnell, Lawrence T. "Money Knows No Master: Market Relations and the American Slave Community," 31–44. In *Developing Dixie: Modernization in a Traditional Society*, edited by Winfred B. Moore, Jr., et al. Westport, Conn.: Greenwood Press, 1988.

McFeely, William. *Frederick Douglass*. New York: W. W. Norton, 1991.

McGinty, Garnie William. *A History of Louisiana*. New York: The Exposition Press, 1949.

McKibben, Davidson B. "Negro Slave Insurrections in Mississippi, 1800–1865." *Journal of Negro History* 34 (January 1949): 73–90.

McLaughlin, Jack. *Jefferson and Monticello: The Biography of a Builder*. New York: Henry Holt, 1988.

McMillen, Sally G. *Southern Women: Black and White in the Old South*. Arlington Heights, Ill.: Harlan Davidson, 1992.

Malone, Ann Patton. *Sweet Chariot: Slave Family and Household Structure in Nineteenth-Century Louisiana*. Chapel Hill: University of North Carolina Press, 1992.

Martin, Waldo E., Jr. *The Mind of Frederick Douglass*. Chapel Hill: University of North Carolina Press, 1984.

Mathews, Donald G. "Charles Colcock Jones and the Southern Evangelical Crusade to Form a Biracial Community." *Journal of Southern History* 41 (August 1975): 299–320.

Meaders, Daniel E., ed. *Advertisements for Runaway Slaves in Virginia, 1801–1820*. New York: Garland Publishing, 1997.

———. "South Carolina Fugitives as Viewed Through Local Colonial Newspapers with Emphasis on Runaway Notices 1732–1801." *Journal of Negro History* 60 (April 1975): 288–319.

Miles, Edwin A. "The Mississippi Slave Insurrection Scare of 1835." *Journal of Negro History* 42 (January 1957): 48–60.

Miller, Randall M. "The Fabric of Control in Antebellum Textile Mills." *Business History Review* 55 (winter 1981): 475–90.

Moore, John Hebron. "Simon Gray, Riverman: A Slave Who Was Almost Free." *Mississippi Valley Historical Review* 49 (December 1962): 472–84.

Morgan, Philip D. "The Ownership of Property by Slaves in the Mid-Nineteenth-Century Low Country," *Journal of Southern History* 49 (August 1983): 399–420.

———. "Work and Culture: The Task System and the World of Lowcountry Blacks, 1700–1800." *William and Mary Quarterly*, 3d ser., 39 (October 1982): 563–99.

Morris, Richard B. "The Measure of Bondage in the Slave States." *Mississippi Valley Historical Review* 41 (September 1954): 219–40.

Morris, Thomas D. *Free Men All: The Personal Liberty Laws of the North, 1780–1861*. Baltimore: Johns Hopkins University Press, 1974.

———. *Southern Slavery and the Law, 1619–1860*. Chapel Hill: University of North Carolina Press, 1996.

Mullin, Gerald W. *Flight and Rebellion: Slave Resistance in Eighteenth-Century Virginia*. New York: Oxford University Press, 1972.

Mullin, Michael. *Africa in America: Slave Acculturation and Resistance in the American South and the British Caribbean, 1736–1831*. Urbana: University of Illinois Press, 1992.

Myers, Robert Mason, ed. *The Children of Pride: A True Story of Georgia and the Civil War*. New Haven: Yale University Press, 1972.

Northrup, Solomon. *Twelve Years A Slave, Narrative of Solomon Northrup, a Citizen of New York, Kidnapped in Washington City in 1841, and Rescued in 1853, from a Cotton Plantation Near the Red River in Louisiana*. Cincinnati: Henry W. Derby,

1853. Reprint, edited by Sue Eakin and Joseph Logsdon, Baton Rouge: Louisiana State University Press, 1968.

Oakes, James. *The Ruling Race: A History of American Slaveholders.* New York: Vintage Books, 1983.

O'Brien, John T. "Factory, Church, and Community: Blacks in Antebellum Richmond." *Journal of Southern History* 46 (November 1978): 509–36.

Olmsted, Frederick Law. *The Cotton Kingdom: A Traveller's Observations on Cotton and Slavery in the American Slave States.* Edited by Arthur M. Schlesinger. New York: Alfred A. Knopf, 1953.

———. *A Journey in the Back Country.* New York: Mason Brothers, 1860.

———. *A Journey in the Seaboard Slave States, With Remarks on Their Economy.* New York: Dix and Edwards, 1856.

Parker, Freddie L. *Running for Freedom: Slave Runaways in North Carolina, 1775–1840.* New York: Garland Publishing, 1993.

——— ed. *Stealing a Little Freedom: Advertisements for Slave Runaways in North Carolina, 1791–1840.* New York: Garland Publishing, 1994.

Penningroth, Dylan. "Slavery, Freedom, and Social Claims to Property among African Americans in Liberty County, Georgia, 1850–1880." *Journal of American History* 84 (September 1997): 405–35.

Phillips, Christopher. *Freedom's Port: The African American Community of Baltimore, 1790–1860.* Urbana: University of Illinois Press, 1997.

Phillips, Ulrich B. *American Negro Slavery: A Survey of the Supply, Employment, and Control of Negro Labor As Determined by the Plantation Regime.* New York: D. Appleton, 1918.

———. *Life and Labor in the Old South.* Boston: Little, Brown, 1929.

———. *The Slave Economy of the Old South: Selected Essays in Economic and Social History.* Edited by Eugene D. Genovese. Baton Rouge: Louisiana State University Press, 1968.

———, ed. *A Documentary History of American Industrial Society.* Cleveland, Ohio: Arthur H. Clark, 1910.

———. "The Slave Labor Problem in the Charleston District," 7–28. In *Plantation, Town and Country: Essays on the Local History of American Slave Society,* edited by Elinor Miller and Eugene Genovese. Urbana: University of Illinois Press, 1974.

Porter, Kenneth W. "Florida Slaves and Free Negroes in the Seminole War, 1835–1842." *Journal of Negro History* 28 (October 1943): 390–421.

———. "Negroes in the Seminole War, 1835–1842." *Journal of Southern History* 30 (November 1964): 427–50.

———. "Three Fighters for Freedom." *Journal of Negro History* 28 (January 1943): 51–72.

Preston, Dickson J. *Young Frederick Douglass: The Maryland Years.* Baltimore: Johns Hopkins University Press, 1980.

Proctor, William G., Jr. "Slavery in Southwest Georgia." *Georgia Historical Quarterly* 49 (March 1965): 1–22.

Quarles, Benjamin. "Freedom Fettered: Blacks in the Constitutional Era in Maryland, 1776–1810—An Introduction." *Maryland Historical Magazine* 84 (winter 1989), 299–304.

Rawick, George, ed. *The American Slave: A Composite Autobiography.* 19 vols. Westport, Conn.: Greenwood Publishing, 1972–.

Reuter, Edward Byron. *The Mulatto in the United States: Including a Study of the Role of Mixed-Blood Races Throughout the World.* Boston: Richard G. Badger, 1918.

Rivers, Larry E. "A Troublesome Property: Master-Slave Relations in Florida, 1821–1865." In *The African American Heritage of Florida*. ed. David R. Coburn and Jane L. Landers. (Gainesville: University Press of Florida, 1995): 104–27.

————. " 'Dignity and Importance': Slavery in Jefferson County, Florida—1827 to 1860." *Florida Historical Quarterly* 61 (April 1983): 404–30.

————. "Slavery in Microcosm: Leon County, Florida, 1824–1860." *Journal of Negro History* 46 (fall 1981): 235–45.

Rosengarten, Theodore. *Tombee: Portrait of a Cotton Planter with the Journal of Thomas B. Chaplin (1822–1890)*. New York: William Morrow, 1986.

Rowland, Eron, comp. *Life, Letters and Papers of William Dunbar of Elgin, Morayshire, Scotland, and Natchez, Mississippi*. Jackson: Press of the Mississippi Historical Society, 1930.

Russell, Marion J. "American Slave Discontent in Records of the High Courts." *Journal of Negro History* 31 (October 1946): 411–36.

Scarborough, William K. *The Overseer: Plantation Management in the Old South*. Baton Rouge: Louisiana State University Press, 1966.

Schafer, Judith Kelleher. *Slavery, the Civil Law, and the Supreme Court of Louisiana*. Baton Rouge: Louisiana State University Press, 1994.

————. "New Orleans Slavery in 1850 as Seen in Advertisements." *Journal of Southern History* 47 (February 1981): 33–56.

Schlotterbeck, John T. "The Internal Economy of Slavery in Rural Piedmont Virginia." In *The Slaves' Economy: Independent Production by Slaves in the Americas*, edited by Ira Berlin and Philip D. Morgan. London: Frank Cass, 1991.

Schwarz, Philip J. *Twice Condemned: Slaves and the Criminal Laws of Virginia, 1705–1865*. Baton Rouge: Louisiana State University Press, 1988.

————. "Gabriel's Challenge: Slaves and Crime in Late Eighteenth-Century Virginia." *Virginia Magazine of History and Biography* 90 (July 1982): 283–309.

Schweninger, Loren. *Black Property Owners in the South, 1790–1915*. Urbana: University of Illinois Press, 1990.

————, ed. *From Tennessee Slave to St. Louis Entrepreneur: The Autobiography of James Thomas*. With foreword by John Hope Franklin. Columbia: University of Missouri Press, 1984.

————. "The Underside of Slavery: The Internal Economy, Self-Hire, and Quasi-Freedom in Virginia, 1780–1865." *Slavery and Abolition: A Journal of Comparative Studies* 12 (September 1991): 1–22.

Smith, Ellen Hart. *Charles Carroll of Carrollton*. Cambridge, Mass.: Harvard University Press, 1942.

Stampp, Kenneth. *The Peculiar Institution: Slavery in the Ante-Bellum South*. New York: Alfred A. Knopf, 1956.

Starobin, Robert S. *Industrial Slavery in the Old South*. New York: Oxford University Press, 1970.

Stearns, Charles. *Facts in the Life of Gen. Taylor; The Cuba Blood-Hound Importer, the Extensive Slave-Holder, and the Hero of the Mexican War*. Boston: published by the author, 1848.

Strother, Horatio T. *The Underground Railroad in Connecticut*. Middletown, Conn.: Wesleyan University Press, 1962.

Sweig, Donald M. "Reassessing the Human Dimension of the Interstate Slave Trade." *Prologue* 12 (spring 1980): 5–21.

Syndor, Charles S. *Slavery in Mississippi*. Originally published, the American Historical Association, 1933. Baton Rouge: Louisiana State University Press, 1966.

Tadman, Michael. *Speculators and Slaves: Masters and Slaves in the Old South.* Madison: University of Wisconsin Press, 1989.

Tansey, Richard. "Out-of-State Free Blacks in Late Antebellum New Orleans." *Louisiana History* 22 (fall 1981): 369–86.

Taylor, R. H. "Slave Conspiracies in North Carolina." *North Carolina Historical Review* 5 (January 1928): 20–34.

Toplin, Robert Brent. "Peter Still Versus the Peculiar Institution." *Civil War History* 13 (December 1967): 340–49.

Wade, Richard C. *Slavery in the Cities: The South, 1820–1860.* New York: Oxford University Press, 1964.

———. "The Vesey Plot: A Reconsideration." *Journal of Southern History* 30 (May 1964): 143–61.

Wahl, Jenny Bourne, "The Bondsman's Burden: An Economic Analysis of the Jurisprudence of Slaves and Common Carriers." *Journal of Economic History* 53 (September 1993): 495–526.

Warren, Harris Gaylord. "Vignettes of Culture in Old Claiborne." *Journal of Mississippi History* 22 (July 1958): 125–46.

Webb, Allie Bayne Windham, ed. *Mistress of Evergreen Plantation: Rachel O'Connor's Legacy of Letters, 1823–1845.* Albany: State University of New York Press, 1983.

Weiner, Marli F. *Mistresses and Slaves: Plantation Women in South Carolina, 1830–80.* Urbana: University of Illinois Press, 1998.

White, Deborah. *Ar'n't I a Woman? Female Slaves in the Plantation South.* New York: W. W. Norton, 1985.

———. "Female Slaves: Sex Roles and Status in the Antebellum Plantation South." *Journal of Family History* 8 (fall 1983): 248–61.

White, Shane, and Graham White. "Slave Hair and African American Culture in the Eighteenth and Nineteenth Centuries." *Journal of Southern History* 61 (February 1995): 45–76.

White, William. "The Texas Slave Insurrection of 1860." *Southwestern Historical Quarterly* 52 (January 1949): 259–85.

Whitman, T. Stephen. "Industrial Slavery at the Margin: The Maryland Chemical Works." *Journal of Southern History* 59 (February 1993): 31–62.

———. *The Price of Freedom: Slavery and Manumission in Baltimore and Early National Maryland.* Lexington: University of Kentucky Press, 1997.

Whitten, David O. *Andrew Durnford: A Black Sugar Planter in Antebellum Louisiana.* Natchitoches, La.: Northwestern State University Press, 1981.

———. ed. "Slave Buying in Virginia as Revealed by Letters of a Louisiana Negro Sugar Planter." *Louisiana History* 11 (summer 1970): 231–44.

Wikramanayake, Marina. *A World in Shadow: The Free Black in Antebellum South Carolina.* Columbia: University of South Carolina Press, 1973.

Williams, Samuel. "Ann Robertson [Cockrill]: An Unsung Tennessee Heroine." *Tennessee Historical Quarterly* 3 (June 1944): 150–55.

Williamson, Joel. *New People: Miscegenation and Mulattoes in the United States.* New York: Free Press, 1980.

Wilson, Carol. *Freedom At Risk: The Kidnapping of Free Blacks in America, 1780–1865.* Lexington: University of Kentucky Press, 1994.

Wilson, Theodore B. *The Black Codes of the South.* University: University of Alabama Press, 1965.

Windley, Lathan Algerna. *A Profile of Runaway Slaves in Virginia and South Carolina from 1730 Through 1787.* New York: Garland Publishing, 1995.

Wish, Harvey. "American Slave Insurrections Before 1861." *Journal of Negro History* 22 (July 1937): 299–320.

——. "The Slave Insurrection Panic of 1856." *Journal of Southern History* 5 (May 1939): 206–22.

Wood, Betty. *Women's Work, Men's Work: The Informal Slave Economies of Low-country Georgia.* Athens: University of Georgia Press, 1995.

Wood, Peter H. "Whetting, Setting, and Laying Timbers: Black Builders in the Early South." *Southern Exposure* 8 (spring 1980): 3–8.

Wright, Donald R. *African Americans in the Early Republic, 1789–1831.* Arlington Heights, Ill.: Harlan Davidson, 1993.

Young, Jeffrey R. "Ideology and Death on a Savannah River Rice Plantation, 1833–1867: Paternalism amidst 'a Good Supply of Disease and Pain.'" *Journal of Southern History* 59 (November 1993): 673–706.

Credits

Page 58: Broadside, William Rogers and Townshend McVeigh, Middleburg, Loudoun County, Virginia, 25 December 1855, Chicago Historical Society, Prints and Photographs Department, #ICHi-22006, ADH #027, Chicago, Illinois.

Page 161: Courtesy of The Board of Trustees of the National Museums and Galleries on Merseyside (Walker Art Gallery, Liverpool, England).

Page 162: "Shooting Scene," ca. 1860, LCWZ62-056053. Reproduced from the Collections of the Library of Congress.

Page 171: Broadside, George G. Ashcom, St. Mary's County, Maryland, 3 November 1825, Broadsides Portfolio, 29-#23, Rare Book Room, Library of Congress.

Page 180: The Charleston Work House, *Harper's New Monthly Magazine* (July 1865), p. 145; Katharine Du Pre Lumpkin, *The Emancipation of Angelina Grimké* (Chapel Hill: University of North Carolina Press, 1974), pp. 3–4; Edward Ball, *Slaves in the Family* (New York: Farrar, Straus and Giroux, 1998), pp. 56, 151, 305; Kenneth Severens, *Charleston: Antebellum Architecture and Civic Destiny* (Knoxville: University of Tennessee Press, 1988), p. 160.

Page 193: "The Author writing down the narrative of several freeborn people of color who had been kidnapped," engraving by Alex Lawson. In Jesse Torrey, *American Slave Trade; or, An Account of the Manner in Which the Slave Dealers take free people from Some of the United States of America, and Carry them Away, and Sell them as Slaves in Other of the States* . . . (London: J. M. Cobbett, 1822), opposite p. 47. #LCWZ62–30837. Reproduced from the Collections of the Library of Congress.

Page 221: *Tennessee Republican Banner*, 26 December 1838.

Pages 265, 267: Broadside of Marshal's Sale of Runaway Joshua, Louisville, Kentucky, 6 November 1854, in Records of the Circuit Court, Jefferson County, Kentucky, Case Files, Case #9,884, Box 2-145, Kentucky Department for Libraries and Archives; Report to the Court, H. Dent, 26 October 1854, with ibid. See also Petition of George and Elizabeth Ghiselin to Louisville Chancery Court, July 1854, with ibid.

Page 270: Affidavit, William L. Shields and William A. Dickson, Bourbon County, Kentucky, 7 August 1830, Natchez Trace Collection, #CN09879, Center for American History, University of Texas Austin.

Page 271: Affidavit, Albemarle County, Virginia, 21 November 1829, Natchez Trace Collection, #CN09880, Center for American History, University of Texas Austin.

Page 284: *New Orleans Picayune*, 9 April 1856; Jail Form for Runaway Jim, Claiborne County, Mississippi, 25 September 1858, Natchez Trace Collection, #CN09877, American History Center, University of Texas Austin; Jail Form for Runaway Emily, Adams County, Mississippi, 5 September 1857, Natchez Trace Collection, #CN09878, Center for American History, University of Texas Austin.

Page 288: Account of Expenses to Recover "negroes run off," 2 June 1846, Natchez Trace Collection, #CN09876, Center for American History, University of Texas Austin.

Index

Italic page numbers indicate illustrations.

BENEATH THE DOVER SKY

GALE
CENGAGE Learning®

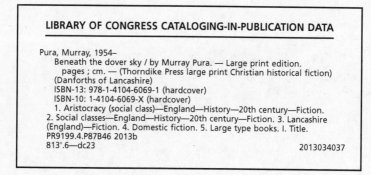

LIBRARY OF CONGRESS CATALOGING-IN-PUBLICATION DATA

Pura, Murray, 1954–
  Beneath the dover sky / by Murray Pura. — Large print edition.
    pages ; cm. — (Thorndike Press large print Christian historical fiction)
  (Danforths of Lancashire)
  ISBN-13: 978-1-4104-6069-1 (hardcover)
  ISBN-10: 1-4104-6069-X (hardcover)
  1. Aristocracy (social class)—England—History—20th century—Fiction.
2. Social classes—England—History—20th century—Fiction. 3. Lancashire
(England)—Fiction. 4. Domestic fiction. 5. Large type books. I. Title.
PR9199.4.P87B46 2013b
813'.6—dc23
                                                          2013034037

Published in 2014 by arrangement with Harvest House Publishers

Printed in Mexico
1 2 3 4 5 6 7 18 17 16 15 14

THE DANFORTHS OF LANCASHIRE

BENEATH THE
DOVER SKY

MURRAY PURA

THORNDIKE PRESS
A part of Gale, Cengage Learning

GALE
CENGAGE Learning·

Detroit • New York • San Francisco • New Haven, Conn • Waterville, Maine • London

For Debbie and Brian
and Larry and Karen.
Family through the blessing of marriage
Family through the blessing of Christ.

ACKNOWLEDGMENTS

My biggest thanks go to Nick Harrison, who not only worked on this project with me but really inspired it with his love of the genre and of England. Thanks as always to the Harvest House crew who worked on the editing, marketing, book cover, etc. People like Barb Gordon, Kim Moore, Shane White, Katie Lane, and Laura Knudson. Thanks to my family who put up with the long hours of typing and word processing and creating. And thanks to my great dog Alaska, who stuck by my side when I wrote this book in our backyard last summer and fall. He was always there and made sure I never wrote alone.

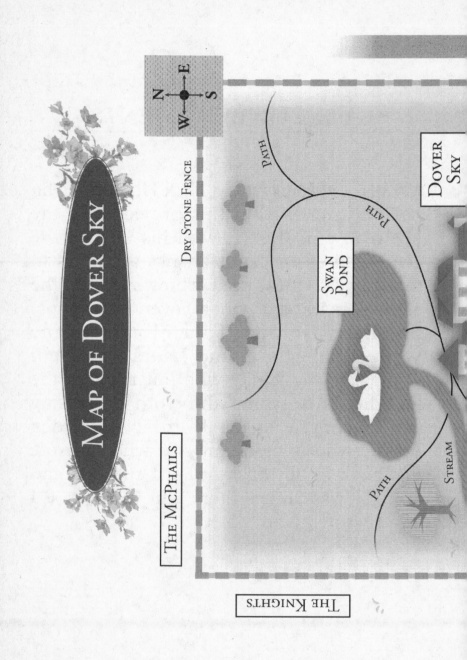

MAP OF DOVER SKY

THE McPHAILS

DRY STONE FENCE

N
W · E
S

PATH

PATH

SWAN
POND

PATH

STREAM

DOVER
SKY

THE KNIGHTS

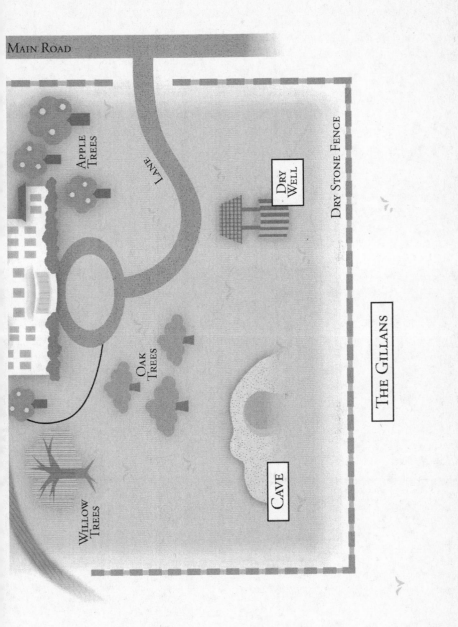

MAIN ROAD

APPLE TREES

LANE

DRY WELL

DRY STONE FENCE

OAK TREES

WILLOW TREES

CAVE

THE GILLANS

THE CHARACTERS

William Danforth — Lord Preston, Marquess of Preston; husband to Lady Elizabeth; father; Member of Parliament (MP); head of Ashton Park, the family estate in Lancashire, as well as Dover Sky, the family summer home in the south of England
Elizabeth Danforth — Lady Preston; William's wife; mother

Sir Arthur — Lady Elizabeth's father
Lady Grace — Lord William's mother

Edward Danforth — William and Elizabeth's eldest son
Charlotte Danforth — Edward's wife; former employee at Dover Sky
Owen — their eldest son;
Colm — their youngest son

Kipp Danforth — William and Elizabeth's middle son; pilot

11

Christelle Danforth — Kipp's wife; French
Matthew — their son

Robbie Danforth — William and Elizabeth's youngest son; serves in British Army
Shannon Danforth — Robbie's wife; Irish
Patricia Claire — their daughter

Jeremiah (Jeremy) Sweet — Anglican clergyman, married to Emma
Emma Danforth Sweet — William and Elizabeth's daughter; married to Jeremy
Peter and James — their fraternal twins;
Billy — their youngest son

Catherine Danforth Moore — William and Elizabeth's daughter; widow of Albert
Sean — her son

Michael Woodhaven IV — American; pilot; married to Libby
Libby Danforth Woodhaven — daughter of William and Elizabeth; married to Michael
Jane — their daughter
Montgomery — Libby's maid; American

Ben Whitecross — pilot; Victoria Cross recipient (WWI); former employee at Ashton Park; married to Victoria

Victoria Danforth Whitecross — youngest daughter of William and Elizabeth; married to Ben
Ramsay — their eldest son;
Tim — their youngest son

Calvert Harrison — groundskeeper at Dover Sky; married to Holly
Holly Danforth Harrison — William's sister; married to Harrison

Lady Caroline Scarborough — daughter of Danforth family friends Lord Francis and Lady Madeleine Scarborough; longtime friend of Kipp Danforth
Charles — her son

Tavy — butler
Skitt — butler and groundskeeper at Dover Sky
Norah Cole, Sally, Harriet, Nancy, Bev — servants at Dover Sky
Mrs Longstaff — head cook
Fairburn — groundskeeper

Baron Gerard von Isenburg — Danforth family friend; German
Albrecht Hartmann — theologian and professor; German
Terrence Fordyce — Royal Navy officer;

serves on *HMS Hood*
Tanner Buchanan — nemesis of Danforth
family; MP

1

June, 1924
Dover Sky estate, Southern England

"All right, Father, you can open your eyes now."

"Are you sure?"

"Quite sure."

"Very well then."

The older man in the back cockpit of the biplane took a look, adjusted his goggles, looked a second time, and laughed. "I've never even seen them by boat!" he shouted. "Never mind by air!"

The pilot turned his head and leaned back. "The gulls see this every day, Father. Not so bad a life, is it? Soar, glide, dive for fish — the white cliffs of Dover for your world."

"The white cliffs and the blue sea and sky. Thank you, my boy, thank you. This is quite the view."

"An early birthday present."

"Is that what this is? It's very early then. The date's over a month away."

The pilot grinned. "I didn't want to miss this chance. My plan was to do something special for you. It's not every day a man turns sixty."

The older man snorted. "I thank God it isn't or I'd have been a relic by the time I was twenty, Kipp."

"You look terrific, Dad."

"Thank you, my boy. For sixty I suppose I'm not so bad off. I can keep up with the grandchildren, and my eyes are still like a hawk's."

The plane swooped over the high, chalk cliffs and the wheeling white gulls. Late June sunlight made the whitecaps in the English Channel beneath the aircraft leap with a brightness the older man never saw on land. The blue sky and sea seemed that much deeper by contrast. He took it all in, white on white on blue, thanked God, and suddenly put his hands outside the cockpit, letting his fingers trail through the swift flow of air as if he were dangling them in a stream of water.

"There's Dover Sky, Father!"

The plane banked over long, green fields and the town of Dover, with its miniature buildings and streets and cars. Further out

16

in the countryside, set solidly on a hill, was a house of windows and verandas and pillars that seemed whiter than the whitecaps and the white cliffs, taking the day's light into its walls and sending it back twice as strong so that the two men in the biplane had to squint.

The older man reached forward and tapped his son on the shoulder of his leather flight jacket. "I've never seen it look so lovely."

"It's a diamond from up here, an absolute gem."

"Whose car is that by the house? Ours is not half so long."

"I don't know, but let's take a closer look."

Kipp put the plane into a dive.

"My boy, my boy, you are not going to buzz the house?"

"Mum doesn't mind."

"But we must have guests if that strange car is there."

"Well, now we'll find out who they are."

They roared over the house. The older man recognized his wife, Elizabeth, his daughter Catherine and her son, Sean, and Norah Cole, their maid. There was also a tall, narrow figure with a sweeping moustache and a ramrod straight back.

17

"No one ran for cover, Dad. That's a good sign."

"I did not expect my family to run . . . or my servants. They are used to airplanes. And now that I see who our guest is, I wouldn't expect him to run either."

"Who is it? The car is a Mercedes Benz 400K, by the way. This year's model. Not cheap."

"Yes, the baron would drive a vehicle like that. Or rather, like me, have it driven for him."

"Baron? Which baron?"

"Von Isenburg. Gerard von Isenburg. A good chap. He gave us our German shepherds before the war."

"Has he come to bring us new ones?"

"I pray not. Gladstone and Wellington have years in them yet."

"Right. Here we go. Coming in for a landing. Hang on."

"Your son still loves the flying, doesn't he, Lady Preston?"

"Please, baron. I'm Elizabeth to you. It's a relief to hear someone call me by my Christian name now and then."

Baron von Isenburg inclined his head slightly. "As you wish. But then I must insist in return that you use my Christian name."

18

"I'm happy to do so, Gerard. Yes, our Kipp has never lost his love for airplanes and the sky."

The two of them watched the biplane land in a field beyond the house.

"William will be surprised to see you," Lady Preston said as the plane came to a stop, propeller whirling. "Surprised and pleased. It has been altogether too long. The war's been over for years. We really ought to have had you up to Ashton Park before this."

"Now is soon enough. I have much to share. And to tell you the truth, I prefer visiting at Dover Sky." He reached down and scratched behind the ears of the two blonde German shepherds who sat on their haunches beside him, tails slowly swishing as soon as he touched their heads.

"Should I be insulted at that remark, Gerard? What on earth is the matter with Ashton Park?"

"There's nothing wrong with it. I simply find it too, well, baronial. I see so much of that in Germany. Dover Sky is quite different — clean, white, shining like jasper. I much prefer it to your Lancashire estate."

"I see. So did you time your visit so it would coincide with our summer escape to Kent?"

The baron laughed and leaned on a cane

19

with a silver pommel. "I am not so much of a schemer. I had a person to visit at Westminster, and a friend asked me to accompany him to England."

"I only see your chauffeur with you."

"No, Albrecht is not with us today. He hopes to come by later in the week, if you can spare a room."

"Spare a room?" Lady Preston glanced back at the manor. "What room can't we spare? Only Catherine came down for the summer with her boy. The others are too busy up north with their work and their families."

"A shame."

"We'll see them all for William's sixtieth birthday celebration at the end of July. Until then it shall be rather quiet . . . too quiet. We shall be glad to have a visit from your friend."

"I'll wire him. He'll be most grateful. He's wanted to meet your husband for some time."

"Really? Is he in politics?"

"Not at all. Albrecht is a theologian. He admires William's Christian convictions."

"Ah." Lady Preston waved as the biplane took off without her husband in it. "There goes Kipp. I'm sorry you two couldn't meet. He was just a boy when you last saw him.

20

He has the Royal Mail for Liverpool and Manchester to deliver today."

The baron watched the plane grow smaller and more distant. "Another time. I am sure of it."

"Ah, Gerard! I spotted you when we flew over the house," William said before kissing his wife on the cheek. "We circled the cliffs, Elizabeth. It was marvelous."

"The way you came at us here on the ground, I'm glad you didn't fly into them."

"Ha!" William said with a smile.

"Lord Preston." The baron clicked his heels together. "It's wonderful to see you again after so many years. Yes, I thought you meant to pluck the hat off my head, your plane dove in so low."

"I very nearly could have done it."

The two men smiled and shook hands vigorously.

"What brings you to England, Gerard?"

"As I was telling your wife, Lord Preston, I had a person to see in —"

"William," interrupted Lord Preston. "You know I wish you to continue to call me William . . . or *Vilhelm,* if you prefer. I hear Lord Preston quite enough."

The baron bowed. "As you wish. I congratulate you on your new title Marquess of

Preston."

Lord Preston nodded. "Thank you. Your cable of last summer was much appreciated. But now tell us why you are here. And how did you get that long, black Mercedes across the Channel?"

"Well, I have my own boat — a barge, really — and it could probably carry three of these. As for my visit, I had a man to see in Westminster."

"Westminster? Someone in the government?"

The baron held up a hand. "Over brandy and cigars?"

Lord Preston snorted. "You and your brandy and cigars. I'll have my tea while you make smoke." He smiled and knelt to pet his dogs. "So, just a man in Westminster to see, is that it? A mystery man?"

"Well, as I was telling your wife, I accompanied a friend here by the name of Albrecht Hartmann. He is a professor at Tubingen . . . a theologian."

"Is he? Wonderful, wonderful! Has he written anything I may have read?"

"He has written several books that have been well received. Alas, only one of them has been translated into English — and American English at that."

"I can tolerate American English. We now

have a Yank in the family, you know. Married my daughter Libby. Do you remember little ginger-haired Libby? The pair are in the United States right now, though we hope to see them back here this fall or winter."

"Splendid. If you wish I can give you a copy of the book and you might be able to read some of the chapters before Albrecht arrives."

Lord Preston stood up. "He is coming to Dover Sky?"

Lady Preston put her arm through his. "I assured Gerard we had plenty of room."

"Plenty of room? I should say we have since our children and their spouses have abandoned us . . . but for Catherine." Lord Preston glanced about. "Have you seen her yet, Gerard? She was so young in 1911."

"He's only just arrived, William," said Lady Preston. "Catherine's off on a walk with Sean. She can meet Gerard at the evening meal."

"Why, I saw her from the plane. She was close by."

"I expect she was, but she's probably drifted since then. You know her moods."

"Yes, of course."

The baron's face behind his moustache grew somber, his eyes darkening. "My condolences once again. Her husband's death was a shock. Civil wars are always the worst for shedding blood."

Lady Elizabeth put a hand on his arm. "The flowers you sent were beautiful, Gerard. Quite the largest arrangement we received. Even the king noticed them."

"A small thing. One always wishes one could do more."

"Catherine will be glad to see you. I have no doubt of it. But she is a bit lost these days. She left Belfast to live at Ashton Park, but she doesn't seem content with us there either. Perhaps it's too lively for her with so many of her siblings having houses nearby. We are hoping a peaceful summer at Dover Sky will help."

"I pray so." The baron stared at the apple trees at the side of the manor. "You never stop worrying about your children. No, never. So much can happen in a lifetime."

"I know, Gerard." She gently squeezed his arm. "I'm sorry for what you've been through."

"Now, mind you attend, young Master Skitt. Next summer you'll be handling matters on your own."

Skitt looked at the map Fairburn was sketching. "I thought the estate here was just the land on the hill."

"A common misconception." The stocky man with a ginger-colored beard, moustache, and sideburns continued to draw, the pencil clutched in his red, stubby fingers. "Of course it's nothing like Ashton Park, but we have a hundred acres running east, west, north, and south. The swans are here — you must pay attention, Master Skitt. There have been poachers, and the police'll not mind if you nab 'em."

Skitt was glancing all about him as the two men sat on a boulder near a narrow stream. "I've not been here before, Mister Fairburn."

"We'll have a long walk today and get you acquainted with the lie of the land. But you must memorize this map. See —" Fairburn made several sharp strokes with a piece of charcoal he yanked from the pocket of his tweed coat. "I've been working on a dry stone fence for years to mark off our boundaries. The Gillans are to the south — good people, salt of the earth. To the east is the main road into Dover. Those fences are done. Of course I'm connecting 'em all together so Dover Sky's in an enclosure, like. So those two have met up. And the east fence is linked with the north fence and the McPhails — rogues, that lot, every last one of them. I've toyed with pointing cannon in their direction, I tell ye. I wouldn't be surprised if they're the ones poaching the swans and geese and deer. I've built that fence a foot or two higher on account of their general nastiness. Now to the west are the Knights — fine people, handsome daughters, no sons. That's the fence we need to complete before the leaves turn in September or October."

Skitt pointed to a spot on the map. "What's that?"

"Grove of oak trees. None near as old as any in Lancashire."

"And that?"

"An old well. We've boarded over the top so's a child won't fall in. The well's dry."

"And this here?"

"A cave. The Lord only knows how long that's been there. Found an ancient yew bow in it fifteen years back. The sinew was gone — y'know, the bowstring — but the wood was sturdy enough. I have it in me groundskeeper's hut if you'd like to see it. Now, by the Gillans' property — Lad, lad, where's your head at this time?"

"It's Cathy — I mean Lady Catherine."

Fairburn craned his neck. "Where?"

"Coming up the slope from the swans."

Fairburn saw her. "Tall and dark. I remember her. How is she then?"

"Why, for long stretches she's right as rain. Then a black mood just takes over, and she's down in the dumps for a good spell."

"A cruel fate, no mistake. So young and a widow with a young boy to raise. How old is he now?"

"About fourteen months."

"Has she shown any interest in, well, meeting another man who can be a father to the lad and a good husband to her?"

"They bring lords and dukes and whatnots 'round to Ashton Park on a regular basis to meet her. She's taken no interest in any of them. Polite enough to 'em, she's all of that, still a lady, but never encourages any of the men to call again."

They watched Catherine make her way towards them. Sean was asleep in her arms.

Fairburn smoothed down his moustache quickly. "I don't recall her being so comely."

"She's lost a good deal of weight since her husband's death. And she's let her hair grow as long as the Thames. That's what you notice."

"It's glossy-black as a raven's wing."

Skitt nodded. "Aye."

Catherine glanced up and saw them on the boulder. She flashed a smile. "Gentlemen, excuse me. I didn't notice you there."

Skitt and Fairburn got to their feet and whipped the flat tweed caps from their heads.

"Ma'am," Fairburn greeted.

"Lady Catherine," said Skitt.

"Oh Skitt, Lady Catherine — that's too much for down here, isn't it? We're hundreds of miles from Ashton Park."

"It comes to you with your father's title. It's a question of respect. Imagine if your mother caught me calling you just plain Catherine."

"*Just plain Catherine?* Now that does sound drab, doesn't it?" She smiled at Fairburn. "Mum tells me this is your last summer with us."

Fairburn clutched at his cap in his hand. "That's so, m'lady. I'll be serving an English family in the south of France. Old friends of your father and mother, y'see, and in a bit of a bind for a competent groundskeeper."

"Well, you'll certainly fit the bill. When do you take up your new post?"

"In November, Lady Catherine. After I've set everything to rights at Dover Sky, and young Master Skitt here's fairly squared away."

"I'm so glad we have you for a final summer."

28

"Thank you, m'lady. I'm grateful as well."

Catherine lifted Sean higher on her shoulder. "I'll see you gentlemen later then. I'm just going to get my boy here to his bed."

Skitt reached out with his hands. "I can help you with him."

"Thank you, Skitt, but I can manage. Ta."

The two men watched her carry on up the slope towards the house.

"How long do you reckon she'll remain unwed?" asked Fairburn.

"Not long," responded Skitt. "You see she's pleasant enough despite everything. Ah, to be a lord and win her hand . . ."

Fairburn erupted in a laugh that sounded like coal rumbling down a chute. He planted his cap back firmly on his head. "We really are daydreamin' today, aren't we, lad? Enough with this map for now. Y'need something to get the steam out of your system. Ever built a dry stone fence? No mortar a'tall?"

"No, I haven't."

"Today's the day then. Right. Let's head over to our property line with the Knights to the west."

Why do men look at me now? I'm so used to them staring at Victoria. Or my brothers' wives Charlotte and Christelle. What has happened?

Do they feel sorry for me? Does my being a widow make them feel like they want to take care of me? Well away from Skitt and Fairburn and still distant from the house, Catherine spoke out loud. She glanced down at young Sean cradled in her arms. "It takes all the energy I have to put up a cheerful front. God, You know I can't do any more than that. When I think of loving another man I simply get weary. I don't have it in me. Maybe five years from now . . . or ten . . . but not now. Not yet." *Thank goodness the baron is an old man. He will not gape at me and pester me like the sons of lords do at Ashton Park.*

"There. Steak and kidney pie. They've all turned out perfect. Lord Preston will be happy with that." The short, round woman with curly hair the color of rust glanced about her. "Norah Cole? Sally? Where have you got to?"

Norah rushed into the kitchen. "Just setting out the bread and butter, Mrs. Longstaff."

"And the crystal? You've laid out the crystal as I asked? He's a baron, you know."

"And a German."

Mrs. Longstaff clicked her tongue. "Never you mind about that. The war's over and

30

done with years ago. He's paid a price himself, you know. Two sons killed fighting the Russians. His wife dead of a cancer. Only the one daughter left. Have some Christian charity."

Norah tilted up her chin. "All right."

"In any case, he is an old friend of the Danforth family, and so was his father and his father's father. That's reason enough to treat him with a good measure of grace and respect."

"Yes, Mrs. Longstaff."

"And he gave Lord Preston those beautiful dogs."

"Yes, ma'am."

"Where's Sally got to?"

"In the wine cellar with Tavy. He's choosing a red, and she's choosing a white."

"Well, run and tell them to make up their minds and be done with it. I'm calling the Danforths to tea in five minutes. Help me with the pies, love. One to a plate. Mind you, Sir William — Lord Preston, I should say — be sure he gets two."

"Yes, ma'am."

Each of them picked up a wooden tray of the steaming pies and headed up a ramp to the dining room. Mrs. Longstaff's eyes took in everything as she placed pies at each place setting.

"You've remembered the high chair for Sean? Good. And you've got Lord Preston's knives and forks and spoons arranged for his left hand. Now did you know the baron is left-handed, as well?"

"I didn't."

"I thought I'd mentioned it. No matter. Only takes a moment." She moved the baron's cutlery around. "There. And we have spare pies in the oven just in case."

"You have some for our men?"

"For Tavy and Fairburn? 'Course I do."

"And young Skitt? He's a growing boy."

Mrs. Longstaff chuckled. "Boy? I daresay he's a man now, Norah Cole. You watch out for him this summer."

Norah sniffed. "I'm old enough to be his mother."

"His mother?" Mrs. Longstaff raised her eyebrows.

"Well, an older sister then. There'll be no to-do between the pair of us, I assure you."

The dining hall shimmered with light from a crystal chandelier that made all the crystal goblets, glasses, and side plates dance. The baron got to his feet after grace and raised his wineglass in a toast. "To my hosts! May nothing ever separate our families. Not war, not peace. God bless you all."

"Hear, hear!" Lord Preston rose. "May I return the blessing? In my best German? *Gott erhalte unsere Familien in der Einheit — für immer!* I think I have that right, Baron."

The baron bowed. "Excellent. Unity forever. I shall drink to that." He sipped from his glass of red wine and sat down. "Good English food, *ja?*"

"Indeed. Steak and kidney pie. Mushy peas. Fried potatoes and tomatoes. All a man needs, Gerard."

"I think so." He placed a white napkin in his lap and smiled at Catherine and her toddler. "You look wonderful, Lady Catherine. How is your health?"

Catherine returned the smile as she broke open her piecrust with a fork. "I am very well, Baron. Thank you for asking."

"Your boy is coming along well."

She smiled at Sean, who was stuffing mushy peas in his mouth with his hand. "He is, isn't he?"

"His looks seem to favor you."

"People say that. But in some of his mannerisms he reminds me of his father. Such as now."

Her father and mother and the baron laughed.

Catherine drank from her glass of water. "I suppose we will find out who he really takes after by the time he is eleven or twelve."

The baron chewed and swallowed while shaking his head. "Oh, much before that, my dear. Believe me, much before that."

The household staff sat in the kitchen and ate together.

"This is right good, Mrs. Longstaff," said Skitt with his mouth full. "Is there much more of it?"

She watched him eat. "If the baron doesn't want seconds and Lord Preston is content with two, there should be plenty left over."

"That's good news."

"And there's plenty of bread and butter and yesterday's coney stew if the pies are gone."

"The rabbit stew? It wasn't all eaten?"

"Not a'tall."

"We were building a fence you see — dry stone — no mortar. Had to fit them tight together just so. Fairburn wanted to get it all done today —"

Fairburn bit into a heel of dark bread. "I haven't had decent help in years. I didn't want to waste the opportunity."

"Which fence is that?" asked Sally.

"We're bounding the property. East,

south, and north are done. So this is to the west."

Tavy wiped the corners of his mouth clear of gravy. "What family is that? To the west?"

"The Knights."

"Short chap? Striking daughters twice his height?"

"That's the one."

"Have they been to Dover Sky for tea? Lady Preston wants me to put together a guest list. She finds the manor altogether too quiet without the other family members."

Fairburn dug into his pie. "Hmm. Years ago they've been, but not recently. It wouldn't be a bad idea. And the Gillans should be invited over as well. It pays to cultivate good neighbors in the country."

"Will there be a ball?" asked Norah. "I've never been to one here."

Fairburn grunted. "There are balls and balls. Servants can't attend all of them. But if they have a servants' ball, well then you're in."

"Certainly. It's the same up north."

Sally grinned and swayed back and forth in her seat. "I'd love that."

"Can I suggest it to his lord?" asked Norah.

"Oh no." Tavy shook his head. "It wouldn't

be proper."

"Isn't anyone allowed to put a bug in his ear?"

Mrs. Longstaff got up and fetched another pie to the table, putting it down in front of Skitt. "There you go." She wiped her hands on her apron. "I'll drop a hint, if you like, to her ladyship. She's so lonely down here this summer I'm sure she'll agree to it."

Norah's face gleamed. "Now wouldn't that be something, Sally? A grand ball and us dolled up in the latest fashions from London and Paris."

Sally cocked her head to one side and fluttered her eyelids, striking a pose. "Rahlly, my dahling, I should find that enchanting."

Norah had forgotten her food. "Neighbors from north, south, east, and west. *Men* from north, south, east, and west."

"Never from the north," rumbled Fairburn. "Never any men from the north, my dear."

"Why not?"

"The McPhails are ugly as rubbish bins. Brute beasts. And they cannot dance." He looked at Norah, who was staring at him in surprise. "Depend upon it, Miss Cole. They would trample you into marmalade with their monstrous great feet."

■ ■ ■ ■

"So do you honestly want brandy, Gerard?"

"I do."

Lord Preston placed a short, fat bottle on the table in the library with a thump. "There you are."

"Excellent." The baron brought out a cigar from the inside pocket of his suit jacket. "I know you don't indulge, Vilhelm, but may I?"

Lord Preston waved his hand and took a seat in a white wicker chair. "Be my guest. I opened all four windows in preparation."

"Danke." Gerard slipped a cutter out of his pocket, snipped off the end of his cigar, placed the cigar in his mouth, and lit it. He sat near a window and across the room from Lord Preston. "Let me say that your daughter looks wonderful, Vilhelm. It is good to see her recovering so well."

Lord Preston nodded. "It will be two years this December. Her mother and I are anxious she begin to develop a new life for herself. Physically she seems to be doing better, but in her spirit? She covers up well, but she has a long way to go. We pray without ceasing for her, of course. If only one decent man would catch her interest . . . but we have yet to see it." He drummed his fingers on the arm of his chair. "Do you have that book for me? The one written by your friend?"

"It is in my room. I will drop it off at your door at bedtime."

"Very good. What is his theme?"

"The suffering Savior. He relates how Christ's sufferings establish a unique bond between the human race and God. That He has embodied the pain of His creation, not only of men and women, but of everything God has made. Because of this, He can never be distant or aloof to our struggles because they are in Him too."

"I should very much like to read that. When will your friend be joining us?"

"I wired him to join us Friday night or Saturday. He has his own car, and I'm confident he'll be able to find the estate."

"How did you get the telegram out?"

The baron turned his head and blew a stream of smoke out the window. "My chauffeur took it into Dover."

"Has your man eaten?"

"Your cook put a plate together for him, and he ate in his room. He's a bit of a loner, so he was quite happy with that." He got up. "I've forgotten my brandy." He went to the table, turned a brandy snifter right side up, and poured several ounces from the bottle into the glass. "Albrecht is at Oxford today. He's already been to Cambridge. He has guest lectures at Manchester and Liverpool as well." The baron took his glass to his seat. "I think I mentioned he teaches at Tubingen?"

"Yes."

"Professor of Protestant Theology."

"And you a good Catholic, Gerard."

"Appearances and history to the contrary, the two are not mutually exclusive."

"Hmm. How are things in Germany?"

The baron shrugged. "Not as bad as 1919 or last year. Inflation has been high. So has unemployment. We see some signs of improvement now, but the terms of the treaty were too harsh, Vilhelm."

"I know it. You've read my speeches in *Hansard.* I felt the same way about Ireland in 1916. I argued for magnanimity then, and I argued it for Germany after the armistice. Each time I was ignored."

"The reparation payments are absurd. When we asked for a reprieve, the French refused and sent their troops to occupy the Ruhr in '22. The German workers went on strike so that Paris could not make money off them. Berlin supported the workers while they were on strike. You remember?"

"Yes."

"The new chancellor of Germany came into power last summer. He agreed to resume the reparation payments to France and ordered the workers in the Ruhr to end their strike. There was a great deal of anger at this. He had to declare a state of emergency. Bavaria in particular refused to obey his orders."

Lord Preston nodded. "Certainly we were preoccupied with our own family matters in 1923, but I read the newspapers."

The baron leaned forward in his chair, brandy in one hand, cigar in the other. "When a situation becomes black as night — a night that has little or no hope of dawn — people become desperate for a savior. One they can see in front of them with their own eyes. They look for a man who will take control and fix everything. They don't care how. They just want light at the end of the tunnel regardless of how it is provided."

Lord Preston drummed his fingers again. "Like Mussolini marching on Rome and taking over in '22?"

The baron lifted his glass. "Exactly like that. You've heard of this Hitler fellow?"

"No."

"He tried to take over the government last fall. He and a group of thugs now called the

Nazi Party. There was a great deal of furor over ending the Ruhr strike and resuming payments to France, and Adolph Hitler took advantage of that. He attempted to kidnap the rulers in Bavaria because he felt they were weakening in their opposition to the French and to the German chancellor. He stormed into a beer hall where they were meeting, waved a gun, and demanded they join his revolution to overthrow the chancellor, defy France, and march on Berlin as Mussolini had marched on Rome."

"What happened to him?"

"He was arrested and sentenced to prison for five years. We should not see him out again until 1928. But I don't think Germany will be much better off in five years. That worries me because I'm sure he'll try to take advantage of a black situation in '28 just as he did in '23."

"He may change, Gerard. Men change in prison."

"Or become even more fanatical and hard-hearted. I have discovered he is dictating a book while he is behind bars. The first volume is due to be published early next year."

"What is it about?"

The German inhaled on his cigar. "His ideology, his beliefs, his politics. I'm afraid he will gain a great following if the book touches on any of Germany's raw nerves. Others dismiss him, but I don't. A few of your people in Westminster don't either."

"Who are you seeing in London?"

"I'm not at liberty to say."

Lord Preston nodded. "What do you want of me?"

"I am hoping you will become directly involved in keeping Herr Hitler in prison. Or directly involved in preventing him from trying to seize power again. We must have your help."

"There is little I can do about the internal affairs of another country."

"We must figure out together what we can or cannot do."

"Baron —"

"Lord Preston." The baron's eyes were an icy-gray that cut through the haze of cigar smoke. "Are you willing to risk another war if this man gains control of Berlin just as Mussolini has gained control over Rome?"

2

June, 1924

Catherine noticed that the sporty red car had come up the drive to their house a second time, stopped, and was sitting there. The wide brim of her sunbonnet shielded her eyes from the afternoon sun so she could see the driver clearly since he had the top of the car down. He was young and clean-shaven. He had light-brown hair, a red woolen scarf about his neck, and brown leather gloves on his hands. He was wearing a brown leather jacket and dark sunglasses. The man gazed in her direction. Then he turned the car around and headed back to the main road. It was easy to spot him speeding south to Dover because all the other cars were dark in color.

I wonder what he's looking for? Catherine thought as she bent down and continued to pinch dead roses off their stalks. The manor was surrounded by white roses of different varieties. While Sean had his nap, she'd decided to pull on gloves and get rid of the brown-edged blossoms that detracted from the overall appearance of the bushes. She placed the dead ones in a basket that hung off her arm. The basket was almost full.

In what seemed like only moments later, she heard the roar of an engine. She turned quickly when a man's voice called out, "Hello? Hello?"

The red car was almost at the house again, and the driver was waving to her and calling as the car slowed to a stop by the rosebush she was working on.

"I'm terribly sorry."

His English was accented in a similar fashion to the baron's — not exactly, she noticed, but very close.

"You must think it odd to see me approach your house and then drive away again. I apologize for that. It appears I'm lost. Can you help?"

Catherine set down her basket and pulled off her white cotton gardening gloves. "I'll certainly try." She walked up to the car, tugging at the bow that held her sunbonnet in place. "What or who are you looking for?" Her bonnet finally came off, and her long, black hair, unpinned, came tumbling down over her shoulders as she shook her head to free it.

The driver stared at her and stumbled over his words. "I'm . . . well . . . I'm not sure . . ."

She was puzzled. "You're not sure what or who you're looking for?"

"I–I didn't think — I didn't think a young woman like yourself — I–I didn't know you were young, you see . . ."

"What?"

He took off his sunglasses. His brown eyes were almost golden in the sunlight. "Excuse me. I'm babbling. I thought you were an older woman, that's all."

Catherine felt a sudden rush of heat as his eyes remained on her. It astonished her. "Oh. Is the person you're looking for older?"

"An older woman? Not at all. I'm much happier to have found you." He put up his gloved hands. "Forgive me. I'm sure I'm making little sense. If you could direct me to Dover Sky, I'll be on my way and leave you to your rosebushes. They're lovely, by the way."

"You're looking for Dover Sky?"

"Have I got the name right? Isn't there a summer estate roundabouts that goes by that? It belongs to the Danforth family. You must have heard of the Danforth family.

Lord and Lady Preston?"

Catherine stared at him and began to laugh. "Why, this is Dover Sky. This is the Danforth summer home."

"It is? You mean this is the right place and you're part of it?"

She felt a blush coming up from her neck at his burst of enthusiasm. "I expect I am. I'm Lord and Lady Preston's daughter Catherine."

"Catherine. What a wonderful name. So you're not the wife? You're not Lady Preston?"

"I am not."

"What a relief."

"Really?"

She saw his eyes glance at her left hand.

"I'm Albrecht. Albrecht Hartmann. Please call me by my first name — Albrecht."

"Ah, the baron's friend. The theologian."

"Has he been talking about me?" He turned off the engine. "Somehow I had the idea in my head the house would be blue. You know, a summer blue like the sky over Dover in fair weather."

"No." She smiled. "White like the cliffs."

"I see that." He opened the car door and stepped out. "Pardon me. How do I address you? You are the daughter of an English marquess?"

"Believe me, I'm quite happy with Catherine."

"But if this were a formal occasion?"

"A formal occasion?"

"A ball. A concert. An affair at Westminster. How would I be expected to address you?"

"Lady Catherine, I suppose."

He reached out his hand. Without thinking, she put hers in it and he raised it to his lips. "Then Lady Catherine it is. I'm so pleased to make your acquaintance."

"Thank you. Do you . . . do you have any title I should address you by?"

"Well, professor, I suppose. But I'd rather you didn't. This is the summer holiday, after all, and you are not one of my students."

"Doctor then?"

He shook his head. "Not yet. I have master's degrees in divinity and theology. Those will have to suffice for now."

"So I may call you Master Hartmann?"

"Oh no! Please don't. I much prefer hearing Albrecht roll off your — excuse me, but I must say it — your perfect lips."

The blush expanded from her neck into her cheeks and around her eyes. "My goodness, thank you, Albrecht. *Danke schön.* That's very kind. But it doesn't seem fair that I am free to call you Albrecht while you must go about putting *lady* in front of my name every time you wish to use it."

"I wouldn't want anyone to think I was treating you with any sort of disrespect. What if I call you Catherine when it is just the two of us and Lady Catherine if other people are around?"

"I'm fine with that." She dropped her eyes suddenly. "You must be eager to see the baron. Shall I show you to the back porch where he and my father are chatting?"

"I'd rather not."

Her gaze came up. "You'd rather not?"

"I've seen a lot of the baron, and I'll see a lot more. But I haven't seen Lady Catherine before. May I not spend more time with her?"

"I — I'm doing the roses." She hesitated, her mind whirling. "But . . . but if you wish."

"Perhaps you're free to show me around the estate?"

"My son is napping . . ."

Albrecht's face went white. His arms went to his sides and he bowed stiffly. "My apologies, Lady Catherine. I didn't know you were married. Here I am offering gallantries and pleasantries, and all the while thinking you were an eligible young woman. Please show me the way to the baron, and you shall quickly be rid of me. You must think me quite the brute. Never mind, Lady Catherine. I'm sure I can find my way to the back of the manor myself . . ."

"Albrecht!" interrupted Catherine. "I am not in the least bit insulted. Quite the contrary." She took a deep breath. "You have not been crass or rude. Forward, yes, but I, well, I find you charming in a very continental way. I was going to say my son is napping and he usually likes a three-hour rest. I'm certain that will give me plenty of time to give you a short tour of the estate. If you are still interested."

"But your husband?"

"Please walk with me, Albrecht. I'm going to show you the apple trees first." She started forward. When he didn't follow, she looked back at him. "Join me. Honestly, it's so rare that I meet new people I actually like."

He continued to hesitate. "It would not do for us —"

"My husband was killed, Albrecht. Almost two years ago now."

"I see. I'm very sorry, Lady Catherine. He cannot have been very old."

"He was an Irishman killed in Belfast. Gunmen targeted him because he wanted Northern Ireland to remain attached to Britain. He didn't want to be part of an independent Irish state. That's all it took."

Albrecht was silent a moment. "Often it takes much less."

"Now that is out of the way, shall we walk? I find you refreshing. You were drawn to me simply because I was a young woman out among the rosebushes. I find that appealing. So many people have been introduced to me in the hopes of making a match. But you didn't know me when you drove up. Nothing was prearranged. You are not Lord So-and-So's heir or Lady Push-and-Pull's youngest son coming to meet me at one of the balls I've attended lately. The whole business seems rather flat to me. But you? You just pulled up in your natty red convertible and asked for directions. You didn't know me from an acorn. As I said, I find that very refreshing. So would my late husband, to tell you the truth. He hated all the stuffed shirts."

"Well, if you insist." Albrecht relaxed. "How do you know I'm not one of those stuffed shirts?"

"I should hardly think so. Not the way you've been acting for the past ten or fifteen minutes." She smiled, her black hair shining in the warm sun. "Mum and Dad would be overjoyed to look out a window and see me strolling with a refined-looking man like yourself. So please don't be worried about how this will look. The staff will whisper, of course, but they always whisper. Just so long as you understand I am not agreeing to anything beyond a stroll on the grounds. I have made a new friend, the friend is a man, and I am enjoying that friend's company. Are you satisfied with this?"

He lifted an eyebrow. "You mean if I ask you to visit me at my castle on the Rhine and stay over for a month, you will refuse?"

"Most certainly."

"Then I will not ask." He joined her, and they walked into the apple orchard at the side of the house.

"You don't actually have a castle on the Rhine, do you, Albrecht?" she asked, the play of light and shade under the trees dappling her face.

His hands went behind his back as they walked. "In fact I do. Or rather my father does. But I'm afraid my older brother Walter will get it."

"And what will you inherit?"

"The old mountain chateau in Pura, Switzerland, with its sweeping views of the mountains and Lake Lugano and Italy."

"Now you're teasing me."

"I'm not actually. We really do have the chateau. Would you like to see it?"

"This estate will have to suffice for the both of us for now. Come, let me show you the swans."

"She said yes!"

"She didn't!"

"Aye, she did!" Norah grinned. "Lady Preston promised Mrs. Longstaff we'll have a dance in a fortnight — a servants' ball, though we'll not call it that. Can you imagine? The regular families from all around will be invited."

"What about the bluebloods?" asked Sally.

"No, no, they'll have their moment later in July when we celebrate Lord Preston's birthday. This is just for us common folk and the Danforths." She chewed on her thumb. "You can be sure Skitt will ask Lady Catherine for a waltz."

"A waltz? He don't know how to waltz."

"Neither do you. Neither do I. We'll have to learn before July twelfth. Such a time we'll have. They say the Gillans have two strapping sons, though I've never met them all the years I've summered here with the lord and lady."

"What makes you think the Gillan boys will look at the likes of us?"

"Oh, they'll look all right. We'll dress in such a way as'll turn their heads right 'round. You'll see."

"What are the pair of you up to?" Mrs. Longstaff came bustling into the kitchen. "We have to serve in fifteen minutes. How is the schnitzel?"

"Perfect." Norah opened the warming door of one of the large ovens. "You see?"

Mrs. Longstaff bent over and looked in. "Lovely." She straightened. "What about the roast potatoes? What about the cabbage soup?"

"The potatoes are done to perfection as well. The soup needed more salt, so Sally tended to that."

"Let me see!" Mrs. Longstaff took a large spoonful of the soup that was bubbling on the stove. "Mmm . . . well done, Sally."

"Thank you, ma'am."

"I'm not sure which you're better at — cleaning the rooms or helping me cook." She glanced about her. "Tavy has the table set in the dining hall. We have another mouth to feed tonight."

Norah groaned. "Have we?"

"Oh, you'll not groan once you've set eyes on him. The baron's friend he is. Handsome young man. Handsome as a prince, I'd say. A theologian from Germany."

"A theologian?" Norah rolled her eyes. "Why, he'd be a little shriveled man with spectacles."

"He isn't a shriveled old anything. He looks like one of the actors in *The Covered Wagon.*"

"I've not seen that film."

"Norah Cole, how is it an old woman like myself has seen it four times and you've never seen it once?"

"We're ready, ma'arm." Tavy stood in the doorway. "Not a minute to waste."

"Right! Norah, you run along with Tavy to the dining hall and see the shriveled-up theologian for yourself. Sally and I will send the soup up by the dumbwaiter."

"Are you sure?"

"Of course I'm sure. On your way now."

"I've not had better schnitzel in Munich or Berlin." Albrecht tucked into a second helping. "Who's your chef?"

"Mrs. Longstaff." Lord Preston lifted a forkful to his mouth. "She's an absolute wizard."

"Longstaff? She's not even European?"

"Not a hint of it. Good Lancashire stock, though there may be a touch of Viking."

"The soup was exceptional as well." The baron leaned back in his seat and sipped his red wine. "Tomorrow's Sunday. Where do you go for services when you're down here,

Vilhelm?"

"St. Mary's. It's been in Dover since just after the Norman Conquest."

"Do you mind if Albrecht and I join you?"

"Of course not. It's Church of England, mind you."

The baron waved a hand. "A change of scenery is good for the soul." He smiled at Catherine who was helping Sean with his soup. "Lady Catherine, will you attend the morning service with our crowd?"

"Certainly, Baron. It's a beautiful stone church, and the choir and messages are inspiring."

"How does young Sean do?"

"Very well, sir. He — whoops!" Sean spat up some soup and laughed. She dabbed at his face with a napkin. "He seems awed by the interior — all the light and stained glass — so he's generally quiet."

"Good for him. Perhaps he'll make a fine theologian, eh, Albrecht?"

Norah appeared over Albrecht's right shoulder. "Coffee, sir?"

"We can always use fine theologians, Baron. The Lord knows we have few enough of them." Albrecht smiled up at Norah. "Nice to see you back here with your pot."

"Thank you, sir."

"A half cup would be just right."

"Very good, sir."

Lady Preston interlaced her fingers on the tabletop. "Tell me, Professor Hartmann, how would you sum up the role of the theologian in this age of skepticism?"

Albrecht put cream in his coffee. "What it has always been. To bring the supernatural into the natural world so that it is just as real as anything we perceive with our five senses."

"Bring it in? But isn't the supernatural always here? Isn't it all around us? Angels and devils and God and His Holy Spirit?"

Albrecht drank his coffee. "You're right. When I speak of bringing it in, I mean to say I wish to make it obvious and credible to the human race. That it is as present as water and air, which are vital to us, and that faith in God is equally as vital. Indeed, without it, we are lifeless and without a proper path so we do not attain to our destinies."

"Do you distinguish between orthodoxy — right teaching — and orthopraxis — right living?"

"I don't, Lady Preston. To me it is a false distinction. You cannot have a Christian faith that is all in your head or all in your intellect. That is meaningless. It must be lived out in your actions. By the same token,

a body without a head is a monstrosity —
your actions must be guided by your
thoughts and prayers and beliefs. So there
is only the one thing, orthodoxy. And
orthodoxy is right belief. And right belief is
lived-out and thought-out faith in Christ."

"Is it the wine or is my head spinning?"
Lady Preston asked.

The baron smiled. "Perhaps we should
remain at the breakfast table tomorrow
morning and have our message here. I vote
for a passage from the Gospel of Mark."

Albrecht shook his head. "I've gone too
far. Forgive me. I return my lecture notes to
my briefcase. Let us have our coffee and
dessert in peace."

Peaceful silence permeated the room as
everyone sat back in comfort.

"And here is our dessert now," Lord Preston announced.

"Really, Vilhelm!" protested the baron. "I
am stuffed, as you English say."

"Pass on it if you wish. Mrs. Longstaff
swears it's a traditional recipe from southwestern Germany."

Sally carried in a large cake on a tray and
set it in the middle of the table. It was
covered in whipped cream and cherries.
Both Albrecht and the baron looked at it in
astonishment, their mouths open but no

words coming out.

Finally the baron sputtered, "Black Forest cake! Surely not with the cherry liquor *Kirschwasser*?"

"She swears it's traditional, Gerard."

"There is one way to find out!" Albrecht held out his side plate. "May I have a generous piece, Sally?"

"Of course, sir."

"I think Sean will have a wonderful time with this German delicacy, Lady Catherine."

Catherine bit her lip. "I hate to give him any, Professor Hartmann. He will just waste it. It will be all over his eyes and ears and mouth. And all through my hair."

"Believe me, Lady Catherine, that is not wasting it."

"You raised a few eyebrows with that remark," Catherine commented.

Albrecht was leaning on the railing of the front veranda and looking out over the fields barely discernible in the dark. He stood up straight as Catherine approached. "What remark was that?"

"About Black Forest cake in my hair."

"Well, it was true, although I did not mean to start a rumor with it."

Catherine put her hand on one of the

thick, white posts. "Never mind . . . I'm just teasing. Gallant remarks seem to pop out of you naturally."

"Do they? That makes me sound insincere."

"No, I think you're very sincere. I guess it's a gift you have."

Albrecht went back to leaning on the railing. "Is your son asleep?"

"Yes."

"Are you . . . would you . . . take a stroll with me along the drive?"

"Perhaps not."

"I'm sorry. I didn't mean to make you feel uncomfortable."

"I love hearing your table talk, Albrecht. And I enjoyed our walk across the estate this afternoon. But I . . . well, I want to slow down a bit. I feel like my head is spinning, and I didn't have a drop of wine."

"I see." He laughed. "You're right, of course. I go too fast. Like a racing car driver." He cleared his throat. "I apologize. It is because the baron informed me a few minutes ago we would be leaving immediately after lunch Sunday."

"I thought you'd be with us until after breakfast Monday morning."

"So did I. Something's up in Munich, and

both of us need to be there as soon as possible."

"But you teach at Tubingen."

"Yes, but there is no more teaching until the fall. This has nothing to do with being a professor of Protestant theology." A smile came to his face in the dark. "By the way, I caught that *Professor Hartmann* title you used at the table." He wagged his finger. "Never again."

"You called me Lady Catherine."

"We agreed on that."

"I like calling you professor."

"Do you?"

"I do, yes." She gazed over the fields just as he was doing. "I should not say I wish you were staying on. After all, I haven't known you but twelve hours. It's madness. But there you have it. I wish you were with us till Monday or Tuesday. It's like a huge roller has washed over me. I'm a bit stunned, I think. I suppose you'd better go. I need to sleep on what I've been feeling. Maybe I'll feel nothing after a few nights' sleep . . . or maybe I'll feel more of everything."

He didn't respond for several minutes. "Do you wonder why we must up and go just like that?"

"Of course I wonder. But it's really none

of my business, is it?" She glanced at him. "It's a very hard life in Germany right now, I think."

Albrecht shrugged. "We see improvement every month. Inflation is on the decrease; employment is on the rise."

"Well then, that's good."

"So it seems. But that is why we must return. Foolish decisions are made in times of change, especially change for the good. There is a man who was imprisoned for trying to seize control of the government a year ago when times were much worse. Now that matters have improved, some of us are worried he will be released early. He is like a stick of dynamite rolling around that no one can quite get his hands on to throw away. Yet the wick is beginning to smoke." Albrecht's lips were in a straight line. "As it is, he is afforded special treatment in prison. It's almost as if he is on holiday at the castle prison in Munich."

"Who is this man? Are you worried he has a following?"

"His name is Adolph Hitler. He has a following, certainly. I am worried that he seems to be able to appeal to a broad spectrum of the German people. The man is a revolutionary when Germany doesn't need a revolutionary. We need peace and stability and growth. So we are working against him, Catherine, even though others say he is nothing and that the uproar he caused is over."

"Who is this *we*?"

"There are a number of us. We call ourselves 'The Brotherhood of the Oak,' *die Bruderschaft der Eiche.* The oak is one of Germany's national emblems. You English use the oak as well." His eyes looked impossibly deep to her when he looked up. "I tell you this in secret, Catherine. Please do not share what I have told you. I'm not sure why I've spoken about it. Am I trying to impress you? I hope not. Perhaps I wonder if you might understand. You seem like a woman who would understand and come alongside people in a time of struggle."

Catherine felt heat in her face. "Albrecht, I —"

"Lady Catherine, excuse me."

"Yes?" Catherine turned away from Albrecht and faced Norah. "What is it?"

"Young Master Sean is awake and crying for you. We're having difficulty settling him."

"I see. Thank you, Norah. I'll be right there."

Norah went back into the house.

Once Norah had gone, Catherine put her hand briefly on Albrecht's arm. "I would like you to tell me more about this. May we speak alone after breakfast before we drive into Dover for church?"

"Of course!" He gave her a smile. "I hope Sean is all right."

"I'm sure it was just a bad dream. Thank you for asking. Ta, Albrecht."

"Auf Wiedersehen."

"Good morning, Papa."

Lord Preston put down his newspaper. "Ah, there you are, Catherine. How did you and Sean sleep?"

"Not well at all. Sean is still in his crib. Where's Mum and our guests?"

"Your mother is under the weather. It'll just be you and me heading to St. Mary's this morning. And Mrs. Longstaff." He picked up a bell by his elbow and rang it. "Sally will bring you some coffee and scones."

"But the baron was to be joining us. And Professor Hartmann . . ."

"Yes. They had to leave earlier than expected. Urgent business in Munich. You know how Germany is these days, my dear."

"I see." Catherine sat down at the breakfast table that was in an alcove off the dining hall. Rain tapped against the tall windows. "Is there any chance we'll see the pair of them again this summer?"

Lord Preston had his newspaper up to his face again. "Mmm? This summer? I wouldn't think so. Next summer is a good possibility however. Would you like that? Did you enjoy the baron's company?"

"W—was there a note left . . . or anything?"

"A note? Why on earth would the baron leave a note? The telegram came for them at four this morning, and I saw them off at four-thirty. Ah, here's Sally with your coffee, scones, and jam."

June
Berlin, Germany
"I expected you two much earlier."

"We were in England. I met with the man in Westminster you asked me to contact. And I recruited Lord Preston. This was as quickly as we could reach Landsberg Castle by car and rail."

"You're here now. Let's get down to business."

Baron von Isenburg, Albrecht Hartmann, and a third man were seated in the baron's Mercedes. A half mile ahead of them the turrets of a castle poked through a dense growth of trees.

"It seems impossible to keep Hitler in

Landsberg Castle the full five years," the third man began, eyeing the battlements. "He has too many well-wishers. We have worked through the channels available to us to insist he serve out his full term. It's no use. He will be released before the end of the year, perhaps as early as this fall, though we are fighting that."

"Their argument?" asked the baron.

"Oh, you know. The Germany of 1924 is a different Germany from the Germany of '22 or '23. Berlin is getting a grip on inflation, the workforce is increasing, wages are improving — all of that. So Hitler will not have the base to draw from anymore; therefore, he does not need to be in detention. Apparently he will renounce violence and his former political beliefs."

"He won't change!" responded Albrecht.

"Of course not. But that is what officials want to believe, and he is only too happy to appear to give them what they want." The man pulled a large envelope from a briefcase at his feet. "We should not stay here much longer. Take this. One of our men inside the castle was able to get his hands on drafts of the book Hitler is writing. He made copies. It will be published in 1925."

The baron examined the envelope. "You have read his manuscript?"

"Most of it."

"Well?"

"It's the same sort of thing we have heard at his street rallies since 1920. Germany for Germans. Purebloods only. No immigration. Death to the Jews. Secure boundaries against the Russians. Down with communism. Open the east for German settlement. It's all there, just more polished and refined. A friend is editing it for him."

"We can't stop the publication?"

"No, Baron. We can only prepare ourselves to argue against his arguments in print." The man turned to Albrecht. "Which is where you come in, Herr Professor. We need a book from you to coincide with the release of Hitler's propaganda."

"I am a theologian," protested Albrecht, "not a politician."

"And Germany remains very religious with its mix of Lutherans and Catholics and Evangelicals. I am not asking you to pen rubbish. Counter Hitler's ideology from the Bible, from your own personal convictions, from the history of the Christian faith, whatever you wish, but write as well and as deeply as you have ever done."

"I have a full course load this coming term."

"Will you or won't you help us? The baron

was sure you could be relied upon."

"It's a question of time."

The man leaned towards Albrecht. "Hitler has an uncanny ability to draw the German people into his sphere. You saw that at his street rallies. Forty thousand people at one."

"I remember."

"So now his ideas will go from one end of Germany to the other with this book. Suppose instead of 40,000 he rallies 40 million to his beliefs? Can you not try to rally those same 40 million to the Christian point of view instead? Is there any possibility you can bring Germany closer to the teachings of Jesus Christ than Herr Hitler's book brings them to the teachings of the Nazi Party?"

June
Dover Sky

"Lady Catherine! Lady Catherine!"

Catherine stood up. She looked beautiful in her white summer dress. "Yes? Sean and I are down here with the swans. Whatever is the matter, Skitt?"

Skitt came running down to the pond, and the swans quickly sailed away from shore.

"A letter just came for you by special post. I didn't want it to sit by your place setting until tea."

67

"A letter? Who is it from?"

Skitt handed it to her, yanking his cap from his head, his face scarlet from his run. "Doesn't say. It's not from England, that's all I know."

"Oh!" Her face turned as white as her dress when she glanced at the envelope. "Germany!"

"Is everything all right?"

"I hope so. Yes, yes, I expect so. Thank you, Skitt. I shall see you up at the manor."

"May I be of further help, m'lady?"

"Oh no. You're a dear for running it down to me. Bless you."

Skitt turned and headed back as Catherine sat down on the grass by Sean. He was playing with a long, white swan feather that had been shed near a tree. She held the letter in her hand, debated about opening it now or waiting. She decided to open it. With one hand on Sean's small back, she read Albrecht's note:

Dear Lady Catherine,
My sincere apologies. The baron and I had every intention of attending services with you and your family until the telegram arrived early Sunday morning. It was rude of me not to leave you with some sort of message, but it was all I

could do to get packed, grab a bite to eat from the kitchen, and jump into my car. Will you forgive me? I very much wanted to speak with you further.

There is something about you. I must say it — I think of you constantly. Here I am at this fancy hotel in Munich, and the baron is snoring like a trumpet in the other room. At any rate, I can't sleep. On the one hand there is the mystery of Lady Catherine to ponder. Why am I caught up with you? On the other hand there is Adolph Hitler to ponder. Why is Germany caught up with him?

I have been asked to write a book to counter Hitler's book that is due out next year. His will be a memoir, and a political rant against the Treaty of Versailles that ended the war, and an attack on the Jews, the communists, and the socialists. Mine will be a volume of theology — but what I call "embodied theology" — a true orthodoxy that is a "lived out" orthodoxy. And it must be alive. The last thing I need to produce right now is a dry, academic treatise on the existence of God.

I've read some of Hitler's book. The Brotherhood I'm involved with has obtained some early drafts. Hitler writes with passion about something he believes in. People will pick up on this. I must write with equal passion about what I believe in. Good must have as much fire and heat as hate because it's to a better end.

I share this in strictest confidence. I wish I could share it with you in person. I fear it will be a long time before we see each other. Am I content with the time I've had with you? No. But I thank God for it just the same.

The blessings of Christ on your lovely head.

Your servant,
Albrecht

Catherine read it through twice. The color returned to her face — more color than had been in it all day. She gazed at the swans as they floated slowly back and forth on the green and silver water. "What is going on, God?" she whispered. "What are You doing in my life now? I have no idea how I feel about Albrecht Hartmann or what he's involved in. How am I supposed to respond to this?"

July, 1924
Dover Sky

"You needn't be so ceremonial, William. This isn't the Magna Carta. Open the letter. It's already sat for a week after Skitt put it in your hand and you misplaced it."

"I merely set it aside, Elizabeth. I was quite conscious of its whereabouts the entire time."

"Yes, yes, dear. Save your speeches for Parliament, please. Just read me Robbie and Shannon's letter."

"Will do." Lord Preston carefully slit the thin envelope with a letter opener that bore the Danforth coat of arms. Setting the opener down, he brought out a sheet of paper thinner than the envelope. "There are no photographs, Elizabeth."

"Well, I didn't think there would be. Oh, read it to me! Is Shannon with child?"

He unfolded the letter and cleared his

throat as if he were about to say, "Mr. Speaker . . ."

Dear Mum & Dad,
Cheers! I'm sending this as quickly as I can. Shannon and I were planning to surprise the two of you by showing up for Dad's sixtieth birthday celebration. We were promised a month's leave from my post here so we were busy packing. On the last day of June I was waiting to speak with an important member of the Jewish community. My adjutant burst into my office with the news the man had just been assassinated. I went to the scene immediately. It was a grim sight. At first we thought Arabs were the assassins, but further investigation made it clear it was one of the Jewish militant groups — the Haganah. Why did they kill one of their own? Simply put, Jacob Israel de Haan wanted a state that included secular and religious Jews in the government, as well as Arab Muslims and Arab Christians, but the Haganah want a Jewish state, period.

I'm used to the Arabs and Jews being at each other's throats. Yet I knew this region had shades of Ireland to it, where

73

Jew might turn on Jew or Arab on Arab just as Irishman had turned on Irishman. However I confess I did not expect the cold-blooded murder of a Jew by other Jews. It has given me a bit of a jolt. Not least because I knew de Haan personally and he was one of my brightest hopes for Palestine's future. Really, the only way we can keep Jerusalem from spiraling down into a cycle of constant violence is to establish a nation that is inclusive of Muslims and Jews and Christians. That is the spirit de Haan epitomized, and he was having successful talks with Arab leaders. Obviously too successful in the eyes of the Haganah and the Zionists.

Well, it could just as easily have been the Arabs who had done it. They too have their hotheads who don't want a Palestinian state that includes Jews in its government. How will the moderates prevail when there are so many with their fingers on the trigger on both sides? And here we British are in the middle. How can I possibly sort all this out when the leaders I have most counted on to bring peace to this region are cut down in their prime?

I'll get this in the mailbag for England straightaway. I am so very sorry we can't make it up for your birthday, Dad, but you see how things are. Perhaps we'll be able to get away next year.

Meanwhile, despite all this, Shannon and I enjoy good health and relish this wonderful climate. God bless you and please pray for us here.

Love to all,
Robbie

Lady Preston was fingering her necklace and staring out the parlor window at the apple trees. "I should like to live to see peace in Jerusalem."

"It has been this way from time immemorial, Elizabeth. One group fighting another. Several Danforths went on Crusades, you know."

"I just don't want them turning on our British troops for lack of something else to do. There's a viciousness in Palestine I had not counted on. I fear Robbie is in harm's way again."

"Nonsense." Lord Preston folded the letter and tucked it back in its envelope. "They have no reason to go after our army. We're there to help."

■ ■ ■ ■

"Now you settle in here behind this bush," ordered Fairburn.

"I'm not *behind* the bush," complained Skitt, "I'm in it."

"All the better. The poachers won't be able to tell you from a thatch of brambles."

The sun had gone down, but there was still enough twilight to see clearly when Skitt crouched down in the brush. Fairburn handed him a cricket bat.

"Now if you spot 'em, holler like the dickens and I shall come running from my hut. Whack them about a bit with the bat and soften 'em up for the constables. Remember, the poachers are on our land so they're trespassing. And if they've come for the swans, they're poaching as well. And they're not just taking anyone's swans."

"I know, I know. They're poaching the swans of the Marquess of Preston."

Fairburn made a sour face. "They're not just the Marquess of Preston's swans, lad. They're the king's birds."

"What do you mean?"

"Have I not told you? The swans of this estate have been under royal protection by edict since 1789. Twenty years back, they were Queen Victoria's swans. Today they're King George the Fifth's. All the more reason to knock the poachers about a bit and give them what for."

"I'll do my best."

"We'll spell each other. You have tonight and tomorrow night. Then it's my go. Have you got your flask of tea?"

"Aye. Mrs. Longstaff fixed me two great ham sandwiches as well."

"Good enough. We'll see you at dawn then, unless you catch 'em. Don't forget to make a great racket that will bring me on the run. Cheers."

"Cheers."

Skitt hunkered down further into the bush, opened his leather flask, sipped some tea, screwed the cap back on, and began to hum "Abide with Me" while he watched the swans glide around the pond. *They look like vessels with all sails set, so they do,* he thought. The great birds settled down as it became fully dark, tucking their bills back under their wings, some remaining in the water, others coming up on land. The July night was warm so Skitt felt no discomfort. He gripped his cricket bat firmly and flicked his eyes from one side of the pond to the other. He thought about the summer ball that was only three nights away. The great hall at Dover Sky was already decorated with white lights and streamers. He almost closed his eyes as he imagined that night . . .

Lady Catherine.

Ah, Master Skitt. To what do I owe this pleasure?

I brought you a glass of lemonade. You look a bit pink.

Why, that's so kind of you. Indeed, I was feeling the heat. How may I thank you?

Well, I was wondering if I might have this dance?

My goodness, you're asking me? A girl should be so lucky. I'd be honored. Please take my hand and let's go onto the floor. Do you know how to waltz?

Indeed I do, Lady Catherine.

Really? You are a man of many talents, Master Skitt. I do hope one dance will not be enough for you.

With a lady as fair as you, I doubt it.

How charming you are. Let us stay partners as long as we possibly can.

"It's not working! I knew it." Sally stood in front of the mirror, lifted up a handful of her hair, and then let it drop. Her eyes were narrowed and her lips tight. "I'm a fright. I can't go upstairs to the ball. I shall spend my night in bed reading a romance."

"Don't be ridiculous!" Norah swished up behind Sally wearing a red gown that flared out from her hips. She began poking pins into her friend's straw-blonde hair. "A few hairpins and you will be absolutely devastating."

"I will not. The night's a disaster."

"The night will be a triumph. Blue eyes, blonde hair, the tiniest freckles I've ever seen — the men will trip over themselves to dance with you. And there are quite a few of them."

"What? Have you gone and peeked?"

"I have. And they all look smashing. There are some soldiers and naval officers too, and their uniforms are lovely."

Sally bounced up and down on her toes. "Oh, I can't wait. Hurry!"

Norah put several pins in her mouth so she could move her fingers about more freely. "Mmm."

"Has anyone danced yet? I can hear the violins."

Norah plucked the pins from her mouth and plunged them carefully into Sally's up-swept hair. "Lord Preston led off with Mrs. Longstaff, if you can believe it."

"Mrs. Longstaff! She said she wouldn't be caught within a hundred miles of here the night of the ball."

"I don't know who or what changed her mind, but she's done up in rose-and-pink ribbons and doesn't even look like our cook anymore. Honestly, she's a woman at least fifteen years younger."

Sally bounced on her toes again. "That's enough. We must get upstairs."

"One minute." Norah jabbed and stabbed. "Skitt's on the floor with Lady Catherine."

Sally whipped her head around and several pins fell out. "No!"

"Now look, we've got to do the right side again," grumbled Norah, bending down for the pins.

"I never thought he'd have the nerve."

"He was fortifying himself at the punch bowl before he asked her."

"But the punch doesn't have any alcohol in it."

"Of course not. Lord Preston's a good religious man. But Skitt didn't think of that.

So he finally marched off thinking he was well fueled for his Waterloo with Lady Catherine."

"Well, if it was his Waterloo, he must have been Wellington if she let him take her out onto the floor."

"Twice that I saw. And you'll also be surprised to know he did us proud."

"What d'ya mean?"

"He glided about like one of those swans of his. Can you imagine?"

Sally almost whipped her head around a second time, but Norah's hands held it firmly this time.

"He did not!"

"You see," Norah said, "all those lessons you gave him made a difference."

"Me? You danced with him more than I did."

"I didn't."

"Three lessons for every one of mine."

Norah snorted. "I can't float like a swan over the dance floor. How could I have taught him how to do it, Sal?"

"Oh, I want to see!" Sally reached up and pulled Norah's hands away from her hair. "Enough. I don't care. Let's go upstairs."

"Sal," Norah said as she peered at herself in the mirror and brushed an eyelash from her cheek, "the ball isn't going anywhere."

" 'Course it is. It's going out the door at midnight. Hurry."

The great hall at Dover Sky was half the size of the one at Ashton Park, but it still held two hundred people comfortably. The walls had sea paintings — some of naval battles in the Channel and others of fishing boats, the background always including images of Dover's white cliffs. A string quartet sat at one end of the hall on a platform erected for the occasion. Tables groaning with meats and cheeses stood at the other end. White lights glowed, strung from one corner of the ceiling to the other, and colored streamers of crepe paper dangled down, stopping eight feet from the floor.

Norah and Sally had helped decorate the hall. Taking it all in at once — the lights in the semidarkness of the room, the string players bent to their task, the red coats of the army officers and the blue coats of the naval officers, the women in their gowns and the men in their morning suits, crystal glasses glittering in people's hands — gave the two young women a sense of being in a different mansion. It didn't seem like their well-known Dover Sky at all.

Sally seized Norah's hand. "There are two men of Nelson's Navy approaching us."

"Nelson's Navy? What in heaven's name

are you talking about? It's 1924 not 1805."

"I like to think of the navy that way. I always have since I was a little girl." Sally stood as straight as she could. "I'll take the tall, dark, handsome one. You can have the other."

"The other one's shorter than me!"

"Shh! Do make the best of it." Sally curtsied as the officers bowed. She made eye contact with the tall one. "Good evening, sirs. May we have the pleasure of your acquaintance?"

"Seven dances! My goodness!" Lady Catherine laughed and fanned her face with her hand. "Who would have thought you had wings on your feet, Master Skitt?"

"I hope you enjoyed yourself, m'lady."

"Enjoyed myself? I don't think I've ever flown about a dance floor like that."

Skitt bowed, his morning suit tight on his slender frame. "My pleasure. And now I'm afraid I must go."

"What? The night's still young. I'd love to have another go 'round with you."

Skitt beamed, his eyes bright amid the shine of the lights hanging overhead. "It would be an honor, Lady Catherine, but it's my turn to be down at the pond. We're trying to nab the poachers, you see."

"Fairburn?"

"He's lending Tavy a hand there by the tables. This would be just the sort of night the rascals would choose to go after our swans, Lady Catherine, what with everyone in here at the party. I do hope I may have the pleasure of dancing with you again one day."

"Oh, of course, Skitt. I'll sneak you into my father's birthday ball in a fortnight."

"But I'm not gentry."

She patted him on the cheek with a gloved hand. "Never mind. We'll have our dance, I promise. Please be careful tonight."

"I will. Thank you." Skitt turned and marched through the great hall doorway.

Catherine snatched a drink of punch from a tray Tavy was carrying as he wandered through the crowd. "I need a drink or I'm going to faint," she announced.

"Are you well, ma'arm?" asked Tavy in his gravelly voice.

"Certainly I'm well, but Master Skitt is so much younger than I am. He would have danced on for another five hours if he didn't have his pond assignment."

"I'm sure you've made his night, ma'arm. Probably his year. Perhaps his life."

"Oh heavens, Tavy. Don't exaggerate. Hardly his life. The year will be done in

84

December, so that might be closer to the mark if he feels anything for me like you're describing."

"Lady Catherine, he dotes on you, he does. Were it a thousand years ago he'd happily mount a horse and joust to win your hand."

"Now I don't know if I'm blushing from the heat or your description of Skitt's adoration. Thank you, Tavy. I'll have another." She returned the empty glass to the tray and picked up a full one. Tavy disappeared among the gowns, suits, and uniforms. Catherine stood and sipped as she gazed over the room.

"A beautiful woman left without an escort? What is England coming to?"

A tall, broad-shouldered officer in a dark-blue uniform was smiling at her, his eyes a brilliant blue and his face tanned like a golden sunrise. He bowed slightly. "Terrence Fordyce. I hope I'm addressing Lady Catherine Moore."

"You are, Leftenant Commander."

"Ah, you recognize the insignia."

"My brother Edward was Royal Navy during the war." She offered him a smile. "Did you come by your tan on Channel duty?"

He laughed. "That's not likely, is it? I was on the world tour with the *HMS Hood.*

Australian sun blessed us, not to mention the Californian sun and the Jamaican sun. I had to leave the *Hood* in Canada and come across to Devonport on another ship. Naval business to attend to."

"When will the *Hood* be back in England?"

"I'd say September." He reached out for her empty glass. "May I take that for you?"

"Thank you."

"Would you like another?"

"I'm quite all right, thank you."

Fordyce went to the tables and returned. "Now your hands are free."

"So they are."

"May I have the honor of this dance?"

"Certainly, Leftenant Commander." Catherine was immediately conscious of the cologne Fordyce was using — a spicy scent she enjoyed. She caught whiffs of it as they moved about the dance floor. His hand on her back was firm but gentle, his footsteps sure and smooth, his grip on her hand warm. He didn't move as spiritedly as Skitt had because he didn't have the younger man's energy, but there was grace and dignity in his large circles over the dance floor that she liked. When the dance was done and he asked her for another, she said yes. This went on for several dances until her father showed up at Fordyce's shoulder.

"May I cut in?" he asked.

"Of course, Lord Preston." Fordyce stepped back. "Enjoy your waltz, sir."

"I shall indeed. Fordyce, isn't it? Family in Dover?"

"Yes, m'lord."

"Your father and mother have been good friends to the Danforths over the years. I'm very glad to see you here tonight."

"Thank you, m'lord."

"I shan't hold on to her long."

Lord Preston swept his daughter wildly into the middle of the room, several couples having to dodge as they swung near.

"What's this about, Father?" she asked. "I was enjoying myself."

"Believe me, the last thing I want to do is spoil your evening. It's a breath of fresh air to your mother and me to see you out on the dance floor."

"Then why did you steal me away?"

"So I could tell you who he is."

Catherine groaned. "I suppose he's a rake."

"Quite the opposite. I know what's going on with his career from my naval connections. He's bound for big things, so my advice is that if you like him even a bit, hang on to him."

"Hang on to him? I've just met him. I don't even know him."

"I am just . . ."

"Thank you so much, Father, but I'm twenty-five. I'll let you know how I feel about him in the morning." She kissed her father on the cheek. "Stop worrying about me."

"Well, your mother and I —"

"And I love you both for it. Now just waltz over and return me to the Royal Navy."

"Where is he?"

"Off by that horrid potted plant. Poor man looks like a boat adrift."

Lord Preston carved a path through the dancers, leaving dresses and suits and uniforms in disarray in his wake. He released Catherine in front of Fordyce with a flourish that embarrassed her and brought red to her face.

"There you are, sir." Lord Preston smiled. "None the worse for wear."

"Oh, m'lord," protested Fordyce, "you didn't even finish the dance."

"I leave that up to you. I must find Elizabeth . . . Lady Preston. I haven't had a go on the dance floor with her all night."

Fordyce shrugged as Lord Preston left. He extended his hand to Catherine. "May I complete this dance for you?"

"Please."

As she placed her arm on his shoulder she said, "Tell me about your cruise, would you?"

"Of course. Well, let's see. We darted down to Sierra Leone right from the start. We left from Devonport on November twenty-seventh last year, so I expect the captain wanted to get as warm as possible as quickly as possible."

She laughed. "A sensible British captain."

"Right. John Thurm is his name. We made it to Cape Town, South Africa, for Christmas, had a break, headed on for Zanzibar, Tanzania, and then anchored at Singapore in February. I remember the dates and times because I keep a journal. After that it was Australia and New Zealand — Adelaide, Melbourne, Sydney, Brisbane, and Auckland. Then full-steam ahead for Fiji and Hawaii."

"You terrible man!" Catherine felt free enough to tease him. "No wonder you have such a golden tan. We're suffering through our English weather, and there you are in Hawaii of all places."

"Defending Britain, Lady Catherine."

"Indeed. And where did the trade winds take you next, Leftenant Commander?"

"All sails set for Canada's West Coast.

Beautiful great trees on Vancouver Island, the cities of Victoria and Vancouver are gems, then down the coast to California and San Francisco —"

"Still defending England?" she interrupted.

"Every morning and every night. And your ladyship, of course."

"Of course."

"So it was necessary to get to Panama and Jamaica to defend you and the flag. Then we went on to South America to do more of the same — Valparaiso, Buenos Aires, Rio de Janeiro —"

"Oh stop!" She was laughing. "I hardly know you and I feel like slapping you. I'd love to see all those places even if it took a lifetime. And you saw them all in a few months."

"We hope to do the tour again next year."

"You do not."

"The Mediterranean, in any case. Why winter here when you can winter in Malta?"

"You're not a man; you're a beast."

He stopped dancing. "There's the song done."

"And that's it?"

"Why, would you like another go 'round?"

"I don't know why, but I do. I want to hear about Victoria and San Francisco and

Jamaica, for starters. I may want to hear about more after that."

The music began again, and Fordyce swirled her about the floor. "I don't think I can figure you out."

"What a dreary woman I would be if you could. We've been together less than an hour."

"Well, isn't Lady Catherine having the time of her life," Sally commented as she stood watching the naval officer whisk Catherine about the floor under the strings of electric lights.

"Thank the Lord, that's all I can say." Norah gulped at her punch. "She moped around Ashton Park for nigh on two years till I thought she'd joined the ghosts in the attic. A few weeks here, and her spirits have gone from night to day. It's wonderful."

"I thought she liked that German fellow . . . the teacher."

"So we all liked him."

"And she clearly likes this naval officer."

"Why shouldn't she? Look at him."

"One minute she's a nun, and the next she's the life of the party."

"Stop fussing, Sally. I'd hardly call her the life of the party. Just a lonely widow who decided it was time to unwrap the mourning band from her soul. I'm sure the lord and lady are thrilled." Norah put a glass of punch in Sally's hand. "Drink up. You're all hot and bothered."

"I am not hot and bothered," Sally retorted, but she drained the glass in a few seconds.

"We've had a fine night, and it's not over yet!"

Sally made a sour face. "We neither of us got two dances in a row from the same man. It's been first this one, and then the other one. I can't remember all their names, and they'll never remember mine. They all want to dance with the Knight girls. Those are the ones what will have the lads coming to call."

Norah watched one of the Knight sisters flash past on the arm of a scarlet-uniformed army officer. "Don't be so sure. They're too tall and thin so far as I can see. Men don't like that."

"They've not been off the dance floor all night, Norah."

"But it's the same few blokes over and over again, d'ya see? A lot of men like sturdier stuff."

"For heaven's sakes, is that what you and I are? You make us sound like Holsteins."

"Didn't I tell you?" Norah suddenly

crowed. "Wasn't I right?"

Sally pushed back strands of damp blonde hair that had fallen into her eyes. "What are you going on about now?"

Two army officers in scarlet greeted them with short bows.

"Ladies," said the one, "we've had our eyes on the pair of you all night and have finally drummed up the nerve to approach."

"Please don't refuse us," pleaded the other man with a warm smile.

"Why, we would never do that." Sally returned the smile and slipped her arm through that of the taller of the two men. "If you've been waiting all night, we must make up for lost time. How will three dances do you, sir?"

"Only three, m'lady?"

"Why, I'm sure there should be more if we find we don't tread all over each other's feet."

Sally and the officer went onto the floor, leaving Norah with the shorter and stockier one who, nevertheless, continued to offer her one of the brightest smiles she had ever seen. He extended his arm. "I'd be honored, ma'am," he said. "You're lovely."

"You don't mean that."

"I do. I truly have waited all night. I've not had a single dance."

Norah put her arm through his. "Not a single dance? I don't know if I believe that, leftenant."

"I swear. I just kept thinking, *What would it be like to spin you about the room?*"

"You're not interested in my friend?"

"Ah, no. Not my type at all. But Squinty, that is, Leftenant Park, he's happy as a clam, isn't he?"

"What about the Knight girls?"

"I don't know them. I just wanted to meet you. Shall we dance?" He took her onto the floor. Whatever awkwardness had existed when he first spoke to her was gone once they moved about. He never stumbled or bumped into others. While he was not what Norah considered a smooth dancer, he was steady and sure-footed. After a few minutes she trusted him enough to let him take her wherever he wanted on the floor.

"What's your name?" he asked.

"Norah Cole, sir."

"And I'm Leftenant Bruce Milne. I'm pleased to make your acquaintance, Miss Cole."

"As I am pleased to make yours, Leftenant Milne."

"Bruce."

She smiled. "Bruce it is."

■ ■ ■ ■

Fairburn strode down to the pond as dawn swept over the fields. He found Skitt huddled in his bush gripping his cricket bat. "No luck then?"

"Not with the poachers." Skitt's eyes and face were bright. "My night on the dance floor was another matter."

Fairburn squatted by him. "Ah, your grand moment with Lady Catherine. Well, not to burst your bubble, but she didn't exactly pine away after you left."

"What d'ya mean?"

"Others asked her to dance. She couldn't very well turn them all away."

"Who? Who did she dance with?" Skitt's eyes narrowed. "Did she dance with you?"

"Me? I didn't set a boot on the dance floor all night. Oh, it was a host of army officers and navy men."

"Who in particular?"

"Why, what are you planning to do with him? Pistols at dawn?"

Skitt's eyes grew darker. "What's his name?"

"Steady as she goes, lad. A naval officer named Terrence Fordyce. He serves on *HMS Hood*."

"Does she like him?"

"Well now, you know I didn't think to march up and demand that information from her, Master Skitt. But you can if you like."

Skitt suddenly stood up clutching his bat, a blanket, and his leather flask. "It doesn't matter. I shall continue on. We had a wonderful time together last night. We'll have a wonderful time at her father's birthday party as well."

"How do you, a groundskeeper, intend to get into a party for the nobility?"

"Lady Catherine said she'd slip me in."

"Slip you in? Under the door? Down the chimney? They'll all see you, Skitt. They'll know who you are and who you aren't. D'ya want to risk getting thrown out on your ear or even sacked?"

Skitt tilted up his chin. "Faint heart never won fair lady."

Catherine sat up in bed, sheets at her neck, arms wrapped about her bent knees, and glanced out the window. Two weeks had passed since the servants' ball, and a change had come over her. Last night, after her second official date with Terrence Fordyce, she'd collapsed into bed without drawing the curtains. Now she noticed the first streaks of sunlight winking off the dew on the grass. Her room was on the third floor and faced south so she could just make out the sparkle of the Channel at Dover. It was a perfect summer morning, and she felt like a perfect summer morning inside. It was the most light and joy she'd experienced since her husband's death.

You'd like him, Albert.

Well, Cat, he seemed like a good sort, right enough. You know I've wanted you to get past your grieving and find a man who'll be a good father to Sean. Fordyce might fit the bill.

It's too soon to say anything about that. Albert, I do so miss you still.

But you must have a life, Cat. That's what I want for you.

Would it be Fordyce then?

Mind, I liked the other chap too. Hartmann seems a solid type. If only he wasn't German. That spoils things.

Albert, what does it matter? The war's over. The Germans were our allies once against the French. You do remember Waterloo, don't you?

Albert's voice grew silent in her head. Continuing to gaze out the window, Catherine prayed, thought a bit, remembered Terrence's tanned face as he told her about Vancouver Island, and saw Albrecht's face, white and strong in the dark of the front porch. She closed her eyes. "Life is happening far too fast," she said softly. "One week I'm the grieving widow, and the next week I'm single and flattered by the attention of beautiful men sweeping me in a beautiful silk gown over the dance floor.

"People seem to like the change. Mother and Father certainly do. I don't know how I feel about it all though. Yes, it's spring and summer in my soul. It's spectacular. But marriage in half a year or a year? A father for Sean? I can't see it. I'm not quite sure who Catherine Moore is at the moment, and it's going to take a while to sort her out — never mind choosing between men as lovely as Terrence Fordyce and Albrecht Hartmann." She lay back on the bed, eyes still closed, and murmured, "Quite honestly, I really don't know what they see in me. Maybe I should take my vows — become a nun. That would solve everything, would it not?"

4

"Look, I'd like to win, but the truth is I'm happy if either of us wins."

"Yeah?"

"Yeah. I just don't want that buzzard Wolfgang Zeltner to win."

Kipp Danforth and Ben Whitecross stood by Kipp's SPAD. All around them ground crew darted back and forth between aircraft checking wing struts, wheels, ailerons, and everything else. Now and then an engine would cough to life, run for a minute, and then be shut down.

Kipp checked his watch. "Fifteen minutes to go. Zeltner got the first takeoff slot with two of the French pilots."

"It doesn't matter." Ben stared past the SPAD at the other planes nearby. "The officials time everyone from liftoff. Zeltner could land at Dover Sky five minutes ahead of you or me and it wouldn't make a difference — not if he'd set off ten minutes before us. We'd win." Ben pointed with his chin. "There he is."

They both stared under the wing at Zeltner, who stood tall, blond, and slender in his three-quarter-length black leather jacket.

"He's dressed like it's the Great War," grumbled Kipp.

"Perhaps it still is for him. You know he always regretted not besting Richthofen's record of eighty kills."

Zeltner appeared to feel their eyes on him for he turned and looked directly at the two of them. He lifted the hand holding his leather helmet in half salute.

They each raised a hand in response.

"It's Baron von Zeltner now, you know," said Ben.

"I saw that in the paper. When did that happen?"

"In '22. Your brother Edward said the Weimar Republic was looking for heroes. He was one of the ones they chose to put on the pedestal. Permitted him to add the "von" to his name. Yet a few weeks later von Zeltner joined a right-wing party the Weimar leadership detests."

"Edward is always up on the politics," grunted Kipp. "He fancies himself the first man in the kingdom in ten years."

"What was the name of the party Zeltner joined? The National Socialist . . . hang on . . . the National Socialist German Workers' Party, that's it. Big name, isn't it? Your dad and Edward call them the Nazis. Heard of them?"

"I'm too busy flying mail."

"Well," Ben went on, "they're a pretty violent lot. They go around and beat up people they don't like. Their leader's in prison right now."

"Hmm . . . so von Zeltner's part of that?"

"Right."

"I know he has a cruel streak." Kipp slapped his leather flying helmet against his pant leg. "Never pictured him as a thug though. Not his style, is it?"

"I'm sure he appoints others to do the street work while he sits in an office."

"That doesn't sound like his style either."

Ben shrugged. "He looks the same as when we met him in London in 1920." He leaned on the lower wing and stared at von Zeltner. "Remember that social event for pilots of all sides? He took an interest in your wife, if I recall."

"And to yours. Do you think he knows who we are?"

"Oh he knows."

"Then you can be sure he wants to beat you," said Kipp.

"And you, the son of the man hosting the race."

"But especially you, Ben. He'll never forget how you tore up his squadron and won the Victoria Cross in the bargain."

"Never forget . . . or forgive." Ben thrust his hands into his pockets. "This race needs to be won by an Englishman!"

"Gentlemen! Aviators!" A heavy man in tweed coat and cap stood in the middle of the parked airplanes. "We are about to begin. Your names will be shouted out in groups of three. Those three will take off side by side. Then another three will be called and so on until all twenty of you are up. The winner cannot be announced until time of arrival at the finish line is compared with time of takeoff and the exact amount of flying time is calculated. Obviously the pilot with the shortest flying time shall find himself the winner of the Lord Preston Cup and two thousand pounds sterling."

He consulted a sheet of paper. "Remember your destination is the estate of Dover Sky in Kent. Each of you has been furnished with a map. There are large markings chalked out on the airfield there. In addition red, white, and blue balloons surround the landing strip. Do not go below one thousand feet unless you have engine trouble and must touch down. Pray choose an unpopulated area if that is the case. Any questions?" He paused. "No?" He brought out his pocket watch. "Gentlemen, to your planes. The air race from Liverpool to Dover is about to begin. May the best man win!"

Kipp climbed into his cockpit. Ben ran fifty yards to his SPAD and swung himself up.

Contact! Contact! The words were shouted from one end of the meadow to the other as pilots started their engines. Roars and rumbles and exhaust filled the July air. Suddenly a flare gun was fired, and a red ball of fire arched over the field. The heavy man in tweed shouted through a megaphone above the growl of engines: "Von Zeltner! St. Laurent! Hugo! You are cleared for takeoff!"

Kipp watched the three SPADs taxi, lift off, streak south, and then head east as they gained altitude. Von Zeltner's plane had a distinctive paint scheme of black and yellow. Kipp muttered, "The same colors your squadron used. The same colors you plastered all over your Fokker triplane. It's not 1918, Wolfgang. I suppose if there hadn't been a rule that you had to use a SPAD you'd have a D.VII or an Albatros up there."

Three or four minutes later a second set of names was called, and three more SPADs took to the air. Kipp opened and closed his hand on the stick and gritted his teeth. A third set of names rang out, and another three aircraft took off. He squeezed his eyes shut and counted to sixty. Nine planes were already up and zooming through the sky for Dover.

"Whitecross! Dickens! Danforth! You are cleared for takeoff!"

Kipp waved his hand in the air and gunned the engine. His ground crew whipped the chocks away from his wheels and the SPAD rolled forward. Ben was on his left; Dickens on his right. They left the ground in unison, as if they'd been practicing the maneuver for weeks. Kipp adjusted his goggles and tightened the white silk scarf around his neck. It was the scarf he'd worn in France during the war. He nudged the SPAD higher and higher, leaving Dickens and Ben quickly behind. Then he aimed his plane towards the English Channel.

"All right, Wolfgang," he hissed through clenched teeth, "where are you?"

Dover Sky
Lord Preston stood by dozens of red, blue,

and white balloons — the same colors as the Union Jack that flew from a pole next to a brand-new Quonset hut. He slapped a rolled-up newspaper against the side of his leg as he kept an eye on the northern horizon and glanced occasionally at the crowd of people spilling over onto the airfield.

"Shouldn't they be here by now?" he asked out loud. "Eh?"

Victoria laughed. "Oh, Papa! You haven't got anywhere to go. It's your birthday. Relax and enjoy it."

"I'd relax a lot more if this race were over and done with and no one was injured. Your mother feels the same way."

"Well, you put up the cup and the two-thousand-pound purse, Dad," Victoria reminded.

"In a moment of weakness, I assure you." He glanced about him. "Where have the children disappeared to?"

"You can't expect an empty sky to hold their attention. Only grown-ups are keen on that sort of thing. Aunt Holly and Harrison have the lot of them down to feed bread crumbs to the swans."

"The swans! I hope Harrison keeps his wits about him. The pond is deeper than it looks and —"

"Father, I think Harrison knows a thing or two about ponds. And if he's forgotten anything, Aunt Holly will be quick to remind him. Catherine, Christelle, and Char are at the pond as well. Please don't fret about that along with the air race."

"Hmm . . ." Lord Preston turned to his son-in-law, who was at his left elbow. "Jeremy, you and Emma have news?"

Jeremy looked at him in surprise, sunlight glinting off his round eyeglasses. "Who told you that?"

Emma put a gloved hand on her husband's arm. "I did, Jeremy, dear. But I said we'd tell him at his party when everyone was present — not out here by the airstrip."

"You can tell the others at the party," said Lord Preston. He placed the arm with the newspaper around his wife. "Elizabeth and I prefer to hear about it now. It is good news, I presume?"

"Very good news, Papa," replied Emma. "Though I think reactions will be mixed. Jeremy has been given a pulpit in London — and a very good one."

"London!" Lord Preston was startled.

"Why, that's miles away from Ashton Park!" exclaimed Lady Preston.

"We hear that Jeremy's being considered for the post of bishop, and that if he does well in London he's got it."

"Em," Jeremy reacted quickly, "you didn't need to tell them that."

"I did. It's the only thing that would soften the blow of us packing up and leaving Lancashire."

"A bishop?" Lord and Lady Preston responded together.

Jeremy looked at the ground and shook his head. "I'm sorry, Mum and Dad. I don't have to take the London church."

Lord Preston stared at him. "What?"

Lady Preston put her hands on his shoulders and kissed his cheek. "My dear boy, of course you must take it. God moves in mysterious ways. We're so proud of you."

"Well done, Jeremy!" Edward came over and pumped the cleric's left hand, carefully avoiding Jeremy's prosthetic right arm and hand. "This is excellent news. I fear I must let my own cat out of the bag now."

"What is that?" asked Emma.

"Mother and Father know, but no one else in the family does. The Conservative Party has chosen me for one of its candidates. I'm to run for a seat in Parliament the next election. I'm to run for Dover!"

Emma laughed. "No! Is it true? You and Char only a stone's throw from us in London?"

"If I win, yes."

Victoria hugged him fiercely from behind. "Of course you'll win, old brother Edward. You've always wanted to rule the world, and now you've got your start."

"Ouch! Careful of the pocketbook. I still have to get by Labor and the Liberals."

"That's nothing."

"Well, Vic, Labor took power from the Conservatives and formed the government in January. I can't underestimate them."

"You'll be first past the post, never fear."

"Here they come!" a voice shouted.

The crowd made their way off the landing strip as the judges yelled into their megaphones. Five or six dots could be spotted rapidly approaching, darting underneath a white bank of cumulus clouds and dropping in altitude. As the shapes of the planes grew obvious, the colors of the SPAD in the lead became clear to the people on the ground: yellow and black. Close on the lead plan's tail was a SPAD with a white cross painted on the fuselage.

"Ben! It's Ben!" Victoria exclaimed as she pointed. "He has the cross. He's right behind the leader."

"And Kipp is right behind Ben." Edward grinned. "See the black K?"

Lord Preston struck his leg with the newspaper. "First past the flagstaff wins."

The roar of engines blotted out conversation. For a moment it looked as if both Ben and Kipp would overtake the black-and-yellow SPAD, but its pilot opened the throttle and surged ahead, streaking past the flagpole half a minute before anyone else. A groan swept through the crowd. Victoria closed her eyes and put the back of her hand to her mouth. Lord Preston unfolded his paper and glanced at a list of entrants that included descriptions of their aircraft.

"I see." He shook his head. "A German won. A Baron von Zeltner. I'd hoped to give the Lord Preston Cup to an Englishman first time around. Well, well, can't be helped."

Von Zeltner brought his plane about and touched down on the grass. Ben and Kipp came in for a landing minutes after him. The judges barked into their megaphones and reminded people more planes would be coming in over the next few minutes even as a cluster of men and women waving the black, red, and gold flag of Germany's Weimar Republic rushed von Zeltner's SPAD. He cut his engine quickly and the propeller whirred to a stop moments before the well-wishers reached his plane. Climbing out, he was swarmed by the flag bearers and lifted up onto their shoulders. Once his boots were on the ground again, a teenaged girl in a dress the colors of his plane kissed him on the cheek and presented him with a bouquet of roses. Smiling broadly, he lifted them to his face. Some were yellow, others scarlet, and still others such a bloodred they looked black.

"Shall I bring the trophy from the hut now, Lord Preston?"

Lord Preston nodded, his lips tight. "Yes, Skitt. They've set up a table for it on the other side of the Quonset. Not with red, black, and gold bunting, thank goodness."

"That's not all there is to say about it, surely?" Jeremy looked at Victoria. "Didn't you tell me the planes all took off at different intervals?"

"Yes."

"Then who won must depend on when Ben and Kipp actually left Liverpool."

"If it was the same time as the German, the race is over and done, Jeremy," Lord Preston said.

Edward cocked his eyebrows. "Yes, but they might have taken off long after him. Jeremy's right. The judges will have something to say about this once everyone's touched down."

The Germans moved their celebration to the edge of the field as SPAD after SPAD made its way in and landed. Lord Preston counted every one and was relieved when number twenty bounced over the grass and sputtered to a stop. The children boiled up from the pond, whistling and yelling and waving their arms, Harrison and Holly running after them to herd them away from the airplanes. The judges gathered the pilots into a group by the Quonset where Skitt had placed the award cup on a table decorated for the occasion. The trophy was two feet high with large handles on either side and fashioned out of silver. Von Zeltner finally broke away from the Germans and made his way to the hut, the roses still in his hand.

"Tough break, England," he said as he approached Ben and Kipp. "The wind was in my favor. Perhaps God as well."

Ben said nothing, but Kipp bent to smell one of the roses. "Great bouquet. A very pretty girl put them in your arms. Mind if I take the flowers home, Wolfgang?"

Von Zeltner gave a half laugh. "Take them home? Well, why not? There will be plenty more for me in Berlin. Here!" He handed the bouquet to Kipp. "And if your French wife doesn't mind, you can take the young

111

woman home too. That would spice up your marriage, Danforth."

Ben saw Kipp's right hand ball into a fist, and he stepped in to take the bouquet. *"Danke, Wolfgang,"* Ben said. "But I wouldn't get my hopes up about taking the cup back to the Fatherland. They timed the flights, remember? And we took off *after* you did."

Von Zeltner was quiet a moment. "Not so long after, Whitecross."

"At least ten minutes."

"We'll see."

Von Zeltner stalked away.

"Thank you for that." Kipp was rigid. "I'm sure my father would have been less than impressed at his son brawling with a German baron at the Danforth summer estate. Could touch off another war."

"Ah, but think how much better you would feel right now if you'd permanently hammered his face into the landing strip. You could have walked over that baronial snout of his every time you flew in and out of Dover Sky."

"There's a heartwarming Christian thought."

"Right."

One of the judges, thin as wire and sporting a top hat and tails, walked into the cluster of fliers with a clipboard. "I've just rung up Liverpool and gotten the departure times for every plane. The judges and I have matched those with your arrival times, and I have the final results here." The pilots grew quiet as he flipped through a few sheets. Glancing up, he spotted von Zeltner at the back. "Baron von Zeltner, I congratulate you on being the first across the line. However you were also the first to leave Liverpool."

Von Zeltner's voice was tight. "I took off in a group of three."

"Yes." The judge consulted his clipboard. "With Hugo and St. Laurent." He looked back up and met von Zeltner's gaze. "You had nine minutes and seventeen seconds head start on the second person across the line, Benjamin Whitecross. And he was only thirty-seven seconds behind you. Which means he beat you by eight minutes and forty seconds. Ben Whitecross wins the Lord Preston Cup Air Race!"

Von Zeltner's face whitened. "I demand to see that page of arrival and departure times."

"Certainly. You will notice it is signed and authorized by all four judges."

Von Zeltner pushed his way through the fliers and snatched the clipboard from the judge's hand. The other pilots crowded in and looked over his shoulder as he scanned the page. He dropped the clipboard on the grass and headed towards his plane.

"Are you not staying for the festivities, Baron von Zeltner?" the judge called after him. "It is Lord Preston's sixtieth birthday and there will be fireworks at ten."

"I will have my festivities in Berlin," von Zeltner snapped over his shoulder. "They know who the hero of the hour is."

"I see. Well, don't forget to fill up with petrol on Lord Preston's shilling. We'd hate to have Germany's hero wind up at the bottom of the Channel for lack of fuel."

The rest of the pilots swarmed Ben, shaking his hand and slapping him on the back. "Well done, Whitecross! Well done!"

Another ball of light trailed sparks and then burst overhead, forming a blazing flower with seven golden petals. A great "ahhh-hhh" erupted from the hundreds of people spread around Dover Sky.

"Mum?"

"That one was particularly lovely. Your Father didn't want to spend the money, but I asked him when he intended to turn sixty a second time. Now and then we have to kill the fatted calf and celebrate."

"Mum?"

"What is it, Catherine? Ohhhhhh, look at that — the colors of the Union Jack!"

"I want you to know that I intend to remain at Dover Sky through the winter."

An explosion of green and white lit up the night sky.

"What did you say?"

"I said I plan to make Dover Sky my home. I'm not going back with you and Papa in the fall."

Elizabeth turned to look at Catherine. Red flashed over her face from the next burst of fireworks. "Of course you are returning to Ashton Park with us. There's no one at Dover Sky in the winter but Fairburn and a few other servants, and Fairburn will be leaving in November."

"I want to be in the south."

"Nonsense."

Thump. Thump. Thump. Gold and silver streaks shot through the darkness.

"Mum, do you want me to rent a flat in Dover? I've lived on my own in Belfast when Albert was on business trips, for heaven's sake. Why can't I stay at the summer estate?"

"My dear, no one lives here but the groundskeeper, and as the groundskeeper will soon be Skitt, it's out of the question."

"Why? He won't be a bother."

"A bother? The young man's dotty about you. It simply can't be done."

"Dotty? You have such quaint expressions." Catherine looked up at a particularly vivid burst of yellow. "I will go to Dover then. Or Folkestone. Or perhaps as far south as Plymouth."

"Plymouth? What on earth is in Plymouth?" Lady Preston's mouth opened slightly as Roman candles were lit and pumped dozens of stars into the blackness. "Ah, it's Leftenant Commander Fordyce, isn't it? You want to be closer to him."

"I don't really."

"You've been out with him several times now."

"Just to dinner."

"Devonport is still a long ways from Dover Sky."

Catherine folded her arms across her chest as bang after bang interrupted their conversation. "I'm not going to argue with you, Mum. I'm twenty-five. Certainly I'm well within my bounds to choose where I wish to live."

"I don't understand why you want to stay here."

"It's not a great mystery. Ashton Park pulls me down; Dover Sky lifts me up."

116

"Why?"

"I can't write out all the reasons why, Mother. It's just that way."

Six or seven fireworks broke open one after another.

"Very well since you are so determined." Lady Preston gazed upward at the showers of colored sparks. "There must be more staff. You cannot have Tavy or Mrs. Longstaff, but Norah and Sally have been helping Mrs. Longstaff with the meals so they will be well suited to the kitchen. It's quite impossible to leave Skitt here with you in the vicinity. Harrison must take over as groundskeeper. He will be amenable to that, although he will certainly miss his castle. Holly will fulfill the role of manager of the household staff. Hmm, and we must have more of those. I'll send along Nancy and Harriet. They'll do nicely as chambermaids, but we require a couple of footmen as well. You do complicate matters, my dear. It's bad enough having Emma in London this fall and Edward and Charlotte taking up residence in Dover so he can start ringing doorbells."

"But there's no election scheduled."

"There will be. Ramsay MacDonald and Labor have a minority government. Something always happens with minority governments. It doesn't take long before they topple, and there's another election. You could always room with Edward and Charlotte, of course, and save me all this trouble."

"No, Mum, I need to be on my own. Alone as I can be in a house you're cramming with servants."

"You'll find you need all of them. People will visit if Dover Sky is occupied over the winter months. What am I thinking? You'll require a butler as well. Liscombe? Tarrington?"

"Put in Skitt, Mother."

"What? Skitt as butler? A young man who is a groundskeeper? Ridiculous."

"Let him have a go. Skitt can do the job. He loves it here."

"I'm sure he does with the queen of his heart in her bedchamber upstairs."

"Don't talk rot, Mum. And you'll have Harrison and two footmen at Dover Sky in any case if you're worried about appearances."

"No, no, I'm sorry, my dear. Skitt staying is out of the question."

"So now it's just family and close friends." Edward lifted a glass. "A toast to my father, Lord Preston! May he live to see another sixty years and another Conservative government before the year's out."

People clapped and cheered. Lord Preston disentangled himself from his grandchildren on the library's couch and got to his feet.

"It may be more likely I see one hundred and twenty summers than I see the Conservative Party in power before Christmas." Lord Preston waved his hand. "We've already had a full day and more than enough speeches. I've promised the children angel food cake and ice cream before their special birthday bedtime, their regular bedtime being long past. So pray, I say, let's say grace and get on with it."

"Father." Edward held up several telegrams. "I have cables to read from Michael and Libby in America, as well as Robbie and Shannon in Jerusalem."

"Do you? Bless them for remembering me. But those are easily read out loud while we're eating cake, I think."

After the family and guests had cake and Edward read the various birthday greetings, the majority of the guests left for home. When just close friends and family were left, Edward announced, "There is also a special gift from Lord and Lady Scarborough."

"Is there? Where is it?"

Lord Scarborough stood up. "Difficult to wrap, Lord Preston. But I'll gladly take you to it in the morning."

"Take me to it in the morning? Where is it? At your villa in Portugal?"

"Not quite, old boy. The gift is down at the Port of Dover — berthed."

"What?" Lord Preston stared at him.

Lord Scarborough smiled. "I have not had the opportunity of presenting you with a prize worthy of your attainment to marquess and lordship. Now you are sixty as well. So many milestones. Not to mention our friendship. Lady Scarborough and I picked this out on our own. It is not brand-new, mind you, but it's utterly seaworthy and comes with a glorious history."

"What have you done, sir? It's not a boat!"

"I would not call it that. It is a forty footer with a bow as keen as a saber."

"A yacht, sir?"

"Indeed, a yacht, sir. She is christened *Pluck*."

"I can't wait for morning!" Lord Preston glanced around him. "Do you all understand? I simply can't wait for morning!" He pointed at the couch. "All those six and above, come with me at once. Harrison?"

Harrison got to his feet. "M'lord?"

"You will drive. Bring around the larger Rolls, if you please. Lady Preston, you must join me. And Lord and Lady Scarborough, of course."

"The Silver Ghost with the long chassis then?" asked Harrison.

"Yes, yes. Anyone else want to come along? I know this is highly irregular and the hour is late, but Lord and Lady Scarborough have indulged in a bit of madness and I can only respond in kind. Why, I couldn't get a wink of sleep in any case without going down to the harbor to see this vessel for myself. I trust you are not pulling my leg, my Lord Scarborough?"

Lord Scarborough barked a laugh. "Never entered my head but once or twice."

Lord Preston propelled his wife through the door. "If any of you are joining us, come along, come along! A glance out the window will give you Harrison and the Silver Ghost at any moment so sharp's the word and nimble's the action."

"Lord Kipp, you're not going with the mob?"

Kipp, glass of punch in hand, was staring at a sea painting of an English frigate clashing with a French warship off Dover, circa 1815. The lady's voice was instantly recognizable. He turned quickly, as if he'd been struck from behind. "Lady Caroline!"

She smiled. "*Lord Kipp. Lady Caroline.* Why are we standing on social niceties when the library is empty, and you're the man who saved my life?"

Her beauty filled his eyes and made him stumble over his words. "Don't you — don't you think that's an exaggeration?"

"No, I don't. Who else would have rescued me from France and that ogre Tanner Buchanan?" She was dressed in a gown the color of sapphire that heightened the blue in her eyes. "It's been ages. Do you have a kiss for me?"

Kipp hesitated. Then he leaned forward and put his lips to her soft cheek and wisps of shining blonde hair. "You look extraordinary," he said when he straightened.

She kissed his cheek in return. "Thank you. And you're still my handsome young aviator. You flew well today."

"Not well enough."

"Oh yes, well enough." She traced a white-gloved finger along the side of his face. "You're the one I'd have chosen for the prize."

"Christelle is just downstairs."

"Chris left in the third car with Matthew and Charles. The younger ones put up such

a fuss they took the lot of them to Dover."
She brushed his cheek with the back of her
gloved hand. "Besides, it was Chris who told
me to hunt you down and pamper you, so
I'm doing that."

"Really? She said that?"

"Yes, she did."

"Have you . . . have you heard anymore
from Charles's father?"

Caroline wrinkled her nose. "You do bring
up distasteful subjects. Tanner Buchanan
writes letters to Charles. He comes by to
visit in the company of that Kate Hall lady
of his. He doesn't want me and I don't want
him, if that's what you're wondering. It's
only about his son. He's maneuvering for
custody of him and for a seat in the House
of Commons."

"Where has he set up residence?"

"Scotland. South Ayrshire. Robbie Burns
country."

"What's he doing there? I thought Buchanan fancied himself a highlander."

"So he does. But this is the seat Labor offered him if there's another election. The
other chap will be stepping down. Tanner's
staking out his political turf, much as your
brother Edward is doing in Dover." Caroline pouted, bringing her full lips together.
"Do we have to go on about such a dreary

subject? The last time I saw you was at your Aunt Holly's wedding a whole year ago. I wish you and Chris would come down for a visit to the Scarborough estate."

Kipp swirled the ice cubes in his drink. "Chris thinks the world of you. Your boy and ours get along. It's me . . . I'm to blame. Too much flying. And now Ben and I are doing the racing as well. There's another one next month — Paris to Madrid."

"So no time for your wife or me?"

"There's time for my wife. You're something else again. Why haven't you picked up on another man by now? If it were possible, you're even more beautiful than you were during the war — and at that time your charm was considerable."

"Not considerable enough to keep you."

"Truly, Caroline, you are a marvel. You can't tell me, what with all the guests your parents bring home, there hasn't been an offer or two."

"I'm damaged goods, remember?"

"It's 1925 in a few months. Attitudes have changed."

"Not among us bluebloods." She took the glass from his hand. "Here . . . let's put that to one side, shall we?" Her eyes seemed to catch fire in the lamplight. "Chris and you always say the same thing about me — that I'm getting more beautiful as I push ahead into my late twenties. Is it true or is it just a French kindness on her part?"

"Christelle's honesty is her French kindness."

"I see." Her lips brushed over his. "Then be nice to me, Kipp. Be kind. Just a little."

"Caroline —"

"I'm not asking for the moon and sixpence, Lord Kipp. Just some charity. For a beautiful woman no one wants."

"I'm married to Christelle now."

Her arms went around him. The perfume of her hair and her skin filled his head.

"Oh, Kipp," she murmured, tangling her fingers in his hair. "I love you."

He turned away abruptly. "No, no."

Without looking at her he walked quickly from the room.

She smiled after him. "We'll try again, shall we?"

5

October, 1924
Port of Dover

"The government's fallen! Can you believe it? Ramsay and Labor lost a no-confidence vote, and we're to have an election." Edward swept Charlotte into his arms and kissed her again and again.

Her hair had been bound up in a scarf while she cleaned the flat, but his sudden swoop and the draft from the open door brought her long, black hair down swiftly.

"That's marvelous!" she laughed. "So when is your first speech?"

"Tomorrow night at the town hall. All the candidates will be having a go and introducing their families."

"Their families?" Charlotte pulled back. "You're joking."

"I'm not. The good people of Dover and district shall want to see I am a respectable family man with a wife and child. And

126

where is our little man?"

"Napping."

"Good! I can kiss you some more, you ravishing beauty."

"Come, Edward, not in the middle of the afternoon!"

"What difference does the time of day make? You are spectacular."

"I'm not! I'm all set up for cleaning."

"Really?" He kissed the dark hair that had unraveled from its combs. "You look ready to go door-to-door with me."

"Oh!" She pushed against him fiercely. "You're not getting me out any door when I'm looking like a bucket of slops."

"A bucket of slops? I'd like to know when you've ever looked like a bucket of slops!" He picked her up off the floor and swung her about in his arms. "You're not afraid, are you, my Lady Charlotte?"

"Your *Lady* Charlotte? Of course I'm afraid. You're the one who wanted to be a public figure, not me. I didn't even want to be called *lady,* but marrying you fixed that."

"It wasn't marrying me. It was dad being made a marquess by the king."

"I don't care whose fault it is, I'm quite happy to stay at home, and mop floors, and raise my boy, and brew tea. I honestly am. Now I suppose you want to become the prime minister of Britain and getting elected member of parliament for Dover is the first step."

"It is. And the rocky road to success begins with tomorrow night's speech and the unveiling of the magical and magnificent Lady Charlotte Danforth and her equally magical and magnificent son."

"I shan't say anything. I'll just smile and nod."

"Hair up?" Edward asked.

"Yes, hair up."

"Our lad in his suit?"

She smiled. "He'll be out of it in a month, so the suit might as well go out with a splash. Yes, our boy will be all suited up like his father."

Edward swung her about a final time and planted her on the floor. "It will be the most exceptional month — the most splendid array of days since the reign of Queen Victoria!"

"Oh, will it? Fancy that."

"I need your love to keep me moving forward."

"You always have that."

"And your kisses."

"You and your kisses. You get more than your share. Most men don't get half so many from their wives in a lifetime."

"I haven't had any lately. Not today." Edward raised his eyebrows. "And today is such a special day."

Charlotte put her hands on her hips. "Not today? How can you say that! You've been kissing me nonstop since you walked through that door and took me away from my broom and dustpan."

"There it is! I've been kissing you, but *you* haven't been kissing me."

"Is that so, Lord Edward?"

"It is so, Lady Charlotte."

She gave him a peck on the cheek. "There you are."

"Lip kisses."

"Lip kisses now? We'll be at this all afternoon."

"Excellent! Once I'm properly inspired, I'll write my speech."

"Little Lord Fauntleroy will be up in half an hour."

Edward peeled off his suit jacket with a grin. "Then we'd best get to the lip kissing. What a capital day for it!"

Charlotte shook her head and gave him a sly smile that made her blue eyes flicker with light. "I've never seen such a man for the loving."

"No other man has had you to love."

"Ah, a charmer." She put her arms around

his neck. "Lip kissing it is for the future prime minister of England. Ready . . . set . . . go!" She brought his head towards hers with a sharp tug and kissed him with relish.

She didn't pull away until Edward was sure he was going to drop like a stone to the floor.

He tried to break the kiss, but she wouldn't let him.

Finally she drew her lips away only long enough to smile at him darkly and murmur, "Oh no you don't, Mr. Prime Minister! In for a penny, in for a pound."

October
Dover Sky
"Skitt! Good to see you."

"Leftenant Commander." Skitt's reply was frosty.

"I've come to collect Lady Catherine."

"Is that right, sir?"

Rain pelted Terrence's officer's hat and trench coat. "Uh, may I step inside, Skitt?"

Skitt opened the manor door a bit more. "As you wish."

Fordyce squeezed into the hall, water running off his coat and forming a puddle on the floor.

Skitt glanced down at the puddle. His lip

curled. "I'll have to fetch one of the maids and have her come with a mop," he said in a flat voice.

"Sorry about that. English weather, you know."

"One shouldn't be out in it, sir." Skitt walked away. "I'll get the maid."

"Will you please tell Lady Catherine I'm here?"

Skitt glanced back at him. "To be sure. After I find Harriet or Nancy and help them get the bucket and mop."

Skitt vanished down the hall. Neither Skitt nor the maid appeared as Fordyce stood impatiently by the door. After a good five minutes, he glimpsed Catherine upstairs, moving from one room to another.

"Hullo, Cathy!"

She appeared at the head of the staircase. Peering down, she said, "Terry! What on earth are you doing standing there? I didn't even know you'd arrived."

"I'm not surprised. I don't think your butler approves of me."

Catherine put her hand over her mouth as her eyes crinkled. "Skitt doesn't approve of anyone. I'll be down in a minute. I want to kiss Sean goodbye."

In just a few minutes Terrence watched Catherine float down the stairs toward him.

He helped her with her coat as they discussed the atrocious storm.

Harriet showed up with mop and bucket just as the couple headed out the door.

"Just a bit of water like this?" she grumbled. "Skitt made it sound like I had to mop up Noah's flood."

"Thank you, Harriet," Catherine said just before Terrence closed the door.

As they drove through the rain and the dark, Catherine rested her right hand on Fordyce's arm. "Mum will try Skitt out till Christmas, she says. He's mostly the groundskeeper; however, he's done very well as a butler. It's only my suitors he has issues with."

"Your suitors? You have more than one?"

"Oh, millions, Terry!" She smiled and gave him a kiss on the cheek. "That's all you get for now. Keep your eyes on the road."

"So we'll have time together after the speech?"

"We shall. I'll want a hot coffee and a snack."

"Char is so hospitable."

"She is. But it will be late, they'll have their son with them, and Edward goes on the road again tomorrow with this election flap. So you don't need to worry about losing out on our time alone." She leaned her head against the window. "It's absolute madness — only three weeks for an election campaign. One week gone now, and I'm sure neither my father up in Lancashire nor Edward here in Dover have had a wink of sleep. I just hope it's a happy ending."

"Me too. I've had my fill of Labor and the Liberals both." Fordyce honked as he passed a car. "Listen, I know everything's moving rather quickly between us, Cathy. But —"

She lifted her head. "Oh no! You have that naval 'take charge' sound to your voice. You're not going to ask for my hand in marriage, are you?"

"Nothing so rash. I just want to make sure you will attend the Christmas Ball in Plymouth in December with me. I very much want to show you off."

"Haven't we already established that I'll be hanging off your arm in silks and pearls at that event?"

"Just double-checking, love."

"Why?"

Fordyce hesitated a moment as he concentrated on driving. "It's a dirty night, isn't it?" He honked at a truck. "Those army lorries always take over the entire road if they can get away with it." He glanced at her. "You look lovely, Cathy. Have I told you that tonight?"

She narrowed her eyes and took her hand from his arm. "Come, Terry, out with it. What's up?"

"We're setting off after Christmas. First to Lisbon to take part in the Vasco de Gama celebration they're having. You know, Vasco de Gama the great explorer?"

"Yes, I know who Vasco de Gama was. Then what?"

"The Med."

"The Mediterranean? But the *Hood* just came back from a worldwide cruise last month."

"I know it. But the lads want to go down to the sun belt. It's good for morale, and the Royal Navy has exercises for us to run."

"I'm sure they do. Our fighting navy off to Gibraltar and Malta to save the Empire. I suppose you'll be gone till spring."

"Something like that."

"Something like that? Oh Terry, things between us were just getting onto surer footing." She plunged her head back against the seat and groaned. "Don't fall for a navy man, every young woman is told. It's something we are told never to do. Now look at the mess I'm in."

"It's hardly a mess, Cathy. I care for you very much and —"

"Of course it's a mess! Here I'm living at Dover Sky through a rainy, dreary winter, and the one good reason to be doing it is off to work on his suntan after Christmas."

"Cathy —"

"So I'm supposed to be like the dutiful wife and wait by the window as I look out toward the sea, darn your socks, and pray for your safe return?"

"I don't know about the wife, window, or socks part of it, but I do hope you'll pray for my safe return."

Catherine sighed, her eyes still shut. "I will. You know I will. But Terry, we're not married or engaged. And I'm not saying I want to be right now. It's far too soon for anything like that. But quite honestly I don't want to sit around all winter as if I were. I do want to get out of the house."

"So there is someone else?" he said sharply, giving her a quick glance.

"There is no one else as close to me as you are. I just want you to understand if I go to a concert in London with a gentleman or attend a worship service in Canterbury with another, that it doesn't mean I want to break off with you. I simply have to get out to get some air."

"I understand that, I guess."

"You do?"

"Yes. And what's his name?"

"Terry! There is no one man . . . just some acquaintances." She looked at his worried face. "Horatio Nelson. It's him. Are you satisfied?"

"Not very."

"Well, that will have to do."

They rode in silence for several miles. Catherine finally spoke. "Let's not spoil our evening together. I care for you, Terry. I'm just not ready to start pining away again. I've been pining for more than two years already."

"I know that."

She put her hand back on his arm and gave it a squeeze. "Good. So you understand why I can't go back to that dark hole, not even for you." She stared out through the rain sliding over the windshield and the swipes of the wipers. "In any case, it works both ways. I shan't mind if you see a woman or two when you're in port at Gibraltar."

"I'm not interested."

"Maybe one of them will change your mind." She glanced at him and noted his clenched jaw and tight lips. "Don't be a martyr, Terry. I count on your cheerfulness. Come back to me, but don't come back to me sour."

"We cannot have a trade agreement with the communists in Moscow! Only Ramsay MacDonald could think that was a good idea. Ramsay MacDonald and his Labor Bolsheviks." Edward paused as people in the packed hall cheered. "If I am elected, I will help form a Conservative government with Stanley Baldwin once more at the helm. Then we will tear up that agreement. We will have no trade with those revolutionaries — those assassins whose hands were dipped in blood with the murder of Tsar Nicholas and his family, even his children! I say it again: No trade with the murderers and Bolsheviks!"

The audience erupted into applause again. Edward waited for the roar to subside. "But I don't want you to send me to Westminster just to deal with the Red Menace, important as that is for the future of Great Britain. I also want to do something for Dover. I want to do something for you — the workingman — and for your children and your grandchildren. More shipping, more across-the-Channel traffic. A bigger harbor — a deeper harbor and a more protected harbor."

Men jumped to their feet, clapping and waving their hats in the air. "I want a port second to none in Great Britain! I want a port that will bring prosperity to Dover! I call upon you to send me to Westminster so I may ensure a Conservative government puts money into you and into our harbor. I call upon you to send me to Westminster so I may ensure a Conservative government that will *pour* money into our harbor!"

Edward tried to continue but the applause drowned out his words. He smiled and lifted his hands. Finally he shouted, "A vote for me on October twenty-ninth is a vote for Britain and the British people! God save the king!"

Fordyce made his way through the crush of bodies and managed to shake Edward's hand and slap him on the back. "Well done, Lord Edward. A great speech."

Edward grinned. "Thanks, Fordyce. I have to give another seven or eight tomorrow, so keep me in your prayers."

"We'll pop by the flat after you're free of all this to say hullo, and then Lady Catherine and I are heading out."

Enthusiastic men and women jostled Edward and called out his name. He kept smiling and shaking hands as he spoke with Fordyce. "Actually, I'm not going back to the house. I'm taking the car to Deal. I have a meeting there in an hour and another at seven in the morning. I was going to ask if you wouldn't mind taking Charlotte and Owen to Dover Sky with you. I'll be gone a week, and I'd like them to be with family."

"Why of course! I'll collect them right away. Where are they?"

"Just at the back. I'll be over to say good-bye once I'm finished here. I won't be but five minutes."

Fordyce struggled through the well-wishers. He'd just broken clear when Catherine slipped up beside him and kissed him on the cheek.

"There, that's done. I'm ready for my coffee right after we say hullo to Char."

Fordyce gave her a cold look. His voice was clipped. "We're to ferry Char and Owen to Dover Sky straightaway. Your brother is driving over to Deal when he's done here, and he'll be gone a week. He wants his wife and child safe and sound at the estate."

"I see." She hesitated. "Well, that only makes sense, doesn't it?" She held his arm. "Cheer up. I'll have Norah fix us up a pot of coffee when we get home, and we'll squirrel away in the den. It'll be better than a coffee shop or restaurant. And you'll have me all to yourself."

"Will I? We can't leave Charlotte on her

own, can we? How hospitable would that be?"

"I thought you liked her."

"I do. She's wonderful. Edward married a gem. But I'll not be able to get away for another month — not until Guy Fawkes — and I'd hoped you and I could have a good talk."

"Terry, we can. I —"

"Oh, there you two are! Cheers!" Charlotte stood in front of them wearing a red dress with a matching red hat and feather. "I hear you're my cab. I really don't want to put you two out. We'd be perfectly happy at our flat while Edward's gone. He gets terribly old-fashioned about things like this."

Fordyce found his best smile quickly. "Nonsense, Char. If it were me, I'd want the same thing for my wife and son. Where's your boy? Where's the luggage?"

"Owen's with the Conservative Party's secretary for this district and probably getting horseback rides on Mr. Tippin's back, I'm sure. Poor man." She smiled. "I'm afraid we'll have to drop by the flat for the luggage, Terry. It's all terribly inconvenient. Edward just came up with this plan before he got up to speak so there's nothing packed."

"That's all right. We'll wait while you get ready."

"I'm dreadfully sorry."

"Not at all." He glanced about. "I'll fetch Owen and give Edward a wave. That'll be his cue to make his way through the multitudes to the parking lot. Come along, you two."

Charlotte walked beside Catherine. "He's a lot more chipper than I'd be if someone had ruined my plans for the evening."

"Yes," Catherine replied. "Terry can reach deep down into his sea chest and usually find the right hat to wear."

"What do you mean by that?"

"I mean he rises to the occasion."

"Well, the very least I can do is leave you two to yourselves once we're at Dover Sky. I'll tuck Owen in and read to him. Then I'll —"

Catherine put her arm through Charlotte's. "I shouldn't bother hiding away on our account. I doubt Terry will stay very long after he's seen us safely home."

"Why not? It's only eight now."

Catherine shook her head. "He'll be on his way back to the fleet."

"Something up? I thought he'd move heaven and earth to be with you for a few hours."

"We had . . . um . . . we had a bit of a disagreement on the way here. The *Hood*'s going south to the Med after Christmas and won't be back till spring."

"What? Then all the more reason for the pair of you to spend all the time you can together."

"Yes, well, once Owen is settled in and Terry leaves, you and I can have tea together and I'll explain the winter and rough weather of taking a fancy to Lord Preston's daughter Catherine. At the most unfortunate times, I get my Danforth up."

When they arrived at Dover Sky, Terry pulled up to the front door. He escorted the women and boy to the front door, went back and brought Charlotte's bags in and left them with the poker-faced Skitt. Then he tipped his officer's hat to Charlotte and Catherine, and headed back into the sheets of rain. He got behind the steering wheel and drove away.

"You were right about that, weren't you?" Charlotte sat in a corner of the library ten minutes later, a model of the clipper ship *Cutty Sark* on the shelf above her head. "Terry didn't let any grass grow under his heels."

Catherine poured from a Royal Doulton teapot. "He's hurt."

"Will you explain?"

Skitt had started a small blaze in the fireplace, and a log snapped twice and hissed.

Catherine wrapped her hands around her teacup but didn't drink. "It's not hard, really. He wanted me to wait for him faithfully with a stiff upper lip while he's down at Gibraltar and Malta and who knows where. I told him I couldn't. And I can't, Char. We're not married. We're not even engaged. We've scarcely kissed."

"I —"

"One moment. I've been two years in the tomb waiting for Albert to resurrect. I walked out of that tomb with Sean in my arms this past summer when I realized I was the one who needed the resurrection. I can't go back into the tomb, Char. Not for Terry, not for anyone. It would kill me."

Charlotte didn't drink either. "I think I understand."

"Terry doesn't. But then he scarcely knows me. He thinks he does, but he doesn't. I'm more stubborn than he realizes. I'm not in a hurry to find a man, not even for Sean's sake. And I've got a fighter's streak running through me as thick as the cable that holds *HMS Hood* in place. I can't sit at Dover Sky all winter waiting for him to return from sea with Drake and Raleigh and Nelson. I want to go to the theater, eat at restaurants where crystal chimes and forks and knives make a great clatter because people are happy all around me. I want to go to concerts in London, get a glimpse of the king and queen in their royal box, and walk under the cliffs at Dover with someone other than Aunt Holly."

Charlotte slipped her a smile. "And other than your sister-in-law?"

"I adore you, Char. For that matter, I adore Holly too. But yes, I want to hear a man's footsteps beside me. I want to smell his cologne, have his hand take my arm if I stumble, take in that lovely man scent I've missed so much — the tweed, the pipe tobacco, the leather gloves and shoes. I miss manliness, Char. I'm starved for it, and I shan't be without just because the navy likes a Mediterranean sun more than four months of English rain."

Charlotte put her teacup to her lips. "Why didn't you stay at Ashton Park if you wanted people and men around you?"

"No, no, no!" Catherine put her teacup down. "Not brothers and sisters and aunts and uncles and lords and ladies. Different people . . . different men."

"What men?"

"I don't know. There's a couple of nice chaps who attend the church in Dover. Also an army officer or two. A sexton from Canterbury Cathedral I met seemed nice. I don't want anything serious or dramatic, Char. But I want to be treated like a lady by a man. Once a week would be just perfect . . . or twice."

"So you don't love Terry?"

Catherine was silent for a moment. "I love his easy ways and his big smile and his uniform, but I don't want a ring or a proposal from him anytime soon. I won't wait by the pier for his return. I'm no nineteenth-century painting with the title 'A Woman Longs for Her Sailor.' " She lifted her cup and drank. "Not much of a widow, am I?"

"You were a very good widow in '22 and '23 and most of '24."

"Was I? What am I now?"

"A very good lady."

"Hmm." Catherine glanced at the ship model as another log cracked and spat. "I suppose I've changed, but I can't help it. It was either change or turn to dust." She smiled at Charlotte. "What about you?

145

You're an election widow. How does that feel?"

Charlotte rolled her eyes to the ceiling. "I'll be so glad when I don't have to be introduced to noisy crowds anymore." She glanced at Catherine. "Election night will be a fright, but I can't wait for it to arrive. What a relief to have the campaigning over and done."

"Will Edward win in Dover, do you think?"

"Don't I pray for that? I hope God doesn't mind, but an unelected Edward will drive me 'round the bend. He needs to be in the House making his speeches and arguing with whomever dares to cross swords with him. Please, Lord, not a mansion on the hill like Dover Sky or a yacht at the dock like Lord Preston. Just a plain, ordinary seat in the British Parliament is all I'm asking for Edward."

"Amen! Well, here's to election night and that God's will be done. Only two weeks left to go. More tea?"

"Please. Is it still hot?"

"Very. I parked it by Skitt's fire."

Election Night, 1924

"Hullo, Mum. It's Charlotte. I've been trying to reach you all night."

"The lines are jammed all over Britain with the election," Lady Preston replied. "Are you calling from Edward's office?"

"It's a complete madhouse in that headquarters of his. I finally fled an hour ago. The nanny's with us overnight, so at least Owen didn't have to endure all those cigars and cigarettes and pipes. My eyes are still red and puffy."

"I understand. For years I attended election night frenzies with William until I'd had enough and decided to stay home with the children. I'd advise you to remain at home until Edward finally wanders in at four in the morning. How are things looking for him?"

"I don't know. Edward's crew is happy one moment and worried the next. They keep changing numbers on the chalkboard. Newspapermen dash in and out as if they're delivering military communiqués that will determine the fate of the Great War. The battery of phones is always ringing off the hook. Clouds and clouds of smoke. Everything made me quite dizzy. I have no idea what's going on, but I'm sure we're holding our own against Labor. How about Dad? What's happening with him?"

"He thought he could manage things from Ashton Park with the one phone. Well, he kept losing the connection or else he couldn't get through to his people in the city. I finally shooed him out the door. Todd drove him into Liverpool to his campaign office. I've heard from him once since then. He said he thought things were a bit dicey. Then he got cut off."

"Oh, Mum, I don't know what we'll do if we lose. Edward has his heart set on joining his father at Westminster."

"Don't fret, my dear. Believe me, I've been through plenty of close elections in my time. The Lord has a way of working things out one way or the other. Even if Edward doesn't win, he'd still be his father's parliamentary assistant."

"That won't satisfy Edward anymore. He wants to debate, make speeches, cast a vote in the House, make policy."

"Yes, yes, just like William — down to the nose on his face. We can only wait and pray, Charlotte. The votes are being counted all over the kingdom. It will be the wee hours of the morning before anyone gets a good grasp of things. Call me the minute you know anything for certain."

"All right."

Election Night
Port of Dover

Charlotte Danforth lay on her back on the bed. The clock in the hall downstairs struck three. She punched her pillow, put it under her head, put it over her head, and then finally tossed it onto the floor. She cradled her head on her arms. She was able to drift off for a few minutes in this position, but the dream was unpleasant. Edward had lost and had taken to drink. She found him wandering by the Dover docks with a bottle of gin in his hand and tears rolling down his face.

"Ah, don't cry, my love," she pleaded, throwing her arms around him. "We'll be all right. We'll get back on our feet."

"We won't," he rasped.

"We will! I swear we will. How many elections have we had in the past few years? Three? Four? Another's bound to come along soon, and when it does you'll run again and win. You'll win, Edward!"

His watery eyes struggled to focus on her. "Are you . . . are you a . . . a lady of the evening?"

Charlotte sat up and put a hand to her face. "That was nasty," she mumbled. She got up and got dressed. *I'm not going to risk another dream like that, Lord. I'm going down*

149

there. And whatever's happened, we'll deal with it, that's all.

The door to Owen's room was ajar, and she peeked in. The nanny was asleep in the bed by Owen's crib. The two-year-old was curled up under his quilt, eyes shut, breathing softly. She made her way quietly downstairs, took her woolen peacoat from the rack, tugged it on, added a black scarf, and headed outside.

"Brrrr." She brought black leather gloves out of the pocket of her coat and pulled them on. "What a time of year to have an election."

Her boots made a *snip-snap, snip-snap* sound on the cement as she walked. The streets were dark and deserted. She put up the high collar of her jacket against the cold. Finally she reached an avenue lit by lamps and slowed down, enjoying the amber glow in the cold blackness. She dreaded turning into the narrow side street that made its way to the waterfront and Edward's tiny office. She'd been there earlier in the evening, and but for the light from the office windows it felt like being in the coal mine she'd visited as a little girl. She could almost taste the coal dust. The empty shops looked like the shored up walls of the mine. It made her feel hemmed in.

"Ma'am? Mrs. Danforth? Lady Charlotte?"

She'd barely emerged into the open by Edward's office when a man barreled into her. His hat was crooked, his tie askew, his eyes wide and a huge, a wild smile creased his face.

"Mr. Gibbons!" She was startled by his appearance. "Are you all right? Is anything wrong?"

"Wrong? Wrong?" He gripped her shoulders and laughed, his breath almost knocking her over. "A landslide! Right across the country! More than four hundred seats. That's how it's shaping up, m'lady! Labor's out and the Liberals . . . why, the Liberals have lost three hundred seats and are down to forty! It's not settled yet, but that's what's shaping up. That's what the phones and the newspapermen are telling us!" He let out a whoop and hurled his hat into the night. "We have a Tory government!" Running past the silent shops he disappeared into an alley still hollering with joy.

"What about my husband?" she called after him, but he didn't turn around or offer an answer.

Edward's office was only a block away now. Light was spilling out of the open door into the street, and people were milling about, arms waving, voices loud, laughter and squeals and singing echoing off the buildings. She heard her husband speaking, his words ringing out. She pushed through the crowd to get inside.

"An amazing evening, an historic evening! Yes, a miraculous evening! Don't you think so? A miracle happened in Britain tonight!" Edward's voice was strong with certainty. The people's roar was so overwhelming Charlotte instantly thought of a rugby game or football match. The room was packed with bodies, and she could get no further than the doorway. She stood as tall as she could while the cheering went on, even going up on her toes hoping Edward would notice her. He didn't. He was reaching down to shake hands while women hugged him and newspapermen were shouting in his ear.

You look so handsome, so young, so alive, so ready to take on the world! Charlotte thought. She unwrapped the scarf from her neck and pulled the high collar of her pea-coat down from her face. She drew her hair out from under her coat, shook her head, and let the blackness fall over her shoulders. *I'm here, my darling. I'm with you!* Looking up, she saw him staring over the crowd in her direction.

Stretching a hand out, Edward said, "My friends, ladies and gentlemen, the greatest support I have in my life — may I present my wife and the mother of my son, Lady Charlotte Danforth. Please make a way for her. Thank you! Please let her through."

A lane opened for her lined with people who smiled as they continued clapping. She'd hardly started forward before Edward came to her, took her in his strong arms, and kissed her. The clapping grew in intensity.

She broke the kiss and put a hand to his lips. "There are more than a hundred people here, Edward. Don't do anything rash."

He grinned. "I'm MP for Dover, love! I'll be as rash as I like tonight." He kissed her again, lifting her off the floor.

She pushed against his arms for a few moments but finally laced her arms around his neck and returned the kiss with as much passion and abandon as she'd ever shown in public. The cheering shook the windows as her hair spread like a shining wing over her back.

November, 1924–April, 1925
Dover Sky

My dear Catherine,
I hope my note finds you well. I regret I will not be able to get to Dover Sky as planned for Guy Fawkes on November 5. I fear I will have to cancel on the Christmas Ball as well. A great deal must be done to prepare the *Hood* for another long voyage, and I am expected to do more than my share. I hope to stay in touch, and trust I may be able to call on you once we have returned in April or May.

With profound apologies,
Terrence

Terry,
I received your note this morning. I should have preferred a phone call. I'm

sorry you are so busy we can't see each other even for a Christmas dance. Are you seriously going to be rushing about making everything shipshape right through the holiday season? I can't help but believe there are other reasons for this change in the weather.

Terry, I grieved as a widow for two years. You were one of the people who helped me get out from behind shuttered windows and into the light of day. I counted on you to understand I cannot be a widow again while you go to sea, but I do not think you do.

I'm not trying to hurt you. I'm not asking for liberty to "play the field" while you are gone. I simply ask you to see things from my perspective. I must get out. I must get around. I will need escorts who are not brothers or uncles. I intend to be here when you return, and I very much want you to call.

I'm sorry Guy Fawkes and the Christmas season couldn't have been all the merrier for being spent in your company, my dear.

Catherine

"Ah, splendid! Splendid!" Lord Preston raised his hands over his head and clapped. "You've outdone yourself, Master Skitt! See what a fine butler he is turning into, Elizabeth."

Lady Preston squinted as flames leaped up. "If building and burning effigies of Guy Fawkes is what makes a fine butler these days, then yes, I expect Skitt is well on his way. It's a good thing he escorted Catherine home for this celebration."

The effigy was a man's figure in a tall black hat and beard. It stood about fifteen feet high and was mounted on a rough wooden sled. Skitt and Harrison were tugging it towards Lord and Lady Preston and their family. Yellow flames curled up the legs of the effigy. The men pulled it up to a high mound of dead brush and pruned branches right in front of the Danforths. It immediately ignited the wood and created a bonfire. Fire shot up to the effigy's nose and eyebrows, giving it a glowering, sinister look.

"Look at that wicked fellow!" exclaimed Lord Preston. "Just think, Edward, had he succeeded in blowing up the Parliament buildings — and he certainly had enough kegs of gunpowder to do it — you might be giving your maiden speech in a shack come the new year."

"Surely not, Father." Edward lifted up his son, Owen, so the boy could see the effigy's smoldering face better. "We'd have put up something wonderful by now to replace it, don't you think?"

"Well, well, I expect so." Lord Preston glanced at Victoria, who had her son snuggled against her shoulder. "How are you holding up, my dear? Would you like me to take young Ramsay?"

"He's half asleep, Dad, bonfire or no bonfire. Two-year-olds can only last so long. I'm all right so don't worry. I'm only three months into my pregnancy, and I'm from sturdy Lancashire stock."

"I see. I pray so. I'm only sorry Ben couldn't make it back from that race of his in France. Kipp is here, after all."

"Kipp didn't qualify, Dad. That's why he made it back for Guy Fawkes Night."

"He told me the race would be finished yesterday afternoon."

"It was. But, well, there was an accident, you see. Not Ben. He's fine. But a mate of his and Kipp's bought it . . . excuse me, he crashed and was killed. He hit power lines. It's dreadful, really. I didn't want to bring it up and trouble you and Mum."

Lady Preston was aghast, her face a mask of fright in the reflection of the flames and the shadows. "How terrible! The poor man and his family. But Ben is all right, you say?"

"Yes, yes, as fine as he can be seeing a friend flip over and blow up. Excuse me, I talk like a pilot all the time now. Ben is returning with the body tomorrow. The young widow lives in Canterbury. Kipp went to see her this afternoon."

Lady Preston placed her hand on her daughter's arm. "How did that go?"

"Kipp didn't say much about it. He took Jeremy with him, and he said Jeremy's presence helped a great deal. There was a lot of fuss — a lot of crying. They were the first people to tell the young woman about there being any accident, you see."

"That's awful. Is that why Jeremy and Emma didn't come down from London with the boys for Guy Fawkes?"

"Possibly. Kipp overnighted with the Scarboroughs at their estate before coming here to be with Christelle. I'm glad Mrs. Longstaff is nursing Chris back to health. That is a nasty bug she picked up."

"It really is." Lady Preston turned back to the blaze. "Well, we'll see Emma and Jeremy tomorrow when we get Edward and your father settled into the flat just down from the Parliament buildings. Fancy them living

158

together when the House is sitting."

Victoria gave a sharp laugh. "The cooking and cleaning will be masterful, I'm sure."

"I expect they will eat out at Tollers a good deal and hire old Mrs. Brill to do the cleaning. She needs the money, in any case. She has five young ones to support since her husband was killed in the war. She gets along pretty well even though she has a bad eye."

Victoria looked into the soaring flames and thought about this. "I met her at Jeremy's church, didn't I? The very thin woman with the eye patch and the biggest smile?"

"That's Mrs. Brill."

"Was her husband Royal Navy?"

"He was, dear, yes."

The bonfire flared and plucked everyone out of the shadows, illuminating them as if they were statues on display. Victoria spotted Catherine, who had been standing further back.

"Hullo, Cath!" she called out. "We were speaking of the navy, and now I'm wondering where your naval officer is. Wasn't he supposed to be here for Guy Fawkes?"

Catherine folded her arms over her chest and kept gazing into the bonfire. "He couldn't make it. Something came up."

"I'm sorry to hear that. You'll see him before he ships out to the Mediterranean, won't you?"

"It looks like not. The *Hood* needs his attention before they weigh anchor for Gibraltar."

Victoria smiled. "Surely you need his attention too?"

Catherine didn't look away from the effigy of Guy Fawkes that suddenly popped and sparks erupted. "I don't, you know."

Dear Mum,
A quick note to let you know we'll not be driving up from Dover Sky as planned for Christmas. I'm so sorry, but Sean seems to have that on-again off-again bug Christelle has been fighting all fall. I really don't want to move him. You don't need to worry though.

We'll have a fabulous time here. Skitt and Harrison have finished winterizing the house up and down, and we're as cozy as hedgehogs in their burrows. Holly has promised a special dinner Christmas Day, and she's had Norah and Sally working away as if the king and queen are paying a visit. Best of all, we'll see Edward and Char on December

22 before they take the train to Liverpool. We'll also see Jeremy and Emma on December 23 before they head back to London for the church services.

I'll have presents for the boys, and Holly and I have bought gifts for all the servants here too so we'll be ready for everyone.

As for Sean, well, the men here are going to spoil him rotten. You know they are bringing down a pony for him? He's from Old Todd Turpin's mare. They'll hide him in the barn they put up in August. Sickbed or not, my Sean will be up on his feet and begging to ride him without so much as a hot biscuit in his tummy, I'm sure. Not quite two but going on twelve, that's him.

So you see, it will be quite wonderful here, Mama, though we will miss you and Dad and the crew at Ashton Park terribly. I'll ring you up on Christmas Eve before you attend the candlelight service at church.

I love you and Dad very much, and the

two of you are always in my prayers.

Best wishes this Christmas season,

Catherine

P.S. Please let me know how Christelle is getting along. When Kipp was passing through on his way to see Lord Scarborough about some sort of investment in the airline he looked troubled. And Kipp seldom looks troubled. Please keep me up-to-date about absolutely everything, Mum. God bless and keep you.

Dover Sky

"How was your Christmas, sir?" asked the courier.

"Very well, thank you," replied Skitt. "What do you have for me?"

"Not for you exactly. It's a message for the lady of the manor — for Catherine Moore."

"She's not home at present."

"It's from Leftenant Commander Fordyce of the *HMS Hood.*"

"Ah."

The motorcycle courier lifted his goggles and held up the letter. "See here — see the stars? That means it's an important message — really important. I brought it up from Dover as fast as I could." He handed the note to the butler.

Skitt held the telegram. "If it's so important, why didn't the Leftenant Commander phone?"

"I don't know the contents of the cable, o'course, but I do know there was something about the phone lines out of Plymouth and Devonport acting up."

"I see."

"Lady Catherine Moore needs to see that right sharp, sir. Right sharp, I say."

"I know my business. Thank you for doing yours. Good day."

The courier tipped his hat and stepped back from the door. "I know my place just as you do."

"Good."

Skitt closed the door. He looked at both sides of the telegram, glanced about, and then quietly opened it with a pocketknife.

MY LOVE
PLEASE FORGIVE ME. I BEG OF YOU TO COME TO DEVONPORT BEFORE WE SAIL WHICH WILL BE IN 24 HOURS. I'VE BEEN A FOOL. I WILL MAKE IT UP TO YOU. I BEG OF YOU NOT TO IGNORE THIS PLEA DEAREST. IF YOU CAN SEND A CABLE AHEAD SO I WILL KNOW

WHEN TO EXPECT YOU THAT WOULD BE GRAND. I DON'T WANT TO SAIL WITHOUT SEEING YOUR BEAUTIFUL FACE ONE MORE TIME.

> WITH ALL MY HEART
> TERRY

Skitt read it through twice. He glanced about again before walking to the peat fire flickering in the grate in the parlor. He tossed the telegram in, and a corner quickly took on a yellow edge and was engulfed in flames. In an instant it was charred paper and then ashes.

Parliament, Westminster, London
Edward Danforth paused after he rose. He glanced up at the visitors' gallery and saw his mother, his sister Emma, and her husband, Jeremy. Looking across at the Opposition benches, he saw only a blur of faces until his eyes focused on one — Tanner Buchanan. Staring over Buchanan's head, Edward began his speech.

Mr. Speaker, as proud as we are of our nation and our Empire, I say we cannot afford to rest on our laurels.

Hear, hear! came from his fellow MPs in

the Conservative government seats around him. He could distinctly make out his father's voice.

While it is true that we have peace in our time, it is also true we have a Bolshevik menace to the east that some members of Parliament sought to bring into our bosom before this last election.

Members of the Labor Party across the aisle began to shout and point at him. Edward noticed Buchanan remained in his seat, his face calm and composed.

The result should scarcely have been different to Great Britain than the effect achieved by Cleopatra when she coaxed the asps to fill her body with their poison.

The roar from Labor grew. Edward spoke over the cries.

Shakespeare declared it: "With thy sharp teeth this knot intrinsicate of life at once untie: poor venomous fool be angry, and dispatch." Bolshevism would have been Britain's death.

Shouts of fury and defiance from the

Labor Party swirled about the chamber amid the yells of "Hear! Hear!" from the Conservatives. Edward waited for the tumult to die down, but it didn't. He spoke as loudly as he could.

We must guard our freedom. We must remain vigilant. Not only against Moscow but with an eye always on Europe, which often as not boils over once or twice every century. We are grateful that borders are secure once more on the Continent. We thank God Germany has crawled out of the ash heap of defeat and degradation the Kaiser abandoned it to. It now has a workforce that is employed and an economy that grows sounder each day. Nevertheless, I say the world requires a strong Britain, a free Britain, in order that the world itself may be free. To that end, we must maintain our navy. Britain must continue to rule the waves!

Men pounded their hands on wood for him, and other men pounded their hands on wood against him. Edward used his strongest voice to finish.

Vigilance in time of peace so there may

be victory in time of war. We should deepen our harbors and build at Portsmouth and Plymouth and Devonport; and build at Dover and Clyde and Scapa Flow.

The navy has always been Britain's lifeline. We cannot neglect it. I say no to any treaties that would limit the construction of our warships. No, no, and a thousand times no shall the heirs of Nelson's legacy — the race who won at Trafalgar and the Nile — be left like beggars on the shore, cap in hand, hoping other navies will defend them! "Rule Britannia! Britannia rule the waves! Britons never, never, never shall be slaves!"

With tumult all around him, Edward sat back in his seat. In the pandemonium of *nays* and *yeas* his eyes locked onto those of Tanner Buchanan. He'd not opened his mouth, or thrown paper, or pounded his fist. In fact, he'd remained motionless. Nor did his eyes flinch from Edward's stare. Finally Edward glanced up at the gallery. Noticing his gaze, both Emma and his mother blew him kisses. Jeremy raised his hand and briefly nodded.

Dover Sky

Catherine looked out the window as the February sleet turned the ground white. It wouldn't last, but she found herself thinking about mountains — snowcapped mountains with sunlight flashing off the peaks. Then she found herself daydreaming about long stretches of ocean with curling whitecaps. *I thought you would at least write. Are you so angry you won't even drop me a line or wish me happy birthday? I know I hurt you, but I thought you were a bigger man than this. I honestly did, Terry.*

The Bible was open in Catherine's lap as she sat on the window seat in her room. She flipped a few pages and her eyes fell on Nahum 1:15: *"Behold upon the mountains the feet of him that bringeth good tidings, that publisheth peace!"* Catherine had scarcely read it before there was a knock on the door.

"Lady Catherine? There is a telephone call for you."

She frowned at the interruption but kept the annoyance out of her voice. "Very well, Skitt. I'll be right down. Who is it?"

"Baron von Isenburg, m'lady."

"Baron? Hullo?"

"Yes? Lady Catherine?"

"Yes, this is she. How are you keeping,

168

Baron?"

"Ah, very well, thank you. This year has been good to Germany in terms of less inflation and much more employment."

"I'm so glad to hear it."

"Listen, Lady Catherine, Professor Hartmann has been given leave from the university to complete his book. Do you know about his book?"

"I remember him mentioning it."

"In any case, he asked specifically if you might join us in Switzerland to help him write it."

Catherine felt heat rush into her face. "What?"

"We are going to his family's chateau in Pura, Switzerland. It's quite lovely and peaceful. Cool in February with plenty of snow. The mountains — astonishing and magnificent! We truly wish you to join us and see them for yourself."

"That's . . . that's gracious of you, Baron. But I have my boy —"

"Naturally he will be most welcome as well."

"He just received a pony for Christmas. I don't think I can tear him away."

"Nonsense. The pony will be at Dover Sky when he returns. There is a stable by the chateau filled with beautiful horses your son will find fascinating, I'm sure. That will certainly take his mind off his pony. They have Lipizzans there. Do you know that breed?"

"No."

"Dark-colored at birth but milky white at maturity. They are strong, noble creatures who are great jumpers and often trained in dressage. I'm sure we can persuade Herr Salzgeber to let Sean ride a stallion or two under supervision."

"A stallion?"

"Under strictest supervision, I assure you."

"I don't know, Baron. How long of a trip are you planning?"

"Six to eight weeks. You could return in April or May. The chateau is fully staffed, and you would, of course, be assigned your own servants."

"I'm grateful you've thought of me, but I'm not sure why you or the professor would want me along on an occasion like that. I'm no writer or scholar."

"You are extremely intelligent and strong-minded. Herr Hartmann values that. He believes your opinions would ensure his book had adequate depth, was thorough, and was . . . *harten Gleichgesinnten* . . . how do I say this in English? Ah, tough-minded."

She didn't know how to respond.

After a moment, the baron added, "You appreciate how important this book will be to Germany?"

"Yes, yes."

"That subversive, that man Hitler, was released from prison just before Christmas. His autobiography will be published in July."

Catherine put a hand to her forehead. She felt warm and flushed. "Honestly, I don't know what to say. I'm flattered Professor Hartmann thinks so highly of me, but it is a lot to take in. I should like to think about it."

"Naturally. May I call this evening? We intend to set out tomorrow."

"This evening would be fine."

"We would, of course, come to Dover Sky and escort you and Sean to Pura."

"Thank you for the invitation, Baron. I'll consider it carefully."

"Okay, then. I'll phone you tonight. Good day."

"Good day, Baron." Catherine set the phone in its cradle and leaned a hand against the table it rested on. *What's the matter with me? It's a simple request. And the reply is also simple: No thank you.* She opened the door and left the parlor. Skitt was standing by the staircase.

171

"Everything all right, m'lady?" he asked.

She gave him a quick smile. "Fine, Skitt. I wonder if you could get Nancy to bring me up a spot of tea?"

"I'll take care of that personally, Lady Catherine."

"Thank you. How is Sean? Do you know?"

"Still with Harrison and Holly."

"Good. Very good."

In her room she sat and waited for the rap on the door. When it came she called, "Enter." Skitt came in and she nodded toward her writing table. He placed the tray with tea and biscuits there before leaving. Catherine set herself up at the table near the fireplace. She poured her tea and watched the rain slide along the window-pane. *Mountains. Sun on the snow. How lovely.* She'd scarcely thought of Albrecht Hartmann since she'd met Terrence Fordyce. Now, at the mention of Albrecht, not only her mind but her entire body had reacted just as it had when she first met him in his red sports car the summer before. His golden-brown eyes, light-brown hair, and dark tan stormed her senses. She could almost smell the eau de cologne on his body. She drank her tea quickly and poured another.

The book. Yes, the book to offset this Hitler

fellow's book. But was the invitation really about the book? Or was it about Albrecht and her? About them as a couple? She picked up a pen and opened the journal she'd named Cornelia.

My dear Cornelia, my diary,
I was just sitting here thinking how dreary the weather is in February. I was also thinking about Terry and wondering why he hasn't sent even a birthday card. At the back of my mind I was admitting a long line of escorts is all good and well, but that loses its charm after a while. What I want is a man I can really speak with and listen to and explore absolutely everything in heaven and earth with.

I suppose that is why I was pining after Terry and moaning about the rain and sleet. By chance — chance? — my Bible opened to the book of Nahum, and I read about someone on the mountains bringing good news just when I had been longing to see sun on the snow of a tall peak. How amazing of God is that? Then to complete the string of unusual events, the phone rings and it's Baron von Isenburg asking me to spend two months in the mountains of Switzerland with him and Professor Hartmann. Mountains! Sunshine! And a stable of white stallions too!

But here is the tricky part. The baron says the invitation is for me to help Albrecht write his book. My opinion is valued apparently. Rot or not? It may well be my opinion is valued. It may also be the professor values my womanhood just as much. After all, he came on very strong when we first met — saying how lovely I was, how sweet I was, how beautiful my eyes were. But we never saw each other again.

Then it was all Terry, Terry, Terry.

Now, eight months later, the baron mentions Albrecht Hartmann in a phone call, and I blush like a schoolgirl. Either this is all in my head or even over a phone line I'm picking up on something between the handsome academic and myself. Do such feelings cross land and sea and know no loss of force due to time and distance?

I want to jump in one of their German

Mercedes and go with them to Switzerland! Sean would adore riding a white horse. But another part of me just wants to stay squirreled up in my room and wait on Terry Fordyce. Will he write, send a telegram, post a gift, show up at the door, come to call in April or May?

Catherine put down the pen abruptly. *Why, I* have *become the sea widow yearning for her sailor after all!* She stood up and pressed the buzzer. Skitt was at the door in minutes.

"M'lady?"

"Skitt, please get Nancy and Harriet. I'd like them to help me get packed. Sean and I are going to Switzerland for a few weeks, and we will need the warmest clothing we have."

"Switzerland! Why Switzerland? Aren't you comfortable here, m'lady?"

She patted him on the cheek and then quickly withdrew her hand. "I'll be back, Skitt. I'm sure you'll keep Dover Sky clean and cozy against my return."

Parliament, Westminster, London
"Ah, Lord Danforth, there you are." Tanner Buchanan approached Edward on the busy street outside the Parliament buildings

where politicians and automobiles and carriages were rushing back and forth.

Edward kept his hands behind his back and his top hat on his head. "Mr. Buchanan."

"Lord Buchanan actually. My dear old papa's earldom finally made it through the gates and chutes."

"Earldom?"

Buchanan tugged on his black leather gloves while he gripped his silver-headed walking cane under his arm. "Indeed. You never knew much about my father up in Scotland, did you? He has benefactors and allies who are now my benefactors and allies."

"Congratulations."

"Thank you. What did you think of my maiden speech today?"

"About the same as what you thought of mine the other week."

Buchanan barked a laugh in the chill gray air. "True! We are met on the field of battle and neither shall be the first to cry 'Hold! Enough!' How will it play out in the end, Lord Danforth?"

"Since you are fond of *Macbeth,* I expect with you yielding 'to kiss the ground before young Malcolm's feet and to be baited with the rabble's curse.' "

"Do you think so? And who will this young Malcolm be? You? Do you intend to be the ruler of the realm?"

"Here's my cab."

The driver got out and opened the door for Edward.

"Tell me, Lord Buchanan, do you really think you will bless England and these islands by scrapping our capital ships and securing relations with Moscow as a bulwark against a resurgent Germany? Or was your speech merely crafted to be in direct opposition to my own?"

"What does it matter?"

"It matters to me if you mean it. I'd rather you actually meant it, to tell you the truth, than to hear you were making speeches as part of an ongoing duel with me and my family. Governing Britain is no place for personal games."

Buchanan smiled and shook his head. "On the contrary, the House of Commons is the perfect place for games. It always has been. Fox and hound. I being the hound who shall rend you limb from limb."

Edward got into the hack, and the driver shut the door.

Buchanan stood tall and dark on the sidewalk, tapping the silver head of his cane in a gloved palm and nodding. "Limb from limb, Lord Danforth. How I enjoy blood sport."

Scarborough estate, Southern England
"Kipp." The warm hands came from behind and slipped under his arms and over his chest in the dark. "I didn't know where to find you! Dad said you'd gone walking in the rain, so I said I'd take a peek at the horses." He felt her lips press lightly against the back of his neck and closed his eyes. "So then I knew you'd be in our secret place — our little tack room beyond the stables that is warm, dry, and delicious with the scent of leather." Her mouth found his ear and her breath made his skin tingle. "Every time Dad tells us you've come on business, my heart leaps. I can't help myself. You do love me, don't you?"

"Caroline, the Lord knows how attracted I am to you. I don't even know all the reasons why. But I love Christelle. She's my wife."

"You love us both, Kipp."

"No I don't," he said as he swung around within her embrace to face her.

"You do." Her lips touched his ear, his neck, his cheek, and hovered near his mouth.

"No man can love two women."

"You can." Her lips brushed his. "Push me away if you don't want me."

"I do want you, but I love Christelle."

"You don't think you love me?"

"I shouldn't be caught up with you, but . . ."

She kissed him softly. "But here we are in each other's arms."

His hand reached up and stroked the long blonde hair that was loose about her shoulders. "I can't get you out of my blood."

"Good. That's where I want you to stay." She kissed him again.

"Two women. My life revolves around two women and a son."

"Only two women? Are you sure?"

"Believe me, Christelle and you are enough. A man can only handle so much beauty." He placed his lips against her hair. "I wish it were ancient times — ancient biblical times — when men had more than one wife. That would work for me."

"In a way you do have that."

"I know you genuinely care for Christelle and our son, Matthew."

"I adore them. Just as you do. And I know you love my son, Charles."

He leaned his head against hers. "This makes no sense, does it? I don't want to hurt Christelle. I don't want to hurt my family. And I don't want to hurt you. I've done that enough." He kissed her forehead.

"You're not hurting her." She smoothed back his blonde hair. "And I'm certainly not feeling hurt right now."

"Christelle is hurt; she must be hurt. She knows there is something between us. Chris is no fool. She's always told me I still care for you. Even when I object she shakes her head and says it doesn't bother her because she knows that you may have part of my heart, but she has all of it."

"Shh."

Their eyes had adjusted to the darkness of the tack room. For the first time, he noticed she was wearing a tweed jacket, and rain-drops had beaded on its shoulders.

She took his hand and sat on one of the English saddles resting on a wooden stand. She gestured to the saddle on a stand next to her.

When he sat down, she turned away from him and shook her head, letting her hair fall over her shoulders to her waist.

"Will you brush it for me, Kipp?"

Kipp ran a hand over her hair's rich thickness. It was damp in some spots and wet in others. He took the brush she gave him and began to pull it gently through. The rain brought out the scent of her hair, and it came to him along with the leather of the saddles and traces, the wax and polish, the musk of horses and ponies, and the dryness of the wood on which the bridles and halters and lead ropes and saddles were hung. He sank his face into the softness and the richness. He placed his hands gently on her shoulders and guided her around until she was sitting up and facing him. Then he gathered her into his arms.

"I suppose I do love you. I love you both. There's nothing I can do about it. God help me, it is not the Christian thing. But Christelle and you are rubies and diamonds to me. You both are silver and gold. I can't walk away from either of you."

He fumbled in his pocket for matches. When he found them, he struck one and held the amber flame a foot from her face.

"What are you doing?" she whispered.

"I just had to see your eyes."

The flickering match filled her eyes with brightness and shadows. The blueness was a sky at early morning, and he could almost feel the cool breezes moving over him. Tears came from her eyes and spilled onto her cheeks, glistening from the light of the flame. Then the match went out.

"Don't light another."

"I want to see you."

"No . . . don't . . . please." Her hand folded over his in the dark.

"Your parents will worry."

"They were already turning in when I walked out into the rain." She brushed his nose with her hair. "You didn't get very far. It's still wet and matted from our April showers."

"I got as far as I could. Your beauty is overwhelming when I'm with you. I'm helpless, really. It's the same way with Chris. One can only do so many chores. Then one has to love."

"My goodness, is my hair a chore now?"

"It's your crowning glory. I love you. It's wrong; but I don't know what else to say. God forgive me."

She traced his mouth with her finger. "And I love you. And we both love Christelle and care for her very much."

"Yes."

"Hold me. I'm afraid."

"Of what?"

"How strong my feelings for you are. I don't know where they're going to take us, Kipp."

He brought Caroline into his chest. Once again the scent of her hair mixed with the straw and leather and wet and now he heard the tapping of the rain on the roof. The moment seemed to make everything fall into place. Caroline, Christelle, Charles, Matthew, God, love . . .

"I won't ever abandon you, Kipp," she said quietly. "I bind you to me tonight. You'll never be lost, never be alone as long as I have breath. I swear it. I'll care for your son just as I care for my own. My love for you won't stop . . . ever."

"That's a lot to promise."

"Kipp, I make this promise to you *and* to Chris."

"What do you mean?"

She reached into the pocket of the riding pants she was wearing. She pulled out a small envelope and placed it in Kipp's hand.

"Christelle sent this to me, and I need to share it with you. You'll need a light to read it."

"What is it? You want me to read this right now?"

"Yes."

She sat up and unhooked a lantern from the wall. "Perhaps you'd better use this."

"Why? Have you given me a book?"

"The ink is faint."

"What were you using to write with?"

"I didn't write it."

He flicked a match with his thumbnail. It caught and he pushed the match inside the lantern as she held it. The wick took the flame and lit up the shed.

Caroline hung the lantern back up. The glow revealed her tweed jacket and the pants and boots she wore. The tumble of her hair about her shoulders and the blue-and-gold of her eyes shone.

He stopped what he was doing and took in her beauty. Then he looked at the note in his hand. "I don't understand . . ."

She avoided his gaze and glanced at the tack hanging on the walls. "Read it, Kipp. It's from Chris."

He looked at the blank envelope. He pulled out the notecard that was covered with barely legible writing. He recognized his wife's hand. "Caroline, what's going on?"

She didn't look at him. "Read it, please. You'll understand."

My dear Caroline,
As we've discussed, you know I'm gravely ill. The doctors say I will prob-ably not live long past April. I need your help . . . Kipp will need your help.

I know this may be awkward, but please let Kipp know you love him. Take him in your arms and kiss him. Tell him everything you feel. At first he will push you away. But keep trying.

I know what is in your heart for him. I know you've held back because of our marriage. But he still loves you, just as he still loves me, even if he will not admit he has feelings for you. I want you to help him find that love for you again. I don't care how hard it is. Reach out to him. Use all the words you have inside you. Be beautiful for him. Touch him. Let him discover what is in his heart for you.

Kipp loves me, and he will always love me. Long after I am gone, he will love me. But he has enough love in his heart for both of us. The last thing I want is for him to be alone in his grief. I don't want him to wander off to try to find solace in the arms of someone who will care nothing for his soul.

There is only one person I trust him — and our son, Matthew — to, and that's you.

Love him, Caroline. Love him forever. For me. For our son. For you. For him.

When the time is right, show him this letter. Thank you for this, Caroline. This is such a difficult time.

Your friend always,
Christelle

7

CHRIS
I HAVE TOLD HIM.

CAROLINE

Christelle sat on the couch with the telegram in her hand. Todd Turpin had brought it, his collar turned up against the May Day rainstorm as he trudged through mud puddles to the cottage in the ash grove. He'd asked how she was feeling, and she'd told him she was much better. He had not been gone five minutes before pain cut into her stomach. She bent double as she tried to get her breath.

Her three-year-old looked up from where he was sitting on the floor playing with wooden blocks.

She forced a smile. "I'm fine, Matthew,

my darling. Just a game, *oui*? A game mommy likes to play." She rested on the couch until her breath came smoothly and deeply. Then she put her son down for his nap, returning to the couch to think as she stared into the flames in the fireplace. She heard the front door of their cottage open. She turned, thinking it might be Victoria or Lady Preston.

Kipp caught her up in his arms, the wetness of his clothes pressing against her cotton dress as he kissed her. His blonde hair had been flattened and darkened by the wintry storm. The moisture was cool on her face, but she also felt the heat of his tears. She patted him on the back.

"Shh . . ." she soothed. "Shh, my love."

"I don't understand." He could hardly get the words out. His voice was rough and low, making it difficult to hear. "I don't understand any of this," he whispered.

"Sit with me." She took him to the couch and held him as she spoke, now and then kissing his head and face softly, moving her fingers over his cheeks and through his wet and tangled hair. "The doctor made the diagnosis in the fall. I asked him to keep it in strictest confidence because I wanted the winter to be happy. I wanted you flying, Victoria to be joyful about having her baby in

188

May, and Lord Preston and Edward in London making their speeches. What good would all the moping and fussing have done if I'd announced it sooner, my love? It would not stop the cancer that is all through me. So as long as I could tell everyone it was a bad illness that was hard to treat during the cold weather, I decided to do that."

"We have to tell Mother and Father," Kipp choked out. "There may be places we can take you in Paris or Madrid . . . or in America." He stroked her hair in a clumsy fashion, his eyes dark. "I will cable Michael and Libby right away. In New York we can —"

"*Non, non,* Kipp. I told you. The cancer is everywhere. It cannot be cured. It's not in just one place where you can feel. It's inside me all over. I can feel it everywhere. It was this way when the doctors discovered it."

"Chris, I can't just watch you die in front of my eyes without trying something . . . without doing something."

"I want you to love me, and cherish me, and rock me. Trust me, that will be the best blessing."

"A blessing?" Kipp framed her small face with his damp hands. "How can you say that?"

"Christians say they wish to be with God,

oui? But when it comes time to die, they do not want it to happen so soon. If I cannot stay here with a good mind and a strong body, I wish to be with God. It's better for you, and me, and Matthew."

"No! No, it's not."

"I will become less and less of me, so yes it is, my darling." She kissed each of his eyes. "That is why I asked Caroline to love you. You will need her after I am gone. You will need someone who loves you. She is someone I trust, and knowing she will be helping you makes this easier for me."

His body stiffened. "How can you expect me to turn to her, to betray my love for you?"

"You will not betray me. I want you to return her love, to love her. I asked her to let you know she still loves you and will love you when I'm gone."

"How could you ask her that?"

"I do not want you and Matthew to be alone. And I don't want you bringing home a woman I don't know to love you and Matthew. I think a great deal of Caroline. Matthew likes her and he likes Charles."

"I want nothing to do with Caroline. I feel as if she played with my heart, trying to draw me to her when I still have you."

"How can she play you if she loves you?"

190

Christelle gripped his face with sudden strength. "Caroline did not want to approach you. She did not want to hurt me or hurt you. She didn't want to do this for me. I argued with her. I pleaded with her. I cried, yes, until she said she would try. She did not think you loved her anymore."

"I don't."

Christelle smiled softly. "We must be about the truth now, my love. There's no time for lies. Caroline is a good woman, and it is right for you to love her."

Kipp's face grew dark with anger as blood rushed to his cheeks. "No, I can't. Not now."

"Kipp, I *want* you to love her."

He shook his head. "I can't accept that."

"I prayed for you to understand you have this love in you, do you know that? God knew I would be taken early. He knew Matthew would have no mother around and you would have no wife, no lover. I do not want a stranger in my house. I do not want a stranger holding you and saying she loves you when she does not. I do not want a woman I don't know raising my son. I love Caroline, and you love her. She loves both of us, and she loves Matthew. I see that in her. I want you and Caroline to be with each other when I'm gone."

"No one in my family will accept such an

arrangement, Chris. We don't have your French way of looking at things, your ability to accept one person loving two people at the same time. I can't lose you one day and take up with another woman the next. Certainly the Scarboroughs wouldn't approve either. This wild plan of yours will not work." He ran his hands through her now silver hair. "What I need is for you to live."

She put her hands on his arms. "My love, I will not live. Not here on this earth. I will be in a different place. Here, you will need another to hold you. I know you, and I know you need that. So let a year go by if you must, but let the love blossom while you must be apart. People and their foolish notions! Let Matthew play with Caroline's Charles often. Visit a lot. Make sure there are family gatherings where you can talk discreetly. A year after I am gone, marry her."

"I won't."

"You must! If you love me, you will marry her. I have told you — I trust her. I trust her with you and Matthew. I have said this again and again, and you do not want to hear me. If you love me as much as you say, you will do this for me. You will be honest with yourself and admit the love you've always had for Caroline even while you loved me with all your heart. You will put a ring on her finger, cherish her, make a home with her, and create a loving family. If you do this, you will make me the happiest woman in heaven." She ran her fingers down the side of his face.

She suddenly grimaced and doubled over. Kipp clutched her as well as he could, supporting her through the pain.

"How often is this happening?" he demanded. "Are you all right?"

"Just . . . just hold me," she said through gasps. Finally she caught her breath. "It doesn't happen . . . that often."

"You should be in a hospital."

"No! I do not want to die in a hospital room."

"They can control the pain much better than anything you or I can do here."

"I have medications here — opiates. It looks worse to you than it feels to me, I'm sure."

"So that's why."

"Why what?"

"Your calmness. The way your eyes are now and then. I didn't see it often, but when I did I didn't know what to think."

"I have not used large doses. And I have not used some every day. Only recently have

193

I needed more." She rubbed his arm. "I'm sorry, Kipp. Perhaps I should have told you a long time ago. But *non,* I did not want you worked up for so many months. *Non . . .*"

He kissed her hair and closed his eyes. "You're so beautiful, love. This is not right. God knows this is not right."

"Jesus was crucified and died slowly after being whipped, yes? Paul was *décapité.* Andrew faced crucifixion. Peter a crucifixion also. We are not spared suffering, but it does not mean we are not loved by God."

"Your calmness confuses me. You're dealing with something terrible. We can't keep pretending it's a winter illness. This is a crisis! We must tell my family."

"No, it would change everything."

"You are already sick, and everyone is worried. Do you think letting my father and mother wake up one morning to find you dead is going to bless them or be any easier on them?"

She patted him on the back. "Shh . . . shh. Matthew needs another hour of sleep or he will be *un monstre — très difficile.* Hold me more tightly, my love. I like to listen to your heart beating." She snuggled into him. "Of course you are right. They are family. It is important there comes a day when they will be told. I turn thirty on the second of June. You could arrange a party — a grand party. Everyone will be happy. Everyone will act normally. A few days after that, I will tell the family. Oh, but I do not look forward to them moaning and groaning over me, but I see it must be done."

"What about your parents?"

"S'il te plaît, amène-les ici pour moi."

"Would they let me fly them to your party?"

"Fly? No. Someone must help them get here on the train or by car."

"I will take care of that."

"I want you here with me."

"I will see to it. Harrison is at the estate in Dover. It's just a short hop from there. Someone can take him, and he can come back by car or train with your parents. I'll do anything that will please you."

"It will please me to have Caroline and Charles here for the birthday also."

"No."

She lifted her head. "You said *anything.*"

"She made me feel like I was betraying our love."

She held his jaw in her hand. "She reached out to you as I asked her to do, as I prayed for her to do. Now I am asking you for this. Will you bring her and her son to my

195

birthday party? *Oui?*"

"Chris, I can't do that — even for you."

"Will you bring her? *Oui?*"

May, Pura, Switzerland

Catherine glanced out the window as her son was led about on a tall, white Lipizzaner stallion. The baron kept his hand on the young boy's leg as he walked beside the horse while Herr Salzgeber, the stallion's owner and trainer, led the horse along the beach. Behind them Lake Lugano was a blaze of blue and white in the spring sun. She watched for a few moments, smiling. Then she turned and looked at the sheaf of papers on her desk.

Das Wesen des deutschen Geistes ist nicht Gewalt sondern Schöpfung . . . The essence of the German spirit is not violence but creation, it is not exclusion of the races but inclusion, not fear of the Jew but friendship with the Jew. It is not simply ensuring industrial capitalists have the liberty to generate wealth for themselves, but that those they employ also have the means to secure housing, food, clothing, knowledge, and the assistance of a physician when there is illness or injury. What makes Germany great is a vast and generous involvement with Europe and the human race — not a retreat from the European nations or the peoples of the earth or a desire to make war against them under misguided notions of Teutonic pride and identity.

A hand lightly touched her shoulder. Recognizing the touch, she leaned her cheek against the hand and arm. "As usual, your writing is eloquent," she said. "I see you took my advice to be more forthright."

Albrecht, red scarf around his neck even though the day was warm and the house comfortable, sat down on the arm of a couch near her. "*Ja, ja. Ich glaube, Sie haben recht.* I believe you are right." He ran a hand through his messy hair and adjusted his reading glasses. "Are you almost done do you think?"

"A few more pages. Why?"

"I have translated my next-to-last chapter for you. I hoped you could read it before dinner."

"Next to last? Really? That's quite an accomplishment. Of course I can. Sean only wants me around if he skins his knee." She laughed as she watched him on the stallion again. "Even then he probably wouldn't cry out. Instead he'd look to the baron or Herr

Salzgeber to help him. Or perhaps he'd simply bite his lip and tough it out."

Albrecht took a look over the top of his glasses. "It's true. The boy acts like a ten-year-old who wears a saber at his waist. Your young cavalryman. How he has grown up since February!"

"His grandparents probably won't recognize him at the birthday party for Christelle. And yet he's just two." She leaned back in her chair and gave Albrecht her warmest smile. "I wish you would reconsider. The family has included you and the baron in the invitation."

He was looking at the chapter in his hand and turning over the pages. "I hope my grammar in the English is correct." He glanced at both sides of one sheet. "Yes, your sister-in-law's thirtieth birthday, hmm? She is French and from Amiens, isn't she? Or somewhere close to Amiens? It is only seven years since the armistice, and France harbors a great deal of hatred towards Germany. I don't think she will want to see me there."

"If you knew Chris, you wouldn't say that. What an amazing soul she is! She loves everyone — yes, even a nasty German such as you." She kicked him gently with her bare foot. "Please reconsider."

"We have much to do before my book can be published."

"A few days at Dover Sky — what will that cost you? Besides, I have two kings I have not played."

He continued to peer at the pages scrawled with handwriting. "Ah, a card playing reference . . . Liverpool Rummy or American poker?"

"She has read your book — the one on suffering."

"What?" Albrecht lifted his head sharply. "Christelle has?"

"Yes."

"She has not. How could she?" He took off his glasses and stared at her.

"The baron gave my father an English translation of it last year. Chris found it at Ashton Park and read it. She said she liked it very much. Her English is excellent, so she didn't have any problem understanding it."

"She read it?"

"Yes! I promise you. She'd be dazzled if her German theologian showed up at her party. Can you imagine?"

"Hmm . . . that is quite a card to play. What is your other one?"

"Well . . . me."

"You?"

She leaned forward and put a hand on his knee. "More than three months we have been together here. I have grown used to all your little habits and quirks, as well as your constant gallantries. And none of them irritate me. I have grown quite fond of them." She paused and then decided to say it. "And quite fond of you."

"You have never said a thing about this! I thought we agreed in February we would be good friends and working partners and nothing more during this time together."

"That's what we said in February. Now it's almost June. I've decided to change my mind."

Albrecht put the pages he was holding on the floor. "How much of a change are we talking about?"

"A great deal of change. A sharp change in the weather — and for the better. A distinct change of seasons."

"You are being as bold as I usually am."

"Bolder! I guess I have picked it up from living in this chalet with you. If you come to Dover Sky that will tell me I mean something to you too. That I am more than just a friend or working partner."

"*If* I come? This sounds very manipulative . . . almost Machiavellian."

"It *is* very manipulative and is bordering

on the Machiavellian, I grant you that. But it's not a game of rummy, professor. The reader of your chapters and the editor of your book has taken a very deep interest in you."

"As a writer?"

"As a writer and theologian . . . and a man."

"We've never even kissed."

"Yes . . . well . . . come to Dover Sky with me, and I'll see what I can do about that."

Half of his mouth curved upwards. "That sounds like a third card."

"I suppose it is."

"An ace?"

"Certainly not a joker." She patted his knee again and sat back. "Have I thrown you off your game?"

"I admit it will take a great deal of concentration to get back to my final chapter, Catherine."

"So then it means something to you when I say these things?"

"Means something?"

"It matters to you that I care about you?"

Albrecht gazed at her. "Of course! I've always liked you . . . only there was this sadness in your eyes — you were like a dark moth. I did not know if it could be chased away or by what means a person could help cause it to vanish."

"So is it gone?"

He nodded. "For the most part. I'm not sure if it was the mountain air, or your son taking to the white horses, or the Swiss cooking and chocolate, or —"

She kicked him with her bare foot, a bit harder this time. "Stop it!" she commanded before laughing. "I'm serious."

"So am I. All those things bless a person and take one out of tunnels and caves. I'm at a loss to say what I may have done that I had not already done to encourage you to be intrigued with me. The same old flirting, the same old teasing, the old-world Prussian charm. Nothing was new here in Pura. In fact, there was less of it because I was so caught up in writing the book."

"Well, I suppose that was why. I was captured by your devotion to a cause. I was fascinated by what I read, chapter after chapter that you translated into English because you cared so much what I thought. Only an extraordinary man can write this well, this profoundly, this passionately. I have feelings for you because the book allowed me to read your heart."

"Is this another card you're playing?"

"It may be another card, but all my cards mean something, Herr Hartmann." She drew a circle on his pants-covered leg with her toe. "I feel quite like a young woman of twenty-one again when I'm here with you. I wanted to leave a dungeon behind and get out into the light of day, and I did! I thank God in my prayers every night for your invitation to come here. My late husband may be in heaven, but I haven't been any-where remotely close — until this winter and spring." She pushed her toe against his leg. "It wasn't just the snow and the moun-tains and the sunshine and fresh air, Herr Hartmann. Or the cooking or the Lindt chocolate. It was *you*."

Her eyes took on a golden light Albrecht had never seen.

"I want you to come to Dover Sky, my theologian. I want you to come as my man as well as my writer and my professor. Will you do that? Or is Berlin more important? Is Tubingen more important?"

He breathed out noisily. "What a bomb you drop on my head! I can scarcely think."

"Good!"

"Good?"

"If I didn't matter to you one way or the other, what I've just said wouldn't have knocked you off your stride. Is that not true? I care about you, Albrecht. It matters a great deal to me that I see you also care about me. That I affect you." She stood up. "Come with me, please."

"Pardon me?"

"Can I make it any plainer? *Komme mit, bitte.*" She glanced out the window and saw that the white stallion with her son astride was far away, moving along the lakeshore. She held out her hand. "It will only take a moment, and then you can get back to your book."

"I wonder if I will be able to do that. Are you going to play another card?"

"I expect I might. Don't be afraid of me, Albrecht. I want you — I need you — at Dover Sky by my side, that's all. A very simple need, really."

Gripping his hand she led him down the hall towards the study where he worked. Books were stacked everywhere, and his desk was overflowing with paper. They'd hardly stepped through the doorway when she turned and pushed him up against the wall.

"This is my final card. Are you coming to Dover Sky?" She narrowed her eyes. "Why do you have those glasses on again? Did you think we were going to read a book?"

"I wasn't sure what we were going to do."

She removed the glasses, reached back her arm and placed them on the desk. "It won't take you long to understand my intention, professor. Believe me." She placed her hands on both sides of his face and ran her thumbs over his skin. "When was the last time you shaved?"

"Sunday . . . for church."

"Five days. I don't mind." She rubbed hard against his cheekbones. "This won't hurt, I promise." Her lips brushed his, and then she pressed against him with more force before pulling away. "You see?"

He caught his breath. "Is that all, Lady Catherine?"

"No, it's not, Professor Hartmann."

She tugged his head towards hers. This kiss was stronger, and she didn't release her grip on his face or stop pressing in with her thumbs. Breaking away a second time, she took the measure of him through his eyes.

"Do you understand me?" she asked him.

"I think so, *ja.*"

"Because this is my ace." She leaned forward and kissed him again. When she finished, she continued to grip his face in her hands.

Albrecht felt warm and tired and weak.

"I haven't felt this way about a man in a long time," she said.

"You surprise me, Lady Catherine."

"I hope I do." She smiled. "You do look a

little flushed." She kissed him softly, letting her lips linger near his when she was finished. "Four of a kind," she whispered.

"Yes?"

"I'm alive again, and I'm not going to die if I can help it. No more sitting alone in the dark. Will you help me with that?"

"Ja."

"Will you?"

"Ja — ich helfe. Yes, I will."

"Then we're agreed. We will go to Dover Sky. And if there is more work to do on your book, we'll do it there." She kissed him gently. "And if there is more work to do on us, we will do it there also."

He finally raised his arms up and around her, pulling her in with a sudden burst of strength that made her inhale sharply.

"That is my prayer," he replied. "May God answer it!"

She caught her breath and ran her fingers over his lips. "Oh, He's answering it, *Herr Hartmann.*"

8

June, 1925
Dover Sky

A rap on the door was followed by a woman's voice calling, "Christelle? Are you all right?"

"I'll only be a minute, *Maman.*"

"Please, dear, let us not stand on ceremony in a bedroom. I'm Mum to all my daughters-in-law and sons-in-law, especially when your own mother and father could not be here." She opened the door a crack. "May I help you? Everyone is wondering where the birthday girl has gotten to."

Christelle braced one hand against the bed and held the other over her stomach as she fought a wave of pain. "*Oui, oui, je suis désolée,* you needn't come in. I'll be right down."

Lady Preston stepped inside. "It's no trouble. Do you —" She saw Christelle bent over and rushed to her side. "What is it, dear? What's happening to you?"

"Just a stomachache, nothing more. I've been having severe cramps when my time of month comes since Easter —" She suddenly drew in her breath sharply. *"Oh, mon Dieu, aie miséricorde. J'ai besoin de ton aide et puissance . . ."* she prayed through a moan.

Lady Preston gripped Christelle's hands. "Squeeze mine. Go ahead. I'm years younger than my husband, and my bones are still strong."

"Non, non."

"Go ahead! I am not fine china. I won't break." She winced slightly as Christelle tightened her grip. "That's fine. Go on. I'm fine," she encouraged.

"Non, Maman."

"I'm fine. Let me help." Lady Preston shook her head as Christelle doubled up again. "It's not cramps, is it? And it's not this bug you say you've been fighting all winter and spring."

"Yes, of course it is — it's both. I only need another minute."

"No one in the family believes you. We don't know what it is, but it's certainly not the flu or an ordinary illness." Her eyes were sharp. "Back at Ashton Park I talked to the doctor about you."

"What?"

"He was tight-lipped. No amount of threatening or pleas could get him to speak. He cited physician–patient confidentiality and a lot of rubbish. I told him, "Listen, every month she is thinner — and she was thin enough to begin with. Something is making her waste away, something serious. What is it?""

"He didn't — he didn't tell you though?"

"No."

"Good."

"By his very evasiveness, the doctor has convinced William and me that whatever it is it must be very bad indeed — worse than we had feared. And seeing you like this makes me quite afraid. Is it your heart? Is it your stomach or intestines? Come, my dear, we love you. You are family. Please don't continue to leave us in the dark. Do you think you're sparing us some pain? Seeing you this way doubles and triples my anxiety. Please tell me what's happening to you."

"*Non, Maman.* I will, but not yet."

Lady Preston put her arms around the young woman until the spasms ceased. "Please, Christelle, listen to me. Kipp is saying nothing even though he looks like death with his worry over you. Ben has told us you must be using opiates. He saw a bottle at your house once. I chose to ignore him."

"Non, non."

"I've been worried. I've seen the way you . . . well, the way you drift in your speech now and then, and even more over the past few months. Once or twice your eyes were different — your pupils were so small — when you spoke with me."

Christelle sank her head against Lady Preston's shoulder. *"Maman,* do not be mad at the doctor or Kipp. I did not want anyone to know. I didn't want to be placed in the hospital to die. I wished to be among all of you and for everything to be as normal as possible for as long as possible."

"To *die*? What is wrong with you? What has the doctor said? With the proper treatment and medicine, you will get better, will you not?"

"No, *Maman.* It is cancer."

Lady Preston's body stiffened. "How long have you known this?"

"Since the fall."

"Why . . . why on earth did you keep this a secret? It should have been operated on long ago. It should have been cut out."

"They could not, *Maman.* Even back then it was growing all through me. It would be — how do you say it? *Etriper un poisson,* like gutting a fish."

Lady Preston's eyebrows darted inward.

210

"The doctor said that?"

"*Non*, he was very polite, but that is what he meant. He said the surgery would kill me. So I said, 'Tell no one. Keep this in strictest confidence. Let me live as ordinary a life as possible for as long as possible.' He reluctantly agreed and prescribed opiates for the pain. He has been most kind."

"He lied to us."

"*Non*, Doctor Pittmeadow did what I wished and what a physician must do, *Maman*. It was between him and me, correct? He had no choice. Please do not be angry."

"Still we can do something, check out more options and new treatments."

Christelle kissed her on the cheek right where she'd spotted a tear slowly making its way to her mother-in-law's chin. "You can pray, *Maman*. And you can go back out to the party with me. It is time for the children to have cake and ice cream. I want to hold Victoria and Jeremy's baby boy, sweet Timothy. Please help me enjoy those I love. If we talk about the cancer now, it will ruin the day. Tomorrow or the day after I will tell the family. But not now. Not today. I want this day to be special and joyful."

"How long — how long do you have then?"

"The doctor said six to eight months last

fall — if I am lucky . . . if I am blessed. So I am happy to still be here."

"When did you tell Kipp?"

"Last month."

"He is not doing well with what you told him."

Christelle bit her lip. "*Non.* He is angry with God and angry with life." She shrugged one shoulder. "And angry with Lady Caroline."

"With Caroline? Why?"

"Because of me again. I am doing all these things and making all these decisions for when I am no longer here, and he is not happy with them."

"What have you said to him?"

"That I adore Caroline. That our children get along so well. That there was a time he loved her, and I believe he still has love for her. I want him to marry her, *Maman.* I want them to become husband and wife and raise our children after I am gone."

"Marriage!"

She took Lady Preston's hands. "I trust her. I do not want Kipp to be with someone I've never met. I do not want Matthew to be raised by a stranger. Kipp is fighting me on this, but this is so much what I want for him. Can you help me?"

"Oh Christelle!"

"Will you help me, *Maman*?"

"Child, child, I don't think Kipp will listen to anyone if he is as angry and upset as he seems. He is long past the age when he will happily listen to his mother's counsel, especially when it goes against his will. I don't like to even think about him being wed to a woman other than you. This is much to take in so quickly . . . far too quickly. I see it matters to you though. If it will put you at some measure of ease, I will speak with him. Caroline is a wonderful girl and, yes, there was a time William and I were sure Caroline and Kipp would be husband and wife. I'm astonished you are the one who wants to bring the two of them together again."

"*Maman,* if I am not here I believe she will be the right woman for him and the right mother for our son."

Tears came more swiftly to the older woman's eyes. Lady Preston hugged Christelle. "You've always been one with such a large heart that few can understand. I confess I still don't understand. But if it pleases you, I will sit down and talk to him. Who knows? Perhaps he will change his mind. I will do this, but I don't even like to think of such things with you in front of me with your beautiful smile."

213

"*Merci, Maman.* I am sure Kipp will listen to what you have to say."

"I'm not as sure as you are, but I promise I will do what I can."

"Kipp?"

Kipp didn't turn around.

"Kipp? Are you going to go on avoiding me all day?"

"It's been working so far."

"Chris has asked to see us both."

"I'm busy." He sliced a lemon. "How did you find me?"

"Mrs. Longstaff said you'd be down in the kitchen making punch. She said you insisted on doing it." Caroline moved to within his line of vision. "It's Chris who is asking, not me."

Kipp glanced up at her, his gaze flat. "A request you put her up to, no doubt."

"Kipp, since when has anyone been able to put Chris up to anything? You know your wife better than anyone. She's a free spirit. She goes where she wants and does what she thinks is right."

"For the most part, yes. But the illness has affected her judgment."

"Meaning in regard to *me*?"

"Who else would I mean?"

"Kipp, stop treating me like a witch. I

214

never wanted to do what your wife asked me to do. I never wanted to reach out to you like that and force the issue between us. But how could I say no to a dying woman when she pleaded with me over and over again?"

"You probably didn't need much convincing, right?"

Caroline folded her arms over the front of her summer dress. "The attraction seemed pretty mutual when we were last together."

Kipp chopped limes loudly and rapidly with a large knife. "Sometimes I lose my way. Big blue eyes do that to me. Unfortunately, I can be pretty weak."

"Is that what it was? You said you loved us both."

"I don't, Caroline. I only love Chris."

"So the wrong words just popped out of your mouth?"

"Like I said, it was a weak moment."

She brushed at her tears with a finger. "So I mean nothing to you?"

"That's right. Nothing."

"And Chris was mistaken to think I might be a good companion for you after her death and a good mother to Matthew?"

Kipp laughed bitterly. "A hooker from East London would be a better mother to my son than you."

Caroline's face whitened and tears shot down her cheeks. "I don't deserve that, Kipp! I can understand your pain and anger over your wife's cancer, but I won't forgive what you've just said to me. I love you, Kipp. Everything I've done has been out of love for you and for Christelle. You can't blame me for the fact she's dying, but you're going to anyway, I see. Just throw all the blame on Caroline, is that it?"

Kipp poured water into a large crystal bowl. "I don't blame you for Christelle's cancer."

"Are you sure? You seem to want to blame someone very badly. God isn't readily at hand, but I am."

Kipp said nothing as Caroline brought a white cotton handkerchief out of a pocket in her dress and dabbed at her eyes.

"Then it's come to this, Kipp. You've broken my heart enough times, but you won't get any other opportunities after this. I'll tell my parents I don't wish to overnight at Dover Sky. I don't care if we have to book a hotel room in Liverpool. I will leave you to your anger, Kipp. You'll never see me again. Do try to have a good life. If not for yourself, at least for Chris's sake . . . and for your son's." Caroline turned and walked swiftly towards the kitchen door.

Kipp laid down the knife and leaned on the tabletop with both hands. "Where are you going?"

She paused in the doorway. "I'm going to say goodbye to your wife. I'm going to spend a good while doing it because I won't be at Dover Sky or Ashton Park again. When I came into this kitchen there was still the possibility of a love between us. Now there is not. You are a cruel and hard man, Kipp Danforth. I feel very sorry for you, but not sorry enough to watch you destroy the remaining years of your life — and that of your son."

"So tell me, professor," Edward settled next to Albrecht on a couch in the library, "how are things in Germany these days?" He dug his fork into a piece of cake on a plate in his hand. "What about Herr Hitler? What's he up to?"

Albrecht sipped his coffee before replying. "The economy is much better, so fellows like him have a harder time stirring up the populace. He is out of prison now, and his autobiography is due to be published next month. Even though he has been out of the political picture for a while, his book is bound to make a few people sit up and take notice."

"How many seats does his Nazi Party have in the government?"

"Only fourteen."

"I see. What will be in his book?"

"He attacks the Jews and the Slavic people. He rails against the trade unions, the Communists, and the Socialists."

"Does he?" Edward reached for his own cup of coffee. "Then he can't be all that bad, can he? Perhaps we should bring him over to straighten out the Labor Party."

"His ways are very violent, Lord Edward."

"Yes? Well, we don't have the Bolsheviks as close to us as the Germans do. We have our wonderful moat — the English Channel. I can understand why Herr Hitler might resort to force."

Albrecht set down his coffee. "He will not unleash his street gangs against only the communists and socialists, Lord Edward. Anyone Hitler considers his opponent is fair game."

"Hmm." Edward set down his coffee, wiped his mouth with his napkin, and put aside his plate. "My sister tells me you are working on your own book."

"Yes. It is meant to coincide with the release of Herr Hitler's. I challenge him on many of his political positions."

"Not on his stance against Bolshevism surely?"

"On the way he means to recreate Germany and the power he wishes to exert to achieve his vision. It is very much like Mussolini's fascism."

"Mussolini's not all bad, is he? He's brought a certain strength and honor back to Rome."

"He seized power, Lord Edward. He didn't form the government by means of a democratic election. I very much fear Hitler may one day look for an opportunity to do the same. Such people think alike."

"I cannot wholly blame them. Democracy can be a very tedious and toadying process where people ingratiate themselves to all manner of rank and file in the hopes of gaining votes. Imagine if Labor had gotten the majority, Herr Hartmann. Just on a whim of the dockworkers or hog farmers who turned out to vote. What then? We'd have Bolshevism in the House of Commons and trade between London and Moscow. That would be unacceptable! What could a person do if that happened? Wait another four or five years in the hopes of ousting the Reds by means of the democratic system? And what if my father and I and the Tories didn't grovel enough to suit the dockworkers and pig farmers and coal miners? Another five years of Bolshevism and Labor after that?"

Edward shook his head and reached for his coffee. "We would have to march on Westminster in the same way Mussolini marched on Rome. We'd have to seize power in the name of all that is holy and good. There would be no other choice if we wanted to save England." He chuckled. "Forgive me, Albrecht. I get too intense. Father is always warning me about that." He leaned back. "So my sister assisted you and the baron with your book?"

"Yes, she was quite valuable."

"I'm glad to hear it. Would you make use of her skills again?"

"Certainly."

"And it goes no further than that?"

Albrecht wrinkled his forehead. "Pardon me?"

"Come, Albrecht! We're grown men. Let's not play parlor games. We're perfectly alone and can say what we mean without fear of others repeating our words in the wrong places. I'm glad you offered Catherine an opportunity to get out of the house and do something that required her intelligence. She's mourned too long . . . far too long. Truly she had become rather sallow in appearance. The Swiss air and food obviously did her good. Her countenance is greatly improved. I am grateful to the baron and you for that."

"Thank you."

"You understand it must end there though. If she marries again, she must marry an Englishman."

Albrecht sat up straight. "Excuse me, Lord Edward?"

Edward smiled. "I've seen the way she looks at you. I thought she was going to take your hand when we were singing happy birthday to Christelle an hour ago. I'm glad Germany is getting back on her feet. I sense Germany can be our ally against Russia and the spread of communism. But a German — even a good German theologian — as part of the Danforth dynasty? Impossible. I think you understand that, don't you?"

"Yes, I think I do understand you."

Edward patted the arm of the couch. "Excellent. I didn't think there would be any trouble. Mind you, I don't intend to stand in the way of any working relationship between Catherine and you. That's just what Catherine needs. Let her help you with a thousand of your books. But no more than that. She has her castle, and you have yours. All right?"

Albrecht inclined his head. "This might be something you should raise with your sister, Lord Edward."

"I may do that." Edward got up. "Thank you for a stimulating insight on European politics, professor."

"It was interesting."

"How is Matthew?"

"He's all wound up from the big day, and he's disappointed Charles left so early with his mother."

Kipp buttoned his pajama top. "Couldn't be helped."

Christelle sat on the edge of the bed, the dark lines under her eyes and her tightly clasped hands revealing her tension. "He says he won't sleep until you kiss him good night."

"Are you all right then, Chris?"

"No, I am *not* all right. We'll talk when you come back." After Kipp left, Chris dragged herself under the covers and turned off the lamp by the bed. She looked out the window and in the moonlight she saw Skitt walking toward the pond carrying a paper bag, a cricket bat, and the thermos Catherine had brought him from Switzerland. She wondered what he was doing, but she soon drifted off. When a spasm jerked her awake, she clenched her fists against the pain and prayed.

Seigneur, I took so much medication today to get through the celebration. Must I take more now just to sleep? *Dieu,* I love Kipp and my son. I love my English family. But I think it would be better if You take me now rather than after I become an opium eater. I have no wish to end my life as an addict. *Aie pitié, Seigneur.*

"Are you asleep?" Kipp asked in the semi-darkness.

"Non." She patted the bed beside her. "Come and lie beside me, my love. Are you afraid I am going to throw the clock at you?"

"I might be," he said as he climbed into bed.

"Well, I don't have the energy for that." She turned on her side to face him. "You will have to decide for yourself what you will do about Caroline Scarborough. I have said enough. In any case, I don't think what I wished for — and asked for — will ever happen. She did not tell me what you said to her, but whatever it was hurt her deeply. There was no need of you to do that, Kipp. That is not what you do to people. You have never been like that."

"I'm sorry. It was not a good day for me."

"I am not the one you need to apologize to. And perhaps she will not hear your apology anyway. I believe she and Charles are gone from your life for good. I hope this is not something you will regret a year from now."

"I don't know. When I think of a year from now, all I see is there will be no birthday party for you next year. There will be no balloons, no candles . . . and none of your smiles."

"Shh. Look! I am smiling for you in the dark."

He reached out and touched her face. "Yes, I can feel that."

She suddenly drew in her breath. "The pain is a little worse. I will have a restless night. You might wish to sleep in another room."

"I'm not going anywhere."

She took his hand. "Always the gallant one, my knight in shining armor."

"You looked very good today. You did very well. People remarked on your thinness, but you had so much enthusiasm and charm everyone was delighted. How beautiful you are, Chris! Even while you're fighting this monster, how much life you give to everyone. You're radiant."

"Ah, merci."

"You don't really know, you know. You might overcome this cancer."

"*Non,* Kipp. Do not allow yourself to think that way. It is not going to happen. I don't feel that happening inside me."

"You can't be completely sure."

"I don't want you to believe I will recover. It will make it worse when I — when I —" She stopped. "Just pray. Will you pray? That will help. Hold me close and pray."

"I'm not good at that anymore."

"Try. I am asking you."

He kissed her on the lips. "Yes. For you, of course."

"Hush." Catherine put a finger to her lips. "Remember, Skitt is standing guard at the pond."

Albrecht looked. "Your butler? What is that all about?"

"Poachers go after the swans, so Harrison and Skitt take turns standing guard. They've never caught any though, and this is their second summer at it."

"It would be best if we moved away from the pond then, I think."

"I agree." She took his hand in the cozy darkness under the trees. "I thought you

225

might have changed your mind, you took so long to join me."

"Me? No. Your brother would wish me to, however."

"My brother? Kipp?"

"Edward. He made it clear he didn't want German blood in the family. A working relationship with you is fine, he said."

"Don't take Edward personally, Albrecht."

"How should I take him?"

She caught the tone in his voice, stopped, and faced him, still holding his hand. "He fancies himself as the leader of the Conservative Party in ten years and then prime minister. After that, emperor of the world, I suppose. This has nothing to do with you. He's not comfortable with Chris either because she's French."

"So no wedding bells in our future?"

"Do you want wedding bells?"

"I don't know. The chat with him did give my train a bit of a lurch."

"The oddest thing is he had a huge row with Mum and Dad when it came to his marriage. Char was a commoner, you see, and they weren't happy about their eldest son marrying her. But he fought them until he got what he wanted. Now he turns up his nose at my interest in a German theologian? This is one of Edward's little hypocrisies. Perhaps he'll grow out of it."

Albrecht glanced up at the stars. "His political views seem a bit harsh. I hope he grows out of those first."

"What views?" asked Catherine.

"He's a little too approving of Adolph Hitler's ideas."

"Against the Jews?"

"I didn't get any sense of that. It was mostly being against the trade unions and communists where he found common ground with the Nazi Party."

"You have to bear in mind he's taken on the role of scourge of Bolshevism. That's all it is. He's no fascist, believe me. Too much of an Englishman for that." She led Albrecht under an old apple tree. "But we didn't come out here to discuss my brother Edward's idiosyncrasies, did we?"

"No."

"Or marriage. We don't want to make a hash of things when we're just getting started, do we?"

"I agree with you. Talk of marriage is *verboten*."

"Good. Let's keep our relationship uncluttered, shall we?" She kissed him gently on the lips. "Did you get a chance to speak with Chris?"

"Very briefly. The children were playing

out on the lawn while she told me my book on suffering meant a great deal to her. She said it made her able to accept her ongoing illness in a better spirit — even to contemplate death in a less fearful manner."

"Death? I hope that's not on her mind."

"Now and then it's on everybody's mind, Catherine. Even if it's only for a few moments. She hoped we could talk more tomorrow after breakfast."

"I'm sure you can. Didn't you say you were staying over another night? At least?"

"At least? Where did that idea come from?"

"I thought I might persuade you with my English charms." She kissed him on the lips a second time, much more slowly, hands on his chest. "We were allies at Waterloo, remember?"

"Oh? Were you there for the entire battle?"

"Yes. Right next to you."

"Did we kiss?"

"Before and after, yes, quite a bit."

"Remind me."

She put her arms around his neck and kissed him a long time before stopping to brush her lips over his cheek and whisper in his ear. "Remember now?"

"It's coming back to me. I can see Blucher and Wellington. Maybe even a glimpse of

Napoleon."

"Then I'm not doing this right. Let's try this." She kissed him with more force and then released him.

He looked at her in kind of a daze.

"Well?" She cocked her head and smiled. "What do you see now?"

"Why, I must admit, not much. Just you."

"Ah, now we have the chemistry just right, Professor Hartmann. What shall we do with it?"

He ran his hands through her long, dark hair. "Carry on I hope, Lady Catherine. *Die Nacht ist jung.*"

"It is young. But still not a star or the moon or a kiss should be lost. We must use them up."

"Once again I agree with you wholeheartedly."

Kipp woke in the dark. At first he lay still as he listened. Matthew wasn't crying. There was no noise from inside the house or outside on the grounds. He reached over to touch Christelle's arm. It was cold and rigid.

"Chris! Christelle!" he cried.

He threw back the covers. Moonlight revealed her open eyes were lifeless. Her lips were parted in a small smile. Her hair was spread over the pillow like silver feathers.

"Christelle!" he shouted.

He moved to her side of the bed. Sitting down, he pulled her into his arms and looked for any sign of life. He clamped his hand over her heart and then grabbed her wrist. He kissed her and cried out again. Her arms remained stiff as stone. Her entire body seemed as smooth and hard as marble.

"Oh no! Oh no! God, my God . . . no please. Not this . . . no . . . no . . . no!"

He heard the sound of running feet. Switches must have been clicked on because light blazed all around him. Hands gripped his shoulders. He turned his head and recognized Ben. Victoria was slightly behind him, her hand over her mouth as she took in the scene.

"I'm sorry. I'm so sorry, Kipp." Ben's face was wet with tears. "God, please help us."

Then Kip noticed his father and mother looking pale and old. There was Catherine, tears cutting across her face. Emma was clutching Victoria. Edward rushed in with Charlotte, whose hair looked like Christelle's — wild and shining, except it was moving as she moved and Christelle's hair only moved because he was rocking her and weeping into the thousands of soft strands.

"Our Father," Jeremy touched his shoulder and knelt beside the bed, "who art in heaven." Jeremy's round glasses had smeared. He took them off. Grasping his prosthetic right hand with his left hand, he dropped his head onto his hands. *"Que ton règne vienne, que ta volonté soit faite sur la terre comme au ciel. Donne-nous aujourd'hui notre pain de ce jour."* He stopped. His voice became a whisper. "Forgive us our sins. As we forgive those who have sinned against us. Lead us not into temptation. But deliver us from evil. For thine is the kingdom. And the power. And the glory. Forever. Amen."

Matthew stood looking at his mother. Kipp saw that he was very slender and very young and that his eyes were as dark as his mother's eyes had been.

9

Dear Cornelia, my diary,
How many times have I intended to sit down and write? More than a year has gone by, and it's July again. But I am determined to tell you everything this evening.

I must start with our loss of Christelle last summer. None of us knew how sick she was. She kept the truth about her cancer from everyone except Kipp until the day she died. Kipp was absolutely shattered. We all were. It was a tremendous shock.

Then the funeral was scarcely over — we laid her to rest at the family cemetery at Ashton Park — before Kipp was gone.

232

He made arrangements with Mother and Father to take care of Matthew. Then he flew off in his SPAD to enter an air race from the Orkneys to South Africa. The first leg he landed at London a half hour behind that horrid von Zeltner fellow. The next day was a short hop to Paris, and the day after that the contestants overnighted at Madrid. Kipp was still behind, but by the time he reached Cape Town in South Africa he was more than an hour ahead of von Zeltner! He won the race and the purse was five thousand pounds! He sent the money to Mother and Father to use for anything Matthew might need.

The next thing we knew, Kipp was missing. He'd taken off for the return flight. Somewhere over the Sahara he just disappeared. Even von Zeltner looked for him. We were frantic for weeks as people searched. If Victoria's husband, Ben, hadn't been so concerned about Vic and their new baby boy being sick, he would have flown down and hunted for Kipp himself.

Finally we heard that Kipp had been rescued by French Foreign Legion troops after his plane ran out of fuel and crash-landed in the desert. Father rounded up everyone from Ashton Park and Dover Sky, and we attended a special service of praise and thanksgiving at Jeremy's church in London even though Kipp wasn't back yet. It was a wonderful time of rejoicing.

But for all that, we still haven't seen Kipp since he left for the Orkneys last July. He joined the Legion and remained in Africa. He writes his son often, and the letters are read to Matthew. Kipp sends photographs that we frame and hang in Matthew's room. My brother looks fit enough in his funny French hat and desert uniform. We think he's been doing some flying for the French, but he's very vague about his duties.

The news tells us France is siding with Spain in the war in Morocco against the Berbers of the Rif region. The Legion has been sent in. We haven't heard from Kipp in at least a month, and Mum is fretting that he's caught up in the fighting. We know it was very fierce in May. All we can do is pray. Between you and me, Kipp's behavior since his wife's death seems suicidal.

It was fierce enough in England in May too. We had a dreadful general strike that lasted a week and just about brought everyone to blows. Edward was ranting about communists and Bolshevists, and I suppose he wasn't far off the mark. The workers walked out by the millions — especially the coal miners. There was indeed a strong revolutionary element stirring the pot. Prime Minister Baldwin maintained his calm and didn't send the army in with rifles firing. Eventually the awful strike was over and done. Dad says the time of the strike will come back to haunt us in the next election. He thinks voters will punish the Conservative Party for turning a deaf ear to the working-man's plea for better wages and working conditions.

Then there is my life. What do I do about men? How nice if I could just traipse off and marry my man as our servant Sally did with her soldier (and leaving us a maid short). I've come to an understanding of sorts with Albrecht Hartmann. We adore one another but won't speak of marriage. I helped him with his book that came out in August last year. We've remained close ever since, and we grow closer all the time. He writes constantly and has asked me to join him on his sabbatical from the university that begins this fall and carries over into 1927. I don't see how I can join him, at least not for all of it, without causing a scandal. Edward is working hand in glove with the prime minister's office, and he would have me strung up from the yardarm if anything I did cast our family in a poor light right now. I really can't say what will happen, but I have until September to sort it out.

Speaking of yardarms and the navy, guess who popped back into my life? Terrence Fordyce! He came calling a few weeks ago. I hadn't seen him in at least a year and a half. I was taken aback. He is more handsome and tanned than ever and keen on picking up where we left off. We've gone out for dinner a few times and to a naval ball.

Yes, I did tell him about Albrecht. It doesn't seem to faze him. I expect he figures that since I am not engaged or married, I am still on the market, which is true enough, I suppose. I don't know how to solve the marriage riddle when it comes to Albrecht Hartmann and Terrence Fordyce. Edward would have an absolute fit over my marrying Albrecht, whereas Terry would graft nicely into the Danforth family tree.

I confess my affection was all for Albrecht until Terry came to call again when the *Hood* was back from the Mediterranean. I am so fickle and feel I am playing the coquette. This is all rather difficult. It would help if either man grew ugly or boorish or witless but alas, the truth is they are both lovely in all respects. My head spins like a weathercock, and I fear my heart does the same. "Frailty, thy name is woman!" Do shut up, Hamlet!

What else to write about, hmm? My sister Libby and her American husband, Michael, are at long last returning to England. They've been gone far longer than anyone expected, so Mum and Dad are ecstatic. The pair are supposed to show up in Dover this fall. That's very convenient for me because now I can tell Albrecht I can't possibly commit to anything until the new year. After all, I must welcome Michael and Libby back and see them settled. It also permits me to spend more time with Terry and see him off to the Med in January. That will give me ample opportunity to decide what to do about Albrecht and his year-long sabbatical.

One other thing, Cornelia, before I forget. Dover Sky is about to become something of a hive. First, we have Lady Caroline Scarborough planning to move here for a while. She had a falling out with her father over something. What, I can't even begin to imagine. She asked if she could room here temporarily. Mum, Dad, and I were quick to say yes. We love her and want to do anything we can to help. Lord Scarborough made it clear to Dad that while he remained at an impasse with his daughter, he was grateful we had opened our door to her.

Then, as soon as Matthew found out Charles was going to be living at Dover Sky, he wanted to come and live here too. No amount of cajoling from his grandparents or his Aunt Victoria could convince him otherwise. After all, it brings him closer to Owen in Dover as well as to Emma's boys in London. So he's leaving Ashton Park. Poor Ramsay! Vic's older boy will feel quite left out stuck up there at the Lancashire estate all by himself, I'm sure. Perhaps we can convince Victoria to let him board here at Dover Sky with the others.

For whatever reason, Michael and Libby want to lodge at Dover Sky this coming winter after they arrive. Mother and Father are a bit put out by this, but Libby is quite settled on the matter. She says in her letters that she feels it would be best for her and Michael, but she doesn't explain why. What's up there, I wonder. All things will be made clear in due time.

Until then, first things first. Caroline and Charles arrive in the morning, and I want to be up early and be ready for them. Terry is dining with us in the evening so it will be a full day. Things will probably never be the same at Dover Sky, Cornelia.

"I love July. It really is my favorite month." Catherine glanced at Caroline as they walked to the swan pond in the sunset. "It suits you."

"Thank you. Not much has suited me lately, so I'm glad summer does." She bent over and picked a yellow dandelion that was vivid against her blue cotton dress. "I know they're a weed, but the scent is wonderful." As they walked she continued to hold it under her nose. "I enjoyed meeting your Leftenant Commander Fordyce. He's a nice man."

"Yes, that he is."

"Do you see him often?"

"No. He doesn't get away from the *Hood* all that much. And, as you noticed, he has to head back to port while the night's still young."

"Charles loves uniforms just as we ladies do."

Catherine laughed as she played with the string of pearls at her neck. "Terry's quite a friend of the family."

"I see that. Do you mind my asking if the two of you have future plans?"

"Plans?" Catherine stopped and pointed at a large white swan that had just unfolded its wings. "Isn't it spectacular?"

"What a beauty!" Caroline said as she pulled several pins out of her hair. They continued on their walk as she pushed the hairpins back in. "I don't want to intrude, so forgive me if you think I'm being too forward."

"Not really. Terry and I haven't talked much about it."

"I suppose you're wondering what my being here is all about — my leaving Mum and Dad and coming to live with you?"

"Yes, I was wondering but didn't want to ask. I knew you'd share when you were ready."

"It has to do with men. Well, one man in particular. That's why I was asking about your future plans. I hope they are going along better than mine."

They'd reached the benches by the pond. The water and reflections were emerald and scarlet in the last burst of sunlight. Catherine had a paper bag of bread crumbs, and she tossed them a few at a time into the water. Swans and ducks arrowed towards her from all directions.

"To tell you the truth, I wouldn't mind being married again." Catherine handed the bag to Caroline and said, "Have a go." She wiped her hands on her white summer dress. "There are two men who fascinate me right now. One the family would embrace if we were to wed. The other — well, a marriage to him could cause some problems."

Caroline finished tossing out the big pieces and then upended the bag into the pond. Bills snapped and water splashed. "That's how it is with me. Papa threatened to cut me off. I don't care really."

"What upsets your parents about him?"

"They just don't like him. He has a history with the family." She smiled at several ducklings who had fought their way in to grab up some soggy morsels. "I hope you'll let him visit me here at Dover Sky."

"He's not Jack the Ripper surely? Of course he can call."

"I should tell you who he is first. Then you can give me your answer." She tossed the dandelion into the pond. The birds stormed it. One swan took the dandelion up in its bill and quickly spat it out.

"If you wish. I'm certain it won't affect anything."

"No?" Caroline turned her blue eyes on Catherine. "The man is Tanner Buchanan."

"Buchanan? The man who — who took advantage of you?"

"Yes."

"Kipp rescued you from him."

"Sir Kipp of the Round Table and his mighty deeds." Caroline picked another dandelion and plucked its yellow flower to bits as she stared at the birds. "Now you understand why my parents have problems with him and me. And why the Danforths might."

Catherine looked at the ground. "Yes, quite."

Two days later Ben Whitecross landed at Dover Sky with Kipp's son, Matthew, and his luggage. Matthew immediately ran off with Charles, who was waiting at the edge of the airstrip. Ben saw to the plane and eventually made his way to the manor where coffee and Danishes were waiting. Sitting back in his chair in the parlor, he immediately drank off half his cup of coffee. "Ah, splendid! Thank you, Holly. So where are Matt and Charles?"

"At the pond with Harrison," Holly replied as she patted Ben on the knee. "How was he on the flight down?"

"Fine. I told Vic he'd be a flier, but she isn't keen on any of the children getting into it. The planes are getting too sleek and fast for her."

"I'll bet you can't wait for Michael to show up," chimed in Catherine.

"I can't. He's been gone forever it seems. And with Kipp out of the picture, I've had to take on two new pilots to handle the work. None too soon because we'll have our first monoplanes delivered in '27. Business is booming all right, and I need help to keep up."

Holly poured tea into her cup. Her black hair was loose and hung past her shoulders. "What news do you have of Kipp?"

"There was a letter just the other day for Matthew. Kipp can't go into detail, of course, but there's no doubt he's in the thick of the fighting in Morocco. The problem is the letters are always months old."

Caroline sipped from her teacup and glanced through the lace-curtained window.

"I don't understand how the French got into it," Catherine said as she leaned forward and clasped both hands in her lap. "The papers always said it was Spain and the Berbers who were mixing it up."

"The Berbers made the mistake of attacking a chain of French forts they felt were on their side of the mountains back in April of 1925. They killed over 1000 French troops. So France sided with Spain and sent in almost 300,000 men, including Kipp's unit in the Legion. So he's been fighting for over a year in the Rif, the mountain region the Berbers claim is theirs."

"Poor Mum. She has both Kipp and Robbie to worry about. And you too, Ben, with all your wild air racing."

"I've always wanted to be a Methodist missionary and go to Africa. Perhaps she'll be pleased with that."

"You're joking."

"I have, really. There's a bit of Jeremy Sweet in me, along with a dash of jungle pilot."

"I doubt that will calm Mother's nerves very much."

"If it's any consolation, I think the fighting is coming to an end in Morocco. The Berbers will lay down their arms. Some guerrilla warfare is bound to continue though because not all the Berbers will surrender. Kipp will have to keep his head down."

Holly frowned. "I can't see Kipp crawling along the desert with a rifle, can you? Don't you think the French would have him in the air?"

Ben bit into a Danish. "The Legion doesn't have an air force, but who knows? These are good. Did Norah bake them?"

"A new girl actually," replied Catherine.

"Amazing. You're running quite a little show down here now, aren't you?" He smiled at Caroline. "You're looking well, my lady."

She turned her eyes from the window. "Thank you. It's good of your family to take me in."

"I'm sure you'll bless us as much as we bless you." Ben finished his coffee and stood up. "Have to be on my way. I need to stop in at our air base by London before I scoot back to Lancashire."

Catherine got to her feet and hugged him. "Tell Mum and Dad I miss them. I'm sorry they won't be dropping down to Dover this summer."

"They thought it best to stay with Vic and me this year. But they'll be here for a visit once Libby and Michael show up, you can count on that."

"How are Lady Grace and Sir Arthur?"

"They're holding their own. Sir Arthur falls asleep at the dinner table now, but he always has something exceptional to say once he wakes up. And Lady Grace hums hymns to herself and wanders about the rooms speaking with the dukes and duchesses who lived at Ashton Park centuries ago. Actually, it's your father's dogs I'm worried about. They're both failing."

"Oh no! That would kill Dad to lose them."

"I hope they'll live out the year, but I think not. Vic is trying to persuade him to pick

246

up of a couple of puppies, but he won't hear of it." Ben kissed Holly on the cheek. "Cheers!" He took Caroline by the hand. "I hope you have a wonderful time here, Lady Caroline, and that everything falls into place for you. I can tell you that at every family devotional at Ashton Park Lord Preston prays for you and your parents."

"Thank you, Ben. Tell Lord and Lady Preston how very much I appreciate their hospitality. I will ring them up myself in a few days."

Just over an hour after Ben took off in his SPAD S.XX for London, a black Rolls Royce Silver Ghost pulled up in front of the manor. Skitt met the car in the drive and opened the door. Tanner Buchanan, Member of Parliament, stepped out. His chauffeur got out and grabbed two large suitcases from the boot before following the two men into the manor.

Harrison tucked a cricket bat under his arm and led the way down the slope in the last of the evening light. "Every summer we lose one or two, Lord Tanner. We find the feathers where they pluck 'em and that's it, except a boot print now and then."

Buchanan strode beside him, silver-topped walking stick in one hand. "If you've been trying to catch them at night and been unsuccessful why not hide out during the day?"

"Nowhere to hide. Unless I used a drinking straw and crawled under the water. Never fear, we'll catch 'em one day. Eventually they'll slip up." Harrison cleared his throat. "You're welcome to the manor and no mistake, Lord Buchanan. You can stay the weekend, if you like. But it'll have to be the first and last for you. If ever Lord Edward dropped in and found you here, I expect there'd be a brawl."

"We're both gentlemen, Mr. Harrison. Gentlemen don't brawl."

"They have disagreements."

"Something like that."

"Well, whatever you wish to call it, I think you'll agree with me your presence here is a bit of a sticky wicket for the Danforth family."

"I most certainly agree with that, yes. I despise your employers, so I can understand how my visit to their Dover Sky estate could be viewed as an impertinence."

Harrison stopped walking. "They were your employers once. They treated you well enough."

Buchanan's eyes hardened into a cold gray color. "Until I was accused of taking advantage of Lady Caroline. Did anyone stop to ask if she might have been the one who approached me?"

"What d'ya mean?"

"Did anyone ever wonder who had seduced who?"

"Is that what you're saying? That *she* led you astray? A strapping big bloke like you?"

Buchanan grimaced as if he'd swallowed hot tea too quickly. "Strapping or not, her Medusa charms laid me low. And no one asked for my point of view, did they?"

"Medusa charms? Is that how you see her? A woman with a hundred snakes writhing on her head who turned men to stone?"

"I do see her that way, Harrison. Didn't she seduce your Lord Kipp as well?"

"What nonsense is this!"

"Didn't Caroline entice him into an . . . um . . . shall I say an indiscretion while his wife was dying? That's the word going the rounds."

"It's a lie!" Harrison's face was bloodred. "Not another word on those lines or lord or no lord, I'll lay you flat."

"Will you?" Buchanan smiled slowly. "I'd like to see you try."

Harrison stopped, laid down his cricket bat, and turned to face Lord Buchanan. "Why do you talk this way about Lady

249

Caroline when I've heard you have every intention of marrying her? And isn't that why you've come to Dover Sky? To call on her?"

"Why, it's a marriage of convenience, Harrison. I'm hoping my wicked little Medusa will destroy Lord Kipp for his great insult against her. And she allows me closer access to the Danforths."

"That's despicable."

"I despise Kipp Danforth for striking me during a dispute in France. I despise the Danforths for sacking me without permitting me to speak a word in my defense. I despise Edward simply for being a Danforth and being in the wrong political party. So Lady Caroline and I shall get back at you all. I will destroy both father and son in the House of Commons and make them look the proper fools they are. And my wicked little Medusa shall destroy Lord Kipp. She'll turn him to stone."

"You are a madman. He doesn't care for her anymore."

"Ah, but he does, he does. She's convinced of it. And equally convinced the day will dawn when he gets over his grief at his wife's death — such a pity, so beautiful a woman — and his guilt at betraying her by

seeking solace in Caroline's arms and kisses
—"

"Lord Buchanan! I swear by all that's holy you'd better quit now!"

Buchanan grinned but his eyes remained hard and flat. "He'll come to her again. He'll plead with her to hold him, to love him. She'll toy with him a while, get him well into her lair. Then she'll have at him and make sure all of England knows it — the newspapers, the aristocracy, the king, the church, members of Parliament, everyone. The scandal will break the Danforth clan, absolutely break it."

Tanner laughed harshly as he imagined it. "The Conservative Party will be done with them, the Church of England will be done with them, Buckingham Palace and the nobles will be done with them. There will be photographs of the seduction, as many as anyone could like. And to top it all off, Lady Caroline will claim rape. Why, it will ruin Lord Preston's business contracts as well . . . and I hope bankrupt the airline. The Danforths will become paupers, swilling gin by the Liverpool docks and begging for bread in East London. How I'll gloat!"

Buchanan expected the punch Harrison threw and easily blocked it with his hand. The second one he stopped with his arm.

Then he struck Harrison in the stomach and hit him with his walking stick. Tanner lifted Harrison's chin off the grass with the toe of his boot and tapped Harrison's head none too softly with the silver top of his cane. "You're lucky I'm not going to report your impertinence to your employers, Harrison. Next time I won't go so easy on you, old man.

"I don't mind telling you all of it. Who are you going to go to? How are you going to stop me? I'll make my speeches in the House and tear Lord Preston and Lord Edward to pieces. Caroline will marry me and wait in her room for Kipp to come back from his war in the Rif and look for her. *Be a mother to my son,* he'll plead. *Be a wife for my manor.* She'll laugh and turn her Medusa head on him and that, old man, will be that. *Finis,* as the late Christelle Danforth might have said, God rest her soul."

Harrison grit his teeth. "You're mad."

"Not at all. It's merely politics, Mr. Harrison. Politics and pleasure." He turned and walked back toward the manor as the sun disappeared.

"Cathy? Are you up?"

"I'm just brushing out my hair. What is it?"

Holly stepped inside Catherine's bedroom and closed the door, leaning her back against it. She was in a maroon dressing gown. "My husband came up from the pond this morning with a huge bruise on his stomach, a cut on his face, and a lump on his head. His knuckles are bruised too. He said it was poachers, but they got away. I don't believe him."

Catherine put down her brush. "That's terrible! Is he going to be all right?"

"Physically he'll be sore a few days and probably just shake it off. But behind his eyes I see something more. I don't know what's going on, but I am certain Lord Buchanan is part of it."

"What do you mean?"

"I know Buchanan went down to the pond last night with Harrison. I think they had words that led to blows exchanged. Harrison won't budge on his story, so I thought I'd engage Tanner Buchanan in conversation to see if I can discern the truth. He's a brute, but I'm a sly wildcat who might just get the better of him."

"Holly —"

"Don't worry. I won't bring a scandal down on Dover Sky. But my intuition tells me he might try."

"How can you be so sure it wasn't poachers?"

"Because I went down there this morning. There were no boot prints in the muck at the edge of the pond or in the bushes. There were no signs of the fight Harrison claimed took place on the shore. No tracks leading away, no feathers, no dead swans. And no missing birds either. I counted to make sure. But a ways up from the pond there was some blood on the grass. And a handkerchief Harrison always carries in the pocket of his corduroy jacket was on the ground, also bloodstained. He used it to wipe the cut above his right eye, he says. And the welt on his face is narrow — just about the width of a walking stick."

Catherine put a hand to her face. "This is dreadful."

"I want to speak with Caroline about this first. Do you want to come? After all, don't you think it's strange she should want to walk the aisle with the man who dishonored her so many years ago?"

"I asked her that when she told me about him. She said, 'He's my son's father, and he's never been unkind to me.' "

"What!"

"That's what she said . . . and that's all she said." Catherine got up from her vanity.

"I feel very bad about this. Buchanan being here is just asking for trouble. I asked Harrison to speak with Lord Buchanan about his visit here. I asked him to reinforce that it could be this once, but only this once. Can you imagine what Edward will say when he discovers Buchanan slept under our roof? Can you imagine what Mum or Dad will say? Or what Kipp might do when he finds out? Perhaps talking to Caroline and then approaching Lord Buchanan is the best thing to do."

"Harrison can give a good account of himself in a fight, but he doesn't carry heavy walking sticks he can knock people about the head with." Holly opened the bedroom door. "The household's barely stirring. Skitt, the cooks, and the maids are just starting their duties. Will you come to Caroline's room with me?"

Catherine threw on a white housecoat. "She might be still sleeping, Holly."

"Then we'll have to wake her, won't we?"

Caroline was up and dressed in a light-yellow gown the same color as her hair. Her bedroom door was already open, and she was standing by her window, one hand on the white curtain as she drew it aside to peer outside.

"Good morning!" she said, turning very slightly — just enough to glance at the two women before looking back out the window again. "Do you know there was a heavy dew last night? The grass is simply blazing with the reflected sunlight from the dawn."

"I hadn't noticed," Catherine said. "We're sorry to disturb you so early, but we need to talk with you."

"Not at all. Is this about Tanner?"

"Yes, it is."

"I'm sure it's uncomfortable for you to have him here. I hope he hasn't caused any trouble. You must understand the demands that are being made on him by the Labor Party and his constituents in Ayrshire South. He's not had a moment's peace since the new year. Even with the House in summer recess, his phone keeps ringing. He thought a short holiday and visit with me here in Kent would relieve some of the strain. And naturally I wanted to see him as well."

Holly closed the door. "Why should there be trouble?"

Caroline continued to stare out the window. "Oh, you know. Edward hates him. Kipp hates him. The Danforths in general hate him. And here I am at the Danforth estate in Kent, so he has to come here if he wants to visit me. He's bound to be a bit wound up about the situation. Wouldn't that be understandable?" She paused, still not turning towards them. "Has something happened?"

Holly clasped her hands in front of her. "I believe my husband and your fiancé —"

"Not yet. We're not engaged yet," interrupted Caroline turning her head just enough to see them before staring out the window again.

"Whatever the case might be, I believe Lord Buchanan and my husband had an altercation by the pond last night. Harrison was quite bruised up this morning, and his face was cut. It looks like he was hit with a walking stick."

"Did he accuse Tanner?"

"No. He said it was poachers. But down by the pond there are no signs of poachers or a scuffle. And I know Lord Buchanan and Harrison went to the pond together last night."

"And did you talk to Tanner?"

"No. I haven't gone to see him yet."

"So what would you like from me?"

"I did find blood and grass on the toe of one of Lord Buchanan's boots. He took them off and left them in the front hall by the door."

"Not much proof, Holly. Sherlock Holmes could have done better."

Holly raised her eyebrows. "Could he?"

"Yes. There are clues you missed. Have you examined Tanner's walking stick for marks or blood? The cane is resting against the wall on your right, just inside my door."

Catherine and Holly looked, and then Holly walked over, picked it up, and examined it.

"There are no blood or marks on it," Holly said.

"But it is quite polished, is it not?"

"Yes."

"Especially the silver top — almost like a mirror."

"Yes."

"I wonder why?"

Holly stared at Caroline's back as understanding dawned. She closed the bedroom door before turning back to Caroline. "Did he ask you to clean it for him?"

"He did."

"Where is the rag you used to clean it with?"

Sunlight streamed into the room around Caroline as she gazed out on the lawn. "The trash would make it too easy to find, don't you think? I'm sure Scotland Yard would check that and under my bed and under my pillow."

"Where is it then?"

"Why, it's where even Sherlock Holmes wouldn't look if he were a gentleman." Caroline tugged a soiled rag from the bosom of her dress and held it over her shoulder. "I had no opportunity to discard it. Your butler seems to prowl around all night. Doesn't he ever sleep?"

"Perhaps he was concerned for our guests?" Catherine offered.

"Or perhaps he heard an altercation . . ." Caroline responded.

Holly and Catherine looked at each other and then back at Caroline.

Caroline suddenly turned from the window to face them. One side of her face was purple and black.

"My word!" exclaimed Holly as she rushed to Caroline's side. "Did Tanner Buchanan do this?"

"Have you put ice on this yet?" Holly asked.

"How could I do that without your butler or the cooks noticing and having a fit?"

Catherine came forward and grasped Caroline's hand. "Why did he hit you?"

"I noticed the blood on the cane and refused to clean up the mess. I told him I wanted to know what had happened. He told me he'd beaten off a mad dog. I said I'd ask the household staff about it . . . and they would clean and polish his cane for him. He told me to do what he'd asked. When I refused again, he slapped me. I fought back, and he used the cane." She gave the rag to Holly. "Your husband's blood and my blood should be ample evidence."

Holly's face was drawn and white. "I shall ring the police in Dover."

"He's Lord Tanner Buchanan, MP. The authorities won't believe my word against his."

"They'll take my word," Catherine said.

"But you saw nothing."

"Once Harrison hears about Buchanan beating you, he'll speak up," Holly said.

"He won't."

"He's no coward!"

"Even if the police believe us, Tanner is still a member of Parliament. The authorities won't do anything. You know how they are. Tanner told Harrison that he means to destroy the Danforth family and included my part in it. If Harrison tells that, the police will think he's raving mad. Tanner knows that, so he thinks his plans are safe."

"What plans?" Catherine squeezed Caroline's hand.

"Never mind that right now." Holly crammed the bloodstained rag into a pocket in her dressing gown. "Catherine, I'm going down to fetch water and ice for Caroline. You two had better —"

There was rapid knocking on the door.

Caroline's eyes went dark. "Yes?"

"Lady Caroline?"

"Yes, Skitt?"

"Lady Caroline, are Lady Holly and Lady Catherine in there with you, by chance?"

"Indeed they are. We're just having a quick chat."

"I thought your ladyships would like to know that a car has just pulled up at the front."

The women looked at one another.

"I see," replied Caroline. "And who would that be at this early hour, Skitt?"

"It's Lord Edward, my lady. Lord Buchanan has already opened the door to him."

"What are you doing here?" Edward asked, trying to keep from shouting.

Buchanan stood on the porch, his chauffeur and suitcases beside him. "Enjoying your family estate."

"You have no business at Dover Sky."

261

"I do, Danforth. My fiancée is here, so I swung by to see how she was."

"Fiancée? And who is that?"

"Lady Caroline, of course."

"Caroline? You're joking! Why would she wed the cad who ruined her life?"

"Perhaps she decided your brother Kipp was the bigger cad."

"I want you off our property right now!"

Buchanan smiled and pulled on white cotton gloves. "I'm leaving. And don't worry, I'll have plenty to say about your family in a speech I'll be giving in the House this fall."

Catherine suddenly showed up in the doorway out of breath, with Skitt following closely behind.

"What's this about, Cathy?" demanded Edward. "Is it true what he says about Caroline being engaged to him?"

She hesitated, and then she straightened as she stepped forward. "No. No, it is not."

Buchanan whipped around. "She is my fiancée!"

Skitt stepped between Catherine and Buchanan. "Steady on, Lord Buchanan."

"She knows very well Lady Caroline is engaged to me."

"That may have been true until you beat her!" snapped Catherine. "It certainly isn't

262

now. Get your bags and leave Dover Sky immediately."

"I never beat Caroline. Is that what she's telling you? She tripped on the stairs during the night. Let me speak to her."

Catherine blocked the doorway. "No, you will not. Lady Holly is tending to the wounds you inflicted."

"I've done nothing, I tell you." Buchanan picked up his cane from where it leaned against his baggage. "I think it best Lady Caroline leave with me."

"I'm afraid not, Lord Buchanan. She is under our roof and our protection."

He barked a laugh. "Your protection? Do you imagine this the Middle Ages? In any case, who is going to protect her? You? Whelps like your skinny little butler?"

Skitt put his hand up. He looked at the chauffeur. "Please load the luggage in the car at once." He looked at Buchanan. "That will do, sir. You've been asked to go. Please leave at once."

Buchanan seethed and swung his cane. There was a crack, and Skitt clutched his wrist as he fell against the wall of the house. "Don't meddle with me, boy." Buchanan pulled on the silver top of his cane and a sword emerged, glittering in the light. "All of you stay back. I'm going to fetch Lady

Caroline and her bags, and then we're leaving this wretched estate. Stay back, Lord Edward, I say. Stay back, Lady Catherine. I am a dangerous man when crossed."

"Aye, you may be dangerous, but I am even more of a threat, Lord Buchanan." The words were followed by several sharp metallic clicks.

Buchanan turned and saw Harrison walking toward the porch holding a double-barreled shotgun.

Buchanan snorted. "You wouldn't dare. I shall contact Scotland Yard."

"If there's anything left of you to make the call, you'll be welcome to do so on our shilling," Harrison replied. He came closer and pointed the shotgun directly at Buchanan's stomach. "Now be off."

"Not without my fiancée."

"She's not your property."

"Oh, but she is. And she comes with me or I'll tear this godforsaken excuse for a manor down around your ears. Who do you think you are?"

"We're all you'll never be, Lord Buchanan." Harrison jabbed the shotgun at him. "Clear off. I'll not say it again."

"Lady Caroline is my woman, and she comes with me."

"I am not, Tanner." Caroline stood in the

doorway, her yellow dress a stark contrast to the side of her face that was dark red and swollen.

"Caroline . . ." Buchanan said softly. "Bear up and back me up. Remember our plans. Remember what I can help you do." He sheathed his sword and extended a gloved hand. "Come. We'll have a physician in London tend to the bruises from your fall. Then I'll have you as my bride before the day's out."

Caroline remained in the doorway. "Tanner, I loathe you. You're a spider I wish I could squash under my boot. You may thank whatever god you worship that Harrison holds the shotgun and not me. I would have already pulled the trigger."

"Caroline, don't lose sight of what we want to accomplish together."

"You mean what *you* want to accomplish. All I wanted was a peaceful life, an honorable husband, and a good father to help me raise Charles."

"Don't be a fool."

Harrison stepped forward and cut in. "Goodbye, Lord Buchanan. Your car's ready. You and your chauffeur can take off. Now would be a good time."

Buchanan slowly came down the steps of the porch. "You are a brave man when there's a gun in your hands, Harrison. One day it will not be there, but I will."

"And you're a brave man with a sword in your hand."

"I won't need a sword or a walking stick to deal with the likes of you."

"May God speed the day of our next meeting, Lord Buchanan. Until then, be off."

Buchanan looked up at Caroline. "You'll regret this."

"I doubt it. I haven't felt this good in months."

Buchanan and his chauffeur walked to the car. The chauffeur set the luggage by the boot, opened the door for Tanner, closed it, and then loaded the luggage. He climbed into the driver's seat, and a few seconds later the black Silver Ghost headed down the drive toward the main road. Buchanan turned for one last stare. His face was like granite.

"All's well that ends well." Edward smiled at Harrison. "Thank you for your help. Is the gun loaded?"

"It is, my lord."

"Ah. Then, as Wellington said, that was a 'near run' thing." He glanced up at Skitt who was getting to his feet with Catherine and Norah's assistance. "That was well done, Skitt. I'll have more to say to you later, but that was well done indeed."

Skitt was still gripping his wrist. "I would die rather than let a beast like that lay a hand on Lady Catherine, my lord."

"I believe it." Edward nodded at Caroline. "I came by for an early breakfast before heading up to London, but breakfast and London will have to wait. Lady Caroline, we must get you into Dover for medical attention. That goes for you as well, young Skitt. We'll take my car. My driver will have us at the doctor's in half an hour."

Caroline shook her head. "I've been trouble enough. My face will heal in time."

"There could be broken bones. That's true of you as well, Skitt."

"But, sir," Skitt protested, "who will man the door? And what if Lord Buchanan comes back?"

Holly came through the door. "Thank you, Skitt, but Harrison and I shall take care of that. You defend Lady Caroline in case that wretch Buchanan is lying in wait on the roadway. We'll defend Dover Sky."

A gleam came into Skitt's eye. "D'ya think he might try to waylay us, Lady Holly?"

"I shouldn't be at all surprised."

"May I — may I take the shotgun then?"

"Ah." Holly patted his cheek. "Our young

lion. No, we shall have it here, I think. But you have one good hand, Skitt. And Lord Edward will be by your side. I fear for Buchanan if he should attempt to stop the car and carry Lady Caroline off. I truly do."

Dear Cornelia, my diary,
Well, the summer has swept past. After that dreadful business with Lord Tanner Buchanan the rest of July and August were delightful. Caroline's bruised face healed up nicely, and Charles and Matthew are getting along famously. The twins came up from London twice with Emma and Jeremy, along with their little brother Billy. We had a very raucous manor indeed. Sean tries to keep up as best he can, but the twins are nine and he is only three — the youngest of the lot during that time.

Between you and me, I have no idea what will become of Caroline. Terry has offered to introduce her to naval officers, but she begs off every time. If a letter comes to Matthew from Kipp and we read it out loud at the table, she excuses herself and leaves the room. I don't think there is any future for her in that direction. Her face may be better —

well, she is stunning, isn't she? — but under her skin she is far from well. Mum calls her a bird with a broken wing. Now that she has broken off with Tanner, she could return home, but she shows no inclination to do so. She talks to her mother once a week on the phone but appears to be holding a grudge against her father. I pray with her about it, and she's grateful for that, yet it seems to make no difference in her attitude. I continue to pray for her on my own.

Edward saw Lord Buchanan when Parliament commenced, of course. At first Buchanan refused to greet him. Then he delivered a scathing attack on Father in his first speech of the session and another one on Edward a week later. After that he makes mocking bows to both of them when they meet.

Edward says Buchanan has that American woman on his arm again — Lady Hall, or Lady Kate, as she likes to be called. Edward cannot understand Lady Kate's sweetness. It's in such marked contrast to her partner's harshness. But apparently Lord Buchanan is at his most courteous when he's in her company.

No warmth, of course. He is never the hypocrite. He's just cold and correct.

If Caroline is no longer the bait to trap Kipp, will that be Kate's role? Edward says she is quite lovely. I wonder if Kipp will find her attractive? However, when he returns from the Rif it will not be Lady Kate he seeks out. It will be Caroline. I am sure of that. But will she receive him? She's said she won't countless times now. Caroline says Kipp blames her for his wife's death, but we're not sure why he'd do that. Apparently Kipp called Caroline an awful name and said she'd be an unfit mother. I can scarcely believe it, but something happened that set Caroline against him like rock.

One thing we Danforths are united about is praying daily for protection against Lord Buchanan's villainy. He told Edward he still hopes to destroy us. We can only place Christ between ourselves and his darkness. Thank goodness Mother and Father don't know the half of it.

But on to pleasanter things. Terry and

Albrecht. What to do? I see Terry two or three times a month, and I enjoy his company very much. Albrecht writes every week, and his letters are beautiful to read. He's so articulate. Cornelia, I wonder if he isn't in love with me? Not infatuated but actually in love? I haven't given him an answer on going on the sabbatical trip with him. I can't decide what to do. I think I'd adore being in his company every day, just as I was in Switzerland. Terry will be on the *Hood* somewhere in the Med during that time. I'd still need to have a chaperone of some sort or Papa and Edward would become positively unstable. It seems ridiculous at my age, but there you are. Who on earth would the chaperone be?

Well, I can't equivocate forever, much as it seems I should like to. Albrecht and the baron are paying a visit on the tenth of September, a Friday, and staying the weekend, which is grand. What answer I can give Albrecht about the sabbatical is a different matter. I must continue to pray, read my Bible, and go to church. Perhaps God's light will shine in with the answer. Albrecht and I have been very close in the past. Perhaps I gave my kisses too freely, but I did think of him as the only man in my life a year ago. Now I must be more careful and discreet. Explaining why to my theologian won't be easy.

One bright spot! Albrecht's book has been translated into English, and he's bringing me a copy! We can use it to set the mood by talking about it and praying together before we do anything else. That, I hope, will help the rest fall into place. Don't you think?

■ ■ ■ ■

"Here it is! *Voila!* as the French say."

Albrecht handed Catherine a square package. They were standing by a dry fence of fieldstones Skitt and Harrison had erected to the west of the manor of Dover Sky.

"This is exciting!" She ripped at the brown paper and string with her fingers. "Em and Vic always open things so carefully. They try to save the fancy paper Christmas presents are wrapped in. I've never been able to do that." The book finally was in her hands, and she dropped the torn paper and broken string on the grass. "The book jacket is wonderful, Albrecht! Mountains, a sunrise, a cross on a peak . . . is this Pura?"

"Yes."

"*My Spirit*. What a wonderful title. What is that in German?"

"*Mein Geitz.*"

"And Hitler's is *Mein Kampf*, which translates as *My Struggle*. How are your book sales compared to his?"

"I suppose I sell one to every three of his."

"Isn't that still good?"

"*Ja, ja*. It's just a question of how much we're reaching the German people. And while Hitler's message is covering a lot of ground, so is mine." He opened the book to the third page as she held it. "Look here."

This book is dedicated to the German people. And to C.F.D., without whom its grace and breadth and depth would not have been possible.

Catherine immediately felt heat creeping up from her neck and spreading over her face. "My goodness, Albrecht. I haven't blushed like this since I was sixteen and thought I was in love with one of the Coldstream Guards at Windsor Castle. Why did you do me such an honor? All I did was proofreading duties."

"No, Catherine, you did much more than that. I value you as a friend, and as a thinker, and as a woman with a rich heart."

"You're making my blush worse, Albrecht. Who told you what my middle initial is?"

"Your father. He mentioned you once by calling you Catherine Faith. It's an extraordinary name and utterly who you are, so I've remembered it ever since."

"Thank you. I don't know what else to say. I shall read the book, of course."

"And keep a pen and pad of paper by your hand so you can make note of misspellings and poor grammatical structure, yes? Those can be fixed when the book gets reprinted."

She laughed. "I suppose I shall." She opened the book in the middle and read a paragraph. She looked up at Albrecht. "And what is Herr Hitler doing these days?"

"Not much. Germany is coming along well — the best we've been since the war. He's toned down his rhetoric and likes to portray himself as a moderate. Regardless, his Nazi Party continues to hold very few seats in the government, in the *Reichstag,* and no one appears much interested in him anymore."

"That's good."

Albrecht shrugged and gazed at a horse cropping grass on the other side of the stone fence. "Yet his book is selling, and membership in the Nazi Party is growing by tens of thousands each year. So what is really going on in Germany, hmm? Suppose we encounter economic struggles again. Would he gain in popularity?"

"If he does, you'll just have to write another book to counter his influence, won't you?"

"*Oh, ja.* Just like that you think?"

"Why not? You have the mind for it . . . and the spirit."

"Ah, Catherine, you have such confidence in me." He placed his hand over one of hers. "Come to the mountains with me. Please. You mean so much to me. I adore you."

"Albrecht, I — I can't just drop everything . . ."

"I know you have your brother and his wife to welcome back from several years in America. Naturally you must be at Dover Sky for that. And there is that naval officer to see. He will be going south to the Mediterranean in January, yes?"

Her face burned again. "Yes, Terry will be on the *Hood*. I didn't know you knew him."

"I've never met him, but it's no great secret that he's in your life. Catherine, it's not a surprise. How could a rose of such beauty like you go unnoticed year after year?

I can't blame him for falling in love with you. I can't blame any man."

"He has never spoken of love or marriage, Albrecht."

"But his love is revealed in his eyes, isn't it?"

She flipped through pages in the book without responding.

"Catherine, I am not a jealous man. Any attention another pays you is just a confirmation in my heart and mind that what I see in you is not based on some wild Teutonic notion of romance. It pleases me to know others understand what I understand and admire about you. I am acknowledging that you will want to bid him a proper farewell when he leaves for his sea duties." He kissed her hand. "Then please do me the honor of coming away with me to Pura and, in the spring, the Rhine."

"What are you proposing?"

"That the baron and I come and get you after your friend has sailed. We will go to Switzerland together and reside in the chalet until Easter. At that time, we will embark by boat for a spring journey down the Rhine. A delightfully slow journey to appreciate the beauty of the country and our time together. When we reach my family home, we can stay there for some time. My parents would like to meet you. And I promise there will be a few surprises along the way — pleasant ones, I assure you. Please say yes."

"It sounds like you plan for us to be gone a long time."

"Until June or July. And Sean must join us, of course. The horses will be watching for him in Pura."

Catherine smiled into his intense eyes and serious face. "It sounds splendid, Albrecht. And Sean would love to join us, not only for the white horses but to go on a long boat ride. He'd love to see ancient castles. Yet you are speaking of being gone six months. I can't conceive of it without a member of my family along as an escort to save us from public scrutiny and scandal. But everyone has lives of their own, and six months is a long time to ask someone to accompany us. That's half of 1927!"

He nodded. "I understand completely. Are you averse to spending the winter at Pura in the company of the baron and me like you did last year? Our servants would be there as well, of course."

"No, I feel quite all right about that. But to extend our time together another three months on some sort of river cruise? No, I feel that is much too much."

"What if your mother were to join us for the journey down the Rhine?"

Catherine stared. "My mother? You're joking. I don't think she'd leave Father. And she loves having Vic and Ben there. And now they have the baby Timothy Mum dotes on, and young Ramsay, of course. She would never agree."

Albrecht brought a letter out of the pocket of his suit jacket and gave it to her. "Read this," he said with a smile.

My dear Professor Hartmann,
Thank you so much for broaching the subject of the Rhine tour directly to me and not through my daughter Catherine. I have talked things over with Lord Preston and also with my youngest daughter, Victoria. We have all prayed about the matter and are in agreement. I shall join you most gladly. Victoria and her children also accept your kind invitation. We will plan to meet you at Dover Sky the first Monday after Easter.

We look forward to the Rhine journey very much. We will, of course, bring two of our servants to see to our needs and be a nanny to the children. I shall ring up Catherine about the matter.

I do look forward to seeing the baron again and to meeting your mother and father.

You are most kind.

Lady Preston

"I don't know what to say." Catherine read the letter a second time. "Should I be angry that you went behind my back and orchestrated this? Or should I be grateful you cleared up all the messiness that created an obstacle to my joining you?"

"If it's any consolation, it was the baron's idea. He felt it would spare you a great deal of stress and confusion."

"Hmm. Does he tell you what to do, Albrecht?"

"Not at all. But he knows how much I'd hoped to spend time with you. So he suggested I approach the matron of the family herself. I was well aware if she said no that nothing would come of my hopes and plans. Even now with her approval, you are free to say yes or no. I'm well aware of that and accept the risk."

"I see." She handed the letter back to him. "Well, I don't feel any anger whatsoever. If anything I feel relieved. I can sit in the chalet at Pura and look at the mountains if

I like. I can go along the Rhine in a boat if I wish. I can say hullo to my sister Libby and goodbye to my friend the naval officer. As my mother wrote, you are too kind."

A smile moved over Albrecht's lips. "So you are saying yes?"

She swatted him on the shoulder with the book. "It's only so I can have the time to read this through from cover to cover and make notes on it."

"And what about the author?"

She tapped *My Spirit* against his cheek. "You may use the months in Switzerland and on the river to introduce me to him again."

Train Station, Port of Dover

Lord Preston slapped his gloves against his pant leg. "The train should be here by now."

Catherine had her arm through his. "My goodness, Dad, it's not due for another five minutes."

"Are you sure we have the date right?"

"Of course. Tuesday, the twelfth of October. Stop fretting."

"I wanted to be in the House today. Lord Buchanan and Labor are up to more mischief."

Lady Preston had his other arm. "The prime minister can handle the situation. So can Edward."

He peered down the track. "Why all this nonsense? 'Meet us at Dover.' Why couldn't they have taken a ship that docked at Liverpool and be done with it? What does Dover have to do with it?"

"They want to be at Dover Sky, Father."

"Whatever for? Why is the whole world moving to Dover Sky? First you, and then Lady Caroline, and then Kipp's son Matthew, and now this. Absurd." He took out his pocket watch and snapped back the silver lid. "Ha!"

"What, Papa?" Catherine giggled. "Two minutes to go, and you can't see the smoke?"

"It's no laughing matter, my dear. We don't even know where they docked. Why all the secrecy? I feel as if we're in the middle of something cooked up by Sir Arthur Conan Doyle."

"I'm Watson then, Dad. You can be Sherlock. And Mum is the landlady — what's her name?"

Lady Preston patted her husband's arm. "There, William. Is that what you were anxious to see, my dear?"

Black smoke smudged the horizon.

"Ah!" Lord Preston snapped open his watch a second time. "Late."

Catherine grinned and hugged his arm. "By what? Thirty seconds?"

"Thirty-five."

"Think of it, Father. We haven't seen them in three years. How exciting to have the train pulling into the station now."

"Yes — if indeed they are on it. I could do with a little less cloak and dagger and a spot more frank and open declaration of the reasons for the odd nature of their return from America."

"Soon all will be made known. I thank God they've come back to us."

A smile played on Lord Preston's lips. "I do thank Him for that too. I do praise Him."

The locomotive slid past and the brakes screeched. White steam tumbled over the platform. Doors of coaches opened and people climbed out. Lord Preston glanced quickly up and down the length of the train.

"Can you see them?" he asked. "Can you see them?"

"No, they're not . . . There they are!" Catherine pulled free of her father and pointed. "Down near the end."

Lady Preston squinted. "Why, Libby is dressed so . . . so American — her hat, her jacket, her pearls."

"Oh, Mum, she looks pretty. And Michael is such a handsome sight in the suit and hat he's wearing."

"He looks American as well."

"He *is* American. Come on! I can't wait here for them." Catherine rushed down the platform ahead of her parents and caught Libby in her arms. They hugged and laughed and kissed each other's cheeks. Then Catherine put her arms around Michael. "How marvelous you both look!" she exclaimed. "I can't believe it. You're here in England. It's been ages."

Libby smiled. "If we're marvelous, you must be spectacular. Look at her, Michael!"

He kissed Catherine on the forehead. "She's a real doll, all right. Did you miss us?"

"Did we ever! Ben will be doing hand-springs."

"I'm more than ready to help run the airline again." He patted Catherine on the back. "Here's your mum and dad, Libby."

"Ah, Michael! Splendid!" Lord Preston stretched out his hand, and Michael shook it. "How was the voyage? How was the train ride?"

"Fine, William. You're looking very well."

"Thank you! I try to walk every evening when I'm in London."

Lady Preston was hugging Libby. "Your hair is so short, but I must admit it looks just right. My, you've lost weight."

"Hullo, Mum. I guess I've been away from English cooking far too long." She hugged her mother back. "You look younger than when I left."

"Now I know America did something to you, my darling. It's a good thing you're back here to stay."

"Who do we have here?" Lord Preston smiled at a dark-eyed young woman wearing a dark dress who was standing behind Michael and Libby. "Are you with Libby and Michael?"

She curtsied in her dark dress. "I am, sir. My name is Lucy, but everyone calls me Montgomery."

"Ah. And which do you prefer?"

"Montgomery, if you please, my lord."

"Then Montgomery it shall be. And who is this?"

A young Chinese girl in a green dress was holding Montgomery's hand and staring at Lord Preston.

"Father." Libby came and stood behind the young girl, resting her hands gently on her thin shoulders. "This is Jane. She has so looked forward to meeting you and Mum. She's nine."

"All right!" Lord Preston crouched. "Hello, my dear. Welcome to England."

The girl smiled so suddenly and so brightly that Lady Preston exclaimed, "Oh my, how sweet she is! Who is she? Why is she in your company? Where is her family?"

"We are her family, Mum."

"I beg your pardon, dear?"

Michael walked over to take Libby's hand. He stroked Jane's shiny black hair.

"She is Jane Danforth Woodhaven," said Libby. "She is our daughter."

January–May, 1927
Plymouth and Devonport, Southern England
"I feel like I'm going to lose you."

"Don't be so dramatic, Terry." Catherine wiped a raindrop off his cheek with her gloved fingers. "We've seen quite a lot of each other, haven't we? And once you're back from the Med, I'm sure we'll see a lot of each other again."

"Are you positive?"

"As sure as I can be right now."

"A boat trip down the Rhine sounds pretty . . . well . . ."

"With my mother and sister in tow, along with Victoria's two children. Hardly a recipe for a Hollywood romance."

Fordyce held the large black umbrella closer to her head as the wind gusted and the downpour increased. "A man will find a way to your heart. I know I would in that situation."

"Terry, he's very old world, very German, and a theologian from a prestigious university. I'm not going to be stuck on a boat with Don Juan."

"He cares about you as much as I do, doesn't he?"

"Possibly."

"Then how can you say nothing will happen?"

"Excuse me, sir." A sailor in a peacoat came to attention behind them and saluted. "Your presence aboard is requested. We will be weighing anchor in under an hour."

Fordyce turned, straightened, and returned the salute. "Very well."

The sailor saluted again, paused as Terry returned the salute, and then left.

"I have to go." Fordyce put the umbrella in her hands. "Your driver's waiting."

"Harrison can wait a bit longer. He won't mind."

He tipped up her chin with his finger and thumb. "How lovely you are. May I?"

"Of course, Terry. You needn't ask."

The kiss was soft and careful, as if he were unsure of himself. Suddenly he wrapped his arms around her and pulled her into his chest and kissed her with the strength of the storm that was sweeping over them. She almost let the umbrella go in the wind as she responded by throwing her arms around his neck. The rain struck them both but they continued to kiss.

When Terry broke off the embrace, he turned and strode quickly down the pier to the *Hood*'s gangway. He did not look back.

"God go with you, Terry," Catherine said quietly.

"Lady Catherine?"

She glanced at Harrison. He was holding the door of the Rolls open.

"No, thank you, Harrison. I want to watch the *Hood* sail."

"You can do that from the comfort of the car, m'lady."

"I can't actually."

She stood in the rainfall and waited. Hundreds of men scurried back and forth on the *Hood*'s deck. She could hear names being called and caught distinct phrases as they carried over the water. A half hour went by. An hour. Shivers moved up and down her spine. The thick lines that kept the battleship tethered to the shore were released. More orders echoed across the water, sounding like she was in a valley of mist listening to hunters shout to one another. The gray ship and escort vessels slipped through clouds of fog, engines thrumming and rumbling.

Harrison had the door open for her when she turned away from the ship. "My lady."

"Thank you so much, Harrison. I know it was foolish of me."

"Not at all. I would do as much or more for Holly. I hope he saw you wait."

"I don't know. Perhaps he glanced this way from the bridge."

"I'm sure he did."

There was a blanket in the backseat. She pulled it around herself as she settled in. Harrison leaned back and handed her a thermos.

"What is it, Harrison?" she asked, unscrewing the top.

"Hot coffee, m'lady."

"It couldn't possibly be from the manor. We've been gone for ages."

"I went for a stroll while you and Leftenant Commander Fordyce were chatting. That's good Navy coffee. No rum in it, mind you, but that coffee will warm you up like a shovelful of coals in your stomach."

"Thank you, Harrison." She put the thermos to her lips. "You're an absolute lifesaver."

Dover Sky

"What is she whispering?" Caroline asked.

Libby, Jane, and Caroline were in the

parlor visiting. Montgomery, the servant Libby had brought with her from the United States, was attending them.

"She says you're the most beautiful woman she's ever seen." Libby grinned at Caroline. "After her darling mother — me — of course."

Caroline smiled at Jane. "Thank you so much. That is very sweet."

"She means it too. She never says anything for show."

"Jane?" Caroline showed her a large red valentine trimmed in lace. "What do you think of this?"

"It's perfect! I love it, Caroline."

"Shall we make one for your Aunt Holly?"

"Yes, please!"

"What about Bev and Norah and Nancy and Harriet?"

Jane nodded. "I do want to give them something too."

"And the boys?"

Jane grimaced. "Not ones trimmed in lace."

"You're right." Caroline laughed. "Perhaps trimmed in rock. Their valentines will last longer that way."

"Can we send some to Aunt Catherine and Sean in Switzerland?"

"We certainly can," Montgomery replied.

"Are you ready to come with me and make a start? I have scissors and glue and plenty of stiff red paper."

Jane jumped up from where she was sitting. "Do you mean you have all of it right now?" She seized Montgomery's hand.

The maid's dark eyes sparkled as she smiled. "I do! Let's go to the craft room."

"Where are Charles and Matthew?"

"In the big playroom with their toy soldiers."

"Can we visit them later?"

"Of course. But valentines first, all right?"

The two of them left the parlor, and Montgomery closed the door firmly behind them.

"She's nine going on nineteen," Caroline commented as she got up and poured herself tea.

"Jane has always been that way as soon as she's comfortable with the people she's with," said Libby.

"Would you like a cup?"

"Yes, thank you."

Caroline handed Libby a cup of tea on a saucer. Steam curled up from the hot liquid. "You know, I really never heard how you and Michael came to adopt Jane."

Libby sipped at her tea. "It was all rather straightforward. Many Chinese families went to the United States to work on the railroads during the 1800s. In this one Chinese family, a son went to the Klondike in Alaska when gold was discovered there. He made an exceptional strike and the family became wealthy. They made their home in San Francisco. In 1919, the Spanish flu wiped out almost everyone in their family. The grandmother and one-year-old Jane were the only ones who survived."

"You were never in San Francisco, were you?"

"Indeed we were. We'd traveled to the West Coast to visit some of Michael's California relatives. That's when we were introduced to the grandmother and Jane. The grandmother was friends with several of Michael's uncles and aunts. Her health had fallen off dramatically that winter, and after we'd visited with her several times she asked us if we would take Jane.

"Michael and I had gotten on very well with the grandmother and Jane from the beginning. We thought it over and prayed and decided to go ahead. Everything was done properly and legally, and Jane was excited to be with us but so tearful of leaving her grandmother. We thought it best to stay on in San Francisco for several months. The four of us grew quite close. The woman became like a mother to Michael and me. And Jane truly became our daughter. There was no question of changing our minds after that, regardless of Jane's race and the difficulty we knew this would present to us in England. Michael and I both very much believed God had brought us all together. The grand old lady passed away last summer. We wept and made her funeral arrangements; it really was a very special goodbye, and then Jane was more than ready to come back to New York with us." She looked at Caroline over the edge of her cup. "I can't bear children, you see. At least not so far, and none of the physicians held out much hope."

"I'm sorry."

Libby shrugged. "Michael and I have coped with it well enough. Jane has been a gift from heaven. The three of us get along as if she'd been born to us."

"How are your parents with this?"

Libby stared into her cup. "Not good at all. A Chinese granddaughter? *Oriental* is the word they use. Of course it affects Jane. She pretends otherwise, but she sees Mum and Dad doting on Matthew and Sean and it hurts her. She so badly wanted another grandmother. There's nothing we can do except love her more than they ignore her.

Even your son gets more attention from my parents."

"Libby, I apologize —"

"No, that's not necessary. I don't mean to censure you or Charles. He has his own row to hoe without a father around, not to mention what you've been through. I want Mum and Dad to bless you, I honestly do. I just wish they would accept Jane." Impulsively, she reached out to take Caroline's hand. "Thank you for your many kindnesses to her. It helps fill in the gap."

"I adore her. And I'm certain Charles is sweet on her even though he'd never admit it."

Libby sank back in her chair as she tapped her fingernails against the teacup. "To be honest, I worry most of all about Matthew. Since his mother died and Kipp is fighting some dreadful guerrilla war in the Rif, the boy doesn't get much parental support. We thought Kipp would come home once the battles were over and the Berbers surrendered, but the rebels who wouldn't lay down their arms scurried deeper into the mountains. I hate the thought of him out there. But Harrison has been grand with young Matthew, I see. And he quite obviously worships you."

Caroline chuckled. "Not so much, but we

do get along."

"I was told Christelle specifically asked you take on guardianship of Matthew after her death."

"Who told you that?"

"It was in a letter."

Caroline ran her spoon around the inside of her empty cup. After a few moments of listening to the clicking sound she looked up at Libby. "I don't know how much you've heard. Christelle wanted Kipp and me to marry and raise Matthew and Charles together. She believed we still loved each other. She asked us both to honor her request."

"And this was something you couldn't do?"

"Chris wanted me to let Kipp know I still loved him even while she was alive. I argued against the idea, but she was so insistent. She was already suffering so much from the cancer that I didn't have the heart to say no. I approached Kipp. We began to have a relationship again. Only a few kisses, a few words, a few embraces, no more, Libby, I assure you. But it was quite lovely for both of us. Once Kipp found out about Christelle's health, he changed. I believe he was overcome by guilt. It didn't matter that this was what she wanted and even tried to orchestrate. He felt he'd betrayed her by admitting we still had feelings for each other. So he took it out on me. He treated me as if I had been a seductress. Christelle wanted us to love one another again, but Kipp was having none of it. He didn't want me for Matthew's mother and he didn't want me for his wife because he only wanted Christelle. He didn't want to think about life without her."

Caroline's eyes were glimmering with tears. Libby put down her cup and took both of Caroline's hands in hers. "He was grieving," Libby soothed. "You know he was grieving. People want to blame someone when that happens — you, me, themselves, God."

"Kipp called me a harlot, Libby. And he meant it."

"I'm so sorry." Libby pulled Caroline to her feet and took her in her arms. She felt the heat of her friend's tears against her neck. "That's not Kipp. You've known him for years. You loved him. If you really think about it, you know that wasn't his heart talking."

"But it *was* him talking, Libby. No one has ever made me feel so much like dirt. Not even Tanner. When Kipp writes letters to Matthew, I try to care, but it's too painful to think about him. That's why I always get up and leave when they're read aloud for the family. It's very hard. I loved him for so many years, and that love was a big part of who I was. Now I'm confused. I'd rather not have anyone if I can't have him. Yet if he came through the door now and said he wanted to marry me, I'd probably turn my back on him."

"You wouldn't, Caroline. You'd feel differently about him if he stood before you and said he still cared for you."

Caroline pulled back and pressed her fingers into her cheeks. "No, Libby. I don't want him. I don't want anyone."

"Caroline, don't say that! You're so beautiful, any man would want to be with you. Don't let bitterness overtake you."

"I don't want any man to be with me — not even Kipp. I hate my beauty. I wish I could tear the skin off my face. The beauty everyone talks about just brings me misery. If only I had the courage to use acid or a knife or a broken piece of glass to change what I look like."

"No! Don't talk like that!"

"I would do it, Libby. God forgive me, I really think I would do it."

■ ■ ■ ■

My dear Libby,

Here at Ashton Park Easter week is almost over. Father and I so meant to get down to you for a visit but, alas, it is not to be. Victoria, the children, and I need to go directly to Dover from London this coming Monday, April 18th, right after Easter Sunday at Jeremy's church. I do hope to see Michael at church for I know he has a small place nearby. I realize he usually spends his weekends with you at Dover Sky but I was given to understand his presence would be required at the airfield on Good Friday and Easter Saturday, so perhaps he'll show up at the Sunday service? In any case, we are meeting Baron von Isenburg in Dover. He is escorting us to the Rhine in Germany. We are so excited! Catherine and Sean should be waiting for us by the time we arrive.

Your father and I are very sorry we won't get a glimpse of you this Easter, but Victoria and I will be sure to return with Catherine to Dover Sky for a get-together in June or July.

Richest blessings in Christ,
Mum

P.S. I hope Matthew and Charles got the chocolate Easter eggs I mailed down last week. They are the special Cadbury ones, and I was sure they'd love them.

Dover Sky

"Is there anything I can get for you, Lady Caroline?"

"Hmm? No, I'm quite all right, Skitt. Thank you. I was thinking of wandering over the estate with my bag of bread crumbs for the geese and swans."

"Does her ladyship think she is up to that?"

"What do you mean?"

"Well, you were feeling faint just an hour ago. You sent all the others off to the May Day celebrations in London without you."

"I know. I'm much improved now. A little exercise and fresh air will do the trick, I'm sure."

"There was talk of Lord Kipp showing up today or tomorrow on furlough, m'lady."

"Or much later in the week. Yes, I know."

"If he comes while you're out on the grounds, should I direct him to you?"

"If that's his wish, Skitt, you may tell him where I'm gone. But I do relish some privacy."

"Of course, Lady Caroline."

Caroline, in a pale-blue dress, made her way towards the pond. Once she was out of sight from anyone in the manor she turned left and disappeared within a grove of willows showered with bright-green leaves. The trees were bent over what Harrison called "a slither of a stream" that emerged from the ground, trickled several hundred yards, and then flowed back under the grass and earth. She sat down, kicked off her shoes, and dipped her toes in the water. After a minute of this, she unbound her hair and dropped the pins in the stream to watch the ripples. She splashed her face until water streamed off her skin and through her hair. Circles of shadow and saucers of sun created a pattern on her cheeks as light fell through the leaves and branches.

All right. It's not as if I'm doing away with myself. Well, I suppose I am in a way. Doing away with this silly, ridiculous beauty called Caroline Scarborough. Charles will still have a mother — a better one, a plain one. No more men will bother me. No Tanners, no Kipps, no lords, no soldiers, no village idiots, no one who might hurt Charles or me. I'll be free of the lies of flattery and betrayal. A different face means a different life.

She brought a knife out of the paper bag. The blade was about six inches long and glittered where the sun struck it. The Kaiser's eagle was stamped into its base near the hilt. Kipp had given it to her as a gift early in the war, and she had never thrown it away. Ten minutes of steady polishing and sharpening had brought out its luster once again.

If only it were so easy for us to bring back the shine we once had.

She ran her thumb over the dagger's edge. It was sharpened on both sides. Blood sprang from her skin. She smiled. *Sharp enough. Fine cuts like threads of silk will do it. You will not want me, Kipp. No one will want me. I thank God for that.*

There was only the sound of the birds and only the movement of their wings as they slipped from branch to branch. She touched the the dagger to her smooth, white cheek but did not press it in. *I must do this before you come home. When you come, I might weaken. I might love you once more. I might throw the knife into the stream. You might take me in your arms and hurt me again . . . and again. The dagger only hurts once . . . just once.*

■ ■ ■ ■

Heidelberg, the Neckar River, Germany

"Ah, there you are. What do you think of Heidelberg?" Albrecht asked Catherine.

"My goodness, I feel like I'm in a fairy tale. Are we going to stay here for a while or go back to the Rhine?"

"We're on the Neckar right now, and it flows quite a bit further. We'll probably berth here a few days. Mother and Father will want to visit the Heidelberger Schloss. They always do."

"You make it sound like such a chore."

"I've been inside more times than I can count."

"Everyone will want to go into the castle — the boys especially. I want to go into the castle too."

"Your wish is my command, my dear Catherine. Though I must say I look forward to returning to the Rhine and continuing to float those historic waters. There are plenty more castles to see and a special magic seems to hang in the air when we're on the water."

She pushed him. "And there is no magic in Heidelberg? I thought you said the other night there is magic anywhere I am."

302

He gently put his arms around her waist. "That's true. I forgot for a minute. And the Heidelberg sun brings out all your color and delicate features."

"My delicate features?" She laughed and then glanced around. "Where is everyone?"

"Forward or below. Hans has laid out baked treats and chocolates in honor of May Day. The children are hovering about the table like hummingbirds, and their mothers and grandmothers are hovering about them like hawks."

"Not this mother."

"Sean is with Lady Preston."

"She'll probably eat more than he does." Catherine smiled up at Albrecht. "Was this your timing? Hans laying out the sweets . . . you and me alone at the stern of the vessel . . . Heidelberg Castle drifting slowly into view?"

"What mortal can plan such things? I prefer to think it is just meant to be."

"I see." She fingered a button on his shirt. "The journey has been lovely so far, Albrecht, but far busier and noisier than I expected. Two grandmothers, a grandfather, my sister, her baby, two boys, the baron."

"At night —"

"Even at night there is no peace and quiet. By the time there is, I'm too exhausted to meet you for a *tête-à-tête* under the stars. By day we talk books, history, art, religion, and politics. By night we do the same until I am drooping."

He lifted a hand and ran his thumb over her cheek. "That is why I have brought you here now."

"This peaceful moment won't last. Sean and Mama will come looking for me any minute now, and that will be that for our little interlude by Heidelberg Castle."

"They won't."

"Why won't they?"

"I told Hans I must have at least a half an hour with you. I told Martin too. So there are . . . how shall I say it? Ah, guards posted to block all paths to the stern. We have twenty-five more minutes."

She continued to toy with the button. "You sound very sure of yourself."

"Sure of myself? No, I feel very hesitant right now. But I am confident of my guards. The children and grandmothers and grandfather shall not get past them."

"Mama can have a temper."

"My men will charm her."

"Charm her? With what?"

"Roses. Coffee. Mints. Whatever pleases her."

"All to what end?"

"Time alone with you, naturally." He put his lips to hers. When she didn't push him away, he kissed her hair and throat and then went back to her lips. This time with more passion.

She responded with a surge of her own and tugged on his hair with her fingers as she kissed him, tugging harder and harder. His arms were around her back with a sudden force that made it difficult for her to catch her breath. But she had no intention of ending the kiss, luxuriating in it as the boat floated over the water.

Finally Albrecht drew back.

"Oh . . ." she said softly, "I wish you hadn't."

"We have more time. But there is something I want to ask you."

"Ask me? Ask me now? I would rather you brought your lips down to mine again."

"It's the most important thing I have ever asked you."

"Is it?" Her eyes were large and dark and flecked with light. "What are you up to, Albrecht Hartmann?"

Dover Sky
Kipp finally spotted her shoeprints in the mud by the small stream under the willows. She hadn't been at the pond or any of the

305

fieldstone fences and he'd been about to head back to the manor when he thought of the willows.

She loves trees but especially the willows at her family's estate.

There he saw her sitting by the stream.

"Caroline."

She didn't move.

"Caroline. I'm back from Africa. It's been years."

Still she didn't move.

"I'm sorry. It's been more like forever. No letters. No cables. But I need to talk to you alone."

She remained like stone.

"What's happened?"

He ran towards her. She suddenly turned her head and brandished the dagger at him.

"Get back, Kipp. I have to do this. At least four cuts to the face. I just haven't had the nerve."

"Caroline, have you gone mad? Give me that knife!"

He lunged, but she put the dagger to her throat. "I'll do it. I don't care anymore. Life is nothing but a great darkness."

"No, it's not. I want to talk to you. I want to start again."

Her laugh was harsh. "Oh, I knew you'd say that. You don't look like Kipp — you've

306

lost too much weight and your skin is as dark as mud — but you sound just like him. More promises. I'm not interested. And when I'm done with my face you won't be interested either."

"Caroline, please don't. You're so beautiful —"

She laughed again. "My famous beauty. What good has it ever done me? Broken heart after broken heart. You called me a whore."

"I was a fool. I was worse than a fool. God forgive me. Christelle was right."

"Christelle, ah, Christelle, what was she right about?" Caroline put the point of the dagger against her cheek. "You won't love me without a face you can kiss, Kipp Danforth."

"Don't!"

He tried to seize the dagger a second time but she thrust it at her throat again.

"I'll finish myself off, Kipp, I swear it. Stay back."

"All right. Do it. Go ahead, do it. I'll join you." Kipp brought a pocketknife from his pants pocket and flipped it open. He put it to his cheek. "If you can cut your face to ribbons, so can I. I'm to blame for your misery. So if you're going to do four cuts, I'll do eight."

"You won't!"

"I will!"

"Stop it, Kipp!"

"Who do you think I thought about when I flew from the Orkneys to Cape Town? You and Chris. Who did I think about after I crash landed in the Sahara and was half crazy with thirst? You and Chris. All the fighting I've done with the French Foreign Legion in Morocco, all the heat and flies and bullets and killing; who was on my mind hour after hour, day after day? You and Chris."

Caroline saw him press down on the knife. She shrieked and threw herself at Kipp, twisting the pocketknife out of his hand with a fierce burst of strength and flinging it into the trees. He seized her dagger hand and they fell to the ground, rolling over and over in the mud and water, her fingers wrapped tightly around the hilt, his hand bending back her wrist and trying to break her grip. She cried out and slapped him and clawed his eyes but he wrenched at her wrist until she dropped the dagger in the stream.

"That hurt!" she yelled, blue eyes blazing.

"I don't care!" he shouted back.

She went at him again with her nails and tried to pull his hair but his head was so close shaven there was nothing to grasp.

Kicking at his legs and biting at his hands, she pushed him against a willow trunk and started beating him with her fists. He caught her hands and threw her into the shallow stream, immediately launching himself at her and pinning her there so that her hair was under water and the current running over her cheeks and eyes. Unable to squirm loose she lifted her head and tried to bite his ear, finally swinging her head so that her heavy wet hair struck him in the face.

"I hate you!" she cried.

"I love you!"

"Shut up, Kipp Danforth!"

"No!"

He began to kiss her cheek, cold water mixing with the taste of her skin.

"Don't touch me!" she screeched.

But he continued to kiss her, his lips finding her eyes that she screwed shut, and her throat that she twisted back and forth to get away from him, and her lips that she sucked in and held tight against her teeth. He let go of her hands and put his arms under her back and lifted her out of the stream, cradling her and kissing her with more and more intensity. She dug her nails into his back and slapped at his neck and shoulders but nothing stopped him. When she opened her mouth to shout something at him his lips were there quickly, pressing against the softness and fullness that had always been part of the great beauty of Caroline Scarborough. Suddenly she laced her arms around his neck as tightly as she could and began to cry as he held her, kissing back with a fire and abandon as desperate as the blows she had rained on him moments before.

"Oh, Kipp, what are we going to do?" she cried.

"Marry me."

"Don't be mad. What sort of proposal is that?"

"It's the best I can do right now."

"Look at us. Thank the good Lord that Harrison went to London today."

"Marry me, Lady Caroline Virginia Scarborough."

"I can't, Kipp. I hate you, you know I hate you, a lovers' quarrel in a creek doesn't change that." They kissed again, their arms around each other. "When do you want to have the wedding?"

"Tonight."

"Oh, Kipp, why wait for tonight?"

Heidelberg, the Neckar River, Germany
Catherine's eyes remained wide. "Now you've got me frightened, Albrecht."

"It's not a matter involving fear." He pushed strands of hair out of her eyes. "Or perhaps it is."

"What are you talking about? Have you decided to join the Nazi Party? Is Herr Hitler waiting to receive us at his castle on the Rhine?"

"Nothing like that! It is much more pleasant a prospect. I want to say I love you. No more than that. *Ich liebe dich.*"

"No more than that? That's a lot, Albrecht."

His hand moved slowly down the side of her face. "There is also the fact that I find you the most beautiful woman alive."

Her hand reached up to grasp his. She brought it to her lips and kissed it. "Thank you. *Danke schön.*"

"And something else."

She smiled. "Well, the arrival at Heidelberg is turning out to be quite a moment in the lives of Albrecht Hartmann and Catherine Danforth Moore."

"It is, isn't it? Let us have many such moments. A lifetime of such moments." He cupped her face in both his hands. "*Catherine, heirate mich bitte.*"

She let out her breath. "I don't think I need a translation. Albrecht, you can't mean it."

"Of course I mean it."

"I'm not ready to —"

"When will you be ready?" he cut in. "You're still young. You can have more children. Build another home — build a castle! How many more years, Catherine? Five? Ten? I love you. Marry me on this boat. Marry me on the Rhine. Marry me when we reach my family's home on the river. But please, can we stop this yes, no, yes, no, back and forth?"

"Albrecht —"

"Marry me. Marry someone who cherishes you. Or marry Leftenant Commander Fordyce. He loves you too, I'm sure. There is no reason for you to keep living alone. I want you to wed Albrecht Hartmann, but if not me, another man who will treasure you and give Sean a family. No more waiting, Catherine. Please, no more putting it off. You are a woman — strong, intelligent, full of compassion, and beautiful. It is time to choose, don't you think?"

"I don't know what to think."

"Of course you do." He kissed her on the lips. "Give yourself a moment, and then tell me yes or no. One or the other. I will celebrate the one and survive the other. But here on the river at Heidelberg, I must know. You have turned all this over in your

312

heart for years. Tell me what you've found. Today. Here. Now. Tell me what you see in your heart and soul, Catherine. Tell me what you feel for me and how strong that feeling is."

11

June, 1927
London airstrip

The silver monoplane circled the airfield, did a victory roll, and came in for a landing. Michael walked out to it while the plane's three propellers were still spinning. Ben jumped down, a large smile spreading across his face.

"Look at her, Mike! Isn't she a beaut? We've got two of them up in Lancashire, and this is the first of your pair I'm delivering."

Michael reached up and ran his hand over the single wing. "The Fokker F.VII B/3M. Three engines — all of them 220 horsepower. Eight passengers. How's she fly?"

"Like a dream. Let's get some petrol into her and you can take her up."

"I'd love that."

"We've given her a name." He patted the letters painted on the engine cowling —

Dover Sky. "One of ours up north is the *Ashton Park.* Did you get down to Dover Sky last weekend?"

"No, it was too busy here at the London airstrip. But Libby and Jane are doing great."

"I couldn't believe it when you rang me up last month about Kipp and Caroline. I thought that flame had died out years ago."

Michael smiled as he admired the airplane. "I guess it never did. We came back from May Day celebrations in London, and Lord and Lady Scarborough were already there, along with an Anglican priest. Thank goodness Lord Preston had tagged along with us and traveled down from London! Lady Preston is still in Germany with Vic and Catherine, so she'll be sorry she missed it. Anyway, away we went right there and then to the swan pond. I stood with Kipp, and Libby was Caroline's matron of honor. They honeymooned in France before he returned to the Foreign Legion. Now he's back tangling with Berber guerrillas in the Rif. And Charles and Matthew are now brothers, not just best friends."

"Will Kipp ever come back to our airline, do you think?" asked Ben.

"He can't muster out until sometime in '28. Let's keep our fingers crossed that he comes back in one piece. He told me he misses the flying, especially the races. How are you holding up without Vic and the kids?"

"Pretty good, but I miss them. I do miss them." Ben slapped the fuselage with the heavy pair of leather gloves he'd just pulled off. "Speaking of racing, there's an endurance contest being set up to honor Charles Lindbergh's solo flight across the Atlantic. Wasn't that something? You must be proud, Mike! He's a fellow American."

Michael nodded. "It took a lot of guts. So many others went into the drink or crashed and burned up."

"So that's what this race is — a way to honor what Lindbergh's done. Orkneys to Gibraltar nonstop for the first leg. Second leg is Gibraltar to Freetown, Sierra Leone, nonstop. Then it's straight to Cape Town, South Africa. That's the tough part. Fastest time wins. Race is in August. I'm signed up. Do you think you'll have a go?"

"Crewing with you?"

"That's what I had in mind."

"Won't our girls have a fit?"

Ben put his arm around Michael's shoulders. "I always tell Vic, as another Yank pilot put it, *'There are old pilots, and there are bold pilots, but there are no old, bold pilots.'* "

"I'm sure that gives her a great deal of comfort."

Ben shrugged. "When your time's up, it's up whether you're in the air or on the ground."

Hartmann Castle, the Rhine River, Germany

Dear Libby,

Well, my dear, you had your bit of excitement with Caroline and Kipp up and tying the knot on May Day out of the clear blue, as they say. Mum is so disappointed for not being present at the wedding of her son. But she's gotten her revenge. I expect you got wind of the cable we sent to Dad in London. Imagine our surprise when a week after we received your telegram in Heidelberg we had no sooner docked at Hartmann Castle on the Rhine then Catherine and Albrecht announced their engagement!

Mum was floored, I can tell you. On top of that, Catherine insisted they be married at the castle. Dad couldn't get free of his commitments in time, as you know, so that's how everything worked out, didn't it? Father at Kipp's wedding and mother at Catherine's. You acting as

Caroline's matron of honor, I doing my bit as Catherine's. Michael standing for Kipp, and one of Albrecht's brothers standing for him.

The wedding was amazing. Picture a spectacular hall hung with old tapestries that have been cleaned and dusted for the occasion, a ceiling as high as the sky, stained-glass windows like in a cathedral, torches burning in brackets on the stone walls. My goodness, Lib, I thought we'd gone back to 1000 AD in H.G. Wells' Time Machine. And they did the wedding service right through twice — first of all by a Lutheran minister who only spoke German and then in English by an Anglican priest. Heaven knows where they hauled him out from since they only had ten days to prepare.

That's really nothing compared to what our sister was wearing. They had this gown for Catherine that must have belonged to one of Charlemagne's wives or daughters. Do you remember how we were taught about Amaudru, his first child and girl? It was royal purple and scarlet studded with diamonds and rubies. Albrecht looked like a German prince in his outfit. Honestly, what with its sash and medallions. You can imagine how ecstatic Mum was when the parents admitted they could trace their line back to emperors and empresses.

So despite all the snubbing from the British nobility, Mum and dad have almost got all they wanted now. You're married to a Woodhaven, Kipp is married to a Scarborough. Robbie's married to a Dungarvan and Irish aristocracy, Emma's husband is practically a bishop, and now Catherine's wed into German wealth and a royal bloodline. It's just Edward and I who have spoiled things by wedding commoners.

As if Catherine and Albrecht haven't had pleasure enough bobbing along the Rhine all spring, the pair of them are off honeymooning in Austria. Well, I don't begrudge Cathy that or her fairy-tale marriage. She's had a tough life the past few years. God bless her! I hope she never has to grieve over a lost husband again. I don't know how I'd hold up if I ever lost Ben.

I'll drop a line again soon. I have no idea

when we're coming home now.

Love to all, and hugs and kisses to Jane and Michael.

Your Vic

Dover Sky

"You miss him, don't you?"

"Very much, Holly. It seems like all my life I've wanted to be married to the blonde, green-eyed Kipp Danforth. But something always happened to prevent it. Now that we're actually married, I have so much lost ground to make up. I can't bear that he's out in Morocco again with the French Foreign Legion."

Holly was sitting next to Caroline on a swing on the back porch. "Would you really have gone ahead with Lord Buchanan's scheme?"

Caroline glanced at her. "The plan where I was supposed to yell that I was being attacked after I enticed Kipp to my room?"

"Something like that."

"That was why Tanner beat me. It wasn't just because I wouldn't clean the blood off the cane or polish the silver handle. I told him his plan was mad, and I had no intention of trying to destroy a family who cared for me as much as the Danforths did. I confessed all this to Kipp on our honey-moon in France." With a brief laugh, Caroline looked down at her hands. "It seems we spent half our time apologizing to one another for things that have happened over the years."

"I can see your love for him."

"I adore him. He's every dream come true."

"Do you think Tanner still has a plan against the Danforths?"

"Yes, I do."

"Do you have any idea what he intends to do?" asked Holly.

"I don't. For all I know, he means to get back at me as well."

Holly smiled and put her arm around Caroline. "Fear not. We're in this together. We shall fend off his assaults."

"Truthfully, I'd scarcely think of him from one day to the next except for Charles. When I look at my son I can see he's already a brighter soul than his father ever was." She bit her lip. "It's Kipp I worry about. If anything happens to him in that dreadful desert, I shall go to pieces. I know I shall."

"Ah . . ." Holly took one of Caroline's hands and gripped it. "I may be a lapsed Anglican, but I still know a bit about talking to the Almighty. May I? On your behalf?"

Caroline's smile was timid. "I should like that."

"Hullo?"

Libby looked up from the rosebush she was fertilizing. She saw a tall man in a dark-blue naval uniform. "Yes?"

"I came by to see if Lady Catherine was back from the Continent. She expected me to call. I'm Leftenant Commander Terrence Fordyce." He smiled and jerked a thumb over his shoulder. "I asked your butler, but he wasn't a wealth of information. He sent me 'round back here and told me to speak to Lady Elizabeth Woodhaven."

Libby stared at him for a full second before moving. "Ah, yes." She got to her feet and brushed dirt off her dress. Removing a gardening glove, she extended her hand. "I'm Catherine's sister Elizabeth, but please call me Libby, Leftenant Commander. How do you do?"

He took her hand. "A pleasure. A beautiful day for working on roses."

"It is. I must get this done while I can. My daughter is having a birthday party in a week, and my schedule will be an absolute shambles once I start to organize that in earnest."

"How old will she be?"

"Ten — and she's making sure everyone knows it. It makes her the eldest child among the Danforth brood."

He laughed. "She'll rule, will she? Queen Victoria or Queen Elizabeth?"

"Either one, so long as it's not Bloody Mary." Libby removed her wide-brimmed straw hat. "My husband and I were in America for several years. That's why you and I have never met, but Catherine wrote me about you."

"Did she? Good things, I hope."

"Very good. Have you not heard from her lately?"

"No, nothing at all. I realize she was on a journey along the Rhine and may not have been free to post a note or send a cable."

"Yes." Libby glanced about her. "Will you take a short stroll with me, Leftenant Commander?"

She led him west towards the Knight property and the oak trees. He fell in step beside her.

"Unquestionably, Catherine would have tried to send you a message," Libby began. "But you're quite right. She has been in locations that are out of the way, which would make sending telegrams and letters awkward. As soon as she is able, I know she'll write you. Unfortunately, that could be weeks."

"Is everything all right?"

"Well, it is and it isn't." Libby took in a deep breath. "Really, she should be telling you this, but it can't be helped. And it wouldn't be fair to keep you in the dark. My sister Catherine has married. I believe you know of Albrecht Hartmann, a German theologian? He is now her husband."

Fordyce stopped walking as if he'd been caught and held. "Married! For how long?"

"Just this month."

"I see." He remained motionless. "I admit this is a lot to take in."

"I'm sure it is. I'm so sorry. I know you and Catherine had a marvelous relationship."

Fordyce looked at the oaks in the distance and then the stone fence beyond them. "Married to Hartmann. Well, bless him, the lucky dog." He forced a smile. "Will Lady Catherine be returning to Dover Sky, Lady Elizabeth?"

"Libby," she reminded him. Then she shook her head. "Not to live. They'll be living in Tubingen, where Albrecht lectures at the university. Summers will probably be spent in Switzerland or at Hartmann Castle on the Rhine."

"Switzerland and the Rhine, eh? I can't compete with that on Royal Navy pay." He straightened his hat. "I won't take up anymore of your time. Thank you so much, Libby. I'll be heading back to Devonport."

"Please don't run off. I'd like you to meet my husband and daughter. They're down feeding the swans."

"I don't want to interfere with your Saturday."

"Not at all. Michael has good friends in the United States Navy. He's been aboard several of their battleships, including the *USS Arizona* and the *USS Oklahoma.* He'd love to meet you, and you'd have oodles to talk about. Do stay on for a bit."

"The *Arizona* and *Oklahoma,* you say?" Fordyce grinned and shrugged. "Why not? A chat would soften this morning's news. I can drive away with my head full of information about keels and engines and funnels and guns — at least for a while."

She smiled back at him as she brushed damp strands of ginger hair out of her blue eyes. "That's the spirit! Let's head to the pond. We have two dozen swans with us this week. It's quite something to watch."

"Two dozen!"

"Indeed. Twenty-four down to the youngest cygnet. All under the protection of King George himself."

My dear Terry,
I fear this will get to you too late and you will have heard about my state of affairs from other sources. You may think that out of sight is out of mind regarding you, but that is not so. I asked but there wasn't a telegraph station within a hundred miles of Hartmann Castle. Now that I am in Vienna, there are plenty of them but I simply couldn't send you the news that way. It was too cold. So this letter will have to do even though it will take much longer to reach you in Devonport.

Albrecht and I were married early in June. It was not an easy decision to make, but it was a decision I had to make. I dragged my heels on this matter far too long. I care for you dearly, Terry. You have a great heart and a great soul. I doubt that will make you feel better about things right now. I'm certain news of my marriage will come as a slap to the face. I was not rejecting you; I was just saying yes to Albrecht — if that makes sense.

I will continue to pray for you and your safety on the high seas. I have no idea when we shall see one another again, and perhaps that's just as well. You will be in England and the Mediterranean, and I will be in Germany and Switzerland.

God bless you and all the best to you, my dear Terry.

Catherine

"Is the sailor man in the uniform coming?"

Libby brushed her daughter's gleaming black hair and tied a purple ribbon at the top. "You mean Leftenant Commander Fordyce? I don't think so, honey."

"But we invited him, and he said he might."

"He's quite a few miles from here on his big ship. It's not so easy for him to just pop over."

"Grandfather William is coming down from London, isn't he?"

"Yes."

"And Uncle Jeremy and Aunt Emma? And aren't Uncle Edward and Aunt Char coming too? And all my cousins?"

"Of course! It'll be an absolute mob. And there will be gifts from your relatives in

America too. Did you see that huge parcel from Grandpa and Grandma Woodhaven that's on the table on the porch?"

"I did! I'm so excited!"

"Hold still a moment." Libby tied an orange ribbon next to the purple one. "There!"

Jane looked at herself in the oval mirror on the vanity. "Purple dress. Purple stockings. Purple and orange ribbons." She grinned. "I love these colors. What about Grandmother Elizabeth? Is she coming?"

"She's still in Germany with Aunt Vickie and your cousins Ramsay and young Timothy. It's too bad. Grandfather William will have your present, and Uncle Ben is bringing the ones from Aunt Vickie and Ramsay. Here are your purple gloves."

Jane tugged them on, and they went up to her elbows. "Will he really fly in?"

"Yes, he really will. Then he'll be off again after a hug and a kiss and a piece of cake."

"Ooh! I think I could fly without a plane! I'm so happy!"

"Here . . ." Libby gently arranged an orange silk scarf about her daughter's neck. "Go show yourself to your father. He's hanging balloons on the porch with Skitt and Montgomery."

Jane's smile grew sly. "Monty likes Skitt."

"Why, who told you that?"

"No one." Jane made circles like glasses around her eyes with her fingers. "I can see for myself."

Libby laughed. "Is that right? And how is Skitt dealing with this bit of Dover Sky romance, Lady Jane?"

"Ha! I don't think he knows what to do . . . except get tongue-tied."

"You look smashing in purple and orange. They're the colors of our coat of arms."

"Indeed." Jane curtsied. "Thank you, m'lady."

Libby straightened and gently pulled the sides of her blue summer dress as she curtsied back. "You're welcome, m'lady." She opened the bedroom door. "Come, let's go downstairs to your father. He'll be bowled over by the beauty of his princess."

"His *enchanted* princess."

"Quite right. His *enchanted princess*."

They heard car doors slam, and Jane ran to the open window.

"Leftenant Commander!" Libby heard her husband call out. "Hey! It's great to see you here!"

"Wouldn't miss it, Michael. Haven't been to a proper birthday party in years."

Jane swung her head around and laughed. "You see, Mama? He *did* come! He *does*

329

like me."

Libby went to the window and put a hand on her daughter's shoulder. "Well, that's not really a surprise, is it? Everyone adores you, Lady Jane."

"He's my knight."

"Your knight? I thought your father was your knight."

"Dad is my father knight. Leftenant Commander Fordyce is my *knight* knight." She stared, suddenly puzzled. "There is something different about him. I thought I had his uniform utterly memorized." She bolted from the room and down the staircase.

"Jane!" Libby called after her. "Slow down!"

She watched from the window as Jane raced out the front door and practically came to attention in front of Terrence Fordyce.

"There's the birthday girl!" Fordyce handed her a present wrapped in purple paper with orange bows. "For the rest of your life you'll always have two numbers in your age. Unless you live to be one hundred, then you'll have three."

Jane took the gift. "Thank you, Leftenant Commander. You remembered about my favorite colors."

"So I did."

"Do you realize your uniform is not the same?"

"It's not? What's different about it?"

"I'm not sure."

Michael walked up and put his arm around Jane. "Honey, I think it's the same uniform Lieutenant Commander Fordyce wore last Saturday."

"It isn't, Dad."

"Everything's exactly the same."

"No."

Fordyce put his hands in his pockets. "Are you sure you're not mistaken, Jane?"

Jane eyed him up and down. Then she pointed at his hands. "Take them out of your pockets."

"Jane," Michael soothed, "calm down. I know it's your big day but —"

Fordyce grinned and removed his hands from his pockets. He turned them toward her, palms outward. "No rabbits, my dear."

Libby smiled as Jane played with his sleeves and then put her knuckles to her mouth. "Oh Jane," she said before chuckling.

"The cuffs are different!" Jane shouted.

"Jane, no yelling!" her father said.

She challenged Fordyce with the intensity of her dark-eyed stare. "They are, aren't they?"

"Jane!" Michael corrected again.

"It's all right." Fordyce held up his hands as if she'd pulled a gun. "Jane's spot on. I have three thick gold stripes on the cuffs instead of the two thick ones with a skinny one in between."

Jane's dark eyes glittered. "What are you now? An admiral?"

"Not quite. A commander. After that comes captain, then commodore, and then admiral."

"Do you get your own battleship?"

"I can have a ship, Jane, but not a battleship."

"Are you getting a ship?"

"Not yet. I am our captain's right-hand man on the *HMS Hood* now. One of them, anyway."

She turned his present over in her slender brown hands. "Does this have to do with the Royal Navy?"

"It does."

"May I open it?"

Michael laughed and shook his head. "Remember the deal, Jane? First everyone arrives. Then we'll play games. Then comes the cake and ice cream. And then — ta da! — you can open the presents."

"But no one's here but old people."

"The kids are coming. And Charlie and

Matt are around here somewhere."

"They're off doing something secret with Aunt Holly and Aunt Caroline. It's so boring right now."

"Jane!"

"Can't I open this one while we're waiting? It is my birthday after all. Please, Dad?"

Michael rolled his eyes up. "Just one, but only if *Commander* Fordyce says, *'Aye, aye, skipper.'* "

Fordyce nodded and said, "Go ahead, Jane."

She tore the paper off and then opened the box underneath. She pulled out a naval officer's hat. "It's the same as yours!"

"It is, but smaller. I hope it fits you."

She quickly put the hat on her head. "It's perfect . . . only a little tight. Thank you so much."

He saluted her. "Happy birthday, Commander."

Jane ruled the day. Not only was she older than her nearest competitors — Jeremy and Emma's ginger-haired and green-eyed Peter and brown-haired, brown-eyed James, neither of whom would turn ten until December — she was also taller than the other children and much faster on her long legs. After the games that included the pinning of the tail on the donkey and a hotly contested croquet match, they consumed cake, lemonade, ice cream, and dozens of pork sausages called bangers that were roasted over a fire.

Jane soon sat surrounded by mounds of wrapping paper and gifts, her commander hat squarely on her head. Uncle Ben had dropped a basket of dolls by parachute, done a victory roll, and then zipped away. Grandfather William had arrived late with German and Swiss dresses shipped from Grandma Elizabeth on the Continent. He also had bags of Swiss chocolate for all and steel swords with blunt edges for the boys. The gifts from America included a large dollhouse that could be plugged in so the rooms lit up and the fireplaces glowed. At bedtime a raid was launched by the boys against Jane's room. It was led by the twins and their seven-year-old brother, Billy. Charles, Matthew, and Owen were eager recruits. All brandished their steel swords from Grandfather William. But Jane had a sword of her own and no fear. A few lightbulbs were lost before order was restored and everyone marched back to their bedrooms. Skitt continued to keep an eye out as he prowled the halls long after the doors were shut.

■ ■ ■ ■

Michael left Jane's room and entered his through an adjoining door. He closed it and then leaned against it. He let out his breath as he looked at Libby before starting to laugh.

"I think Mary, Queen of Scots, has finally settled."

"I'm glad to hear it. She can be a monster if she doesn't get her sleep."

"I'm pretty sure there's a sword somewhere under her blankets."

"Is there? That's surprising."

Michael stared as her sharp tone registered. "Hey, what's the matter?"

Libby was sitting in her nightgown on the edge of the bed and filing her nails. "I'm just shocked she has a sword of her own. My dad certainly didn't give it to her."

"What do you mean?"

"He had swords for everyone but her. When she asked for one, he said the extras were for Sean and Ramsay and Tim when they come back from Germany."

"So he just brought them for the boys —"

"Only one of the dresses they gave her fit, do you know that? I helped her try them on while the boys were roasting bangers with

Harrison."

"I'm sure your mom did the best she could. She wouldn't know Jane's size."

"She knows it all right. Vic cabled me and I cabled her the measurements back weeks ago."

Michael sat next to her on the bed. "Look, she had a terrific day. I'm sure she's forgotten all about the dresses that didn't fit."

Libby examined her nails. "Until next week. Then the tears will come."

"She has that incredible dress from Kipp and Caroline — the one from Morocco. She looks like a sultan's queen in that."

"She does. With her skin color, high cheekbones, and dark eyes and hair she's stunning."

"She'll be all right."

"She won't be all right. She knows my mother and father don't approve of her being our daughter."

"They need time, Lib."

Libby flared. "Time? It will be a year in October. It's precisely the sort of thing that happened when they didn't approve of Victoria and Ben or Edward and Char."

"So they'll come around eventually."

"You don't know that. Mum and Dad went through years of being snubbed by their friends because of Vic and Edward's 'low' marriages. I'm sure neither of them is interested in a repeat of that experience, and certainly not over a little, lost Chinese girl from America."

He rubbed a hand over his face. "I'll talk with them."

She smiled even as she shook her head. "Dear Michael, my American hero." She kissed him on the cheek. "They'll listen politely to their precious son-in-law from the United States. They'll nod. They'll offer you tea or coffee. And a week later . . . maybe two weeks . . . nothing will have changed."

"Jane's status doesn't seem to bother anyone else in the family —"

"With the exception of Edward. But then he doesn't approve of Catherine marrying a German, so why should he approve of you and I adopting an *Oriental*?"

"If Jane were among the schoolchildren in London or Liverpool, they would be merciless because she's different."

"And that's why she's not among the schoolchildren in London or Liverpool!" snapped Libby. "That's why we're at Dover Sky and a tutor comes from Dover three days a week. How do I protect my daughter from her British grandparents?"

Michael gripped her hand and put it to

his lips. "We love her. She knows that."

"Of course we do."

"And the day will come when your mom and dad will too. I believe that."

"Darling, you believe anything. You're always on the up and up."

"Ever since I met my English nurse during the war."

Her blue eyes lost their fire and softened. "Yes, that's true. Ever since her." She leaned her head against his chest and his arm went around her. "I expect you're right. They'll become proper grandparents one day. I just don't know what it will take."

12

August, 1927
The Orkney Islands, northern Britain
Ben Whitecross peered out of the cockpit at a black and yellow airplane also idling on the runway. It was the same kind of three-engined Fokker he was sitting in. "Von Zeltner again. Doesn't that bloke ever give up?"

Michael Woodhaven leaned over from his seat and looked back past Ben's shoulder. "He probably wonders the same thing about us."

Ben glanced at his brother-in-law's neck. "A bit flashy for an endurance race, don't you think?"

Michael patted the orange silk scarf. "Jane asked me never to take it off, so here it stays. You can always put on sunglasses if it's too bright for you. I'm sure Ramsay had something for your pocket."

"He did." Ben grinned and tugged out a large wooden soldier dressed as a fighter

339

pilot, complete with goggles and a white scarf. "It does look like me, don't you think?"

"With its wooden head? You bet."

They both laughed and returned to checking the dials and gauges.

"Oil looks good." Ben tapped the face of one of the gauges. "Petrol is topped up."

"Well, it won't be if they don't get this show on the road. We've been idling for ten minutes already."

"Looks like something's up."

A tall man in a long trench coat waved his arms. Another man beside him had a blue flag that he was unfurling.

"Right. Here we go. We're fourth in line. The Belgian is first, then the Dutch lad, then Zeltner, and then us. I've got the first leg to the Channel. After that it's your stick."

Michael settled himself into his seat. "We'll go over Dover Sky as we agreed?"

" 'Course we will. Won't cost us any time. The whole crew'll be there except Catherine and Albrecht."

Michael checked the map on his knee. "No reason we can't do a flyover of Tubingen. It's within the flight path."

"I doubt they'll be on the rooftop watching for us."

Michael shrugged. "I'll do it anyway."

"It'll probably be dark."

He shrugged again.

"Our turn." The man with the blue flag was waving it at them. Ben opened the throttle. "In any case, we can't play cricket with the whole clan. Robbie's still in Palestine, and we'd have to go well out of our way to fly over his head."

"Can't have that. We should visit him after."

Ben grunted. "Could do."

"There's Kipp in Morocco."

"African landfall's Algeria, one country over. Then we land in Sierra Leone for our second leg. We'll not see Kipp anymore than we'll see Robbie."

Michael rustled around in a paper bag at his feet and pulled out a large ham sandwich. With a wink at Ben he bit into it.

"Hey, mate!" Ben protested. "That's for later."

Michael shook his head. "I'm famished."

The Fokker roared into the sky.

Lord Preston paced back and forth in the library at Dover Sky.

"Where are the children?" he suddenly asked Victoria.

She put down her teacup. "With Harrison and Holly, of course."

He glanced over the faces in the room. "What about Caroline?"

"On a stroll with Jane," said Libby who was sitting next to Victoria.

Edward had both arms along the back of a couch he was sprawled in. "Relax, Dad. The BBC will broadcast if there's any news of the race. The planes were all there at Gibraltar."

"Two days ago. No news from Sierra Leone. Africa is the rough spot, Edward. None of them will have enough fuel."

"They've all strapped on extra containers of petrol they can release into the main tank if they need it."

Lady Preston's hands were clasped tightly in her lap. "Do stop this pacing and fretting, William. You're making me anxious. I was quite all right after you and Jeremy prayed an hour ago. Now you follow it up with your lion in the cage restlessness, and now I'm on pins and needles."

"Sorry, my dear. Forgive me." He cocked his head. "What's that?"

Jeremy was sitting next to a radio that was housed in a cathedral-shaped wooden cabinet on four legs. He'd been listening to weather reports and music with the volume turned down. Hearing the broadcaster's voice at the same time as Lord Preston, he turned a knob.

"This is the BBC. We've heard by cable from colleagues at Cape Town Radio," the announcer said.

Outside the library windows that had been opened to let in the summer breeze and the salt air from the sea, a boy shouted, *"I'm a plane! I'm Daddy."*

"Two airplanes have landed. At the time the cable was sent to London from Cape Town, another aircraft was spotted approaching the landing site from the north and west."

"Vrooooom. Vroooooom."

"There are reports of at least one plane going into the sea as it followed the African coastline. Fishing vessels attempted to reach the aircraft before it sank, but they were unsuccessful. It remains unidentified."

"Ramsay! Watch out! You almost ran over your brother!"

"Right, everyone! Round to the back of the manor for oatmeal cookies with chocolate chips! Missus Norah and Missus Bev have baked up dozens!"

"Another telegram from Cape Town Radio has reached us at our studios here in England. The news in it is at least an hour old. A plane has crashed upon arrival at the Cape Town airfield. Cape Town confirms it is one of the four British planes entered in the endurance race in honor of Charles Lindbergh. There are no further details."

"Yaaaaaaaay!"

"Hurry! Last one gets the horse's oats!"

"Lord Preston?" Skitt had entered the library.

The family members were hanging on every word the broadcaster spoke. Libby and Victoria held each other's hands. Head down, Lord Preston merely grunted in response to Skitt's summons.

"It's the telephone, m'lord. Do you want to take it in the parlor?"

"Who is it, Skitt?"

"It's the prime minister, m'lord. He says he has important information for you."

ALBRECHT AND CATHERINE AIRCRASH AT CAPE TOWN LANDING SITE. MICHAEL KILLED. SURGEONS IN CAPE TOWN REMOVED BOTH OF BEN'S LEGS. IT IS STILL TOUCH AND GO WHETHER HE WILL SURVIVE. AT HIS PARENTS' REQUEST MICHAEL'S BODY IS BEING SENT FROM SOUTH AFRICA TO NEW YORK. AS YOU CAN IMAGINE WE ARE QUITE DEVASTATED HERE. VICTORIA AND

LIBBY ARE BEARING UP BUT WE
ALL COULD USE YOUR PRAYERS.
IN PARTICULAR PRAY FOR BEN.
WILL SEND ANOTHER TELEGRAM
WHEN THERE'S MORE NEWS.
JEREMY

Dover Sky

"I feel old, quite old, my dear." Lord Preston awkwardly patted Libby's hand. "I don't know what else to say."

Libby looked down at her hands in her lap. "I don't suppose any of us have words for some of these things, do we, Father?" She tried to smile. "I could have lost him during the war. We had almost ten years together because he wasn't shot down like his brother. That's something, isn't it?"

"It is, yes."

"You are in agreement that Jane and I travel back to New York to see the gravesite? And attend the special memorial service in September?"

"Of course."

"I don't want to leave Vic's side, but we must go, Father. Mum doesn't seem to understand."

Lord Preston closed his eyes a moment. "It is a great blow. Two years ago Christelle and now this. And Kipp still fighting with the Foreign Legion in Africa. It's too much for Elizabeth."

"I asked Ben, and he said it was the right thing to do."

He patted her hand again. "Never you mind about Ben. We all have our eyes on him. His leg stumps are healing up nicely, and he gets around very well indeed in his wheelchair. The doldrums have passed, and his spirits are much brighter. If he thinks you should go to New York and be with the Woodhavens, then that is what you should do."

"He wrote a lovely card about Michael for Mr. and Mrs. Woodhaven."

"Wonderful. And so have your mother and I. We expressed our condolences by telegram, of course, but a card is so much more personal."

Libby wiped at one of her eyes with a handkerchief. "You have all been very kind." She put the cloth to her nose and blew softly. "I don't know what I'd do without family."

"Times like this remind us why the Lord gives us one another — not to quarrel with but to be nurtured and defended by."

"Please keep Jane in your prayers too."

Lord Preston nodded. "Naturally we do."

"I fear Mum and you still have a problem

with her Chinese background."

"Nonsense."

"Michael loved her dearly." Libby put the handkerchief to her nose again.

"We all do, my dear."

"Commander Fordyce has been very nice to her since Michael's death."

"Indeed."

"He always has a gift for her."

Lord Preston was silent.

Her tears came. "I just want Mum and you to see she is as much a Danforth child as Ramsay or Peter or Owen. She so badly needs your love now that her father is gone."

"She has it, my dear. She has it unreservedly."

Dear Libby,
Now that you have been in New York several weeks and it is more than two months since Michael's passing, I pray a good many of your wounds have healed. I do not expect you to be on top of the world, of course. I only hope you see some light at the end of the tunnel.

You know how long your sister Catherine grieved over the loss of her husband, Albert. And Kipp almost threw himself off a cliff when Christelle died. We are still reaping the bitter fruit of his reckless-ness — a crash landing in the Sahara and enlistment in the French Foreign Legion putting him right back in another war. Terrible. I fret over him every day. Please do not take Catherine's or your brother's route in your sorrow.

Grieve, yes, but not as one without hope. I trust that a year from now you shall see your way clear to engagement with a man as fine as Michael. You are still very young and must look to the next fifty or sixty years of your life.

This brings me to the matter of Jane. I know you and Michael felt it was a good deed while you were in America to adopt her. Indeed, it was a gracious act of Christian charity. But now you must forge a new life for yourself. Surely the Woodhavens will take her in and give her a home? It is one thing for Catherine to hang on to Sean. He really is her son and our blood runs through him. But you cannot move ahead and look for a husband of your station with a girl from the Orient calling herself your daughter and a Danforth. For one thing, it simply isn't so. For another, no Englishman will accept you with Jane at your side. She is a sweetheart, and you have done your best by her. Let the Woodhavens take her in and raise her in remembrance of their son.

You need to begin again with a clean slate. I am certain that within months of it being known your mourning period is over and that you are unattached to Jane, any number of excellent men will be calling at Ashton Park or Dover Sky for you. I am convinced of it.

Forgive me for being forthright. I know you won't like it, but someone must say these things while you are deciding what you will do and where you will live. Your father will not talk about these matters, so it is left up to me. Spend as much time in New York as you need, and then return to England alone. Believe me, such a course of action is the best way to begin again. It is the best route for you to follow.

All my love, my dear Libby. God bless you.

Mother

October, 1927
London hospital

"I could feel a buzzing or tingling in my legs. When I looked down they were both twisted at impossible angles. There was no pain at all. I looked over at Michael, and I could tell he was dead. People worked to yank the canopy back and then reached into the cockpit. Some men hauled out Mike. It was Zeltner who cut away my harness and got his hands under my arms. He and his copilot pulled me free. I was in and out of consciousness over the next few days. They used morphine and heart stimulants to keep me going. By the time I was in the clear, they had already shipped Mike's body to New York City. Once I was strong enough, they started flying me in short hops back to England."

Jeremy sat in the chair by Ben's hospital bed. He was dressed in black clothes with a white clerical collar at his throat. Ben didn't look at him as he spoke, and Jeremy stared at the floor.

"I've tried to put up a bold front, but it's hard, Jeremy. Every day is very hard. They say I won't walk again, that it'll always be a wheelchair for me. They've scratched flying so there's not much to look forward to. I keep wondering how Mike would have

350

stood up to this. Lib says he was an absolute bear when he crashed during the war. Maybe he learned from that and would have been more chipper than I am."

Jeremy cleared his throat without looking up. "You don't know that. He may have been much worse having gone through this twice."

Ben, sitting up in the bed with a pillow behind his back, kept on talking as if Jeremy hadn't spoken. The sun was going down, and the room was darkening but neither moved a hand to turn on the bedside lamp. "Mum and Dad have no idea I'm feeling this way. Neither do Vic and the boys. It's bad enough losing Michael. They don't need me moaning and groaning and adding to the gloom. So whenever I see them I play 'the man.' "

"Surely you can be honest with Victoria."

"I can't. She said she's reminded of losing our first baby, and that she feels wretched when she sees me without my legs. *I thank God every day you haven't lost heart,* she said. So I've got to soldier on. I need *your* help for that."

"What can I do to help?"

"Just what you're doing. Listening. Giving me a few upbeat words now and then. Saying a few prayers. Since you lost your right arm and hand while fighting in France back in 1914, I know you understand some of what I'm going through. That helps too, along with the other things."

"I'll come over from the church as often as you like, Ben. Once or twice a day if you want."

"I won't be here forever. What's the date today?"

Jeremy looked up. "Wednesday, the twelfth of October."

Ben glanced at him. "They've taken plaster casts of my stumps now that they've shrunk down. They'll start fitting metal legs with cushions and straps in about a week. I'm going to make myself walk, Jeremy."

"You'll do it."

"And once I get the hang of walking, I'm going to fly again."

Jeremy nodded, his eyes strong and dark behind his glasses. "Right. You will."

"I need you to put the backbone in me."

"Believe me, Ben, you've got plenty of it."

"I need more. They'll adjust the legs until the fit is just right, give me some walking lessons, and then after that I'm on my own. They want me close enough so I can drop in if there's a problem. I plan to take up residence at Dover Sky."

"Just you?"

"No. I'll bring Vic and the boys down. They'll have Charles and Matthew to play with, not to mention Jane. She can be their big sister."

Jeremy sat up in the chair and took off his glasses. "That will be fine. Emma and I would love to bring Peter, James, and Billy to Dover Sky once a week. Overnights on a Friday would be best. We'd head back on Saturday afternoons so I can be ready for church on Sunday." He pushed the right temple and earpiece of his glasses under his wooden hand so the lenses were upright. Then he polished them with a white cloth from his pocket. "Ben, I take it you're not aware Libby and Jane won't be returning to Dover Sky? They'll be wintering in Germany with Albrecht and Catherine."

"What?"

"They are heading straight there from New York. I gather she's supposed to be in Tubingen by the end of the month."

"But why isn't she returning to England? My Ramsay loves Jane. He finds her quite the tomboy."

Jeremy smiled. "My lads feel the same way. Though Jane plays the princess well when it strikes her fancy. In any case, Lady Preston wrote a letter to Libby in New York City telling her to have done and leave Jane with the Woodhavens. Something about starting afresh without being encumbered by Jane now that Michael is gone."

"You're joking."

"I'm afraid not. You can imagine how well that went over. Libby's heartbroken. She loves Jane, and Jane is a strong link to the life she had with Michael. Lib dashed off a letter in reply, certainly not the kind Lady Preston wanted to get. Now there's a great row going on between the pair of them. Catherine invited Libby to Germany, and Lib accepted straight off. Now it appears Jane will be big sister to Catherine's son, Sean, instead of your boys and mine. She'll have a friend in Baron von Isenburg's daughter, Eva, too. The von Isenburg girl is twelve, so they're close enough in age."

"I can't believe what you're telling me. It never rains but it pours."

Jeremy finished cleaning his glasses, put them back on his face, and returned the cloth to his pocket. "All the more reason we'd be happy to come to Dover Sky once a week. We'll work on keeping the family together rather than permitting these squabbles to break us apart. And for you and I to stick together and get you back on your feet and up among the clouds and swallows."

"I'll make it, Jeremy — with your help and God's. What I can't control is what's going to happen next. This family gets bad news in bunches. It'd be a deathblow, wouldn't it, if Kipp came back from Morocco in a pine box or Robbie got a bullet in the back in Palestine?"

"Let's not believe in deathblows," Jeremy said.

13

March–June, 1928
Jerusalem

I was glad when they said unto me, Let us
    go into the house of the LORD.
Our feet shall stand within thy gates, O
    Jerusalem.
Jerusalem is builded as a city that is
    compact together:
Whither the tribes go up, the tribes of the
    LORD, unto the testimony of Israel, to
    give thanks unto the name of the LORD.
For there are set thrones of judgment, the
    thrones of the house of David.
Pray for the peace of Jerusalem: they shall
    prosper that love thee.
Peace be within thy walls, and prosperity
    within thy palaces.
For my brethren and companions' sakes, I
    will now say, Peace be within thee.

Because of the house of the LORD our God
  I will seek thy good.

"Thank you." Robbie leaned back, loosened his uniform collar, and closed his eyes. "I need to hear that every day of my life."

"Shall I read it a second time?" asked Shannon.

"Can't hurt."

She read Psalm 122 again from the Bible on her lap.

Robbie and Shannon were sitting together on a terrace that overlooked the Old City of Jerusalem. For miles the green tops of palm trees stirred in the warm breeze. Walls and buildings made of large square stones the color of honey sprawled between the palms. Directly in front of them was the Dome of the Rock, its gold roof flaming in the afternoon sun. Below them men and women in various types of robes crowded the streets. As Shannon read, voice after voice called out in Hebrew or Arabic as donkeys brayed while the harnesses on their necks and shoulders jingled from the attached small silver bells.

"Your voice is sweeter than those shouts," Robbie said, opening his eyes and looking at Shannon.

"Only because I'm not selling anything. If

357

I were, then the Dublin fishmonger in me would come out soon enough."

"Do you think so?" Robbie ran a finger over both sides of his dark moustache. "You look splendid. How are you feeling?"

"As splendid as I look, kind sir." She placed a hand over the roundness of her stomach. "I think it's time you wrote your mother and father."

"Well —"

"Come! I am almost four months along. Doctor Schultz says I am as healthy as a horse — a Connemara horse at that."

"Still I worry."

She closed the Bible and smiled at him. "My silly British soldier. What happened to me happened so many years ago. Yes, back then they were worried about a miscarriage. Not anymore."

"You were badly hurt."

She reached across the space between them and ran a hand down the side of his face. "I was. Now I'm healed. And the man who beat me so badly is dead and gone. Write your mother and father. Heaven knows they could use some good news."

"Very well."

She pinched his cheek gently. "That's not the only thing that's worrying you, is it? What happened today?"

"What happens every day. This time it was a group from the Grand Mufti. They are concerned that the Jews are planning to take over the Temple Mount. You know, where the Dome of the Rock is. They fear they'll rebuild a temple like Solomon's."

"What do you think?"

"Really, I can't see it. But every now and then one of the Jewish leaders spouts off about a Jewish nation that extends from Dan to Beersheba and about erecting a new temple on Mount Moriah — the site of the Dome of the Rock. And then the Muslims get agitated, and their mullahs whip them into a frenzy. There's bound to be trouble."

"So did you talk to any of the Jewish leaders about this?"

Robbie stared at the Dome of the Rock. "Of course. But what can they do? They can't control every Jew in Palestine anymore than the Grand Mufti can control every Muslim. I'm constantly getting reports of imams ranting about wiping out all the Jews in Jerusalem, and not only Jerusalem, but the entire length and breadth of Palestine. So the Jews smuggle in more guns to defend themselves. And the Muslims smuggle in more guns to defend themselves. I only have a hundred British soldiers, Shan. I can't stop a war. If they want another Belfast, I expect they are going to get it."

"Surely things aren't as bad as all that, love. We have many Muslim and Jewish friends, and we all get along well together at our dinner parties."

Robbie drummed his fingers on the arm of his chair. "Yes, because we're all moderates, aren't we? But moderates never run revolutions or uprisings. And when the day of trouble comes, they are swept away by the fanatics and hotheads who will murder anyone or blow up anything for their great cause. Moderates never kill like fanatics do. That's why they never last, and the position they take for peace and goodwill vanishes with them."

Shannon took his hand. "So what's your next step?"

He sighed. "Just housekeeping chores. I've asked the Jewish leadership to remember the ruling in '25 that forbids the use of chairs and benches and prayer screens at the Western Wall of the Second Temple where the Jews gather to pray.

"The Muslims are anxious that nothing be left there on a permanent basis. They're afraid it will become the start of a synagogue, and a synagogue will be followed by a full-blown temple going up."

Shannon laughed. "That sounds rather ridiculous."

"Yes, well, what sounds ridiculous in another country or up here on our terrace makes complete sense on the streets of Jerusalem. And it usually ends up with someone getting beaten or shot."

Tubingen, Germany

Catherine stood by the window with the letter in her hand. "The big news is that Shannon is five months along now."

"What!" Libby turned away from her bedroom mirror. "Five months? That's wonderful! But why are we only hearing about it now?"

"I don't know. She's due in September."

Libby waited another moment before going back to applying her lipstick. "Boy or girl? Do they say?"

"They don't say."

"What's your guess?"

"Heaven knows we have enough boys to populate a private school in Oxfordshire. I say we need a girl to be a proper cousin to Jane."

"That's sweet, but Jane will be in university by the time this little one is six."

"No matter. They can catch up to each other when they're in their twenties and thirties."

"Maybe." Libby gazed into the mirror and puckered her lips. "We need to send Shannon a card."

"We do." Catherine picked up another letter. "Ben is coming along better than hoped, Vic says. He's gotten the hang of those artificial legs and can move about on his own pretty well, though he still uses a cane."

Libby stepped back from the vanity and slipped her arms through the sleeves of a long, blue woolen coat. "That's marvelous. It really is."

"Jeremy and Emma swing by every Friday night. The children have a grand muck up together, Vic and Em and Caroline have a terrific chat, and Jeremy closets himself with Ben. No one knows what those two go on about since they've never been that close."

Libby wrapped a dark-blue scarf about her neck. "Mmm."

"Oh dear. Papa's lost the dogs."

"No."

"Gladstone in January and Wellington at the beginning of March. What a shame. Vic says he's absolutely devastated."

Libby came to the window and peered over her sister's shoulder at the letter. "I feel so bad for him. He loved them so much. Well, we all did. Does the baron know?"

"I doubt it. Unless someone wrote him or

362

cabled him separately."

"He gave Papa those German shepherds."

Catherine nodded. "I remember." She kept reading, her lips moving.

Libby craned her neck. "What's the rest of it about?"

"Little things." Catherine paused. "She mentions a letter from Kipp. He's well. Sent Matt and Charles a couple of Foreign Legion caps in the mail. Y'know — with those flappy things at the back. Caroline's stuffed the sweatbands with newspaper, and the boys are marching up and down the estate with wooden rifles Harrison carved for them."

"No. Before that."

"Nothing, I told you."

Libby's eyes snapped to indigo blue. "I can read, thank you. I didn't know Dad and Mom were having a big row over me."

"I tried to spare you the news. Why carry that around in your head?"

Libby took the letter from her sister. "It actually does help to know he's taken my side. No, I'm not happy about them having a long drawn-out fight. But yes, it is nice to know one of them thinks enough of Jane to fight for her." She kept reading. "Ben is determined to fly again. You skipped that part too."

"Look, you told me all this reminded you of how you helped Michael get back on his feet and back in the air after his crash during the war. I didn't see the point of making the comparison even sharper."

"I'm a big girl, Cathy, I can handle it. I cried myself dry in America."

"Mum! What's taking you so long?" Jane stepped through the doorway, her arm linked through another girl's. "The sun is going to go behind a bunch of clouds. You said we could shop in the old part of Tubingen before we go to Switzerland this weekend." She half sang, "It's a beautiful day in May . . ."

Libby handed the letter back to her sister. "If Uncle Albrecht has finished all his marking and all his student interviews, we can go."

"The students are gone, Mum. The streets are empty. There's never been a better time to go to the shops."

"Yes, I'm ready then." Libby put a hat on her head and looked in the mirror. She smiled at the reflection of Jane and her friend. "Good afternoon, Eva. You look exceptional."

Eva was the same height as Jane. She had dark skin similar to Jane's. Eva's flaxen hair was separated into two braids that framed her face, and her blue eyes shone like suns out of dusky cheeks. She grinned. "Thank you, Mrs. Woodhaven." She glanced down at her black coat and black leather boots. "Papa said he would spoil me because I did so well at school this spring." She pouted, her lower lip pushing out from her mouth. "But I cannot come up to Pura with him for another four weeks."

"We shall have your rooms perfectly ready for you and the baron and be counting the days," Catherine announced.

Jane bounced up and down on the balls of her feet. "Montgomery is waiting at the front door, Mama."

"Good. So we're all ready to walk by the riverfront and those colorful old houses?"

"More than ready."

"Downstairs to Montgomery then." Jane and Eva were gone in a flash, giggling as they raced down the steps to the front door.

"Girls!" Libby called after them, "A herd of wild elephants couldn't make more noise than the pair of you!" She glanced at Catherine. "We'll be back in a few hours but not in time for tea."

Catherine nodded. "Don't rush. You've never enjoyed the city without the mob of university students. You'll have Eva here in time to attend mass with the baron? At St.

Joannes Evangelist?"

"Of course. I promised Jane and I would join them."

"That's splendid." Catherine held up an envelope. "There is a letter for you when you find the time."

Libby stopped in the doorway. "For me? Not for both of us?"

"Certainly not for both of us."

"Who's it from?"

"A secret admirer, I believe."

Libby came back into her room. "What rot. I'll be ready for a man in my life when the clock strikes midnight for 1941." She took the envelope from her sister's hand and read the return address. "I don't know anyone in the Royal Navy. Oh!" Her cheeks flamed immediately. "It's not what you think it is."

"Isn't it? And what do I think it is?"

"Terry. Terry Fordyce. He quite adores Jane. And the feeling is mutual. Even Michael remarked on how the two of them hit it off from the first."

"So why isn't the letter addressed to Jane?" Catherine asked.

"Why, he — he naturally . . . she being so young . . . he obviously thought it best to correspond with her through her mother so

366

there would be no hint of any sort of impropriety."

"Impropriety? She's a child." Catherine folded her arms over her chest. "Why don't you open it and read the first page aloud?"

Libby's face reddened. "Why would you ask such a thing?"

"I don't really care to hear the first page, Lib. I just want you to be honest with me. You know very well to whom Terry is writing. My guess is this isn't the first letter you've received from Terry Fordyce, is it?"

"No."

"But you didn't think to mention it to me?"

Libby's temper flared and her blue eyes suddenly sparked with color and heat. "Well, why would I? The two of you used to be . . . well, an item, as the columnists would say. I didn't want you to get the impression I was going around with him behind your back."

"Is that what you're doing?"

"We're friends, that's all. Just friends. How on earth could I go behind your back with him anyway? You're married to Albrecht, and you haven't seen Terry in a year and a half. You're not interested in him anymore, right? He's out of your life. I don't need your permission to post him letters or receive them from him."

"I am married — happily married. But Terry was and is very dear to me. It could have been him in my life. You know that."

"I do. That's why I haven't talked about the letters."

"I wouldn't want him coming for a visit, Lib."

"He's not going to come for a visit. He just got back from the Med on the eighth of May."

"How do you know?"

Libby licked her lips and kept her eyes on Catherine's. "He sent a telegram the other day."

"I see."

Libby suddenly thrust the envelope at her sister. "Go ahead, read it then."

"I won't."

"You want to know what he's saying to me? You think you still own him?"

"I don't think that."

"Of course you do. You may be married to Albrecht, but you still think of Terry as your property. Is that just in case things don't work out with Albrecht?"

Catherine's face stiffened like granite. "How dare you."

"Terry and I are friends, no more. I have no intention of taking him out of Jane's life just because you can't let go. And if he should want to visit one day, why can't he?"

"It would be very awkward. I don't want him here."

"Then if he comes you can throw me out. Throw Jane and me out into the street. We'll find lodgings somewhere else in Tubingen. Or we could head for Stuttgart or Heidelberg . . . even take the train east for Munich and be out of your life completely. Father will see us properly set up."

"I don't want you out of my life."

"Then you will have to let me have my own friends, including males . . . even old men friends of yours."

Catherine's face was pale. The light in the window whitened as the sun moved into a cloudbank. "I don't know if I can do it, Libby. I think it's too much to ask of me."

Libby stared before she whispered, "You still love him."

Dover Sky
Edward smacked his fist into the palm of his hand.

"It was a scurrilous attack directed at me and my alleged pro-German sympathies."

His father looked up from his newspaper. "Labor attacks the government for what it considers our pro-French stance. Lord Buchanan would have found a way to go after you even if your sister hadn't married Professor Hartmann. Besides, Hartmann is well respected at our universities. You must ignore Buchanan."

Edward paced back and forth in the parlor. "How can I ignore him? Did you catch his snide remark about my ties to the Orient and the Boxer Rebellion in Peking in 1901? About the massacre of missionaries and Chinese Christians?"

"I did."

"First he lays Germany and its problems at my feet because of Catherine's marriage to Hartmann. Then he smears me with the Boxer Rebellion because Libby is rearing an Oriental girl as her own. My own family is working against me."

"For heaven's sakes, Edward." Lady Preston set her cup in the saucer in her hand. "Your father and I come to Dover Sky for the summer to get away from politics. Must you go on and on?"

"There will be an election next year, Mother. Suppose I lose my seat due to the antics of my sisters?"

"You are not going to lose your seat. What that vagabond from the Hebrides has to say is of no consequence, especially when it comes to matters of the family. We will decide what is right and wrong among us. The voters will respect that. Catherine has married a prince — there is no other word for Albrecht. And we have absolutely nothing to be ashamed of in terms of her conduct."

Lord Preston was back to reading his newspaper. "In any case, the German economy is doing very well indeed."

"And the Chinese economy? How well is it doing?"

Lady Preston's eyes flamed. "If anyone is going to take Libby to task for her choices, it will be your father and me. Not you, Edward, and certainly not the Labor Party. I am not in agreement with what Libby has done. I pray she may still change her mind, but the poor girl has been through more than her share of tragedy and grief. Imagine losing her husband in a plane crash!"

"I know, Mother."

Lady Preston lifted the teacup to her mouth, her face still cut by lines and wrinkles of rage simmering just under her skin. "Your father and I are having our own row about Libby and Jane. We don't see eye to eye on this issue, but I will say that Jane is a beautiful girl who deserves every opportunity to develop into a lady. I simply hope it happens somewhere else and with a different family — preferably American."

The pop of a cricket bat striking a ball came through the open window. Edward bent and looked out, keeping his hands in the pockets of his striped trousers. "Ben's just made a hit. Ramsay is running for him."

Lady Preston's sharp lines smoothed and rounded into a full smile. "Ben is exceptional. All week I've watched him when he didn't think anyone was about. Working on climbing stairs. Walking on the grass and falling a dozen times. I understand it's much more difficult than getting about on concrete walkways. But he climbs to his feet and carries on no matter what. I could see the sweat on his face. And how it must hurt! He went back to London twice in the past fortnight, Victoria tells me, to get his artificial limbs adjusted. He never quits, does he? A good lesson for our family. And for you, Edward."

"Yes, yes, all for England, tallyho, Mum."

She glared at him over the rim of her cup before changing the subject. "How is Charlotte feeling?"

Edward finally smiled. "She's a great beauty, isn't she? Three months along and such color in her eyes and cheeks. I've fallen head over heels with her all over again." He glanced out the window again. "She's chatting with Victoria, Emma, and Holly. Ben's still at the bat. Harrison's bowling. Owen's doing very well for himself fielding." He let out a lungful of air and nodded. "Quite right, Mum. The fight must go on. Our family's worth fighting for, isn't it? And our country, of course."

"I should hope so, dear." She set her cup and saucer on the white wicker table beside her. "That's more like the Danforth spirit."

Lord Preston glanced up from his newspaper again. "I'd like to take *Pluck* out to blue water tomorrow morning. Are you game?"

Edward scooped a handful of cashews from a glass dish. "I'd like that, Dad. Can I bring Owen?"

"By all means. Short rations and weak grog, but I hope the salt air and enemy action will make up for it."

Edward popped a large cashew into his mouth. "I'm absolutely certain it will."

Jeremy and Ben stood under the willow trees in the dusk. The lights of Dover Sky could not be seen from where they stood.

"One of the stumps had shrunk a bit more. They had to make some changes in London."

"How do your legs feel now?"

"Never better. I can't say I'm pain-free, but it's much improved from a few months ago."

Jeremy smiled. "You've made a lot of progress."

"I'm doing it for Vic, Ramsay, and Tim. But I'm doing it for Michael as well."

"I understand that."

"So it's time for the next big step, Jeremy. I've got to go up."

Jeremy squatted by the thin stream of water and took up some pebbles with his left hand. "When?"

"This summer." Ben gazed west through the willows at the last line of red light where field and sky met. "Look, I've got to do it on the day we crashed in August. Not before and not after. In one of our Fokkers. I have to be ready on that day."

Jeremy tossed the pebbles in his palm. "How will Victoria feel about it? Or your mum and dad?"

"They're bound not to like it. They'll be superstitious about the date and say I'm tempting fate. But you don't believe that, do you, Jeremy? You're a Christian minister. God's bigger than our doubts and fears, isn't He?"

Jeremy kept tossing the pebbles.

Ben glanced at him. "Or are we prisoners

of fate?"

Jeremy shook his head. "Not in Christ." He dropped the pebbles and stood up, brushing off his pants. "You have a destiny that's in God's hands. We all do. So how do we go about getting you up?"

"It's mostly hand movements. I just need a few run-throughs with the rudder while I'm on the ground because that's what is operated with my feet. The chaps we have managing the airline are going to drop in with one of the Fokkers on that day. Then they'll take it back to London because we have a lot of business these days."

"Will that be enough time for you to get a feel for the controls?"

"More than enough. I'm thinking it will be far easier for me to fly than to walk or run."

"All right."

"Jeremy, will you go up with me? I need a copilot."

Jeremy looked at him in surprise. "I've never flown. Why are you asking me? Get one of your flying chaps to crew with you."

"You've helped me get this far. I want you up with me. Nothing's going to go wrong. My hands are steady as rocks. All I need is to walk through the basics with you in case I need your help with the stick. I want

Jeremy Sweet up there with me." Ben grinned. "You're my good luck charm."

Jeremy smiled. "An Anglican good luck charm? What happens when they take the Fokkers away? How do you keep up your flying skills then?"

"Our SPAD S.XXs have been mothballed. They're bringing in one of those as well and leaving it here at Dover Sky. I'll keep flying with it." He paused. "So what do you say, Jeremy? Will you go up with me? Will you fly?"

Jeremy nodded. "I will, Ben. Why not?"

The English Channel, near the Port of Dover
"What do you think, Owen? How d'ya like it?"

"I love the sea, Grandpa. Dad says he misses being a sailor on a battle cruiser."

"Does he indeed?"

Edward laughed and wrapped a line tightly around a cleat on the mast. "I don't like going into the drink. I like it best when I'm on top of the waves and not underneath them."

Owen smiled and closed his eyes as spray broke over *Pluck*'s bow. "I like the wind and the water, Dad."

"I see that. I expect you're a bit of a sea dog. Likely in your blood. What say, Father?

376

Didn't we have seamen on Mum's side as well as the Danforth side?"

Lord Preston, in a dark-blue peacoat like the ones Owen and Edward had on, had both hands on the spokes of the wooden wheel and an eye on the mainsail as he steered. "We did. Sailed with Drake and Nelson — officers, privateers, explorers."

"Who, Grandpa?"

"Too many to mention. Your grandmother is a Cornwall, and they have as many sea dogs as the Danforths."

The yacht slit through the Channel waters and chop, the waves like cold iron, the sky a mix of gray and blue and white, gulls turning in wide circles above their sail. The boat was trimmed in navy blue, burgundy, and white like the Union Jack that flapped at its stern.

"You must tell me one story." Owen tugged on a line slick with salt water. "I am your crew."

Lord Preston barked a short laugh. "Indeed you are. I have one tale then. I can tell you more when we're ashore. This is from your grandmother's side, mind. A Cornwall. A midshipman. Perhaps five years older than you are now. On board a British frigate right in this Channel. Got into a fight with a French warship with more guns.

After a lot of smoke and flame and noise, Cornwall's ship only had two working cannon, while the French had more than a dozen still in play. So what to do, Owen? Two guns, powder and shot running low, the Frenchmen bearing down on you. Do you turn tail and head for England or strike your colors and go to a French prison?"

Owen puzzled this out. His blue eyes were so much like his mother's as they remained motionless even as his dark-red hair, just like his father's, was whipped about by the wind. "I wouldn't want to do either, Grandpa."

"Ha! Duck your heads. Coming about." The boom swung across the boat, and Edward and Owen stooped. "Spoken true like our brave Cornwall midshipman. Sheet her home, if you please, Master Edward." Edward sprang to secure the line for the mainsail. "They surprised the French, Master Owen, by coming right on and ramming them, bowsprit to bowsprit. The French cannon were useless to inflict harm. Then they boarded her, screaming like devils, cutlasses slicing the air, pistols flashing, and after ten minutes they had her! Indeed, sir, they had her. They kept a prize crew on board, and sailed both side by side back to an English port. Might have even been Dover. In the great hall at Dover Sky you will see a painting of this very thing. When we are back and have our tea and jam I shall point it out to you."

Owen's cheeks were red and his eyes bright as wind and wave lashed them. "You must tell me another, Grandpa."

"On shore in the officers' mess. But I have a grand sea poem for you. Fragments of it, mind you, bits and pieces, windblown spume and hard hurled sea spray, but extraordinary for all of that. Now this poem must be memorized, Master Owen, word for word. Are you ready?"

"I am, sir."

"Very well then. *Ulysses* by Alfred Lord Tennyson."

Lord Preston began to recite as *Pluck* continued to press ahead through the sea.

I cannot rest from travel: I will drink
Life to the lees: all times I have enjoyed
Greatly, have suffered greatly, both with
    those
That loved me, and alone; on shore, and
    when
Through scudding drifts the rainy Hyades
Vexed the dim sea: I am become a name;
For always roaming with a hungry heart
Much have I seen and known; cities of men

And manners, climates, councils,
   governments,
Myself not least, but honored of them all;
And drunk delight of battle with my peers,
Far on the ringing plains of windy Troy.

There lies the port; the vessel puffs her
   sail:
There gloom the dark broad seas. My
   mariners,
Souls that have toiled, and wrought, and
   thought
with me — That ever with a frolic welcome
   took
The thunder and the sunshine, and
   opposed
Free hearts, free foreheads — you and I
   are old;
Old age hath yet his honor and his toil;
Death closes all: but something ere the
   end,
Some work of noble note, may yet be done,
Not unbecoming men that strove with
   Gods.
The lights begin to twinkle from the rocks:
The long day wanes: the slow moon climbs:
   the deep
Moans round with many voices. Come, my
   friends,
'Tis not too late to seek a newer world.

Push off, and sitting well in order smite
The sounding furrows; for my purpose
    holds
To sail beyond the sunset, and the baths
Of all the western stars, until I die.
It may be that the gulfs will wash us down:
It may be we shall touch the Happy Isles,
And see the great Achilles, whom we knew
Though much is taken, much abides; and
    though
We are not now that strength which in old
    days
Moved earth and heaven; that which we
    are, we are;
One equal temper of heroic hearts,
Made weak by time and fate, but strong in
    will
To strive, to seek, to find, and not to yield.

"Hurrah!" Owen clapped his hands. "That
is my poem! To strive, to seek, to find, and
not to yield! I shall never yield! But what is
windblown spume, Grandfather?"

"The thick white foam that gets in your
hair and eyes like dandelion fluff. Will you
have it memorized for me by the time we
sail again, Master Owen?"

"I shall. Will you tell it to me again?"

"Over tea and jam, sir, over tea and jam."

Edward smiled as a large wave broke over

the length of the yacht, soaking them all. "I think you told me the very same poem at the very same age. Only it wasn't on a boat."

Lord Preston gazed up at the set of the sail. "It was on the Liverpool docks."

Dear Caroline,
The heat can just about drive you crazy out here. Heat and hate. It takes me places I don't want to go in my thoughts. Should I have married you after the war instead of Chris? Why couldn't I understand how much I cared for you? How was it possible for me to love both of you at the same time? The long stretches of inaction are as murderous as the fighting with my head spinning around like this. But I pray, I think of how sweet a person you are, I remember how much we both loved Chris, I think of Matthew and Charles and I know how lucky I am . . . how blessed.

In case you wonder where that picture is of you on our wedding night, the one where you're indoors by the candles at Dover Sky with the biggest smile I've ever seen on anyone, well, it's here in Morocco with me. I look at it all the time. It's a bit curled from being in my pocket, and I suppose faded by the sun, but it's still you — the most beautiful woman in the world, a beauty that never ended with what I saw but carried over to what I always knew about you within and without.

I miss you very much.

Kipp

My love,
Please don't keep going back to the past. Yes, there was a lot of pain and confusion. But you loved a lot too. And now you are loving me with all your heart. I know that. We also have two sons we adore. And me, well, I have loved you since I first saw you at that Christmas ball at our estate when I was sixteen. Nothing has changed since then no matter what I've said or how I've acted or how disappointed I've been. God blessed me with a family and a friend I loved named Chris, who sees us from heaven and who wanted us to love each other and be together for the rest of our lives. Oh, Kipp, we have lived such an exceptional story! Look at what's happening for us. I wouldn't want to change anything because if I did I might change

what we're experiencing right now.

I'm waiting for you. Come back to me, Kipp Danforth. Our honeymoon was too short. We need another as soon as you return to Dover Sky. The boys can come too. We have to go somewhere and just be the two of us and sometimes the four of us. I look forward to that very much.

I am so in love with you!

Caroline

Dover Sky
Victoria lay beside her husband in the dark, turning things over and over in her mind. Finally, unable to drop off, she placed a hand on his shoulder.

"Darling?" she said softly.

"Mmm?"

"Are you asleep?"

"Mmm."

"I just want you to know because I don't think I've ever said it in so many words, that I think you are amazing."

Ben opened his eyes and lifted his head. "What?"

"You crashed and lost one of your best friends. The doctors removed both of your legs below the knee. But you didn't give up.

You're walking. Most importantly, you didn't give up on your wife or your children."

"My wife and children? How could I?" He sat up. "Were you afraid of that?"

"Yes."

"It hasn't been easy, Vic —"

"I know that."

"But it never entered my head to abandon you or the boys. Not once did I dwell on that."

"Do I have Jeremy to thank for that?"

"Partly."

"I need a hug, love."

He gathered her into his arms.

She reached down and touched one of his stumps. "This doesn't matter, you know," she whispered.

"Shh."

"It doesn't, Ben. You're more of a man than most of those walking about on their own two legs. You're magnificent, honestly."

"You shall give me a swollen head, and then I'll have problems with that part of me too."

She played over his chin and lips with her fingers. "Tim and Ram are so proud of their father. Are you aware of how much they love you?"

"I think the world of them. I'm glad they

feel the same way."

"Ramsay asked if there was another war if you would enlist and fight. I said no, that you couldn't fly in the military again. Then he asked if you might not fight on the ground like Uncle Kipp is doing. I said probably not. He wept, Ben, how he wept. I held him but I couldn't comfort him."

Ben said nothing for a moment. "You know, don't you?"

"I do know."

"How?"

"A woman's intuition. Comparing notes with Emma. Jeremy didn't let anything out of the bucket, if that's what you're thinking."

"I have to do it, Vic. I love flying. It's a bigger part of me than my limbs were. I can't let it go. And I owe it to Mike. I do. He fought back and flew again after his crash and his brother was killed. Well, Mike was my brother too, wasn't he? So I owe him the same. I've got to go up. I've asked Jeremy to go with me."

"Jeremy? He's never flown a plane in his life. Why can't you go up with someone who can take the controls if something goes wrong?"

He stroked her hair. "Nothing will go wrong."

"How can you say that?"

"Look, it's easier for me to fly than to walk. Almost everything I do up there is with my hands. The rudder's the only thing I work with my feet. I will practice on the ground with that until I'm confident my metal feet know their place. Vic, climbing stairs is more difficult than manipulating a rudder. And I'll show Jeremy how to do that just in case I need help."

"But why Jeremy?"

"Because his words helped me get this far — along with everyone else's, of course. Yes, along with your words and prayers too. But I took my darkness to him, unloaded it on him, and he bore it."

"Is that the only reason?"

He ran his hand over her back, up and down, up and down. "Perhaps it's because he lost his arm in a war so he understands what I've been going through and what still lies ahead. I want us both up there on the anniversary of the crash."

She dug her fingers into his arm. "The anniversary? Ben, what on earth are you thinking?"

"I'm not going to be ruled by fear, Vic. I simply won't. God is bigger than the finger of fate, isn't He?"

"Ben —"

"Isn't He?" He kissed the top of her head and her soft auburn hair. "I'm going to change a day of darkness into a day of light. I'm going to take a day of mourning and make it a day of celebration. I have to, Vic. And God will help me."

"My lord?"

Lord Preston swished his razor in the basin of water in his bedroom. "Yes, what is it, Skitt?"

"I thought you might wish to come downstairs, m'lord."

Lord Preston stroked away foam on his cheek with the razor. "I'm in my robe. Why should I want to go downstairs right now?"

"There is something you should see."

"Can't it wait?"

Yips suddenly sounded through the window.

"What is that?" He rushed to the window. Three puppies were romping about on the grass with Harrison. Baron von Isenburg stood watching and leaning on a cane. Lord Preston ran to the door and threw it open. Skitt stood there in his butler suit.

"Why on earth didn't you tell me, Skitt?"

"I did, m'lord."

"Next time it's a dog, shout, *'Dog! Dog!'* And then I shall respond far more appropriately."

"Very good, sir."

Lord Preston rushed down the staircase, lather flying from his face as he tightened the belt about his maroon robe. "Elizabeth! Elizabeth!"

She popped her head out of a doorway just as he reached the front door. "Whatever is the matter, William?"

"Dogs! The baron is here with dogs!"

"The baron? He's supposed to be in Switzerland with Catherine and Libby!"

Lord Preston swung open the front door and let it bang against a wooden holder for canes and umbrellas. Running down the steps to the lawn, he became an instant attraction for the puppies.

The pups, one black, one brown, and one brown-and-black — tumbled towards him, their tails thrashing.

"Gerard, what is this? What is this?" Lord Preston went to both knees and the puppies scrambled all over him, licking his face and hands until he laughed. "Praise God, what is going on? Where are you going with these rascals? Why are you here?"

"These are Belgian shepherds, Vilhelm. The black one is the Groenendael kind, the brown one a Malinois — you see it has a short-haired coat while the other two are longer haired — and the brown-and-black one is a Tervuren. I have named her Poppy since the breeder is in Flanders, and there is that famous poem from the war about that area. Indeed, I've given the black male that very name — Flanders. His coat reminds me of the long fields of dark soil. It is up to you to name the Malinois."

"I?"

"The puppies are home, Vilhelm. That is to say, wherever you hang your hat is their home."

"Impossible."

The baron lifted his cane. "I saw your family to the Hartmann Castle on the Rhine, and then I came back as quickly as I could through Belgium to the coast. My chauffeur drove, and I watered and fed and pampered the beasts." He lowered his cane and watched his friend play with the puppies. "Once I heard you had lost Gladstone and Wellington, I set the wheels in motion. I know the breeder well, and these will be extraordinary dogs. I expect them to be with you at least until 1945. I have also had them blessed."

"No."

"Yes! By a priest in Ypres. I hope they will in turn bless you, my friend."

The black puppy had his face right in

Lord Preston's and was washing the statesman thoroughly.

"They shall, Gerard. I have no doubt of
it."

14

July–December, 1928
Dover Sky

"Who was that at the door, Skitt?" Lady Preston asked.

"It's a cable, m'lady." He brought it into the library and presented it to her on a silver tray as she sat with her tea in the library.

"A silver tray, is it, Skitt?" she asked as she put her teacup in the saucer and set both on the small table next to her.

He smiled.

She picked up the envelope. "It's from Germany, I expect."

"Paris, m'lady."

"Paris? What on earth?" She examined the envelope more closely. "It's addressed to Lady Caroline Danforth. Why have you brought it to me?"

Skitt's smile was gone. "It bears a government stamp, ma'am."

"It bears a —" Lady Preston's face whitened. "Oh no! Dear God, please, no." She bowed her head and closed her eyes. "Pray, give me a moment. Fetch Lord Preston."

"Yes, m'lady."

Lord Preston was at her side within ten minutes. "I was running the puppies about with Harrison. We must keep them away from the pond and the swans."

Elizabeth was slumped in her chair, her face drawn and looking ten years older.

"What in heaven's name is wrong?" He saw the cable in her hand. "Bad news? Where from?"

"France."

"France . . ." His mind raced. "No . . . not Kipp!"

"Of course Kipp. What other member of the family rushed off across the Channel to enlist in the French Foreign Legion?"

"May I see it?"

She lifted her hand, and he took the envelope.

"Why haven't you opened it?"

She put a hand over her eyes. "It's addressed to Caroline. Even if it wasn't, I really don't think I could, William. I can't bear more bad news. Can you imagine what this will do to Caroline if it's what we think it is?"

Lord Preston turned the envelope over in

his hand. "It's not addressed to us so I don't feel comfortable opening it."

"Would you feel more comfortable giving it to Caroline without reading it first so we are unprepared to help her cope?"

He tapped it against his pant leg. "There is a teakettle in the front parlor. I shall steam it open."

She pushed herself wearily out of the chair and followed him. The kettle was plugged in and once the water came to a boil, he held the envelope over the spout. "Thank goodness it is not a whistling kettle," he said.

Lady Preston watched him from the wicker chair she'd sat in. "A small mercy God has granted us, yes."

"There we are." He unplugged the kettle and the cloud of vapor vanished. Peeling back the seal carefully, he brought out the telegram. He waited a moment. "Lord, help us." He glanced at the words. "The cable is in French."

Lady Preston made a fist and gasped. "Of course. And I don't know French and you don't know French. I do know the word 'mort' means dead. Can you see it there?"

"I don't know what I can see or can't see. Holly!" he called as he noticed his sister walking past the doorway. "Holly, how is your French?" he asked when she stepped inside the room.

"*Magnifique.* I learned a great deal from Christelle."

"Are you able to make sense of this?"

Holly, dressed in trousers and a coat, took the cable. "I was just about to go over the grounds with Harrison," she said, noticing her brother looking at her clothes. She scanned the telegram.

Lord and Lady Preston stared as they waited impatiently.

Holly frowned in concentration. "Ah . . ."

"What is it?" demanded Lady Preston. "Is he dead? Is Kipp killed?"

Holly looked up. "Not at all. He's been wounded. He was treated in Paris and is being honorably discharged from the French Foreign Legion. *La libération honorable.*"

"Discharged?" Lady Preston's face and eyes took on color as she smiled.

Holly smiled back and handed the cable to her. "He's coming home, Elizabeth."

Caroline saw Kipp from a distance when he returned, stepping out of a cab, right arm in a sling, the puppies and children running up to the car. He was taller and thinner than she remembered and his skin was much darker than May of 1927 when they had married. Matthew, who was six, threw his arms around his father's neck as Kipp scooped him up with his good arm. Her son Charles, seven, stood off to one side, stiff and awkward, smiling, but not sure what to do. Kipp put Matthew down and offered Charles his hand. Charles shook it. Kipp patted him on the shoulder and said something she couldn't hear that made her son laugh. A warmth went through her.

He was a man absolutely without fear. I think he's the only man I have ever met who was incapable of fear.

She remembered reading the words in a newspaper. The American pilot Eddie Rickenbacker had said it about Canadian ace Billy Bishop but it had made her think of Kipp from the beginning, even after they broke up. His blond hair blazed in the morning sunlight as he spoke with Ramsay and Owen and knelt to pet the Belgian Shepherds.

So finally you have let your beautiful hair grow back.

His mother came quickly across the lawn from her white rose bush by the front porch, tugging off her gardening gloves, and Kipp put an arm around her and hugged her with enough force to knock the broad-brimmed straw hat from her head. She put her fingers to her mouth and laughed as Kipp kissed her on both cheeks, French style. Lord Preston hurried out the front door with Skitt and Norah.

Caroline smiled to herself. *It is all right for you to have him now. I know he wishes to greet you. But he wants me most of all. After he is done at the manor house he will find me. And then it will just be the two of us.*

She was standing in a cluster of red poppies that had sprung up a hundred yards north of the house and to the east of the pond. Walking slowly, hearing voices calling out to Kipp as Harrison and Holly came up from the stables, she headed away from the manor and towards the northern end of the property. The poppies streamed ahead of her to an old dry stone fence spattered with orange lichen that separated Dover Sky from the McPhail acreage. She trailed her fingers over blossoms that began to show pink, white, and orange as well as scarlet among the tall blades of green grass.

Did Harrison do this? Or Holly? I'm sure they didn't just sprout here on their own.

She followed the stone fence to the west, getting farther and farther from Kipp and the house. The McPhail fields were overgrown but pleasant enough despite that, bending and rippling in the July breezes like long hair. Without thinking about what she was doing, Caroline took off her sun hat and shook her hair loose from its pins so that it fell over her shoulders and back and began to move with the breezes like the tall grass.

"Caroline Virginia Scarborough."

She looked up in surprise at a figure standing in a copse of young oak trees by the fence.

The man put a finger to his lips. "Shh. Don't say a word."

He emerged from the shadows in his sport coat and pants, arm in a khaki sling. "They think I'm freshening up in my room, you see. I slipped out the back door."

She opened her mouth to reply but his hand went over her lips gently. "No. No words. The first thing I want from those perfect lips is a kiss. And a long one at that." He put his arm around her. "It's like water to me. And I've been in a desert, you know."

She tried to respond again, her lips moving against the palm of his hand, but he shook his head. "Really. There's nothing to say."

Her eyes softened to a pale blue.

"Do you know my hand over your lovely mouth has the effect of a Moroccan veil covering the lower half of your face? It accentuates the blue in your eyes and the

398

bright gold of your eyebrows. As if there's nothing else in the whole wide world." The corners of her eyes moved. "Do you know, I think you're smiling at me beneath that veil."

Her lips kissed his palm.

"Ah, thank you, but I shall need a great deal more than that if I'm to survive."

She kissed his palm a second time.

"I'm grateful. But it isn't quite what's needed." He put his head by hers and whispered in her ear. "Most beautiful woman in the Empire and the world, your dress and your eyes and the sky over your head are exactly the same color right now. Did you know that?" He closed his eyes, taking in the scent of her blonde hair and skin. "Most beautiful woman in the Empire and the world, if I remove the veil, do you promise not to speak?"

Her eyes softened to a lighter blue so that they looked as if they were the color of clear air.

"I'll take that as a yes."

He removed his hand. Gazing down at her face he entwined his darkly tanned fingers in long strands of her thick hair. Her eyes were still and unmoving and fixed completely on his. He took in as much of her beauty as he could without doing anything more than twine her hair around his fingers and feel her warmth against his chest and breathe in the smell of the perfume at her throat and shoulders. Then he closed his eyes and put his lips to hers, slowly and almost awkwardly as if he had never kissed her before, then adding more energy and force until he heard the air leave her body and felt her fingers dig into his arms and move higher and higher to finally grip his back with all the strength she had. She refused to let go or lighten her hold, drawing him farther and farther from England and Dover Sky to a place that was all Caroline Scarborough and her sapphire eyes and golden hair, all her cloud white skin and poppy red lips.

Dover Sky
"What did you do? Sell tickets to the event?"

"I did. There's a grand prize."

"And what is that then?"

"A free hop over the Ditch to Holland — with you at the controls."

"Terrific prize!" Then Jeremy looked sourly at the control panel of the Fokker, a three-engine aircraft. "I'd like to win it myself."

"Maybe you will." Ben continued to taxi the plane over the grass airstrip while working the rudder with his metal feet. "I think I have the hang of this."

"We could crack up, and you're as chipper as a lark."

Jeremy stared through the glass at the people standing shoulder to shoulder nearby. Everyone in the family except Catherine and Libby were watching. All the servants were out, along with dozens of neighbors.

"I don't see any other way of doing this except with a bit of levity." Ben glanced at Jeremy's white face. "Our roles have reversed over the past few weeks, haven't they? You were always on the positive side of things and telling me to take everything on. You prayed with me. Read the Bible with me. Now I'm walking, and today we're in a plane. And you're the one who looks like he's a fog bank."

Jeremy's smile was thin. "And you're the sunshine?"

"We're going to be fine." Ben grinned. "Can't help myself, Jeremy. I love being in an airplane again. Love the feel of it, love the smell of the cockpit and the leather gear, love the throb of the engine. I thank God I'm here. I can't do the stark and stoic look today, mate. Sorry." He turned the plane around and headed east, keeping tabs on the red windsock. "You're one of the reasons I'm in the plane at all a year to the day after the crash at Cape Town. That's why you're along for the ride. My crazy way of honoring you."

Jeremy stared straight ahead. "It felt like an honor a fortnight ago. Now I feel like I've been asked to take over a coronation at Westminster Abbey without a shred of advice from the Archbishop of Canterbury."

"I *have* given you advice. Showed you how to work the stick and watch the gauges. In fact, the only thing that really can go wrong is my feet not being able to handle the rudder. In that case, you just do the dance with your feet like I tell you to do. I'm not going to keel over and pass out, Jeremy. Heart and lungs are fine. Stop fretting. It's going to be the kind of day that redeems the day everyone remembers so far as a tragedy." Ben laughed and shook his head. "Can't believe I'm about to fly again. It's marvelous." He opened up the throttle and the engine roared. "Enough fooling around. I'm more than ready. Whisper a prayer, my good vicar. We're up and away to where angels soar."

"I wish you wouldn't put it that way."

The Fokker streaked along the grass. Victoria clamped her hands onto both her sons, and Emma put her knuckles to her mouth. The aircraft lifted smoothly and gained height rapidly, soon disappearing to the south over the Channel.

Kipp kept a pair of Zeiss binoculars trained on it until the plane was a black dot. "Well, at least they're up and away safely," he said.

No one else spoke. Even the children were silent, picking up on the nervousness of the adults. Harrison had the three shepherds on leashes, and they were quiet as well, sitting on their haunches, tongues out, sensing the mood, and waiting for a different moment to arrive. Six or seven minutes went by before the plane's engines could be heard again, this time coming from the direction of Dover. Kipp raised his binoculars to his eyes and laughed.

"What do you find amusing?" snapped his father.

"Jeremy's at the stick, and he's doing very well for himself — for an Anglican cleric, I must say."

"What!" Emma reached for the binoculars. "I don't believe it."

"Go ahead. Take a look. You can see right into the cockpit."

Victoria's dark-green eyes were on Kipp. "Is Ben all right? What's happened? Why is

Jeremy flying the plane?"

Kipp smiled and put his hands in his pockets. "No doubt Ben is sitting up straight and tall and grinning ear to ear."

"I can see Jeremy!" Emma shouted holding the binoculars to her face. "It is him! Why, he's doing splendidly!"

The Fokker howled over their heads. Lord Preston clapped a hand to his straw hat to hold it on. "Good heavens, sir!" he yelled. "Slow down! You're a man of the cloth!"

Kipp took the glasses from Emma. "Right. They're coming in. Jeremy is leaning back with his eyes shut so Ben's back at the helm. This is the tricky part. Let's see how he does with the landing. After all —"

"Do stop, Kipp. Please." Victoria was staring at the Fokker as if she could make it land perfectly by force of sheer will. "I'm trying to pray."

The Fokker touched down, bounced once, and then all the wheels met the grass together.

"A three-point landing!" Kipp chuckled. "Marvelous."

A number of people clapped.

"Well, sis?" Kipp looked at Victoria. "God or Ben's skill?"

Victoria was standing with her eyes closed and her hands still clamped tightly on Ramsay and Tim. "The two should never be far apart, Kipp Danforth, should they?"

Hartmann Castle, the Rhine River, Germany
Libby found her sister high up on one of the Hartmann Castle's battlements, wind blowing her dark hair straight back.

"How on earth did you get through that door?" Libby asked. "It's been locked tight ever since we arrived."

Catherine was leaning with her arms folded on the parapet and taking in the view of the Rhine River Valley. "To keep the children out. All of the turrets are locked up, but I have the key."

Libby stood beside her. "It's breathtaking."

"I agree. I never tire of it. I don't know which I prefer — Pura or the Rhine."

"Fortunately you don't have to choose. You can have both."

Catherine nodded. "I can."

"The summer's almost spent, and we've never returned to the conversation we had in Tubingen, Cath."

Catherine didn't reply immediately. She kept looking out over the valley. "Maybe there's a good reason," she finally said.

"What's the good reason?"

"I love Albrecht."

"I know you love Albrecht."

"So there's nothing more to discuss."

Libby folded her arms on the parapet next to Catherine. "So you don't mind if Terry pops over for a visit?"

Catherine's jaw tightened. "I wish you wouldn't do that."

"Do what?"

"Start fights."

"If you love Albrecht and don't have a problem with Terry —"

"I love Albrecht, and there is no problem with Terry."

"Except you love Terry too."

Catherine's face darkened. "I don't. I can't."

"Oh Cath. *Don't. Can't.* What do they do to help you when you have feelings that frighten you?"

Catherine put a hand to her face. "Please don't bring this up. I honestly don't have answers for you."

Libby watched a rolling swarm of blackbirds swirl past the top of the castle. "Soon it will be autumn." She leaned over and kissed her sister's head. The wind was blowing Libby's ginger hair and Catherine's dark hair about their faces. "If the day ever comes when I want to see Terry, I will not bring him to Tubingen, Pura, or to this castle on the Rhine."

Catherine didn't respond. After a moment she lifted one of her hands off the parapet and grasped Libby's shoulder.

"And if a day ever comes when there is much more emotion between Terry and me," Libby went on, "well, that day is far, far away. Michael still has my heart. But should life happen again with another man, and if that man is Terry, we will not live within a thousand miles of you, my dear. I would not wish to see you in turmoil and pain over things you can't control or understand."

Catherine whispered, "I wouldn't want that — wouldn't want you so far away. Please. There's conflict between Mum and you, and Mum and Dad, and Edward is in his high-and-mighty snit because I married a German and you adopted a girl from a Chinese family. No more rifts."

"You've been hurt enough in your life, Catherine. I don't need to add to it."

Catherine turned her head and touched her other hand to her sister's cheek. "You said once you were a big girl. So am I. We've both lost so much. I've tried to make a new start. You deserve a chance too. How can I stand in the way of something like that?"

"Just so you understand Terry and I are

talking — only talking. There's no hand of God in this, Cathy. No touch of the divine driving us forward."

Catherine smiled crookedly. "You don't know that."

DEAR MUM AND DAD
WE HAVE A BABY GIRL AS BEAU-
TIFUL AS SHANNON AND AS BIG
AS HER FATHER. NINE POUNDS
FOUR OUNCES. BORN ON 3 OF
SEPTEMBER. MOTHER DOING
FINE BUT IT WAS A LONG DELIV-
ERY. WE HAD TO COAX OUR GIRL
OUT. JANE FINALLY HAS A FE-
MALE COUSIN. WE'VE NAMED
HER PATRICIA CLAIRE. SHE
REALLY IS LOVELY. WE HOPE TO
HAVE FURLOUGH NEXT YEAR SO
WE CAN BRING HER TO EN-
GLAND TO SEE YOU. GOD BLESS
AND THANK THE FAMILY FOR
THEIR PRAYERS.
ROBBIE

Old City, Jerusalem
Robbie nudged the toe of his boot against the shattered panel of wood. "Tell me what you saw, Sergeant."

They both looked as nurses and doctors

helped wounded men and women into ambulances. Above the massive stones of the Western Wall, hundreds of Muslim worshipers gazed down from the Dome of the Rock at the splintered wood and wounded bodies and listened to the cries of pain. British soldiers and police were everywhere.

"Sir." The sergeant had a strong Scottish accent. "The worshipers here at the Wall — the Jews — they had brought some chairs for the sick and the elderly, which they've done before. But they also brought a prayer screen covered in a kind of cloth — this is it here at your feet — so's men and women could pray together; the screen separating one group from the other."

"Who took exception to this?"

"Well, sir, the sheikhs did so far as I could see. I know they were warning the Jerusalem commissioner who was visiting up on the Rock there. He came and told the rabbi to take the screen down. I overheard that part of it word for word. The rabbi asked if they could leave it up until the prayer service was over. The commissioner, Mr. Keith-Roach, he said that would be fine."

"So did they take it down?"

"They understood from the commissioner they could finish their prayers first. Ten minutes later a great shouting starts: 'Death! Death! Kill the Jews! Strike down the Jewish dogs!' "

"Who was doing that?"

"Muslims on the Rock and others in the streets here."

"Then what?"

"The prayers were over, but the rabbi didn't take the screen down immediately. Not sure why. He was tending to other matters, talking with the people who had been praying at the Wall, and so forth. Suddenly the shouting became like screams — bloodcurdling screams — and the commissioner sent in ten or twelve armed men to get ahold of the prayer screen."

"Armed? Are you sure?"

"Armed, sir."

"Did the Jews have any weapons?"

"None. They were just ordinary folk."

Robbie squinted into the light over the Dome of the Rock. "I take it the Jews tried to protect their prayer screen?"

"Aye, sir. It was a sacred object, like."

"Of course."

"They fought back, wouldn't let the men Keith-Roach sent in to take it. So heads were broken. The prayer screen, as you can see for yourself, was torn apart."

"Was anyone shot?"

The sergeant shook his head. "I thank the good Lord, no."

Robbie put his hands behind his back. "Very good. I'm grateful for your report. Keep the peace here as best you can."

The sergeant saluted. "Yes, sir."

Robbie returned the salute and bent to pick up a fragment of the screen that measured four or five inches across. Several Hebrew letters were carved into the wood. He ran his thumb over them. He stood up and put the broken piece of the prayer screen in the chest pocket of his uniform.

Dear Catherine,

Here I am writing you from Jerusalem, sis. It seems the family is divided between England, Germany, and the Holy Land these days. How are you getting on there in your new life? What does Sean think of it all? A five-year-old like him must be overjoyed at seeing the castle in Tubingen every day and watching custodians polish suits of armor to a gleam. Of course, he's seen the old castle at Ashton Park, but he was very young when you left there to take up residence at Dover Sky. He can't remember much of Ashton, I'm sure.

411

I want to ask after Libby, as well. Please send her my regards and Shannon's. I pray things work out between Mum and her, and I'm glad you've given Jane and Libby a place to stay until then. How do the two of them like Germany? How are their language lessons coming along? "Sprechen Sie Deutsch?" is all I know.

Shannon and Patricia are doing so well. I wish I could say the same about Jerusalem. Things are not so holy in the Holy City. Back in September we had a bad incident at the Western Wall where the Jews pray. Then in October the Grand Mufti, Haj Amin al Husseini, made matters worse by ordering new construction near the Western Wall. He purposely had mules laden with building supplies led through the area while the Jews were praying. The drivers made every effort to ensure the mules dropped their excrement right at the Western Wall. Filthy water was thrown on the Jews as well. Can you imagine how the Muslims would react if that were done to them at the Dome of the Rock?

Now we even have a Muslim holy man, a muezzin, doing the call to prayer just a few steps from the Western Wall precisely when the Jews themselves are praying. I doubt you've ever heard an Islamic call to prayer. It is loud and long and stark, a plaintive cry that carries over every other sound. Quite understandably, the Jews are upset at all this.

The Jerusalem commissioner has his hands full. So do we. There are not many of us soldiers. We're just a token force really — the British Palestine police also have all they can handle. How well the police will handle the unrest I don't know. They certainly overreacted when the Jews set up a simple prayer screen at the Wall back in September. By last count over 1200 of the police officers are Muslim Arabs. Less than 500 are Christian Arabs, and only about 320 are Jews. I don't know how evenhanded the justice they mete out is bound to be in 1929.

Listen to me prattle on. A month from Christmas and what sort of good cheer am I bringing you? My purpose in writing is to tell you we had Patricia Claire baptized Roman Catholic shortly after her birth. This was Shannon's wish, and

I felt no inclination to say nay. After all I was ready to be baptized a Catholic when I was stationed in Ireland years ago. So were you before you and Albrecht patched things up.

Do you ever give a thought to picking up where you left off? I suppose not. Albrecht is Lutheran. I understand the baron is a practicing Catholic, though I doubt that will have any bearing whatsoever on your situation. Well, I wanted to share the news about my baby's baptism with you because I felt you'd be interested and sympathetic. I'm quite happy about it, but please not a word to Mum and Dad right now! I think that might really drive them 'round the bend.

We'll certainly send you and Libby and Sean and Jane a few Christmas cards from Jerusalem. I might even get a chance to get down and pick something up from Bethlehem. Some camels and a nativity scene carved out of olive wood perhaps? It's a lovely wood, and I'm sure the children would love the donkeys, shepherds, magi, and all the other figures that go into the Christmas story. Even sophisticated eleven-year-old Jane might like setting it up.

That's all for now. Must get this off in the post. Love to all. God bless you in every way during the remaining weeks of 1928.

Cheers,
Robbie

Christmas Eve
Tubingen, Germany
"Catherine?"
"Yes, Albrecht?"
"What do you think of this sentence?" he asked as he came into the library, reading glasses on and hair askew, holding a sheaf of papers covered with typing:

As the Christmas tree was removed from the realm of pagan ritual by Martin Luther and redeemed and made whole to honor the love of God we find in Jesus Christ, so the German heart must also be released from any vestiges of a Nordic pagan past, and be redeemed and made new in Christ, so that a true and spiritual Germany may emerge from our confusion once again.

She closed the book she was leafing

through and smiled. "It is a long sentence, love."

"I know but —"

"Nevertheless, I like what you say and how you bring things together. How will it sound in German?"

His head was down as he reread the sentence to himself. She watched for a moment — the movement of his lips, the shape of his fingers on the sheets of paper, the tangle of his light brown hair, the slender strength of his body. Light and warmth moved swiftly through her as if she'd drank hot tea. She stood up and took the pages from his hands.

"It is Christmas Eve, Albrecht. We have that lovely fir tree from Bavaria downstairs."

He stared at her. "Yes, of course. But I —"

"Time to put away pens and thinking caps. Time to celebrate the love of God in Jesus Christ you like to write about."

"Another half hour." He half-smiled. "It may seem to you that I am obsessive, but we want this essay published to coincide with New Year's Day. Hitler has been yammering about an economic crisis to try to draw attention back to his political ideas. We cannot ignore him. Membership in the Nazi Party continues to grow."

"But he still has hardly any seats in the *Reichstag,* correct?"

"That can change with one election. A bad year for Germany, and his party could go from fourteen to fifty or sixty seats overnight. Do you know how many stormtroopers he's recruited — those thugs of his in brown shirts? We estimate at least 400,000. That's almost half a million, Catherine! And the Treaty of Versailles restricts the German army to only 100,000 troops. Hitler could take over the government with a snap of his fingers."

"He won't, Albrecht. You know he won't. Hitler's smart enough to understand he needs far more than half-a-million brutes to govern Germany. He needs the German people behind him. He doesn't have that. He'll never have that."

"You don't know that for sure. History turns like a weather vane in the wind. One moment east, the next moment north."

"Albrecht —"

"Just a half hour."

"Your half hours are hours and your hours are days." She ran her hands over the sweater on his chest. "I have many confusions about many things, but one thing I have been successful at sorting out is that whatever else I feel, I know I feel great love

417

and affection for you."

"Do you?"

She removed his glasses and placed them on a table. "I do." She gently put her lips to his. "No more academics. Or rather, if you must be theological, live out your theology in your marriage. Right now. Right here. The house is empty for a few hours . . ."

"Catherine —"

"Begin with a kiss. Don't you find a kiss pleasant?"

"Naturally."

"Especially mine?"

"Only yours."

"Ah . . ." She continued to kiss him. "I've found the year difficult in many ways, Albrecht, not least of all because of Mother's unkindness towards Libby's daughter and Edward's hostility towards our relationship. Often I didn't know what to think or do about anything. But when I look at you and I hear the students singing carols outside our house for their favorite professor —"

"Come, you exaggerate."

"I realize whatever else may not be settled in my life, I know you are my favorite professor too."

"Catherine —"

"Albrecht, tomorrow is Christmas. Show

me I mean something to you."

He didn't speak again. He framed her face in both of his hands even though his fingertips were smeared with ink from replacing typewriter ribbon. He put his lips against her eyebrows, her eyes, her cheeks, and finally her mouth. She slipped her arms over his back, and her fingers found their way to his soft brown hair.

"I understand so little from one moment to the next," she said in a quiet voice. "But I understand this."

15

March–August, 1929
St. Andrew's Cross Church

Ben peered closely at the stained-glass window depicting Jesus speaking with the centurion. "When was this one made?"

"The 1700s. Early on, I believe, in the history of St. Andrew's Cross Church." Jeremy, in his clerical robes and a white collar at his throat, stood behind Ben. "Kipp took a great interest in this particular window as well when he was here for the baptism of Edward's newborn."

"Yes. Sorry I missed that. Colm Alexander Danforth. Handsome baby?"

Jeremy smiled. "With his great shock of black hair and brilliant blue eyes he takes after his mother certainly."

"And now Caroline's with child, hmm?"

"She is. The baby's due in the fall."

"I've been flying too much. Vic says I'm trying to prove something." He walked away from the window and sat in a pew. "We're back to Ashton Park. I'll take up the reins in the north, and Kipp will handle the airline in the south. He'll be doing much the same thing Michael did, dodging back and forth between the airfield and Dover Sky."

Jeremy sat next to him. "That's what you wanted to chat about?"

"No, no, actually not. I wanted to thank you again for helping me get back on my feet and up in the clouds. It's been a great thing . . . a great blessing."

"And I got to fly and see you return to your natural element. It was a great blessing for me too."

"Speaking of natural elements. Well, I was wondering what, ah, what you would think of me . . . taking holy orders."

Jeremy's eyes opened wide behind his glasses. "What did you say, Ben?"

"Not in the Church of England. That's beyond me, and my background is Methodist — the Wesleys, you know. Even when I was a stable boy I fancied having a pulpit and saying the good words."

Jeremy couldn't think of a response.

"It's always been in my head to go to Africa — to see the jungles and the animals — rhinos and lions and giraffes. I used to think of combining the two — Africa and being a missionary. And now, well, I could fly, couldn't I? I could be a missionary pilot or something like that?"

"Have you talked with Victoria about this?"

"No, not yet. She'd think I was off to prove myself on a grand scale. I wouldn't act on any of this for another year. But then I'd want to step down from the airline and start to train with the Methodist Church, with an eye to heading to British East Africa and lending a hand in matters of the spirit and everything else."

"You've never mentioned any of this before, Ben. There hasn't even been a hint."

Ben shrugged. "I've brought it up now and again, but life swept me up in its rough-and-ready current like it does everyone. I had no intention of going to France during the war, but there I was. Had no idea of flying a plane, and one day there I was up in the clouds. Didn't know I'd win the Victoria Cross or marry William and Elizabeth Danforth's youngest daughter or have children with her, but that's how it turned out. Back of my mind I held onto the Methodist Church and Africa and missionary service even though I couldn't see how it might come together."

Jeremy raised his eyebrows and blew out a mouthful of air. "I see."

"I know you're Church of England, and I expect you don't approve of my being a Methodist minister, but —"

Jeremy waved a hand. "This is not 1780, Ben. I know many fine Methodist clerics. That doesn't matter to me one bit. I'm just a bit taken aback by everything you've said. It's like standing on the beach at Brighton and suddenly getting slammed by a monstrous ocean wave."

"You don't think I'm suited?"

"I don't think that at all. You're a fine man. I'm just trying to take it all in. Look, I can't say it's right or it's wrong. It's your life, and it's your decision to make. But you are going to have to bring Victoria in on this — and the sooner the better."

Ben glanced away. "I know, I know. But I don't want her thinking I just came up with this off the top of my head so I could show the world what a man with two tin legs was capable of. The dream's been a part of me for a long time."

"Explain that to her."

Ben looked up at the arched ceiling of stone. "Perhaps in the spring."

"It won't get easier."

"Not with Victoria Anne Danforth it

won't, right enough."

Jeremy rubbed his hand over his mouth. "But there's something more important. Is this just an idea you've been carrying around since you were a lad? Or do you feel a call?"

"A call?"

"Do you . . . do you think God is part of this? That He's speaking to you about becoming a minister?"

Ben folded his arms over his chest. "And what would that sound like?"

"I really can't describe it."

"This happened to you?"

"It did, yes."

"The impression has always been with me. Since I was a schoolboy. It's never left me alone. Always nagging, always pestering, always tugging at my sleeve and grabbing me by the arm — even when I flew during the war and even when I did all the air races. It's got a grip on me like a fever. Or like a dog with its teeth sunk into my leg."

Jeremy's smile grew.

Ben looked at him. "No music. No angels in white. No pleasant warmth tingling through my body. Just this constant at me, at me, at me. I don't suppose that sounds at all like God, does it?"

Jeremy laughed. "Actually, it sounds a

good deal like Him."

Dear Cornelia, my diary,
April fool's! I thought I was coming
along quite nicely as far as love and marriage were concerned. I adore Albrecht,
I absolutely do. And after those chats
with Libby last year I thought I'd gotten
this whole issue of her having a relationship with Terry Fordyce off my chest.
Now she's off to Cartagena, Spain,
where the Royal Navy ships have berthed
for two weeks. He cabled her, she
thought about it for five seconds, and
then she went downtown and sent back
a telegram accepting his invitation. Jane
remains here with Albrecht, Sean, and
me. She's pouting quite a bit. I think
our almost-twelve-year-old has a bit of a
thing for Commander Fordyce.

I have no wish to rush off to Spain, and
I have no desire to see Terry. I'm looking forward to traveling to Pura with
Albrecht very much, and that's only six
weeks away. But I must confess I still
don't like the idea of Libby spending
time with Terry. She continues to tell me
it's no more than friendship, but what
woman takes a train hundreds of miles

to see a man for two or three days simply for the purpose of developing a friendship? Why not wait a bit until his ship is back in English waters in May or June?

Of course she wants to see him as soon as possible. Of course she has every right to see him. But this man was once very precious to me. I don't know if what I'm feeling is jealousy or possessiveness or what. I can only say it is very hard to think of her spending hours in his company — dining with him, making him laugh, enjoying his gallantries. I don't wish to be with him, but I don't wish for her to be with him either.

I pray all these confusing and conflicting feelings I have will be gone when I wake up. I pray that Terry will become no more than any other man out there floating around on the sea in a boat.

Danforth flat, Port of Dover
Charlotte watched as her husband smacked his fist into his palm over and over in the front parlor of their Dover flat. "Lost! And now Labor holds the reins of the greatest nation on earth in its grip! The greatest nation and the greatest empire!"

426

"You and your father have retained your seats. That's something."

"So did Tanner Buchanan."

"Still, you won reelection, and we all know it was a difficult campaign. I'm very proud of you, persevering right through the swamp and heat of May and June."

"We may still be MPs, Char, but we have no power."

Charlotte leaned forward on the couch. "I spoke with your father at some length, Edward. Yes, Labor has more seats in the House — but barely. And they didn't win the popular vote. They don't have a clear majority. The day will come when they will need to cross the aisle. Ramsay MacDonald is prime minister for a year or two, but eventually there will be a hung Parliament. At that point, if MacDonald wants to form a government capable of passing legislation, he must patch together some sort of national coalition. That's how your father put it."

Edward threw himself into an armchair. "I have no desire to be on the same side of the aisle as Tanner Buchanan."

She smiled, reached over, and rubbed his shoulder and back. "Love, if you wish the Conservative Party to continue to exert a positive influence on British politics, I doubt you'll have much choice. Of course you could sit on the Opposition benches and glare at Lord Buchanan from there, perhaps shake your fist at him now and then, and even occasionally pitch a wadded ball of paper at his head."

"They'd escort me from the chamber *tout de suite* for that."

"But how exciting. You might actually bop him between the eyes. Then he'd challenge you to a duel of honor and you'd run him through. No more evil Lord Tanner. Triumph! His last words? *'Why, I am justly killed by mine own treachery.'* "

Edward laughed. "Here I am, tired and flustered by it all and yet how is it possible that my Pendle Hill beauty can still make merry with me?"

She took his hand and curled her strong fingers tightly around it. "After ten years of marriage too."

"Well, you look ten years younger, Charlotte Squire, not ten years older. Are you sure we're not traveling backwards in time on H.G. Wells' invention?"

She tugged his arm over to her and kissed his hand while keeping her dark-blue eyes focused on him. "What if we were? Would you still have me? Still marry me in that great heap of rocks and battlements in Scotland?"

"I'd do it a hundred times over — a thousand times over."

"Prove it, Lord Edward Danforth, MP."

"Prove it?"

"Take me to our room, hold me in your arms, and tell me in exactly a thousand different ways how and why you still love me." She stood up, and still holding his hand dragged him to his feet.

"You're joking! Colm will be up and wailing in two hours. You need what little bit of sleep you can get."

She pulled him across the room. "Yes, well, that's what nannies and warm bottles are for. Do put some effort into it, Edward. I feel like I'm trying to heave anchor on that great new battleship they just put into service."

"The one named after old Admiral Rodney? How I'd love to sail on her. Sixteen-inch guns!"

"There, we got some life out of you with that. Come along. You can do it. Only two or three more sea miles, and you can snuggle up to your new berth. Rule Britannia, Lord Edward. Britannia rule the waves."

He grinned as she yanked him into their room and shut the door.

"You're as mad as a hatter," he said.

Old City, Jerusalem

"Death to the Jews!"

"Strike for Allah! Strike!"

Thousands of men boiled from the Dome of the Rock into the streets.

"Right!" snapped Robbie. "Leftenant Kirke!"

"Sir."

"They're bent on murder this time. Go after them with your platoon. Work with the police. Arrest the leaders."

"Yes, sir."

"Leftenant Skilling!"

"Sir."

"Follow him with your men."

"Yes, sir. What if — what if the mob won't let us arrest their leaders, sir?"

Robbie's eyes were like rock. "Fire weapons to warn them. If they're killing Jews or they assault your troops, direct your fire as seems most appropriate."

Robbie turned to the British soldiers still at attention behind him, their eyes fixed on the Western Wall. "Leftenants Stark and Kettle!"

"Sir!" the two officers responded in unison.

"Take a pair of armored cars. I shall be in another. Follow me. Bring your platoons. We are heading to the Mea Shearim neighborhood."

"Yes, sir!"

Robbie leaped into an armored car. The engine roared and the car shot forward. The driver threaded it swiftly through the narrow and crooked streets of the Old City. Eventually the convoy and troops were forced to a standstill as hundreds of men in robes called Thawbs jammed the roads and lanes. Robbie saw a Jewish man and his wife hauled from their house and stabbed to death. He unholstered his Webley revolver and fired two shots into the air. The mob shrank back, shouting. Jumping to the ground, Robbie pointed his pistol at the killers who glared back at him in a mixture of fear and rage, deep and dark frown lines crisscrossing their faces. The rest of the soldiers joined him.

"Corporal Reynolds. Sergeant Ward."

"Major Danforth?"

"Sir."

"Arrest these three men on a charge of murder. Chain them and put them in one of the armored cars."

"Yes, sir."

The tallest of the three Arabs sneered, bent down and wiped the blood from his knife on the dress of the woman he'd stabbed, and spat at Robbie. "British pig.

431

You and your Balfour Declaration. This is holy war, a *jihad.* Beware."

"There were Jews living here thousands of years before Mohammed was born. And they shall continue to live here side by side with their Arab neighbors. Drop your knife."

"In fifty years there will be no Jews in Jerusalem or within a thousand miles of Palestine."

"They are 'people of the Book' according to the Qur'an. They are to be accorded tolerance, respect, and liberty under Islamic law. Have you forgotten the Prophet's words?"

The man spat again.

Robbie thumbed the hammer back on his revolver. "Are you ready to die for breaking sharia law?"

"You would not do it."

The mob around Robbie, the armored cars, and the other British soldiers seethed as people shrieked, "Death to the Jews! Kill the Jewish dogs!"

"They are 'people of the Book'!" Robbie shouted above the clamor. "Do not defile your faith! Obey the Prophet and return to your homes!"

"The Mufti has blessed us!"

Robbie thrust the revolver at the three men. "Corporal Reynolds! Sergeant Ward!

Do your duty!"

"Sir!" The corporal and sergeant stepped forward with manacles.

The crowd reacted by throwing stones and sticks at the soldiers.

Robbie swung his pistol quickly over to the men in the mob who were closest to him. "Are you ready to die violating the words of the Qur'an? Are you ready to die defying the words of Mohammed?"

A man lunged at him with a sword. Robbie shot him in the shoulder, and he collapsed with a scream. Then Robbie shot the man next to him in the foot. The mob fell back, cursing and breaking apart as men fled into alleys and arched doorways. Robbie aimed his pistol back on the three killers, including the tall Arab who had spoken before.

"Drop the knife or I will shoot. All three of you — drop your knives. If you do not, I will open fire."

The tallest man's eyes remained full of black fire but he laid his knife down on the body of the dead woman. So did the other two. The sergeant and corporal rushed up with the chains.

"You will regret this, British!" the tall man said between clenched teeth as the manacles went on his wrists with a loud snap of iron.

Robbie glanced at the window of the house the Arabs had dragged the man and woman from. A small girl with dark curls and round brown eyes gazed at him. He thought of his daughter's eyes and face.

"I doubt it," he replied.

Dover Sky

"Dad! I think you'd better come in the house and listen to this."

"Yes, what is it, Edward? I'm rather busy here." Lord Preston was covered in soap and water as he and his grandchildren washed the year-old Belgian shepherds on the lawn amidst loud squeals and shouts. "We've decided on a name for the brown one instead of calling him Shepherd all the time. Now he must learn to answer to Charlemagne. Isn't that a grand name? Doesn't it suit him?"

"Dad, it's the BBC," Edward said, leaning out the window. "They're announcing a second day of riots in Jerusalem and Palestine."

Lord Preston hesitated as he was about to run a brush over the squirming Flanders' long, black coat. "A second day? Why, we've heard nothing about it." Covered in water, he ran up the steps of the manor and through the front door. The radio was playing in the library. Charlotte was walking up and down in front of the stacks of books, eight-month-old Colm Alexander in her arms. Edward stood near the radio with his hands in his pockets and head down.

We continue to receive cables and signals from the Old City and outlying areas of Palestine. Fatalities have mounted since the unrest broke out into open violence yesterday, August twenty-third. Mobs of Arabs are assaulting Jews in their neighborhoods and homes in Jerusalem. There have also been attacks in Hebron. Dozens of Jews have been killed, the pharmacy in a medical clinic destroyed, and a synagogue desecrated and set ablaze. There are reliable reports of massacres on an unprecedented scale. We shall continue to provide updates as they become available.

"Dear God!" Lord Preston stood perfectly still as the water ran off his clothing and spread across the polished hardwood floor. "We must pray now! Skitt?"

Skitt was right behind him. "My lord?"

"Pray, fetch Lady Preston and other members of the family. Have them gather here." He looked at Edward. "Please get the prime minister on the phone."

435

"MacDonald? Why he's Labor, Father. He won't talk to you."

"Of course he'll talk to me. He'll need you and me if he hopes to form a national coalition government in a year or two and stay in power. More to the point, we've never had cross words. Ring him, please."

"All right."

Lord Preston's shoulders sagged after Edward left the room. Charlotte moved quickly to his side and put a hand on his arm.

"Da, are you all right?"

"Just overwhelmed, my dear. How quickly we move from happiness to fear." He leaned over and kissed her infant's forehead between his wide, blue eyes. "But God is great."

Old City, Jerusalem

"Get back!" Robbie grabbed a Tommy gun from inside the hatch of the armored car and fired a burst over the heads of the men in the mob. When they failed to react, he sprayed bullets at their feet so that stone chips sprang into the air. Shaking their fists, they retreated.

"Death to the Jews!"

"Kill the dogs!"

"Strike the infidels! Praise Allah!"

The mob surged toward the Jewish shops and houses once again. Robbie, who had only had two hours of sleep in the armored car the night before, saw dead children lying in their own blood in the road. This was the third or fourth time he'd witnessed that atrocity since they'd arrived on the scene. A flame of anger shot through him. "Leftenant Kettle!" he barked.

"Sir?"

"Your men will fire a volley over their heads. If they fail to fall back, aim low and shoot the men in front."

"Sir."

Chunks of wood and rocks bounced off the armored cars. The sudden blast of rifle fire made the Arabs in the back of the mob scatter, but the leaders still pushed towards the Jewish homes, trampling the bodies of the murdered boys.

Robbie aimed the Tommy gun at a heavily bearded man holding two swords whose white Thawb was streaked with blood. "Get out of here! *Yella, yella!* Hurry up."

The man continued to edge past the armored car.

"Leftenant Kettle! Fire at their feet!"

The officer shouted the command, and British rifles blazed. The leaders cringed, suddenly shouted, began to chant, and ran

437

past the armored car — three or four dozen of them, the heavily bearded man in front. Robbie vaulted from his armored car and chased them as they swarmed a house. They broke the door and windows and seized two women by their hair.

Robbie struck several men with the stock of the Thompson submachine gun, knocking them to the pavement. The bearded man swiped at him with a sword, and Robbie rammed the barrel of the Tommy gun straight into his face, crushing his nose. He fired two rounds into another man's leg and another two into the shoulder of a man who was beating one of the women.

"Kettle! Arrest them! Every one of the devils you can lay your hands on. Knock them flat if they won't hold still for the manacles!"

"Sir!" The officer turned to his platoon. "Men, seize the Arabs directly in front of you. Stick your gun barrel in their guts if necessary. March each man off to the side and chain him up. If your man won't go with you voluntarily, give him a rifle butt to the head to wake him up. These are murderers, lads. No kid gloves now. He takes the chains or you flatten him. D'ya hear me?"

As the soldiers sprang forward, the Arabs fled. Several of the privates made rugby tackles and brought their men down. Others chased rioters into back alleys and along empty streets where families cowered behind locked doors. Robbie kicked the bearded man in the ribs as he tried to get up and brandished one of his swords. Robbie placed his boot on the back of the Arab's head and pressed down with his body weight to keep the man in place. He glanced at the two women who had been assaulted.

"Go to a neighbor's house," he ordered. "Bar the door. If you have any weapons, don't hesitate to use them."

"We have nothing," one of them said.

"You have axes to chop wood, don't you? Knives to slice bread and meat? Use those if you must."

"Are — are you going to leave us alone, sir?"

"No. A section of my men will stay to guard this street — ten or twelve men. You won't be left unprotected. I have to go to other neighborhoods to see what is happening. There is rioting everywhere. Where are your men?"

One woman's face looked as white as snow and ice. "Dead," she responded. "They were killed at the synagogue."

Robbie tugged a knife from his boot and

tossed it to the woman, sheath and all. "Keep that by your side. If you have to protect yourself and your children, remember Deborah and remember Jael. Bear in mind how Jael slew Sisera, the enemy general, by driving a tent stake through his head. If you have to do the same, do it. A child's life is worth a thousand of these murderers' lives."

"*Toda raba.* Thank you."

"How old are you?"

"Eighteen."

"That's young to be married."

She shrugged. "Not among us. In any case, I am one of the daughters — not a wife."

"I see. Do not lose the knife."

"I will not."

"What is your name?"

"Michal."

"Like the wife of King David."

She offered him a fragment of a smile. "One of them."

"A fiery one, if I recall."

"With good reason, sir."

"Yes. Well, put that spirit to use if men try to slay you and your household." He pointed at the knife. "I shall be back for it."

"I will keep it in my hand until you return."

"That's an excellent place."

Robbie bent down and dragged the bearded man to his feet. The Arab growled through fingers dark with his own blood as he held his nose. Robbie manacled him and then shoved him roughly towards the armored car. Looking back over his shoulder at Michal, he said, "I will not cease to pray for you . . . and your people."

She bowed her head briefly in thanks.

Dover Sky

Lord Preston paced his study while Edward and Kipp watched. "A week of killing, rapes, mutilations, and desecrations. Hundreds of people killed, and hundreds of arrests. Still no word from Robbie! The prime minister assures me there have been no reports of British fatalities. I thank God for that, but what of the others? Mostly women and children — unarmed, defenseless, posing no more threat to the Arabs than a cloud in the sky. Attacks totally unprovoked as far as the reports Mr. MacDonald has read. The viciousness utterly without cause except hatred. Exceptional hate — where does it come from? How does it live in people's breasts, in people who were made in the image of God, the people who were sons of Ishmael?"

441

Kipp and Edward kept their eyes on him but didn't reply. They noticed their father's face was haggard and gray, his white hair uncombed.

Lord Preston paused in his pacing to look at a painting of Jesus in the Garden of Gethsemane. "Well, the worst is over I'm told. The prime minister assured me he would ring us with information on Robbie the moment he hears anything. So we shall wait on that and trust God." He looked at his sons. "What would I tell the families of the murdered if I were there? What would I say to them of the ways of the world and the ways of God? How might I possibly bring them a morsel of comfort? What words could someone use that could make any difference at all?"

Safed, Palestine
The colonel slipped into the back of the car next to Robbie. He tugged off his leather gloves and stared straight ahead. "How long have you been sitting here, Danforth?" he asked.

"Ten minutes, sir."

"Saw all you could stomach of Safed and Hebron?"

"Yes, sir."

"Yet you were in Ireland, weren't you?"

"Even at its worst, Ireland was never like this, sir. There I didn't walk into houses and find twenty or thirty men, women, and children murdered in cold blood. I didn't find young girls raped and tortured and stabbed to death. I didn't walk into orphanages and see the horrors I saw here in Safed."

"No. I expect not." He sighed with a low groan. "At least some Arabs hid Jewish neighbors in their homes."

"Yes, sir. I take some measure of hope for the future in that."

"Do you? I wish I could be as sanguine as you."

Robbie shook his head. "I don't feel sanguine, sir. It's one straw to grasp on to, that's all. Not much."

"What does your crystal ball tell you?"

"My crystal ball? I wish I could say I see one nation of Arab Christians and Arab Muslims living side by side with religious Jews and socialist Jews, forming a kind of coalition government just as we would do back in Britain, sir. But massacres like these — pogroms, really — just ensure the Zionists will argue other Jews into the desire to establish a totally Jewish state. Muslims will hate them for it, so the fighting will carry on regardless of the peace that moderates and well-wishers dream of."

"Why not form two separate nations, Danforth?"

"That would be like Ireland and England, sir. Never the best of friends."

"Well, I shall continue to hope for some sort of miracle." He glanced at Robbie. "You're right. You are not as sanguine as you first appear." He patted the back of the seat in front of him. "Corporal. Let's leave this place and get back to Jerusalem."

The driver started the engine of the car. "Very good, sir." The vehicle stirred up dust as it headed off. Army lorries full of troops and police followed them.

"Nevertheless, I should like your full report on my desk in two days, Danforth. Sanguine or not."

"I will have it for you, Colonel."

MUM AND DAD
WE ARE ALL RIGHT HERE. SHANNON AND THE BABY ARE DOING FINE. I WAS NOT INJURED DURING THE RIOTING. WILL WRITE A LETTER IN A FORTNIGHT. AS YOU CAN IMAGINE THINGS ARE PRETTY HECTIC HERE IN THE AFTERMATH. PRAY FOR THE

PEACE OF JERUSALEM.

OUR LOVE
ROBBIE SHANNON
AND PATRICIA CLAIRE

Jerusalem
In summary:

As far as we can ascertain, between the dates of August 23rd and August 29th, 133 Jews were killed and some 300 injured. During the same period, 115 or 116 Arabs were killed and more than 230 injured.

The Jews were killed and wounded by Arab rioters for the most part, though there is evidence some were victims of British gunfire. The majority of Arabs were killed and wounded by soldiers of the British Army and officers of the British Palestine Police Force who were trying to halt the massacres. A small number of Arabs were killed by Jews defending themselves or retaliating for Arab assaults. In the worst case, an Imam and six others were slain. For the most part, Jews neither attacked rioters nor defended themselves.

Casualties occurred in Jerusalem, Hebron, Safed, Motza, Kfar Uria, and Tel Aviv.

124 Arabs have been charged with murder, 50 with attempted murder, 250 with arson and looting, and almost 300 with less serious offences.

70 Jews have been charged with murder, 40 with attempted murder, 31 with arson and looting, and 21 with less serious offences.

Jews and Arabs — Arab Muslims in particular — have become more firmly entrenched in their positions as a result of the riots. Jewish proponents of an all-Jewish nation now dominate the political landscape. By the same token, Muslims who desire an all-Arab or even all-Muslim Palestine under sharia law hold sway among their population.

Recommendations:

The British military garrison must be reinforced in 1930. One hundred soldiers is not a sufficient complement to deal with the tensions in this region.

Talks between Jewish and Arab leaders must continue, mediated by British officials.

The British military and police in Palestine and the British Government in Westminster must brace themselves for increased hostilities between Arabs and Jews over the next decade. Nothing will appease Zionists except a fully Jewish state. Nothing will appease Muslims except a fully Muslim Palestine.

The Grand Mufti bears watching. He could have quelled the rioting before it began, but it appeared to me he was whipping the Arabs into a frenzy against the Jews at the Dome of the Rock. He does not have the best interests of Great Britain at heart and certainly not the best interests of those among us who desire an amicable solution to the Jewish–Arab problem.

"Shalom, Michal."

"Shalom . . . major."

"You may call me by my Christian name please, Michal. I'm Robert, but you can use Robbie if you wish."

She stood in the doorway and smiled, her eyes and hair dark. "I prefer Robert." She handed the knife in its sheath to him. "You have come for this."

Robbie took the knife. "This and to see how you are."

"Frightened like the other Jews here. Hoping it will not happen again, but knowing it will. Trusting the British will protect us, and realizing we must also protect ourselves."

He pulled the knife from its sheath. "You used it?"

She dropped her eyes. "I tried to clean it well."

"What happened?"

"That night a man came through the back window. Your soldiers didn't see him. He put a hand over my mouth and tried to force himself on me. I put the knife into his back. His finger jerked the trigger on his pistol several times. Your men rushed through the door, knocking it down. They saw what had happened. A corporal ordered the man's body be carried away and placed in the street far from my house."

"He didn't report the incident."

She kept her eyes on the ground. "He said I acted in self-defense, and he did not want me charged with murder."

"You would have been exonerated."

"The corporal wasn't sure."

Robbie looked at her a few moments. "So in the end you were like Jael."

"In the end I was a frightened Jewish woman grabbing whatever came first to her hand."

He tossed the knife in his palm and then slipped it into its brown leather sheath. He handed it back to her. "Good Sheffield steel, that. You'd better hang on to it. You might need it again."

"I hope not."

"Hope but be prepared to defend yourself against those who have different hopes."

She lifted her eyes to his and took the knife. "Thank you, major."

"Robert."

"Yes, Robert. *Toda raba.*"

Robbie touched his fingers to his officer's hat. "Perhaps I will see you again, Michal."

"Perhaps."

She watched him climb into his armored car. He remained standing in the hatch as it drove away. She followed him with her eyes as the vehicle negotiated the street between vendors selling kosher meat, vegetables, and baked sweets. It slowed down, sped up, slowed down, sped up according to traffic. He looked back once and they saw each other.

16

November, 1929–April, 1930
Tubingen, Germany

"Now Hitler has what he wanted — economic chaos!"

"Please calm down, Albrecht."

"Calm down? Let me explain the situation." After moving a stack of books, Albrecht sat next to Catherine on the couch in his study. "So long as our economy was doing well, Hitler had no real power to attract the German people. I was alarmed by the number of his stormtroopers and the fact that Nazi Party membership kept growing, but I was comforted that he wasn't drawing in the majority of the population. Germany was at work, and our money was good. However, a great part of this was due to massive loans from the United States that helped us get back on our feet. The money was used to subsidize various employment schemes and businesses and to shore up our currency, not to mention shore up the government."

He paused to remove his reading glasses and run a hand through his hair.

Catherine waited.

"Now with the stock market crash in America in October, everything has changed drastically. Fortunes have been lost, wealth has vanished overnight, millionaires are throwing themselves out of windows in New York City because they are suddenly penniless. And because they are paupers, America is in danger of becoming a pauper too. So with this financial crisis, America is already making sounds we don't want to hear in Germany — that they are short on cash, that they need to deal with the economic disaster in their own country, that they need to recall their international loans. Yes, every single loan. They are going to take them back."

"Has this actually happened yet?"

"My sources tell me the tremors are certainly being felt in Berlin. It's not noticeable to you or me at this point, but employment is being affected and the Deutschmark is losing ground rapidly. It will be quite obvious in 1930. In any case, the working-man who has lost his job or had his wages cut already sees it. The financiers and capitalists who are taking it on the chin see it. And what do you think they are saying on the street, in the beer halls, in the private clubs, in the business meetings? That if Hitler was smart enough to predict this economic collapse in 1928, then maybe he is smart enough to fix it in 1929 and 1930."

Catherine felt an uncomfortable coldness in her body, and she clasped her hands together. "I see."

Albrecht gazed out the study window at the slow spinning fall of snowflakes. "Hitler is already making more speeches, already saying democracy doesn't work — certainly not for Germany. That the Fatherland has always done well with a strong man at the helm, like Charlemagne or Bismarck . . . like himself. He and his henchmen are trying to manipulate the situation and have him appointed chancellor over the nation. So far he hasn't succeeded in budging von Hindenburg on the matter. The day may come when our elderly statesman and president has no choice but to bow to Hitler's demands. If the economic situation worsens and the Nazi Party continues to grow, and if Hitler wins more seats in the *Reichstag,* well, von Hindenburg will be backed into a corner."

"Your views do not cheer the soul, Albrecht. I hope you exaggerate the threat facing Germany."

"If it faces Germany, it faces Europe as well." Albrecht squeezed her shoulder. "I shall be late for dinner. Do not wait for me. The Brotherhood of the Oak are meeting in half an hour at a small room in a museum."

"The Brotherhood? You have not met for years."

He stood up and took his suit coat off the back of a chair. "That tells you others share my rosy outlook."

"That suit coat is badly wrinkled. Let me iron it for you."

"No time. It is just men with cigars and pipes and fear in their eyes, Catherine. Believe me, they will not be looking at my coat and its wrinkles."

"No? Exactly what do these men look for from you?"

"Fight." He wrapped his red scarf about his neck. "They look for the German fighting spirit. Hitler and his brownshirts, with their swastikas and their fists, have it. The Brotherhood look for it in those who have a different vision for Germany and a totally different heart. And they hope to God they can find it."

Lord Preston jingled coins in his pants pocket as he held the phone to his ear and patiently repeated his words. "No, Longbottom. No shipyard worker in Liverpool or Belfast will be asked to pick up and go home, ending his employment with us."

"But, my lord, the economic crisis in America has touched us all. You are losing profits. If you wish to ensure a fairly high cash flow despite international circumstances, you must trim expenditures."

"Out of the question. The pound has already lost buying power for my workers."

"And for you."

"Nevertheless, we shall weather the storm without putting anyone out of work. The most I will agree to is a ten percent wage cut across the board for office workers as well as those on the docks. They must be told this is to ensure Danforth Shipyards and Shipping continues to stay in business so they can keep their jobs. We've taken the same steps at the textile mills in Preston. Baxter and I tried to ease the sting of this by initiating the provision of hot lunches for employees. This will keep more food on the table at home. I should like you to set up the same sort of thing in Liverpool and Belfast."

"Such an arrangement cannot be brought about cheaply, my lord."

"I know that."

"Some will see it as charity and refuse it."

Lord Preston jingled the loose change in his pocket again. "I can do nothing about that, Longbottom. They will have to look to themselves and to God as far as that is concerned. The hot meals will be available for all employees of Danforth Shipyards and Shipping if the workers wish to enjoy them and bring some relief to their economic hardships. Have you seen what the price for a loaf of bread is now? Heaven knows the farmer and the miller feel the pinch as well as the grocer, but still it is outrageous. My people in my companies must keep their wages at home and take care of their sons and daughters."

"Very good, my lord. I see your mind is set."

"It is indeed." Lord Preston smiled as he watched Caroline walk past the parlor door with a baby wrapped in white blankets in her arms. His voice changed completely. "Ah, Longbottom, if only you were down Dover way this weekend. My son Kipp — you remember Kipp the pilot — Kipp and his lovely wife, Lord and Lady Scarborough's daughter Caroline, have had themselves a child — a girl as beautiful as a sunrise, I swear it. Well, you know how we grandfathers are. I shall send a photograph up to you."

"Pray convey my best wishes, my lord. That is marvelous news. May I ask after your granddaughter's name?"

"Cecilia. Cecila Printemp. A bit of poetry in that, eh?"

"It's wonderful, my lord. Isn't 'printemp' French for spring?"

"It is. There is a story behind that. My son's first wife, Christelle, was from France, you will recall . . ."

"Of course."

"Well, she was great friends with Caroline. Before her death, she asked if my son and Caroline might not marry and create a family. It took a while, but that is precisely what came about, and it has turned out splendidly."

"Ah."

"Cecilia has the fairest hair and the bluest eyes I've ever seen, Longbottom. The black-and-white photographs don't do her justice, really not, I say. Someone should go about looking into manufacturing color film."

"I believe there are projects afoot, my lord, even in these hard times, in Europe and in the United States. Should I look into an investment on your behalf?"

"Do that, yes! Do that. It may be shares can be had at a reasonable price at this time in the development. Certainly color photography is something I would like a hand in bringing to the world. Even if it is only to help grandfathers show off the God-given beauty of their grandchildren."

"Not a small thing, surely."

"Indeed not! Most certainly not."

My dearest Catherine,
Your father and I congratulate you and Albrecht on your announcement. A child is due to arrive! What a fine way to cheer up a dreary February of rain and clouds. How God has blessed us with grandchildren of late — Patricia Claire to Robbie and Shannon in Jerusalem in September in '28, Colm Alexander to Edward and Charlotte in January of '29, beautiful Cecilia to Kipp and Caroline just this past October, and now you tell us we are to have yet another grandchild in August 1930! A grand way to start the decade off.

I haven't been to Germany since that tour of the Rhine several summers ago when you and Albrecht wed at Hart-

457

mann Castle much to everyone's surprise and delight. It is time for another visit, especially now that you are with child. I shall certainly not wait until August. I want to see you as soon as possible. It has been far too long. Naturally I look forward to seeing Sean Albert. He's seven years old this Easter, imagine that! And I look forward to seeing dear Libby as well. It really has been ages.

Father cannot come. He and Edward are both on the Opposition benches now and challenging the Labor government for every inch of ground. Lord Buchanan baits them without mercy. What a to-do whenever Edward and that man lock horns. How long the present situation shall last is anyone's guess, but for now the two Danforths are sequestered at Westminster and sharing their flat in London. It does make me smile to think of that — as if they were a pair of bachelors.

I shall arrive at Tubingen by rail just before Easter then. Skitt will accompany me. Yes, Skitt. Old Harrison can play the butler and see to Dover Sky's needs. A maid from Ashton Park will come too.

Do you remember Margaret? I hope I shall not put you out too much, but it is past time I saw the Teutonic side of the family (as your father calls you all).

God bless. I am counting the days.

Mum

Tubingen, Germany

"Ah! There you all are!" Lady Preston smiled as brightly as she could as she took first Catherine and then Libby into her arms on the platform at the train station. "My girls! How I have missed you!"

"And we you, Mother," said Catherine, hugging her back.

"You are coming along quite nicely, I see," Elizabeth said, looking at Catherine's bulging abdomen.

Catherine rubbed her hand over her stomach. "I am. Plenty of kicks too."

"Wonderful."

"Hullo, Skitt," said Catherine. "It's been a few years, hasn't it?"

He bowed his head as he held Lady Preston's luggage. "You look well, m'lady."

"Thank you. Do you remember Jane's maid, Montgomery?"

A short slender woman with flashing black eyes dressed in a long, dark coat smiled at him. "Hullo, Skitt. How have things been at Dover Sky?"

"Never a dull moment, Lucy."

"Please. No one uses that name. I like it when people call me Montgomery. I think it sounds very distinguished."

"Montgomery it is then. This is Margaret, maid to Lady Preston."

Montgomery extended her hand to the orange-haired young woman. "How do you do, Margaret?"

Margaret took the hand. "Very well, thanks, Miss Montgomery. It's a pleasure to meet you."

Lady Preston spotted Sean standing back a ways looking a bit awkward in his dark suit and tie. "Sean Albert Hartmann! How handsome you are! Come, give your grand-mother from England a hug and a kiss, my dear!" Sean smiled and came forward, duti-fully putting his arms around Lady Preston.

"Willkommen," he greeted.

"Why, thank you. *Danke schön,* isn't it?" She hugged him again. "You are getting so tall. What are they feeding you?"

"Schnitzel." He grinned. "And beer."

"Beer? I should hope not!" She looked over his shoulder at two tall girls. "And who do we have here?"

Jane stepped up and kissed Lady Preston

on the cheek. "Hullo, Grandmother. It's so nice to see you again. I hope your journey was pleasant."

"Thank you." Lady Preston put a hand on each of Jane's shoulders and pecked her on the cheek. "Except for the waves in the Channel, everything was splendid. Who is this beautiful girl with you?"

"Grandmother Elizabeth, this is my very good friend, Eva."

"Eva. Such a lovely name."

"She is Baron von Isenburg's daughter, Grandmother."

"The baron's? Of course! Eva, your father is an old and dear friend of the family. Come, let me give you a hug." Eva dutifully let the older woman put her arms around her. Lady Preston held the girl at arm's length after the hug and gazed at her. "Eva von Isenburg. How tall and straight you are — as straight as your father. And how becoming your blonde hair and blue eyes are."

"Thank you."

"I must take you shopping. There are so many things I should like to buy the daughter of Baron von Isenburg." She glanced at Jane. "And you too. I must take the pair of you Easter shopping tomorrow or the day after. What do you say to that?"

Jane smiled. "I'd like that, Grandmother Elizabeth."

Eva nodded. "Jane and I know the best shops, Lady Preston. It would be a delight."

"Oh no, no Lady Preston, Eva. Grandmother Elizabeth will do for you as well. All right?"

Eva bowed her head. Even under the dark tone of her skin everyone could see the blush spreading over her face. "As you wish. It is an honor."

"I'm sorry, Libby."

"For what?"

"She doesn't mean anything by it. Mum is just set in her ways."

"Is that what it is? Suppose she had snubbed Sean like that? Would you still be so forgiving?"

Catherine sighed and placed her hands on Libby's shoulders from behind. "Perhaps not."

Libby bit on her thumbnail and looked down through the window in her bedroom to the street rippling with cars and trucks and wagons. "Oh, Eva, how beautiful you are! Oh, Eva, how tall and straight you are! Oh, Eva, how I'd love to take you Easter shopping. Oh, Eva, you must call me Grandmother Elizabeth."

"I know."

"The old bat."

"Hush."

"I wish she would turn around and go back to England. I'd pay for the cab to the train station out of my own pocket."

"I think she's settling in for several weeks, Lib. She loves being with the baron."

"And with your husband, the German prince."

"Shh."

"And with your son, and with the baron's daughter, and even with Montgomery, Jane's maid, for heaven's sake. But Jane? Ah, well . . . Jane, you can come shopping with Eva and I . . . if you wish, Jane."

"Bear up as best you can. Everyone else treats Jane like gold. The baron is everything Mum is not when it comes to your daughter. He's with Jane constantly. Mum is in and out of our lives like the wind from the Channel."

"Jane feels the rejection keenly."

"I know she does, and I'm sorry. But Mum's only a small part of our family tree. Just a branch, really."

Libby continued to bite at her thumbnail. "Just a grandmother."

"Perhaps we should have Mr. and Mrs.

Woodhaven over here. Extend an invitation."

Libby shrugged. "They're wonderful people, but they can't hop over to Germany on a ship in half a day like Mum can. They'd visit once, have their long ocean voyage, and disappear again for a few years. Jane is thirteen this June, Catherine. She needs a grandmother now. A real one."

Catherine rubbed her sister's back. "Perhaps the baron can have a talk with Mum."

"He wrote her once about Jane. She claimed she treated all her grandchildren the same and adored Jane. She told him I had the problem, not her."

"I see. Well, I'll pray with you, if that helps."

"Certainly, it helps. For a few minutes. Then it's back to the real world."

"Lib —"

"Honestly, Catherine, I have prayed up and down and all around. Mum's still the same year after year. She considers Eva von Isenburg more family than her own granddaughter. She bent over backwards on the marriages of her children and even felt she bent too far. Now she refuses to bend an inch regarding a granddaughter just because she has Oriental blood in her veins. And that is that. Not even God can budge her.

I've done everything but wear a hair shirt and lie on a bed of nails to get His help. If you want to pray with me, go ahead, but it's not going to change anything. I'm stuck with Lady High-and-Mighty Preston as a grandmother for my child."

Libby suddenly turned to face her sister, tears coursing down her cheeks, her blue eyes shot through with fire. "And if I want to marry Commander Terrence Fordyce, I'm going to marry him. If you don't like it you can lump it. I'm tired of going through all this turmoil alone."

Lady Preston stepped out of the hat boutique and linked an arm through Eva's. "The yellow hat with the small blue flowers was absolutely perfect for you. It brings out the colors in your eyes and your hair."

"Thank you, Grandmother Elizabeth. It is, yes, a lovely hat but so expensive. You are spending too much on me."

"Nonsense. It's Easter. We celebrate Jesus Christ's resurrection." She glanced at Jane, who was walking by her side but a few steps back as they headed down the crowded sidewalk. "Don't you agree, Jane?"

"Certainly, Grandmother."

"You mustn't fret. We've found the right dresses for Eva and the perfect hat, and we will soon do the same for you."

"It's all right. I just like being with you and Eva."

"Trust me, Jane. The right dress is in a window somewhere. If not today then tomorrow."

"Oh!" Eva tugged Lady Preston towards the shops. "Now we are seeing these young men in Tubingen. Give them plenty of room, Grandmother, please. They are always spoiling for a fight."

"Who do you mean, dear?"

"The men with the brown shirts and armbands. Don't stare at them. Just look in the shop windows." Eva looked at Jane. "Get out of their path, Jane. Come and look at this toy train running through the Alps. Hurry!"

But the six young men were already upon them, taking up half the sidewalk as they strode through the crowds. People stepped into the street to avoid them. One brownshirt spotted Jane as she moved away.

"Look at this!" he called to his friends. "Can you believe it? One of these creatures is on our sidewalk!"

The other five men glared at Jane.

"A China dog is not fit to stand where we stand!"

"What are you doing desecrating German

soil, China dog?"

"Get out of our country! Germany is for Germans only!"

"*Ja, ja,* Germany is for purebloods only! No filth bloods, no mongrel bloods!"

One of the men grabbed Jane by the arm and swung her into a lamppost. There was a loud crack as Jane hit her head. She cried out, and the same young man punched her in the stomach. "Shut up, China dog!"

Another brownshirt seized Jane's long, dark hair and pulled until in her pain she struck out at him. She screamed, and he laughed and jerked so hard blood sprang out along her hairline.

"What are you doing! What are you doing!" Lady Preston ran towards Jane and the six men, pushing them aside and slapping at their arms. "Let her go! Do you hear me? Let her go!"

They laughed and shoved Lady Preston back against the building.

One of them sneered at Eva. "Hey, little beauty, tell your mother to stay out of this or we'll use her skull for an ashtray."

Eva's eyes were dark-blue slits. "You really are pigs."

His face darkened. "Be careful or we will smack you into a wall and ruin your pretty face."

Lady Preston struck out at them with her hands and shopping bags. "Get away from Jane! Leave her alone!"

The one with his fingers twisted in Jane's hair gave her another sharp yank and Jane fell to her knees.

"Please stop! Please stop," Jane cried through her sobs.

"Police!" Lady Preston threw herself at the one who had Jane by the hair. She pummeled him with her fists, not caring when the shopping bags ripped open and the contents spilled onto the cement. "Someone help! Help!"

The young man shoved her so hard she fell. "Get out of here, you mad woman! No one is going to help you! No one helps a China dog!" He kicked Jane in the ribs. "All we do with China dogs is kill them!"

"No vermin allowed in our cities!" another one yelled.

"Purify Germany!"

Lady Preston didn't understand German, but when two other men in brown shirts and swastika armbands joined the first six and began kicking Jane, she hurled herself over Jane's body so that the toes of the black boots cracked into her sides. "Help us! Help us!" she cried in English. "Someone help us!"

None of the bystanders made a move to help. Most just walked on, heads down. Some hung back, faces set like stone as they watched. When Eva realized no one in the crowd was going to act, she ran at the eight Nazi youth, shrieking curses in German, pounding them with her fists, and tearing at their faces with her fingernails. Blood streaked their cheeks and foreheads. Flying into a rage, they slapped her as hard as they could, threw her to the sidewalk next to Lady Preston and Jane, and kicked all three women as savagely as possible.

Lady Preston wrapped her arms tightly over Jane's head as the blows rained down. "My baby, my poor baby! Oh Jesus, help us! Help us, Jesus!" She reached out a hand to Eva. "Come here, girl. Come here, my poor girl! God, help us! God, God, please help us!"

Suddenly police whistles blew and officers charged the eight Nazis. Fists smacked into heads and police clubs crunched against legs and arms. Bystanders finally jumped in and beat the Nazis with their walking sticks, umbrellas, and rolled-up newspapers. The brownshirts fled, holding their arms and putting hands to the cuts on their faces, shaking their fists and vowing revenge as they ran down the street and into an alley.

Lady Preston was weeping. "Jane, my dear. Oh, my poor child. There is so much blood. Say something to me — anything. Please open your mouth and talk. Eva, look at me. Are you going to be all right? Oh God, help us!" Lady Preston focused on the Germans standing around them. "Please help us! We need a doctor and a nurse. These are my granddaughters, and I need help getting them to a hospital. Please have pity and help us."

Albrecht and the baron stood stone-faced and stiff as they waited for the doctor to open the door and come out of the hospital room where Lady Preston, Jane, and Eva had been taken. Catherine and Libby were in the room with the patients, doctor, and nurses. The sound of a grandfather clock in the waiting room was loud. Montgomery sat on a couch against the wall. She was leaning forward, and dried streaks of tears crisscrossed her handsome face. Margaret sat next to her staring into space. Skitt stood beside the couch, his face a thundercloud. Sean sat several feet away in a chair. He stared straight ahead, barely taking in the framed picture of the Black Forest.

Finally Libby and Catherine came out of the examination room, followed by the doctor — a young man with coal-black hair and a small, coal-black moustache.

"Baron von Isenburg, the staff at the hospital cared for the women very well. I only needed to adjust a few of the bandages." The doctor nodded at Skitt and Montgomery. "I would like to speak with the family privately in my office. Will you two sit with the women and keep an eye on things? All three are heavily sedated and shouldn't wake till morning."

Montgomery shot to her feet. "Of course, doctor."

"If you spot any fresh bleeding, call a nurse right away."

"We will," promised Skitt.

The doctor led the others downstairs, Sean trailing the procession, his face the color of ashes. The doctor ushered everyone into his office. Once they were seated by the fireplace, the doctor paced and told them what the physicians at the hospital had already told them. All three had cracked ribs. In Lady Preston's case, the injuries were more serious due to her age. Time and rest would heal their wounds. Jane had unfortunately lost some of her hair because it had been pulled out by the roots.

"As for the wounds inside . . . time and prayer and the love of family must help with

471

that. I caution that you will have to be patient. Recovery could take a long time. Please avoid any of these Nazi brutes in the future even if you must cross the street. Don't go near any of their street rallies, not out of curiosity, not out of anger, not for any reason whatsoever. These brownshirts will not go away any time soon. If you must take young Jane out in public, consider having her wear a veil. You might consider getting her out of Germany. Another such attack would be extremely destructive to her spirit. Today the police and a handful of people helped out. Another day no one may help." He stared at the baron and at Albrecht. "Such is Germany in 1930."

Early the next morning, Catherine and Libby arrived to sit with the patients. They sent Skitt and Montgomery away to rest. The two sisters sat side by side facing the beds. The curtains were drawn, but a thin slit let a few rays of pale white light into the room. The beds were close together, and sometime during the night Lady Preston and Jane had linked hands. Both were sound asleep but their grip held.

Libby wiped her eyes with the back of her hand. Catherine squeezed her arm. "They will get better," Catherine whispered. "In a few weeks they'll be up and about and getting on with their lives. You'll see."

"It's not that. I don't understand the ways of the world, and I'm like Father in that I certainly don't understand the ways of God. I never thought the Nazis would be the ones who brought Mother and Jane together."

17

July–November, 1930
Hartmann Castle, the Rhine River, Germany

Dear Cornelia, my diary,
We are at Hartmann Castle on the Rhine. We left Germany for Switzerland as soon as Mum and the girls were on their feet. We stayed in Pura through May and June and then came here.

Mum is still with us, along with Skitt and Margaret, Jane's maid Montgomery, Eva and the baron, my Sean and my Albrecht. Mum wants Jane and Eva to go to England to live. This is being debated right now, though no longer with Libby present. She's at Dover Sky visiting with Terry under the watchful eyes of Holly and Harrison and Caroline and Kipp.

First things first. Mum and Jane and Eva are all right — but not really all right. Their bodies are healed for the most part and their spirits seem strong. But Mum will not return to Tubingen, and Jane is hesitant about going back as well. It's impossible to keep the German news from them. We may be on the Rhine, but we are not on the moon. We are all aware that the economy remains in rough shape and that Herr Hitler and the Nazis are taking full advantage of the bleak situation. Just the other day two boats drifted past heading south, hours apart, each with large red-and-black swastika flags flying from their sterns. Any thought that the Nazis are a passing phase is dashed. Clearly some Germans are looking to them to bring the country into a golden age of prosperity and success.

The great blessing has been how Mum and Jane have come together because of the attack by the brownshirts. No more talk of Jane being adopted or not being of English blood and all that rot. Mum says she is a Danforth through and through. Jane cries when she talks about how Mum fought to protect her, putting her body over Jane's and absorbing the blows. The two are inseparable now. It does the heart good to see. You can imagine the happiness this has brought Libby.

So now my feelings about Libby and Terry. I can truthfully say the street incident with Mum and the girls and the Nazis shook me awake. If God means Terry to be part of the family, who am I to stand in His way or, indeed, in the way of my sister's happiness? Jane could have been beaten to death, and Libby would have been left with no one. Any lingering feelings I may or may not have for Terry Fordyce simply have to be locked in a steamer trunk and stored away in the attic. My sister comes first. If she marries my navy man, God bless her, and may she have a new start on a life that is filled with love and miracles. In any case, they wouldn't be making their home in Germany — not with Terry being an officer on the *Hood.* So I shan't see him unless I go to the wedding. I find I am quite strong enough to do that now — if they get to that place — and I look forward to it. No wedding has been announced — not even an engagement — but if I were betting on the horses, I would be betting on Libby and Terry.

Finally I must mention my pregnancy. It is much easier than Sean's was, but I don't think that necessarily means it's a girl. I crave strudel, so whoever is coming into the world has a very strong sweet tooth. I intend to give birth in this lovely old castle, which has Albrecht on needles and pins. He has a doctor and midwife standing by. And, as I reminded my German prince, it is not so many years ago that most babies were born in the home, not in hospitals. We'll be fine. These castles represent some of the best of the German spirit, and I want a child crying its first cry and taking its first breath in one of them. That is my fairy tale.

Jerusalem

"How is your Arabic coming along?" the man asked.

Robbie poured his friend some sweet strong coffee. The windows in his office were shuttered against the bright Jerusalem sun. *"Jayed."*

"Glad to hear it." The slender man in the

477

white Thawb and keffiyeh lifted the small cup of coffee to his mouth. "You have made it exactly the way I like it, major. Just the right amount of sweet; just the right amount of bitter."

"It sounds like you're talking about Palestine, Azad."

The Arab laughed. "I suppose I am." He set the cup down. "Did you attend the hangings on the seventeenth of June?"

"Yes."

"Did the three men die well?"

"They died, Azad."

"Only Arabs were executed."

"Many other Arabs and Jews received life sentences. The three who were hung were convicted of multiple murders and mutilations."

Azad picked up his cup again and sipped. "It won't matter. The Palestine Arab Congress will twist it to suit themselves. So will the Zionists."

Robbie drank from his own small cup of coffee. "Let's talk about your writing. What sort of novel are you working on?"

"Two friends in Jerusalem. One Jewish, the other from an Arab family that has moved into the city from a village. The story is tragic."

"I'm just working my way through your

first novel with an Arabic–English dictionary by my side. There is a good deal of *joy* in that book."

"I wrote it fifteen years ago, Robert."

"I've read portions of it to my wife. You know how the Irish are about literature. They believe they created it. She quite likes your prose, even in my rough and ready English translation."

Azad bowed his head briefly. "Convey my thanks."

"We must have you over for dinner."

"I should like that. Please, let us do it sooner rather than later."

"Why? Is something about to happen?"

"Something is always about to happen, Robert. My fear is that eventually too many things will happen. The British will leave, Jews and Arabs will be at each others' throats, and we will have half a dozen countries in this region at war with each other. Arab Christians in one place; Arab Muslims in another; Orthodox Jews in Safed and Jerusalem; Jews who no longer believe in God in Tel Aviv and Haifa."

Robbie leaned over the table between them and poured more coffee into Azad's cup. "Where will you be?"

"England. Where else does a nonpracticing Muslim run to?" He wrapped both hands around his small cup of fresh coffee. "But the believers will come there too eventually and find me. So then I will flee to America or Canada."

"I suppose if we miss the dinner date here we can always make arrangements at my family's estate at Ashton Park."

Azad smiled. "If there is a great deal of green, I will come."

"Lancashire is as green as a *keffiyeh* full of emeralds."

"Count on me then." Azad drank from his cup. "You opened fire on Arabs during the riots. You testified against a number of them at their trials."

"Azad —"

He held up one dark hand. "It is true you arrested several Jews as well. One was attempting to burn down a mosque. Your testimony put several Jews behind bars. They should have been hung for what they did."

"Several Arabs as well as Jews had their death sentences commuted to life imprisonment."

"I do not say this to incriminate you in any way. Those on both sides who still choose to see clearly understand you are fair and evenhanded. But others only see what they do not like. You will be surprised to learn I don't come to warn you of what the Arabs might do but the Jews."

"What do you mean? No one has attacked British troops or officers. Not Jews, not Muslims."

Azad took a biscuit from the tray next to the coffee. "You spoke with members of the Hope Simpson Royal Commission this past year, didn't you?"

Robbie nodded. "I was ordered to co-operate. I spoke with the Members of Parliament who drafted the Shaw Report as well."

"Do you know Sir John Hope Simpson?"

"Yes. He's a friend of the family in England."

"I understand the report will be presented this fall. There are rumors about what is in it. The rumors have the Palestine Arab Congress singing praise to Allah and Jews gnashing their teeth. Hope Simpson will recommend Jewish immigration be restricted."

"The Shaw Report was made public in March. It said the same thing."

"So Hope Simpson will push the line that much harder."

Robbie was quiet a moment. "How reliable are your sources?"

"Very. The reason Hope Simpson will give

is that there is not enough farmland to support the influx."

"Nonsense. The Jews have planted eucalyptus trees to drain swamps. They've irrigated desert no one wanted. They've taken the worst land Arabs have sold them and raised crops."

"I grew up in this region. Many Arabs living here now did not. They are immigrants just as a large number of the Jews are immigrants. From what I understand the report does not go into great detail about Arab immigration." Azad spread his hands. "Hope Simpson had to give some rationale. That is what he chose — insufficient arable land. If true, Zionists will never accept such a proposal. Should your prime minister, Ramsay MacDonald, implement it, British officers will be targeted. So I ask you to be careful, my friend. Vary your driving routes. See there is security keeping an eye on your home. Perhaps MacDonald's hold on power is too weak for him to act on the report. Or perhaps he will find the support he needs close at hand."

"Or perhaps your sources are inaccurate. Perhaps Hope Simpson will not recommend a hard line on Jewish immigration. Perhaps Westminster will pay no attention to either Shaw or him." Robbie smiled. "Or perhaps you exaggerate the threat to the British army and myself."

Azad sipped at his bittersweet coffee. "Perhaps."

Ashton Park

At the dinner table, Lord Preston was cutting into his mutton when Ben cleared his throat. The older man glanced up and cocked a white eyebrow as he chewed and swallowed. "Mmm? What's on your mind?"

"I was wondering if you were heading to Dover Sky for the summer, sir? Or are you remaining here at Ashton Park?"

"I will go down. But first I'm waiting to hear from Lady Preston on the birth of Catherine's child. Once I have that cable in my hand, I'm on my way to Germany and the Hartmann Castle on the Rhine. I have never seen it, and I very much want to take Catherine's son or daughter into my arms among those crenellations and merlons. I must say I am looking forward to a trip abroad."

"Will Elizabeth be returning with you?"

"She'd better be!" Lady Grace darted a glance at Ben. She held her soup spoon firmly. "She's been in that dreadful country since Easter and all because of a Chinese girl!"

"Thank you, Mother." Lord Preston wiped the corners of his mouth with a white napkin as Tavy hovered over him with a silver coffeepot. "The Chinese girl is our granddaughter, and Catherine is happily married to a German professor of theology."

"You're making all that up." Lady Grace's attention returned to her soup, eying it suspiciously. "Tavy, did you exchange my soup bowl for this one?"

"No, ma'arm."

"Because I had more soup than this."

"Shall I ladle a bit more into your bowl, Lady Grace?"

"No, thank you, Tavy. You will not. Having my own soup returned to me will be sufficient, if you please."

"Very good." Tavy brought a fresh bowl of soup curling with steam from his cart and placed it before her. He removed the bowl. "There you are, m'lady."

"Ah." She half-glared and half-smiled at him. "Now that wasn't so hard, was it?"

"What's that?" Sir Arthur looked up from his plate on the other side of the table.

"Someone took my soup. I have it back now. All's well."

"Grace, it's the same soup, year in, year out. What bowl it's in hardly matters."

"It matters a great deal who has been sipping at my soup. I want my own bowl, untouched, unspooned, thank you."

Sir Arthur sawed away with knife and fork. "The cook tests the soup by putting it to her lips. That's what you're eating, and you've been eating it since 1909."

Lord Preston laughed. "Ben, you're going to get lost in the shuffle. Speak up, my boy, before there's another incident with soup or dumplings or mutton."

"The mutton is fine." Lady Grace's voice was rimmed with frost. "I'll trouble you to mind your manners and keep to your own plate, William."

"Sir!" Ben blurted. "William, I have intentions of going into the ministry. I've talked it over with Victoria, and she's in agreement."

"Ministry? What?" Lord Preston put down his fork. "Ben Whitecross an Anglican priest like Jeremy here?"

"Not exactly Anglican —"

"Please, my boy, enough. I much prefer to hear 'father' from you."

"Yes, of course. It's just that this is something of an announcement I want to make."

"Not Anglican? What then? Baptist? Presbyterian?"

"Methodist, Father."

Both of Lord Preston's eyebrows shot

upward. "Do you say so? You mean like John and Charles Wesley? Like circuit riders on the American frontier? Count von Zinzendorf and the Moravians?"

"Yes, sir."

"What's this about, eh?" Sir Arthur looked back and forth between Ben, William, and Jeremy, who was sitting at the table next to Emma. "Not another air race?"

"The Wesleyans, Sir Arthur," Jeremy said, still working on his soup. "Ben is thinking of being ordained with them after a period of training."

Sir Arthur narrowed his eyes at Jeremy from behind his glasses. "And what will you do, sir?"

"I?"

"Are you thinking of becoming a Wesleyan as well? Is this going to be a family thing?"

"Not at all. I'm content in the Church of England."

" 'Amazing Grace' is a fine hymn, very fine."

"Yes, well, that's by John Newton, Sir Arthur, an Anglican."

"O for a Thousand Tongues to Sing; Love Divine, All Loves Excelling; Christ the Lord Is Risen Today."

"Quite right, Sir Arthur." Jeremy smiled and laid down his soup spoon.

Tavy whisked spoon and empty bowl away.

Jeremy continued. "We use those hymns by Charles Wesley all the time at our church in London."

Emma folded her hands under her chin. "I adore 'Hark! The Herald Angels Sing.' Charles Wesley wrote those words too."

Lord Preston nodded at Emma and then looked at Ben. "What about the airline, young man?"

"Kipp is buying me out for my share of the partnership. With Michael and I both gone from the picture, he'll become the head of the business. I expect he will hire more managers."

"But you've always loved flying."

"Part of the plan is that I will keep one of our old SPAD S.XXs. It's quite lovely to fly, Father."

Lord Preston smiled at the use of the term. "Thank you. And you feel a call to preach the gospel?"

"Yes, sir."

"You wish for a Methodist church or are you content to be a lay preacher?"

"I should like a church to pastor. Victoria shares with me a certain enthusiasm for missionary work in Africa, so perhaps we'll wind up there in due course."

"Africa? The Dark Continent?"

"There have been Methodist missionaries going there for generations."

Victoria put a hand on Ben's. "I was shocked when he first raised the subject with me, Father. But when I thought back, I did remember he used to talk about the Methodist Church before he left for the war. So it's been in his head and heart even before flying."

"Has it?" Lord Preston caught Ramsay's eye. "What does the eight-year-old think, hmm?"

Ramsay's somber face suddenly brightened with his smile. "I should like to see lions and gazelle and wildebeest, Grandfather William."

"Ha! And what about Timothy?"

The five-year-old with his mother's auburn hair and green eyes didn't smile at all. He looked at his grandfather with a serious face. "I should like to see giraffes and elephants and God in Africa."

Lord Preston chuckled. "And so you shall. Undoubtedly, so you shall." He turned back to Ben. "Sounds like the Lord's hand is on your entire family, Ben." He went back to his mutton. "Capital."

"Shall I reheat that in the oven, m'lord?" Tavy asked, now standing at William's shoulder. "Or bring you a fresh portion piping hot?"

"Hmm? Not at all. I don't mind cold mutton." He glanced up from his plate a moment. "Well, well, Jeremy, did Ben bring you up here to play the role of *HMS Rodney* to Ben's *HMS Hood*? Are you the big guns meant to ensure the First Sea Lord's opinion is properly swayed to support his endeavor?"

Jeremy sipped his water. "Ben and I have talked about this, naturally. He sought out my advice as a clergyman. Ben is a fine man, but I wondered if he truly was, um, *cut out* to be a man of the cloth. Just like most in the family, I saw him as a dashing pilot and, after the accident, as a man who simply wouldn't quit. I ought to have expected God had his hand on Ben's life for him to come so far and surmount so many obstacles."

"So the two of you have discussed this?" asked Lord Preston.

"Yes."

"And prayed together?"

"Indeed we have."

"So you are in support of his desire to train as a Methodist minister? You see the Divine spark in him?"

"I do. I most certainly do. I am sure God is in this, Father."

Lord Preston pushed himself back from

the table and walked around the table to Ben.

Ben slowly got to his feet.

Lord Preston wrapped his arms around the younger man. "My boy, I praise God. I am overjoyed! Elizabeth will be as filled with rejoicing as I am. Have you said anything to the servants here at Ashton Park? Anything at all to our good Baptist, Mrs. Longstaff?"

"No, sir."

"Well, that is something we must announce when they bring us our cobbler and ice cream, eh? But first let me offer up a prayer for you. This is a great thing — an extraordinary moment. We must go to God with it and thank Him. Don't you agree, Reverend Whitecross?"

"Why, of course, sir. But I'm no reverend yet. Far from it."

Lord Preston kept his arm around Ben's shoulders. "Man looks on the outward appearance, but God looks on the heart."

Hartmann Castle, the Rhine River, Germany
The mist rose up like a grey ship from the Rhine and moored itself over Hartmann Castle. Lord Preston walked around an inner courtyard with his new granddaughter in his arms, his daughter Catherine at his side in a cloak and hood. They spoke quietly

with each other and laughed just as quietly. After half an hour, the sun had still not won out over the haze. While he conversed with his daughter, Lord Preston found his mind drifting away to Danforth Castle and the age of chivalry that had touched both England and Germany with a strong but gracious hand. He looked at the babe in his arms, then he kissed the sleeping child's forehead and murmured, "Angelika."

"Ah. There you two are."

Catherine put a finger to her lips as her husband approached. "Shh. She's sleeping."

He smiled and looked at the baby in Lord Preston's arms. "That's because she was up all night singing."

"Oh . . ." Catherine stifled a laugh. "Is that what you call her screeches?"

"I have heard far worse from choirs, believe me." He turned to Lord Preston. "Lord Preston, after much discussion, Jane and Eva have decided to weather the storm for now by returning to Tubingen. Next week Jane will meet with her tutor and Eva will return to school. It's true the Nazi presence is not great there, and they feel the incident at Easter was one that will not be repeated."

Lord Preston's features grew rigid. "I pray not."

"Libby will remain in Germany with her daughter. In addition, Lady Preston wishes to linger till the New Year, another month or so, if you have no objections. She is welcome to remain with us as long as she likes."

"Elizabeth must have found something wonderful in the German air, to want to stay that long. Well, I have Ben and Victoria and their children at Ashton Park, so I shall not get too lonely. I suppose you will have a grand celebration at Christmas, Albrecht?"

"With our new baby girl? Of course! You can count on us having an especially large tree in the great hall."

"You mean to enjoy the holiday here?"

"Yes. The area is magical, especially if we are blessed with a fall of snow."

"I should like to see that some year." Lord Preston gently handed the infant to Catherine. "What news of the election?"

Albrecht's face lost its new-father glow. "I just received the paper. With the stock market crash last year and the economic downturn, the Nazi Party and its goblins, including Goebbels and Himmler, have picked up momentum. I feared this. They have one hundred and seven seats now. A day ago they only had fourteen. This makes them the second largest party in Germany."

"I'm very sorry to hear it. You still think Jane will be safe?"

"I would not take her to Munich or Berlin. It's my hope that if financial conditions improve over the next twenty-four months we will see Herr Hitler and his cronies fade into oblivion once again."

"Hmm." Lord Preston gazed up at rooks that had flown into the courtyard and found several window ledges to perch on. "I hope you're right. The Labor government of Ramsay MacDonald will be forced to make unpopular cost-cutting measures this Parliament. And it seems clear from what I've read in the papers from New York and Toronto that the United States and Canada are heading into a serious depression."

Albrecht put his hands behind his back. "My sense of it is that the German people mistrust Hitler and his brownshirts. He may have won more seats this election, and he may be straining at the leash to gain the presidency or chancellorship of the nation, but he will not get either. People see what happens in the streets and at political rallies when his Nazis are present. They represent absolutely the worst side of the German character."

Lord Preston nodded and put a hand on his son-in-law's shoulder. "Nor can Britain ever let down its guard. Bullies and fascists lurk in the corners of every democracy. Only good men like yourself keep them at bay." He suddenly smiled. "You should write another book."

"That very thing was raised by the Brotherhood last week. Frankly I didn't think they would go forward on the idea, but Bruno Dressler rang this morning and said they very much want me to begin working on a first draft for publication in the spring or summer."

Catherine laughed as she cradled Angelika. "That's marvelous, Albrecht!"

"Indeed." Lord Preston shook Albrecht's hand. "What will be the theme? How shall it differ from your other book released to offset Hitler's propaganda?"

"They wish me to challenge Hitler directly, as if he and I were engaged in a public debate at the university. Toe to toe and blow for blow, so to speak."

"That sounds fairly aggressive and combative, but perhaps that's the very approach needed. Have they suggested a title for this work?"

Albrecht nodded. "They wish to play off the success of Hitler's title and raise sales as well as eyebrows. His, as you know, is called *Mein Kampf*, which means 'My Struggle.'

Mine is to be entitled *Mein Krieg,* which means 'My War.' "

Parliament, Westminster, London
"Danforth. Fancy meeting you here. You're so far away on the benches in the House I thought you'd fallen into the Thames." Buchanan strode across the empty foyer in the Parliament buildings, silver-headed walking stick in hand. "Waiting for Daddy, are you?"

Edward kept his hands clasped behind his back. "Stanley Baldwin, actually."

"Baldwin? Old Has-Been Baldwin? You've hitched your cart to the wrong star, Danforth."

"Do you think so? Your minority government will fall soon enough, Buchanan. And when it does, Baldwin will be first man in the kingdom once again."

Buchanan lifted his thick eyebrows and curled his lip. "The Conservative Party is finished as a political force. So are you and your father. What will you do when Dover finally tosses you out on your ear? Sell pencils to the reporters on Fleet Street?"

Edward turned his back on Buchanan and gazed through a window at the November rain coming down in long, gray streaks. "Run for Ayrshire South, of course. That would be the easiest plum for me to pick from the Labor tree. They have a slacker as MP, no mistake about that."

"Insult for insult, blow for blow, eh?" Buchanan's voice was low. Edward half expected to get cracked over the head by the walking stick. "I'm far from finished with your lot, Danforth. Everything continues to fall into place. Hold fast to what you have. Soon enough you'll not even have that left."

Edward grunted. "You won't live to see the day, Buchanan." He turned his head slowly and their eyes locked. "Believe me, you won't."

December, 1930–May, 1931
Christmas Eve, Tubingen, Germany

Stille Nacht, heilige Nacht!
Alles schläft, einsam wacht
Nur das traute, hochheilige Paar.
Holder Knabe im lockigen Haar,
Schlaf in himmlischer Ruh,
Schlaf in himmlischer Ruh.

Stille Nacht, heilige Nacht!
Gottes Sohn, o wie lacht
Lieb aus deinem göttlichen Mund,
Da uns schlägt die rettende Stund,
Christ, in deiner Geburt,
Christ, in deiner Geburt.

The baron bent and poked the logs in the fireplace. "Sean, will you get me some more wood from the basket?"
"Ja, Opa."

"Now we must have a song from Britain, Elizabeth . . . and then America, Jane. But Elizabeth first; she must begin it."

"Me?" Lady Preston laughed, her fingers fluttering to her mouth and face. "Don't be ridiculous, Gerard. Catherine and Libby can do that far better than I can."

"They will have their turns."

"Oh heavens."

"Mum," Catherine said as she rocked Angelika in her lap, "you have a lovely voice." Angelika was mesmerized by the firelight.

"Victoria has the voice, my dear."

"Where do you think she got it from?"

Libby jumped in. "Oh come, Mother. You'd think he'd asked you to sing *The Messiah.*" Libby got up from her chair and plopped down next to Lady Preston on the couch. "I'll help you. I have the perfect song. I'll start but you have to come in."

"Of course, my dear."

"You all have to come in, all right?" She raised her eyebrows at Jane and Eva. "All right?"

Jane smiled. "Yes, Mum. We'll raise the roof."

"*Ach,* don't do that." Albrecht was mixing hot apple cider in a pot by the fire. "It's snowing."

Libby started singing an old French carol, and soon the other women joined in:

The holly and the ivy,
Now both are full well grown.
Of all the trees that are in the wood,
The holly bears the crown

Oh, the rising of the sun,
The running of the deer.
The playing of the merry organ,
Sweet singing in the choir.

The holly bears a blossom
As white as lily flower;
And Mary bore sweet Jesus Christ
To be our sweet Savior.

Oh, the rising of the sun,
The running of the deer.
The playing of the merry organ,
Sweet singing in the choir.

The holly bears a berry
As red as any blood;
And Mary bore sweet Jesus Christ
To do poor sinners good.

Oh, the rising of the sun,
The running of the deer.

The playing of the merry organ,
Sweet singing in the choir.

The holly bears a prickle
As sharp as any thorn;
And Mary bore sweet Jesus Christ
On Christmas Day in the morn.

Oh, the rising of the sun,
The running of the deer.
The playing of the merry organ,
Sweet singing in the choir.

The holly bears a bark
As bitter as any gall;
And Mary bore sweet Jesus Christ
For to redeem us all.

Oh, the rising of the sun,
The running of the deer.
The playing of the merry organ,
Sweet singing in the choir.

The holly and the ivy,
When they are both full grown,
Of all the trees that are in the wood,
The holly bears the crown.

The rising of the sun
And the running of the deer,

The playing of the merry organ,
Sweet singing in the choir.

Montgomery and Skitt stood just outside the alcove in the great hall where the family had settled in with cider to sing carols and open presents.

"Well, they won't be needing us for a while," Montgomery said in a low voice. "Come on, I want to show you something."

"What if they ask for something?"

"They have German staff who are always at their beck and call and come at a quick march as if trying to show us up." She seized his hand in her strong grip. "Come on!" She led him down a stone hall that still held centuries-old iron brackets for torches. Dropping his hand, she used both of hers to tug on the handle of a huge oak door. "They made 'em this thick to hold up against arrows and axe blows and fire."

"Do you need a hand?" Skitt put his hands next to hers and pulled. "Oh! It's stuck."

"It'll open. It always does."

"How many times have you been here?"

"Enough." She glanced at his face. "And all alone, don't worry."

"I wasn't worried."

The door finally gave with a long moan. A

gust of cold air spinning with snowflakes blew over them.

"What does this open to?" asked Skitt.

"A turret." Montgomery went outside, hugging herself with her arms. "Brrr. It's nippy but the view is worth it."

"What you can see of it. It's dark as pitch."

"The lights of the village are far below. Look."

Skitt had his hands in his pockets and his shoulders drawn up around his ears. "Lovely," he said.

"Don't tease."

"I'm not. I like the sheer drop of thousands of feet. You think I'd land near the sweets shop?"

She punched him in the arm. "Running off on me?"

"Never."

She opened her fist and ran her hand up and down the sleeve of his butler jacket. "I shall miss you, Skitt. I feel I got to know you better here than I did in England. Especially after we nursed Lady Preston and young Jane together."

He smiled. His eyes were used to the darkness now so he could make out her petite features clearly. He brushed a cluster of snowflakes off her maid's cap.

"It strikes me that you haven't seen much

snow, have you?" she asked, still moving her fingers up and down his arm.

"Not much, no. I did see a snowfall once when I was a boy. It was in the Welsh mountains."

"It snows all winter in New York State."

"Is that still home?" He brushed at her cap again. His fingers strayed and touched the dark hair pinned up underneath.

"Home's wherever Jane winds up. Dover Sky. The Rhine. Perhaps Ashton Park one day."

Now his fingers touched her cheek. "It's snowing all over you."

"Have you ever caught snowflakes on the tip of your tongue, Skitt?" she asked.

"I confess I haven't."

"You should try."

"I'd rather try this." He kept his hand on her face as he bent slightly and kissed her softly on the lips.

"Oh how I shall miss you when Lady Elizabeth returns to England, my lovely Skitt. I pray Libby, Jane, and I will visit England this summer. I'll do everything in my power to convince her she ought to marry Commander Terry and move us back across the Channel lock, stock, and barrel."

"That's a good plan. You could stir up the

Nazis as well. That might help your plans along."

"Those gangsters! I prefer a wedding between Commander Fordyce and Lady Libby be the reason for our move."

He put his lips against her neck and shoulder. "I would prefer a wedding too."

"Now, my dear Jane, I have a special gift for you."

"But it's not Christmas morning yet, Grandmother Elizabeth."

"We won't tell the others, will we? Jesus was born on Christmas Eve, wasn't He? So that is a wonderful time to give someone a gift."

"Unless He was born at two or three. Then that really would be Christmas morning."

Lady Preston laughed. "You and your wit. Please shut the door, Jane."

Jane got up from the bed where she'd been sitting next to her grandmother. The air current caused the candle that lit the room to flutter. The girl closed the door, and when she turned to come back Lady Preston was holding up a necklace of rubies that flamed brilliantly in the candlelight. Jane stopped and put a hand to her mouth.

"Merry Christmas, my dear!"

"Grandmother! Not for me?"

"Yes, for you. And this as well." She patted a hand on a red dress folded up by her side. "Both came from the Far East long ago. You know what the Far East is known as today?"

"China and Japan and —"

"The necklace and dress are from China and fairly traded, I must say, by my great-great-grandfather Welcome Cornwall. He was a great seaman, Jane. Twice he circumnavigated the globe. He was an extraordinary man. We have one of his ship logs and three of his diaries."

"I should like to read those."

"I thought you might, and so you shall when you come to Ashton Park, which I pray will be soon." She set down the necklace and lifted up the dress. It gleamed in the candlelight. "Pure silk. Come. You must try it on. I want you to wear it with the necklace Christmas morning in the great hall."

"I can't, Grandmother Elizabeth."

"Nonsense! Of course you can. You will be fourteen this coming year, but you already look like a lady. You are so tall and perfectly proportioned. You will turn all the men's heads when you come of age. Why, you already do. Don't think I haven't noticed."

Jane could feel a blush rising from her neck. "Grandmother, that's not true."

"Of course it's true. You will soon grow into the kind of exceptional beauty men paid a king's ransom to woo and wed in the days of the great dynasties. Emperors would have courted you with pearls and gold. Now, alas, you shall have to settle for Germans and Englishmen. Hopefully a dashing one!"

Jane giggled. "You're such a storyteller. I should like very much to wed a naval officer like Terry Fordyce."

"I don't blame you one bit. He cuts a fine figure. Hopefully your mother will grasp the fact and make him her husband — the sooner the better."

"I think he's very close to asking for her hand."

Lady Preston's mouth formed a perfect circle. "Oh? And what will your mother say?"

"Yes, yes, a thousand times yes."

"Are you sure?"

"I am."

"Well, praise God if we have a wedding to look forward to. But now here we are prattling on, and it's past midnight. Come, off with the old and on with the new." She shook the dress so that it seemingly burst into fire in the flickering light.

Jane quickly removed her outer clothing and slipped on the sleeveless dress. It held to her figure perfectly.

"Ah, my beautiful child." Lady Preston gazed at Jane and sighed. "With your long, dark hair and lovely legs and face — well, there are no words adequate for your beauty. You're stunning, my dear. What a grand way to celebrate the birth of our Savior. You look royal! I wish your grandfather were here to see you." She stood up and placed the necklace of rubies around Jane's neck. "I saved this for my first granddaughter, and that's you, I'm happy to say. It will ride on your throat just above the neckline of the dress. Oh, you look like a queen! These are from Burma, or so the good Captain Cornwall recorded in his diary. The rubies are of the finest hues of scarlet and vermilion." She kissed Jane on the cheek. "Walk about the room and let me look at you."

Crimson and gold rippled up and down the silk as Jane moved about the room shyly. Lady Preston clasped her hands together at her chest and nodded her head. Finally Jane stopped in front of a large, freestanding, oval mirror rimmed in dark wood.

"I — I scarcely recognize myself." Jane's eyes were dark and wide. "I look so much older."

"You do. You do indeed. And tomorrow you shall have black high-heeled shoes, and we shall arrange your hair by sweeping it back and add a red poinsettia. I purchased long red gloves for you to wear. We shall add some eye shadow and mascara too. You must meet me here at seven, and we'll make you the toast of Hartmann Castle!"

Jane turned from the mirror. "I am very happy, Grandmother Elizabeth. You should not love me so much."

"Yes, dear, I should. This much and more, so much more."

DEAR LIBBY
YOU WILL NOT WANT TO HEAR
HOW WARM A MARCH DAY IS ON
THE SOUTH COAST OF SPAIN SO
I SHALL NOT TELL YOU. INSTEAD
I WILL SAY HOW MUCH I ADORE
YOU AND THAT I LOVE YOU WITH
ALL MY HEART. AND SOMETHING
ELSE. YES I KNOW THIS OUGHT
TO BE DONE IN PERSON AT A
FINE RESTAURANT OR BY A
LOVELY SEASCAPE BUT I CAN'T
WAIT FOR MAY! I AM LOOKING

508

AT WHITE CLOUDS OVER A BLUE SEA WITH WHITE BIRDS IN A BLUE SKY AND I AM THINKING OF THE ASTONISHING BEAUTY OF THOSE BLUE EYES GOD GIFTED YOU WITH — AND GIFTED ME WITH FOR I AM FREE TO GAZE INTO THEM AS A SAILOR GAZES INTO THE VAST IMPENETRABLE DEEP.

MY DEAR LIBBY I WANT TO MARRY YOU. I WANT YOU TO BE MY BRIDE. I WANT TO LIVE WITH YOU FOREVER AND A DAY. YES I AM ASKING YOU BY TELEGRAM! I MEAN IT WITH ALL MY HEART. PERHAPS BY ASKING YOU IN MARCH IT MEANS WE CAN BE MARRIED THIS SUMMER AS SOON AS I STEP OFF THE SHIP IN GOOD OLD ENGLAND. LIBBY I LOVE YOU! I LOVE YOU! PLEASE SAY YES YES YES!

YOUR GALAHAD
TERRY

GALAHAD
YOU ARE ABSOLUTELY MAD BUT YOU'RE RIGHT. I'D LOVE TO

MARRY YOU AS SOON AS YOU SET FOOT ON SHORE. WE CAN EVEN BE WED ON THE GANGWAY OR ON THE DECK IF YOU'D LIKE. OR RIGHT IN THE WATER WITH WAVES BURSTING OVER OUR HEADS. I DON'T CARE. THE IM-PORTANT THING IS TO DO IT. I SHALL MAKE ALL ARRANGE-MENTS. SEE YOU IN MAY MY LOVE.

YOUR LIBBY

OH AND THE ANSWER IS YES YES YES!

Plymouth and Devonport, Southern England
The *Hood* docked in May, and Libby was there to welcome Terry home. She waited by the car with Skitt and Jane for two hours as they watched sailors scramble over the huge deck securing the battleship. Finally Terry walked down the gangway in uniform, a sailor behind him toting a seabag over his shoulder.

"I've missed you!" Libby cried as she threw her arms around him. "Look at your tan! I'm jealous."

"You look wonderful. A woman like you doesn't need a tan. Besides, ginger-haired

510

women burn and peel."

"Not this ginger. Our honeymoon is still on, isn't it?"

He laughed and stroked her cheek. "As long as the wedding's still on."

"Oh, it's on all right. I can hardly wait to get away with you to the Mediterranean and take in some very hot sun."

"Mum!" Jane was at Libby's side, pulling on her dress. "Are you the only one who gets hugged?"

Terry wrapped his arms around the young woman dressed in a red coat and hat. "How tall you are now. And how lovely you are. You must grow a foot every month."

"I will be fourteen next month. I have to keep growing to keep ahead of the Sweet boys. They're holy terrors."

"Are you still one up on them?"

"I am." Jane smiled up into Terry's face. "You're almost as dark as me."

"But not as pretty."

"Thank goodness. I want a father, not a flower." She dropped her eyes and played with the brass buttons on his uniform. "I know the wedding's not till next week, but can I — may I — call you Dad now?"

He put his fingers under her chin and tilted her head. "I'd love that."

"Really?"

"Yes, really. Let's start right away. How is my daughter today?"

Jane's smile opened up her face. "She's fine, Dad. She's very fine indeed."

They hugged again. Looking on and thinking of Michael and then the death of Jane's birth father, Libby's eyes glittered with tears she brushed at with her fingers. *Thank You, God. Thank You for this miracle. Thank You, my God.*

Dover Sky

Lord Preston put his glasses on his nose to read the list in his hand. "The photographer arrives the morning of the wedding. We must get the family pictures taken after the ceremony. And special baby pictures — Catherine with Angelika and Shannon with Patricia Claire."

Lady Preston was at a table nearby with a pen and a pad of paper. "For heaven's sakes, William. Patricia is hardly a baby — why, she's almost three."

"How big can she have gotten?"

"You'll find out soon enough. Aren't you and Harrison picking them up at the pier in Dover?"

"Yes, yes, after lunch." He glanced over his glasses at his wife. "What are you jotting down?"

"These are meal suggestions for Mrs. Longstaff. She and Norah have matters quite in hand, but I didn't see Harrison's Cock-a-Leakier soup here or your Welsh rarebit on the menu."

"But the pheasant — we have the pheasant? There are hundreds of guests coming."

"We have dozens of pheasants. Not to worry, Dear. Stick with your own list, please."

Lord Preston removed his glasses and placed them in his coat pocket. "I must see how my aviation room is coming along. Ben and Victoria are flying down with the children before supper."

Lady Preston scribbled on her pad. "Oh you and your aviation room. By all means, look in on it, William. There's nothing more pressing than that."

The day of the wedding began with a May shower, but by noon the sun was shining. The ceremony was held down near the pond, the swans keeping their distance and paddling about in the middle of the water. Kipp and Caroline's daughter, Cecilia, who would be two in October, and Robbie and Shannon's daughter, Patricia, who would turn three in September and was quite noticeably not an infant anymore, were the flower girls. Jeremy and Emma's twins, Peter and James, both thirteen, their younger brother, Billy, ten, along with Caroline's son, Charles, aged nine, Kipp's son, Matthew, aged eight, Ben and Victoria's son, Ramsay, also eight, and Edward and Charlotte's Owen, who was eight too, were chosen to usher the lords and ladies and other guests to the chairs arranged neatly on the lawn by Harrison and Skitt. Jane held the rings on a red-velvet cushion by the outdoor altar where Reverend Jeremy Sweet, St. Andrew's Cross, Church of England, London, assisted by Ben Whitecross, Methodist Chapel, Lime Street, Liverpool, brought Commander Terrence Fordyce and Libby Danforth Woodhaven into holy wedlock before God and people on the late Queen Victoria's birthday.

After the ceremony, the photographer was trying to arrange the large Danforth family on the grass for family photographs but the children kept bolting and chasing each other across the large expanse and the adults kept edging towards tables groaning with soups, meats, and greens placed amid crystal bowls filled with crimson punch.

"Now Ben and Kipp, you are the fliers in the family. You see what we've done with this room here? There are so many sea paintings at Dover Sky, I decided it was time to balance out the equation."

Oil paintings and watercolors of aircraft covered the walls. In some, the planes were lined up on the ground or warming up for takeoff. In most, they were in the air darting through clouds, flying over the white-caps of the Channel, or navigating above the patchwork quilt of the Kent countryside. Four or five were paintings of war with Sopwith Camels pitted against Fokker triplanes, SPADs looping and rolling in aerial combat with Fokker D.VIIs. Kipp examined one of a Sopwith Camel taking on the red triplane of Baron von Richthofen.

"Is this supposed to be the Red Baron and Roy Brown going at it on April 21, 1918?" he asked as he bent down to peer at the brass plate on the frame. "Well, he's got the planes and the weather right, but from what I understand, the two never went at it head-on. The baron was after one of Brown's chums, so Brown dived on him from behind and cut loose with his guns. The baron carried on for a few more miles and crashed behind our lines stone dead." Kipp straightened and grinned as he glanced about the room. "But it's marvelous, Dad! Really quite something. I'll make this my official headquarters when I'm home for the week-end. I'll do all my airline paperwork in here." He walked behind an oxblood leather armchair and tapped a watercolor that showed Sopwith Camels with the morning damp rising off their wings like steam. "That brings back memories, eh, Ben?"

Ben nodded. "It does. Whoever painted that one had to have been there."

"He was." Lord Preston stood with his hands behind his back. "Whenever possible I employed veterans who had an eye for detail and knew pilots' movements and moments."

"It's brilliant." Ben was taken by the portrait of an officer standing by an SE5a. "I love this one. Is that Ball?"

Lord Preston smiled. "I'm so glad you're pleased. It is Ball, yes."

Kipp dropped into the oxblood armchair. "A welcome respite from that madness on the lawn. I wish someone would fetch us some cold drinks."

Lord Preston pressed a buzzer by the door. "There's bound to be someone in-doors. Let's see who shows up."

"You'll have to do something for Robbie now, Dad," Kipp said. "You do know that, don't you?"

"What do you mean?"

"The great hall has sea paintings for the likes of Edward and Terry. Now Ben and I have this aviation room. But what about Robbie? He's British Army. What are you going to do about that?"

"Hmm, it will take some time to plan, won't it? You're right, of course. Absolutely right. There should be a room with its feet firmly planted on the ground."

"How long's Robbie's furlough?"

"Six months."

"Then he has plenty of time to help you with it. Waterloo, Agincourt, Crecy, the Somme — a proper mud-and-blood room."

Lord Preston hummed as he glanced about at the airplane paintings. "Do you know, I was thinking, we don't quite have it right any longer. With our song 'Rule Britannia,' I mean. 'Rule Britannia, Britannia rule the waves, Britons never shall be slaves.' There is something else we must rule if we're to keep our heads above water, so to speak. The air — am I right?"

Ben slowly lowered himself into an armchair like Kipp was sitting in. "I think you have it, sir. Enemies don't require boats to cross the Channel now."

"Exactly, so I thought of this." He hummed again. "Tell me what you think."

Rule Britannia, we rule the skies and
waves.
Britons never, never, never shall be slaves.

Lord Preston laughed. "My voice is not what it used to be."

Kipp and Ben clapped.

"That's excellent, Dad," said Kipp. "It really works."

Ben was grinning. "Well done."

"Do you think so?" Lord Preston smiled and admired an oil painting of a Nieuport 17 dropping into a dive. "Now if we can only convince the BBC to give it some airtime, hmm?"

"Cath?"

Catherine glanced up from the cradle Angelika was sleeping in. "Cheers, Lib. I'm just settling her down for a nap, otherwise she'll be a German–English bear this evening. How are you holding up with all this madness? Where's the groom?"

"Terry's off with Jane and Eva and the boys. They're on a march around the whole estate."

"That will take forever and a day. No worries though. It'll all be over tonight, and Terry can whisk you away to the Med."

"He can't actually. He's due to sail tomorrow with Dad and a crew of eight or ten."

"Eight or ten? My goodness! Does he fancy he's back on the *Hood*?"

Libby smiled down at nine-month-old Angelika as she slept, hands curled in a pink blanket. "He finds he can't say no to Jane or the older boys, including Sean. Your son was a bit put out not having been included in the ceremony —"

"Oh Sean's fine. He wouldn't have liked ushering old ladies to their seats anyway."

"Well, be that as it may, he's skipper of the *Pluck* at the crack of dawn tomorrow. He gets the wheel for two hours."

"He doesn't!"

Libby sat on the new swing that had been placed on the front porch. "They'll make a sailor out of your boy yet."

"His father was around the Belfast docks all his life, so I suppose Sean comes by it honestly." Catherine sat next to her sister and made the swing glide back and forth. "Are you never going to have a honeymoon? Marches and sailing and fireworks tonight and that's it?"

"Terry promises me the moon by the weekend."

"The moon by the weekend? Any woman should find the patience in her to wait for that, Lib. Imagine! The moon, you lucky girl." She moved the swing faster. "I want you to know I'm happy for you. No cheek, I really am. I'm madly in love with Albrecht, and that's where my heart wants to stay. There's no point in denying a certain fondness for our dashing naval officer, so I'm glad you've brought him into the family. It's so nice to have him on board. He'll do us all good. Terry always brings out the best in everyone, especially the children." Catherine's eyes glimmered. She smiled and gave Libby a quick kiss on the cheek. "You and I have both lost husbands. But I looked at the crew today with the children racing over the fields, and I feel I've recovered at long last. We're one happy family. I truly feel that. God bless you, sis. God bless your marriage."

Libby leaned her head against Catherine and put her arms around her.

Skitt closed the door and made a show of dusting his hands off. "That's that then. Lord Preston said I am free to turn in. He intends to be up with the baron quite a bit longer. I've given the old German a bottle of brandy and a decent supply of cigars. For all I know, they'll be at it all night."

Montgomery took his hand. "Good heavens. What on earth are they going on about?"

"German politics."

"Ah."

"We both know what a nasty topic that can be."

Montgomery nodded. "We do. But it brought us together, didn't it? I remember how I loved you as you tended Jane and Lady Preston with me day after day. Not many men can do that, you know — be strong and be sweet."

"Is that what I am?"

She pressed his hand to her lips. "Yes."

"Fancy a walk to the pond?"

"I'd love that."

They headed out the door and down over the lawn under the May stars, holding hands. Skitt was in his black-and-white butler uniform, and Montgomery was in her black-and-white maid outfit and cap. She laughed but quickly covered her mouth with her hand.

Skitt smiled at her. "What's that?"

"I'm just thinking about you and your ponding."

"My ponding? What?"

"Sitting all night in the rushes with your cricket bat and flask."

"Oh that. Well, it's over and done with.

Haven't made my blind in the reeds for years."

"You were still at it when I arrived here from America."

"There was still poaching going on then. It stopped, so Harrison and I finally gave up on the summer vigils."

She giggled with her hand over her mouth again. "Did you ever whack anyone with your bat?"

"Mosquitoes and gnats and midges, that's about all."

"And the swans have been all right since you stopped lurking?"

"Yes, Monty. They've been all right. God save the king's swans."

The moon was at half as the swans, white and starlike, floated silently, heads tucked back under their wings.

"Dreaming," whispered Montgomery as she watched them drift. "Just dreaming. Them and me."

"Am I to ask about your dreams?"

"My dreams are you, love. My dreams are all you."

"It's absolutely brilliant." Terry swung the door back and forth. "I mean, who would have thought?"

Libby sat up in bed, smiling, her arms

wrapped about her knees. "None of us children, I can tell you that. And we were up and down all these hallways on rainy days. To us it was just a locked door. We picked it once and got in, and it was like a horrid old closet heaped with ratty coats and mothballs. The smell was wretched. We couldn't stand it, so we never went back. If only we'd thought to pick the lock hidden behind the coats and swung the second door open. And then got through the third door into this room here. My goodness, what a triumph that would have been! All these oils of great ladies and grand dukes to stare at. Sabers hanging on the wall to take down and swing through the air. Daggers to play with. That suit of armor in the corner there — what a mess we would have made. And we'd probably have taken off a few fingers or heads with the swords. It doesn't bear thinking about on my wedding night." She stretched out a hand. "Come to bed, love. There are better things for you to do tonight than open and close a secret door over and over again."

"It's a marvel of engineering. We're quite safe here from the whole brood. Even the evil twins Peter and James."

"We are, so let's make the best of it. Remember that you're shipping out early in the morning on the good ship *Pluck*. They'll storm this room with pikestaffs and maces if you're not at the front door at five."

"And in full uniform too."

"What?" Libby laughed. "Who on earth asked you to do that?"

"Who do you think? She'll have the commander's uniform on I had tailored for her, so she insisted we be look-alikes tomorrow."

"The things you get yourself into over *our* girl." She patted the quilt. "Come along now. Or is the brave naval officer afraid?"

"I am a bit, you know." Terry came over and sat on the edge of the bed. "Mum always told me to watch out for ginger-haired women."

"Well, it's too late now. You're stuck with one."

"Sounds ominous."

"Oh, it is — very much so." She took his chin in her hand. "I love you, Commander."

The baron opened the window wider to let more of the smoke out of the room. Then he promptly lit another cigar and took another sip of brandy.

"You believe he has the support of the upper classes?" asked Lord Preston, putting down his tea.

The baron nodded and blew out a stream

of white-and-gray smoke. "And the middle class too, which is more worrisome. He promises one thing to one group and promises something else to another. Hitler keeps hammering away at the failure of democracy and pointing to the successes of strong monarchs and emperors in Germany's past. He holds up the need for another Bismarck. He makes remarks about the success of Benito Mussolini in Rome. People are listening as the economy and employment continue to decline into a pit no one seems able to pull us out of. It's the same in America, in Britain, and in the whole of Europe."

"Yes, I'm afraid some draconian measures will be coming down from the Labor government. I can't fault them, but it will not go over well. Even in Parliament's corridors and foyers I hear mutterings about the need for a strong man to lead us and implement strong measures. I suppose there are fascist groups everywhere these days, not just in Spain, Italy, and Germany." Lord Preston poured himself another cup. Steam curled up like smoke from the match the baron had just blown out. "But now, Gerard, what about the military? Isn't Herr Hitler afraid of them just a bit?"

"Not at all. As I've mentioned, his personal army — his brownshirts — number close to half a million now. The Treaty of Versailles restricts Germany to 100,000 soldiers, and Hitler's forces could overwhelm them in a matter of hours. But that's a moot point because the army is on his side for the most part. If he gains control of the government, the soldiers will simply fall into step with the Nazi Party. To them Hitler is like another Blucher, the victor of Waterloo along with your Wellington. *Ran wie Blucher* — charge like Blucher, they say. They already see Herr Hitler's aggressiveness in that light. Germans admire courage from the top."

"Is it courage?"

"Certainly he has that along with his fanaticism. And the state of the world's economy is slowly bringing him to power."

"What does the Brotherhood of the Oak intend to do?"

The baron shrugged. "You're one of us, Vilhelm. What do you intend?"

"Our navy is strong. Should Hitler take over, we could keep him blockaded on the water."

"Hopefully it won't come to that." The baron gazed at his friend through the cigar smoke. "What about the air? How is England fixed there?"

"We're not on a war footing. The RAF is not much to speak of these days. Neither is the army. Everything is reduced and restricted. No one expects trouble. Everyone is watching the pound and the shilling. Few care about Berlin. Germany is considered a broken reed."

"That could change overnight with one election. Hitler would tear up the Treaty of Versailles. That much is clear from his rants. He would rearm Germany. You know that."

"I do, and a few others see it too. But we aren't listened to." Lord Preston tapped his teaspoon on the rim of his cup. "What do the Germans and Austrians of the Brotherhood plan to do?"

The baron kept his eyes on Lord Preston. "If the economic depression continues to play into Hitler's hands and he gains more and more ground, our only option would be to stop him before he forms a government."

"How would you do that?"

"Assassination."

Lord Preston set the spoon down sharply. "Assassination? Are you mad, Gerard? It was the assassination of the Archduke that set off the Great War."

"There would be unrest in the aftermath, certainly. The Nazis would run amok for a few days. Blood would be spilled. But it would be limited and over quickly. Ultimately the Nazis would be headless and wither on the vine." The baron turned to look at the darkness through the window. "Better a week or two of civil war than two or three years of war in Europe."

Lord Preston stared at his friend's back then reached for the small bottle of brandy and poured a capful into his tea. "I shall pray, Gerard. Ask for guidance and wisdom. I know we're dealing with serious matters. I know sometimes great risks must be borne. But I'm not comfortable being an assassin. I'm not comfortable with overcoming darkness by using more darkness."

The baron continued to gaze out the window. "The Lord has placed us in such a world where the choices available to us fall far short of heaven. The dark choices are often the only way to regain light."

"I pray not," replied Lord Preston.

19

"Right, then." Edward paced the flat he shared with his father in London. "Now that Ramsay MacDonald has resigned, we can have a proper election and get the Conservatives back in power."

His father sat in a chair sipping tea. "Labor is split over the budget and Ramsay has stepped down, that much is true. But the prevailing mood amongst Conservative and Liberal MPs is to get MacDonald back in the prime minister's chair right away at the helm of a National Government."

"What?"

"The economic crisis worldwide is simply too serious to put party before country, my boy. An election we must have, yes, but with a national coalition vying for votes against Labor, not all the parties split up into their usual bits and pieces. So when we go back to the House in a few minutes, it is Stanley Baldwin's wish that we support MacDonald as head of a National Government."

"What about Lloyd George and the Liberals? They hold the balance of power."

"They do now. If the British people back a National Government in this time of crisis, which I believe they will, I doubt the Liberals shall keep that hold."

"It's a mess," Edward fumed. "I look at where Germany is headed, and now we have a golden opportunity to do the same. But you're saying we want to put that deadweight Ramsay back in the prime minister's chair."

"And where is Germany heading that we should be following after it?"

"A moratorium on democracy. You're right, it is an unprecedented financial crisis and must be met with unprecedented measures. But not dead men like Ramsay leading the dead men of a National Government. No, Father, we must thrust democracy aside for the time being."

"I beg your pardon?"

"Have the election, yes. But place Baldwin back at the helm of a Tory majority. Give him sweeping powers. No more elections for ten years. Strong trade ties with Italy and Germany. High tariffs for trade with those not part of the Commonwealth or the Empire. Cut relations with the League of Nations. Build up our navy and army and air force. Make our ships the size we want them to be. Put the British laborer to work on tanks and fighter planes and battle cruisers. Our economy will be revived in half a year, and Great Britain will be back to work and happy."

Lord Preston set down his cup. "A moratorium on democratic government Englishmen have fought and died for since the Magna Carta? How do you propose to get the support for that even if we're facing a financial crisis?"

"We need a strong man now, Dad. We need a monarch or we won't weather the storm. This democratic pattern of voting and revoting every few years is rubbish. We put a good man in and we keep him there until everything is sorted out."

"What if it takes decades?"

"So be it."

"Who put all this into your head?"

Edward smacked a fist into his hand. "It is going to work for Germany, and Germany has been in a far greater hole than we've been. It must work for us."

"The elimination of democracy will work for Germany? You would replace the free vote of the people with a dictatorship?"

"The baron was adamant about this back in May, and he was right."

Lord Preston's face sharpened. "Baron von Isenburg promoted this line of thinking? I don't believe it."

"The strong man, the clearheaded man, the man with unprecedented powers wielding them wisely and ably without the nagging hindrance of opposition parties or debate or national elections is the man best able to steer his country out of economic chaos. Freedom to act decisively. That is the thing, Father. Liberty to act in order to bring this nation the very liberty it requires and deserves."

"Whether the baron was goading you to get a reaction, I don't know. But if you wish to have a future with the Conservative Party, you must support Mr. Baldwin's wishes for a National Government with Ramsay MacDonald at its head and put away this rubbish about a moratorium on democracy."

Edward went back to pacing. "We do what we need to do and win a National Government with a majority of Conservative seats. Then we oust Ramsay, replace him with Baldwin, and vote in necessary and extraordinary powers for the government that give him — and us — a free hand to do what needs to be done to put Britain back on her feet strong, free, and unrestrained."

Lord Preston stood up and straightened his suit jacket with a strong pull from both his hands. "It's time to return to the House and support Ramsay MacDonald's return to the office of prime minister."

"By all means. It's what we do after winning the election that counts."

Lord Preston nodded. "Indeed it is."

"Elizabeth?"

"Ah, William. It's a very good connection. How did you get on with your speech in Liverpool?"

"We have mutiny at Invergordon in Scotland."

"Mutiny! Not on the *Hood*?"

"Yes, on the *Hood* and many other vessels as well. It is a black thing. I gather there were rumblings for days, but it got under way in earnest on the fifteenth of September — yesterday — and is still going today. Turn on the BBC this evening, and they will tell you what they're permitted to broadcast about the events."

"Why haven't the Royal Marines on board the ships put it down?"

"The Marines have joined the mutiny."

"Oh no!"

There was a rustling of paper at Lord Preston's end. "There is no mention of officers joining the mutiny. Indeed, they've done their best to get the sailors to return to their duties."

"Libby will be frantic down at Dover Sky."

"I have no word on Terry."

"I shall call her. Robbie and Shannon are with her. And Caroline."

"Well, don't panic her. There are no reports of violence. No shots fired. No beatings. No one hurt. No officers assaulted."

"Of course I won't panic her. The minute you hear anything else, please ring me."

"I shall. I have another election rally tomorrow. How is Edward's campaign getting on, do you know?"

"Charlotte reports he's on top of the world and prophesying Baldwin's return to power."

"He's saying that? When will the boy learn to keep his mouth shut? If Baldwin or Ramsay MacDonald get wind of it, they'll throw him out of the party."

"Please, William."

"It's true, Elizabeth. They will skin him alive."

"All right, Dear, that's quite enough. Go back to your speechwriting. I shall call

Libby up straightaway."

Dover Sky

Robbie tugged a white-faced Libby into the library where Kipp was adjusting the dials on the large, wooden radio set. "I'm telling you, the news is good, Lib."

"You're only saying that."

"I'm not. The BBC is saying that."

"They only tell us what the Royal Navy permits. Heaven knows what they're holding back. They always held back casualty reports during war. Remember how they covered up the losses at Jutland?"

"It's 1931 now, Lib, not 1916. Listen."

The *Hood* has sailed from Invergordon as ordered. All mutinous activities appear to have ceased on board the flagship. No casualties have occurred. This is true of all the other ships as well. After two days of unrest and disobedience, we have no record of fatalities or serious injuries. All ships have followed the *Hood* out of port as ordered. All ships are away. The mutiny has ended without resort to force.

"There you have it."

"I admit it does sound hopeful, Robbie. But I shall feel better when I get a cable from Terry. Certainly he would have gotten one away before they sailed."

"I should think so. And I shall stay up with you until it arrives, dear girl."

"That's not necessary, but thank you."

"I'm on six-month leave, remember? I have nothing better to do but to pester you until the courier arrives at the door. Kipp can't wait up because he has an airline to run."

Kipp smiled as he stood by the radio. "That's the truth."

"Shannon can't because she has to be available for Patricia Claire when she wakes at five or six."

"Available?" Shannon raised a golden eyebrow. "Is that what I'll be?"

"You will. And Caroline has her hands full with little Cecilia."

Caroline laughed. "Indeed I do. No stretch there."

Robbie bowed. "So you see, Lady Libby, there is only myself, but I shall be sufficient to keep you awake and alert until the good news comes to the door. We shall play checkers."

"I detest checkers."

"Chess then. Chess and we'll snack on coffee and biscuits."

Libby made a face at him.

"Chocolate biscuits." He mussed her hair and she slapped his hand. "Lib Danforth, lady or no lady, could never resist milk chocolate digestives."

"I'm no lady."

"We can discuss that until three or four in the morning."

She wrinkled up her mouth. "How happy that makes me."

The cable arrived at two thirty-seven. Robbie had put Libby in check for the third move in a row. Libby was at the door first, followed by Robbie, who tipped the courier and then read the cable out loud over her shoulder.

DEAREST LIB
YOU WILL HAVE HEARD THE NEWS. THIS WAS MY FIRST CHANCE TO DASH OFF A NOTE. WE WEIGH ANCHOR IN TWO HOURS. THE LADS HAVE RETURNED TO THEIR DUTIES. THERE WILL BE CONSEQUENCES BUT AT LEAST NO ONE WAS HURT AND THE NAVY AND ARMY DID NOT SEND IN TROOPS. I WILL SEE YOU AND JANE VERY SOON

INDEED. ALL MY LOVE.

TERRY

"Such good news!" Libby turned and slung her arms about Robbie's neck. She kissed him on the cheek.

"It is. And it means I can go to bed now. I'm tuckered."

"I'm not. I ate too much. One more game of chess?"

He laughed and groaned. "You lost all the others."

"I won't lose this one. I'm sharp now. I always do well at chess when I've had welcome news. Isn't it the same for you, Robbie?"

"It's not. I simply sleep better."

"Capital! Then I shall beat you up one side and down the other." She put her arm through his. "Come on. I feel like a stick of dynamite."

"Well, blow up quickly then and be done with it so I can go to my pillow as soon as possible."

Election Night, 1931
"Dad? Is that you?" Edward held the phone to one ear and put his finger in the other as people cheered and shouted behind him.

"It is. Congratulations, my boy. Another

538

October election, another Guy Fawkes on the horizon, and once again you've come out on top."

Edward laughed. "I have indeed. So have you. So have we all. Imagine, Baldwin has four hundred and seventy seats and Labor only forty-six. It's a miracle! Really it is! And that villain Buchanan is out. We have James Orr MacAndrew in Ayrshire South now — our own man."

"It's a great blessing. But now, my boy, you must keep your opinions to yourself. Ramsay MacDonald will continue on as prime minister —"

"Surely not, Father!" blurted Edward. "We have all the seats! Baldwin should lead the government!"

"Nevertheless, MacDonald will carry on. Mr. Baldwin and the party think it best in these troubled times. And you must think so too, Edward, and voice your support so that everyone can hear. Recall what happened when MacDonald agreed to head up a National Government of all parties — Labor threw him out permanently. If you are perceived as being an opponent of the National Government the Conservative Party helped bring into being, Mr. Baldwin will have you ousted in like fashion. Stick with your party, Edward. You can do much good there and eventually be rewarded for your loyalty."

"How rewarded? I've been in office seven years and haven't been offered a cabinet position."

"Your time will come, dear boy. Persist and your time will come. My best to lovely Charlotte and my two wonderful grandsons. Tell Owen to keep *Sea-Fever* fresh in his mind. We will get another sail in before Guy Fawkes. I shall drop down to Dover Sky on the weekend. Tell Colm I'll see him soon."

"Yes, I'll tell them, Dad."

"Good night, my boy. Once more, congratulations. Keep what I've said before you at all times."

"I will, sir. Thank you. Love to Mum."

London

Danforth,
Let us put our differences aside and talk. You see what is happening in the government and the country. Believe it or not, you and I share a number of the same concerns. Come to Tollers tomorrow afternoon at three. Ask for Edmund Henson's private room and give out your name as Jack Thistle. Do not fail to arrive at the appointed time. It will be to

our mutual benefit and certainly offer you an opportunity for political advancement.

Buchanan

Edward entered the crowded Tollers, but he didn't recognize any of the men at the tables amidst the haze of pipe smoke. He shook his umbrella so that water drops spattered the carpet just inside the door. He folded it shut and removed his silk top hat.

"May I assist you, sir?" A uniformed waiter asked and then smiled. "I'm afraid all the tables are occupied."

"I'm here to see Edmund Henson."

"Your name?"

"Tell him Jack Thistle has arrived."

"One moment."

The waiter vanished into the back. Edward stood by the door staring straight ahead. The waiter returned quickly.

"This way, sir."

Edward followed him down a short hallway that had doors on either side. They came to the last one. The waiter knocked, opened the door, and stepped aside. Edward went into the room and immediately saw Buchanan seated at a wooden table smoking a white, long-stemmed pipe.

"Danforth." Buchanan removed the pipe

stem from his mouth. "Good of you to come."

The waiter closed the door.

"What the devil are you playing at?" snapped Edward. "Why all the cloak and dagger?"

"Gently, Danforth. We need to be discreet." He indicated a man Edward hadn't noticed seated at the far end of the table. "I presume you've met Sir Oswald Mosley, the Sixth Baronet?"

Edward briefly inclined his head. "Sir Mosley. I didn't expect to see you here with Lord Buchanan."

The slender man with a dark moustache and flashing black eyes smiled. "Why not? He and I both admire Mussolini and Hitler and their ideological inclinations. As do you."

"As do I, sir?"

"Death to the communists. No trade with Moscow. A strong man at the top rather than the weak and slow action . . . or rather inaction . . . of the democratic process. High tariffs to protect British manufacturing from international trade. Nationalization of our major industries. A solid and innovative network of public works to reduce unemployment. A strong army, navy, and air force." Mosley patted a sheaf of papers in front of him. "All of your thoughts are on paper. In addition, a person may track the development of your thoughts by means of your speeches that are recorded in *Hansard.* Like many other good people in Europe, you are a fascist, Lord Danforth."

Edward took a chair opposite Buchanan. "I've never called myself that."

"The left would make it a dirty word, but the fascist movement has worked wonders in Italy and Rome. In time it will work wonders in Madrid and Spain, as well as Berlin and Germany. Soon enough it will change London and Britain if true Englishmen like yourself join our cause."

"Your party was wiped out in the election, Sir Mosley. You lost your seat in Smethwick."

"A temporary setback. I plan to spend time with the fascist leaders in Rome and Berlin to sharpen my strategies and tactics. They began in the streets and won the people to their side. So shall we."

Edward placed his top hat on the table. "Herr Hitler may have the second largest party in Germany, Sir Mosley, but he is far from winning the German people to his side."

"Do you doubt he will go further, Lord Danforth?"

Edward drummed his fingers on the arm of his chair. "I shall be kicked out of the Conservative Party if I consider this, let alone have to deal with what my father will say."

"Let us not rush things. We meet in private for now. In a year or two, once the time is ripe, we come forward. My plan is to unite all the fascist groups in Britain to make one formidable force. Until then, we do what we do out of the public eye." Mosley nodded at Edward. "I see a cabinet position for you, Lord Danforth. And for you too, Lord Buchanan." His dark eyes remained on Edward. "Can we bury the hatchet?"

Edward glanced at Buchanan. "How is it you have summoned me to this meeting when you know the bad blood that exists between us?"

Buchanan shrugged. "I'm willing to abide by a truce until the nation is back on its feet again."

"But you were with Labor, the lovers of communism and socialism."

"I had no other choice, Danforth. I couldn't join the Conservative Party because you and your father were in it. The one party that most actively opposes your own is Labor, so it wasn't a difficult decision to make."

"Labor's policies are utterly at odds with the agenda Sir Mosley proposes."

"I'm out of Labor now, Danforth, so all of these issues you raise are moot. I can now show my true colors and not kowtow to the Labor line in order to strike out at the Danforth clan."

"And what will keep you from striking out at us if I join forces with Sir Mosley and you?"

"I will," Mosley stated, his voice having the ring of iron on iron. "There can be absolutely no infighting. We must provide a united front against our foes if we are to pull Great Britain out of this economic depression. Is that clear, Lord Buchanan?"

Buchanan inclined his head. "Very much so."

"Lord Danforth?"

Edward nodded. "I will abide by the truce, Sir Mosley. I will abide by the truce for king and country so long as Lord Buchanan stays true to his word."

Buchanan grunted. "No fear of that, Danforth."

20

April, 1932–January, 1933
Lime Street Chapel, Liverpool

Ben Whitecross looked over the congregation in the small room. The place was packed. Officials and bishops from the Methodist Church in England sat in the front row. His wife and two sons were right behind them, seated next to Lord and Lady Preston. At the back, with all their children, sat Jeremy and Emma and Kipp and Caroline. People Ben had been caring for the entire two years he'd been at Lime Street Chapel were watching him closely, eyes fixed on his face and the small movements of his hands. He turned a page of the large Bible that lay open on the pulpit in front of him.

"I suppose I have an adventurous spirit," Ben said. "God uses that. He certainly used it in the life of the apostle Paul. Paul wanted to go everywhere with the gospel, including

Europe, Spain, and Asia. My text today is from his words in his second letter to the Corinthians: *'To preach the gospel in the regions beyond you, and not to boast in another man's line of things made ready to our hand.'* I've loved being among you here. The Lord has fulfilled a dream I kept hidden for years — to minister to people in His name. Up until now, I've worked with horses and flown airplanes and been blessed with marriage and children. I could successfully argue that my entire life has been a blessing. Coming to the pulpit was one way of thanking God. Going to East Africa, to Kenya specifically, is another. Christians have been serving there for a century, but many places remain untouched. Many live and die and pass into eternity without hearing about the God of love and His Son, Jesus Christ. So that's where I need to go. Regions beyond that need someone to preach, to pray, and to fly in medical supplies and Bibles. With the gracious support of the Methodist Missionary Society, your tithes and offerings, and the help of my family and our own resources, I'm on my way to Kenya in a fortnight. My wife and children will join me at the end of the year once I have everything prepared. I praise God for the opportunity to take His light and His love to the African people. It will be the grandest adventure of what has already been a very grand life."

The Methodist officials got up and gathered around Ben. They prayed over him.

Lord Preston nudged his daughter Victoria. "Isn't this something, my dear?" he whispered. "Who would have guessed it? Ben Whitecross VC a missionary to Africa. You must be very proud. One accomplishment follows another accomplishment in his life. And they said he would never walk again after that airplane crash. But no, one adventure comes swiftly on the heels of another with him."

Victoria stared straight ahead at the bishop who had placed his hands on her husband's bowed head. "Ben Whitecross's adventures will be the death of me, Father," she replied without whispering or keeping her voice low.

Tubingen, Germany
"Baron?" Catherine opened the door and smiled. "What brings you to the house on such a fine summer day? I thought you'd be out on a long nature hike with Eva."

"She's on some sort of outing with a few of her friends." The baron's face was etched in sharp lines and tense. "I must see Albrecht right away. Is he at home?"

"Of course. Is everything all right?"

"The election results are official. Herr Hitler won two hundred and thirty seats. He now has the largest party in the government."

"Oh no!" She stepped aside. "Please go directly to his study."

"*Danke.* I apologize, Catherine."

"For Hitler? It is certainly not your fault, Baron. Please come in. Albrecht will want to discuss this news with you."

The baron found him behind his desk, hair uncombed, a day's growth of beard showing on his face. Papers and books were stacked higher than his head.

Albrecht looked up from the pad he was writing on. "Ah, Gerard. What brings you here? You know, you were right after all. We should have fled to Pura or the Rhine instead of remaining in Tubingen for July and August. What was I thinking? All because of this new book the publishers are hounding me for after the success of *Mein Krieg* and *Mein Geist* —"

The baron interrupted him. "Have you listened to the news?"

"The news? No, I haven't had the time. I've been chained to this desk since six this morning."

"The votes have been officially counted."

Albrecht took off his reading glasses. "What has happened?"

"The Nazis now have the greatest number of seats in the *Reichstag*."

"Impossible!"

"Hitler's star is rising. Now he is demanding that von Hindenburg make him chancellor."

"Will von Hindenburg do it?"

"Today? No. He detests Hitler. Next week, next month? Who knows?"

"We must act."

The baron took a seat and removed his hat, a fedora with a feather in its band. "A meeting has been called for this evening at Schultz's home. We've already set a number of things in motion. It remains to determine the right place and time. There will be several target shooters in place at whatever outdoor location is selected. A grenade will also be thrown, possibly two. However we don't want any bystanders injured or killed. Only Nazi Party members."

"Perhaps Goebbels or Himmler can be eliminated at the same time."

"If those sycophants are standing close to him, yes."

Albrecht lifted a piece of paper on his desk and glanced over it. "I do not do this lightly,

Gerard. I am just now writing a chapter on following in the footsteps of the Prince of Peace."

"Yet our Lord also drove the merchants out of the Jewish temple with a whip."

"Yes, but He killed no one."

"Do you wish to halt the assassination attempt?"

"God forgive me, I do not. And I will have to answer to Him for my decision. But what else can be done? The more powerful Hitler gets, the more danger he puts Germany in. When is the meeting?"

"In an hour."

Albrecht stood up and tugged on the gray blazer that hung on the back of his chair. "We should leave now."

The baron also got up. He locked the door with the twist of the latch.

Albrecht frowned. "What are you doing? An hour is not a great deal of time to get to Schultz's villa out in the country."

"We're not going there. The Brotherhood is betrayed."

Albrecht stared at him as if he'd been punched in the stomach. "Betrayed?"

"Yes, betrayed. Hitler's brownshirts are going to surround Schultz's villa and burn it to the ground. Whoever escapes will be beaten to death."

"How do you know this?"

"I have betrayed them. Wegner and I betrayed them."

"You?" Albrecht moved towards the door. "Don't spout nonsense, Gerard. If what you say is true, we must phone Schultz and the others immediately."

The baron thrust a hand against Albrecht's chest. "There will be no phone calls. Sit down."

"Are you mad? How else can we reach them in time?"

"We aren't going to reach them in time. That was the deal I struck with Wegner and Ernst Rohm, the leader of the *Sturm Abteilung.* The stormtroopers get the Brotherhood, I join the Nazi Party, and you and your wife and children stay alive."

"What?" Albrecht's face lost its blood. "I have not agreed to any such terms. Let me by."

"No."

The two men struggled, and Albrecht quickly pinned the older man to the wall. The baron quit struggling, and Albrecht stepped back and turned to unlock the door.

The baron struck him from behind with the butt of a luger pistol he'd pulled from his pocket. Albrecht fell to the floor, and the baron pointed the gun at him. "Stay there. Do not attempt to get up. Your wife and children are at risk, man. Think of them. It is open warfare on the streets between the Nazis and the communists. Scores have been killed. Do you think anyone will care about you or me or a dozen more at Schultz's home?"

With blood running down the side of his head, Albrecht glared up at the baron. "How could you do this? You of all people?"

"Survival. Mine, Eva's, yours, Catherine's, Sean's, Angelika's. Wegner was an infiltrator from the beginning. Once talk turned to actual plans for assassination, he told me in confidence that the brownshirts had marked all of us for execution. Because of my prominence as a member of the upper class, I was permitted to renounce my affiliation with the Brotherhood and swear allegiance to Adolph Hitler. I did that with the understanding that you and your family would be under my protection and not be harmed. You will not go to the villa to die tonight with the others."

"Eva will hate you for this."

"She already knows. Once I explained I was joining the elite of the Nazi Party and not the brownshirts she was in agreement. In fact, she has joined the League of German Girls, the young women part of the

Hitler youth. That is where she is today . . . out of harm's way."

Albrecht sprang for the gun, but the baron struck him on the head with it again. The professor fell back against the desk before dropping to the floor.

"Enough of your heroics, Albrecht. Do I have to kill you to save your life and your family?" The baron could see that Albrecht was almost unconscious. Setting down his pistol on a chair by the door, he quickly removed his suit jacket, shirt, and dress pants. Underneath he wore black pants and a brown shirt with a red swastika armband, along with a black tie and black strap that ran across his chest from right shoulder to left hip. "This is in case Rohm forgets about the bargain. I am one of Himmler's SS, you see. Untouchable, really." He picked up the Luger again. "We'll remain here until I receive the phone call that the villa is gone and the Brotherhood finished with."

"How can you talk that way about our comrades?" groaned Albrecht.

"They were fools mostly, weren't they? Do you seriously think they could have pulled off the assassination? And even if they had, would that have helped Germany or hindered it? The time for killing Hitler was five years ago. Now he is our future. There is no one else who has his vision. What I am helping you do is imminently practical, Albrecht. We shall have to do away with your books, however. I am sorry for that. There were many good and patriotic chapters."

"Lord Preston will be furious with you."

"I expect he will. But he has the luxury of living across the Channel. You and I must make the best of things here. Support Hitler, that is the route to take. And we are taking it."

"Do you seriously believe Catherine will support this?"

"If she wants you and her children to live, yes. You know what the brownshirts are like, Albrecht. Wild dogs. They will catch you on the street and slaughter you all."

"Not the children."

"Oh yes, certainly the children."

"Even tonight . . . what you're allowing at the villa . . . there will be a storm of protests."

"There won't be. Right now large communist cells are being eliminated in Munich and Berlin. The villa will be one small part of the news tomorrow morning. More communists will be killed tonight than the tiny band in the Brotherhood. No, the greater slaughter will get the greater attention. Few will care about what happened to men who were planning to overthrow the government with bombs and bullets. Yes, that is the story that will be given out, my friend."

"Don't call me that. Don't ever call me that again."

"As you wish, but you have a poor way of thanking someone who kept you from being burned alive and your family shot."

"They would not have dared kill Catherine and my children."

"Certainly Rohm would have dared. Hitler already considers you an enemy because of your books."

"You are everything I have written against that is wrong with our country. You are the bad German who will lead us into more misery."

For the first time anger cut across the baron's face. "If there are bad Germans, you can lay the blame at the feet of the British and the French. The Treaty of Versailles was without grace or magnanimity to a fallen foe. It not only spawned Hitler but our need for Hitler. If worse comes to worse in Europe because of Hitler, the blood is on the hands of those who threw the German people in the dirt and ground them down under their heels."

There was a soft knocking at the door and then it opened. Catherine stuck her head through the opening. "Baron?"

"Yes, Catherine?"

"I'm sorry to interrupt your talk with Albrecht, but there was a phone call for you. The gentleman only wished to leave a message."

"Ah, yes. What was it?"

"*Deutschland uber alles.* That's all he said. Does that mean anything to you? He was a bit of an odd duck."

"Thank you, Catherine. I agree the man who called is indeed a strange one. But his message makes perfect sense."

"All right. We'll see you two in a bit." She closed the door.

The baron kept his hidden pistol on Albrecht and nodded. "The Brotherhood of the Oak no longer exists."

"I suppose it gives a man like you pleasure to say that."

"It gives me no pleasure at all, Albrecht. It was something that had to be done if Germany is to experience a resurrection."

Dover Sky
The motorcycle came to a stop and the rider climbed off.

"I'm looking for Lord Preston."

Lord Preston was sitting in the shade by the manor and brushing his three Belgian shepherds. "I'm Lord Preston, young man. Do you have a cable for me?"

"Yes, m'lord. It came to us marked highest priority so I was sent up from Dover at once."

"I see." Lord Preston got to his feet and took the telegram from the courier.

Lady Preston sat upright on the porch swing. "Is it from Jerusalem? Another baby, I hope."

"It's from Germany, my dear." Lord Preston gave the courier a five-pound note. "Thank you very much indeed." He watched the courier turn and leave before opening the telegram as the motorcycle roared off.

Lady Preston watched him battle the urge to ball the note in his fist once he'd finished.

"What is wrong, William? Is Catherine all right? Is it the baby?"

"Nothing is all right now. Nothing."

"Please tell me what the cable says."

He slowly turned to face her and read it aloud:

LORD PRESTON
THE BARON HAS BETRAYED US. HE PERMITTED STORMTROOPERS TO MURDER THE BROTHERHOOD OF THE OAK WHEN THEY

MET LAST WEEK. IN ADDITION HE HAS JOINED THE NAZI PARTY AND IS NOW A HIGH-RANKING OFFICER WITHIN HIMMLER'S SS.

MY FAMILY AND I ARE NOT IN DANGER AS LONG AS I FOLLOW THE NAZI PARTY LINE. FUTURE BOOKS I WRITE CAN ONLY DISCUSS THEOLOGY PROPER NOT THEOLOGY AND POLITICS AND CERTAINLY NOT THEOLOGY AND HITLER. I MUST WATCH WHAT I TEACH AT THE UNIVERSITY IN THE FALL. ALL THIS AND ADOLPH HITLER IS NOT EVEN IN FULL POWER. THERE ARE GRIM DAYS AHEAD FOR GERMANY. THE BARON CLAIMS HE IS OUR PROTECTOR AND SAYS THAT IS WHY NONE OF US WERE HARMED BY THE BROWNSHIRTS. HE SAYS WEGNER WAS A NAZI PLANT IN THE BROTHERHOOD. WE HAVE SEVERED RELATIONS WITH THE BARON AND HIS DAUGHTER. EVA HAS JOINED THE NAZI YOUTH. I AM SORRY I CANNOT SEND YOU BETTER NEWS.

ALBRECHT

Lady Preston left her husband and walked into the manor. Passing Skitt, she asked if he'd seen Jane.

"I believe she's feeding the swans with Lady Caroline and Lady Holly," Skitt responded. "Do you wish to speak with her?"

"I do."

"I shall go down to the pond at once."

"Send one of the footmen, Skitt."

He left through the front doors as if she hadn't spoken. Lady Preston shook her head and carried on up the staircase to her room. Sitting at her reading desk, she pulled a large scrapbook towards her that she'd been working on. The first page had fine gold script across its black surface: *Libby's marriage to Commander Terrence Fordyce, May 24, 1931.* She lingered over the black-and-white photographs that followed, especially the ones of the baron posing with her and her husband, ones of Eva linking arms with Jane. For a moment she felt she should remove the pictures. She went to another set of photographs instead.

The gold script read, *Robbie and Shannon off to Palestine again with Patricia Claire in October. I long for the day Robbie will be based in England.* There were photographs of Robbie and Shannon and their daughter at the dock, and others of the three of them walking up the gangway, looking back at the camera. Several showed them standing on the deck and waving.

"Too far away," murmured Lady Preston. "You three in Jerusalem. Catherine and Albrecht and Sean and Angelika in Germany. All of you too far away. All of you in danger."

She put a hand to her face and closed her eyes a moment. She prayed. Then she looked back at the scrapbook and turned pages until she found the picture she wanted. It took up an entire page and was mounted sideways. Tugging it away from the corners that held it in place, she glanced at the families standing on the lawn shoulder to shoulder: Caroline with Cecilia in her arms, Kipp beside her, arm around her waist, Matthew and Charles standing in front of them; Edward and Charlotte to their left, Owen sitting with two-year-old Colm in his lap on the grass; Emma and Jeremy with the twins, Peter and James, and their young son Billy; Victoria, Ben's arm around her shoulders, Ramsay and Timothy standing at attention and not smiling like everyone else; Catherine and Albrecht holding hands, Sean gripping his mother's other hand, Albrecht cradling Angelika in his free arm; Libby and Terry with Jane standing between the two of them, beaming, their hands resting on her shoulders; Robbie and Shannon and Patricia Claire at the end of the row, each of their faces darker than anyone else's, including Terry's. Behind all of them stood William and herself, as well as Harrison and Holly. At her husband's feet, unseen by the camera lens, were the three Belgian shepherds — Flanders, Poppy, and Charlemagne. Turning over the photograph she saw her handwriting in India ink: *All together in one spot at the same time. Miraculous.*

"I hope this happens again soon," she said out loud. "I don't know how, but soon, Lord."

"Grandmum?" Jane stood in the doorway, flushed from running in the summer heat. "Skitt said you wanted to see me and that it was important."

Lady Preston nodded and smiled. "Indeed, I do wish to speak with you, and yes, it is a matter of some importance, my dear. Please sit down in that chair there."

Jane took her seat. "Is something wrong? What did I do?"

"You didn't do anything, my dear Jane. Set your mind at ease about that."

"Then why do you have such a serious

look on your face?"

"Because I have serious news to tell you. We just received a telegram from Germany."

"Oh . . . is the baby all right?"

"The baby is fine. It is something else. I want to say first of all that I am sorry, so very sorry, but you may not correspond with Eva von Isenburg anymore."

"Skitt, may I see you for a moment, please?"

Skitt had just stepped into the manor, humming under his breath, an engagement ring from a pawnshop in Dover in his pocket. Thoughts of meeting Montgomery that night by the pond and what he would say to her dominated his thoughts. He slipped into the small room Holly used as an office and smiled.

"How may I help you, m'lady?" he asked.

"Well, you're quite chipper, aren't you? I suppose a day off agrees with most of us. Please have a seat."

Still smiling, Skitt hitched up his pant legs and placed himself in a chair. "So what's this about then?"

Holly appeared reluctant to begin, glancing at a ledger open on the desk in front of her and tapping a yellow pencil against her teeth. Finally she turned to face the butler.

"We've had an amazing run at Dover Sky,

Skitt. Almost ten years we've been using it as a year-round home for members of the Danforth family, and you've been butler for all of them. You've done an extraordinary job."

"Thank you, m'lady. It's hard to believe a decade has gone by."

"Near to it. An astonishing set of years. Marriages, births, the children growing like weeds. I'm sorry to tell you it must now come to an end."

"What's that?"

Holly met his gaze without enthusiasm. She turned the pencil around and around in her fingers. "Lord Kipp has purchased a home in London. He's had enough of only seeing Caroline and the children on weekends. We can't blame him, can we? It so happens Lord Edward has done the same. I imagine sharing a flat with his father whenever Parliament was in session finally wore thin. Both of them bought places within a few blocks of each other and of Jeremy and Emma, so they'll have a bit of a village going on amongst themselves."

"I see."

"It's much the same story for Commander Fordyce and Libby. He's weary of driving from Plymouth and Devonport whenever he has shore leave. He'd much prefer to have his wife and daughter closer to hand. It's true there are the four months he's in the Med each winter, but the rest of the time he's in British waters and would dearly love to be able to pop in and see his loved ones whenever the opportunity presents itself. He's in the process of securing a house near homeport. He wants Libby and Jane moved in by the time he returns from winter maneuvers in May. Montgomery, naturally, will move with them."

"Of course."

Holly half-smiled. "All of this is months away so far as Commander Fordyce and Libby are concerned. It's only September, and Libby and Jane shall be remaining here for the winter. However at Easter they will move into their new house. Once they're gone, any reason for Dover Sky to remain open year 'round is gone. Harrison and I will be returning to Ashton Park at summer's end next year, as will the rest of the staff. Tavy is senior butler at the Lancashire estate. We'd like to keep you on, but I'm afraid the only position available would be senior footman."

"Footman?"

Holly's face reddened. "I'm so sorry, Skitt. Both Harrison and Todd Turpin will be handling grounds at Ashton Park, so there's no opening there, I'm afraid."

"What about groundskeeper here at Dover Sky?"

"Ah, well, Fairburn is returning."

"What? Fairburn?"

"His services are no longer required at the estate where he was employed in France. He applied to return here to his former duties at Dover Sky some time ago, and naturally Lord Preston could not refuse."

Skitt stared at her. "Where does that leave me, Lady Holly?"

"You are a valued family servant, Skitt. We wish to see you employed here through the fall of 1933. Once the families have left and Lord and Lady Preston have completed their summer holiday, you will be released from your duties. Harrison and I shall remain until Fairburn arrives. If you don't wish to take up a position as senior footman at Ashton Park, perhaps you might wish to serve as assistant chauffeur or in some other capacity."

"Assistant? I expect I might find that a bit difficult, Lady Holly, after having been my own man for so long, so to speak."

"I well understand that, Skitt. If you wish to move on to another family, no one will think the worse of you for it. The Danforths will provide excellent references and assist you in finding suitable employment. Good butlers are worth their weight in gold. It would not be long before we found you another family."

Skitt cleared his throat. "Thank you, but there is the matter of Montgomery. We have reached an understanding, you see."

"Have you?"

"Well, I hope we have. I expect I shall find out soon enough. Has she been told about her move to Plymouth and Devonport in the spring, do you know?"

"I believe Libby spoke with her this morning."

"This morning?"

"Yes. Libby was at a loss to explain why Montgomery seemed down at the mouth with the news. What you've just told me makes her reaction perfectly understandable. I'm so sorry, Skitt, but there's no reason to keep Dover Sky open after Easter."

Skitt's mood hadn't improved by the time he made his way to the pond to wait for Montgomery. The moon was a thin slit cut by a silver blade, the stars like the small diamond in his pocket that he had half a mind to toss in the water. The September night was as soft as cashmere, yet his mind was jagged with ruined plans and a bleak future. When he saw Montgomery approaching silently over the lawn, he tried in vain to put a smile on his face and hold it. She took his hands and gazed up at him.

"You look absolutely shattered, love," she said. "It's good to see that."

"It's good?"

"I should have felt devastated to come down here and find you dancing a jig what with the news. I felt horrible this morning after Libby spoke to me. She was puzzled for I'm no better at hiding my emotions than you are. I told her it had nothing to do with her or Jane or the Commander. Honestly, I adore them. Don't be angry, but I had to let the cat out of the bag a bit. I said you and I had come to an understanding, and it would be difficult to have you at one place and me at another. Was it wrong of me to tell her that?"

Skitt let the air out of his lungs and shook his head. "Not at all. I did much the same thing. It changed nothing. I got her sympathy and little else. The Commander's household is too small to require the services of a butler."

"I shall go with you, Skitt, wherever you have a mind to go. I shall. Cheer up. We're not going to be separated."

"You can't let Libby down. They count on you to help them with Jane. She needs you. She'll be a young lady soon enough."

"There are plenty of English maids who can fit the bill."

Fit the bill? Skitt laughed. "You act and speak so much like one of us it takes a quaint expression like that to come along and remind me you're American. I love you dearly, Montgomery, but you can't let Libby and Jane down. You really can't. You might feel all right about it for a day or two, but then you'd think of Jane's tears and fall apart."

"I wouldn't, you know."

"You would, you know. Imagine if we got a letter saying Jane was having a rough go and was down in the dumps and they couldn't bring her out of it? Don't tell me you wouldn't feel it like a dagger to the heart. That's the sort of woman you are. It's one of the reasons you're a treasure. You can't abandon the Fordyces and trail after me to heaven knows where. It won't work."

She wrapped her arms around him. "Then what are we going to do? I might not be able to live without Jane, but I can't live without you either."

"I don't know. I swear I don't."

"What's in your pocket?"

"What d'you mean?"

"You keep playing with something. You won't even put your arms around me."

Skitt took his right hand out of his pocket and embraced her. "There. Will that do?"

"I'm not a chore, surely."

"I'm distracted by the day's events. Even Fairburn, the former groundskeeper who quit and worked for another family, warrants more attention than I do. They've rehired him as groundskeeper here."

"He doesn't warrant my attention!" She kissed Skitt on the lips and darted her hand into his pocket. They wrestled briefly, but she pulled away and ran off towards the water. She opened her hand, and the moonlight glinted off the ring. "Oh!"

Skitt watched her. "It's not much."

"Not much? It's adorable. I utterly love it." She smiled at him. "Who's it for? Norah Cole?"

"Don't be mad. You know who it's for. But what's the point?"

"What's the point?"

"We can't do anything about it. You shall go to Plymouth, and I shall wind up in northern Scotland or Wales or the Isle of Man, for all I know. I might as well be on the moon and you on Neptune."

"We'll work it out, my love."

"How?"

She came back to him and put the ring in his hand. "I don't care about *how* right now. I just want to receive my ring properly, that's all. If it is to be my ring."

"Of course it's your ring. There's no one I love half so much as you. But it's such a small thing . . . all I could afford."

"It's a great thing. I want to wear it with all my heart."

"Very well." Skitt turned the ring over in his hand and watched the wink of light hit the diamond. "I'm at a loss for words, really."

"Come on, Skitt. You can go on about rugby scores till everyone's asleep in their ale."

"Rugby scores are easy. It's just numbers. A beautiful woman is something else again."

"Well, that's a good start. Carry on."

Skitt put his hands behind his back. "I've asked for some help."

Montgomery looked around quickly. "From whom? Not Harrison."

"From William."

"What! Lord Preston?"

"I have it here." Skitt unfolded a piece of paper. "Shall I go ahead?"

"Yes, yes, go ahead. I'm going to die if we keep up this dance."

Skitt squinted and read the words slowly as one of the swans, waking up, flapped its wings.

Let me not to the marriage of true minds
Admit impediments. Love is not love
Which alters when it alteration finds
Or bends with the remover to remove
O, no! It is an ever-fixed mark
That looks on tempests and is never
    shaken
It is the star to every wandering bark
Whose worth's unknown, although his
    height be taken
Love's not Time's fool, though rosy lips and
    cheeks
Within his bending sickle's compass come
Love alters not with his brief hours and
    weeks
But bears it out even to the edge of doom

If this be error and upon me proved
I never writ, nor no man ever loved.

Montgomery smiled. "Wonderful. Your voice is perfect. And you did write it out, after all."

"So I did." Skitt brought the ring out from behind his back. "Your eyes flash just like it flashes, you know."

"Do they?"

"Black jewels. I've been fascinated by them ever since I first saw you years ago when you came to Dover Sky with Michael and Libby and Jane."

"Really?"

"They dazzled me. I used to have a fancy for Lady Catherine y'know. But not after I had a look at you."

"I'm astonished and flattered. But was it just the eyes that brought you to me, Skitt?"

"You know it wasn't. You have a beauty like a starry night, yes. But a spirit just as brilliant."

"Ah, now that's sweetly said. As good as anything from your friend William Shakespeare."

"I don't have anything else to add. Will you marry me, Montgomery?"

"You know I will."

She held out her hand, and he slipped the ring over her finger. It was loose.

"Arrr," he growled. "It doesn't fit proper."

She twined her arms around his neck. "There are ways to fix that."

"I don't want you fat. I love you exactly the way you are."

"I have no intention of getting fat." She ran her lips over his. "Enough talk. We're to be married. Let's kiss to that for the rest of the night."

Gloom descended on Skitt once again. "What good is all this, Montgomery? We can't do anything about it. How can we be married if we can't even live together?"

"You must pick up the habit from the Danforths. They seem to be very good at that sort of thing. The husband's in the one place and the wife's in the other. Like Ben in Africa and Victoria here. Or Kipp in Jerusalem and Caroline pining away for him at Dover Sky."

"I don't want to be good at that sort of thing. I want you in my arms every night."

"And I want to be there. Now no more of this." She began to plant short, sharp, fiery kisses on his lips and cheeks. "We shall be happy, you and I. Something will work out, my lovely man."

"I don't see how." But Skitt closed his eyes and responded to the sparks landing rapidly on his face and mouth with pleasant stings.

Terry showed up at Dover Sky the day before Guy Fawkes with bags of sweets and strings of firecrackers for everyone at the estate. As far as children went, with Caroline and Kipp living in London, only Jane remained, who at fifteen thought of herself as a woman, not a girl. Nevertheless, she

574

grabbed candy and firecrackers with a squeal, popping the first in her mouth till her cheeks bulged and tossing the others all about her as they exploded overhead and in the grass.

"Skitt!" Terry called as the butler stood on the front porch of the manor. "Harrison is busy with pruning. Will you give me a hand with the effigy?"

He and Skitt, a rough tweed coat over his black and white uniform, stuffed large pants and a large gray coat with straw, filling both sleeves, as well as a tall hat that bulged to reveal a head with button eyes and a button mouth. Keeping Guy Fawkes upright with a long wooden pole they ran through his back and up to his neck, they placed him in the middle of a large mound of brush that Harrison had been collecting all week as he cleaned up hedges and groves and thickets.

"Do you think it needs anything else, Skitt?" Terry asked.

"Well, Commander, perhaps if we could find logs and some thicker limbs the bonfire would burn a great deal longer."

"Good idea. Let's fetch a barrow and see what we can find."

As Skitt pushed the barrow along, twice having to take it back from the naval officer dressed in corduroy pants and coat and shirt, Terry clapped a hand to his shoulder. "Libby tells me you're engaged."

"Yes, sir."

"That's wonderful news. Congratulations."

"Thank you very much, Commander."

"Now that you're settled on Montgomery and I'm settled on Libby, perhaps we can let the Catherine business go the way of the wind. What do you think, Skitt?"

Skitt's face quickly turned scarlet. "Lady Catherine was a young man's fancy and folly, sir."

"And I was the unwelcome rival."

More blood filled Skitt's cheeks and he kept his head down, pushing the barrow ahead with renewed vigor.

"I don't mind, Skitt. Lady Catherine is a fine woman. But I'm head over heels with Libby's ginger-blonde hair and ocean-blue eyes, just as I expect you can't get enough of Montgomery's shining black locks or flashing dark eyes."

Skitt couldn't keep himself from smiling. "Aye, there you have it, sir."

"I have a proposal for you. Once we're living close to the Royal Navy docks, I shall be entertaining considerably. Captains, commanders, leftenant commanders, commodores, even the odd admiral. There will be some busy seasons when I'm ashore. Too much for Libby to handle on her own, and Montgomery will have her hands full with Jane turning sixteen and seventeen and, eventually, twenty-one, Lord help us. What do you say? Is butlering that sort of crew something that piques your interest at all?"

"What, sir?"

"Do you want to work for me, Skitt? I could use you, and heaven knows I trust you with the lives of everyone in my family. You can think it over if you'd like, but I'll be shipping out in a couple of months and it would be nice to know how you feel about it one way or the other before the *Hood* weighs anchor after New Year's Day."

"Think it over?"

"Certainly. We're not going to be one of the large Danforth estates you're used to serving, but you'll still have a lot to look after, not to mention —"

Skitt dropped the barrow handles and seized the commander's hand, forgetting for a moment where he was and who he was. "With all my heart! With all my heart, sir. Montgomery and I shall be married and serve your family together with pride and distinction. It's a brilliant plan if you don't mind me saying so, sir. Absolutely brilliant."

Terry laughed and pumped his hand.

"Why, then, the bargain is sealed . . . sealed and done. You're a Royal Navy butler come Easter, Skitt. A butler in the tradition of those who served Nelson and Rodney and Jellicoe, though I am a minnow compared to those leviathans. You shall have an outfit suited to your station — dark-navy trimmed with deep burgundy all set off by the crisp white of your shirt. How does that sound?"

"Capital, sir, capital! May I leave you for a moment? Only for a moment, mind. I must run and tell Montgomery. She is just on a walk with your daughter along the northern boundary of the estate. I must catch them up. I must tell her what's happened."

"By all means, go, man. Faint heart never won fair lady. Run as if your life depended upon it."

"I will do, sir. Thank you. Bless you!"

Terry saluted as Skitt vaulted the barrow and raced for the stone fence to the north of them. "England expects every man to do his duty!" he called after him.

British East Africa, Kenya
"May I open my eyes now, Ben? Honestly, we're not youngsters in the stables anymore playing our silly games."

"Just a moment. I have to position you

just so. There. All right, Lady Victoria, you may take a good look."

She opened her eyes to a tall mountain peak rising out of the jungle and grasslands white with snow at its summit. She put her knuckles to her mouth.

"My heavens, Ben! How high is that?"

"More than 19,000 feet — almost four miles."

"It's magnificent. I never expected something like this. And what are those beasts moving across the fields? Not giraffe?"

"What other creature has such a long neck?"

"I'm amazed. Utterly shocked and amazed. Have the boys seen this yet?"

"Not at all. They've been with the bishop — Stevenson. He's introducing them to some of the African children. I wanted us to look at Mount Kilimanjaro together."

"Kilimanjaro. What a beautiful name. What does it mean?"

"I've heard so many stories about that: mountain of caverns, mountain of whiteness, mountain of greatness. I prefer mountain of greatness."

"Of course you would."

He put his arm around her. "Though calling it mountain of whiteness ties in with the name Whitecross much better."

"Can it be climbed?"

"It can. One day we shall do it. For now it's good to gaze at it and to think of God and give thanks."

She leaned into him and took his hand. "Only you would do this. Only you would bring me here. I didn't want to come to Africa even though I acted as if I did. I didn't want another 'Ben Whitecross and God' adventure that involved airplanes and skies and dangers known and unknown. But now I'm so grateful. This is a spot of extraordinary beauty. And truth be known, I feel much safer here than I did back in Europe and England."

"Really? Why do you say that?"

"That Hitler fellow taking over as chancellor of Germany. Dad's in a flap about it and his old friend Baron von Isenburg joining the Nazi Party. Mum is terrified and wants Catherine and Albrecht to get out of Germany with Sean and Angelika before something happens."

"What's going to happen?"

"I don't know, really, but everyone is expecting something to blow up. I hate all the rumors and gossip. Nasty memories of when I was young and the Great War started: you disappearing to the Western Front, Folkestone being bombed, and Mr.

Seabrooke getting killed. I feel much safer here among the lions and gorillas and snakes actually."

Ben laughed. "I'm glad to hear it. I must thank Herr Hitler for his part in making Kenya so amenable to you. Half my battle's won because he's created such a threatening environment in Europe."

"Don't joke, Ben Whitecross. The Europe situation leaves me with an ugly feeling."

He kissed the top of her head. "Don't worry, Vic. Nothing in the world is going to happen. Europe and Germany and Britain will sort themselves out like they always do. We already had our world war and no one wants another. So while the great leaders of the great nations huff and puff and move pieces about on the checkerboard, you'll be here serving God and gazing at Kilimanjaro every morning and evening. Think of the sunrises and sunsets on that peak. Think of how it will bless Ramsay and Tim to live in a magical world with magical beasts far from the English rains and fogs."

She smiled. "When you put it that way it fills me with peace. I never thought Africa could do that."

21

Ten-year-old Sean Hartmann locked his fingers around Albrecht's hand. "I don't feel comfortable with you going to Berlin, Papa. I feel like Herr Hitler is watching you whenever you set foot out of Tubingen."

"I am not so important, son. No one is wasting time putting binoculars on me, I assure you. But I promise to watch what I say at the university. There will be no politics, no rants, no roars."

"You roar like a lion at the dinner table."

"The dinner table is a German man's pulpit, podium, and lecture hall. But there the roaring stays. What I do at the table, I will not do at the university. Don't fret. Instead pray and, of course, while I'm away you must take care of your mother and baby sister. Especially your sister. She is almost three and gets into everything. And she wanders off! Angelika will go out the door and walk all the way to Berlin to see the tigers at the zoo if you let her."

Sean laughed. "I won't let her, Papa. I'll watch her like a hawk."

"That's my knight. What color is your horse today?"

"Still dapple gray."

"A good color. Ride well. Make sure the sword is large enough. Nothing less than a two-handed broadsword will do."

"That's what I have. Don't be afraid for your family, Papa."

A cable arrived for Albrecht as he kissed Catherine and Angelika goodbye. He placed it in his coat pocket and pulled it out to read as the cab darted in and out of traffic on its way to the train station.

ALBRECHT
WHETHER YOU READ THIS OR NOT ONCE YOU SEE IT IS FROM ME I DO NOT KNOW. I IMPLORE YOU TO BE CAREFUL ABOUT WHAT YOU SAY AT HUMBOLDT UNIVERSITY. BERLIN IS BERLIN AND NOW THAT HITLER HAS COMPLETE POWER ARRESTS AND DEPORTATIONS OCCUR DAILY.

THIS INCLUDES ACADEMICS SUCH AS YOURSELF. THEY KNOW WHO YOU ARE. THE GESTAPO WILL MOST CERTAINLY ATTEND EACH OF YOUR GUEST LECTURES. DO NOT GIVE THEM ANY EXCUSE TO REPORT YOU. THINK OF YOUR WIFE AND CHILDREN. STAY WITH TOPICS LIKE THE ATTRIBUTES OF GOD AND THE VIRTUES OF THE CHRISTIAN LIFE.

WHETHER YOU BELIEVE IT OR NOT I REMAIN YOUR FRIEND AND GUARDIAN. HEIL HITLER.

GERARD

On the train to Berlin, Albrecht opened a newspaper that summed up and praised the events of the twenty-third of March, the day the *Reichstag* passed the Enabling Act. It gave Hitler and his Nazi Party broad, sweeping powers. "All for the good," the paper crowed. "Look at how well off the nation is six weeks after the fact."

"So Goebbels, minister of propaganda," murmured Albrecht so other passengers couldn't hear him, "tell me why dictatorship is better than democracy."

The article didn't immediately weigh in

on why a strong man at the top was the best form of government. Instead it printed parts of Hitler's speech on the day the Act was passed and he became absolute ruler of Germany:

> By its decision to carry out the political and moral cleansing of our public life, the Government is creating and securing the conditions for a really deep and inner religious life. The advantages for the individual that may be derived from compromises with atheistic organizations do not compare in any way with the consequences that are visible in the destruction of our common religious and ethical values.

> My Government will treat all other denominations with objective and impartial justice. It cannot, however, tolerate allowing membership of a certain denomination or of a certain race being used as a release from all common legal obligations, or as a blank check for behavior that is difficult to punish, or for the toleration of crimes.

> My Government will be concerned for the sincere cooperation between Church and State.

My struggle against materialistic ideology and for the erection of a true people's community serves as much the interests of the German nation as of our Christian faith.

The national Government, seeing in Christianity the unshakable foundation of the moral and ethical life of our people, attaches utmost importance to the cultivation and maintenance of the friendliest relations with the Holy See.

The rights of the churches will not be curtailed; their position in relation to the State will not be changed.

Why, Herr Hitler, Albrecht thought as he folded the newspaper and put it away, *"you have become a theologian."* He watched the trees and fields and towns slide past. *We must meet and write a book together on the German Jesus. What would he look like, I wonder? Would he wear a swastika or a cross?*

Humboldt University, Berlin
Albrecht always liked walking up to Humboldt University by crossing the large plaza to its front and taking in the stately build-

ings and columns and statues. But something had changed. He'd expected to see the Nazi flags with the swastika draped over government buildings around Berlin. He didn't expect to see them flying from flagstaffs on the university campus. Nor did he expect to see students wearing swastika armbands or faculty members giving one another the stiff-armed Nazi salute. With a tightness in his stomach, he made his way to the office of the head of the Faculty of Theology.

"Dr. Mueller," Albrecht said as he bowed his head and offered his hand, "it is good to see you again."

"Ah, Professor Hartmann." The large man, a head taller than Albrecht and twice as heavy, pushed himself away from his desk and rose to grip Albrecht's hand. "I'm glad you arrived safely. How are you?"

"I'm very well, Herr Doktor. How is your wife?"

"Splendid. I trust your wife and children are in good health?"

"They are, thank you." Albrecht set down his briefcase and unwound the red scarf from his neck. "I was surprised to see the university had become so . . . politicized."

"Hmm? Oh, you mean the flags. There is a cultural event tonight. Goebbels is giving a talk as well. The student body is quite excited about it. So is the faculty, truth be told."

"But these are Nazis, Dr. Mueller. They are not in support of free thought or free speech."

"They are our legal government, professor."

"Why the armbands? Why the Nazi salute?"

Dr. Mueller smiled. "You have been around students long enough to know how quickly they jump on bandwagons and rally around causes."

"And their teachers?"

"The salute is Roman in origin. Jacques-Louis David's *Oath of the Horatii* inspired it, I suppose, based on what he knew of Ancient Rome. No doubt that is why the Italians are so comfortable with it."

"Excuse me, Herr Doktor, but few faculty members should be comfortable with that salute. Many of them have read Hitler's *Mein Kampf.* You have read it. You told me when it came out that it was the worst thought the German mind could produce."

Dr. Mueller's face grew rigid. "I never said that."

"I have it in a letter."

"Then I ask you to destroy that letter. I

was in error when I wrote it."

"Dr. Mueller —"

"Professor Hartmann, the Nazi Party is our legal government. Adolph Hitler is our greatly esteemed leader. There will be cultural events at universities across the nation tonight that are inspired by good Nazi ideology and theology. I trust you will linger long enough after your evening lecture to take part in ours. Now, let me escort you to the lecture hall where you will be giving your first talk at the top of the hour. Heil, Hitler!"

"Hitler is a high school dropout, Herr Doktor. He has always despised deeper thought and intellectuals. And his stormtroopers are even worse. How many of them have had a university education? They scorn us."

"Heil, Hitler!"

Albrecht retorted, "Hail, Caesar!"

"What!"

Albrecht hesitated and then responded in full. "Hail, Caesar, we who are about to die salute you."

Mueller's eyes almost spat fire.

Albrecht smiled. "Merely an academic exercise, Herr Doktor. *Ave Caesar, morituri te salutamus.* Weren't you just talking to me about Ancient Rome?"

Mueller brushed past Albrecht on his way to the door and into the corridor. He marched ahead of his guest to the lecture hall. When they arrived, Mueller took Albrecht's arm. Dozens of students were already seated and waiting. Two men in black leather coats sat at the back.

"You see the police are here, Albrecht. The *Gestapo,*" Mueller warned in a low voice nodding slightly toward the back row of seats. "Be careful what you say, professor, or you will find yourself arrested and taken somewhere far away. We've already lost several members of our teaching staff. Play the Nazi game, and you will weather the storm. If you remain ramrod straight and self-righteous, the winds of change will surely break you. I shall meet you for supper. Heil, Hitler."

"Jewish professors, Herr Doktor? Jewish colleagues? Are they the ones the Nazis have purged from among you?"

"Heil, Hitler."

"Friends like Mandelbaum in chemistry and Goldstein in physics? And you let them? You did nothing?"

"I say again, 'Heil, Hitler.' "

Albrecht could not resist. "Hail, Mary."

Mueller stared at him in shock.

Albrecht continued. *"Hail Mary, full of*

grace, the Lord is with thee. Blessed art thou among women and blessed is the fruit of thy womb, Jesus. Holy Mary, Mother of God, pray for us sinners now and at the hour of our death."

Mueller snapped his head away. "We will skip the formal meal with the faculty. You can see yourself out after your last lecture this evening. Don't expect any visits from the other professors. Associating with you puts us all at risk." He turned and walked quickly from the room.

A spirit rose in Albrecht he refused to quell. He greeted the students as he arranged his notes at the podium by saying, "You know, I am going to change my lecture altogether. I have a sudden inspiration to forgo my scheduled talk on the historical Jesus and to examine the "Mary Prayer," which I'm sure you are all well acquainted with. *'Ave Maria, gratia plena, Dominus tecum. Benedicta tu in mulieribus, et benedictus fructus ventris tui, Iesus. Sancta Maria, Mater Dei, ora pro nobis peccatoribus, nunc, et in hora mortis nostrae. Amen.'* "

He spoke for an hour, took the numerous questions that came his way, bowed when the students applauded, and remained at the podium for the next lecture as the first group of students left and a new class made their way in. He looked toward the back and noticed the police hadn't moved. Both were still in their seats. The dark-haired one was scribbling rapidly in a black notebook.

His second lecture was on Paul's letters to the Corinthians, and Albrecht emphasized the chapter on love. The third lecture Albrecht had entitled "The True Cross," and it centered on the sacrifice of Jesus at Calvary. At the end of the lecture, he compared the broken cross of the swastika with the unbroken cross of Christ. By the time he gave his final talk, it was dark. He lectured on one line from the gospel of John: "He then having received the sop went out immediately. And it was night."

The police left when the last few students finished speaking with Albrecht. They didn't look his way or say a word.

The dining hall was deserted and there wasn't much left to purchase when Albrecht arrived, but he was able to get a hot bowl of cabbage soup, a large portion of rye bread, and a wedge of hard cheese, along with a cup of coffee. Shouts and singing filtered into the hall from outside, and he asked a waiter what was happening.

"A cultural event, sir," the waiter responded. "You would be most welcome to join in, I'm sure."

Albrecht finished his meal and went out to the plaza. The first thing he saw was a bonfire in the middle of the large, open space. It was surrounded by thousands of students and stormtroopers singing Nazi marching songs. He spotted Mueller tugging a cartload of books from the direction of the library, laughing with two *Gestapo* who were helping him — the same men who had taken notes at the lectures. Albrecht thought they were going to set up a display in the plaza. To his horror, once the men reached the bonfire, students grabbed the books and hurled them into the flames. Mueller and the police officers helped them.

"You heard Reich Minister Goebbels!" Mueller shouted. "No to decadence and moral corruption! Yes to decency and morality in family and state!"

The students cheered and then began to chant. Albrecht saw a large microphone from a radio station being adjusted so listeners at home could hear the chant clearly. Trucks pulled up with cargoes of books that the students and professors took up by the armload and threw into the heart of the fire.

"Destroy the un-German spirit!"

"Cleanse the nation! Cleanse the universities! Cleanse our blood!" Singing erupted again.

We will continue to march,
Even if everything shatters;
Because today Germany hears us,
And tomorrow, the whole World.

And the elders may chide,
So just let them scream and cry,
And if the World decides to fight us,
We will still be the victors.

They don't want to understand this song,
They think of slavery and war.
Meanwhile our acres ripen,
Flag of freedom, fly!

We will continue to march,
Even if everything shatters;
Freedom arose in Germany,
And tomorrow the world belongs to it.

No sooner had one song finished before professors and students and stormtroopers began to thunder out another.

Germany awake from your nightmare!
Give Jews no place in your Empire!
We will fight for your resurgence!
Aryan blood shall never perish!

All these hypocrites we throw them out!

Judea leave our German house!
If the native soil is clean and pure
We united and happy will be!
To the swastika, devoted are we!
Hail our Leader, Hail Hitler to thee!

Students rushed by Albrecht loaded down with books. He grabbed one of them and shouted, "What are you doing? Think of what is happening here! This is a great university! Do not tear it down in one night!" Volumes spilled from the youth's arms. Albrecht saw the names *Helen Keller, Albert Einstein,* and *Victor Hugo* on the spines.

The youth cursed and punched Albrecht in the face so hard he staggered backwards, clutching his briefcase. Then the student knelt, scooped up the books, and ran towards the fire.

"I will deal with this!" seethed Albrecht. He headed towards the blaze. "Before God, I will stop this!"

A young woman dressed completely in black seized his hand. "Do not fight them, Professor Hartmann. They are wild enough to throw you into the flames along with the books."

He tried to shake his hand free, but she held it with a grip like iron.

"What are you doing?" Albrecht raged. "Let go of me! I do not fear them!"

"You should fear them. They are many, and you are but one."

He looked at her gray eyes, blonde hair, and tense face. "I can make them listen."

"No, you can't. Not unless you are Goebbels or Himmler or Adolph Hitler himself. You have family, don't you? A wife and children? Do you want them all to be picked up by the *Gestapo*? They have already done it to other teachers here in Berlin — and not all of them were Jews."

She released his hand. He could still feel the pressure from her strong fingers.

"Write us another book instead," she told him. "You will have to publish and distribute it in secret, but it will eventually find its way into all corners of Germany. People will read it. Fight the Nazis that way . . . and the professors who have forgotten what they represent."

"Who are you?"

"My name is Stefanie Brecht. Write the book for me, if for no one else."

She vanished into the dark. He couldn't tell which way she'd gone. He turned back to the fire. His mind much calmer, he walked towards the sheets of flame. Thousands were singing the Nazi songs now. The plaza was full.

"Our Father which art in heaven," he prayed under his breath. The winds of the fire sent pages whirling into the night, along with ashes and sparks. One after another flew over Albrecht's head or landed at his feet. He stopped and picked up several. He recognized names of American writers such as John Dos Passos, F. Scott Fitzgerald, and Ernest Hemingway, along with British writers Rudyard Kipling, D.H. Lawrence, and H.G. Wells. There were German writers too — Erich Maria Remarque and his novel *All Quiet on the Western Front,* Bertolt Brecht and his *Threepenny Opera,* and the Austrian psychoanalyst Alfred Adler's *Understanding Human Nature.* A page from Tolstoy's *War and Peace* lay across his shoe.

The man next to Albrecht bent down for a sheet curled from the heat, muttering that he had his hands on a piece of Franz Kafka rubbish. Albrecht made a sudden decision to get away from the plaza. He kept his head down as he passed some SS officers whose eyes glittered like fire stones. A number of charred papers were scattered over a hedge, speared by the sharp points of the pruned branches. He plucked several free that were stuck together and glanced at them as he made his way through the crowds and off the campus.

"Heinrich Heine's play *Almansor,*" he said out loud. Reading over the pages one after another in the streaks and flares of light, he dropped each on the pavement once he was finished. Near the bottom of the last page his eyes caught a phrase he went over twice. Three SS men hurried past him towards the bonfire, coming from the direction of a bookstore that had all its windows shattered. The men's arms were crammed with books. Albrecht's quick glimpse revealed that several of the volumes were titled *Mein Geist.* Albrecht saw a photograph of his face on the back cover of one and quickly looked away. He placed the charred sheet from Heine's 1821 play into his coat pocket. The words he'd noticed ran through his mind like a line of fire as he made his way through traffic and across roadways, getting further and further from the red-and-black flames:

"Das war ein Vorspiel nur, dort wo man Bücher verbrennt, verbrennt man auch am Ende Menschen."

He wanted to remember to tell Catherine about this so he mentally translated the words, *"That was only the beginning. Where they burn books, in the end they will burn people."*

22

July, 1933
The English Channel, near the Port of Dover

Push off, and sitting well in order smite
The sounding furrows; for my purpose
   holds
To sail beyond the sunset, and the baths
Of all the western stars, until I die.
It may be that the gulfs will wash us down:
It may be we shall touch the Happy Isles,
And see the great Achilles, whom we knew
Though much is taken, much abides; and
   though
We are not now that strength which in old
   days
Moved earth and heaven; that which we
   are, we are;
One equal temper of heroic hearts,
Made weak by time and fate, but strong in
   will
To strive, to seek, to find, and not to yield.

"Capital! You still remember it!"

"I remember all of Ulysses by Tennyson, Grandfather. But I have another surprise for you."

Lord Preston put his hand on Owen's shoulder as the eleven-year-old steered the yacht. "Steady there, steady. You have a surprise, do you? And what is that?"

"Are you ready for it?"

" 'The sun is shining, the ship is heeling to port and responsive to the helmsman, fair stood the wind for France. Fire away."

Owen's red hair blew straight back, dark with wet where sea spray had struck. Owen kept his blue eyes focused straight ahead as he recited a different poem:

Whither, O splendid ship, thy white sails
    crowding,
Leaning across the bosom of the urgent
    West,
That fearest nor sea rising, nor sky
    clouding,
Whither away, fair rover, and what thy
    quest?
Ah! soon, when Winter has all our vales
    opprest,
When skies are cold and misty, and hail is
    hurling,
Wilt thou glide on the blue Pacific, or rest

In a summer haven asleep, thy white sails
    furling?

Lord Preston laughed. "Aha! Well done, Commander! I don't think I know the piece, but it's full of salt water and sails, isn't it? Who wrote the poem? How did you come by it?"

"Dad gave it me. It's called 'A Passer-By' and a dead man named Robert Bridges wrote it."

"Dead, was he? Well, he did remarkably well for a dead man."

"There's more to it, but I haven't memorized all of it yet. Except for the ending."

"Let's hear it then. If it's a good ending that is, one full of hope and promise."

"It is a good ending, Grandpapa. Look at those gulls swoop!"

"There's a school close to the surface. Carry on, Commander."

And yet, O splendid ship, unhail'd and
    nameless,
I know not if, aiming a fancy, I rightly divine
That thou hast a purpose joyful, a courage
    blameless,
Thy port assured in a happier land than
    mine.
But for all I have given thee, beauty enough

is thine,
As thou, aslant with trim tackle and
   shrouding,
From the proud nostril curve of a prow's
   line
In the offing scatterest foam, thy white sails
   crowding.

"Extraordinary! *"A purpose joyful, a courage blameless, thy port assured in a happier land than mine."* Let us hope he is right, Owen, and the ship he sees has all that. Let us hope you and I and *Pluck* have it. Let us pray our whole family has it!"

"Aye, aye, sir."

Lord Preston looked out over the whitecaps in the Channel as the yacht cut through the hard-blue of the water. The poem Owen had recited, especially the last lines, made him think of his far-flung family. He wondered about their courage, their joys, and their situations in the places where they'd settled and called home.

He had an image of Robbie and Shannon sitting with their daughter under a grove of palm trees in Jerusalem. Robbie was in his uniform, Shannon in a pale-yellow summer dress, Patricia Claire in shorts and a light, white cotton shirt. Patricia was playing in the dust. Around the three of them stood great stones of the great city thousands of years old. Almost as old, he sometimes thought, as civilization. And the dust that whirled in the hot winds seemed as old as the human race itself.

Another image came but this time of Victoria. Victoria and Ben with zebra running nearby because of lions. And there were Ramsay and Tim, growing tall and dark under the African sun, watching the zebra and the lions, their eyes keen and sharp and clear. Young Tim pointing beyond to the fine line of the horizon, where sky and earth touched at an edge slim as a thread of gold. The elephants were moving slowly there, tall, majestic, silhouetted against the long brightness.

Catherine and Sean and Angelika at the castle on the Rhine and at the chateau in Pura, Switzerland, were next. They were far from the turmoil in Germany, from the marches at night and the burning torches, Albrecht joining his family in the mountains, red scarf about his neck, papers under his arm, pen in hand. He was writing, writing, with Catherine reading each page and tracing each line of script with her finger.

Libby and Jane at the Channel, like he and Owen were, watching the mighty *Hood* steam in and out of port, gulls streaming over its wake. Terry was on the deck at attention and smiling as his family waved. Their lives were solid and sure and impenetrable, strong as dawn over the Atlantic, ribbed with steel like a battle cruiser's hull slipping over the long, grey depths.

Dover Sky stood basically empty but for a few summer days. Ashton Park was empty but for Elizabeth, Holly, Harrison, and himself. Jeremy and Emma in London with their twins Peter and James and their little brother Billy at play in streets and alleys and on patches of grass. Edward and Charlotte a block away, with Owen and Colm running with their cousins — not under palm trees or African skies or the ramparts of German castles, but in the shadow of Big Ben and the Tower of London and Buckingham Palace, still free, still unharmed. Kipp and Caroline with them all, and their children Matthew, Charles, and Cecilia growing as tall and straight as any of the others, books and schools and pencils and the rumble and rattle of cars and lorries and motorcycles, roadways teeming with traffic and people, sunlight coming through cracks between the high buildings of stone and brick finding them, lighting on them, blessing them.

"We have come this far, I thank God,"

Lord Preston murmured as a wave split in two over the bow. "We have come this far, and we are still together. We have lost some but not all, praise God. Not all. The Lord has granted us a future. I see it just there like I see the coastline of France."

"What did you say, Grandfather?" asked Owen. "Do you want me to come about?"

"Just indulging in a little of my own poetry, Commander. No, carry on to Calais. We'll sup with French fishermen this evening."

"Are we really going all the way to Calais?"

"It is only twenty-five miles . . . but perhaps not. Your grandmother would have a fit if we didn't return in time for high tea. Still, carry on! We won't come about just yet."

"Do you have a poem for me, Grandfather?"

Lord Preston thrust his hands in the pockets of his peacoat and whistled between his teeth, drawing the flying clouds and blown spume into him along with his breath and all the colors of the sea. "I do! It's from the Bible — Psalm 19. Mind the wheel and take these words to heart, my sailor."

"I shall, Grandpapa."

The heavens declare the glory of God; and

the firmament showeth his handiwork.

Day unto day uttereth speech, and night unto night showeth knowledge.

There is no speech nor language, where their voice is not heard.

Their line is gone out through all the earth, and their words to the end of the world. In them hath he set a tabernacle for the sun,

Which is as a bridegroom coming out of his chamber, and rejoiceth as a strong man to run a race.

His going forth is from the end of the heaven, and his circuit unto the ends of it: and there is nothing hid from the heat thereof.

The law of the LORD is perfect, converting the soul: the testimony of the LORD is sure, making wise the simple.

The statutes of the LORD are right, rejoicing the heart: the commandment of the LORD is pure, enlightening the eyes.

The fear of the LORD is clean, enduring for ever: the judgments of the LORD are true and righteous altogether.

More to be desired are they than gold, yea, than much fine gold: sweeter also than honey and the honeycomb.

Moreover by them is thy servant warned:

and in keeping of them there is great reward.

Who can understand his errors? cleanse thou me from secret faults.

Keep back thy servant also from presumptuous sins; let them not have dominion over me: then shall I be upright, and I shall be innocent from the great transgression.

Let the words of my mouth, and the meditation of my heart, be acceptable in thy sight, O LORD, my strength, and my redeemer.

ABOUT THE AUTHOR

Murray Pura earned his Master of Divinity degree from Acadia University in Wolfville, Nova Scotia, and his ThM degree in theology and interdisciplinary studies from Regent College in Vancouver, British Columbia. For more than 25 years, in addition to his writing, he's pastored churches in Nova Scotia, British Columbia, and Alberta. His writings have been shortlisted for the Dartmouth Book Award, the John Spencer Hill Literary Award, the Paraclete Fiction Award, and Toronto's Kobzar Literary Award. Murray pastors and writes in southern Alberta near the Rocky Mountains. He and his wife, Linda, have a son and a daughter.

Visit Murray's website at
www.MurrayPura.com

The employees of Thorndike Press hope you have enjoyed this Large Print book. All our Thorndike, Wheeler, and Kennebec Large Print titles are designed for easy reading, and all our books are made to last. Other Thorndike Press Large Print books are available at your library, through selected bookstores, or directly from us.

For information about titles, please call:
  (800) 223-1244

or visit our Web site at:
  http://gale.cengage.com/thorndike

To share your comments, please write:
Publisher
Thorndike Press
10 Water St., Suite 310
Waterville, ME 04901